Custer's Luck

CUSTER'S LUCK

by *EDGAR I. STEWART*

UNIVERSITY OF OKLAHOMA PRESS

NORMAN

Library of Congress Catalog Card Number: 55-6368

 Manufactured in the U.S.A. First edition, 1955; second printing, 1955; third printing, 1957; fourth printing, 1964; fifth printing, 1967; sixth printing, 1971; seventh printing, 1980; eighth printing, 1983.

FOR JANE

of whom it might almost be said that she "lost" her husband in the Custer Fight

CUSTER'S LUCK

Preface

To ATTEMPT to tell again the much discussed story of the Battle of the Little Big Horn requires a great deal of courage, and at least a word of explanation. Probably no other event in American military annals has provoked so much contradictory statement or more acrimonious "analysis" than this fateful fight. It is only an item—and a small one at that—of frontier history, but it has been attended by more speculation and by more surmising than many other engagements of far greater magnitude. It has become almost completely engulfed in myth and legend, and the blood spilled on that eventful Sunday has been exceeded many times over by the ink from the fountain pens of historians and military experts who have written about it. There is so much about the subject that we do not know and so much that we shall never know, that it will remain a subject of speculation as long as the American people have a history. For after Custer sent Martin back with the "bring packs" message to Benteen, and waved his command down into Medicine Tail Coulee, no one knows what happened, for of the members of those five troops none came back. And as has often been observed, both before and since, "dead men tell no tales."

Judged by the standard of actual losses the battle was a comparatively minor affair, but many attendant circumstances have tended to make it one of the most tragic and controversial campaigns in the folklore of the United States. It has become an American epic, believed by at least one writer to take equal rank with the classic story of the Iliad.

Of the white actors in the tragedy, many lips were sealed, first by a sense of gallantry, and then by death. Much that could have been told apparently was not, some of it out of a feeling of respect for Mrs. Custer; some of it out of loyalty to the regiment and to brother officers. The widow of the Little Big Horn idolized and worshipped her soldier husband, and devoted the years of her widowhood to a consecration of his memory. It was long axiomatic among students of the battle that no further light would be shed on its obscurities as long as Mrs. Custer lived. It was expected that when she died the lips of many might be unsealed and new facts brought to light, and that then there would be an explanation for much that was hitherto unintelligible. But Mrs. Custer confounded them all, and by the time she died, most of the participants in the battle had traveled that lonely way before her, and what information they had, died with them. As a result there are doubtless many stories that will remain forever untold, many questions to which we shall never know the answer.

Much of the evidence that does exist is so contradictory that it is impossible to tell even from the accounts of participants and eyewitnesses exactly what did happen, and what did not. Many stories which at first were told quite simply were later elaborated in detail, some of it quite fanciful while other parts were undoubtedly true as details long forgotten recurred to mind. Memory plays strange tricks at times, and then there is the very human love of notoriety which often causes those who tell a story to tell it in the most sensational manner possible. Many persons who have written on this subject have refused to use the accounts given by the hostile Indians on the ground that they are so fragmentary, inconclusive, and contradictory as to be almost worthless. But in common fairness it should be noted that they are no more so than the accounts of some of the white survivors which often disagree on even the most elementary details. And Thomas B. Marquis, one of the ablest students of the American Indian, believed that the veracity of the Indian warriors was higher than that of the old soldiers although admitting that allowance had to be made for the Indian idea of spirit interference in Indian affairs. Also, Stanley Vestal, in his researches, adopted the splendid model laid down by George Bird Grinnell, his friend and frequent correspondent, and gave the testimony of Indian eyewitnesses to great events the credibility that they had long deserved. The testimony of the Indian does need to be used with caution: they were interested parties and many of their stories were told at a time when they fully expected to be punished for having had a hand in the affair. Even as late as fifty years after the battle some of the Indians who were in it professed fear of being punished, and One Bull, a half-brother of Sitting Bull, refused to attend the semicentennial celebration for fear of being hanged. As a result they quite naturally told what they thought their white auditors wanted to hear.

The accounts of some of the soldiers who survived are also open to the charge of forgetfulness and rationalization. As a result of these disagreements, many details of the fight have undoubtedly been permanently obscured and will never be recovered. Much of the writing on the subject has been extremely controversial, and while it has been objected that this has shed more heat than light, such is not necessarily the case since heat is necessary to separate the true metal from the dross whether the problem be one of metallurgy or of historical research. There are very few aspects of the controversy upon which there is agreement; Reno, Custer, and Benteen have alike had their defenders and defamers and in too many instances the cloth has been tailored in accordance with the prejudices of the writer. Upon one thing there is agreement—that it was a battle and not a massacre, unless we accept the distinction which the Indian sometimes makes: when the white man wins, it is a battle; if the Indian wins, it is a massacre.

This battle—and all accounts agree that it was a fierce one—provided a smashing crescendo to the vacillating policy of the government of the United States towards the Indians of the Great Plains, a policy which was so vacillating that it constituted almost a total lack of policy. But the tragedy of the Little Big Horn River availed the Indian nothing, his day was already past, and it was nothing more than a last defiant gesture, an expression of the determination to go down fighting to the last, and it constitutes one of the most glamorous and heroic passages in the history of the American nation.

In telling the story I have attempted to tell it as objectively as possible without passion or prejudice, utilizing the contributions of recent scholarship as well as the accounts of those who wrote many years ago. Where the recital of events gives way to conjecture I have so indicated, and have attempted to state the contradictory as well as the positive evidence. I have also essayed the task of interpretation since I conceive it to be the task of the historian to explain and interpret as well as to relate. Faults must be presented along with virtues, and minor slips and aberrations must be faithfully reported when they affect the record. With these interpretations there will be many that will disagree, and I will cheerfully concede that they may be right and I wrong. No one expects agreement on very many facets of the Custer fight, and in this case disagreement is the spice of history.

In the spelling of tribal and band names, I have been perhaps arbitrary, but in each instance, there is abundant historical, and often linguistic, justification for my choices, e.g., "Uncpapa," "Minneconjou," "Ogallala." These are conscious choices which my publisher, the University of Oklahoma Press, has accepted for the purposes of this book, despite its adoption for all other volumes in the Civilization of the American Indian Series of the corresponding versions, "Hunkpapa," "Miniconjou," "Oglala."

My debts and obligations are legion. The summer of 1946, spent as Historical Aide at the Custer Battlefield National Monument, reawakened an old interest in the battle and gave me some ideas as to the way in which it possibly developed. Major and Mrs. Edward S. Luce, in charge of the Monument have been of unfailing assistance at all stages of this study, and without their interest this book would probably never have been brought to completion. Various western libraries have made their facilities available to me. These include the University of California at Berkeley, the Public Library of Billings, Montana, the Western Collection of the Denver Public Library, the State Historical Library at Bismarck, North Dakota, and the Historical Library at Helena, Montana. In the former Miss Jennie Margaret Rose gave much assistance while at the latter I am indebted to Mrs. Anne McDonnell and Miss Rita McDonald. My local library at Eastern Washington has been of especial assistance in procuring otherwise unobtainable books through the facilities of the Inter-Library Loan Service. Mr. Ray Schulenberg of Bismarck spent the better part of two extremely warm days in guiding me to historical sites in the vicinity; and I am grateful to Miss Mary Godfrey, daughter of General Edward S. Godfrey, for making many of her father's letters and papers available to me, and to Mr. Charles Booth for his assistance in the drawing of the maps. My colleague, Dr. Robert Lass, has read the entire manuscript and given me the benefit of his criticism. My greatest debt is to my wife who has sacrificed vacations that we might follow Custer's trail up the Rosebud or across the Dakota prairie, has had her home in perpetual disorder due to the presence of notes and manuscripts, and has also done a large amount of the typing.

To one and all I am deeply and sincerely grateful—to the men and women who carried out valuable researches in this field, to fellow Custer students from whom I learned much, to the tourists at the Monument who asked questions that had never before occurred to me—to all of these I extend my thanks. In the eight years in which the manuscript has been in progress, in the five or six revisions it has undergone, it is too much to hope that some mistakes have not crept in, that some footnotes have not wandered away and got lost, or that some citations have become multiple. For all and any of these I crave pardon. With all of my debts and obligations, this should have been a better book. For the fact that it is not, I am solely responsible.

EDGAR I. STEWART

Contents

Illustrations & Maps

MAPS

Custer's Luck

CHAPTER I

The Plains Tribes

THE NEWSPAPER OFFICES were dull and unexciting on that hot and sultry July night. The eyes of the nation were centered on the Centennial Exposition in Philadelphia where the Republic celebrated one hundred years of existence as an independent nation dedicated to the immutable principles of freedom and justice for all. The Democratic and Republican conventions had passed into history with the nomination of two almost equally obscure and colorless personalities, and the canvass for votes had not yet begun in real earnest. But over all there was a tension of anxiety.[1]

General George Armstrong Custer, reputed the greatest Indian fighter in the army, together with several less glamorous commanders, was campaigning in the Sioux country against the band of hostiles led by the notorious Sitting Bull, whose unusual name furnished the newspapermen with considerable amusement since they often referred to him hilariously as "Slightly Recumbent Gentleman Cow." There were in circulation a few vague and unconfirmed stories originating from frontier posts in the West to the effect that the Custer expedition had met with disaster. On the sixth the *New York Herald* had published two accounts, both based on dispatches from Salt Lake City dated the fifth of July, one originating at Stillwater, Montana Territory, on the second and quoting the special correspondent of the *Helena Montana Herald*, who described the arrival of "Muggins" Taylor with news of the battle.[2] The second dispatch had originated at Bozeman at 7:00 P.M. on

[1] Joseph Mills Hanson, *The Conquest of the Missouri; Being the Story of the Life and Exploits of Captain Grant Marsh*, 307; *Time*, Vol. XLVIII, No. 8 (August 19, 1946), 108.

[2] *New York Herald*, July 6, 1876. This account is also to be found in the *Army and Navy Journal*, July 8, 1876.

the third and was also based on the Taylor message. The same edition of the *Herald* carried a sketch of General Custer in which it spoke of him as having met his fate in one of those characteristic dashes which gave him his reputation as the most reckless cavalry leader of the war.[3]

Although the *Herald* seems to have accepted the accounts at their face value, the general tendency was to accept them with reluctance mixed with anxiety. Possibly, because the wish is father to the thought, the War Department was inclined to discredit the information since no official dispatches had been received, and the Adjutant General's Office felt that the whole story appeared to be improbable. General Sherman was of the opinion that it must be exaggerated since it seemed too terrible to be entirely true, and Sheridan, commanding the Division of the Missouri, called attention to the fact that the report did not come from any accredited source, neither from headquarters nor from a special correspondent with the expedition, but had appeared in two far western newspapers. Moreover, it was based on the account of a frontier scout, and this, in his opinion, entitled it to be regarded with the gravest suspicion. To this another officer added that the reputation of the scout who brought the news was not such as to justify the acceptance of the story without considerable reserve. But this opinion was contradicted by General D. S. Stanley, who from personal experience declared his opinion that the scouts were reliable and nonexcitable men and that any of them coming in with such news was worthy of belief.[4]

Then suddenly the telegraph from Bismarck, Dakota Territory, began tapping out the message:

> General Custer attacked the Indians June 25, and he, with every officer and man in five companies were [*sic*] killed. Reno with seven companies fought in intrenched position three days. The Bismarck *Tribune's* special correspondent was with the expedition and was killed.[5]

Then followed column after column of notes, comments, interviews

[3] *New York Herald,* July 6, 1876.

[4] *New York Herald,* July 7, 1876.

[5] Hanson, *The Conquest of the Missouri,* 307; *Time,* Vol. XLVIII, No. 8 (August 9 [1946]), 108.

with members of Reno's command, and, finally, the list of the dead and wounded. In all, more than fifteen thousand words were transmitted at a cost of upwards of three thousand dollars to the *New York Herald*, which thus scored one of the greatest "scoops" of newspaper history. This newspaper promptly proceeded to adopt Mark Kellogg, the newspaper correspondent with the expedition, as its own, although in reality this was not the case, for Kellogg had gone along at the last moment as a substitute for C. A. Lounsbury, editor of the *Tribune*, who was the official correspondent.

Coming as it did like a thunderclap out of a clear sky, the authentic account of the disaster left the American people stunned and bewildered, and the humiliation felt by both the army and the nation was as great as the shock of the massacre, if not greater.[6] The effect was heightened by the fact that the country was celebrating the completion of its first one hundred years of independence, and admiring, with complacent but pardonable pride, the progress that had been made in a century. Not since the assassination of President Lincoln (and some contemporary accounts insisted not even then) had public opinion been so profoundly shocked. The first reaction was one of disbelief—such a thing simply could not be: Custer, "the Murat of the American army," the "Beau Sabreur," and his regiment, the glorious, incomparable Seventh Cavalry, could not have met such a fate. But disbelief was overcome by certainty, and bewilderment gave way to grief, and grief to resentment. One writer quite justifiably viewed it as a "public humiliation" at the height of national exultation and concluded:

> It is a standing disgrace to us, that a nation of forty millions of civilized, and to a great extent, Christian people, is utterly unable to deal in any creditable manner with a few thousands of so-called savages within easy reach.[7]

This writer was able to realize, as many of his fellow-Americans were not, that the Battle of the Little Big Horn was only one of the

[6] Struthers Burt, *Powder River, Let 'er Buck*, 179.

[7] Reverend Edward Jacker, "Who Is to Blame for the Little Big Horn Disaster?" *American Catholic Quarterly Review*, Vol. I, No. 1 (January, 1877), 713. The same author saw it as the greatest misfortune of the Sioux that the Jesuits of the period had never gained a foothold among them. *Ibid.*, 714.

final scenes in a historical drama which had been going on for more than two centuries—in fact, ever since the white man had first set foot on the shores of North America, and more especially since the settlers at Jamestown brought the aggressive civilization of the Anglo-Saxon into a life-and-death struggle with a savagery so primitive that in many respects it had advanced but little above the level of the Stone Age. John Smith and his reputed adventure with Pocahontas, King Phillip's War, "Mad Anthony" Wayne and the Battle of Fallen Timbers, Black Hawk and his pitiful remnants of a once mighty tribe—all were characters and episodes in that grim story of the white man's advance and the futile resistance of the red man, a story that was to have one of its greatest chapters written in blood on that dusty ridge overlooking the valley of the Little Big Horn. And this chapter, although seemingly telling the tale of an Indian victory, was in reality only that of a last despairing and futile gesture against a fate that the red man could not hope to escape.

The first two centuries of the struggle had been localized for the most part east of the Mississippi River, a fact that was due somewhat, although not entirely, to the widespread belief, first advanced by Lewis and Clark but ably seconded by Lieutenant Pike, that the land to the west of that stream was largely desert and unfit for white habitation and development. The Americans had been perfectly willing to leave it to the Indian and the buffalo, and as late as 1832 it was viewed as permanent Indian territory where the American aborigines could pursue their ancestral way of life without interference.[8] As a result it was not until the decade of the forties was well advanced that the Indians of the Great Plains and Rocky Mountains really began to feel the full impact of the advance of white civilization.

By 1840 the Indian frontier was practically complete, and the tribes established west of the Arkansas and Missouri rivers. By Congressional enactment, whites were not allowed to enter this Indian domain without a license and were expressly forbidden to sell or give spirituous liquors to the Indians. To look after the welfare of their red charges, superintendencies, agencies, and subagencies were established, while a line of forts extending from Fort Snelling on the north to Fort Smith in the south was constructed for the double

[8] E. Douglas Branch, *The Hunting of the Buffalo*, 105.

purpose of preventing white encroachment on the lands of the Indians and affording protection against the Indians to the farm frontier.[9]

Prior to the 1840's the tribes of the plains had known the white man chiefly as a trader and trapper who came among them for the purpose of securing furs either by his own trapping or by bartering with the natives. But in 1840 the Rocky Mountain fur traders held their last great rendezvous. This event, which usually goes unnoticed in the history books, meant that the western country had been largely trapped out, that fur-trading expeditions on a large scale were no longer considered profitable, and that in the future the taking of beaver and other skins would be for the most part a small-scale enterprise. But many of the mountain men knew no other way of life, and despite the decline of the fur trade they continued to live in the mountains among the tribes with whom they had intermarried. They went where the beaver were to be found, and as a result most of them lived among the Crows and the Shoshones and the other tribes who ranged between the mountains and the Great Plains proper, rather than among the tribes of the plains such as the Sioux and the Cheyennes. By taking the side of their hosts in the recurrent intertribal wars, they incurred the wrath of the Sioux, for since the turn of the century, and perhaps even before, the Crows and the Sioux had been almost perpetually at war.[10]

In 1841 the hostility which the tribes were beginning to feel for the whites who lived among and fought on the side of their enemies was intensified and transferred to a new object, for in May of that year the first emigrant train passed westward along the Platte River.[11] In the years following, these columns of white-topped wagons passed with increasing frequency along the Oregon Trail, which to the Indians was "the Great Medicine Road" of the whites, and which by that time had become a well-defined highway. There were two principal routes, the first of which followed the Platte

[9] Dan E. Clark, *The West in American History*, 567.

[10] George E. Hyde, *Red Cloud's Folk: A History of the Oglala Sioux Indians*, 51.

[11] This party, which was composed of about eighty-one persons, had thirteen wagons in addition to some small carts. It included the celebrated missionary, Father Pierre Jean De Smet, and two other priests, as well as a Methodist preacher, the Reverend Joseph Williams. LeRoy Hafen and W. J. Ghent, *Broken Hand; the Life Story of Thomas Fitzpatrick, Chief of the Mountain Men*, 130.

and the North Platte, the Shell River of the Indians, to the junction with the Sweetwater, and then along that stream to the Continental Divide; the second followed the Platte and the South Platte to the vicinity of the present city of Denver, then north to Cheyenne and then to the Green River. The first route was that of the historic Oregon Trail, the second was the Overland route, the path later to be followed by the Union Pacific Railroad. This Platte River country was the historic hunting grounds of the Sioux Nation since it abounded in all kinds of game and was the range of enormous herds of buffalo.[12]

It was not only that the white trespassers cut down and wasted the scanty wood supply of the prairies, that their draft animals ate the grass along the streams, but that they drove away the buffalo upon which the Indians depended for practically everything in their domestic economy. The flesh furnished food; the horns, glue, spoons, and other tools and implements; the dried droppings of the animal, the familiar "buffalo chips," were used as a fuel; while the hide furnished robes for his bed, a covering for the tepee, and was also made into leggings, bowstrings, moccasins, and sacks.[13] Not only did the white man butcher these animals recklessly but by mere force of numbers frightened the others away from their customary range and thus forced the Indians to go farther and farther afield to hunt.

The Indians loved the country with a depth of primitive feeling of which the white man of that period was stupidly unappreciative. Vast, strange and illimitable plains, more changeful and mysterious than the Sahara, filled them with the great awe and admiration distilled from their own peculiar brand of piety and superstition.[14]

Each tribe occupied a fairly definite area, and the members of one tribe did not hunt in the territory of another except at considerable

[12] Charles Edmund DeLand, *The Sioux Wars*, 33. "The Sioux were rovers, camping wherever fancy or the fortune of war dictated. They were noted for intelligence, superior morals, stature, and manner of living." Maurice Sullivan, *Jedediah Smith, Trader and Trail Breaker*, 15–16.

[13] Carl Coke Rister, *Southern Plainsmen*, 6; James McLaughlin, *My Friend, the Indian*, 97.

[14] Lieutenant Colonel Frazier Arnold, "Ghost Dance and Wounded Knee," *Cavalry Journal*, Vol. XLIII, No. 183 (May–June, 1934), 19–20.

risk. War parties might, and did, invade the territory of rival tribes for the purpose of stealing ponies or lifting scalps, but the hunters more often confined themselves within the limits of the region which was theirs from custom and long occupancy. Had there not been this feeling toward the land, there would have been few Indian wars, since these were generally the result of attempts to dispossess a tribe of its traditional hunting grounds.[15] And the Oregon Trail, which represented "an American idea as well as a road," the idea of colonizing the agricultural lands of the West and Far West,[16] cut the great hunting range of the Sioux and the buffalo herd in two, and "turned that great pasture land along the Platte into a barren desert."[17]

It was a matter of real concern when the buffalo began to desert their accustomed range, and the Sioux, who at first had watched the passing of the white-topped wagons with a fascinated interest that was almost childish, began to grow increasingly resentful and to talk more and more about driving all of the white men from the country. Their hostility against the emigrants was increased by the talk of the traders who had almost as much to lose as the Indians and who, in addition, sought to divert hostility from themselves. The emigrants thus became the favorite whipping boy of both, and the blame for everything that went wrong on the western frontier was laid at the door of these people, who, with their families and all their earthly possessions, followed the trail that led westward.[18]

But there was another aspect to the opposition of the Indians. This was the fact that they came to realize at an early date that they were fighting not only for a living, but for a way of life, to preserve a culture as well as a princely domain.

> . . . with the buffalo went the whole basis and reason of the Plains Indians' culture. Their traditions and their characteristic life were fading away. They felt degeneration creep over them. All the while the greedy and pre-emptive whites, in inexhaustible numbers, kept trooping in,

15 Stanley Vestal (comp.), *New Sources of Indian History, 1850–1891; A Miscellany*, 164; McLaughlin, *My Friend, the Indian*, 17.

16 Branch, *The Hunting of the Buffalo*, 114.

17 Stanley Vestal, *Jim Bridger, Mountain Man; A Biography*, 168–69; Rister, *Southern Plainsmen*, 6.

18 Hyde, *Red Cloud's Folk*, 51.

changing and despoiling the country and desecrating the face of nature. This was the Indian point of view, as it would have been the point of view of any war-like and self-respecting race of men under similar circumstances.[19]

In 1842 the party of Dr. Elijah White, newly appointed Indian agent for the territory of Oregon, who was being guided by the famous trapper and scout, Thomas Fitzpatrick (he of the broken hand), was stopped just west of Independence Rock, "a large rounded granite mass that rested like a huge turtle on the plain," by several hundred Sioux. After some disagreement among the chiefs as to the course of action to be taken, the party was allowed to proceed, but the Indians gave notice of their intention to prevent any more wagon trains from passing through their country.[20] Among other things Dr. White carried instructions from the American Board to its missionaries at Waiilatpu and Lapwai making several far-reaching changes in the disposition of its missionaries in the Oregon country. The next year when Dr. Marcus Whitman made his famous trip east in a successful attempt to secure a modification of these orders—an overly publicized and overly dramatized episode which is best, although incorrectly, known as "Whitman's Ride to Save Oregon"—the hostility of the tribes was so great that he was advised not to proceed along the Oregon Trail any farther east than Fort Hall. As a result, he and a companion made a long detour to the south by the way of Taos, Santa Fé, and Bent's Fort on the Arkansas River, before going on to St. Louis.

But the Indians were struggling against destiny as well as against the white man. For the famous migration of 1843—which Dr. Whitman joined but did not lead—followed the usual route up the Platte in numbers so great that the hostility of the tribes availed little, and the succeeding years saw an ever increasing number of emigrant wagons crowding the westward trail. This same decade witnessed the great Mormon migration during which Brigham Young and thousands of the faithful made their way toward the

[19] Arnold, "Ghost Dance and Wounded Knee," *Cavalry Journal*, Vol. XLIII, No. 183 (May–June, 1934), 19–20.

[20] Hafen and Ghent, *Broken Hand*, 134–37. Fitzpatrick received his name from the bursting of a rifle which took off a finger and otherwise crippled his left hand. *Ibid.*, 71; see also page 46.

promised land of Deseret, although they followed the north, rather than the south, bank of the Platte. The Indians raged, but could do little else to arrest the ever mounting tide that flowed westward toward the setting sun. Attacks upon individual wagons, upon stragglers, and upon small parties constituted more of an annoyance than a hindrance except to those directly involved. But these scattered raids definitely contributed to the bad reputation which the tribes had had throughout the East ever since the stopping of Dr. White's party.

In 1849 came the rush of gold seekers to California, and in the same year the government transferred the Indian Bureau from the War Department to the Department of the Interior, apparently on the assumption that the needs of the Indian could be better understood by civilians than by army officers. For its part, the War Department established a post near Fort Hall and also built Fort Kearny on the Platte at the upper end of Grand Island, 190 miles from Omaha, and on the recommendation of John C. Frémont purchased Fort Laramie from the American Fur Company.[21] This post, which was nearly 600 miles from Omaha, was located on the left bank of the Laramie River at its confluence with the North Platte, and at the foot of the Laramie Range of the Rocky Mountains. By 1842 it was already well established as a major stopping place on the great western trail.[22] When the government garrisoned these posts with small detachments of infantry, the Indians were at first naïve enough to believe that the purpose was to protect them from the whites, only to discover that the real object was to prevent them from molesting the emigrants. But it is not apparent that the presence of the soldiers had any effect upon the conduct of the Indians, either among themselves or in their relations with the whites.[23]

Indian resentment was further increased by the outbreak of epidemic diseases among them. One of these was the Asiatic cholera, which was first introduced into North America from Europe in 1832 and which spread with fearful rapidity throughout the country. Carried by the emigrants, it was soon communicated to the Indians along the Platte. While it took a fearful toll among whites

[21] Hyde, *Red Cloud's Folk*, 64.
[22] Vestal, *Jim Bridger*, 143; Hafen and Ghent, *Broken Hand*, 210.
[23] Hyde, *Red Cloud's Folk*, 69.

and Indians alike, the inroads made among the whites were largely unknown to the Sioux, who imagined that they were its only victims. Nor was this all, for the Indians also contracted smallpox, measles, and venereal diseases from the whites. To the most of these the white man had developed at least a partial immunity, but they played havoc among the red men. The Indians, long accustomed to explain everything that they could not readily understand in terms of the supernatural, believed that these diseases were a form of special "medicine" or magic which the whites were employing in order to decimate the natives and acquire their lands.[24]

Disorder on the plains continued. One scheme that had been urged for several years was that of a great Indian council in which representatives of the various tribes would meet with officials of the government in the hope that the Indians could be induced to sign a treaty of peace and friendship that would result in greater safety for travelers along the Oregon Trail. Although most of the frontiersmen scoffed at the notion, officials in Washington were enthusiastic about the scheme and in 1851 finally brought it to pass. Representatives of most of the northern tribes of the Great Plains and Rocky Mountain area, including the Sioux, Assiniboin, Arikara, Gros Ventre or Hidatsa, Crow, Shoshone, Cheyenne, and Arapaho,[25] who had been rounded up very largely as a result of the activities of Father Pierre Jean De Smet, met with Colonel D. D. Mitchell and Thomas Fitzpatrick. Fitzpatrick, who knew the mountains as no other white man before or since, except Bridger, was now government agent for the Indians of the upper Platte and Arkansas rivers.[26]

The meeting, held on Horse Creek, a tributary of the Platte, about thirty-five miles east of Fort Laramie, is said to have been attended by one of the greatest assemblages of Indians in history,

[24] *Ibid.*, 63–64. The comparative freedom of the trail from Indian attacks, during the summer of 1849, is said to have been caused by the Indians' fear of coming within range of the cholera epidemic. Hafen and Ghent, *Broken Hand*, 221.

[25] "The Comanches, Kiowas, and Apaches refused to attend. They had too many horses and mules, they said, to risk such a journey and among such notorious horse thieves as the Sioux and the Crows." Hafen and Ghent, *Broken Hand*, 223.

[26] Hyde, *Red Cloud's Folk*, 64–67; Vestal, *Jim Bridger*, 168–70; DeLand, *The Sioux Wars*, 341. In 1846 Fitzpatrick had been appointed Indian agent for the tribes at the head of the Arkansas, Platte, and Kansas rivers. The idea of an upper Platte and Arkansas Agency with headquarters at Bent's Fort was somewhat impractical. Hafen and Ghent, *Broken Hand*, 191–92.

and had for its main purpose the formulation of an agreement with the Indians which would result in greater safety for the emigrants on the Oregon Trail. It lasted two weeks and accomplished precisely nothing, and well deserved General Harney's characterization of a "cracker and molasses treaty," although at the time it was trumpeted far and wide as a great victory for the peace party,[27] since the assembled Indians had agreed that the United States government had the right to build roads and forts in the Indian country. The reason for this poverty of result was a simple one, but one which no white man could bring himself to understand, namely, that among the Indians no chief had any real authority except over a very small group of immediate followers. Except in times of dire emergency—and generally not even then—there was no such thing as a real head chief. The Indians were too ruggedly individualistic for that, and for any chief to even attempt to claim any authority was simply an invitation to assassination.[28] The Indians who signed the treaty signed only for themselves, a fact that the white man could not or would not understand.

Such was the treaty of Fort Laramie, or Fitzpatrick's Treaty, which the Sioux knew as the Treaty of the Long Meadows. It attempted to set up certain definite boundaries within which the Indians could preserve their tribal way of life with some degree of permanence, although it did not recognize the right of the United States to construct forts and to build military and other roads within the Indian territory, a fact which apparently was not fully understood by the Indians. The United States also undertook to protect the tribesmen against white depredations, and promised to make an annual payment of goods to the tribes concerned for a period of fifty years. Later the Senate, without obtaining Indian ratification of the change, reduced this period to fifteen years, so that technically the treaty never became effective. When the issuance of annuities was terminated at the end of the fifteen-year period, there

[27] Corporal Percival G. Lowe, writing from memory fifty-four years later, put the number of Indians present at sixty thousand, which is an impossibility. It was probably closer to ten thousand. Hafen and Ghent, *Broken Hand*, 228. Stanley Vestal estimates the number at not less than eight thousand. Vestal, *New Sources of Indian History*, 194. He also says that both Sitting Bull and Red Cloud were there as young men. Vestal, *Jim Bridger*, 170.

[28] Vestal, *Jim Bridger*, 180.

was considerable misunderstanding and a great deal of recrimination which was at least a contributory factor in the outbreak of Red Cloud's War.

This treaty also attempted to define the territorial boundaries between the various tribes and to secure their acceptance by all concerned. The Powder River[29] country, where the buffalo were exceptionally plentiful, was given to the Crows, the line of demarcation between them and the Uncpapa Sioux farther to the east being the divide which separates the valley of the Powder River from that of the Little Missouri. But although this Powder River country was traditionally the land of the Crows, actually they found the region unsafe for their hunting parties because of the persistent hostility of the Uncpapa, who were the fiercest and most recalcitrant members of the Sioux Nation. But in turn the Crows were able for a time to keep any other tribe from occupying the valley, and the result was that the region became a sort of Indian "no man's land" over which a hunting party traveled only at enormous risk with the ever present possibility of sudden attack from war parties of the enemy.

In 1851 the Uncpapa had stubbornly refused, despite a great deal of coaxing, to make peace with the Crows, a fact which was *not* reported at Washington. To have told the truth about such a situation might have meant an end to the "presents" which the government so generously provided, and which the Indian agents regularly distributed among the tribes to the great profit of the agents. This distribution was accompanied by a great deal of chicanery, if not downright dishonesty, and not a few Indian agents are suspected—to put it mildly—of having acquired a considerable competence in the process. To have reported the continuance of even the intertribal wars might have caused the officials in Washington to conclude that the money of the government was being spent to no good advantage, and might have resulted in a decision to discontinue the distribution of presents. Such a discontinuance would have inconvenienced the Indians very little, but it would have put an end to the agents' lucrative side money.

[29] The Powder River was named the Redstone by William Clark in 1805. It acquired its present name because of the fine, black sand along its banks which resembles gunpowder. The best account of the stream and its history is probably that of Struthers Burt, *Powder River, Let 'er Buck.*

The stated idea behind the meeting had been to bring peace to the plains, not only between the Indians and the whites, but also among the various Indian tribes as well. However, the tribesmen took the presents which the government representatives distributed with such a lavish hand, and then returned to their hunting grounds to hunt buffalo, to quarrel among themselves, to continue their intertribal wars, and to carry on their sporadic attacks on the whites just as if there had been no meeting and no treaty.[30]

But actually the officials in Washington were not primarily interested in peace among the tribes. For all they cared, the Indians could continue to exterminate one another with impunity as long as that extermination was confined to the Indians. What the government was interested in was the protection of the Platte road and in obtaining the right to construct military roads and posts in the Indian country. It was this last that the Sioux were increasingly determined to prevent, treaty or no treaty.[31]

In 1849, when the War Department had garrisoned the newly acquired Fort Laramie with a small force of infantry, Fitzpatrick, whose experience in handling western Indians was inferior to none, had made a vigorous protest, maintaining that it was ridiculous to expect a small detachment of foot soldiers to protect emigrants against the attacks of mounted Indian warriors. Instead, he recommended that an adequate force of cavalry be maintained on both the Platte and the Arkansas rivers for a few years in order to impress upon the minds of the Indians the power and strength of the United States government. That his advice was not followed was due to two facts. In the first place, "brass hats" in Washington, who had had little or no experience in Indian fighting—and who probably had never seen an Indian outside of a sideshow—were unwilling to admit, even to themselves, that anyone, especially an uncouth frontiersman, could possibly know more about anything than they did. The second reason was economy of the penny-pinching sort. The cost of transporting grain to the western posts was very high, and for that reason it was cheaper to garrison the posts with infantry rather than with cavalry. It also cost a good deal of money to trans-

30 This council is especially well covered in Hyde, *Red Cloud's Folk*, 64–67. See also Hafen and Ghent, *Broken Hand*, 228–45.

31 DeLand, *The Sioux Wars*, 32; Hyde, *Red Cloud's Folk*, 67.

port the necessary supplies for foot soldiers, and the result was that economy was further served by maintaining only a small garrison.[32] The effect upon the Indians and the ability to carry out the policies of the government were apparently extraneous matters which were not to be seriously considered. Lives and the success or failure of a policy apparently meant less than the saving of a few dollars, a policy of false economy that was to characterize the relations of the government of the United States with the Indian tribes until the day when the Indian ceased to be a military problem.

But despite the predictions of Fitzpatrick and others, there was comparatively little trouble at Fort Laramie until 1854, when an ill-advised attempt to arrest a Sioux warrior of the Minneconjou tribe led to a fight in which Lieutenant Grattan and several soldiers were killed. Grattan's temperamental unsuitability for the position he held is shown by his declaration that with ten soldiers he could whip the entire Cheyenne Nation, while with thirty he could put to flight all the tribes of the plains. Although the killing took place under circumstances which largely, if not entirely, exonerated the Indians from blame, and practically everyone admitted that Grattan was solely responsible for the fight and its consequences,[33] the War Department and the eastern public in general refused to believe it. On their part, the Indians felt that they had been unjustly imposed upon, and as a result the incident uncapped a great amount of latent hostility, fanned some smoldering resentments, and directly precipitated a whole series of raids undertaken by the Indians in retaliation. So serious did the situation become that the next summer General Harney was sent with a body of troops on a march up the valley of the Platte. In the course of events, he attacked and massacred a small group of Brulé Sioux in a rather disgraceful affair at Ash Hollow.[34] This incident furnishes an illuminating example of the governmental method of dealing with the recalcitrant Indian tribes. None of the hostiles who were guilty of crimes and depredations against the whites would have been so foolish as to camp within easy striking distance of the soldiers, and the village that General Harney attacked was inhabited by "friendlies" who were guilty of

[32] Hyde, *Red Cloud's Folk*, 69.
[33] *Ibid.*, 72–76; DeLand, *The Sioux Wars*, 36.
[34] DeLand, *The Sioux Wars*, 35.

Fort Abraham Lincoln, Dakota Territory, established in 1872.

Courtesy North Dakota Historical Society

Lieutenant Colonel George Armstrong Custer, about 1867.

"By far the most important cause of dissension in the Seventh Cavalry, and one which was limited to that regiment alone, was the character and personality of its lieutenant colonel."

Courtesy Custer Battlefield National Monument

no offense and whose main desire was to live at peace with the whites. But the expedition did clear the road of hostile Sioux and make it safe for emigrant travel at least for the time being. Just how long it would remain so was another question.

By this time the various Sioux tribes that had formerly lived and hunted along the Platte were being forced to the reluctant conclusion that the white man had come to the valley to stay, and that the Indians could remain only by submitting to the rules and the regulations of the conquerors. The alternative was migration, and the Indians took it. Both the Cheyennes and the Sioux split up temporarily, one group going south into what is now the state of Kansas, while the other and much larger group began to occupy the region to the west of the Black Hills and around the headwaters of the south fork of the Cheyenne River. There were already Indians in this territory, and the newcomers reinforced those of their people who had been driven westward from the Missouri River. It is doubtful if the increased population put any serious burden on the food supply, for even twenty years later enormous herds of buffalo and other game animals were reported.

For once the Indians attempted unity of action, and the result was the great council of the Sioux Nation at Bear Butte on the northern fringe of the Black Hills. This huge extinct volcano which stands opposite present Fort Meade was one of the favorite gathering places of the Indian tribes. They were fully aware of the seriousness of the situation which confronted them and not at all ignorant of the strength of the whites. They appraised the situation, counted the cost, and determined on a course of action. And from that summer until their final defeat and surrender more than two decades later, resistance to white encroachment in every form was the one consistent policy of the Sioux.

That they meant business is shown by the fact that immediately after the breakup of the council, the Minneconjou and Uncpapa groups moved into the territory just west of the Black Hills to hunt buffalo. Here they encountered a surveying party under the command of First Lieutenant G. K. Warren of the United States Army. Warren, a topographical engineer, had left Fort Laramie and proceeded northward to the western slope of the Black Hills, mapping the area and especially seeking sites for forts and routes for military roads, thus making the first extended exploration of the region. At Inyan Kara Mountain he was strenuously opposed by the Sioux. Having only a few soldiers, he would have stood absolutely no chance had the Sioux determined to attack. But after a violent argument among themselves in which the Sioux with difficulty restrained some of their more ardent and impetuous young men, it was decided to let the white men go. Lieutenant Warren was told to leave the country and not to come back, and to warn the other white men that upon the pain of death they must stay out of the Sioux country.[35]

But still the white man came. That he did not settle west of the Missouri River in the land which the Sioux claimed as theirs was not so much because of the Indians' warning as because the region was not too attractive or desirable for white settlement. There was much better land to be had elsewhere, in the east as well as farther west. At this time the legend of the Great American Desert still persisted, and it was widely believed that the region lying between the Missouri River and the Rocky Mountains was largely unsuitable for white habitation. Consequently, most Americans who thought about the subject at all were quite willing to leave it to the Indians and the buffalo. The result was that those emigrants from farther east who did not take the trail to either Oregon or California filled in the fringes of the already established settlements in the valley of the Missouri and left the Sioux temporarily at peace.

But there were many tiny pinpoints of friction. In June of 1857 a number of white citizens living near Spirit Lake, Iowa, were massacred by a marauding band of Indians. This was not in any sense the work of the entire Sioux Nation, but rather the act of a small band of renegades and outlaws who happened to be Indians but who might just as well have been whites, Negroes, or Chinese. They were led by an Indian gangster known as Inkpaduta, or Scarlet Top. To hold the Sioux responsible for this outrage was just as sensible as it would be to hold the entire population of the city of Chicago responsible for the excesses of the Capone gang. But that was precisely what the representatives of the United States government did.[36] The Indian annuity payments were due, and the officials now attempted to make payment conditional upon the surrender of

[35] Hyde, *Red Cloud's Folk*, 35.
[36] DeLand, *The Sioux Wars*, 13.

Inkpaduta and his gang. It was impossible for the Sioux to comply with this demand since they had no control whatsoever over the outlaws. But the white officials pretended to be unable to understand this rather elementary fact, and the only result was to further embitter the relations between the two peoples.[37]

The next year gold was discovered in Colorado, and the lure of the yellow metal brought emigrants by the thousands swarming across the plains, probably upwards of a hundred thousand gold seekers crossing to Pikes Peak in a single year. The traffic became so heavy that a stage line was established along the Republican River and through some of the best buffalo country remaining to the southern tribes. This further alarmed the Indians, who felt that history was beginning to repeat itself and that the white man would leave the red man alone just as long as it was to his advantage to do so.

The coming of the Civil War in the United States temporarily distracted the attention of the American people from the problems of the frontier and gave the Indian a priceless opportunity, of which he failed to take advantage. There is no better evidence of the desire of the Indian merely to be let alone than the fact that during the four years of the Civil War the tribes failed to capitalize on the advantage that was presented to them. The regular troops were all withdrawn from the Indian country, and if the Sioux had had any intention to exterminate the whites among them, this was obviously the time to carry such a scheme into effect. And it cannot be argued that it was due to a lack of knowledge of the situation, for most of the traders were Southern, at least in sympathy, and at the outset of the struggle had attempted to align the Indians against the federal government; indeed, in the North there was a widespread fear of a successful Confederate plot to foment an Indian uprising. But the Sioux were not to be tempted and seem to have given the war but little attention.[38]

In 1862 the eastern, or Santee, Sioux, under the leadership of Little Crow, perpetrated the so-called "Minnesota massacres" in which about eight hundred settlers and soldiers lost their lives, and which soon involved almost the entire Sioux Nation in war. The causes of the outbreak were almost entirely local in character and

[37] *Ibid.*, 17.

[38] George Bird Grinnell, *The Fighting Cheyennes*, 121–24.

had nothing to do with the war between the North and the South.[39] Nor did they concern the western, or Teton, Sioux in any way. But following the attacks, the Santees abruptly left the country and moved westward, hoping to find refuge among the more nomadic tribes beyond the Mississippi. But the Tetons were under few, if any, illusions, and when the Santees arrived in the western country bringing captives and plunder, they correctly surmised that the soldiers were in pursuit and that the Santees had not made the journey "merely to tell them the news."[40] But the Tetons, by merely sheltering the fugitives, invited attack and thus inherited a war which was not of their making, for General Sully and his troops were unwilling, if not unable, to make distinctions between the various tribes. To the soldiers, all Indians looked alike, and most of the Indians were supposed to be hostile. So the soldiers shot first and inquired afterwards. Soon after the pursuing column reached the western country, the Santees moved farther north and took refuge among the belligerent Uncpapa Sioux, whose great leader, Sitting Bull, never accepted white domination. Once again it was the innocent bystander who was punished because the hostile tribes would not wait for the soldiers to catch up and attack.

Although most of the plains tribes remained quiet, and by the exercise of a little tact and discretion could have been kept that way, the "Minnesota massacres" alarmed the settlers along the entire western frontier. The saying that the only good Indian was a dead one was unconsciously or consciously subscribed to in every ranch house and military station along that far-flung border. These settlers felt, and not without reason, that their turn might be next, and they began to demand that troops should be sent to defend them. The result was that General Patrick E. Connor was placed in charge of defending the Overland route and that several regiments, including the Eleventh Ohio Volunteer Cavalry under Colonel William O. Collins, which was sent to Fort Laramie, were ordered to the frontier to guard the stage and telegraph lines as well as to hold the Indians in check.

[39] DeLand, *The Sioux Wars*, 19–28; Doane Robinson, *History of the Sioux*, 256; Fred Dustin, *The Custer Tragedy; Events Leading up to and Following the Little Big Horn Campaign of 1876*, 6.

[40] Hyde, *Red Cloud's Folk*, 101.

It was the coming of these soldiers that was largely responsible for the trouble that ensued. They were volunteers and had enlisted in the quite natural expectation of seeing action in the Civil War. Consequently, garrison duty on the western frontier had even fewer attractions for them than it did for the regular troopers. As a result they were continually craving excitement, and when none seemed to be coming their way, they did what they could to create some. Most of the officers were of a similar stripe, the chief difference between them and the enlisted men apparently being that the latter had less political influence; an abysmal ignorance of the Indian and of his way of life was common to both.[41]

The northern group of Sioux and Cheyennes was, by this time, largely concentrated in the Powder River country of eastern Montana. Here the tribesmen hunted buffalo and other game and carried on their never ceasing warfare with the Crows. There were no white men in the region, and the closest ones, those along the Platte and Missouri rivers, were too far away to cause any real concern. So the Indians continued to live in much the same fashion that their ancestors had, although with the advantage of new and improved weapons such as the metallic cartridge and breech-loading rifles which they acquired from the white traders. They hunted, fished, loafed, and quarreled, and refused to worry about the menace of white aggression, which to them no longer existed since it had ceased to be an immediate threat. However, they had not relaxed in the slightest their determination not to allow the construction of military posts or roads in what they regarded as their particular territory.

But in the region south of the Platte, the story was different. Not only was the white man rapidly overrunning the land with the construction of roads and stage routes, but he was also beginning that senseless slaughter of the buffalo for their hides alone which constitutes one of the most disgraceful blots in American history, a proceeding in which he was ably assisted by the Indians themselves. For despite the maudlin sentimentality that has been wasted on the subject, the Indian did kill buffalo in enormous numbers and sell their skins to the white traders. They, as well as the white man, killed for commercial purposes as well as for food. But regardless of who did the actual killing, the buffalo were being rapidly

[41] *Ibid.*, 102–103.

eliminated from the Southern Plains, and since this animal represented life itself to the Indian, he could not view the disappearance of the herds with anything except foreboding. As a result, he attempted to strike back; and it was only natural that he should seek a redress of grievances by the only method that he understood, a direct appeal to arms.[42]

It was this resentment of the Indians plus the excitement-seeking troopers that led to a series of attacks, recriminations, and misunderstandings in which stage and freight service across the plains was almost completely disrupted and which culminated in the famous (or infamous, depending upon the point of view) Sand Creek or Chivington Massacre of November 19, 1864. Even today it is impossible to assess the blame for this occurrence. Colonel Chivington, who can be, and has been, viewed as a frontiersman of the worst stripe, or as a sincere patriot striking a blow to free the frontier from the menace of the red man, was the commander of a regiment of Colorado volunteer cavalry. On the day in question he led an attack on a village of from eighty to one hundred lodges of Cheyennes and Arapahoes under the leadership of Black Kettle.[43] This camp was located on Sand Creek, not far from Fort Lyon, and it had been assigned as a reservation to the Cheyennes and Arapahoes. There is still widespread uncertainty about the justification for the attack, inasmuch as the Indians had camped on that spot with the specific permission of Major Anthony, commanding Fort Lyon, and Black Kettle had run up a large American flag with a white flag underneath to show that the village was friendly. But many of the warriors in the village were fresh from the warpath, and the troops later asserted that they found the fresh scalps of white women and children in some of the lodges. Whether it was a justifiable attack on a hostile village that was masquerading as peaceful in order to escape punishment, or the wanton massacre of peaceful tribesmen,

[42] Rister, *Southern Plainsmen*, 7–11; Branch, *The Hunting of the Buffalo*, 67–125. "A great deal of nonsense has been written concerning the care wild Indians took never to waste a particle of the buffalo they killed. This was the version set forth by the reservation Indians after the last buffalo herds had been destroyed by the white hunters." Hyde, *Red Cloud's Folk*, 62.

[43] There were apparently eight lodges of Arapaho under Left Hand in addition to Black Kettle's band of Cheyennes. Myra E. Hull (ed.), "Soldiering on the High Plains; The Diary of Lewis Bryam Hull, 1864–1866," *Kansas Historical Society Quarterly*, Vol. VIII, No. 1 (February, 1938), 29.

probably never will be known. Chivington took no prisoners, and his report stated that from five to six hundred Indians were left dead on the grounds. There were many who escaped, however, including Black Kettle.[44]

But while Chivington's deed met with almost universal approbation on the frontier, it was greeted with almost the same proportion of condemnation in the East. The Commissioner of Indian Affairs described it as a brutal and barbarous massacre, and most Easterners regarded it with horror. And what was most important, the Indians were not long in learning of the Commissioner's reaction[45] which agreed with theirs, although it is doubtful if their subsequent actions were in any way affected by the fact that a very substantial portion of the American public sympathized with them.

If Colonel Chivington had deliberately attempted to stir up Indian hostility, he could have followed no better course than he did. During the winter a war pipe was sent around and was accepted by most of the tribes north as well as south. The result was that long before spring the whole western frontier was ablaze, and one of the greatest mass uprisings in American history was under way. The entire Platte route was practically in a state of siege, and for one period of six weeks no mails passed either east or west. By June every tribe from the Canadian border to the Red River in Arkansas was on the warpath. And a Congressional Committee of Inquiry headed by Senator Doolittle of Wisconsin attributed the trouble entirely to the Chivington affair.

It was this "massacre" which also brought the southern tribes to the conclusion that they could not hope to remain where they were and escape white domination. They decided on migration, but before leaving, they gave the white settlers an unwelcome "surprise party" as a small token of their power and ferocity. On the seventh of January they looted the town of Julesburg on the South Platte and threatened Fort Rankin a mile west of the town. The supply depot at Julesburg was thoroughly and efficiently ransacked, and the troops at the fort were so effectively intimidated that they were afraid to leave the protection of its walls. The Indians remained in the vicinity for over three weeks, apparently in the for-

[44] Hyde, *Red Cloud's Folk*, 109; Grinnell, *The Fighting Cheyennes*, 159–69.
[45] Grinnell, *The Fighting Cheyennes*, 170–71.

lorn hope that someone might decide to come out and give them battle, but in this expectation they were disappointed. They then started north, leaving a trail of havoc and consternation through the valley. They moved over familiar and well-established trails, crossing the rivers at the usual places and generally acting as though engaged in the most peaceful and law-abiding of pursuits.

Their march to the North Platte was almost without interruption or interference. For some mysterious reason the cavalry regiments sent in pursuit were unable to locate them despite the fact that the Indian camp extended for four miles along the Platte, that their war and signal drums could be heard for long distances, and that hunting parties which had become lost were able to locate the camp by the reflection of its fires against the sky. The ignorance and incapacity displayed by the military at this time is so great as almost to rule out all other explanations except that of cowardice. The officers seem to have concluded that if "he who fights and runs away, will live to fight another day" is true, then he who avoids battle altogether has a still greater chance of survival. Although there were a few brushes, such as the pitched battle at Platte Bridge in which the Indians defeated the soldiers, there were almost no engagements on a large scale and nothing at all that was conclusive. The hostiles moved north and northwest across what is now eastern Nebraska and western South Dakota to the Black Hills, then around their northern fringe and westward to the Powder River.[46] Encumbered as they were with women, children, and other noncombatants, vast herds of captured horses, mules, and cattle, as well as other booty, their march of over four hundred miles during severe winter weather and over some of the most difficult and desperate terrain in the entire United States must take rank as one of the greatest exploits of western history, comparable only to the more famous retreat of Chief Joseph and his Nez Percés over the Lo Lo Trail.

In the meantime the northern tribes, though restive, were peaceful. In July, 1864, Brigadier General Alfred Sully, still in pursuit of the perpetrators of the Minnesota massacres of two years before,

[46] Hyde, *Red Cloud's Folk*, 110–13; Grinnell's *The Fighting Cheyennes* has a good map of the northward march of the allied Indian tribes opposite page 176. These raids are also described in a very interesting article by Leroy W. Hagerty, "Indian Raids Along the Platte and Little Blue Rivers, 1864–1865," *Nebraska State Historical Quarterly*, Vol. XXVIII, No. 3 (1947), 176.

fought a running and somewhat indecisive battle with the Sioux that lasted for the better part of three days. This engagement, known as the Battle of Kildeer Mountain, was fought in the badlands of the Little Missouri River by one of the most powerful and best-equipped expeditions ever sent against the Indians. Sully had four thousand cavalrymen besides eight hundred foot soldiers, as well as several pieces of artillery and nearly three thousand wagons. So well prepared was he that it is said to have required the services of fifteen river steamers merely to carry his supplies. That he was unable to win a decisive victory is adequate testimony to the difficulty that confronted army commanders operating against the western tribes.[47]

But generally the northern Indians were guilty of few depredations. The news of the "massacre" at Sand Creek had produced considerable excitement for a time, but generally the chiefs succeeded in controlling their young men, and there were few attempts at retaliation. On the other hand, Colonel W. O. Collins, the commandant at Fort Laramie, had been able to keep his troops well in hand, and there would probably have been no serious trouble except for influences from the outside.[48] Winter set in before the tribes became too restless; and unless the provocation was especially great, few Indians ever cared to take the warpath during cold weather. But in March of 1865, the arrival of the southern hostiles with their vast herds of captured animals and other plunder, and, above all, their tales of looting and conquest during the raids on the stations along the Oregon Trail, made war in the spring almost a certainty.

On their side the whites were becoming surfeited with Indian depredations and were convinced that something had to be done to bring them to an end. Some of the stage and freighting companies which followed the Platte route had been hard hit, and since they were not without political influence they were able to make their complaints heard. Now that the Civil War had come to an end, they argued that there were plenty of soldiers to put the Plains Indians in their place and keep them there. Accordingly, a great military expedition was planned against the hostiles.[49] It called for

[47] These difficulties are well described in Hyde, *Red Cloud's Folk*, 115–22.
[48] *Ibid.*, 115.
[49] *Ibid.*, 117–18.

several columns of troops, moving from different directions, to converge on the Powder River region. In addition, two forts were to be built and garrisoned as bases of operations, one to be located on the Yellowstone River, the other on the upper Powder. Had this ambitious project been carried out as planned, it could scarcely have resulted otherwise than in the permanent subjection and control of the Indian tribes.

But like so many other well-laid plans of mice and men, it was not carried out as planned. Although the expression had not then been coined, it was a case of too little, if not too late, and although costing the people of the United States upwards of forty million dollars and widely advertised as a great success, the Powder River expedition of 1865 was really one of the greatest fiascoes of American military history.[50] The idea was for three columns of troops to converge on the Indian country. All were to be under the command of General Patrick Edward Connor, a redheaded and hotheaded Irishman with "blood in his eye," whose reputation as a fighter dated back to the Mexican War. He had been given command of the District of the Plains, a division of the western command that had been created especially for him in March of that year, and had signalized his advent to power by issuing a general order to his troops: "You will not receive overtures of peace and submission from the Indians but will attack and kill every male Indian over twelve years of age."[51]

The plan of campaign was for one column under the command of General Sully to march westward from the Missouri toward the Powder River, another to march from the Black Hills toward the Powder, while the third under the command of General Connor himself was to move northward from the Platte toward the headwaters of the Tongue. The three columns were to rendezvous on the Yellowstone River at or near its confluence with the Tongue.[52] In essentials this was the same plan that was to be used eleven years later when the Seventh Cavalry rode to death and immortality; and the purpose was the same: somewhere in that great unmapped region the hostile Indians were to be trapped—and destroyed.

[50] *Ibid.*, 133.
[51] Vestal, *Jim Bridger*, 221.
[52] *Ibid.*, 220.

But at the last moment, owing to the officious interference of Major General E. R. Curtis, Sully's column was diverted on a wild-goose chase into the region north of the Missouri River, where for two months the troops marched and countermarched without as much as seeing a hostile Indian.[53] On the thirtieth of July, General Connor, according to plan, marched northward from Fort Laramie with a force of about nine hundred men and a considerable number of Pawnee, Winnebago, and Omaha Indian scouts. There were also a number of other scouts headed by "Jim" Bridger and including the latter's famous protégé, Minton "Mitch" Bouyer.[54]

This expedition reached the Powder River on the eleventh of August, and there, at the junction of the Dry Fork and the Powder, on the broad level bench on the west bank and between the river and the bluffs,[55] twenty-four miles above the mouth of Crazy Woman's Fork[56] and one hundred and sixty-nine miles northwest of Fort Laramie, they began the construction of a fort, temporarily named Fort Connor. Using this as a base of supplies, the expedition marched across the foothills of the Big Horn Mountains and deeper into the Indian country. During this march the battalion of Pawnee scouts, on the seventeenth of August, pursued and apparently wiped out a Cheyenne war party of twenty-five with the loss of only four horses. That the enemy force was completely annihilated is indicated by the fact that the Cheyennes have no record of the encounter.[57] On the morning of August 29, the com-

[53] Hyde, *Red Cloud's Folk*, 135. It has been claimed that General Sully remained at Fort Rice because he knew that he did not have the strength to punish the Sioux and that his marches and battles had served no other purpose than to antagonize the Indians. Stanley Vestal, *Warpath and Council Fire: The Plains Indians' Struggle for Survival in War and in Diplomacy*, 82.

[54] J. Cecil Alter, *James Bridger, Trapper, Frontiersman, Scout, and Guide; An Historical Narrative*, 410. Vestal, *Jim Bridger*, 221. Robert B. David, *Finn Burnett, Frontiersman: The Life and Adventures of an Indian Fighter*, 62, makes no mention of Bouyer as one of the scouts. Neither officers nor men took the expedition too seriously, often riding off to hunt buffalo, getting lost and "setting the prairie afire so that every Indian within sixty miles knew they were coming." Vestal, *Warpath and Council Fire*, 84.

[55] Vestal, *Jim Bridger*, 223; Grinnell, *The Fighting Cheyennes*, 196.

[56] David, *Finn Burnett*, 72. The Crazy Woman Fork of the Powder River was so named because of the fact that some fifteen years before a poor demented Indian woman lived in a wickiup near the bank, and finally died there. Alter, *James Bridger*, 413.

[57] George Bird Grinnell, *The Two Great Scouts and Their Pawnee Battailon*, 90–94; Vestal, *Jim Bridger*, 225–26; Grinnell, *The Fighting Cheyennes*, 197–98. How-

mand attacked an Arapaho village of about fifteen hundred persons, said to have been that of Black Bear and Old David, who up until that time had apparently not been hostile to the whites. Although the troops were outnumbered, the element of surprise was in their favor and in a hand-to-hand fight that is reminiscent of Sand Creek, they succeeded in destroying the village of 250 lodges, with all of its winter supplies, killing sixty-three warriors, putting the rest to flight, and capturing the pony herd, all at a cost of six troopers killed. The troops, because of a shortage of ammunition, were unable to follow up their victory, and moved down the Tongue toward the projected meeting with Cole and Walker, set for the first day of September on the north side of the Wolf Mountains, but could find no trace of either.[58]

In the meantime the Black Hills column, consisting of some two thousand soldiers with forty-six mule wagons and a pack train, under the command of Colonels Nelson Cole and Samuel Walker, had marched westward toward the Powder. It was this detachment that encountered the larger share of the trouble, and much of it was of their own making.

Neither Cole nor Walker had had any experience in fighting Indians. Cole's men were all from the eastern states and were sick and tired of Indian campaigning long before they had ever seen a hostile, and according to their commander's own admission they never fought unless they had to. Men of both commands had mutinied before the expedition started, arguing that they had enlisted to fight in the Civil War, and now that that war was over they should be discharged and sent home rather than be forced to participate in an Indian campaign. In the case of Walker's men, it had been necessary to bring cannon to bear on them before they could be brought to terms. But the chief drawback was the fact that the column was poorly supplied with guides and had no officers who

---

ever, David, *Finn Burnett*, says this party was Sioux and that it consisted of forty-two braves and two Indian women, all of whom were killed. The scouts found much equipment and several fresh scalps, possibly from an emigrant train, 75.

[58] Grinnell, *Two Great Scouts*, 105–12; Alter, *James Bridger*, 416–21; Vestal, *Jim Bridger*, 229–36; Vestal, *Warpath and Council Fire*, 85; David, *Finn Burnett*, 83–89. Hyde says that this attack was on the Arapaho camp of Medicine Man and that there is no evidence that his people had been with the hostiles. *Red Cloud's Folk*, 128.

were familiar with campaigning on the plains. Connor had taken all, or nearly all, of the scouts, leaving Cole and Walker to get along with maps, which were both inaccurate and inadequate.[59] All in all, a more poorly prepared or planned expedition can hardly be imagined.

It was a case of the blind leading the blind; the reconnaissance of the troops was so poor that they actually passed between a large camp of the hostiles—some fifteen hundred to two thousand lodges—on the Powder River, and the Uncpapa camp of Sitting Bull and Black Moon[60]—which was even larger—on the Little Missouri without being aware of the existence of either camp, and without seeing a hostile Indian. But the reconnaissance of the Sioux was little better, for they failed to discover that the soldiers were in the country until several days later. The Sioux were holding many ceremonies and social dances in their camps, which partially explains their lack of vigilance. Their failure does, however, set at rest the old theory that the Indians were always vigilant and kept a guard against surprise at all times. On the contrary, the Indians were often taken by surprise as the result of their own carelessness, and on many occasions their first suspicion of the proximity of the soldiers was when the troops came charging into their camp.[61] But if the Indians had a partial excuse, the soldiers had none, for they were supposed to be actively hunting for the eighteen thousand Indians who were in these two camps and who, moreover, were to be taken by surprise.

The toiling and bedeviled column finally reached the lower Powder, and then proceeded to get lost in the Bad Lands, where the horses almost starved since there was little or no grass. Here, to add to their other troubles, the soldiers were finally discovered and attacked by the Sioux. After losing both men and horses to the enemy, the expedition began to move up the Powder, the main idea being to get out of the country as quickly as possible. Colonel Cole is said to have concluded from the great number of Indians

[59] Vestal, *Jim Bridger*, 221; DeLand, *The Sioux Wars*, 48; Hyde, *Red Cloud's Folk*, 130. Connor's orders to Colonel Walker may be found in *War of the Rebellion, Official Records of the Union and Confederate Armies*, Vol. CII, 1045–49.

[60] Black Moon literally was Black Sun and referred to a total eclipse of the sun. The name came from the phenomenon once seen by a war party as it was setting out on a foray. The war party turned back. Grinnell, *The Fighting Cheyennes*, 278.

[61] Hyde, *Red Cloud's Folk*, 131.

attacking his force that General Connor's command had been wiped out, and to have decided to retreat toward Fort Laramie.[62] At the mouth of the Little Powder they blundered into an Indian village of from fifteen hundred to two thousand warriors, including both Sioux and Cheyennes. Here again both sides had poor reconnaissance, for neither soldiers nor Indians seem to have had the slightest suspicion that the other was anywhere in the vicinity, and it is difficult to say which was the more surprised. The Indians, possibly because they were in familiar surroundings, recovered first, and a battle ensued in which both sides suffered significant loss.[63]

The expedition continued its march up the Powder, and after a series of desperate adventures, in the course of which they were reduced to slaughtering the pack mules for food, finally established contact with General Connor on the nineteenth of September. When found, they had been out of rations for nearly two weeks and the men resembled tramps more than soldiers, being ragged and half-starved as well as disgusted and discouraged.[64]

This ended the fiasco of 1865, and although General Dodge tried to maintain that the expedition had been a glorious success and had pictured the ragged, footsore, and frostbitten column as driving the enemy triumphantly before it,[65] it is doubtful that very many people were deceived by his extravagant claims. The blunders, and there had been many of them, were caused mostly by the lack of exact information concerning the geography of the country north of the Platte and by the difficulty of campaigning over this unknown terrain without competent guides.

For the Indians it had been a glorious summer. They had taken many scalps and counted "coup" many times, the young men had possessed themselves of many fine carbines taken from the soldiers, the pony herds had been augmented by many fine cavalry mounts and government mules, and quantities of food and miscellaneous supplies had fallen into the hands of the tribes.[66] It had been a sum-

[62] Alter, *James Bridger*, 423.

[63] Hyde, *Red Cloud's Folk*, 132.

[64] Alter, *James Bridger*, 423–24. See also Myra E. Hull (ed.), "Soldiering on the High Plains; The Diary of Lewis Bryam Hull, 1864–1866," *Kansas Historical Society Quarterly*, Vol. VIII, No. 1 (February, 1938), 29.

[65] Hyde, *Red Cloud's Folk*, 133.

[66] *Ibid.*, 133.

mer long to be remembered, and the Sioux can hardly be blamed for hoping that the pony soldiers would come back again and soon.[67]

[67] For the Indian version of the Powder River expedition, see Grinnell, *The Fighting Cheyennes,* 195–206.

CHAPTER II

The Peace Policy

THE INDIAN POLICY of the United States in these years vacillated between beating the Indians to death and loving them into submission. Beating had been tried and had accomplished nothing; if anything, the Indians were more powerful and arrogant than they had ever been before; resort was now to be had to the opposite extreme. This was the period which American historians know as that of Reconstruction, when the long-haired men and the short-haired women, the crackpots and the lunatics, the zealots and the self-seekers, along with many honest and sincere persons, were attempting to remodel the United States and human nature along the lines of what they imagined to be a Utopia. From plans to introduce the black man to a more abundant life, it was an easy step to include his red brother, and the advocates of Negro equality found little difficulty in accepting the conclusion that the "noble savage" was destined to better things than he had heretofore experienced. But it goes almost without saying that few, if any, of the people who held this point of view had ever lived on the frontier or in close proximity to wild Indians.

The advocates of peaceful persuasion were now allowed to see what they could do, and even while the footsore and hungry soldiers of the Cole and Walker command were making their tragic way through the Bad Lands, commissioners were dispatched to meet the Indians in council. By a mixture of cajolery, bribery, and downright misrepresentation they succeeded in getting a treaty, which gave the government the right to construct roads and establish military posts in the Indian country. But—and it was a large but—it should be noted that not a single chief from any one of the hostile bands, numbering over four thousand lodges, "took the stick" or "touched the pen" to the treaty, a fact of which the commissioners were not unaware. And the hostiles were hostile precisely because they were determined that military roads and posts were not to be constructed in the Indian country. The treaty, despite the enormous cost of the presents that had been freely distributed in order to get it signed, was absolutely worthless. But the commissioners persisted in their absurd attempt to delude the public as well as themselves into believing that the Indian troubles on the Great Plains were at an end, and that hereinafter peace and harmony would prevail over the region, world without end. This, despite the fact that at the very moment Sitting Bull with two thousand lodges and another village of about equal size were located in the region south of the Yellowstone River, their occupants refusing to have anything to do with the white man or his treaties.[1]

Various attempts were made to lure the recalcitrants in to sign the treaty, but they all failed; finally, in the spring of 1866 the peace party sent Mr. E. B. Taylor of the Indian Office to Fort Laramie in a final attempt to pacify the hostiles, and in June some of those tribes, led by Red Cloud and Man-Afraid-of-His-Horses, came in to see what the white man had to offer and to accept the presents, especially the guns and ammunition, which rumor said had been provided. But when it came to signing the treaty, the Indians procrastinated and delayed, but only a few of the old-timers, like Jim Bridger, detected the element of ill faith and distrust among the Indians. They scented a familiar Indian trick, the willingness of the real chiefs such as Sitting Bull to allow their lesser chiefs to play at the game of talking peace while the others prepared for eventualities. Bridger and the others like him were not willing to accuse the Sioux of duplicity, nor were they willing to accept his professions of peace; they would simply wait and see.[2] Finally the Indians insisted upon having the treaty read and explained to them, item by item. When the clause giving the government the right to build forts and roads in the Indian country was read, the chiefs refused to agree to it. Thereupon Mr. Taylor had to resort to trickery and explained—which was untrue—that the treaty did not contemplate the construction of any new roads, but merely referred

[1] Hyde, *Red Cloud's Folk*, 134–37.

[2] Alter, *James Bridger*, 426.

to the one road, the Bozeman Trail or Powder River Road which already existed—in theory if not in actuality.[3]

The Bozeman Road,[4] or Trail—it can be called either or both—had been provided for by an act of Congress dated March 3, 1865,[5] and was named for John M. Bozeman, who had first "blazed" or explored it. This road was the answer to the demand for a more direct route to the Montana mines. Gold had been discovered there in 1860, and as usual, prospectors and adventurers stampeded into the district. It was virgin territory, and as a result practically all of the necessities of life had to be shipped in. The two existing routes, the first along the Oregon Trail to Fort Hall and then north and east to Virginia City, and the second which followed the old Lewis and Clark Trail along the Missouri River, were alike uneconomical, from the standpoint of both time and mileage. The Bozeman Road left the Oregon Trail about 135 miles west of Fort Laramie and proceeded north and west along the eastern side of the Big Horn Mountains, crossing the headwaters of the Powder River above Pumpkin Buttes, then across Crazy Woman Fork and the Tongue River to the Big Horn River, and then west across many streams and creeks to the Yellowstone River, which was crossed on a ferry only a few miles from Bozeman Pass. Then the road followed through the pass to Bozeman City, up the Madison River for a short distance, and then west to Virginia City. It was a much shorter route than either of the others, but practically all of it lay in the land of the Sioux, and it was this road which the Indians were determined that the whites should not be allowed to use, and which the United States had promised would be kept open. Mr. Taylor was on the horns of a dilemma, and it is interesting to speculate just how he would have extricated himself from his predicament had not outside events over which he had no control performed that service for him.

Early in that same spring of 1866 it had been decided to send

[3] Hyde, *Red Cloud's Folk*, 139.

[4] This account is based largely on Grace R. Hebard and E. A. Brininstool, *The Bozeman Trail: Historical Accounts of the Blazing of the Overland Routes into the Northwest, and the Fights with Red Cloud's Warriors*. See also Stanley Vestal, *Jim Bridger*, and Cecil Alter, *James Bridger*.

[5] DeLand, *The Sioux Wars*, 43. There is an interesting account of a trip over the Bozeman Trail in Benjamin Ryan, "The Bozeman Trail to Virginia City, Montana, in 1864, A Diary," in the *Annals of Wyoming*, July, 1947. He says that the Bozeman cut-off was about 135 miles west of Fort Laramie.

troops into the Powder River country and to construct a series of forts which would bring protection to travelers using the Bozeman route. Whether Mr. Taylor knew of this or not is uncertain, but he probably did; for at the same time that he was holding high powwow with the tribesmen, a large force of infantry under the command of Colonel Henry B. Carrington had been moving slowly up the Platte. Carrington, who was a high-minded, idealistic officer totally without experience in Indian fighting and who had not served in the field during the Civil War, had a force of some seven hundred men of the Twenty-seventh Infantry, of whom considerably more than half were raw recruits. He also had 226 mule teams, besides ambulances, horsemen, and a band of 25 pieces. While the infantry soldiers were equipped with the old-fashioned muzzle-loaders, the carbines of the bandsmen were of the very latest model. In the Colonel's charge were 260 noncombatants, including officers' ladies, children, and Negro servants who had come along on the assurance of General Sherman himself that the expedition would be a peaceful junket. Carrington's instructions, however, belied these circumstances, for he was ordered to open a wagon road around the Big Horn Mountains to the Montana mines but, "if possible," to avoid war with the Sioux.[6]

On the evening of June 16 these troops were camped a few miles below Fort Laramie when a friendly Sioux chief dropped in for a "visit," and was told by the commander, who had never made any secret of his destination or purpose, the reason for the presence of the soldiers.[7] It did not take long for the news to reach the Indian camps, and it effectively broke up the council, the chiefs accusing Taylor of treachery and double-dealing, a charge which unfortunately was true, although there is, of course, the scant possibility that it was unintentional on the Commissioner's part. Whether with Mr. Taylor's knowledge or not, Colonel Carrington was introduced to the Indians as the "White Chief" who intended to occupy the Powder River country, and its effect upon the Sioux may well be imagined. Although a few of the older chiefs seem to have favored capitulation, Red Cloud is said to have drawn his blanket more closely around him and refused to acknowledge the introduc-

[6] Vestal, *Jim Bridger*, 246–47; Grinnell, *The Fighting Cheyennes*, 222.
[7] Hyde, *Red Cloud's Folk*, 139.

tion, while Standing Elk, one of the Brulé chiefs, bluntly told the Colonel that the region he proposed to occupy was Sioux country and that the Indians would not give him the road unless he whipped them.[8] The tribesmen then departed in high dudgeon, pausing only long enough to send back a message emphasizing their determination to keep all white men out of their territory. Taylor's lack of sincerity—indeed of elementary honesty—is shown by the fact that he misrepresented the situation to his superiors in Washington and declared that all had gone well, even going so far as to say that most of the hostile chiefs had signed the treaty and that Red Cloud, who admittedly had not, was only the leader of a small band and largely without influence. Nothing could have been further from the truth, and Taylor knew it when he wrote his report.[9]

The government was now fully committed to an Indian policy in which it attempted to carry water on both shoulders. No white man could enter the Powder River country except at the risk of his scalp, and also perhaps of precipitating an Indian war. Yet at the same time the citizenry were being assured that travel through the Indian country was perfectly safe, while the frontiersmen were told that this road which traversed the favorite hunting grounds of the Sioux must and would be kept open. Just how this highly contradictory situation was to be resolved no one seemed to know, but that many persons accepted the statements of the government at face value is shown by the fact that several parties of emigrants, assured that travel along the trail was perfectly safe, insisted upon traveling through the Indian country without either guns or ammunition. In fact, one contract train with supplies had thirty-one wagons and only five firearms in the entire party.[10]

Carrington had wanted to wait until the conclusion of the treaty but had been ordered to go ahead immediately. He left Fort Laramie on the seventeenth of June with a force of about seven hundred men, although he had only one thousand rounds of ammunition for his infantry rifles, despite the fact that he had requisitioned

[8] Vestal, *Jim Bridger*, 248. McLaughlin says that Spotted Tail, who was more inclined to treat diplomatically with the whites than to resort to the warpath, promoted this treaty opening the Bozeman Trail even after practically all his people had deserted him to follow the fortunes of Red Cloud. *My Friend, the Indian*, 70.

[9] Hyde, *Red Cloud's Folk*, 139–40.

[10] DeLand, *The Sioux Wars*, 68.

one hundred times that amount.[11] The command reached Fort Connor on the twenty-eighth. This post, which had been built as a temporary supply base for the Powder River expedition, was located on the left bank of the Powder at the confluence with Dry Creek and about twenty-four miles above the mouth of Crazy Woman Creek.[12] It was not far from the present town of Sussex in Johnson County, Wyoming.[13] The site has been described as an unusually fine one, the only serious drawback being an almost total absence of good hay land. Crude buildings stood on the mesa which rose more than one hundred feet above the river and extended to a line of white bluffs over five miles to the west.

Colonel Carrington garrisoned this post for a short time only and then began the construction of a new fort near a spring of sweet water about a mile farther up the river. It consisted of a log stockade with blockhouses and bastions and was so designed that the fire of its defenders could sweep the surrounding plain. It was first named Fort Carrington but was later changed to Fort Reno, in honor of General Jesse Lee Reno, who had lost his life at South Mountain, Maryland, in 1862. But while the location was a good one from a military point of view, the country roundabout was bleak, with no redeeming characteristics, and it must have been anything except a desirable place in which to be stationed.[14] Here 160 men of the small force were left as a garrison while the remainder marched northward to a site about midway between the present towns of Buffalo and Sheridan, Wyoming.

Here they began the construction of the second of the Bozeman forts which was named Fort Phil Kearny. The place selected was only about forty miles in a direct line north of Fort Reno, but the distance that had to be traversed between the two points was sixty-seven miles of hostile territory. The site of the new fort, which was selected personally by Colonel Carrington over the adverse recommendation of Bridger, who pointed out the superiority of a site on either Goose Creek or the Tongue River,[15] was between

[11] Vestal, *Jim Bridger*, 248–50.

[12] DeLand, *The Sioux Wars*, 68.

[13] *Ibid.*, 64.

[14] Cynthia J. Capron, "The Indian Border War of 1876," *Illinois State Historical Society Journal*, Vol. XIII (January, 1921), 481. She says that in addition to the other drawbacks the water was alkali.

[15] Vestal, *Jim Bridger*, 253.

the two forks of Piney Creek but nearer to the Little Piney—so close, in fact, that the stream was diverted and the waters brought within the stockade. It had a natural defense, being built on a plateau which sloped away from the fort in all directions, and had abundant grass, water, and timber. When completed, the fort consisted of an enclosed area six hundred by eight hundred feet, surrounded by matched palisades of logs some sixteen feet in length sunk six feet into the ground. It was intended to be a permanent establishment and was provided with cavalry stables, warehouses, and barracks—in fact, all of the appurtenances of a first-class frontier post.

While the troops were engaged in its construction, they were visited by a delegation of Cheyenne chiefs, led by Black Horse and including, among others, Dull Knife, Two Moon, and Red Arm,[16] who rode into the camp and begged the Colonel to take his troops back to Fort Reno and not make any further attempts to enter the Powder River country, for the Sioux would surely fight and would probably force the Cheyennes to join them. These chiefs, who seem to have been trying to preserve a precarious neutrality between the white soldiers and the Sioux and were undecided about what course of action to pursue, also reported that the Sioux were holding a sun dance and making active preparations for a fight. Colonel Carrington made no promises, but he tried to pacify the chiefs and seems to have fairly well convinced them that no serious interference with the Indian way of life was contemplated.[17] After leaving the fort, the Cheyennes went to a near-by trading post, where they were later set upon by a war party of Sioux who accused them of traitorous conduct and struck the chiefs repeatedly across the head and face with their unstrung bows, at the same time crying "Coup" as when counting coup on the body of an enemy. This was the most calculated insult that they could devise, but the Cheyennes were not strong enough to fight the Sioux and so had to endure the taunts and insults in silence and without any attempt at retaliation.[18]

[16] Alter, *James Bridger*, 447; Vestal, *Jim Bridger*, 254.

[17] DeLand, *The Sioux Wars*, 67.

[18] Hyde, *Red Cloud's Folk*, 142–43; DeCost Smith, *Indian Experiences*, 161. "Mr. Frank Zahn, the Upper Missouri interpreter, states that the Sioux in punishing a member of their own tribe used the same expressions as when counting *coup* upon the body of an enemy. . . . I have been unable to find any old warrior who had heard the Sioux yell 'Coo' or 'coup' on such an occasion." Vestal, *Jim Bridger*, 320.

A further evidence of the determination of the Sioux to keep the whites out of the country is the fact that several soldiers who had deserted from the post with the expectation of making their way to the Montana mines were met by the Indians and forced to return to the fort. They were not harmed in any way, but were compelled to carry back a message ordering Colonel Carrington to abandon the post and take his soldiers out of the country.[19]

The War Department was equally insistent in its determination to protect travelers over the Bozeman Road, and, with Bridger as guide, two companies of the Eighteenth Infantry under command of Lieutenant Colonel N. C. Kinney were sent to the Big Horn River, where, on August 12, on a site ninety-one miles from Fort Phil Kearny, they began the construction of Fort C. F. Smith, named in honor of General Charles Ferguson Smith, who had won distinction in the Mexican War.[20] It was built on a bluff, or tableland, five hundred yards east of the river and a mile above the great canyon that extends westward one hundred miles to the Shoshone River. Here the Big Horn flows a little north of due east, and the fort was built between the two tributaries, Spring Gulch and Warrior, or Battle, Creek. The attractive site, which had an elevation of thirty-seven hundred feet, overlooked a broad, fertile plain. So well situated was this fort that if the guard were on duty, no one, neither friend nor foe, could approach within a mile without being seen.[21]

Although Fort Smith suffered less from the depredations of the hostiles than did either Reno or Phil Kearny, owing to the fact that it was built at the extreme western edge of the hunting grounds claimed by the Sioux and that many of the Indians in the vicinity were friendly Crows, the garrison had at best a precarious existence, living most of the time in a state of siege. A man going from the stockade to the river took his life in his hands, and although the stream was full of fish and the country abounded in game, fishing and hunting were indulged in only at the risk of sudden and merciless Indian attack. During the winter the garrison lived for the most

[19] Alter, *James Bridger*, 442.

[20] DeLand, *The Sioux Wars*, 69.

[21] Granville Stuart, *Forty Years on the Frontier*, Paul C. Phillips (ed.), II, 119. See also DeLand, *The Sioux Wars*, 178–80 and David, *Finn Burnett*, 161.

part on corn since no supply trains came through, and thousands of Indians had established winter quarters on the Big Horn.[22]

The Eighteenth Infantry, which garrisoned the post, was there, according to one story, as the result of the irascibility of Secretary of War Stanton, who became exasperated when the regiment's commander repeatedly requested a transfer from Louisville, Kentucky, preferably to a more eastern post. Upon receiving one of Colonel Thompson's frequent requests, Stanton is said to have asked a clerk: "Where, next to hell, is the worst place to send a regiment?"

"To the Powder River country," was the reply.

"Then order the Eighteenth Infantry there at once."[23]

Fort Phil Kearny was under almost incessant Indian attack, and, as at Fort Smith, to leave the walls even for a short distance was to risk death, and so successful were the Indian attacks that the military cemetery is said to have been the most rapidly growing feature of the new post.[24] In August, Colonel Carrington made another attempt to negotiate a peace, but his efforts had no tangible results, the reply of the Indians always being the same, that the troops must get out of the country before the attacks would cease. In the late autumn the depredations eased off somewhat while the Indians were absent on the annual fall buffalo hunt, but as soon as that was out of the way, the raids were resumed with full vigor. Colonel Carrington did not have a force adequate for the many duties that it was expected to perform, most important of which were guarding and policing the route from Fort Laramie to the Montana mines, but his reports to that effect and his requests for reinforcements were only met with the suggestion that Fort Smith be abandoned. This was preposterous and idiotic, but it is a good example of the official military mind which was to be found in Washington. To have abandoned the fort on the Big Horn would have brought travelers and emigrants to Fort Phil Kearny, in the heart of the Indian country, and left them there to continue the

22 Martin F. Schmitt (ed.), *General George Crook, His Autobiography*, 192 n., (hereinafter cited as Crook, *Autobiography*); John G. Bourke, *On the Border with Crook*, 249.

23 DeLand, *The Sioux Wars*, 181–82.

24 *Ibid.*, 181; Alter, *James Bridger*, 450. During a period of six months the Indians had made more than fifty hostile demonstrations, more than 150 white men had been killed in the vicinity of the fort, and several hundred head of stock had been run off.

remainder, and most dangerous part, of their journey without protection.[25]

The Indians at this time were camped along the middle reaches of the Tongue River, their villages being strung intermittently along a good twenty miles of that stream.[26] When two of Carrington's officers conceived the crack-brained plan of taking fifty mounted men and fifty citizens and "surprising" their camps, the Colonel merely showed them his morning report, which revealed that he had less than fifty serviceable horses at the post since General Hazen, who had recently been there on an official visit of inspection, had taken twenty-six horses and an equal number of men with him as an escort. This proposed scheme afforded the veteran Jim Bridger a great deal of amusement; he admitted that by an unlikely miracle the troops might surprise the Indians at the upper end of the camps, but he was confident that after that it was the Sioux who would do the surprising.[27]

Carrington continued to maintain his precarious position between the hostility of the Sioux in front of him and the indifference of the government at home. Then on the twenty-first of December came the famous Fetterman Massacre. This attack by the Indians seems to have been planned well in advance and to have succeeded only after two previous attempts had failed. On one of these, made on the sixth of December, when the white signal flags of the Indians indicated a line almost seven miles in length, Chief Red Cloud commanded in person. On this occasion an attack was made on the wood train, but the troops refused to ride into the ambush which the Indians had set for them, although Lieutenant Bingham and Sergeant Bowers were killed in the fight which resulted.[28] On the morning of the twenty-first, Two Moon, "the dark, sawed-off chief with the big mouth," and a party of so-called "friendly" Cheyennes visited the fort ostensibly to beg for supplies, especially ammunition, but actually to spy out its weaknesses preparatory to a mass attack.

[25] Hyde, *Red Cloud's Folk*, 144.

[26] One probably exaggerated account says that the Sioux lodges "stretched in close array for nearly forty miles" and that it took the Crow scout, Half-Yellow-Face, nearly two days to travel the length of the camp. *Contributions to the Historical Society of Montana*, VIII (1917), 223.

[27] Vestal, *Jim Bridger*, 269–73.

[28] Alter, *James Bridger*, 460; Vestal, *Jim Bridger*, 274–76.

However, Bridger, whom the Indians knew as "Big Throat," was at the fort and in the course of a long conversation adroitly showed Two Moon the strong features of the stockade, and succeeded in convincing him that it was impregnable and could be taken only at the sacrifice of hundreds of lives, if at all. After returning to the hostile camp Two Moon apparently brought about an abandonment of the original plan, and it was decided to make an attack on the wood train instead.[29]

This affair, which is said to have been the only occasion upon which the Indian strategy of decoy and ambush was completely successful,[30] was made possible by the fact that the fort's wood-cutting camp had been located in the hills some miles to the west. The train which brought the wood into the fort was frequently attacked, so that it was nothing new when about eleven o'clock on the morning of the twenty-first, the wood train signaled that it was under attack.[31] A detachment, consisting of eighty-one officers and men under the command of Captain William J. Fetterman, was thereupon ordered to its relief. Fetterman, who had arrived at the fort only a few weeks before and was without experience in Indian fighting, was a brave but somewhat truculent officer who had a deep and abiding contempt for the ability of the Indians as warriors. He had often stated his belief that one company of regulars could whip one thousand Indians and that a regiment could clear the plains of all the hostile tribes.[32] He had also been heard to declare that with eighty men he could ride through the entire Sioux Nation. This was the number he had with him when he rode out shortly before noon on the twenty-first of December to relieve the wood train.[33]

Colonel Carrington was well aware of his subordinate's im-

[29] Alter, *James Bridger*, 461; Vestal, *Jim Bridger*, 278–79.

[30] Hyde, *Red Cloud's Folk*, 148. It is, of course, entirely possible that at the Battle of the Little Big Horn River, General Custer led his troops into just such an ambush.

[31] A signal station had been set up on a near-by hill. The signals are given in some detail in Vestal, *Jim Bridger*, 321–22.

[32] *Ibid.*, 279; DeLand, *The Sioux Wars*, 81; Alter, *James Bridger*, 457.

[33] Lewis F. Crawford, *Rekindling Camp Fires; Exploits of Ben Arnold (Connor)*, 242. Fetterman had seventy-eight officers and men, and two civilians, Fisher and Wheatley, who had Henry repeating rifles. Vestal, *Jim Bridger*, 150–51.

petuous disposition and seems to have attempted to give the command to Major Powell, who was apparently a more levelheaded officer, but Fetterman claimed the honor by reason of his seniority. Thereupon Carrington ordered him specifically to relieve the wood train and escort it to the fort, but not to pursue the Indians, and under no circumstances to go beyond Lodgepole Ridge, which is the divide separating the waters that flow into the Powder River from those flowing into the Tongue River. As if peculiarly impressed with some anticipation of rashness on the part of his subordinate, the General repeated the orders, this time in the presence of the detachment, and Bridger also warned Fetterman that the Indians were not to be taunted or tempted.[34] Two other fire-eating officers, Captain Frederick W. Brown, who seems to have joined without orders, and Lieutenant George W. Grummond, were with the party. Possibly at the prompting of Captain Brown, whose orders detaching him from duty at the fort had already been received and who was anxious to engage the Indians in battle before he left, Fetterman, disgruntled as the result of previous trouble with Carrington[35] and confident in his own conceit, allowed his enthusiasm to get the better of his good sense and disobeyed orders. Instead of taking the west road toward the Piney where the wood train was corralled, he headed toward the northwest, and when the Indians retreated along Lodgepole Ridge, he followed and "rode over a beautiful ridge trimmed with Indians in war paint and thence into the dismal valley of death,"[36] leading his command into an ambush from which not one trooper escaped alive. The annihilation of the command took less than an hour, during which the wood train made its way almost unnoticed to the comparative safety of the fort.

[34] Alter, *James Bridger*, 460. "Lieutenant Wands as Acting-Adjutant relayed Carrington's orders to Fetterman. 'Support the woodtrain, relieve it and report to me. Do not engage or pursue the Indians at its expense. Under no circumstances pursue over Lodge Pole Ridge as per map in your possession.' Afterwards Carrington crossed the parade ground and from a sentry platform halted the mounted party and repeated his orders. 'Under no circumstances must you pass Lodge Pole Ridge.'" Vestal, *Jim Bridger*, 280–81. This volume also has an excellent map of the vicinity. *Winners of the West* (October 20, 1924) has a letter written by Louis Zinzer concerning the Fetterman fight which is especially interesting.

[35] David, *Finn Burnett*, 126.

[36] Alter, *James Bridger*, 460; Vestal, *Jim Bridger*, 281–82.

Fetterman and Brown, who had often declared that they never would be taken alive and would save the last bullet for themselves, are believed to have shot each other, although many years later Chief American Horse declared that he had killed Captain Fetterman by stabbing him to death.[37]

A rescue party was sent out from the fort as soon as it became apparent that Fetterman had not only disobeyed orders but had also taken on more than he could handle. Captain Ten Eyck, who commanded the relief detachment, found the bodies of the command but not a living survivor. The battlefield lay between Lodgepole Ridge "where the road to Virginia City followed down a high narrow ridge running a little northwest of north parallel to Peno Creek. . . . Here and there along the road a few large rocks or boulders lay in groups. This narrow ridge fell away steeply from the road on both sides to the bottoms below." Ten Eyck found plenty of Indians—there are said to have been two thousand in the battle,[38] and White Elk, a Cheyenne who was present, believed that there were more Indians here than were in the Custer fight,[39] but as the soldiers showed no inclination to leave the ridge and go after them, the hostiles gradually withdrew. The troopers were then able to recover the bodies of Fetterman's command, although not all of them were brought into the fort until the next day. Most of them had been killed with arrows, knives, spears, and clubs, only six or seven of the bodies showing bullet wounds.[40] Bridger learned afterward from the Crows and Cheyennes that the soldiers fought hard to the end. It had been a great mix-up, and in the excitement the Indians had killed several of their own number. How many Indians were killed no one knew, but the Sioux are said to have told Frank Grouard later that they lost 185 killed and wounded in the encounter, although Bridger's information put the total killed at 14 or 15 Sioux and 3 or 4 Cheyennes, and others might have died from wounds later. Bridger was also told that Red Cloud was not present

[37] Hebard and Brininstool, *The Bozeman Trail*, I, 312.

[38] Vestal, *New Sources of Indian History*, 136.

[39] Grinnell, *The Fighting Cheyennes*, 235.

[40] Grinnell, *The Fighting Cheyennes*, 235, says that only six of the dead had bullet wounds. Crawford, *Rekindling Camp Fires*, 242, makes the number seven, while in the opinion of the post surgeon, a large number were wounded and slowly tortured to death by mutilation. David, *Finn Burnett*, 135.

at the fight and that Crazy Horse led the Ogallalas and Black Shield, the Minneconjou.[41]

The news, carried to Fort Laramie, 260 miles away, through Indian-infested territory and with the temperature hovering between twenty and twenty-five degrees below zero, by John (Portygee) Phillips, a frontiersman and civilian quartermaster employee, reached the outside world on Christmas Day[42] and caused a great deal of excitement, all of those in authority immediately busying themselves in an attempt to place the responsibility on someone else. The event effectively ended Colonel Carrington's military career, although a subsequent Court of Inquiry set up to determine "who, if any, were to be punished for the Fetterman massacre" acquitted him chiefly on the ground that he had specifically ordered Captain Fetterman not to pursue the Indians beyond the ridge, but to relieve the wood train and escort it into camp, and that his orders had been disobeyed. Later Carrington charged that his detailed report to General Grant was suppressed because it contained evidence of the maladministration of Indian affairs.[43]

Colonel Carrington was immediately relieved of his command and succeeded by Colonel H. W. Wessels, who had orders to take the field immediately in a winter campaign to punish the hostiles. But his force was too small and the weather too severe, so the order was never carried out. For their part, the Indians confidently expected attack. They felt that a disaster of the magnitude that had overtaken Fetterman's command would never be countenanced by the whites and that a desperate retaliation would be attempted. But just what they did about it is a subject of contradiction. One account says that despite the severity of the weather the great camp on the Tongue River broke up into many smaller units which then proceeded to scatter in all directions,[44] while another one says that they remained on the Tongue River for a considerable time expecting retaliation but prepared to repel an attack.[45]

41 Vestal, *Jim Bridger*, 287–92; Grinnell, *The Fighting Cheyennes*, 225; Bourke, *On the Border with Crook*, 291. *The Rocky Mountain News* (Denver) for March 25, 1867, has an Indian account of the battle and massacre.

42 A. B. Ostrander, *After Sixty Years*, has an appendix giving the story of the ride made by John Phillips.

43 Hebard and Brininstool, *The Bozeman Trail*, I, 339–40.

44 DeLand, *The Sioux Wars*, 127.

45 *Contributions to the Historical Society of Montana*, VIII (1917), 223.

Despite the Fetterman disaster the position of the troops in the various stations along the Bozeman Road was far from hopeless. Three forts had been established in the heart of the Indian country and were being held despite incessant Indian attacks. All that was needed was to reinforce them to whatever extent was necessary in order to carry out the purposes for which the forts had been constructed, namely, the protection of travelers using the Bozeman Trail. But to have expected a realistic policy of that sort from the government as it was then constituted was to expect the impossible. The unfortunate quarrel between President Andrew Johnson and the Congress was then at the height of its bitterness, and any common-sense policy toward the Indian was certain to be anathema to the Utopians of the Indian Bureau, who did not have to fight Indians and who persisted in believing, despite adequate evidence to the contrary, that a policy of turning the other cheek would persuade the Sioux to desist from their hostility. These Utopians refused to consider as valid the fact that more than 54 soldiers and citizens had been killed by the hostiles during the first six months of occupation of the three forts along the road, that over forty had been wounded, and that some seven hundred head of horses, mules, and cattle had been lost to Indian depredations.[46] Instead, the Bureau accepted the explanation that the Sioux were essentially peace loving and had been forced, by hunger and the callous refusal of Colonel Carrington to furnish them guns and ammunition for the hunt, into the attack which culminated in the Fetterman Massacre. Needless to say, no one who had ever lived on the frontier or had any practical experience with Indians accepted any of this pious nonsense. But serene in its own ignorance, and pursuant to an act of Congress of the twentieth of July to establish peace with certain Indian tribes, the Bureau appointed a peace commission of three civilians and four army officers which was sent to negotiate once again with the Indians in the region north of the Platte and south of the Yellowstone River.[47]

Despite the presence of this group the summer of 1867 saw

[46] DeLand, *The Sioux Wars*, 181; *Wyoming, A Guide to its History, Highways and People*, 272 (hereinafter cited as *Wyoming Guide Book*).

[47] The members of this commission were N. G. Taylor, commissioner of Indian affairs, J. B. Henderson, S. F. Tappan, and Generals Sherman, Harney, Terry, Sanborn, and Augur. See DeLand, *The Sioux Wars*, 194.

several developments on the military front. The first of these was the establishment of Fort Fetterman ninety-five miles beyond Fort Laramie. It was built in July of that year by Major William Dye on the right bank of the North Platte River at the mouth of La Prele Creek, and was destined to be the last army outpost along the Indian border after 1868 and to constitute an important supply depot in the Sioux wars.[48]

Much more spectacular, although not as important in the long run, were two of the most interesting Indian fights in American history, the famous Hayfield fight three miles east of Fort C. F. Smith on the first of August and the better-known Wagon-Box fight near Fort Phil Kearny the next day. In each case the technique of the hostiles was the same, in fact, the Indians seem to have planned both attacks at the same time and to have intended them to occur simultaneously, but the difference in distance from the main camp of the hostiles prevented this. In each case small parties of civilians and soldiers at some distance from their respective stations were attacked by overwhelming numbers of Indians. The whites took refuge, in one case in a brush corral,[49] in the other in a stockade constructed of wagon boxes, and beat back the attacks with the help of newly arrived breech-loading rifles—which proved a great and painful surprise to the attackers. The Indians withdrew at length, neither side having suffered any considerable number of casualties, although tales of enormous Indian losses are still credited in some quarters. This is especially true of the Wagon-Box fight where one author puts the number of Indian dead at fifteen hundred warriors, a figure which is pure fantasy since there were probably not more than one thousand engaged in the battle.[50] In both cases soldiers from the forts seem to have known what was going on—indeed they could hardly have remained ignorant of it even if they had wanted to—but at Fort Smith they appeared to have been afraid to venture forth from the protection of the walls because of the fear of an ambuscade,

[48] Crook, *Autobiography*, 192n.; Bourke, *On the Border with Crook*, 249.

[49] David, *Finn Burnett*, 161–95, has a vivid, firsthand account of the Hayfield fight.

[50] Vestal, *New Sources of Indian History*, 132, has this comment on such fantastic figures: "If all the Indians killed on paper in those wars could be laid end to end they would extend from the House of Ananias to the Castle of Baron Munchausen."

and at Fort Kearny a column of about a hundred men was sent to the relief of the besieged troops.[51]

The Peace Commission which journeyed to the Great Plains in 1867 was actuated by several motives. Probably the most dominant was the realization that time was running against the Indian. The historic policy of the United States had been to establish an Indian frontier and to make definite allocations of territory to the tribes, which was precisely what the Sioux did not want and which they were determined to prevent. But this could be brought about by indirection as well as by direct military action, so the commissioners seem to have reasoned. The return of peace on the frontier would permit the more rapid construction of the Union Pacific Railroad, and the construction of a branch line northward into Montana would permit the abandonment of the Bozeman Trail and the bypassing of the hostile tribes. In fact, there is some reason to believe that the single aim of the government in these negotiations was to get the hostile tribes as far away as possible from the main line of the Union Pacific.[52]

Red Cloud's solution for the problem was simplicity itself. He declared that his war against the whites was for the purpose of saving the Powder River country for his people as the only good hunting ground that they had left. He assured the peace commissioners that his war against the United States would cease when the garrisons were withdrawn from the three hated forts along the Bozeman Road and not before.[53]

The troubles and vicissitudes of the commission were many. The Indians from long experience had learned to be suspicious of the white man bearing gifts or offering a treaty to be signed, and it was not until April of 1868 that a representative body of chiefs could be assembled at Fort Laramie. The resulting treaty gave in completely to the Sioux demands; in fact, it has been said to be the only treaty ever signed by the United States in which nothing was asked of the other side except peace.[54]

[51] Hyde, *Red Cloud's Folk*, 159–60. Vestal, *Jim Bridger*, 293, says that there were about a thousand Sioux and Cheyennes in the battle and that six members of each tribe were killed. For the story of enormous casualties among the Indians, see Colonel Richard I. Dodge, *Our Wild Indians; Thirty-three Years' Personal Experience among the Red Men of the Great West*, 485–89.

[52] *Wyoming Guide Book*, 112.

[53] DeLand, *The Sioux Wars*, 197–98.

This treaty[55] is rather lengthy, but, in view of its fundamental importance for subsequent events, it deserves a rather detailed consideration. After declaring that all war between the two parties should cease, and that malefactors of either race committing depredations against the other were to be punished, the treaty went on to set aside a permanent reservation for the Sioux. This was to be composed of that part of the present state of South Dakota lying west of the Missouri River and is described as follows:

> . . . commencing on the east bank of the Missouri, where the 46th parallel of north latitude crosses the same, thence along the low water mark down the said east bank to a point opposite where the northern line of the state of Nebraska strikes the river, then west across said river and along the northern line of Nebraska to the 104th degree of longitude west from Greenwich, thence north on said meridian to the point where the 46th parallel of north latitude intercepts the same, thence due east along said parallel to the place of beginning . . .[56]

Other articles provided for the enlargement of the reservation under certain conditions, for the erection of buildings, and for the education of the Indian children, and specifically called for a "full and exact census of the Indians" to be taken annually by the agent.

On their part, the Sioux agreed to withdraw all opposition to the railroad then being constructed across the plains (the Union Pacific) and to permit the construction of any other *railroads not passing over their reservation as herein defined.* [italics mine]. They also withdrew "all pretense of opposition" to the construction of railroads, wagon roads, mail stations, or "other works of utility or necessity," which may be ordered or permitted by the laws of the United States. In case roads or railroads should be constructed on the lands of their reservation, the government was to pay whatever damages might be assessed by three disinterested commissioners to be appointed by the president, one of whom was to be a chief or headman of the tribe.

[54] Vestal, *Jim Bridger*, 294–95.

[55] Charles J. Kappler (comp. and ed.), *Indian Affairs. Laws and Treaties . . .* vols. I–II; 57 Cong., 1 sess., *Sen. Doc. 452*, III; 62 Cong., 2 sess., *Sen. Doc. 719*, II, 998–1007. Kappler was secretary of the Senate Committee on Indian Affairs. See also the article by Thomas B. Marquis in the *Billings* (Montana) *Gazette*, July 17, 1932.

[56] Kappler, *Indian Affairs*, II, 998.

The Indians also agreed to cease their attacks on "persons, wagon trains, coaches, mules or cattle belonging to the people of the United States or to persons friendly therewith." They also promised not to capture white women or children or to carry them away from the settlements, nor were they to kill or scalp white men or attempt to do them harm.

Could the Commissioners have foreseen the consequences of Article XII, they would doubtless have prevented its insertion in the treaty. For this article provided that no treaty for the cession of any portion or part of the permanent reservation would be valid unless signed by at least three-fourths of all the adult male Indians occupying the same. The United States also stipulated that the country north of the North Platte and east of the summit of the Big Horn Mountains should be held to be "unceded Indian territory" upon which *no white person should be permitted to settle, or to pass through the same without the consent of the Indians first had and obtained.* Within ninety days after the conclusion of peace the military posts in the territory, Forts Reno, Phil Kearny, and C. F. Smith, were to be abandoned and the road to the Montana mines closed.

For the United States, all of the commissioners, except J. B. Henderson, signed. Many Indians representing nearly all of the Sioux tribes as well as the Arapahoes, "touched the pen" to the treaty although at different times. Among the more prominent and outstanding chiefs were Iron Shell, Standing Elk, and Spotted Tail for the Brulés, and Red Cloud, Man-Afraid-of-his-Horses, and American Horse for the Ogallalas. Among the signatures of this last-named band is one of Sitting Bull, who is not to be confused with the Uncpapa medicine man of the same name, who did not sign but who definitely broke with Red Cloud on the issue of the treaty. Among other prominent chiefs who did not sign were Crazy Horse, Gall,[57] and Black Moon. They were the leaders of the "hostiles," the recalcitrants who wanted nothing to do with the white man or his ways. Thus Red Cloud's War, which had its origin in the intense

[57] One biographer of Sitting Bull says that Gall signed this treaty, which caused Sitting Bull to remark contemptuously, "You must not blame Gall. Everyone knows he will do anything for a square meal." Albert Britt, "Sitting Bull, War Chief or Swindler?" in his *Great Indian Chiefs,* 198.

dissatisfaction of the Indians at the attempt of the government to open a new road from Fort Laramie to the gold fields of Montana,[58] resulted in "a solemn dedication of a tract of country of vast extent to barbarism—a country larger than any of our first-class states—upon which no American citizen shall ever be permitted to set his foot or pass through without the consent of the autocrat Indian."[59]

The surrender of the Bozeman Road had another result in that it finally "convinced the Cheyennes that their only safety lay in an alliance with the Sioux," and in the years which lay ahead the two were to make common cause against the Americans, in the course of which we were to learn that Indian fighting can be a very serious business.[60]

The problem of how to build the projected Northern Pacific Railroad across the northern part of this Indian territory without incurring the hostility of the Sioux was not an immediate one and could, perhaps, be left to the healing hand of time, or the road might go north of the Yellowstone River. Some similar solution was doubtless hoped for in case the persistently recurring rumors of gold in the Black Hills should prove to be true. In other words, for the present the policy was peace, the future would be allowed to take care of itself, and to be on the safe side the Commissioners inserted an article, to which the Indians apparently agreed, to allow the construction of rail and wagon roads through the territory and to permit "other works of utility and necessity." But it is doubtful if the Indians ever knew that they were agreeing to this. Red Cloud was later to contend that he and the other chiefs had signed the treaty without its having been read to them, and the explanation probably is that the Sioux had been so interested in getting rid of the hated forts that they failed to pay any attention to the other provisions, being satisfied with the explanation that the document they were signing was a peace treaty. So—it was hoped—peace would come to the prairies until, in the course of time and history, the Indian way of life would be obliterated by the onrushing Juggernaut of white civilization.

58 DeLand, *The Sioux Wars*, 195, for the report of C. H. Norris, United States Indian agent at Omaha, Nebraska.

59 *New York Tribune*, July 15, 1876.

60 Smith, *Indian Experiences*, 161.

CHAPTER III

The Gathering Storm

THE SIGNING of the treaty of 1868 was expected to bring peace to the Indian country. That it failed to do so is further illustration of the fact—if such be needed—that there is often a great gulf between theory and reality, between the expectations of men and their realization. But the treaty was to be given a chance to prove itself, and the advocates of the idea that it was better and cheaper to feed the Sioux than to fight them were not to be denied the opportunity to put their idea to the test of performance. What few, if any, seemed to see was that it might be necessary to do both, to fight the Indians after having prepared them for war.

The ink on the treaty was hardly dry before new trouble began. The anger and consternation of the Montana miners was great, for they felt that they had been basely betrayed by their own government. Deprived of their most convenient route to the outside world, most of them soon showed the frontiersman's characteristic indifference to any governmental acts that he considered inimical to his interests and displayed an inclination to ignore entirely the closing of the Bozeman Road and to go on using it regardless of the Sioux tribes or the government of the United States.

But the reaction of the miners was feeble compared with that of those other frontiersmen who made their homes in the vicinity of the Oregon Trail. The "nonceded area" set apart as a hunting preserve for the tribes was not only enormous in acreage but it contained many tracts of land, especially along the Powder River, that the white man felt would make desirable homesteads, and there was no way of telling without actual exploration what precious metals might be discovered in the mountain fastnesses of the Big Horn Range. Since these frontiersmen adhered almost religiously to the doctrine that no Indian had any rights that the white man was bound to respect, they soon began to trespass on the reserved area, and the government found itself unwilling, if not unable, to restrain the activities of its more aggressive citizens, so the penetration of the Indian lands continued, thus adding weight to the later contention of Colonel John Gibbon that there had not been a single treaty made with the Indian tribes which had not been violated by the whites.[1] The Indians, on their part, viewed these violations as merely another example of the bad faith of the white man. These were pinpricks of irritation, but they carried the germs of disaster.

And if some of the whites were dissatisfied with the treaty, the same was true for some of the Indians. Most of the Sioux were pacified, but a portion—the exact number varied from time to time—remained implacable and continued their old nomadic existence in the region of the Powder River. These were the "hostiles" led by Sitting Bull and Crazy Horse, and they ranged themselves in open opposition to Red Cloud, who had advised signing the treaty. From this time on there is a steady diminution in the power and influence of that great Ogallala chieftain. Many of the malcontents were renegade outlaws who seldom went near an agency. They roamed over a vast extent of territory, and since they were closely connected by intermarriage and interest with the agency Indians, they found little difficulty in making the agencies a base of operations from which they secured recruits as well as arms, ammunition, and other supplies. In the winter these renegade bands dwindled to only a few hundred warriors, but in the spring they were reinforced by all of the restless young men from the different reservations who were attracted by the lure of the old, carefree life of their ancestors and the opportunity to hunt and plunder the frontiersman, so that by midsummer most of the bands had been increased in size from less than a hundred to many times that number.[2]

While the disorder on the plains continued, someone in Washington had a "great idea" which in retrospect seems to have been more idiotic than inspired—that of bringing Red Cloud and a dele-

[1] Colonel John Gibbon, "Hunting Sitting Bull," *American Catholic Quarterly Review*, Vol. II, No. 3 (October, 1877), 691.

[2] *Report of the Secretary of War, 1876*, 499. In 1868 the Sioux Nation was composed of many distinct families or tribes amounting in the aggregate to fifty thousand people, of whom eight thousand were said to be warriors. *Ibid.*, 27.

gation of his henchmen to the national capital, ostensibly for a conference with President Grant, but in reality to attempt to overawe and intimidate them by a display of the power and progress of the white man. In all, twenty-one Indians—seventeen men and four women—made the trip. Highly indicative of the state of public opinion along the frontier was the fact that the delegation was put aboard a Union Pacific train at the tiny station of Pine Bluff rather than at Cheyenne, which was the logical place. The avoidance of the latter city was due entirely to a very well-founded fear that the citizenry of that brawling place would fail to treat the chief as a guest of the government and might possibly lynch him in accordance with the frontier belief that the only good Indian was a dead one.[3]

If the officials of the Indian Bureau had expected to intimidate Red Cloud and the others to the extent that they could persuade them to go home and behave themselves, they were disappointed, for the chief refused to budge in his opposition to white encroachment on tribal lands. He denounced the treaty of 1868 as a swindle when it was read to him, and declared (he was undoubtedly telling the truth) that he and the other chiefs had "touched the pen" to the treaty without knowing its contents since it had never been read to them, and they had been told only that it was a peace agreement which provided for the abandonment of the hated forts along the Bozeman Road. The entire entourage was then taken—almost by force—to New York City, where Red Cloud made a sensational appearance at Cooper Union. Then they returned to the Indian country.

They had surrendered nothing and had made no concessions but had received a rich trainload of presents. Eastern pacifists had been provided with substantial new ammunition and were more convinced than ever of the inherent nobility of the "noble savage," without realizing that the Indians regarded the giving of presents and the issuance of rations as an indication of weakness and interpreted it to mean that the government was afraid of the tribes. Red Cloud and his companions were equally obtuse, for, despite the overwhelming character of what they saw, they failed to realize that

[3] Hyde, *Red Cloud's Folk*, 174–75. One writer claims that Sitting Bull was a member of this party. Charles A. Eastman, *Indian Heroes and Great Chieftains*, 118.

the power of the white man was too great for the red to combat. Sitting Buli was not a member of the party, but he had a very easy explanation of the wonders that were related to him: they were simply figments of the imagination, phantasms of the air which had no reality, being induced by the powerful nature of the white man's "medicine" to which Red Cloud and his companions had fallen victim.[4]

Spotted Tail, who was with the party, had realized years before that the day of the old, free life of the Indian was almost a thing of the past and that the problem of readjustment had to be faced. But Spotted Tail was a statesman and a prophet, not a charlatan and a faker, and his fate was the usual one of prophets in their own country. Red Cloud, possibly partly because of his personal opposition to Spotted Tail, persisted in believing that the sun could be made to stand still. Had he had a greater breadth of vision and been less petty, he would have realized that the old Indian way of life was doomed and that the big problem was that of transition to the white man's way rather than a stubborn attempt to turn back the clock of time. Had Red Cloud been the statesman that Spotted Tail was, the subsequent history of his people might have been much happier.

There was never peace on the frontier, but the next few years were devoid of any sensational happenings, although there were many storm clouds along the horizon. One question that was certain to cause plenty of trouble was that of the advancing Northern Pacific Railroad, which was steadily extending its tracks westward. In 1871 it reached the Red River at Moorhead, by March of the next year the western terminus was Fargo, and by 1873 it had been completed as far as Bismarck on the eastern bank of the Missouri River. This was as far as it could go without entering the region which the Sioux regarded as peculiarly theirs, and which was set aside for them by the treaty of 1868. The Depression or Panic of 1873 kept the question in abeyance for several years, and Bismarck remained the terminal point for six years. But the surveyors were always ahead of the construction gangs and never, even at the worst of the depression, entirely ceased their activities although their presence was an open violation of the treaty (a violation not only ap-

[4] *New York Tribune*, July 15, 1876.

proved by the United States but aided and abetted as well since soldiers were provided to protect the surveying crews). In 1871, the Whistler expedition, led by the father of the celebrated artist, had traveled up the Little Missouri and then on into Montana in search of the most practical railroad route to the Pacific Ocean. By the fall of that year the surveyors, after much exploration, had decided that the best route lay up the valley of the Yellowstone River. Although that valley ranges in width from one hundred to three hundred yards, it is generally all on one side of the stream, while on the other, high bluffs come down to the water's edge so that at least a part of the route would lie along the south bank. This was a part of the "unceded" territory guaranteed to the Sioux by the treaty of 1868, and it was certain that the Indians would resent the intrusion. Whether that resentment would lead to war only time could tell, but serious trouble was expected to follow any attempt of the railroad to build through the area.[5]

In order to protect the settlers, to keep the Indians in order, and later to guard the railroad, the government began the erection of a series of forts along the Missouri River frontier. Fort Rice, located on the west bank of the river about sixty miles from Standing Rock Agency, had been established in 1864. Its site has been described as one of the most Godforsaken spots on earth and is said to have seemed like the conception of a nightmare.[6] Two years later, Fort Buford, at the confluence of the Yellowstone and the Missouri rivers, was garrisoned, to be followed during the next year by Fort Ransom on the Cheyenne, Fort Totten near Devil's Lake, and Fort Stevenson on the Missouri at the mouth of Douglas Creek. In 1870, Fort Pembina was added, and in 1872, Fort Seward, originally called Fort Cross, was built at Jamestown. That same year, 1872, also saw the erection of Fort McKeen across the river from Bismarck and not far from the present site of Mandan, North Dakota. This was later enlarged and renamed Fort Abraham Lincoln; and in 1874, in order to call a halt to the overwhelming arrogance of the Sioux who had even refused to allow the agent to fly the American flag over the agency, General John E. Smith of the Fourteenth Infantry built

[5] Lieutenant James H. Bradley, "Journal of the Sioux Campaign of 1876 under the command of General John Gibbon," *Contributions to the Historical Society of Montana*, IV (1903), 156–57 (hereinafter cited as Bradley, *Journal*).

[6] Katherine Gibson Fougera, *With Custer's Cavalry*, 162–63.

Forts Sheridan and Robinson at the agencies of Spotted Tail and Red Cloud.[7]

The over-all threat of these forts and the government's policy of encirclement was not lost upon the Sioux, who attacked with increasing frequency. It was these attacks, especially those upon Fort Lincoln, that led Lieutenant General Philip H. Sheridan, commanding the Division of the Missouri, to request that the Seventh Cavalry be transferred from duty in the South to the Indian frontier. His request was granted, and by order of Brigadier General Alfred H. Terry, commanding the Department of Dakota, the regiment was stationed at Fort Lincoln and Fort Rice.[8]

Fully aware that the Sioux bands of Sitting Bull and Crazy Horse constituted the "hard core" of the hostile tribes, Sheridan had also recommended the construction of two forts in the heart of the Indian country, one to be located on the Big Horn River and the other at the junction of the Tongue and Yellowstone rivers. But Congress failed to act, and the two forts, which would have provided an efficient base of operations against the hostiles, were not constructed. Later Sheridan was to express the opinion that had his recommendations been followed, the Sioux War of 1876 would have been avoided.[9]

In the summer of 1873, ten troops of the Seventh Cavalry,[10] with Custer as leader, accompanied the Stanley expedition in support of the Northern Pacific's surveying parties which explored westward along the north bank of the Yellowstone River as far as Pompey's Pillar, an expedition which aroused the opposition and resentment of the Sioux, especially since the construction of a rude fort—known as Stanley's Stockade—several miles above the mouth of Glendive Creek seemed to indicate that the white man had come to the country to stay.

On August 4, the regiment had a brush with hostile Indians almost opposite the confluence of the Tongue and the Yellowstone,

[7] Bourke, *On the Border with Crook*, 242.

[8] Elizabeth B. Custer, *Boots and Saddles, or Life in Dakota with General Custer*, 289.

[9] Carl Coke Rister, *Border Command: General Phil Sheridan in the West*, 202.

[10] Troops D and I were not on the Stanley expedition. They were doing escort duty to the commission that was surveying the boundary between Canada and the United States. See Edward S. Luce, *Keogh, Comanche, and Custer*, 45.

and a running fight developed with the Indians retreating westward. Again on the eighth they saw a large Indian village near the mouth of the Rosebud, but at the approach of the troops it broke up and began to scatter. The regiment pursued a group of the hostiles to a point about three miles below the mouth of the Big Horn, where the Indians managed to escape by crossing the river in skin boats and on rafts, and the regiment could not follow. On the night of the tenth and morning of the eleventh, a large number of warriors recrossed the stream, and at dawn made a surprise attack while others fired on the soldiers from across the river and from the bluffs to the rear but were driven off after a hard fight. The hostiles were estimated to number between 800 and 1,000 warriors and were believed to be Uncpapa Sioux for the most part, under the leadership of Sitting Bull. Custer's force numbered about 450 including both officers and men.

From the civilian clothing, the coffee, sugar, and bacon dropped by the Indians, and from the cartridges and two new Winchester rifles found on the field, it was known beyond the possibility of a doubt that the Indians, who were present in the area in large numbers, were the recipients of the bounty of the United States and that they "had at no long time since, come from that center of iniquity in Indian Affairs, Fort Peck."[11]

From the beginning Custer had acted as though he were in command of the expedition, much to Stanley's exasperation. It was not long before the latter recorded his conviction that Custer was a "cold-blooded, untruthful and unprincipled man," who was "universally despised by all of the officers of his regiment" with the exception of his relatives and a few sycophants. Stanley complained not only that Custer had brought a trader into the field without permission, but that by bringing along an old Negro woman as his cook, together with a cast-iron stove, he delayed the expedition with his extensive packing up in the morning.[12] The inevitable blowup came when Custer, being separated from the rest of the expedition by some four miles, sent word to Stanley to send him forage and rations and then marched his regiment off for another fifteen miles. This was presuming too much, and Stanley sent a messenger

[11] South Dakota Department of History *Collections*, XI, 372.

[12] *Personal Memoirs of General D. S. Stanley, U. S. A.*, 239.

ordering Custer to halt where he was and to send for his own rations and forage and never to make another movement without orders.[13]

But Stanley's advantage over his subordinate was soon lost. Stanley was excessively addicted to alcohol, and his being found drunk on several occasions gave Custer his opportunity.[14] Even so, Custer had discovered the limits of his superior's forbearance and thereafter behaved himself with such circumspection as to win Stanley's praise, and on the return journey Custer was allowed to strike out across the country north of the Yellowstone and to make his way back to the stockade by way of the Musselshell River, a distance of about 150 miles. Although authorized to destroy what property might be necessary, he—as he wrote to Mrs. Custer—with "Custer luck" struck the most favorable country for marching and succeeded in bringing in every wagon.[15]

It was while on this expedition that Dr. Holzinger, the veterinarian of the Seventh Cavalry, its sutler, a Mr. Balarian, and a private soldier by the name of Ball, were cut off and killed by the Indians. The two noncombatants were both men of scientific tastes and interests, and often left the column in search of the fossils which abounded along the Yellowstone, although the scout, "Lonesome Charley" Reynolds, had warned them on several occasions of the dangers involved in such a practice. On this particular occasion, when the two men had dropped behind the regiment, they were detected by a small party of Sioux, said to have included the celebrated warrior, Rain-in-the-Face. Accounts of what happened differ, one saying that the two men were killed from a considerable distance and without the warriors exposing themselves, and without the victims apparently knowing the whereabouts of their assailants, although Mrs. Custer states that Dr. Holzinger was shot first and rode a short distance before falling from his horse. Then the Sioux beat out his brains with an iron mallet and filled his body with arrows. Meanwhile Mr. Balarian had managed to hide in some bushes, but was soon discovered by the Indians. He held up his hand as a gesture of peace and later gave Rain-in-the-Face his hat as a petition for mercy, but it availed him nothing. Neither man was scalped, as

[13] *Ibid.*, 240.

[14] Marguerite Merington (ed.), *The Custer Story: The Life and Intimate Letters of General George A. Custer and His Wife Elizabeth*, 252, 265.

[15] *Ibid.*, 262.

Holzinger was bald and Balarian wore his hair close cropped, but both bodies were shot full of arrows and otherwise badly mutilated.

Although responsibility for this episode is generally attributed to Rain-in-the-Face, there is a strong possibility that he was not even present since the fighting was said to have been with the Ogallala Sioux and a few Cheyennes. Rain-in-the-Face, who was an Uncpapa and a member of Sitting Bull's band of nonreservation Sioux, was probably with the band which was hunting buffalo some one hundred miles to the northeast at the time of the affair and knew nothing at all about it.

Although both men were technically civilians and were not in uniform, they were members of an armed expedition which was invading the land of the Sioux, and the Indians may be excused for being unable to draw fine distinctions between noncombatants and actual belligerents. During the winter that followed Charley Reynolds heard Rain-in-the-Face, who had come in and was spending the winter at Standing Rock Agency, boast of the murder. The news was relayed to Custer and a detachment of cavalry sent to arrest the culprit. The party, guided by Reynolds, was in charge of Captain Yates and included Tom Custer, who was one of a party of four making the actual arrest after Rain-in-the-Face had been pointed out by a Ree scout.

The captive was incarcerated in the guardhouse at Fort Lincoln, but after a good deal of hocus-pocus, including a secret interview with Custer and visits from his brother and other relatives who expected him to be killed out of hand, he made his escape in company with a soldier who had been placed there on a charge of desertion. The circumstances of the escape itself, the fact that there was no pursuit and no action was ever taken against the sentry from whose custody the two men escaped, makes it look very much like a simple case of collusion—in short, that Rain-in-the-Face was allowed to escape as the best way out of an almost impossible situation. But Rain-in-the-Face is said to have blamed Tom Custer for his predicament and to have threatened to cut the Captain's heart out and eat it.[16]

[16] This incident is covered in Custer, *Boots and Saddles*, 208; Dustin, *The Custer Tragedy*, 185; and David F. Barry, *Indian Notes on the Custer Battle*, 25. Like so many other events connected with the Custer fight, it is surrounded by extensive

While the railroad was one very serious menace to the continuance of the more or less armed truce which prevailed along the frontier, another and even greater danger was the ever persistent rumors that there was gold in the Black Hills, a report that had been current ever since "Jim" Bridger was supposed to have found traces of it in 1859.[17] By the early seventies these reports had gone far beyond the stage of rumor, for on more than one occasion Indians had brought small nuggets and grains of gold into the trading posts, and then under the influence of the trader's whiskey revealed that these came from various streams in the hills. That the Indians were fully aware of the implications of such a discovery is apparent from the report of Father Genin, a missionary among them for over thirty years, who told of a great Indian council held one summer at Lake Traverse, in which it was decided that any Indian who revealed the presence of gold in the Black Hills or any white man who discovered it was to be slain. They reasoned that such a discovery by the whites would mean the loss of the country to the Indians.[18]

The Black Hills—so named by the Sioux because from a distance their heavily forested sides[19] look to be deep blue or black—comprise the territory between the Belle Fourche River on the north and the South Fork of the Cheyenne River and extend 120 miles north and south with a breadth of from 40 to 60 miles. The area[20] covered—nearly six thousand square miles—had been guaranteed to the Indians by the treaty of 1868 and constituted one of the still untouched hunting grounds left to them. There were many species of game—bear, deer, antelope, and elk—and in great num-

controversy. For the story that Rain-in-the-Face was not even present when the killing of Balarian and Holzinger took place, see Thomas B. Marquis, *Rain-in-the-Face and Curly the Crow*. A somewhat fantastic account of the affair is D. J. Benham, "The Sioux Warrior's Revenge," *Canadian Magazine*, Vol. XLIII (September, 1914), 455–56.

17 Alter, *James Bridger*, 333n. Father De Smet is said to have been aware of the presence of gold in the hills almost from the time of his advent into the country as a missionary. Arthur J. Larson, "The Black Hills Gold Rush," *North Dakota Historical Quarterly*, Vol. VI, No. 4 (July, 1932), 302.

18 *Billings* (Montana) *Times*, September 10, 1925.

19 *Wyoming Guide Book*, 373; Crook, *Autobiography*, 189.

20 Walter P. Jenny, *Report on the Mineral Wealth, Climate and Rainfall and Natural Resources of the Black Hills of Dakota*, 44 Cong., 1 sess., *Exec. Doc. No. 51*, 5.

bers. More than that, they were *Pa Sapa*, the sacred hills, the home of the Sioux deities, and it was a foregone conclusion that the Sioux would not abandon them without a struggle. But the government knew that if the reports of gold were true, it would take more than the army to keep the prospectors and miners out. There was always the possibility of buying the region from the Indians, but before taking any steps in this direction, the government decided to do some investigating.[21]

Although the treaty of 1868 prohibited entry into the country without the consent of the Indians, Lieutenant Colonel Custer with ten troops of the Seventh Cavalry, two companies of infantry, a contingent of Indian scouts, and a wagon train, was ordered to make a reconnaissance in the summer of 1874. Custer was apparently given the command at his own request, although in granting it Sheridan limited the period that the troops could be absent from their regular stations to sixty days, on the understanding that only the military, the necessary civilian employees, and a few selected scientists and newspaper correspondents should go with the expedition. The plans for the survey created a great deal of excitement in the Northwest, and there were applications by the hundreds from all over the country, only a few of which could be granted.[22] The expedition as finally composed included Colonel William Ludlow, chief engineer of the Department of Dakota, Colonel George A. Forsyth and Colonel Fred D. Grant, both aides on General Sherman's staff, and a group of civilians, including scientists, newspapermen, two miners, and a photographer.[23]

The ostensible and assigned purpose of the group was to obtain accurate information concerning the trails of the hostile Indians on

[21] Britt, however, attributes the Indian attitude to pure stubbornness since they were not interested in digging the gold and had no real love for the Hills. In fact, they are said to have regarded the spirits that inhabited them as evil. *Great Indian Chiefs*, 199.

[22] Brigadier General Edward S. Godfrey, "Custer's Last Battle," *Contributions to the Historical Society of Montana*, IX (1923), 155 (hereinafter cited as Godfrey, *Montana*).

[23] Grinnell, *Two Great Scouts*, 239. South Dakota Department of History *Collections*, VII, 554–80, is an account of the expedition written by A. B. Donaldson. It is on this trip that Custer is said to have incurred the dislike of President Grant by placing the latter's son, Colonel Fred Grant, under arrest for drunkenness. W. M. Wennett, "Custer's Expedition to the Black Hills in 1874," *North Dakota Historical Quarterly*, Vol. VI, No. 4 (July, 1932), 296.

the Yellowstone, trails which were known to lead through the hills to the agencies on the Missouri River and which, incidentally, were found to follow the divides and streams much as U. S. Highway 14 does today.[24] The instructions were to reconnoiter the route from Fort Lincoln to Bear Butte just north of the hills and then to explore the country "south, southeast and southwest of that point."

Guided by over sixty Indian scouts, most of them Arikaras and Santees, the expedition marched from Fort Lincoln on the second of July, 1874. It was preceded by the regimental band playing "Garry Owen," the "fight song" of the Seventh Cavalry. "To start into supposedly hostile Indian country accompanied by a brass band was a novel experience to some of those who rode with the expedition."[25] Seventeen days later they reached the Belle Fourche Valley, some 290 miles away, having averaged a little better than 18 miles a day, which was a very good rate of progress considering that the infantry companies naturally could not move as fast as the cavalry. Here the Indian scouts objected to going any farther or to entering the hills proper, stating that they understood that the command would only skirt the fringes. They especially urged that the wagons should not be taken beyond that point. But Custer was deaf to their arguments, and the next day the march was resumed, the column traveling over a clearly defined pony-and-lodge trail which led up the valley of the Red Water, a branch of the Belle Fourche.

Few Indians were encountered, but their signal fires were seen almost daily, and it was obvious that they were watching the command. Although the officers with the rear guard observed Indians following their trail, no hostile demonstrations were made. The scouts had a very simple explanation for these occurrences, stating that the signal smokes were probably to let the villages know the location of the command so that they could keep out of the way. One small village, that of Chief One Stab, which had recently returned from the hostile camp on the Powder River, was encountered, but it managed to make its escape despite Custer's efforts to prevent it.

On the twenty-second of July the expedition camped on Spring

[24] *Wyoming Guide Book*, 373.
[25] Grinnell, *Two Great Scouts*, 240.

Creek. Since the valley there contained a great profusion of wild flowers, Custer named it Floral Valley, and the troopers covered themselves and their horses with the fragrant blossoms. Some two weeks were spent in the exploration of the region, during which many members of the expedition climbed Harney Peak, which has an altitude of 7,403 feet and is the highest point in the present state of South Dakota. More important was the fact that the scientists made rather extensive tests for minerals and found evidence of their existence in great abundance, not only "gold at the roots of the grass" but in gravel bars on French Creek as well, and indications that there were extensive deposits of lead, copper, and silver.

On August 2, Charley Reynolds left the command in an attempt to ride through to Fort Laramie with Custer's report. Since his route lay entirely through enemy country and since the Sioux had been worked up to a high pitch of excitement by this invasion, his mission was a very dangerous one. Custer offered him the escort of a small detachment of cavalry, which Reynolds refused, stating that it would be impossible to send a large enough detachment to offer full protection and that a small group would only increase the danger of detection. So traveling by night and hiding by day, he made the trip alone, arriving at Fort Laramie without mishap and bringing to the outside world the first reliable report of the treasures of the Black Hills.[26]

Four days later the command started the return trip, passing around to the east and north and following the valley of the Box Elder in leaving the hills and then retracing the original route with only slight divergence. The Sioux had held a good many councils and powwows, in the course of which they had talked a lot about the violations of the treaty and the invasion of their rights. They referred to the trail which Custer had blazed as "the thieves' road," and to Custer as "the chief of the thieves," but they did nothing about it, again displaying that almost fatal weakness of the tribes, the inability to form a plan and then act in concert to put it into operation.[27]

[26] 43 Cong., 2 sess., *Exec. Doc. No. 32* contains Custer's report of August 2, 1874. This report can also be found in South Dakota Department of History *Collections*, VII, 583–94. Joseph Henry Taylor gives some incidents of Reynolds's ride to Fort Laramie in *North Dakota Historical Quarterly*, Vol. IV, No. 4 (July, 1930).

On one occasion on the return trip Custer was warned by a group of Cheyenne warriors that Sitting Bull at the head of a war party of five thousand Sioux was preparing to ambush the column in the Short Pine Hills. The command was alerted, but no Indians were seen, although they did find the abandoned camp of a very large body of Sioux. The size of the camp caused Luther North to remark that it was probably just as well that the Indians had departed before the soldiers got there, to which Custer replied that with the Seventh Cavalry he could whip all of the Indians in the Northwest.[28] The most that the hostiles were able to do was to burn over a great tract of prairie, thus forcing the command to descend into the valley of the Little Missouri River in order to secure the necessary wood, water, and grass. Here travel was more difficult, and the pace of the troops was correspondingly slowed. But they gradually worked their way out of the burned-over area, and on the thirtieth of August crossed the Heart River less than a day's march from Fort Lincoln.

Although members of the expedition had already reported "gold at the grass roots," and the newspaper correspondents sent out reports which verged on rhapsody in describing the riches of the region, there were many government officials who regarded the evidence as inconclusive. Whether there was an honest doubt is, of course, unknown, but it is altogether probable that it was a desire to avoid collision with the Sioux that actuated the Commissioner of Indian Affairs when he reported in November that not only was there little, if any, gold in the Black Hills, but that the region was almost valueless for agricultural purposes. If it was the purpose of the Commissioner to discourage prospectors who might otherwise flock into the region, that purpose was not realized, for the miners and prospectors had begun to crowd in almost before Custer's troops had returned to Fort Lincoln. A few parties of miners were turned back by the military, but many more of them succeeded in getting through, and some of them spent the winter in the country despite the open opposition of the Sioux.[29]

Agnes Wright Spring, *The Cheyenne and Black Hills Stage and Express Routes*, 17–19, is a description of the effect of the news at Fort Laramie.

[27] Hyde, *Red Cloud's Folk*, 230.

[28] Grinnell, *Two Great Scouts*, 242.

[29] The news of the discovery of gold in the Black Hills came just as the

In this same year, Professor O. C. Marsh of Yale University arrived in the Bad Lands in search of the fossil bones of extinct monsters which had been reported there. The Indians could not understand why anyone should be interested in such things and suspected that his real object was gold. After considerable difficulty with the Sioux, in the course of which he had more than one narrow escape from death, the Professor secured more than two tons of the fossil bones. What was even more important, he secured the Indians' side of the story of their difficulties with the whites. Marsh must have had an unusually forgiving disposition because his experiences had been enough to make him despise Indians for the remainder of his life, but he listened to Red Cloud's recital of his woes not only with interest, but with a steadily rising indignation. The Ogallala chief complained that dishonest contractors robbed both the government and the Indians by furnishing insufficient rations of an indifferent quality. Marsh asked for samples of the rations, and he got them although he was apparently made the victim of a rather barefaced piece of skullduggery.

George C. Hyde describes the incident as follows:

> And here is an unsolved mystery. Who was it that took a sample of the none-too-good Indians' flour and added to it a few handfuls of the gritty White River clay dust? Who picked over several pounds of Indian coffee and carefully selected all the bad berries as a fair sample? Who unearthed that ancient and moldy specimen of long-plug tobacco, and who picked up the piece of mess pork which had once been sweet but after being thrown away by the Indians who did not like mess pork, had lain on the ground until it was no longer sweet? No one will ever know. It looks like a white man's work, and perhaps no one would be far from the truth in pointing to Red Cloud's pet interpreter as the artist who designed this pleasing little joke.[30]

At any event, in the spring of 1875, Marsh took the samples to Washington and demanded an investigation.

For the time being public attention was diverted from the

---

country was beginning to recover from the effects of the Panic of 1873 and therefore probably produced a great deal more excitement than would otherwise have been the case. Arthur J. Larson, "The Black Hills Gold Rush," *North Dakota Historical Quarterly*, Vol. VI, No. 4 (July, 1932), 303.

[30] Hyde, *Red Cloud's Folk*, 227.

matter of purchasing the Black Hills to the subject of irregularities at the Indian agencies, particularly in the matter of rations, especially beef and flour. That there was graft and corruption on a large scale is beyond doubt. The agent would issue a barrel of sugar to a tribe and from an obliging chief get a receipt for ten times that amount, or an Indian would in ignorance sign a receipt for fifty sacks of flour while receiving but one. Three hundred head of cattle driven four times through a corral would be receipted for as twelve hundred head, a part given to the Indians and the remainder sold to a white man, while the proceeds of all the transactions found their way into the agent's pocket. Nor was this all, for soured and damaged foods, moth-eaten blankets, and inferior clothing were issued although billed at the full value of first-class goods.[31]

While there were irregularities, to prove them was another matter. Some of the testimony offered at the hearings before the commission was ludicrous in the extreme and involved forgetfulness that almost partook of the nature of a science, but although the investigators found plenty of smoke, there seemed to be little fire. There was plenty of indication that many suspicious and peculiar things had taken place, but there was little legal evidence of fraud. So things went on as usual; the Indian was promised redress, but the agents kept their trails covered, and the swindling continued.[32]

Then public attention veered back to the subject of gold. Government officials pretended to be still uncertain as to how reliable the Custer report really was and suggested that he had looked at the Black Hills with a jaundiced eye. The result was that in the summer of 1875 another expedition was sent out to investigate. This was headed by Walter P. Jenny, a mining engineer from the New York School of Mines, while the military escort was under the command of Colonel Richard I. Dodge. Their report was very favorable, even more so than that of the preceding year,[33] but long before it was received a great horde of miners and prospectors, not at all deceived by the official propaganda, had stampeded into the region.

[31] Stuart, *Forty Years on the Frontier*, II, 80.
[32] Hyde, *Red Cloud's Folk*, 234–39.
[33] Jenny, *Report*.

This influx was partly due to the fact that Colonel Dodge represented the Indians as being anxious to give the Hills to the whites and blamed "squaw men" for stirring up all the trouble.[34]

To this invasion the Sioux reacted violently; many parties of miners were attacked and not a few lives were lost.[35] But the opposition of the Indians was not enough to stem the tide of adventurers. Although General Terry had been ordered to keep all whites out of the area, his efforts seem to have been rather half-hearted, and he could not have succeeded even if he had tried. When trespassers were seized by the troops, they were taken out of the reservation territory and turned over to the civil courts. The personnel of the court, being sympathetic to the prospectors and antagonistic to the Indians, immediately turned the trespassers loose, and they re-entered the Hills by another route. One man is reported to have said: "I have been captured and sent out from the Hills four times. I give the troops more trouble in catching me each time. I guess I can stand it as long as they can."[36]

In a short time the government realized the impracticability of such a procedure and decided to attempt to purchase the region from the Indians. The plain fact of the matter was that the government did not dare to discipline its own people in this matter and was seeking a way out. The miners could have been kept out of the Hills, but the desperate measures that would have been necessary would probably have resulted in a political upheaval that was exceedingly painful for the party in power to contemplate. And it must be remembered that at this time President Grant was still unconvinced that a third term in the White House could not be his for the asking. Accordingly, Red Cloud and a number of other chiefs were hauled off to Washington with the idea of persuading them by bribes or browbeating, whichever was most efficacious, to sell their beloved Hills. The chiefs were apparently somewhat intimidated, but not enough so to consummate the sale, declaring that they could do nothing without consulting their people. The negotiations were then shifted back to the agencies, and it was

[34] Richard I. Dodge, *The Black Hills*, 137–38.

[35] Colonel T. M. Coughlan, "The Battle of the Little Big Horn," *Cavalry Journal*, Vol. XLIII (January–February, 1934), 13.

[36] Charles Francis Bates, *Custer's Indian Battles*, 27.

arranged that a commission should be sent to meet the Sioux in council.

The government would have liked to acquire the Powder River and Big Horn regions, but the mere mention of this fact produced such an outburst of indignation from the Indians that the last two were discreetly forgotten. The Sioux could not, or would not, agree to anything. They put such an outrageous price on the Hills as to make their purchase impossible and rejected out of hand a more moderate counteroffer by the government. There were several riotous meetings in which the more impetuous young men were with difficulty restrained from open hostility against the representatives of the United States, and finally the council broke up without result, although in their report the Commissioners attempted to minimize the magnitude of their failure and never mentioned some of the most interesting and revealing incidents at all.[37]

The failure to purchase the Hills put an unenviable choice before the government. It could attempt to enforce the treaty of 1868 and keep the whites out of the Black Hills; but this could not have been done except at enormous cost, and the government would not have dared to attempt it. Or it could seize the region on one pretext or another and then use the army to protect the prospectors and settlers from attack by the Indians. But this would have brought down the wrath of the peace party and the professional eastern friends of the Indians. So, as governments often do when confronted by two alternatives, it tried to carry water on both shoulders. A confidential letter from General Sheridan informed Terry that the President had decided, on the third of November, that while there was to be no change in the orders forbidding miners and prospectors to enter the Black Hills, the troops were to make no further attempt to enforce them.[38] At the same time the government had recourse to another line of action—to give the recalcitrants an object lesson by proceeding against a smaller group of Indians and bringing them to terms. The theory was that when the larger group

[37] For a very interesting and illuminating account of this conference see Hyde, *Red Cloud's Folk*, 242–44. "The commissioners were the gladdest people alive to get away from that part of the country that ever visited there. They didn't recover their courage until they got the Missouri River behind them," Crook, *Autobiography*, 190.

[38] Bates, *Custer's Indian Battles*, 27.

saw this display of governmental power they would willingly agree to sell the Black Hills, and all would be calm and peaceful on the western frontier.

In the meantime Indian depredations along the frontier and especially along the line of the Union Pacific continued. Although the Indians complained that the presence of the Northern Pacific's surveying parties along the Yellowstone and the presence of the prospectors and miners in the Black Hills constituted a violation of the treaty of 1868, they conveniently overlooked the fact that they were constantly violating the same treaty by their attacks on white travelers and settlements and furnished the white settlers with at least a reasonable excuse for their activities, since a treaty so "persistently violated by the Indians themselves should not be quoted as a valid instrument for the preventing of such occupation" (of the Black Hills). Indeed, the attitude of the Sioux had become so insolent and overbearing that it was believed that an attempt to hoist the American flag over the Red Cloud Agency, or a persistence in the determination to find out by active count the number of warriors who were out on the warpath would result in the massacre of all the white people at the agency.[39]

The conviction had been growing for some time among persons fully cognizant of the true situation on the frontier, and especially among the higher officers of the army, that these wild bands who infested the Powder River country and formed the nucleus for all the dissatisfied and unmanageable Indians from the various agencies would have to be subjugated and made to feel the power of the government before there could be anything like permanent peace on the Great Plains.[40] To this end, General Sheridan had recommended the construction and garrisoning of two large and permanent military posts[41] in the heart of the Indian country—one on the Yellowstone at the mouth of the Tongue and the other on the Big Horn River—but his recommendations had been disregarded by an economy-minded Congress, perhaps at the suggestion of the Indian Bureau, which had consistently argued that the wild bands were too small and weak to be of any consequence, that they were more

[39] *Report of the Secretary of War, 1876*, 500–501.
[40] *Ibid.*, 502. See also *Ibid.*, 498, and Godfrey, *Montana*, 156.
[41] 44 Cong., 1 sess., *Sen. Exec. Doc. No. 81*, 4.

of an annoyance than a threat, and that the problem, if left alone, would solve itself.

It was the question of the Black Hills that brought matters to a climax and tied together all of the loose threads of American Indian policy. The Indians were already exasperated by many things, not the least of which was the poor quality and insufficient quantity of the supplies furnished them by the government under the treaty, and to which violations of their territory only added further evidence of the duplicity of the white man. The officials of the government, on their side, seem to have felt that the existing situation was intolerable, and could not be allowed to continue. How much this decision to force a reckoning may have been attributable to the influence of President Grant we do not know. But it would not have been the first nor last time that a national leader attempted to distract attention from domestic failures by the device of an outstanding military success.

It would be worse than idiotic to maintain that the government brought on the Sioux War of 1876 merely to obtain possession of the Black Hills. For as General Crook pointed out, the occupation of the Black Hills had not resulted in any increased number of Indian depredations and the people who had gone to the Black Hills had not suffered any more, and probably not as much as they would have, had they remained at their homes along the border,[42] and Mr. McGinnis, the Montana territorial delegate, insisted that there was little real connection between the two, for the Indians had been recalcitrant and hostile long before the question of the Black Hills arose.[43] The President of the United States agreed that the discovery of gold and the intrusion of settlers had not caused the war but only complicated it by the uncertainty of the numbers to be encountered.[44] Rather, the issue furnished an excuse for both sides to bring to an end the uncertain and poorly observed truce that had prevailed for seven years. Few people believed that there would be any serious fighting. It was almost the universal consensus that only a few hundred warriors at most would dare to oppose the

[42] *Report of the Secretary of War, 1876*, 501.

[43] *New York Tribune*, July 15, 1876.

[44] 44 Cong., 1 sess., *Sen. Exec. Doc. No. 81*, 3. See also a letter to Secretary of War Cameron dated July 8, 1876, and published in the *Army and Navy Journal*, July 15, 1876.

troops and that these could be rounded up in a short campaign, "before the grass was up in the spring," as someone expressed it. The peace policy of loving the Indians into submission had failed; the advocates of a more "realistic" policy were to be given the opportunity to see what they could accomplish with a club.

CHAPTER IV

Preliminaries of Conflict

UP UNTIL THIS TIME the Commissioner of Indian Affairs had insisted that the problem of the hostile bands was not a serious one and that it would solve itself if left alone. But now, for some unexplained reason, that officer had a change of heart. Whether it was due to the fact that the charges of graft and corruption levied against the Indian agents were known to have too much truth in them, and that the officials hoped to escape the consequences of their misdeeds by joining in the hue and cry against the tribes, we do not know. Colonel Gibbon, of whose honesty and patriotism there can be not the slightest doubt, later declared that the government through its agents had starved many of the Indians into leaving the agencies, and in his official report stressed the fact that in many cases the malcontents were "driven to desperation by starvation and the heartless frauds perpetrated upon them."[1] Captain Benteen was of the same opinion. It was his belief that the principal cause of Indian unrest was the enormous pilfering and stealing done by the Indian agents, some of whom managed to save from thirteen thousand to fifteen thousand dollars out of an annual salary of

[1] Colonel John Gibbon, "Last Summer's Expedition against the Sioux," *American Catholic Quarterly Review,* Vol. II, No. 1 (April, 1877), 274 (hereinafter cited as Gibbon, "Summer Expedition"). See also Gibbon's Report in the *Report of the Secretary of War, 1876,* 475. General Hugh Scott later wrote, "The Indians were attacked at the insistence of the Interior Department while they were peacefully attending to their own business with no desire to fight." *Custer* (South Dakota) *Chronicle,* July 23, 1936. DeCost Smith adds that "barring minor deviations, Sitting Bull's people were right in the wars the government waged against them; it was the government, not they, who broke the treaties. There was 'gold at the grass roots' in the Black Hills; 'the Northern Pacific must go through.' Treaty or no treaty, 'barbarism must not be allowed to stand in the way of civilization.' It was the old argument of expediency; the shortest way out of a bad bargain." *Indian Experiences,* 213.

fifteen hundred dollars.[2] So it may very well be that to denounce the hostiles was the easiest way out of a bad situation for the men charged with ministering to the welfare of the tribes. Or, to do them justice, it may simply have been that the Indian officials became convinced that their previous attitude had been entirely wrong. In any event, E. C. Watkins, United States Indian inspector, was sent to investigate the situation and under the date of November 9 made a full report, which is of unusual interest in illustrating the change in attitude.

In this report he mentioned that the region inhabited by the hostile tribesmen was probably the best natural hunting ground remaining within the United States. This reduced the need of these tribes to receive governmental supplies, and consequently they had never accepted aid from, or been brought under the control of, the Indian Bureau. He emphasized that they were rich in horses and robes and very well armed with breech-loading rifles and pistols as well as with bows and arrows, and that they were lofty and independent in attitude. While these wild tribes were only "a drop in the bucket" compared to the great number of peaceful Indians, he foresaw the possibility that the young men from the agencies would join the hostiles to such an extent that the hostiles would become a formidable fighting force, although he disclaimed being an alarmist and specifically stated that he did not agree with the sensational articles relative to the strength and belligerency of the malcontents that had been published in some of the western newspapers.

Watkins argued, too, that it was the responsibility of the United States to protect the peaceful tribes, which it was not doing. These latter were very much disgusted and were reported to have said that they "might as well go out and kill white men as to try to be good Indians for they got no protection or extra reward for being good," and when told that the Sioux would be punished, they replied that they had heard that story before and that they would wait and see. Watkins was also of the opinion that efforts to civilize and teach the arts of peace to the tribes on the reservation would

[2] *Reno Court of Inquiry: Stenographic Report of the Testimony, Editorial and Miscellaneous Articles from the Chicago Times, January 14 to February 12, 1879.* William J. Ghent Papers in Library of Congress, Washington, D. C. (hereinafter cited as Reno, *Court*).

be largely wasted effort as long as the hostiles were allowed to defy the government with impunity.

Feeling that everything that could be done peaceably to get control of these Indians or to induce them to respect the authority of the United States had been done, but to no avail, the Inspector recommended that they be turned over to the War Department for appropriate action. He urged the sending of troops against them as soon as possible in order to inflict much deserved chastisement upon the hostiles and to afford protection to the friendly Indians, the agents, missionaries, and frontier settlers, and as the satisfaction of a debt due to civilization and the common cause of humanity, which was strange language coming from a representative of the Indian Bureau. He declared that the hostiles numbered only a few hundred warriors who were never all together, and believed that one thousand soldiers under an experienced officer operating in the wintertime, when the Indians were nearly always in camp and were most helpless, would be able to handle them without difficulty.[3]

At this time, the United States Army was, for administrative purposes, divided into three military divisions: the Atlantic, the Pacific, and the Missouri. This last was composed of all the states and territories located on, or in proximity to, the Mississippi and Missouri rivers and included substantially all of the Rocky Mountain area. Commanded by Lieutenant General Philip H. Sheridan, with headquarters in Chicago, it was subdivided into five departments, only two of which are of importance here. The Department of Dakota, comprising the state of Minnesota and the territories of Montana and Dakota, was commanded by Brigadier General Alfred H. Terry, with headquarters in St. Paul. The Department of the Platte, including the states of Iowa and Nebraska, the territories of Wyoming and Utah, and that part of the territory of Idaho as lay east of a line formed by the extension of the western boundary of Utah to the northeastern boundary of Idaho, was commanded by Brigadier General George Crook, who made his headquarters in Omaha. Both Terry and Crook had won distinction in the Civil War, but the former was entirely without experience in Indian fight-

[3] 44 Cong., 1 sess., *Sen. Exec. Doc. No. 52*, 3–5; 44 Cong., 1 sess., *House Exec. Doc. No. 184*, 8–9 (both contain the Watkins' *Report*). See also *Report of the Secretary of War, 1876*, 28, and the *Army and Navy Journal*, July 15, 1876.

ing, while Crook had added to his other laurels by several successful campaigns against the Apaches in the southwestern United States. In the spring of 1875, Crook had been transferred from the Department of Arizona to that of the Platte and had spent the greater part of the time after his arrival at the new station in a vain effort to keep white miners out of the Black Hills.[4]

Sheridan, who had long been urging punitive measures against the Sioux and who believed that immediate action was necessary to success, insisted that the Indians must be caught before spring or they would not be caught at all and began preparing for action, for he fully realized the difficulties which would be presented by the weather and the country inhabited by the hostiles.

Before his plans had progressed very far, however, he was notified by the Secretary of War that the Interior Department wanted to make one more attempt to bring about a settlement of the issues involved without recourse to military measures. Military preparations were not entirely halted, but were rather in a state of suspended animation while the Commissioner of Indian Affairs, acting on instructions from the Secretary of the Interior, ordered the various Indian agents in the Sioux and Cheyenne country to notify all the Indians then living in the unceded territory that they were expected to come in to the agencies before the thirty-first of the next January. Failure to comply with this directive would, it was announced, result in the recalcitrants' being classified as hostile and in their being turned over to the War Department for appropriate action. Stripped of its official verbiage and reduced to the plain and simple language of everyday life, this order meant that the old order of things had passed, the free and wild life of the tribes of the northern plains was at an end; henceforth the Sioux and Cheyennes would "walk the white man's road"; they would be lodged on reservations and maintained at the expense of the government. The only question remaining was, would the tribes accept their new status peaceably, or would they compel the government to use force in order to inaugurate the new way of life for them?[5]

[4] *Report of the Secretary of War, 1876,* 439; Crook, *Autobiography,* 187–89.

[5] *Report of the Secretary of War, 1876,* 28. The instructions to the various agents may be found in 44 Cong., 1 sess., *Sen. Exec. Doc. No. 52,* 5–6, and 44 Cong., 1 sess., *House Exec. Doc. No. 184,* 14–15.

Sheridan felt that this notifying of the hostiles to come in to the agencies would be regarded as a good joke by the Indians themselves,[6] and the reaction of the tribes was exactly what anyone who knew them might have expected under the circumstances. The message reached the various Sioux agencies just before Christmas, and was at once sent on to the hostile camps by trusted Indian runners, some of whom were themselves unable to return until after the time set for compliance with the order. None of the hostiles themselves came in. Although much has been made of the inclemency of the weather and the fact that the winter was an unusually severe one even for that region, with low temperatures and deep snows, this was not the real reason for the Indian failure to co-operate. Despite the severity of the weather, Sitting Bull had moved his camp twice during the winter, once in December and again in March, and neither the snow nor the freezing temperature was enough to prevent Crazy Horse from moving his camp from a location near Bear Butte to one on the Powder River. The weather was a convenient excuse; the real reason for noncompliance was that none of the chiefs took the order seriously.

In after years Sitting Bull denied ever having received the official notice, and it is probable that most of the roamers could plead a similar ignorance. Nevertheless, most of them knew about the order from unofficial sources and campfire gossip at least, but simply chose to pay no attention to it. They felt that they had a right to be where they were and that no one had a right to order them back on the reservations. They were not bothering any white men for the good and simple reason that there were none in the region for them to bother.[7]

The few chiefs who did receive the order were not at all defiant in their answers; the messengers, in fact, uniformly reported that they had been well received; the answer simply was that the tribesmen were too busy. When spring came, well, that would be a differ-

[6] 44 Cong., 1 sess., *House Exec. Doc. No. 184,* 14.

[7] Patrick E. Byrne, *Soldiers of the Plains,* 27; Hyde, *Red Cloud's Folk,* 250–52; Thomas B. Marquis, *Sketch Story of the Custer Battle, a Clashing of Red and Blue; Billings Gazette,* July 17, 1932. However, on February 12, 1876, H. W. Bingham, one of the agents, reported that the hostiles under Sitting Bull and the other wild tribes received the invitation and warning in good spirit and without any sign of ill feeling. 44 Cong., 1 sess., *House Exec. Doc. No. 184,* 26.

ent matter, and they would have to think about it! The chiefs had had experience with government orders before, and they may have remembered that while the Grandfather talked a lot, he seldom did anything. What the hostiles did not realize was that there had been a change of policy at Washington. However, even if they had been in possession of that information, it would in all probability have meant nothing to them, and their attitude would have been unchanged. As for the threat of the government to send the soldiers after them, that was not too frightening a prospect, and they doubtless argued that there was no sense in crossing that bridge until they came to it.

In the meantime conflicting reports were coming in from the various agencies. Thus on the twenty-fourth of December it was reported from Standing Rock that the Indians there who were closely connected with Sitting Bull's band were trading hides for ammunition. Since there was no game in the vicinity, there was little doubt that this ammunition was finding its way to the hostile camps, but the trader justified his actions on the ground that it was the only way that he had of securing buffalo robes. Although the Indian Office by telegraph ordered these transactions to stop, they continued, and resulted in a long and acrimonious controversy between the agent John Burke, the trader J. R. Casselberry, whose license incidentally had expired, and Captain J. S. Poland of the Sixth Infantry. There was also a great deal of illegal trading, and Captain Poland complained particularly of the activity of unlicensed traders on Beaver Creek who were selling both liquor and ammunition to the hostile tribesmen.[8] Although during the month many lodges, including that of Chief Little Wound, had deserted the reservation and slipped away to join Sitting Bull after stealing government horses and mules, the agent John Burke on the thirty-first reported his belief that many of the wild and lawless Indians would come in and accept the conditions of the Treaty of 1868.[9]

The month of January brought many additional reports. From the Crow Agency in Montana, the agent, Dexter E. Clapp, reported considerable numbers of Sioux in the valley of the Big Horn River, mostly scattered in small bands, presumably hunting buffalo.[10] C. W.

[8] 44 Cong., 1 sess., *House Exec. Doc. No. 184*, 26–43.
[9] *Ibid.*, 17.

Darling at Fort Berthold in reporting a Sioux raid on a Gros Ventre village at the mouth of the Little Missouri on the night of the eleventh, declared that Sitting Bull had five hundred lodges of lawless ruffians, the very worst Indians in the Northwest. The Sioux camp was said to be at Calf's Ear Butte on the Yellowstone River, some ninety to one hundred miles west of Fort Buford in an air line, the camp having removed from the Little Missouri some weeks before.[11] Here the Sioux chieftain exerted a demoralizing influence over the more peacefully inclined Indians by preventing them from hunting and by maintaining a place of refuge for the lawless. In contrast to this, H. W. Bingham at Cheyenne River said that he expected little or no trouble from Sitting Bull and that the Indians had not been so quiet or peaceably disposed for a long time,[12] a sentiment which was seconded by Mr. Hastings at Red Cloud, who reported that Crazy Horse and other Ogallala chiefs were then on their way to the agency with some three to four thousand followers, but that their progress was retarded by the heavy snow.[13]

On the eighteenth of January the office of the Commissioner of Indian Affairs rather belatedly telegraphed the various agents ordering them to stop all sales of arms and ammunition to the Indians and to seize all such articles that were likely to reach the hostiles,[14] which was bolting the door of the barn after the horses had been stolen. Three days later, the Commissioner, Mr. J. Q. Smith, reported to the Secretary of the Interior that enough had already been done to commit the department to the policy of restraining by force any further outbreaks or acts of insubordination on the part of the hostiles, should they fail to return to their agencies within the allotted time. Failure to carry into execution the threats of military action so clearly made would, in his opinion, be very detrimental to the authority and prestige of the government among all of the Indian tribes. As to the danger of a diversionary outbreak by the Indians at the agencies in favor of Sitting Bull and his followers, the Commissioner believed that although this question had not been specifically considered, the army officers doubtless felt that they could

[10] *Ibid.*, 47–48.
[11] *Ibid.*, 23, 46.
[12] *Ibid.*, 22.
[13] *Ibid.*, 25.
[14] *Ibid.*, 20.

restrain any demonstration of this kind with the forces at their disposal as well as move directly against the hostiles.[15]

The thirty-first of January came and went, and despite the optimistic reports of some of the agents, few, if any, of the hostiles had made any move to return to their reservations, so on the following day "the Secretary of the Interior officially notified the Secretary of War that the time given the hostile Indians having expired he formally turned them over to the military authorities for such action as the Secretary of War might deem proper under the circumstances."[16] The campaign was thus begun at the request of the Indian Bureau and did not originate with the War Department, although the latter was not at all unwilling to proceed.

In the meantime, the army had not been wholly idle. Apparently in answer to a question, General Crook, on the twenty-second of December, had notified headquarters that he could take the field against the hostiles whenever in the judgment of the Indian Bureau such action might be considered necessary.[17] General Terry also indicated that he was ready to move on short notice and ventured the opinion that Sitting Bull's band was located near the mouth of the Little Missouri River and that his camp could be reached by a quick movement, which at that time of the year might well be decisive. He also believed that the five companies of the Seventh Cavalry at Fort Lincoln plus the two at Fort Rice would be sufficient for the movement. But he emphasized that it would have to be a surprise attack, for the soldiers would be able to carry only a few days' supply of food and forage and could not follow far if the Indians should scatter. He advised that it would be possible for scouts from Fort Stevenson to discover the exact location of the hostile camp as the garrison there was entirely of infantry, and these scouts would arouse no suspicion since Sitting Bull knew that they could not catch him.[18]

The War Department was known to favor immediate operations against the hostiles, and believed that a quick movement at

[15] 44 Cong., 1 sess., *Sen. Exec. Doc. No. 52*, 8–9.

[16] *Ibid.*, 9; *Report of the Secretary of War, 1876*, 28.

[17] 44 Cong., 1 sess., *House Exec. Doc. No. 184*, 14–15; General Sheridan's Report in *Report of the Secretary of War, 1876*, 440 (hereinafter cited as Sheridan's *Report*).

[18] 44 Cong., 1 sess., *House Exec. Doc. No. 184*, 15.

General George Crook, 1875.

"Crook, who has been described as an ideal soldier in every respect, standing about six feet, straight, broad-shouldered, lithe, sinewy, had won an illustrious reputation as an Indian fighter in the Southwest."

Courtesy National Archives

Hunting and camping party from Fort Lincoln at the
Little Heart River, 1875.

Left to right: *Lt. James Calhoun; Leonard Sweet of Chicago; Capt. Baker, 6th Inf.; *Boston Custer (on ground); Lt. W. S. Edgerly; Miss Watson; *Capt. Myles Keogh; Mrs. Calhoun; Mrs. Custer (in chair); *General Custer; Dr. H. O. Paulding; Mrs. A. E. Smith: *Dr. George E. Lord; Capt. J. B. Weir; *Lt. W. W. Cooke; Lt. R. E. Thompson, 6th Inf.; the Misses Wadsworth; *Capt. Tom Custer; *Lt. A. E. Smith. Those indicated by an asterisk were killed at the Battle of the Little Big Horn.

Courtesy National Archives

this time of the year would be decisive, because, for the Indians, defeat in winter usually meant starvation. Sherman considered midwinter the best time to operate in the latitude of the Yellowstone; and, in addition, the Sand Creek Massacre and the Washita affair both seemed to demonstrate the superiority of winter operations since the Indians were notorious for wishing to avoid action when the weather was cold and inclement. To the Indian, summer was the time for war; in the winter he preferred not to be disturbed. While snow and cold weather did not hamper the movement of the tribes any more than it did that of the soldiers, if as much, there was considerable merit in the well-known contention of General Sheridan not only that it would be easier to catch the Indians during the winter, but that if they were not caught before spring, they would not be caught at all.[19] And, on their part, the Indians, who believed that the white soldiers would not be able to endure the hardships of a winter campaign, were convinced that they were safe from attack during that season of the year.[20]

On the seventh of February, authority was received to commence operations against the hostile Sioux, and the slow and cumbersome machinery of the War Department was set in motion. At the same time General Terry was told that Sitting Bull with his band was no longer on the Little Missouri but on the Dry Fork of the Missouri River some two hundred miles farther to the west. Bloody Knife, one of the Arikara scouts, declared that there were now no regular camps of hostile or other Indians on the Little Missouri. But Terry's information was that the Uncpapa camp consisted of only thirty or forty lodges and not over seventy warriors, while the reports from the Indian agents put it at more than ten times that number of lodges.[21]

Sheridan's plan of campaign was simplicity itself. Departmental lines were to be disregarded and the operations to be carried on without concert, although there was no objection to an understand-

19 Sheridan's *Report*, 440. For General Sherman's opinion see 44 Cong., 1 sess., *House Exec. Doc. No. 184*, 14–15.

20 Hafen and Ghent, *Broken Hand*, 210.

21 Sheridan's *Report*, 441; 44 Cong., 1 sess., *House Exec. Doc. No. 184*, 44–46. Colonel Robert P. Hughes, however, declares that General Terry believed that Sitting Bull's personal following consisted of about five hundred lodges. "The Campaign against the Sioux in 1876," *Journal of the Military Service Institution of the United States*, Vol. XVIII (January, 1896), 16.

ing between the various field commanders. Three columns of troops were to march against the hostile Sioux and Cheyennes. One column would be commanded by General Crook and would advance from Fort Fetterman northward into the Powder River country, while Colonel John Gibbon would lead another detachment, including both infantry and cavalry, eastward from the Montana forts along the Yellowstone River. The third column, to be known as the "Dakota column," would move westward from Fort Abraham Lincoln, roughly paralleling the course of the Yellowstone. The three columns were expected to rendezvous at a common center, probably somewhere on the Big Horn or Little Big Horn rivers.[22]

Just how many hostile Indians might be met with, no one seemed to know, although the officials of the Indian Office estimated that there could not be more than three thousand men, women, and children, off the reservations. They apparently informed the military authorities that there were not more than a few hundred warriors and that they were not united. The commonly accepted figure seems to have been five hundred warriors, while no one apparently put the estimate at more than eight hundred.[23] Although estimates furnished by the agents put the figure much higher, the military was apparently told that Sitting Bull had only about seventy-five warriors in his camp on the Dry Fork, while Crazy Horse's Ogallala village was said to consist of not more than 120 lodges with perhaps 150 warriors at an extreme estimate. The remainder would be made up by various other scattered bands.[24]

These estimates were probably fairly accurate at the time they were made; the trouble was that they had not been revised in the light of later information. It is also a matter of doubt whether or not the military leaders were justified in accepting them, for at every agency there was a small garrison of troops and the commanders of these could not have been unaware of the great numbers of warriors who were slipping away to join the hostiles. Sheridan had anticipated this exodus from the agencies and had asked that the

[22] Sheridan's *Report*, 441. However, the *Report of the General of the Army* (General Sherman) says that Sheridan decided on his concentric movement of the three columns *after* the Reynolds' fiasco on the Powder River [italics mine]. *Report of the Secretary of War, 1876*, 29.

[23] *Report of the Secretary of War, 1876*, 29.

[24] Sheridan's *Report*, 440.

army be given supervisory authority there, but the proposal had no results of any consequence.[25] However, the military leaders seem to have accepted the estimates of the Indian Office without too much question and to have assumed that any one of the three columns could defeat any force of the enemy that it might encounter. The main difficulty, as the army viewed it, would be to catch the Indians and force them to fight or surrender. Lieutenant Colonel Custer, who was expected to command the Dakota column, was of the opinion that the Sioux would not offer very much resistance when faced by the military power of the United States. In fact, there was a general disposition not to take the expedition very seriously, since no one realized that the Indians had decided to die violently rather than starve to death peaceably.[26]

General Terry did not receive his official orders until the tenth of February, and then he projected an expedition against the camp of Sitting Bull. The Seventh Cavalry, which was to carry out the assignment, was badly scattered, Headquarters and Troops A, C, D, F, and I being at Fort Lincoln, E and L at Fort Totten, and H and M at Fort Rice, while the three remaining troops B, G, and K were temporarily assigned to detached service with the Department of the Gulf under command of General C. C. Augur.[27]

Before those troops readily available could be concentrated at Fort Lincoln, the weather became so cold and the snow so deep that it became necessary to postpone the movement. New preparations were begun with the idea that the troops would be able to march early in April, although much depended upon the early spring opening of the Northern Pacific Railroad.[28] General Terry, not unaware of the growing strength of the Sioux, apparently planned to establish a secure base of supplies well up the Yellowstone River. From this Custer could operate, and to it he could

25 *Ibid.*, 443. Both Terry and Crook knew and calculated upon the fact that with the beginning of spring there would be large desertions, chiefly of warriors, from the agencies to the hostile bands. Hughes, "Campaign against the Sioux in 1876," *Journal of the Military Service Institution of the United States,* Vol. XVIII (January, 1896), 6.

26 Bates, *Custer's Indian Battles,* 28.

27 General Terry's Report in *Report of the Secretary of War, 1876,* 455, 459 (hereinafter cited as Terry's Report).

28 General Terry notified Gibbon that he expected to start Custer about the first of April. Hughes, "Campaign against the Sioux in 1876," *Journal of the Military Service Institution of the United States,* Vol. XVIII (January, 1896), 6.

retire if the Indians, at any time, were found to be in too great numbers for the force at his disposal. Terry realized that if the hostiles who regularly passed the winter in the valleys of the Yellowstone and Powder rivers should be able to concentrate their warriors in one camp or in contiguous camps, they could not be attacked by a small force without great risk of defeat. Since the nine troops of the Seventh Cavalry on duty in his department numbered only about 620 men all told, of whom not more than 550 could be put in the field for active operations, Terry wrote Division Headquarters asking that the troops serving temporarily in the Department of the South be ordered to rejoin their regiment in his department.[29] When this failed to accomplish the desired result, he sent an urgent telegram to Sheridan about a month later, asking for the troops in Louisiana and added: "The most trustworthy scout on the Missouri recently in the hostile camp reports not less than two thousand lodges, and that the Indians are loaded down with ammunition." Inasmuch as the ordinary estimate was three fighting men to a lodge, it would appear that Terry should have been under no illusions concerning the number of Indians with whom his command might come into collision. His request was granted, although the three troops did not arrive at Fort Lincoln until the middle of April.[30]

In the meantime, Terry, in carrying out Sheridan's plan for a three-way pincer movement against the Sioux, had sent orders to Colonel John Gibbon directing him to move eastward with all the troops that could be spared from the various garrisons in Montana. Oddly enough, these orders to Gibbon on their way westward crossed with a dispatch from that officer to Terry suggesting a similar movement.[31] Colonel Gibbon was not to seek to destroy the power of the Sioux Nation unless an unusually favorable opportunity should present itself, but was to attempt to hold the Indians south of the Yellowstone and prevent them from crossing over to the north bank either in pursuit of the buffalo, as they often did in the spring of the year, or in an effort to escape if they became alarmed at the approach of either or both of the other two columns

[29] *Ibid.*, 6, 15.
[30] *Ibid.*, 16; Sheridan's *Report*, 442; Terry's Report, 459.
[31] Terry's Report, 459.

of troops. These instructions to Gibbon constitute a further illustration of a policy which was to be in evidence again and again throughout the subsequent months, to surround the Indians and keep them from running away. But, despite the fact that the white man did not seem to be able to comprehend it, the Sioux and the Cheyennes, as time was to prove, had not the slightest intention of running away.

A small segment of Terry's command did take the field, though its action was not connected with the campaign against the Sioux. In 1875, a group of traders from Bozeman, Montana, had built Fort F. D. Pease, named for the leader of the expedition, a former agent of the friendly Crows, on the left bank of the Yellowstone a few miles below the mouth of the Big Horn and at the edge of a wide-open prairie. At the time it was expected that the post would become an important trading point in the river traffic that was expected to develop with the coming of the steamboat to the waters of the Yellowstone. However, during the few months that it was in operation it was used largely as a trapping post, especially in securing wolfskins, the animals taken by the use of strychnine in the winter when the skins were heavy and soft. The fort, which was in no sense a military post, consisted of a series of log huts connected by a palisade of cottonwood logs enclosing an area about two hundred feet square.[32]

The hoped-for development of traffic on the river failed to materialize, and soon the small garrison of traders and trappers found themselves engaged in a life-and-death struggle with the Sioux, who regarded their activities as an invasion of their hunting ground and another example of the perfidy of the whites. Finally, on the eighteenth of February, 1876, an appeal was sent to Fort Ellis for help and referred to General Terry at Department headquarters.

A telegram from Terry authorized the sending of a relief expedition on the twenty-first, and Troops F, G, H, and L of the Second Cavalry, with a detachment from Company C of the Seventh Infantry to serve a twelve-pound Napoleon gun and a Gatling, with a wagon train and rations for thirty days, all under the command of Major James Brisbin, left Fort Ellis for the trip down the Yellowstone. A contingent of civilian scouts accompanied the com-

[32] Gibbon, "Summer Expedition," 272.

mand, and Lieutenant Schofield was sent ahead to the Crow Agency, where he succeeded in enlisting the services of fifty-four Crows and twenty-five citizens as scouts and guides. The march was largely without incident; the Yellowstone was crossed several times, all of the crossings except the first being on the ice.

On the fourth of March the party reached Fort Pease and found that the Indians had lifted the siege, at least temporarily. Of the original garrison of forty-six men, six had been killed and eight wounded, while twenty-one had left the fort at night and made their way to the settlements, so that Brisbin found only nineteen men at the post. Two days later the fort was evacuated, and all of the men started back with the cavalry column. The flag was run up to the top of the flagstaff in the center of the fort and left flying as a gesture of defiance to the Sioux. It had been planned to leave the establishment intact, but one disgruntled member of the party set fire to one of the buildings, which burned without doing any damage to the others. All the valuable property belonging to the men was brought away and taken to the mouth of Stillwater Creek, where it was considered safe from the Indians, and unloaded. The command saw no Indians, although scouts were sent to a point from which they could see the mouth of the Little Big Horn, but there was evidence that small parties of Sioux were about, and the scouts found five war lodges of about sixty Sioux who had fled south. On the seventeenth of March, the expedition reached Fort Ellis, having covered a distance of 398 miles without a casualty and without, in fact, having seen a hostile Indian. On their return to the fort, the cavalrymen found new orders directing them to march again over the road they had just traversed.[33]

Four of the Crows who had accompanied Brisbin reported, after their return to the agency, that a large force of Sioux was moving up the north bank of the Yellowstone, and Mr. Clapp, the agent, reported a great deal of belligerent activity on the part of the Sioux who were occupying the eastern and best part of the Crow reservation. Adding that the Crows had come in to the agency much earlier than usual, he expressed his belief that the Sioux would

[33] *Ibid.*, 273; Terry's Report, 459. For the detailed itinerary of the trip and Brisbin's telegram from the mouth of the Big Horn River, see 44 Cong., 1 sess., *House Exec. Doc. No. 184*, 49–51.

attack the agency. He suggested that a military post be established at the mouth of the Big Horn, to be garrisoned by troops already in Montana, most of whom were stationed at points where an Indian was seldom seen.[34]

While General Terry was being thwarted by the elements in his attempts to move against the hostiles and Brisbin was engaged in rescuing the garrison at Fort Pease, General Crook, whom the Indians called the "Gray Fox," or "Three Stars," won the distinction of being first in the field. Crook, who has been described as an ideal soldier in every respect, standing about six feet, straight, broad-shouldered, lithe, and sinewy,[35] had won an illustrious reputation as an Indian fighter in the Southwest.

On the first of March, after a heavy fall of snow the night before, Crook left Fort Fetterman with ten troops of the Second and Third Cavalry regiments, under Colonel J. J. Reynolds of the Third, two companies of the Fourth Infantry, eighty-six mule wagons loaded with forage, three or four ambulances, and a pack train in five divisions of eighty mules each, one division to each two companies.[36] The weather was severe, but Crook, who accompanied the expedition, not as the immediate commander but chiefly to test by personal experience whether operations against the Indians in winter and early spring were impossible due to the rigors of the climate, did not allow this to deter him. He understood that "the object of the expedition was to move, during the inclement season, by forced marches, carrying by pack animals the most meagre supplies, secretly and expeditiously, surprise the hostile bands and, if possible chastise them before spring fairly opened and they could receive re-enforcements from the Agencies. . . ."[37] And he was attempting

[34] 44 Cong., 1 sess., *Sen. Exec. Doc. No. 52,* 10–11.

[35] John G. Bourke, "General Crook in the Indian Country," *Century Magazine,* Vol. XLI (March, 1891), 652–53, describes the General as follows: "His personal appearance was impressive, but without the slightest suggestion of the pompous and over-dressed military man; he was plain as an old stick, and looked more like an honest country squire than the commander of a war-like expedition. . . . He had an aversion to wearing a uniform and to the glitter and filigree of the military profession."

[36] Bourke, *On the Border with Crook,* 254.

[37] Crook's Report, May 7, 1876, in *Report of the Secretary of War, 1876,* 503. That this expedition was intended to be little more than a scout or reconnaissance in force would seem to be apparent from the following dispatch from Crook to General Terry. ". . . The command under General Reynolds has already started. I intend to accompany the expedition so as to get some idea of the country and the

to put this intention to the test of actual performance, since it was believed that if a single one of the large villages of the hostiles could be surprised and destroyed during the winter, the resulting loss of property and exposure to the elements would cripple the enemy for years and render them unable to escape from an energetic pursuit.[38]

The first night out, Indians attacked the camp, wounding the herder and stampeding the herd, which was not captured but returned to Fort Fetterman and could not be turned and brought back. During the succeeding days there were plenty of Indian signs, night attacks, the flashing of looking-glass signals, lodgepole and pony trails, and puffs of smoke from signal fires, but actual contacts were few.[39]

The expedition followed the familiar Bozeman Trail to the site of old Fort Reno, of which nothing remained but a few chimneys and fragments of adobe walls.[40] From Crazy Woman Fork of the Powder, the infantry and wagon train were sent back to the neighborhood of Fort Reno, where a base camp was hastily improvised, while with the cavalry and scouts Crook pushed on past Fort Phil Kearny and then turned northeast, scouting Rosebud Creek and the upper waters of the Tongue River to a point at the mouth of Red Clay Creek. Here he turned southeast toward the Powder because Black Coal, an Arapaho, had told Crook that the hostiles were encamped on the Little Powder some 150 miles from Fort Fetterman.[41] No trace of a hostile village had yet been discovered, although his scouts had gone as far as the Yellowstone, and all the trails that they had seen led over toward the Powder.

The weather was bitterly cold, from the eleventh of March to the seventeenth, ranging between twenty-three and twenty-six degrees Fahrenheit below zero.[42] For breakfast the cook had to chop

difficulties to be overcome in a summer campaign. I hope to make this scout and get back before so using up my stock as to make them unfit for a summer campaign." Hughes, "Campaign against the Sioux in 1876," *Journal of the Military Service Institution of the United States*, Vol. XVIII (January, 1896), 5.

38 Bourke, *On the Border with Crook*, 247.

39 *Ibid.*, 256–57.

40 *Ibid.*, 259.

41 *Ibid.*, 250. There is also the statement that the wagons were left on the Crazy Woman Fork of the Powder River. Crook, *Autobiography*, 191.

42 Report of the General of the Army in *Report of the Secretary of War, 1876*, 29.

the bacon with an axe and often broke the axe in the process, for overnight the bacon had become as hard as marble. Bread had to be thawed out before it was eaten, and all the eating utensils had to be run through hot water or hot ashes to prevent them from taking the skin off the tongue, and the same practice had to be followed with the bits when bridling the horses.[43] On at least two occasions the mercury congealed in the bulb, showing at least thirty-nine degrees below zero, and for several days the thermometer failed to register.[44]

The command had followed Otter Creek to an abandoned Indian camp about thirty miles from the Powder River. Here the scouts reported a hunting party of Sioux in the direction of the river, and it was surmised that there was a village not far away.[45] The next day, the sixteenth, two Indian hunters were seen on a near-by ridge, and it was obvious that they were watching the soldiers. So, in an attempt to deceive them about his intentions, Crook halted at a point near the mouth of Otter Creek and went into camp. He then sent Colonel Reynolds with six troops, E, I, and K of the Second Cavalry and E, F, and M of the Third,[46] with one day's rations, to follow the trail of the hunters, and if possible to attack and destroy the village from which they came, which was believed to be on the Powder River since there was not sufficient water any nearer.

Colonel Reynolds, a classmate of President Grant at West Point, had been in trouble during Reconstruction days in Texas where he had been accused of collusion with contractors and of having accepted the gift of a house and lot.[47] He was apparently given the command purposely, in order to help him atone for the past. If the trail led to a village, Reynolds was to attack and hold it until Crook could come up with the remainder of the command. If not, the two units were to reunite at a point designated near the mouth of Lodgepole Creek.[48] Crook himself did not accompany the

43 Bourke, *On the Border with Crook,* 265.

44 Crook, *Autobiography,* 191; Bourke, *On the Border with Crook,* 263.

45 Anson Mills, *My Story,* C. H. Claudy (ed.), 166; Vestal, *New Sources of Indian History,* 179.

46 Brigadier General W. C. Brown, "Reynolds' Attack on Crazy Horse's Village on Powder River, March 17, 1876" *Winners of the West,* April 30, 1934.

47 *Army and Navy Journal,* June 24, 1876.

48 Mills, *My Story,* 166; Bourke, *On the Border with Crook,* 270; *Report of the Secretary of War, 1876,* 29.

attacking force in order, according to his own statement, that the detachment might not be embarrassed by any division of command or even the appearance of such in the field, and to free the immediate commander from any embarrassment that he might feel if the Department commander were present.[49]

Colonel Reynolds moved out shortly after five o'clock on the afternoon of the sixteenth, marching up a ravine which must have been either Pumpkin or Owl Creek, following the trail of the two young bucks, who proved to be members of a hunting party of about forty.[50] After an all-night march over the divide and down a creek bed, the troops reached the Indian camp about daybreak. Located in a thickly wooded bottom and close under the bluffs on the west bank of the Powder River about ten miles north of the mouth of the Little Powder—near the present town of Moorehead,[51] Montana—it consisted of approximately 110 lodges and between 500 and 700 Indians, of whom about 250 were warriors.[52] Although generally supposed to have been the Ogallala village of Ta Shunka Witko, better known as Crazy Horse, there is a strong probability that it was the camp of Old Bear, a Cheyenne. Some accounts insist that it was the village of Two Moon and his band of Cheyennes and that only a few Ogallalas were in the camp.[53] Since the village

[49] Crook's Report, May 7, 1876, in *Report of the Secretary of War, 1876*, 503; Crook, *Autobiography*, 191.

[50] Bourke, *On the Border with Crook*, 270.

[51] Vestal, *New Sources of Indian History*, 178–79; Marquis, *Sketch Story of the Custer Battle*.

[52] Brigadier General W. C. Brown locates the place of the battle about seven miles north of the Wyoming-Montana line and on a ranch owned by former State Senator Kelsey. He says that it contained 105 lodges and slightly over two hundred warriors. *Winners of the West*, April 30, 1934. On April 15, 1876, the *Army and Navy Journal* put the number of Indians in the camp at seven hundred although in its previous edition, April 8, it had put the number at five hundred and expressed the opinion that there were only about one-half as many hostile Indians in the country as had previously been supposed.

[53] Vestal, *New Sources of Indian History*, 180. Martin F. Schmitt and Dee Brown, *Fighting Indians of the West*, 116, say that it was a combined village of Ogallala Sioux and Cheyennes under Low Dog and Two Moons [*sic*]. Further, disagreement is provided by the fact that a wounded Indian woman in one of the lodges said that it was the village of Crazy Horse, but that forty new canvas lodges at one end of the camp belonged to some Cheyennes who had only recently arrived. Bourke, *On the Border with Crook*, 277. For the contention that it was the village of Old Bear, see Thomas B. Marquis, *She* [Kate Bighead] *Watched Custer's Last Battle; Her Story Interpreted in 1927*, and an article by Dr. Marquis in the *Billings Gazette*, July 17, 1932.

contained both Sioux and Cheyennes, and a few renegade Arapahoes are also supposed to have been present, the question of whose village it was, while not particularly important, probably never will be settled to the satisfaction of everyone.

What is more important, the attack of the soldiers was a complete surprise. The Indians were well aware that there were troops in the vicinity, and a party of warriors had been sent out to intercept them. For some reason these young men had failed in their mission, and since no guards had been posted, the troops were riding through the camp before the Indians were aware of their presence. The village, including a large herd of ponies, was captured without any trouble, the startled and bewildered occupants fleeing to the high broken hills on the west, leaving the camp in the possession of the attackers, who proceeded to set fire to the more than one hundred lodges, which did not burn but exploded when the flames came into contact with the cannisters of powder stored there. While no great quantity of baled furs was found, there were many loose robes of fine quality, enormous amounts of fresh and dried buffalo meat, and ammunition sufficient for a regiment, besides many other articles which even the white man "would not disdain to class among the comforts of life."[54]

Having recovered from their initial surprise and having taken the women and children to places of safety, the hostiles now returned and began to fire on the soldiers from rocks, bushes, and gullies, taking full advantage of the failure of the troops to occupy near-by bluffs which commanded the village. Up until this time the movement had been a perfect success. Colonel Reynolds had divided his command in an attempt to surround and annihilate the village, but the plan did not materialize when one detachment failed to carry out its assignment on account of the difficult terrain.[55] Moreover, during the latter part of the battle one battalion or squadron—that commanded by Lieutenant Noyes—was permitted to unsaddle, make coffee, and eat lunch within sight of the battlefield.[56]

For some reason—possibly doubt concerning the loyalty of

[54] Bourke, *On the Border with Crook*, 277–78; Crook, *Autobiography*, 191.

[55] Vestal, *New Sources of Indian History*, 179.

[56] *Army and Navy Journal*, April 15, 1876; *Winners of the West*, April 30, 1934.

Frank Grouard, the chief scout,[57] and the fear that he might be leading them into a trap—Colonel Reynolds lost his nerve and decided to withdraw after having been in possession of the camp for about five hours. Factors contributing to this decision, which no one has ever been able to explain satisfactorily, may have been the age and feebleness of Colonel Reynolds and the exhaustion of the troops, as well as the bitter feud which existed among the officers of the command.[58] But the dominant factor seems to have been the mistaken belief that the Indian counterattack was so formidable that the troops themselves were in danger of being surrounded and annihilated. In any event, Colonel Reynolds withdrew so precipitately that the troops practically abandoned the partially destroyed village to the Indians, retreating so rapidly that the bodies of several dead troopers were left in the hands of the hostiles. What was worse, one wounded soldier, Private Lorenzo Ayers of Company M of the Third Cavalry, was abandoned to the Indians and was cut limb from limb. Considering the importance attached to bodies by both the Sioux and the Cheyennes, and the fact that both the dead and wounded soldiers could have been removed easily but were not, this abandonment was the cause of much dissatisfaction among the troops.[59] Later a large number of enlisted men belonging to the units stationed at Fort D. A. Russell (near Cheyenne) deserted, giving as their reason that they did not care to serve under officers who would abandon their dead and dying to the foe.[60]

The magnitude of Colonel Reynolds' mistake is shown by the fact that he not only had possession of the village with its enormous stores of ammunition, meat, and robes, but also had the rest of General Crook's command within supporting distance and could have sent for it instead of falling back. Despite these advantages, about half-past two in the afternoon he began to withdraw, camping that night about ten miles from the mouth of Lodgepole Creek. The next day—the eighteenth—about noon he made junction with Crook at

[57] Vestal, *Warpath and Council Fire*, 212.

[58] Mills, *My Story*, 166.

[59] *Report of the Secretary of War, 1876*, 29; Crook's Report, May 7, 1876, in *ibid.*, 502; Bourke, *On the Border with Crook*, 278–79. Crook, *Autobiography* says that "our *wounded men* [italics mine] were left in the hands of the Indians," 191–92. See also the *Army and Navy Journal*, April 8, 1876.

[60] Bourke, *On the Border with Crook*, 285.

the appointed place. The Indians pursued the retreating troops, who were so exhausted from lack of rest and the continued cold that they neglected to post a guard over the captured pony herd, with the result that during the night many of the ponies either strayed off or were driven off by the hostiles. The troops were so tired that, although the loss of the herd was discovered before the hostiles were out of sight, no attempt was made to pursue and recapture it. But the Indians did run into Crook's four companies and for a second time lost a part of their ponies.

General Crook was quite disgruntled by the conclusion of the affair, especially since the troops had suffered the loss of four men killed and five men and one officer wounded, while the Indians had had only one killed and one wounded.[61] However, there was nothing for the troops to do but return to the forts and attempt to reorganize for a summer campaign. The command was out of supplies—they had destroyed enough in the village to last a regiment for a month—and were encumbered with wounded and with men crippled by the cold because they had not had the foresight to save the furs and skins in the camp. Moreover, the Indians were on the alert, and all possibility of another surprise attack had vanished.[62]

Through the years there has been considerable controversy concerning whether Colonel Reynolds accomplished all that the opportunity afforded. On the success side, he had completely destroyed the village, together with large quantities of equipment and ammunition, including meat and buffalo robes and many articles of food and clothing that must have come from the agencies. His failures were listed by General Crook: neglect to make a vigorous and persistent attack with his whole command, together with the failure of certain parts of the detachment to support the first attack properly; and, most serious of all, failure to secure the provisions that had been captured instead of destroying them and to take proper precautions to prevent the recapture of the pony herd by the Indians. General Crook had intended to remount his command on the captured horses and ponies and use the captured village and its supplies as a base of operations from which to push on and dis-

61 Vestal, *Warpath and Council Fire*, 215; Grinnell, however, says that no Indians were killed. *Fighting Cheyennes*, 334.

62 Bourke, *On the Border with Crook*, 280.

cover what other hostile camps might be in the vicinity.[63] It is uncertain whether Colonel Reynolds was informed of this intention, and in case he was not, he can hardly be censured for using his judgment as the commanding officer and doing what seemed to him best under the circumstances.

General Crook felt that the campaign had been a perfect success up until the moment the troops entered the hostile camp, but that the mismanagement which characterized the actions of portions of the command from then on had destroyed any chance of success that the expedition might have had.[64] The plan literally had "gone up in smoke" when the village had been fired and the lodges and supplies destroyed. Failure to secure the captured horses properly rendered any further prosecution of the campaign at this time abortive, and the expedition retreated toward Fort Fetterman, marching back to the Platte with charges against several officers as their sole accomplishment. The Indians continued to harass the party until Crook in his exasperation ordered all the remaining ponies killed, an action which solved the problem of a meat supply for the scouts and some of the troops. After this the Indians departed and left the soldiers comparatively alone.

The whole affair had been a fiasco, and it resulted in serious charges being preferred against several of the officers, notably the immediate commander of the troops, Colonel Reynolds. After a long trial, full of animosity and countercharges, Reynolds was found guilty and suspended from rank and command for one year. Of the others, Captain Alexander Moore was convicted of neglect of duty and suspended from command for six months, during which time he was to be confined to the limits of the post, while Lieutenant Henry Noyes, for conduct prejudicial to good order and military discipline, "was to be reprimanded by the Department Commander."[65] Crook's failure, together with the fact that General Terry had been unable to get started at all, seemed to demonstrate the futility of winter operations against the northern tribes, and the

[63] Crook's Report, May 7, 1876, in *Report of the Secretary of War, 1876,* 503.

[64] *Ibid.*, 502–503.

[65] *Ibid.*, 503; Crook, *Autobiography*, 191. In January, 1877, Reynolds was tried by a General Court Martial at Cheyenne, was found guilty, and sentenced to suspension from rank and command for one year. President Grant remitted the sentence, and Reynolds was retired for disability on June 25, 1877. *Winners of the West,* April 30, 1934.

complete collapse of military plans brought the campaign against the hostiles to a temporary standstill.

One significant, although somewhat incidental, result of the campaign, was to embitter further the relations between the military and the Indian Bureau. Whether the camp on the Powder River was predominantly Cheyenne or Ogallala Sioux is immaterial, since in either case its inhabitants were from Red Cloud Agency, and many of them had come out to hunt for the good and sufficient reason that there was not enough to eat at the agency. The agent there, Mr. J. S. Hastings, made no secret of the fact that his supplies of both beef and flour were inadequate. Under the prevailing system he could do nothing until Congress passed a deficiency appropriation, with the result that the new supplies did not reach the agency until midsummer. To solve the immediate crisis, the Indians had to hunt or starve.

Crook reported that many of the lodges destroyed by the troops had been new canvas ones issued to them at the agency and that among the supplies destroyed were several cannisters of powder which had been brought from the agency to trade to the hostiles, and implied that such conduct was highly unpatriotic if not treasonable. This provoked an exasperated reply from the agent, who suggested that General Crook's charges were not only untrue but made for the sole purpose of covering up his own incompetency. The agent added that his information was that five pounds of powder, twenty pounds of lead, and six boxes of percussion caps comprised all of the ammunition that had been found in the camp. He claimed to have learned from a half-blood scout that the expedition had been a complete failure, the only Indians killed having been an old Indian woman and two children.[66] From Spotted Tail Agency, Mr. E. A. Howard also protested against the erroneous information given out by Crook concerning the ammunition, war material, and general supplies found in the hostile village and declared that no arms and little ammunition had been sold to the Indians at his agency for the past two years.[67]

The engagement was at first represented as a victory for Crook and had the effect of increasing the self-confidence of the army to

[66] 44 Cong., 1 sess., *Sen. Exec. Doc. No. 52*, 12.
[67] *Ibid.*, 11–12.

a dangerous degree. Thus the semiofficial *Army and Navy Journal* commented that the village which had been destroyed had contained nearly half of all the Indians who were then off their reservations and quoted a telegram to the *New York Tribune* which read: "This engagement severely crippled if it does not entirely break up the only hostile band now infesting this portion of the frontier."[68] A week later the *Journal* suggested that it was probable that the number of Indians who were hostile was nowhere near as great as the War Department had previously supposed.[69]

Most important of all, the Indians were aroused by this failure of the troops, their old feeling of superiority to the white man was reawakened, and they became convinced that they not only could elude the white soldiers but could also defeat them on a battlefield of their own choosing. Once let an Indian be convinced that his own "medicine" is good, and he will stop at nothing.[70] Accordingly, the extent of Crook's failure is to be measured not so much by what he failed to do as by the increased confidence that that failure gave to the hostiles; and the task faced by the army, never an easy one, was now rendered much more difficult and formidable, a fact of which its leaders themselves seemed to be supremely unaware.

[68] *Army and Navy Journal*, April 1, 1876.
[69] *Army and Navy Journal*, April 8, 1876.
[70] Frank B. Linderman, *American, the Life Story of a Great Indian*, 276.

CHAPTER V

The Montana Column

CONGRESS had created the territory of Montana in 1864 by carving off a slice from both Idaho and Dakota territories. Four years before there had been nothing in the region that remotely resembled a settlement. Fort Owen, a trading post operated by Mr. John Owen, was located in the Bitter Root Valley, and the American Fur Company, as the firm of Pierre Chouteau, Jr., was known, had an establishment at Fort Benton. There were also two Catholic missions among the Coeur d'Alene and the Flathead Indians, but otherwise the country was occupied mostly by roving bands of Indians, together with a few white hunters, trappers, and idlers in the Indian camps.[1] The discovery of gold in the following year brought, as it always does, settlers flocking into the region, and various towns such as Deer Lodge and Virginia City soon sprang up. With them came naturally and inevitably the problem of pacifying the Indian tribes, especially the belligerent Blackfeet, whose resentment was aroused at this new threat to their hunting grounds.

To meet this new danger of Indian warfare, and in furtherance of its policy of the encirclement of the tribes, the War Department began the construction of military posts in the territory. In 1866, Fort Cooke on the Missouri River, 120 miles below Fort Benton, was garrisoned by the Thirteenth Infantry, and during the next year Fort Shaw on the Sun River[2] was built to protect travelers over the Mullan Road from the Blackfeet, while a year later Fort Ellis[3] was constructed on the East Gallatin River, both of the new forts being garrisoned by detachments from the regiment at Fort

[1] Bradley, *Journal,* 150.

[2] Stuart, *Forty Years on the Frontier,* II, 80. It was named for Colonel Robert G. Shaw, a veteran of the Civil War.

Cooke. Two years later, however, Fort Cooke was abandoned and its garrison transferred to Fort Benton, but at the same time Camp Baker, later renamed Fort Logan, on Smith's River or Deep Creek, was built and occupied, while four troops of the Second Cavalry were added to the garrison at Fort Ellis. The next year the Thirteenth was replaced by the Seventh Infantry, and the military district of Montana assumed the form that it was to maintain for the next several years.[4]

In 1876 the territory had a population of about fifteen thousand persons, most of them permanent residents, who were concentrated for the most part in the mining settlements in the western part of the state and in the valleys of the Missouri River and west of its three forks, Helena being the capital city and chief metropolis.[5] Fort Shaw, as an outpost against the hostile and treacherous Blackfoot Indians, was garrisoned by headquarters and six companies of the Seventh Infantry; Camp Baker had two companies; Fort Benton, to the east and north, had one; while Fort Ellis had one company of the Seventh Infantry and four troops of the Second Cavalry.[6] All were under the command of Colonel John Gibbon, who had been appointed to the post in 1869. He had made an enviable record in the Civil War and has been described as "a typical officer of the old school, not much given to 'fuss and feathers' but one of the sturdy, substantial sort who could be depended upon to carry out his orders."[7] A pronounced limp resulting from a wound received during the Civil War led to his being known among the Crows as "No-Hip-Bone" or "The One who Limps."[8]

On the twenty-seventh of February, General Terry had ordered Gibbon to prepare for the field all the troops that could be spared from the various garrisons under his command, and then

[3] Fort Ellis was named for Colonel Augustus VanHorn Ellis of the 124th New York Volunteers.

[4] Bradley, *Journal*, 151.

[5] Dustin, *The Custer Tragedy*, 69.

[6] Bradley, *Journal*, 149–51. The headquarters detachment, the noncommissioned officer staff, and the regimental band were stationed at Fort Shaw in addition to Companies A, B, G, H, I, and K of the Seventh Infantry; Companies D and E were at Camp Baker, F at Fort Benton, while C was at Fort Ellis. This last post also housed Companies F, G, H, and L of the Second Cavalry. *Report of the Secretary of War, 1876*, 58, 65.

[7] DeLand, *The Sioux Wars*, 313.

[8] Linderman, *American*, 154; Dustin, *The Custer Tragedy*, 169.

to move eastward against the hostile tribes. On account of the inclemency of the weather and the difficulties of communication, immediate compliance with the order was impossible, and it was not until the fourteenth of March that Company E of the infantry, under the command of Captain Clifford, marched from Camp Baker toward Fort Ellis, digging its way through the deep snowdrifts of a mountain range. Arriving at Fort Ellis on the twenty-second, they took charge of a train of twenty-eight contract wagons carrying one hundred thousand pounds of supplies and marched for the Crow Agency on the Stillwater, where Gibbon planned to establish a supply depot.[9]

Three days later, at ten o'clock on the morning of the seventeenth, the same day that General Crook's command was fighting the Indians on the Powder River, five companies of the infantry comprising twelve officers and nearly two hundred men, with ten contract wagons and rations for ten days, began the march of over 180 miles from Fort Shaw to Fort Ellis. Several inches of snow were on the ground, the weather was extremely cold—a night or two later it was estimated that the temperature was forty degrees below zero—and the men, who had grown somewhat soft during a winter of garrison duty, found the going rather difficult. In addition, there were many cases of frostbite and snow blindness, and the roughness of the road caused the wagons to fall far behind and in some cases to overturn.[10]

Lieutenant James Bradley, whose *Journal* is one of the chief sources for this march of the Montana column as well as a most interesting piece of frontier Americana, had been placed in command of a mounted detachment of twelve infantry scouts.[11] While pursuing two soldiers who had deserted from the command, he was overcome by snowblindness and has left a most graphic description of that horrible affliction:

> It comes on with a feeling such as is created by smoke in the eyes, that, if the case is severe, increases in to the most intense burning pain.

[9] Bradley, *Journal*, 157; Gibbon's Report in *Report of the Secretary of War, 1876*, 471.

[10] The account of the march as here given, except as otherwise noted, is based on Bradley, *Journal*.

[11] *Billings Gazette*, May 15, 1932.

The eyes can not bear the light and the eye-balls seem to roll in liquid fire with a grating feeling as though in contact with particles of sand.[12]

Bradley recovered after a few days and rejoined the battalion, but Captain Rawn, who, in the absence of Colonel Gibbon, was in command of the detachment, was not so fortunate, and after two attacks was forced to turn over his responsibilities to Captain Freeman and to return to the fort for treatment.

By Monday, the twentieth, the weather had moderated and the men marched eighteen miles through mud and slush and that night pitched their tents "in the mud with clothes and blankets wet." The next day saw a march of only five miles, the battalion camping after only two and one-half hours on the road, in order to give the soldiers a much needed rest and to allow them to dry their clothing and equipment. Camp was made at "John's Ranch," at the head of Little Prickly Pear Canyon on the old Helena and Fort Benton stage road, and between the stations of Silver and Mitchell on the Montana Central Railroad.

On the twenty-second a fresh difficulty presented itself, for the road was now hard and dry, and the infantrymen began to suffer from blistered feet. But they made seventeen miles that day before camping some four miles from the city of Helena, which some of the officers and men visited during the evening and where one man deserted. Here Colonel Gibbon overtook and joined the command. The next day's march was over a muddy road, and as one officer expressed it, "The march was eighteen miles long and six inches deep all the way," and the men went into camp thoroughly tired out. The march on the twenty-fourth was easier and the road better; Lieutenant Bradley, who rejoined the command that afternoon at its camp at Indian Creek Ferry, noted that the troops were toughening in to their work, an observation which was borne out on the following day when they made twenty-five miles without apparent ill effects.

On the twenty-sixth they put fourteen miles behind them, in the course of which they crossed the Missouri River somewhat less than a mile below the junction of the Jefferson and the Madison rivers and two hundred yards above the place where the waters

[12] Bradley, *Journal*, 153.

of the Gallatin join the main stream. On the twenty-seventh the men, who now marched like veterans, covered eighteen miles, and the next day a march of twelve miles brought them to the town of Bozeman and four more miles to Fort Ellis.

The whole country around the fort was found to be in a wash of slush and mud with torrents of dirty water sweeping down the slope upon which the infantry had pitched their camp. Here the command remained for one day only, drawing supplies and forage and preparing for the next stage of the campaign.

On the thirtieth the march was resumed with the infantry heading for the Yellowstone River. Colonel Gibbon remained at the fort planning to accompany the cavalry battalion, which was not yet ready to march and which would follow in a few days, being able to overtake the slower-moving infantry without any trouble. Departure from Fort Ellis meant that the troops were putting the settled portion of Montana behind them, marching into a country that was almost devoid of human habitation, its few scattered cabins and ranches being occupied only at the constant risk of their owners' lives. The route followed—across Bozeman Pass, beneath which the main line of the Northern Pacific now tunnels—was a rugged one, through a gap and then over a divide and across the range of mountains which separates the drainage basin of the Missouri River from that of the Yellowstone. It was approximately that taken by Captain Clark on his return from the Pacific some seventy years before. The steep, rocky road was interspersed in places by streams and marshy spots where the heavily loaded wagons sank to the hubs.[13]

The Missouri River is formed near Three Forks, Montana, by the waters of the Madison, the Jefferson, and the Gallatin rivers. The easternmost of these, the Gallatin, rises in Yellowstone Park not far from the headwaters of the Yellowstone River, and the two streams flow parallel to each other and only a few miles apart for a considerable distance. But the Yellowstone turns to the northeast sooner than the Missouri, and the two streams gradually approach each other before merging their waters almost at the North Dakota–

[13] Gibbon, "Summer Expedition," 274. There is a good map of the route followed by the Montana column in Edward J. McClernand, "March of the 'Montana Column' " in Charles F. Roe, *Custer's Last Battle* (New York, Bruce Publishing Co., 1927). It may also be found in McClernand, "With the Indians and the Buffalo in Montana," *Cavalry Journal*, Vol. XXXVI (January and April, 1927), 24.

Montana boundary line, near the site of old Fort Union and the later Fort Buford. Where it turns eastward, the Yellowstone River is only about twenty miles from Fort Ellis at the head of the Gallatin Valley. Because of the nature of the country the Yellowstone has few tributaries entering it from the north, but from the south it receives the waters of Clark's Fork, the Big Horn, the Rosebud, the Tongue, and the Powder, as well as those of many smaller streams and creeks.

Just before leaving the fort, the infantry column learned of Crook's fight near the Little Powder two weeks before.[14] The information was rather sketchy, but indicated that while he had withdrawn his forces from the field and returned temporarily to Fort Fetterman, he had driven the Indians away with considerable loss of life, had destroyed their camp and winter supplies, and had captured the pony herd.

A heavy snow on the thirtieth kept the expedition in camp all of the next day. Advantage was taken of the delay to begin instituting the regulations that were to govern the conduct of the column during the campaign that lay ahead. Instead of a mixed guard as had previously been the case, an entire company was to be detailed for guard duty each night, and its senior officer was to be officer of the day. Since there were five companies, this meant that every company would be on duty every fifth day. The sentinels were to be posted about the camp in groups of three, but only one was required to keep awake at a time. Instead of challenging orally, the sentinel was to whistle at anyone approaching and to fire if he received no reply, a system that Lieutenant Bradley felt was abominable and more dangerous to the troops than to the enemy.[15]

On the first of April the troops marched nineteen miles and camped that night on Shield's River or Twenty-five Yard Creek, which is the only principal tributary of the Yellowstone coming in from the north. A famous beaver stream, it had been named by Captain Clark for one of his men. There were two explanations given for the alternate name, one that it was not twenty-five yards wide, and the other that it headed within that distance of another

[14] Gibbon, "Summer Expedition," 274.
[15] Bradley, *Journal*, 153.

stream, a report that the scientifically minded Bradley admitted that he did not have the time to investigate. Here the infantry overtook a train of contract wagons which had left Fort Ellis several days in advance carrying supplies for sixty days. The next day seventeen miles were covered, and on the third the troops marched sixteen miles, most of it through a blinding snowstorm, before camping at the junction of the Big Boulder and the Yellowstone rivers. Since they were now getting well into the region where they might expect to encounter hostile Indians, Bradley and his mounted detachment scouted the country thoroughly for traces of the Sioux before making camp, and at night the wagons were arranged as a corral and the herd driven inside, while the soldiers were arranged around the outside in approved defensive fashion.

On April 1, the four troops of the Second Cavalry, F, G, H, and L, left Fort Ellis under the immediate command of Major James Brisbin, who at the time was suffering from rheumatism to such an extent that he was on crutches and unable to mount a horse. But he insisted upon going along and Gibbon finally consented, the Major riding in an ambulance for the first part of the journey.[16] Brisbin was an elderly officer who took a great deal of interest in the agricultural potentialities of the district where he was stationed, and who discoursed upon them to such length at every opportunity that he won from the soldiers the good-natured nickname of "Grasshopper Jim."[17]

The command proceeded along the same trail that the infantry had followed, but the condition of the road was so frightful that they were able to make only seven miles before camping at sunset. The second day's march was a repetition of the first, but on the third day they made better progress despite a furious storm of wind and drifting snow, although at the expense of the wagon train, which fell far behind; the battalion spent the fourth day in camp at Shield's River waiting for the wagons to catch up.[18] On the fifth, they made twenty miles, in the course of which they passed the site of the old Crow Agency; the next day they crossed Big Boulder Creek and

[16] Gibbon, Report, 471.
[17] Hanson, *Conquest of the Missouri*, 249.
[18] Gibbon, "Summer Expedition," 274.

that night camped at the junction of Big Deer Creek and the Yellowstone, being only a short distance behind the infantry, with whom they united on the eighth just above the mouth of the Stillwater.[19]

The infantry had halted and waited for the cavalry to come up because of a change in plan occasioned by the news from General Crook. The original intention had been to march the Montana column eastward to the site of Fort C. F. Smith by way of the old Bozeman Trail. From there it was to march directly eastward in the expectation of striking and destroying any hostile camps which might be located in the valleys of the Little Big Horn, the Rosebud, or the Tongue rivers. But the complexion of things had changed greatly with the receipt of the news of the fight on the Powder River. Since the hostile bands were believed to be not numerous, it was felt that they would probably flee northward as Crook began to press them and would attempt to cross to the north bank of the Yellowstone and possibly even of the Missouri, making it necessary for Gibbon to prevent their crossing so that one of the other columns could strike them. The new plan called for Gibbon to press forward as rapidly as possible, keeping on the north bank of the Yellowstone instead of to the south of the river, for otherwise the Indians, if moving north, would cross the Yellowstone and possibly even the Missouri before either the Montana or Dakota columns could interfere.[20] The former river generally begins its spring rise in April, reaches the crest in June, and then subsides, reaching its low water mark in August; since the two principal crossing places used by the Indians were just above and just below the mouth of the Rosebud, it was incumbent upon Gibbon to arrive in that vicinity as soon as possible.

The united command camped on the north bank about twenty miles downstream from the mouth of Bridger Creek, where they had found a party of civilian prospectors preparing to set off for the Black Hills, Sioux or no Sioux. The infantry camp was just above the mouth of the Stillwater, while the cavalry camp was near a ford some four miles farther upstream. Here Gibbon sent word to the Crows at their agency that he desired to meet their headmen in council for the purpose of enlisting scouts. He also asked the

[19] *Ibid.*, 275.
[20] Terry's Report, 460.

famous frontiersman, Minton, or "Mitch" Bouyer, for whose scalp Sitting Bull is said to have offered a reward of one hundred horses,[21] to come in and see him, planning to employ him as a guide for the expedition if mutually satisfactory terms could be arranged.

Bouyer was considered, next to his "teacher," Bridger, the best scout in the country. A half-blood Sioux, who could speak English, Sioux, and Crow, Bouyer had served with troops before, and was reputed to have a minutely detailed knowledge of every local region between Bozeman and the Platte River. Diffident and low spoken, he uttered his words in a hesitating way, as if uncertain of what he was going to say. He looked like an Indian but dressed like a white man. Gibbon later declared that Bouyer was the only half-blood he had ever known who could give the distances to be passed over with any degree of accuracy, in miles.[22]

Bouyer, who was hired, and not enlisted, as a guide, brought word that the Crows were waiting for Gibbon at their agency, and so the Colonel, accompanied by Major Brisbin, Captain Freeman, and Lieutenants Burnett and Bradley, together with the mounted detachment, started for the agency, which was located on Stillwater Fork. They reached that place after a disagreeable ride of eighteen miles, mostly through wet snow. Here they found the mountain Crows assembled for the council. Also there were the officers and men of Company E of the infantry which had come on ahead with its train of wagons and camped here in the belief that the Crow Agency was to be used as the base of supplies for subsequent operations. But the news of Crook's fight with its resultant change of plan made necessary the selection of a new base and with it the transfer of the stores already assembled to a new location on the north bank of the Yellowstone.

The Crows, who were tall and unusually light-complexioned for Indians[23] and handsomest of all the western tribes—the Veren-

[21] Jacob Adams, "A Survivor's Story of the Custer Massacre on the American Frontier," *Journal of American History*, Vol. III, No. 2 (1909), 228 (hereinafter cited as Adams, "Survivor's Story").

[22] Thomas B. Marquis, *Memoirs of a White Crow Indian*, 210; Gibbon, "Summer Expedition," 275; Colonel John Gibbon, "Hunting Sitting Bull," *American Catholic Quarterly Review*, Vol. II, No. 3 (October, 1877), 671. McClernand says that Bouyer had married a Crow woman and lived with her tribe. "With Indian and Buffalo in Montana," *Cavalry Journal*, Vol. XXXVI (January and April, 1927), 16.

[23] Dustin, *The Custer Tragedy*, 3.

dryes[24] seem to have called them the Beaux Hommes—had always been friendly to the whites and seem to have been noted alike for their moral profligacy and for their ability as horse thieves. They were also great buffalo hunters and were especially adept at dressing the robes. Proud and stately, they were generally clean of body and clothing, in contrast to the greasy garb of some other tribes. Their name for themselves was Absaroka, or Sparrowhawk people, which is said by some to mean "chosen people," but whose exact meaning has probably been lost.[25] There are several explanations of how they happened to be called Crows, one being that the early French traders translated the name Absaroka as *gens de corbeaux*, or the "raven people," but the older Crows deny this and declare that it was their enemy, the Sioux, who fastened the name on them.[26] Along with the Arikara they had early become blood or hereditary enemies of the Sioux confederacy, for whom they had an inveterate hatred,[27] and Gibbon knew that it was among them, if anywhere, that he would find the scouts whom he needed for his campaign.

The Crows had gathered at the agency to receive their annuity payments, and the agent, Mr. Dexter Clapp, had arranged a conference or formal council between Colonel Gibbon and the principal chiefs and warriors. To these Gibbon said:

> I have come down here to make war on the Sioux. The Sioux are your enemy and ours. For a long while they have been killing white men and killing Crows. I am going down to punish the Sioux for making war upon the white men. If the Crows want to make war upon the Sioux now is their time. If they want to drive them from their country and prevent them from sending war parties into their country to murder their men, now is the time. If they want to get revenge for Crows that have fallen, to get revenge for the killing of such men as the gallant soldier, Long Horse, now is their time.[28]

[24] LeRoy R. Hafen and Carl Coke Rister, *Western America*, 38.

[25] Branch, *Hunting the Buffalo*, 47.

[26] *Montana, State Guide Book*, 196 (hereinafter cited as Montana, *Guide*).

[27] Dustin, *The Custer Tragedy*, 1–2.

[28] Bradley, *Journal*, 158. Pretty Shield, wife of Goes Ahead, says that the Crows were camped at the mouth of Rotten-Sun-Dance-Tepee Creek (Clark's Fork of the Yellowstone River) when Gibbon asked for scouts. She puts the month as May—"the moon when the leaves were showing"—and says the soldiers came in a "fire-boat" on Elk River, which is obviously impossible. Frank B. Linderman, *Red Mother*, 224. According to Bradley it was Saturday, April 9, when Gibbon visited the Crow camp.

He then said that he wanted twenty-five young men who were active and brave to go along with him and be his "eyes" to find out where the Sioux were so that he could go after them. These young men would be enlisted as soldiers of the government and would receive soldier's pay and soldier's food.

The Crow chiefs pretended to be very much unimpressed, and there followed a long period of wrangling and argument, during which it was apparent that while they feared and hated the Sioux, they were also somewhat skeptical of the white man and his promises. The two chiefs, Iron Bull and Blackfoot, who replied to Gibbon, said that their young men could go if they wanted to, but that the chiefs would not force them to go. They had many complaints about their treatment by the government, the rations furnished them, and things in general, to which Gibbon could answer only that they were not his concern and would have to be adjusted with the agent. There was lengthy discussion which often wandered far afield, and finally Gibbon, apparently in some exasperation, withdrew.

Much of the difficulty was no doubt attributable to the interpreter, a Frenchman by the name of Pierre Shane, who spoke very broken English, and who in the course of his interpretation translated "God Almighty" as "Godulamity." Although the interpreters left much to be desired, they were always a factor in dealing with the Indian tribes, for it was only rarely that the white officials and the Indians could converse together in the native tongue of either. It was this experience which caused Gibbon to record his opinion of them:

These Indian interpreters are a peculiar institution. As a class, they are an interesting study, and will generally bear a great deal of watching. A white man, usually a renegade from civil society, takes up his abode with a tribe of Indians, adopts their mode of life, takes unto himself a squaw, picks up gradually enough of their signs and words to make himself understood, and when the Indians come in contact with the whites becomes, in the absence of any other means of communication, an interpreter. He may not understand the English language, or be able to put together a single intelligible sentence, and it does not mend the matter much if he happens to be a French Canadian, for then broken French, broken English and broken Indian are mixed up in a hodgepodge which defies all understanding, and makes the listener sometimes give up in despair. . . . The one who officiated on this occasion appeared to be making up by gesticulations and a loud voice for any defects in his knowledge of the language.[29]

After the council one fact became quite obvious, that the two chiefs spoke only for themselves, and not for their young men, in their opposition to Gibbon's request for scouts. The warriors, as soon as the nature of the soldiers' errand was learned, gathered about the officers and professed themselves as anxious to join the expedition, and Gibbon had little difficulty in securing the number wanted.[30] There were twenty-three in all, most of them in early manhood between the ages of twenty and thirty, but two were veterans of middle age, while two of the others were over sixty. The older scouts were expected to be of little service beyond giving the young men the benefit of their experience and advice and adding "tone" and "character" to the expedition. One of them was Ee-suh-seé-ush, an inveterate "coffee-cooler" who had no idea of engaging in any of the labors of the group, and who, because of a resemblance, real or fancied, to a senator from Pennsylvania, was known among both officers and men as "The Senator."[31] Of the others, several were quite young, the one destined to become the most famous of all, Curly-Head or Curly, being a boy of only seventeen or eighteen. He was not the youngest, for another, known as Grandmother's Knife, was not more than sixteen.[32] The scouts furnished their own arms, but all except two had modern breech-loading carbines—one of these had a revolver, while the other was armed only with a bow and arrows. The armament of the scouts is sufficient comment upon the apparent ease with which the Indians were able to obtain the best in arms and ammunition.

In addition to the Crows there were two squaw men—LeForge, whom Lieutenant Bradley always referred to as Le Forgey and for whom he seems to have had a good deal of respect, and Bravo, of

[29] Gibbon, "Summer Expedition," 276; Bradley, *Journal*, 162. The famous Crow chief, Plenty Coups, shared the opinion of the white soldiers. He said, "I am always afraid of interpreters. Too many have forked tongues." Linderman, *American*, 162.

[30] Gibbon, "Summer Expedition," 277; Marquis, *Memoirs of a White Crow Indian*, 209.

[31] Gibbon, "Summer Expedition," 278.

[32] Marquis, *Memoirs of a White Crow Indian*, 208–209.

whom his opinion was not so high—who went along as interpreters. The latter is said to have been a particularly notorious character, being a deserter from the army—one account says from the Seventh Cavalry because of his infatuation for a Crow woman—who had never been picked up because he was not worth the trouble, his military service consisting mostly of malingering and dividing his time between the hospital and the guardhouse.[33]

In the Indian wars the service rendered by the scouts was of inestimable value. Although they had their faults, were indolent and mercurial, and often restive under discipline, they were not cowards, and in their capacity as the eyes and ears of the army often displayed a courage and audacity in time of danger that put the white soldier to shame. They guided the troops across wild and inaccessible country and braved blizzards, cold, and heat, as well as the menace of a wily foe. No trial of strength or endurance was too great, and in many ways they were fully as important as were the guns and ammunition, although too often their services were unappreciated and unrewarded.[34]

On the morning of the tenth, Gibbon informed Bradley that he was to have command of the scouts, much to that officer's satisfaction, and the ceremony of administering the oath of allegiance to the Crows was begun. Among that tribe the custom in taking an oath was for the individual to touch the tip of his finger to the point of a knife. All of the volunteers were paraded, and while one of the officers held a large hunting knife toward them, each of the scouts placed the tip of his index finger on the point. When the ceremony was over, the Indians had become United States soldiers for three months and were to receive soldier's pay, rations, and clothing. The scouts then wanted Gibbon and Bradley to take an oath to believe what the scouts told them and to do what they wanted them to do; but Gibbon replied that such a proposition was preposterous, that it was the scouts who were to obey and that the obligation was on their side alone. Apparently wanting only some sort of mutual obligation, the scouts settled for a promise that they would be given the same pay, rations, and allowances as the

[33] Bradley, *Journal*, 163; Fred A. Hunt, "A Purposeful Picnic . . . ," *Pacific Monthly*, Vol. XIX (1908), 446.

[34] Joseph K. Dixon, *The Vanishing Race, the Last Great Indian Council . . . Their Solemn Farewell and the Indians' Story of the Custer Fight*, 129.

white soldiers, whereupon Bradley solemnly touched the point of the knife.[35] The matter settled, Bradley uniformed them by the simple expedient of furnishing each scout with a piece of red cloth, which was to be worn on the left arm above the elbow.

On Saturday afternoon, Captain Clifford and his company had marched to join the other elements of the command in the camp on the Yellowstone. On Monday morning, Lieutenant Jacobs, the quartermaster, arrived with a train of wagons, escorted by Lieutenant McClernand and a detachment of the cavalry for the purpose of transferring the supplies stored at the agency to the new base of operations. The stores were all loaded before nightfall, but by that time a snowstorm had set in, and by morning there were eighteen inches of snow on the ground. Fearful of being snowed in, Gibbon decided to march in spite of the bad road conditions, and by nine o'clock the command was under way. As they got farther from the mountains, the storm became less violent and the snow less deep. In crossing the Yellowstone, two mules were drowned, but without further mishap the detachment reached the remainder of the command, which had moved fifteen miles down the Yellowstone and were camped together for the first time at what is now Columbus, Montana.[36]

In all there were six companies of the Seventh Infantry, an aggregate of thirteen officers and two hundred and twenty men, four troops of the Second Cavalry, or ten officers and one hundred and eighty-five men, a surgeon, Dr. Paulding, the twenty-three Crow scouts and two interpreters, several half-blood and white scouts, and twenty noncombatants who manned the train of twenty-four government and twelve contract wagons. The command also had a twelve-pounder Napoleon gun and two Gatling guns. These were served by a detachment from the infantry commanded by Lieutenant Woodruff.[37]

[35] Gibbon, "Summer Expedition," 277.

[36] Thomas B. Marquis, *Two Days after the Custer Battle*, 1. The command as constituted for the campaign consisted of six companies of the Seventh Infantry, A under Captain Logan, B under Lieutenant Kirtland, E under Captain Clifford, H under Captain Freeman, I under Lieutenant English, and K under Captain Sanno, and four companies, or troops, of the Second Cavalry, F under Lieutenant Roe, G under Captain Whelan, H under Captain Ball, and L under Captain Thompson.

[37] Bradley, *Journal*, 164. Coe Smith Hayne, *Red Men on the Big Horn*, 5, gives the names of twenty-one Crow scouts who went with Gibbon although he says

The troops in the camp had spent the day of their commander's absence in resting and repairing uniforms and equipment. Men and officers alike had spent much time fishing and had taken several hundred pounds of trout from the Yellowstone despite, as Bradley noted with considerable satisfaction, Washington Irving's statement in *Astoria* that the fish were not to be found in Rocky Mountain streams. The wagon train from the agency arrived in camp late on the evening of the eleventh, and the next day was spent in loading, sorting, and reloading the supplies, all of which could not be transported in the number of wagons available. Therefore it was arranged that Captain Logan and A Company of the infantry with one of the Gatlings should be left behind to guard such supplies as could not be taken. That night the Crow scouts, who had been accompanied to the rendezvous by a number of their friends and relatives, had a ceremonial dance, "making medicine," or conjuring for good luck, and it was with extreme difficulty that Bradley was able to restrain them sufficiently to allow the remainder of the command to get some sleep.[38]

The next morning saw the campaign begin in real earnest with the resumption of the march down the Yellowstone. The column moved at seven o'clock in the morning over heavy roads. Bravo, with ten of the Crows, was well out in front, then came Lieutenant Bradley with the remainder of the scouts and his mounted detachment, and the train and column were a few miles to the rear. As LeForge had not yet joined the expedition Bradley was without the services of an interpreter, and as a result most of the Crows hung around the wagon train instead of remaining with the advance. LeForge put in an appearance that evening, and the next day Bradley noted that "the Crows did excellent scouting service, scouring the country ahead for a breadth of ten or twelve miles and keeping well to the front. If allowed they would be mere camp loafers, but if urged and looked after, they will do good work."[39]

The ground was still very soft as a result of the melting snows, and the heavily laden wagons moved ponderously along, slowing

there were twenty-five all told and he fails to list some names which are given elsewhere.

38 Bradley, *Journal*, 164.

39 *Ibid.*, 165.

the progress of the expedition to their own snail's pace. On the thirteenth they made less than twelve miles although eight hours on the road, and on the next day made only a little better time, camping that night opposite the confluence of Clark's Fork and the Yellowstone. On the fifteenth they passed through large areas of sagebrush, about the first that they had seen, and in the late afternoon passed Baker's battleground, where in 1872 the Indians had attacked a body of troops who were escorting an engineering party engaged in making a survey for the Northern Pacific Railroad. They camped that night at six o'clock after making more than seventeen miles.

The command was annoyed by the presence of about fourteen Crows, relatives and friends of the scouts, camp followers who served no purpose at all other than exerting a bad influence over the scouts and encouraging them in neglect of duty. Gibbon's exasperation increased daily until it finally overflowed, and then he gave the hangers-on their choice of returning to the agency or of making a scout down the river toward the mouth of the Rosebud. In this latter event they were to be furnished with rations for three days. They chose the second of the two alternatives, drew their rations, and left, accompanied by two of the scouts, who were to return and inform Gibbon of any discoveries made by the party. At the same time a white scout, "Muggins" Taylor, and one of the Crows were sent to scout toward the Big Horn River. A march of only seven miles on the sixteenth brought the expedition to Pryor Creek, and the next night they camped only a few hundred yards below Pompey's Pillar after a warm and sultry day.[40]

This peculiar formation, which received its name from Lewis and Clark, is an irregular mass of sandstone rising several hundred feet above the valley on the south side of the Yellowstone River, and evidently belonged originally to a corresponding bluff on the opposite bank, from which it had been separated by long years of erosive action.[41] Many of the officers expressed their disappointment at what they saw, having doubtless expected to see a tall, needle-like spire, whereas in fact the rock is broader than it is high and is overtopped by many of the near-by bluffs. Officers and men alike took advantage of the occasion to indulge in the practice of inscribing

[40] *Ibid.*, 172; Gibbon, "Summer Expedition," 278–79.
[41] Gibbon, "Summer Expedition," 279.

their names—for the benefit of posterity?—in the soft rock of this formation.

Taylor and his companion returned to report having seen no sign of any Indians, although they had scouted as far as the mouth of the Little Big Horn. They had discovered enormous herds of buffalo quietly feeding, a circumstance which some of the officers interpreted as constituting further proof that there were no Sioux in the vicinity. But, as Bradley noted, this was not conclusive evidence by any means, for the Sioux were such expert hunters they had been known to kill buffalo daily from a herd without frightening the remaining animals sufficiently to cause them to leave the vicinity. Gibbon added that the presence of these enormous herds was the best evidence in the world that the hostiles were not far away, since the buffalo constituted a moving depot of supplies which the Indians constantly followed,[42] and from past experience the Crows knew that as the spring and summer advanced, the Sioux and Cheyennes would begin coming into the region east of the Big Horn.[43]

The eighteenth of April was spent in camp, but the next day the march was resumed, with no trace of the enemy. During the day the troops covered better than eighteen miles, fording the river twice, a procedure which was slow and difficult as well as dangerous. During the night one of the sentinels reported what he thought was a signal fire on the bluffs farther down the river, but the scouts who were sent to investigate reported that they could find no sign of human presence.[44] During the next day's march the command passed the mouth of the Big Horn and after a march of seventeen miles, camped at 4:45 P.M. in a grassy cove only two miles above the site of Fort Pease.

Here, on the twenty-first, Colonel Gibbon received a dispatch from St. Paul dated the fifteenth and sent to Fort Ellis and from there by courier, stating that General Crook would not be prepared to take the field again before the middle of May, and that owing to the late snows the Dakota column would not start before then, which meant that Gibbon's comparatively small command was un-

42 *Ibid.*, 280.
43 Marquis, *Memoirs of a White Crow Indian*, 241.
44 Bradley, *Journal*, 173.

supported in the middle of hostile Indian country.[45] These dispatches also added the information that the hostiles were in much greater force than the original estimates had indicated and that Crook's "victory" on the upper Powder had been a rather empty one, by no means as decisive as Gibbon had at first been led to suppose. Since General Terry was fearful that the Indians might combine and overwhelm Gibbon, the latter was directed to cease his advance and remain at Fort Pease until further orders. In accordance with these orders the column moved two miles farther downstream and that afternoon camped outside the walls of the fort, some 215 miles from Fort Ellis. They found the soil fertile and the grass plentiful and good. Also the abandoned buildings of the fort made an excellent storehouse for the supplies.[46]

Gibbon's command found the fort in the same condition as it had been left by Brisbin's command only a few weeks before, sure evidence that the Sioux had not returned in the interim or they would certainly have fired it. Here the wagons were unloaded, and, with Captain Freeman's company of the infantry, sent back to bring down the supplies which had been left at Logan's Camp. The rest of the command, after a thorough "policing" of the fort, for the most part settled down to await future developments.

On the twenty-fourth, Captain Ball with two troops of the cavalry,[47] his own and Lieutenant Roe's, a total of about eighty men, and accompanied by two white scouts, "Muggins" Taylor and George Herendeen, and by LeForge and some of the Crows, left for a seven-day scouting trip up the Big Horn River as far as the site of Fort C. F. Smith, to return via Tullock's Creek, which the Indians knew as "the place where the colts died."[48] In order to minimize the possibility of detection by any of the enemy, the start was not made until after six o'clock in the evening, when they crossed

[45] Gibbon, "Summer Expedition," 282; Roe, *Custer's Last Battle*, 1.

[46] Bradley, *Journal*, 174.

[47] McClernand, "March of the 'Montana Column,'" in Roe, *Custer's Last Battle*, 20–23. The same material may be found in McClernand, "With Indian and Buffalo in Montana," *Cavalry Journal*, Vol. XXXVI (January and April, 1927), 7–54, 191–207. McClernand did not belong to either of the troops participating in the scout but went along in his capacity as acting engineer officer for the district of Montana.

[48] Linderman, *American*, 190.

the Yellowstone by a good ford just above the mouth of the Big Horn and five and one-half miles from Fort Pease. They ascended and rode along a high ridge or "backbone," noting that in several places along its summit the channels of streams draining into the Yellowstone and Big Horn rivers almost joined. Camp was made a few minutes before midnight on a tortuous stream which the Indians called Wood Creek, at a place where the water stood in pools. But the grass was poor and the horses had little to eat.

Resuming the march at 9:15 A.M., the little detachment rode sixteen miles before halting on the left bank of the Big Horn. Here the troops rested until nearly seven o'clock in the evening, when they continued the ride upstream, reaching the mouth of the Little Big Horn half an hour later. They came in from the southeast through a green and attractive meadow, and halted briefly a short distance from the present town of Hardin. Lieutenant McClernand noted that on each stream there was an abundance of cottonwood timber. Camp was made at midnight in a small cove on the Big Horn, with a total of thirty-two miles covered during the day.

On the morning of the twenty-sixth they forded the Big Horn and during the day rode through enormous herds of buffalo which were grazing in all directions. Two small streams, Rotten Grass Creek and Soap Creek, were crossed, and the soldiers noted that the water was both clear and cold. Rotten Grass Creek, which was about ten feet wide and quite shallow, flowed through a deep ravine. They crossed about 2:00 P.M. and a few minutes after six o'clock crossed Soap Creek, with its high banks and firm, pebbly bottom. Frequent rests were taken during the day in order to allow the horses to graze, and only twenty miles were covered before halting for the night. At the campsite the grass was both good and abundant, and Captain Ball decided to remain there all of the next day as some of the horses and mules were very weak. He later declared that this was the finest land he had seen in Montana, with not a stone, cactus, or sagebrush, and water in abundance.

Starting again shortly after 5:00 P.M., they moved through the hayfields of Fort C. F. Smith and three miles farther on reached the site of the abandoned fort, seventy-five miles from the mouth of the Big Horn River. Its walls, which had been constructed of adobe on a stone foundation, were still standing as were most of the buildings, although the roofs had fallen in and the flagstaff lay across the parade ground, having undoubtedly been felled by the Indians. The cemetery was little injured, and the limestone monument erected by their comrades to the memory of Lieutenant Sternburg and his companions was still standing, relatively undefaced although its corners were chipped. Near the fort they found a deserted camp apparently made only a few days previously by a party of prospectors on their way to the Black Hills.

The next day the detachment moved slightly east of north and through a district alive with game, reaching the Little Big Horn at six o'clock in the evening. After riding about a mile farther downstream, they camped on the west bank in a pleasant grove of cottonwoods where there was an abundance of grass and good water. The march down the left bank continued the following day through a beautiful meadow, but they noticed that the bluffs across the river were badly cut and scarred by ravines, and a few miles farther on they passed the place where a large Indian village had stood during the preceding summer. Although identified by Lieutenant McClernand, who was present at the time, as Sioux, this village, which was on the west bank of the Little Big Horn just below the mouth of Lodge Grass Creek, was in reality Cheyenne.[49] Just before noon they reached a point where the Big Horn River washes a long, irregular line of hills on the right, hills over which Custer and the Seventh Cavalry were to ride two months later. The command rested almost on the exact site occupied by the hostile village at the time of the Custer attack. Here Jack-Rabbit-Bull, or Bull Rabbit, one of the Crows, took a discarded breadbox and, using a piece of charcoal, covered it with Indian hieroglyphics which he said would let the Sioux know that the Crows and the soldiers intended to clean them out. Then he took a handful of green grass and stuck it in the cracks of the box, adding that that would tell the Sioux that the soldiers intended to do it during the coming summer. Lieutenant McClernand was later to comment that it seemed somewhat strange, considering the number of miles covered during the scout, that this taunt should have been left so close to the spot where the one desperate fight of the campaign was to take

[49] *Billings Gazette*, May 15, 1932.

place.[50] Later in the day, the two troops forded the river, and after crossing the Wolf Mountains camped for the night on a dry tributary of Tullock's Creek.

The thirtieth of April saw them make a leisurely ride of some twenty miles, interspersed with several long halts during which the animals were allowed to graze. Both horses and pack mules were becoming very weak, and some of the latter had had to be abandoned. The next day they rode down the valley of Tullock's Creek, making slow progress, owing to the fact that the stream is very crooked and the banks steep which made frequent fording necessary.

During the trip they had not seen a hostile Indian; indeed, there was no indication of Sioux in the entire region. This was due to the fact that the few hostiles who were in Montana were still farther east, although heading west, in the valleys of the Powder and the Tongue rivers. The great majority of the warriors who were to overwhelm the Custer command several weeks later were still at the agencies on the Dakota reservation and were just beginning to leave there to join the hostile bands.[51]

In the camp on the Yellowstone, life had been very uneventful. The men had raised their beds off the ground and had built roofs of boughs over the tents as though expecting to remain there permanently. Officers and men had hunted and fished almost daily, securing little game but large numbers of catfish, shad, and suckers, which added variety to the diet. Six of the Crows had gone on a scout as far downstream as the mouth of the Rosebud but had returned without seeing any trace of the Sioux, although they reported that there were plenty of buffalo.

This enforced idleness of camp life was especially hard on the Crows, for, though naturally lazy, they preferred to choose their own time and method of indulgence. Restive under regulations and discipline as well as nervous and excitable, they caused Lieutenant Bradley no little trouble. But, as is usually the case, there was right and wrong on both sides. The Lieutenant simply could not get over some of his ideas. A roll call each morning of a band of untamed

[50] Hayne, *Red Men on the Big Horn*, 5; McClernand, "With Indian and Buffalo in Montana," *Cavalry Journal*, Vol. XXXVI (January and April, 1927), 13.

[51] Marquis, *Memoirs of a White Crow Indian*, 217.

Indians was especially ludicrous, but it was only with difficulty that he was dissuaded by Gibbon from attempting it.[52] In general he interjected too much red-tape formality into situations which the scouts considered an absolute hindrance to their efficiency.[53] On the other hand, the Crows either could not or would not understand that the act of enlistment imposed certain duties and inhibited their accustomed free scurrying to and fro over the country. They considered that there were entirely too many rules, and by the first of May six of them had deserted; and Bravo, the interpreter, who, according to Bradley, had a great deal of ill-merited influence over the scouts, and Little Face, whose son was one of the deserters, had gone back to the agency in an effort to induce the absentees to return.

On the twenty-fourth some of the Crows who had gone on a scout were seen returning to camp, riding in single file at a good speed and occasionally deviating from a straight line to describe a small circle, their way of indicating that the enemy had been sighted. Great excitement prevailed throughout the camp, and the scouts who had remained there "formed in line shoulder to shoulder behind a pile of buffalo chips placed for the purpose and stood there swaying their bodies and singing while the riders approached. As the leader of the scouting party came up he paused to kick over the pile of buffalo chips which was equivalent to a pledge to tell the truth." After all this excitement and preparation it was discovered that the Crows had sighted a party of officers and men from the camp who had gone hunting that morning and were now returning.[54] The only result of the incident was to impair the confidence of the officers in the ability and judgment of the Crows, a confidence which was still further diminished when on the first of May four of them were seen running toward the camp and circling. They reported that the Sioux in great numbers were pouring down the valley of Tullock's Creek, but no one took their alarm seriously inasmuch as Captain Ball and his detachment were expected during the day, and by that route.[55] And so it turned out,

[52] *Ibid.*, 211; Gibbon, "Summer Expedition," 282.

[53] Marquis, *Memoirs of a White Crow Indian*, 228.

[54] Bradley, *Journal*, 176.

[55] *Ibid.*, 183.

for by three o'clock the two companies were back in camp, having covered over 180 miles without having seen a hostile Indian or indeed even a fresh sign of one, a circumstance which, added to the reports of the Crows who had scouted toward the Rosebud, caused many of the officers to express the belief that the magnitude of the preparations against them had caused the erstwhile "hostiles" to stampede back to the agencies, where they would be fed and clothed as the wards of a government against which they had planned to wage war.[56]

[56] Gibbon, "Summer Expedition," 282.

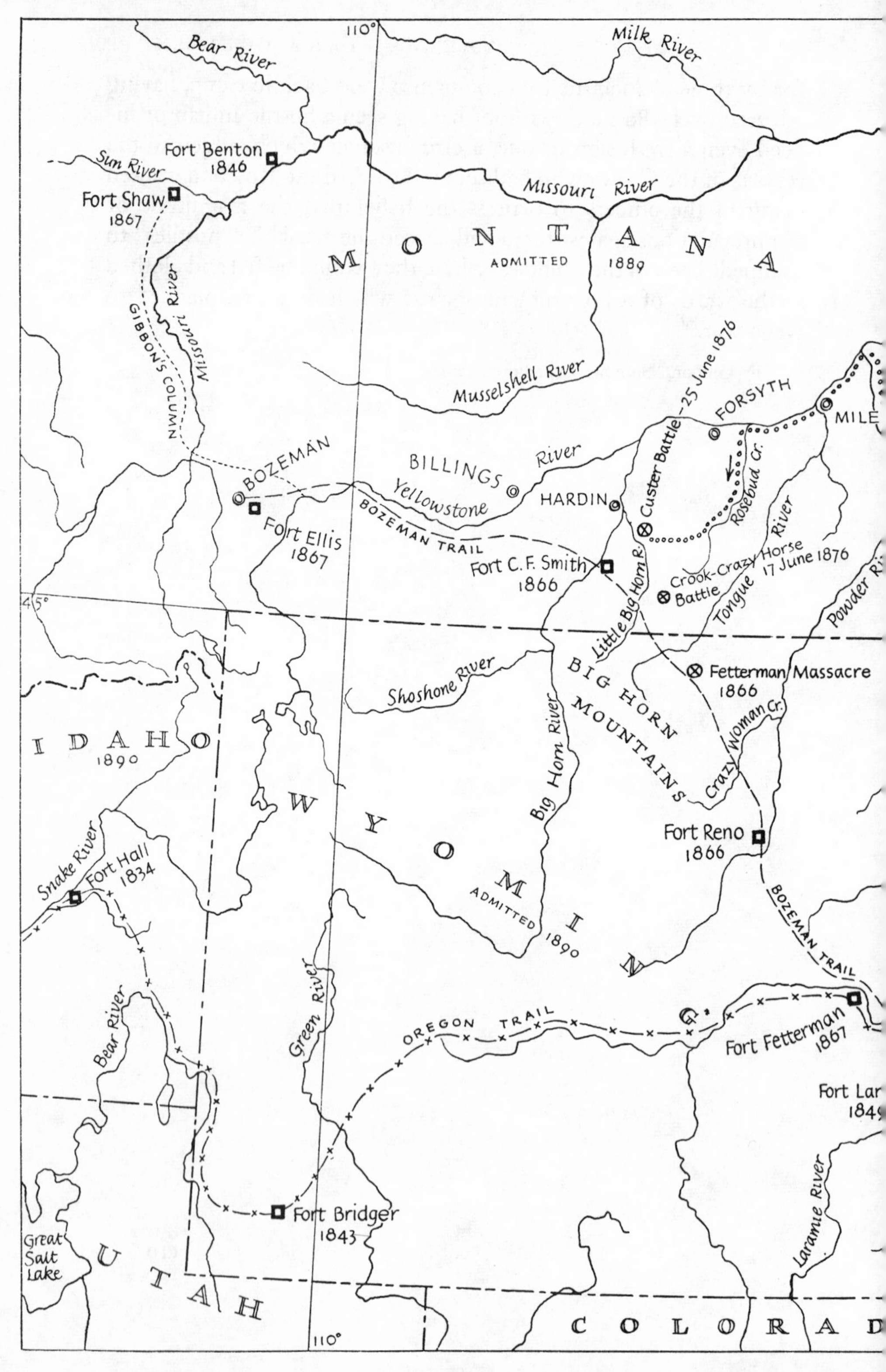

110°
Bear River
Milk River
Fort Benton
1846
Sun River
Fort Shaw
1867
Missouri River
M O N T A N A
ADMITTED 1889
Missouri River
GIBBON'S COLUMN
Musselshell River
Custer Battle — 25 June 1876
FORSYTH
MILE
BOZEMAN
BILLINGS
River
Yellowstone
HARDIN
Fort Ellis
1867
BOZEMAN TRAIL
Rosebud Cr.
Tongue River
Fort C. F. Smith
1866
Crook-Crazy Horse Battle 17 June 1876
Little Big Horn R.
Powder Ri
45°
Shoshone River
BIG HORN MOUNTAINS
Fetterman Massacre
1866
Crazy Woman Cr.
Big Horn River
I D A H O
1890
W Y O M I N G
ADMITTED 1890
Fort Reno
1866
Snake River
Fort Hall
1834
BOZEMAN TRAIL
Bear River
Green River
OREGON TRAIL
Fort Fetterman
1867
Fort Lar
1849
Fort Bridger
1843
Great Salt Lake
U T A H
Laramie River
C O L O R A D
110°

The Yellowstone & Missouri River Areas · 1876
0 25 50 100 150
SCALE
100°
NORTH DAKOTA
ADMITTED 1889
Fort Union 1829
Yellowstone River
Little Missouri River
Missouri River
CUSTER'S COLUMN
BISMARCK
Heart River
Fort Abraham Lincoln 1872
45°
Belle Fourche or Big Cheyenne
Cheyenne River
PIERRE
BLACK HILLS
SOUTH DAKOTA
ADMITTED 1889
White River
Rosebud Agency
Spotted Tail Agency
Niobrara River
Red Cloud Agency
NEBRASKA
ADMITTED 1867
Platte River
BOZEMAN AND OREGON TRAILS
TO INDEPENDENCE
Fort Sedgwick 1864
100°

CHAPTER VI

The Belknap Impeachment

GENERAL SHERIDAN'S plan of campaign had called for three columns of troops to move simultaneously against the hostiles in March and early April. Crook and Gibbon both got their commands away approximately on schedule; only the Dakota column was dilatory, partly because of the weather, but mostly on account of a sudden eruption of party politics over which the army had no control.

In 1866, as the result of many complaints, the office of sutler in the army camps had been abolished and trading establishments substituted, the traders to be appointed subject to the approval of the General of the Army. In 1870 the abrupt dismissal of the trader at Fort Laramie by the Secretary of War brought a protest from General Sherman, and resulted in a change in the law so as to give the power of appointing these traders to the Secretary, and placing them, as camp followers, under his protection and control. By law the traders were given the exclusive privilege of trade upon the military reservations to which they were assigned, and no other person was to "be allowed to trade, peddle or sell goods, by sample or otherwise, within the limits of the reserve." The post commander was given authority to inspect and approve the trader's schedule of rates and prices, "*which should be fair and reasonable*" [italics in the original], and was required to report all violations to the Secretary of War, to whom the trader, if dissatisfied, could also appeal.[1] Thus, in the final analysis, complete control of the appointment of the traders was given to the Secretary of War. The situation created was one which, in the hands of persons so inclined, offered abundant opportunity for graft and corruption, and long before any

[1] 44 Cong., 1 sess., *Index to Reports of Committees of the House of Representatives*, Serial No. 1715 (hereinafter cited as *Reports of Committees*).

official notice was taken of the matter, ugly rumors were afloat involving some of the highest officials in the nation's capital.

On the tenth of February, 1876, the *New York Herald,* whose publisher was James Gordon Bennett, had demanded a full investigation into suspected corruption in the War Department, and had followed it up with the flat declaration that the Secretary of War, W. W. Belknap, was farming out traderships in the Indian country. The newspaper also declared that Orvil Grant, the President's brother, was implicated and suggested that the President ask his brother how much money the latter had "made in the Sioux country starving the squaws and children."[2]

Custer had spent a part of the winter of 1875–76 in New York City, where he had many friends, among them the powerful publisher of the *Herald.* Later, Robert C. Seip, the post trader at Fort Lincoln, was to tell the Clymer Committee that he had cashed a draft on James Gordon Bennett made out to Custer for an amount which he remembered as being in excess of $100. This was supposed to be in payment for an article entitled "Belknap's Anaconda" published in the New York paper on March 31, 1876, and presumably written by Custer. Seip also declared that a telegram appearing in the *Herald* on March 15 contained an expression which he had used to Custer, and as far as he could recollect "only to him" at Bismarck.[3] From this it would seem possible that Custer, who was not without political ambitions of his own, was at least partially responsible for the commencement of the whole campaign against Belknap.

The Democrats had won control of the House of Representatives in the by-election of 1874, and something of this kind was just exactly what they had been waiting for. As a result, a House committee under the zealous chairmanship of Hester Clymer began digging into the records of the War Department, and the resulting odor soon became a stench in the nostrils of an American public which by that time should have been able to stand anything.[4]

On the morning of the second of March, Belknap, who has been described as a "pouchy-cheeked, beetle-browed, curly-haired man with a tremendous flowing beard and the air of an unctuous

[2] Allan Nevins, *Hamilton Fish, the Inner History of the Grant Administration,* 806.

[3] *Reports of Committees,* 234.

[4] Nevins, *Hamilton Fish,* 804–806.

politician,"[5] apparently in an attempt to head off the impeachment which he felt to be impending, visited the President before ten o'clock and presented his resignation in person. Grant accepted it in writing about thirty minutes later, "with great regret." Just why he indulged in such abrupt and precipitate action is uncertain. One explanation is that he believed that Belknap was acting in this way in an attempt to protect his wife. There is the further possibility that the Secretary's statements were so incoherent that Grant did not realize the exact situation, and received the wrong impression.[6] It has also been alleged that Grant did not understand that acceptance of the resignation was not a mere matter of course.[7] This after seven years in the White House, in the course of which even the most inept and bumbling of persons could reasonably be supposed to have learned something of the facts of political life and morality.

Although the Belknap scandal was only one of a whole series of similar affairs, it touched the President very closely, for not only was a trusted adviser involved, but the President's nomadic brother, Orvil, also was deeply concerned. Orvil admitted later, before the Clymer Committee, that in 1874 he had applied to the President for a license as an Indian trader, and had received four posts in that same year.[8] In charge of each he placed a subagent or clerk, who agreed to turn over a large share of the profits, although the War Department circulars of 1872 and 1875 had specifically provided that the post traders were to carry on the business themselves and were not "to farm out, sublet, transfer, sell or assign the business to others."[9] It has also been charged that Orvil made arrangements with the other traders to deliver to them supplies sent as a part of the government's treaty obligations to the Indians. These supplies were shipped up the Missouri River by steamboat, checked out to the recipients but never delivered, and then taken farther up the

[5] *Ibid.*, 806.

[6] William B. Hesseltine, *Ulysses S. Grant, Politician*, 395–96; Claude G. Bowers, *The Tragic Era, the Revolution after Lincoln*, 469–73. On the other hand, President Grant's son, Jesse, says that Grant demanded Belknap's resignation, and although the Secretary protested, Grant insisted, despite his feeling that criticism of his action would be severe. Jesse Grant, *In the Days of My Father, General Grant*, 122.

[7] Nevins, *Hamilton Fish*, 805.

[8] *Ibid.*, 807; *Reports of Committees*, 568–72.

[9] *Reports of Committees*, 151–52.

river and turned over to the post traders, many of whom paid as high as $1,000 a month for the privilege of receiving and selling these goods, the money being split between Mrs. Belknap and Orvil Grant.[10] What was most regrettable in Orvil Grant's eyes was not the sale of his influence but the smallness of the amount he made out of the transaction.[11]

Whatever the truth of these charges, it was obvious that Orvil Grant was deeply involved. In no case had he contributed any time or labor to the job of being a trader, and in only one case did he contribute any capital, in which instance it was at such a late date that it is highly probable that the action was taken in an attempt to head off an investigation, even if nothing could be done to allay suspicion.[12] And the traders, in paying Grant profits, paid him not for any real contribution on his part but merely for his influence with his brother, the President.[13] In other words, Orvil Grant had traded shamelessly on—and received a handsome income from—the fact that he was the President's brother, a situation of which the President could hardly have been unaware.

Lieutenant Colonel Custer, then commanding at Fort Abraham Lincoln, was undoubtedly cognizant of what was going on and had attempted on several occasions to protect his troops against the rapacity of the traders. He also knew of the mistreatment of the Indians, and the hostiles seem to have had his admiration as well as his sympathy. But all attempts to correct existing abuses had been futile, owing to the opposition of "higher-ups," and he was forced to look on in almost helpless, if not inarticulate, wrath while Belknap's parasites exploited the men and officers of the posts on the Indian frontier.

Custer's feelings on the subject were well known, and it was only natural that when Clymer began digging into the malodorous mess, he should summon Custer to Washington to testify.[14] This was an order that the Lieutenant Colonel of the Seventh Cavalry did not want to obey. He was then preparing to take the field against the hostile Indians as the leader of the Dakota column and intended

10 Usher L. Burdick, *Tales from Buffalo Land, the Story of Fort Buford*, 14.
11 *Nation* (New York), March 16, 1876.
12 *Reports of Committees*, 568–72.
13 *Nation* (New York), March 16, 1876.
14 Burdick, *Tales from Buffalo Land*, 15.

to begin operations as soon as the weather made it feasible, in any event not later than the middle of April. Since his presence with the command was almost essential and because he much preferred campaigning in the field to any other form of activity, he telegraphed Clymer explaining the situation and asking if it would be satisfactory for the committee to forward the questions in writing and allow him to reply by deposition.[15] But Clymer was after big game and on a hot trail, and was not to be denied, for with a presidential election in the offing the Democrats were by no means inclined to forego such a heaven-sent opportunity. Therefore Custer's request was refused, and after conferring with the Department Commander and finding that there was no way to evade the summons, Custer left for Washington, a reluctant and unwilling witness.

Before Custer appeared before the committee, Orvil Grant had admitted that he was interested in several post traderships, and that the President had notified him when they would be vacant. These were the Indian licenses at Standing Rock and Cheyenne River agencies and at Fort Peck. He denied that he had any interest at Fort Buford, Fort Abraham Lincoln, or Fort Rice, although William Harmon had told the committee that he was removed as post trader at the last place in July, 1874, because Orvil Grant had had his license canceled, adding that Grant had then offered to buy his stock of goods, giving him twenty-four hours in which to accept or reject. He had accepted, for he considered he had no other alternative.[16] Orvil Grant further admitted that he had secured the post at Fort Berthold for a man named Raymond, from whom he afterwards received $1,000. He had also secured the tradership at Fort Stevenson for A. L. Bonnafon, who was his partner, and the one at Fort Belknap for a man named Conrad, insisting, however, that he had received nothing from these two last-named positions.[17] A reasonable and considered judgment of the whole affair was provided by the *Nation* which said editorially:

> Orvil Grant . . . appeared . . . before the Committee on the War Department and told his own story of his jobs as an Indian trader in

[15] *New York Herald*, May 10, 1876. This telegram in full is reprinted in the *Herald* of July 6, 1876.

[16] *Reports of Committees*, 237.

[17] *Ibid.*, 568–72.

a simple artless way that could be diverting if it were not for the picture it presents of the views entertained by the Presidential family on "the science of politics." Mr. Grant appears to have been an unsuccessful man, who, when all else failed, tried to get a living in some easy way out of the Government and accordingly applied to his brother to license him as an Indian trader. . . . Of course the traders in paying him profits paid him simply for his influence with his brother, the President, and Orvil confessed to the committee in the plainest manner that what was regrettable in his eyes in the whole affair was not his use of his "influence" but the smallness of the amount he made out of the traderships. . . . We are not surprised to hear that General Grant is very much annoyed by their investigations and says they are carried on for "partisan purposes." Orvil appeared . . . to be a man entirely devoid of what is called a sense of honor in matters pertaining to public funds and is well worth study . . . as an illustration of the moral tone of "administration circles."[18]

Lieutenant Colonel Custer first testified on the twenty-ninth of March. He said that the effect of the law of 1870 putting the appointment of the post traders in the hands of the Secretary of War had been to add greatly to the discomforts and inconveniences of frontier life, which was not good even under the most favorable circumstances. The law, by putting the appointment in the hands of a "ring," increased the cost of living at the frontier posts, and it came out of the pockets of officers and men.[19] When Custer assumed command at Fort Abraham Lincoln, the post trader was S. A. Dickey, who managed the business together with one Robert Wilson. Dickey at the time was under fire for alleged violation of the revenue laws and for introducing liquor among the Indians, and Wilson for alleged disloyalty. Investigation proved these charges to be baseless, but Custer had recommended Dickey's removal on the ground that he was an unfit person to hold such a position, that he drank excessively and, although kindhearted and obliging, exercised a bad influence over the younger officers.[20]

On July 1, Dickey was succeeded by Robert C. Seip, but, said Custer, he was not removed on account of his (Custer's) recommendation, and commented that Seip was no improvement, being

18 *Nation* (New York), March 16, 1876.
19 *Reports of Committees*, 156.
20 *Ibid.*, 152–53.

open to the same objection of drinking.[21] Custer testified further that Dickey had told him that he was removed because he did not divide, and that there was not a post on the river except his that did not divide. He expressed the belief that no proposition was ever made to Dickey; the post was wanted for someone else, and so Dickey had to get out.[22] Dickey's partner, Robert Wilson, wrote a letter in which, according to Custer, he called attention to the sale of traderships on the Missouri River and declared that he expected to be able to prove that Belknap, who was the most corrupt official ever to occupy high position, made these posts articles of traffic.[23] Wilson also published a statement in which he declared that Seip was a member of a firm in which the Secretary of War was interested, a statement which Belknap, in a letter to General Sheridan, declared to be a lie.[24]

The prices charged by Seip, according to Custer, soon became so exorbitant and outrageous that the officers and men who could, purchased their necessities elsewhere. Seip thereupon made a written complaint to the effect that army personnel had no right to buy anything elsewhere and bring it to the post, but must buy from him. With this contention the officers naturally disagreed, but when the question was carried to a higher authority, the claims of the trader were upheld.[25] In addition, Seip attempted to impose restrictions on the sale of stores through the Commissary Department, threatening that "if it was not stopped he would use his influence with the Secretary of War, which he claimed to be very great" to cause trouble for the officers responsible.[26] Custer also testified that he had known the post trader to go out and stop an officer's wagon, inspect it to see what it contained, and then threaten to cause trouble because that officer had traded in a town about five miles distant where he could get things for about one half of the trader's prices.[27]

21 *Ibid.*, 157.

22 *Ibid.*, 157. The *Army and Navy Journal* (April 1, 1876) said that Dickey had paid nothing for his place because his brother was a member of Congress from Pennsylvania and chairman of the Military Committee. But when his brother went out of Congress, Dickey went out of the tradership.

23 *Reports of Committees*, 161.

24 *Ibid.*, 153.

25 *Ibid.*, 153–54.

26 *Ibid.*, 155.

27 *Ibid.*, 156.

Custer told the committee that he had not reported these occurrences to the Secretary of War because he was as suspicious of the Secretary as he was of the trader, and that he had no doubt that Seip had enough influence to have his actions sustained;[28] in fact, the one or two incidents that had been carried up had been resolved in favor of the trader. He also declared that he had told General Belknap of Seip's claims to great influence on the occasion of the Secretary's visit to Fort Lincoln, and that Belknap had replied in an unsatisfactory manner, turning the statement off with, "You must not believe all you hear," or something of the sort.[29]

Regarding this visit of the Secretary of War to Fort Abraham Lincoln, Custer testified that he had learned of it only the day before Belknap's arrival and then from the post trader. Seip had sent him a basket containing several bottles of wine for the entertainment of the visitor, but Custer had returned the gift, saying that he did not drink and that he did not propose to use it for the entertainment of the Secretary. Custer added that his knowledge of Belknap's transactions and his opinion of them were such that while the appropriate salute was fired, he, as the commanding officer of the post, did not meet the Secretary at the edge of the reservation as was customary, but merely stayed at the door of his office and waited for him. After the necessary business had been transacted, Custer went to his quarters, leaving his visitor to his own devices.[30] In answer to a question, Custer said that he had heard rumors that this visit of the Secretary had been for the purpose of facilitating the smuggling of whiskey across the Canadian border for the benefit of the traders, but that he had entirely forgotten about them and never would have thought of the matter but for the question.[31]

Custer also testified that it was a matter of common report and information that the trader had to split his profits with outside people. Upon being questioned, he declared that Seip had told him that the yearly profits of the post were $15,000, of which one-third

[28] *Ibid.*, 156. Custer told the Committee that it was common belief among army officers on the North Missouri that Belknap was a silent partner of the traders and that the corrupt bargaining of the latter could not have been continued without Belknap's knowledge and connivance. *Army and Navy Journal* (April 1, 1876).

[29] *Reports of Committees* 155.

[30] *Ibid.*, 157.

[31] *Ibid.*, 160.

was paid to a man named Hedrick, who was a brother-in-law of General Belknap[32] and a supervisor or collector of internal revenue residing at Ottumwa, Iowa,[33] while another one-third went to General E. M. Rice, an attorney in Washington,[34] who was supposed to be an intimate friend of the Secretary of War.[35] After all the payments had been made, the trader had had only $2,000 or $3,000 left for himself and had declared that he was getting tired of it.[36] Custer said that the trader had added that while he only knew positively that money was paid to Hedrick and Rice, he was under the impression that a portion of it went to the Secretary of War.[37]

Concerning the relations existing between the traders and the Indian agents, Custer said that they seemed to be very much interested in each other, but that the officers on the post felt a good deal of hesitancy about calling attention to anything wrong in the Indian Department, resentful as it was of interference; Custer cited an illustrative case at Standing Rock Agency where the supplies had been exhausted, but despite this fact the agent would not accept a loan of supplies from the army post at Fort Lincoln, with the result that the Indians had been left to shift for themselves for two months.[38] He then told of refusing to accept a shipment of corn in sacks branded with the name of the Indian Department, as there had been other occasions upon which goods intended for distribution to the Indians had been sold to the troops or to civilians. However, he had been ordered by higher authority to accept the corn, and he expressed the belief that the order came from the Secretary of War.[39] The situation had progressed even to the point where an attempt was made to keep a Mrs. Galpin, a full-blood Sioux, from trading with the Indians at Standing Rock. All means short of force were used to keep her from trading; force was not used only because of the fear of arousing the hostility of the tribesmen. Application was

32 *Ibid.*, 30.

33 *Ibid.*, 176–77.

34 *Ibid.*, 176–77. See also the *Army and Navy Journal* (April 1, 1876). This led to the claim that Custer had "caned" Rice as a result of an argument regarding whether or not Rice had ever received post tradership money. *Army and Navy Journal* (April 8, 1876). This was vigorously denied by Rice. *Ibid.* (April 15, 1876).

35 *Reports of Committees,* 154.

36 *Ibid.*, 156.

37 *Ibid.*, 154–56.

38 *Ibid.*, 160.

39 *Ibid.*, 158.

made to the Department of the Interior, but its order to her to move was disregarded; an appeal by the agent to Custer for troops to remove her and close up her store was not granted, and even the United States Commissioner refused to interfere on the request of the agent.[40]

Regarding Orvil Grant and his activities, Custer told the committee that he had met him and his partner, a Mr. Bonnafon, on a train trip from St. Paul to Bismarck at a time when the two men were going out to take possession of certain Indian trading posts. The President's brother had asked if they could be furnished with an army ambulance for the trip, while Bonnafon had requested that Custer recommend someone familiar with the country whom they might employ as a guide. Orvil Grant failed to show any authorization for his request but said that he had it. Custer complied with both requests and furnished an ambulance, four mules, and a driver, but no provisions, for the trip. He did so, he said, not to Orvil Grant as a trader, but "to any member of the President's family . . . out of courtesy to the President of the United States, I would render any facility I could."[41] Custer had been absent from the post on other duty when the two men returned to Bismarck, but it was at this time that Orvil Grant was said to have sent a telegram to Washington in the form of an order that J. W. Raymond be appointed a trader at Fort Berthold. A return telegram had promised that the appointment would be made, and Raymond had shown a copy of the wire to several people in Bismarck, stating that he had paid Orvil Grant $1,000 for the appointment.[42]

When asked about the extension of the Great Sioux reservation to include the east bank of the Missouri River—an extension which had been brought about by executive order in January and April of 1875—Custer replied that he inclined to the belief that while the ostensible and alleged object was to suppress the liquor traffic and to prevent the Indians of the region from obtaining unlimited supplies of rum, the real motive was not so much to improve the morals of the Indians as to improve the profits of the traders by giving them a monopoly of the trade of the region. The orders

[40] *Ibid.*, 156. See also p. 237.
[41] *Ibid.*, 155.
[42] *Ibid.*, 155, 179.

had removed and suppressed all competitors and had given these favorites of the President almost a complete monopoly of the trade, even to the extent of dispossessing many persons who claimed to have acquired land titles there.[43] Custer also testified that when some of his officers were in Kentucky for the purpose of buying horses, they were approached by a Dr. Tomlinson and asked about the profits of Fort Rice, the doctor stating that he was interested since a friend of his had been appointed to the post tradership there and that he (Dr. Tomlinson) was to have a share of the profits.[44] Tomlinson, who was a brother of Mrs. Belknap, had put $1,500 into the business, but died before the post showed any profit, although his partner, James G. Pitts, declared that no improper means had been used and no money paid in order to obtain appointment to the post.[45]

Custer concluded his testimony by declaring his belief that had the Secretary of War been a man of integrity and honesty, these frauds could not have occurred. He was insistent that their occurrence and continuance were attributable solely to the fact that the persons responsible were protected and shielded by General Belknap.[46]

Recalled to the stand on the fourth of April, Lieutenant Colonel Custer testified to an order of the Secretary of War dated March 15, 1873, which provided that "no officer, either active or retired," should "directly or indirectly, without being called upon by proper authority, solicit, suggest or recommend action by members of Congress for or against military affairs." Furthermore, all petitions by officers to Congress relative to military matters were to be sent through the office of the General of the Army and the Secretary of War "for their action and transmittal." Any officer visiting Washington for any reason while Congress was in session was required to register at the office of the Adjutant General, and in addition to

[43] *Ibid., xiv,* 155, 158.

[44] *Ibid.,* 154.

[45] *Ibid.,* 569.

[46] *Ibid.,* 162. ". . . unhappy Grant was surrounded by thieves from the very start of his administration, and nowhere was corruption more rampant than in the War Department. Custer, hot-headed and out-spoken, waxed increasingly furious as he watched his men sicken and die from rotten food and saw the junk rifles and cartridges that were sent him." George Creel, "To the Last Man," *Collier's,* Vol. LXXIX (January 22, 1927), 12.

notify him in writing of the purpose of the visit, the length of time he expected to be in the city, and the authority under which he was absent from his regular command or station. This order, which was strictly enforced, sealed the lips and tied the hands of the officers of the army about as thoroughly as it was possible to do it.[47] Custer declared that this order was "about the most effectual safeguard that he [Belknap] could have thrown around his conduct to prevent exposure." He added that General Hazen, for daring to make a communication relative to Fort Sill business, had been "exiled" to Fort Buford, a lonely and forlorn post approximately one thousand miles to the west of St. Paul. Thus any report which was in any way critical of or opposed to the personal interests of the Secretary of War could, and would, be effectively pigeonholed when it reached his hands, and, in Custer's opinion, would probably result in the officer's being pigeonholed as well.[48]

In his testimony before the committee, Mr. Seip contradicted Custer on some points and declared that Custer had misunderstood him on others, especially in regard to remarks that Seip was supposed to have made. He admitted that Hedrick and Rice were interested in the profits of the post, although neither of them seems to have invested any money in the enterprise. The money had been furnished in equal amounts by Seip and his partner, Alvin C. Leighton, each of whom received one-fourth of the profits, according to Seip, the remainder being paid to Hedrick and Rice.[49]

Custer expected and hoped that he would now be permitted to return to Fort Lincoln and lead the Dakota column in the great campaign that was being prepared against the Sioux. But on the seventeenth of April, when the actual impeachment trial of Secretary Belknap began, he was still in Washington, chafing at the delay. On the twentieth, Custer advised Terry by telegraph of his intention to leave for St. Paul, stopping at Detroit under orders. Four days later he telegraphed from New York that his departure for St. Paul had been postponed because of a summons to attend the impeachment trial. He also asked Terry to telegraph the impeachment managers, stressing the readiness of the expedition against the

47 *Reports of Committees*, 162–63.
48 *Ibid.*, 163.
49 *Ibid.*, 183–87.

Sioux and the desirability of Custer's presence at Fort Lincoln. Later he wired Terry that J. D. Cameron, Belknap's successor as secretary of war, had consented to intercede with the impeachment managers and request that Custer be allowed to depart for Fort Lincoln at the earliest practicable moment. On the twenty-eighth, Sheridan, who probably had a very good idea why Custer's orders did not come through, wired Terry that orders had been received to send someone other than Custer in command of the expedition and asked whom Terry wished to go. Terry suggested two names, Colonel Sykes of the Twentieth Infantry and Colonel Crittenden of the Seventeenth, adding that although both were anxious to go, he preferred Crittenden, who was the senior and had indicated a desire for such duty. The following day Sheridan suggested that Terry lead the expedition in person. Terry immediately agreed.[50]

Custer was not unaware of what was going on, for on the same day (April 29) he telegraphed Terry informing him that the President had instructed the Secretary of War not to ask the impeachment managers to discharge Custer from attendance upon the Senate, but to send some other officer in command of the expedition. Custer had then visited the managers and obtained their consent to leave, but at Sherman's request he postponed his departure until Monday in order to see the President. Custer added that he would leave Monday for Fort Lincoln and duty with his command.

Custer had, however, reckoned without the President. His testimony before the committee had had much to do with the decision to proceed with the impeachment trial,[51] and in daring to testify against one of the favorite henchmen of the administration, Custer had incurred the hostility and hatred of one of the most petulant, smallest-souled men who ever sat in the seat of the mighty.

Personally honest, incorruptible, and thoroughly loyal, Grant was one of the poorest judges of men who ever lived. Naïve and trusting to the point of incredulity, he either could not or would not believe that anyone to whom he had given his friendship and trust could be other than scrupulously honest. In 1876 he was approaching the end of an administration which on the domestic side

[50] Hughes, "Campaign against the Sioux," *Journal of the Military Service Institution of the United States*, Vol. XVIII (January, 1896), 16.

[51] Dustin, *The Custer Tragedy*, 240.

was distinguished almost entirely by venality and corruption, and which has been declared one of the rottenest—if not the rottenest—in American history. Scandal had succeeded scandal—one had not ended before another began. With the Belknap affair the political bankruptcy of the administration was complete, and the President's chances of a third term, never very robust, flickered out in despair and desperation.

The President considered Custer's testimony to be a reflection on his character, and when Custer, in accordance with Sherman's request, tried on May 1 to obtain an interview with the President, he was unsuccessful. After cooling his heels in the President's anteroom for several hours, he became an object of solicitude on the part of a fellow-officer, General Ingalls, who personally told Grant that Custer was waiting to see him. Grant replied that he did not wish to see Custer. Custer then sent in a note stating that he desired the interview merely to correct certain unjust impressions that he understood were held concerning him, but Grant still refused to give him an audience. General Sherman, general of the army, was out of town and Custer could not see him, but, apparently in accordance with a schedule agreed upon in advance, Custer, feeling that he was no longer needed in Washington and that his presence in the field was required, left Washington for St. Paul after penciling a note to Grant protesting the treatment he had received and reporting his proposed departure to both the Adjutant General and Inspector General of the army. That he had some sort of advance agreement with Sherman is borne out by the fact that on the same day, R. B. Marcy, the inspector general, in an official letter to Custer informed him that he would not be required to perform certain duties at Detroit, as previously suggested, since it was the desire of the General of the Army that he return to his regiment without delay.[52]

The fact that Custer, although released by the committee which had summoned him to Washington, left without securing official War Department authorization, gave Grant the opportunity he sought, and he ordered that Custer not be allowed to accompany the expedition against the Indians. Upon his arrival in Chicago on the

[52] Jacob P. Dunn, *Massacres of the Mountains; a History of the Indian Wars of the Far West,* 602.

morning of May 3, Custer was met at the station by a member of Sheridan's staff, who informed him that he was under arrest by order of General Sherman. Custer then wired Sherman for permission to continue to Fort Lincoln but not to accompany his regiment into the field.[53]

For some of the antiadministration newspapers, the affair was almost too good to be true, and the *New York Herald*, a bitter foe of the President, in particular had a field day. On the second of May, it had denounced Grant for conduct which appeared "to be the most high-handed abuse of his official power which he has perpetrated yet."[54] Four days later it referred to the fact that no official charges had been preferred and declared that Custer was being disgraced "simply because he did not 'crook the pregnant hinges of the knee' to this modern Caesar," and declared that Grant's theory of government was that of an "irresponsible despot . . . with an absolute power to decapitate anybody offending his Highness or his favorites." The newspaper also stressed the fact that Custer was being punished for obeying an act of Congress when the President felt that such action was likely to injure a personal friend.[55] On the ninth, the *St. Paul Dispatch* joined in the general chorus of denunciation by observing that the significance of the attack on Custer lay in the fact that the White House had served warning that any attempt "to expose and correct the evils which have grown in the public service under the administration will be punished to the full extent of the powers which Ulysses S. Grant holds for ten months longer as President of the United States."[56]

But Grant had his defenders as well as his detractors. A writer signing himself "Bayonet" defended the President's action on the ground that to have released Custer, even temporarily, from attendance at the impeachment proceedings would have been equivalent to dispensing with his testimony altogether, since once in the field he would have been beyond the reach of telegrams or messengers. It was the writer's argument that President Grant, aware of the

[53] Hughes, "Campaign against the Sioux in 1876," *Journal of the Military Service Institution of the United States*, Vol. XVIII (January, 1896), 12; Frederick Whittaker, *A Popular Life of General George A. Custer*, 554–55.

[54] *New York Herald*, May 2, 1876.

[55] *New York Herald*, May 6, 1876.

[56] *St. Paul Dispatch*, May 9, 1876.

impropriety of allowing Custer to leave, had expressed his disapproval because the command of the expedition against the Sioux was not one which Custer, under any circumstances, could claim as a right. Custer's action in getting released by the committee and starting to rejoin his command, without permission of either the President or the War Department, savored of insubordination and made imperative the President's order detaining him at Chicago.[57] Others were even more emphatic and bitter in their criticism of Custer, and a leading western newspaper referred to him as "an extra-ordinary compound of presumptuous egotism and presumptuous mendacity which makes him the reckless and lawless being he is."[58]

In the meantime Custer was eating humble pie. The worst thing that can happen to a man in public life had happened to him; he had become a political martyr for the benefit of an opposition.[59] Seeking a way out of his unenviable predicament, he induced the Department commander to intercede for him, and finally sent the following telegram:

Headquarters Dept. of Dakota
St. Paul, Minn., May 6, 1876

The Adjutant General
Division of the Missouri, Chicago.

I forward the following:

To His Excellency, the President:

(Through Military Channels)

I have seen your order transmitted through the General of the Army directing that I be not permitted to accompany the expedition to move against the hostile Indians. As my entire regiment forms a part of the expedition and I am the senior officer of the regiment on duty in this department I respectfully but most earnestly request that while not allowed to go in command of the expedition I may be permitted to serve with my regiment in the field. I appeal to you as a soldier to spare me the humiliation of seeing my regiment march to meet the enemy and I not share its dangers.

/S/ G. A. Custer

57 *Army and Navy Journal*, May 27, 1876.
58 *St. Paul Pioneer-Press*, May 11, 1876.
59 Dunn, *Massacres of the Mountains*, 603.

In forwarding the above I wish to say, expressly, that I have no desire whatever to question the orders of the President or my military superiors. Whether Lieutenant Colonel Custer shall be permitted to accompany the column or not, I shall go in command of it. I do not know the reasons upon which the orders given rest; but if these reasons do not forbid it, Lieutenant Colonel Custer's services would be very valuable with his regiment.

/S/ Alfred H. Terry
Commanding Department.

Just why General Terry took this action, we do not know. He may have realized his own inexperience in Indian fighting and recognized Custer's ability, or he may have felt that Custer was being unfairly punished, if not persecuted, and that such an action on his part would offer a solution of the problem acceptable to all concerned. It has been reported on good authority that Custer actually got down on his knees and begged Terry to get the orders changed,[60] and Terry himself later told a group of officers that Custer, with tears in his eyes, actually begged for aid.[61] In any event, Sheridan in Chicago supported the recommendation and immediately sent the dispatch on with the following endorsement:

Brig. General E. D. Townsend
Washington, D. C.

The following dispatch from General Terry is respectfully forwarded. I am sorry Lieutenant Colonel Custer did not manifest as much interest in staying at his post to organize and get ready his regiment and the expedition as he now does to accompany it. On a previous occasion in eighteen sixty-eight I asked executive clemency for Colonel Custer to enable him to accompany his regiment against the Indians, and I sincerely hope if granted this time it may have sufficient effect to

60 Colonel Hughes maintains that every word of this dispatch, including the part signed by Custer, was Terry's own composition. Hughes, "Campaign against the Sioux in 1876," *Journal of the Military Service Institution of the United States*, Vol. XVIII (January, 1896), 12. Hughes was General Terry's brother-in-law and, consequently, was in a position to know.

61 Eli M. Huggins, "Custer and Rain-in-the-Face," *American Mercury*, Vol. IX (November, 1926), 341; Hughes, "Campaign against the Sioux in 1876," *Journal of the Military Service Institution of the United States*, Vol. XVIII (January, 1896), 12.

prevent him from again attempting to throw discredit on his profession and his brother officers.

/S/ P. H. Sheridan, Lieutenant General[62]

President Grant now relented and ordered that Custer be allowed to accompany the expedition, but only in command of his own regiment, the command of the Dakota column, which was to have been Custer's, to be in the hands of the Department commander.

Although Custer's moderate and sober appeal, ably seconded by Terry and Sheridan, is generally held to have been responsible for Grant's change of attitude, there are other factors which must be considered. Grant was notoriously thin skinned, and the chorus of criticism directed against him for his treatment of Custer showed no signs of diminishing. Custer's appeal afforded him a dignified retreat from a position which was rapidly becoming impossible to maintain.[63] And he took full advantage of the opportunity.

Another factor which was undoubtedly of importance was that the Seventh Cavalry was already deplorably short of officers, and had Custer not been allowed to march with his regiment, the problem of command might have become serious. For one reason or another, eleven of the forty-one officers of the Seventh were not on duty with the regiment at that time. Besides its colonel, who was on recruiting duty, two majors, four captains, and seven lieutenants were missing. While Custer had been in Washington, the command had devolved upon Major Marcus A. Reno, who, although he had won distinction in the Civil War as a brave and able officer, was like General Terry, totally without experience in Indian fighting. When it became apparent that Custer might not be allowed to lead the regiment against the Sioux, Reno had telegraphed General Terry: "From Custer's telegrams and the papers it seems that he will not be back soon. In the meantime the expedition here is making large expenses and S. Bull waiting on the Little Missouri.

[62] Frazier and Robert Hunt, *I Fought with Custer*, 134; Hughes, "Campaign against the Sioux in 1876," *Journal of the Military Service Institution of the United States*, Vol. XVIII (January, 1896), 13.

[63] McGillycuddy, *McGillycuddy, Agent*, 41, maintains that Grant acceded to Custer's request to be allowed to fight with his regiment only through the influence of Generals Sheridan and Townsend.

Why not give me a chance as I feel I will do credit to the army."[64] Terry had returned a soft though noncommital answer, and the suggestion was apparently never referred to again.

That Custer was ungrateful and self-seeking is shown by two facts. In telling Terry that Custer might go along on the campaign in a subordinate capacity, Sheridan had warned against his talking too freely to newspapermen; yet Custer took along Mark Kellogg, of Bismarck, as a substitute for the regular correspondent of the *New York Herald*. Kellogg was with the expedition when it left Fort Lincoln, and again when it started up Rosebud Creek in pursuit of the hostile Indians. But there was no attempt at concealment of Kellogg's presence, and General Terry, who could certainly have ordered the reporter back, must have known of his presence with Custer's command.

Although Terry had been largely instrumental in securing the partial revocation of Custer's "banishment," Custer was apparently planning, within a few hours after he knew definitely that he would be allowed to participate in the campaign, how he could elude Terry and win a great victory for himself, for he is said to have told Colonel Ludlow of the Corps of Engineers of his determination "to cut loose from and make my operations independent of, General Terry during the summer" and that he had "got away from Stanley and would be able to swing clear of Terry" without any difficulty.[65]

On receipt of the official orders from Washington, Terry and Custer left almost immediately for Fort Lincoln. The plan had been for the Dakota column to take the field against the hostiles early in April, but it was the seventh of May before the official orders came through setting the command in motion, and it was three days later that the officers arrived at Fort Lincoln, where preparations for the expedition were well advanced. As a consequence of the delay several thousand Indians who had wintered at the various agencies had accepted Sitting Bull's invitation to join him and have one more big fight with the soldiers, and had slipped away and joined the hostiles. How many of these had actually departed no one seemed to know, but their morale had been given a terrific boost by Crook's defeat on the Powder, and their hostility further

[64] Bates, *Custer's Indian Battles*, 28.
[65] DeLand, *The Sioux Wars*, 430.

fired by the revelations of the Clymer Committee that the traders had been systematically defrauding them for years.[66] In any event, the number was sufficient to throw all earlier estimates of hostiles who might be encountered entirely out of line, but this was a fact which the Indian agents, for reasons of their own, attempted to conceal from the military. The military leaders, however, were not working entirely in the dark, for Major Reno, who during Custer's absence had been commanding at Fort Lincoln, had reported the exodus of large numbers of the Indians from the agencies,[67] and Terry on the eve of starting against the hostiles had wired Sheridan: "It is represented that they have 1,500 lodges, are confident and intend making a stand." From this message it is obvious that Terry appreciated the strength of the enemy and should, from an estimate based on the number of lodges, have expected to encounter a force of between 4,500 and 6,000 warriors.[68]

From many independent sources Terry had received information which led him to believe that the main force of the hostiles would be found concentrated either on the Little Missouri River or between that stream and the Yellowstone, and the campaign was planned accordingly. The Dakota column would march almost directly west, while orders were sent to Colonel Gibbon telling him to march down the north bank of the Yellowstone as far as Stanley's Stockade, there cross the river, and move eastward following Stanley's Trail to meet the column coming from Fort Lincoln.[69]

66 Burdick, *Tales from Buffalo Land*, 15.

67 44 Cong., 1 sess., *House Exec. Doc. No. 184*, 16.

68 Coughlan, "The Battle of the Little Big Horn," *Cavalry Journal*, Vol. XLIII (January–February, 1934), 13.

69 Terry's Report, 460.

CHAPTER VII

Gibbon Guards the Yellowstone

ALTHOUGH neither the Crow scouts nor Captain Ball's detachment had been able to find them, there were hostiles in the immediate vicinity, a fact of which members of the expedition soon became all too painfully aware. On the afternoon of May 2, a heavy windstorm set in, and all that night the camp was swept with driving clouds of dust, through which objects could be seen only at a short distance and then very indistinctly. It was just such a night as the Indians preferred for their horse-stealing expeditions,[1] and the next morning a horse and mule belonging to Bostwick were missing. They had been picketed to a stake just outside of the line of sentries, only about three hundred yards from the camp. Nor was this all, for the ponies of the Crow scouts, which had been turned out to graze overnight just above the camp, had all disappeared. Investigation disclosed that the raiding party had been composed of about fifty persons, of whom twenty had reconnoitered the camp and escaped with the horses, while the others held themselves in reserve a short distance back. These raiders had shown extreme daring, coming in very close to the sentinels. Almost universally credited to the Sioux, this exploit was really the work of a band of northern Cheyennes under the leadership of their famous chief, Two Moon.[2]

After discovering their loss, the Crows assembled in camp "and

[1] Gibbon, "Summer Expedition," 283. The Indians had probably discovered the trail of Ball's scouting party and followed it to the camp on the Yellowstone River. *New York Herald*, July 8, 1876.

[2] Marquis, *Memoirs of a White Crow Indian*, 212; *Billings Gazette*, May 15, 1832.

cried like children whose toys had been broken," a proceeding which caused Colonel Gibbon to remark somewhat acidly:

> There is nothing unnatural in a crying child, and the manly grief of a broken heart excites one's sympathy but to see a parcel of great big Indians standing together and blubbering like babies with great tears streaming down their swarthy faces because they had lost their horses, struck everyone as supremely ridiculous.[3]

This raid meant that not one of the seventeen Crows remaining with the command had a horse, which definitely impaired their usefulness as scouts and caused Lieutenant Bradley to criticize his commanding officer for being too lax in his discipline of the Crows, a laxity which Colonel Gibbon made no effort to deny.[4]

The trail of the raiders was followed down the valley to a point eight miles below. Here it was found to cross the stream, and the Crows insisted that they had heard shots on the opposite bank, which indicated that the hostiles had little fear of being followed and were in no hurry to leave the vicinity. Being afraid to cross, the Crows returned to camp. In the afternoon a report, afterwards proved to be false, that the Indians had stampeded the horse and mule herd spread through the camp. A heavy fog overhung the valley of the Yellowstone and a light snow was falling, reducing visibility to a minimum and making almost anything seem possible. In addition, one trooper who had gone hunting before the discovery of the raid failed to return to camp although his companions had put in appearance, and it was feared that he might have been killed by the raiding party. He was found unhurt the next day, although he had had a very narrow escape since the trail of the enemy had crossed his, but either it was at night or else the Indians had not been curious enough to investigate, for no attempt at pursuit had been made. All together, it was a day of wild, confused excursions and alarms which were extremely trying on the nerves of both officers and men.

The next day two couriers came with mail and dispatches and reported that, although they had been fired on about ten miles from

[3] Gibbon, "Summer Expedition," 284.
[4] *Ibid.*, 283.

the camp, they had not been chased, an indication that the hostiles were ranging all around the command. Colonel Gibbon attempted to persuade the Crows to go in search of the enemy, but they refused, insisting that the disparity between them, on foot, and the Sioux, mounted, was too great; the Crows did scout for a short distance up and down the stream without learning anything definite concerning the strength and whereabouts of the enemy.

On the sixth of the month, Bradley, tired of working almost entirely on instinct, mounted two of the most reliable of the Crows, Half-Yellow-Face and Jack-Rabbit-Bull, on cavalry horses, the Lieutenant's own and one other, and sent them downstream to see what they could find. They were able to ascertain that the trail of the raiders did not come from the interior towards Fort Peck as had been suspected, but that the horse thieves had crossed the river a few miles below. They concluded that there was probably a hostile village farther downstream on the south bank of the Yellowstone. The two scouts also encountered three hostiles whom they charged and drove off, and in so doing secured three horses which the Sioux abandoned in their haste to get away. These the scouts brought back to camp with great pride.

This episode convinced Bradley that there was a substantial war party on the north bank of the river, and that the three warriors who had been put to flight by the Crows had merely been scouts for the larger band. He secured permission to make a night march downstream with his detachment and the scouts in the hope of being able to discover and strike the enemy camp. Gibbon was somewhat reluctant but finally agreed to the plan, although postponing the time of departure until the next night. He and most of the other officers seem to have agreed with Captain Clifford, who wrote in his *Journal*: "The entire force of scouts went down the river and are very likely to be scooped up by an overwhelming force of Sioux."

Six miles out, Bradley's scouts found fresh pony tracks, proving that the enemy was still in the vicinity. These were followed until a low wolf cry from the scouts out in front—so excellent an imitation that it would have deceived almost anyone—signaled that the enemy had been sighted. Advancing to the attack, Bradley's little group found three abandoned war lodges, the occupants having been gone probably not more than twenty-four hours. The site was only about a mile beyond the place where the two Crows had captured the horses, showing that Bradley's theory was correct: the scouts had really been in considerable danger. Probably the fear of being led into ambush had kept the Sioux from pursuing them. It was now about three o'clock in the morning, and the detachment rode on, fording Froze-to-Death Creek and continuing downstream until they found the place where the war party had crossed to the south bank. An observation taken from one of the highest bluffs failed to yield any sign of smoke or other indication of an enemy camp in the vicinity. After unsaddling and resting for about five hours, the party went on to the Great Porcupine Creek, where they found immense buffalo herds. Before Bradley could restrain them, or before he really knew what was taking place, the Crows had killed several of these animals, much to the disgust of the Lieutenant, for while the fresh meat was most welcome, the sound of the firing might have brought the Sioux down upon them. But nothing of the sort happened, and the return trip to camp was made without incident and without any further sign of the hostiles. They arrived about noon on the ninth after having traveled some eighty-five miles.

On Monday, the eighth, during the absence of the scouting party, Captains Freeman and Logan, with their respective companies, arrived at Fort Pease, bringing the supplies which had been left at Logan's camp. Freeman had marched on the twenty-third of April; Camp Supply had been reached on the twenty-eighth; the next day was spent in loading the train; and on the thirtieth the return trip was begun, minus Lieutenant Kendrick and ten men, who continued on to Fort Ellis, escorting a number of discharged contract wagons.[5]

The command was now all together again, and Gibbon decided to move farther down the river on the assumption that the enemy would probably be found farther east if he were to be found at all.[6] The march was begun on the morning of the tenth, the trail followed being the one which Stanley had explored in 1873. The ground was extremely soft, and the heavily loaded wagons made progress

[5] Bradley, *Journal*, 185–88.

[6] Gibbon, "Summer Expedition," 284.

slowly amidst continued signs that the hostiles were watching every movement of the command. On the twelfth, Bravo and Little Face overtook the column, bringing with them the six deserters. This pleased Lieutenant Bradley highly, for it increased the number of horses available to the scouts.[7] Various attempts by officers and scouts to locate the enemy village failed, and on the fifteenth the detachment camped on the Little Porcupine, the "Table Creek" of Lewis and Clark, a short distance above the mouth of the Rosebud but on the opposite bank; they were fifty-two miles from Fort Pease, a distance that it had taken them five days to cover, so frightful were the roads.[8]

Here some of the Crows came in with the news of having discovered a trail of about thirty mounted Sioux on the south bank; and Bradley, who believed that they might have come from a village on the Tongue River, won Gibbon's reluctant consent to go village hunting. Although Bradley's standing with his commanding officer had risen as a result of his correct diagnosis of the week before, Gibbon was still fearful that his subordinate might be taking needless chances which would endanger the lives of his command.

The traders who had built and then abandoned Fort Pease had left several small boats behind. These had been repaired and made serviceable by the troops and had been navigated downstream by the members of Captain Clifford's company, who doubtless preferred that method of traveling to marching. The boats were now used to ferry the scouting detachment and a number of volunteers—a total of twenty-seven men—across the stream, a trip which took only about twenty minutes in all. All of the volunteers were from the infantry, the cavalry having furnished none despite the promise of Major Brisbin that some would be forthcoming. Nor could any of the Crows be persuaded to volunteer, so Bradley was forced to order five of them to accompany the party; and they, together with Bravo, the interpreter, went along with extreme reluctance.

The route followed was along steep and slippery hillsides, down muddy ravines, and then over precipitous ridges. So terrible was the trail that Bradley rightly suspected that the Crows were seeking to discourage him and to tire out the command by selecting the

[7] Bradley, *Journal*, 188.

[8] Gibbon, "Summer Expedition," 284; Gibbon's Report, 472.

Sitting Bull, Chief of the Uncpapa Sioux.

"The greatest instrument in uniting the various tribes of the Northern Plains in resistance to the whites, his name has led all the others in the calendar of infamy."

Courtesy Custer Battlefield National Monument

Indian sign left by the Dakota Sioux on the Custer trail, 1876.

"On several occasions the Crow scouts saw fresh Sioux signs, indicating that every move made by the troops was under enemy surveillance."

Courtesy North Dakota Historical Society

Seven Sioux Warriors who participated in the Battle of the Little Big Horn.

Left to right, top row: Iron Hail, age 90; High Eagle, age 88; Iron Hawk, age 99; Little Warrior, age 80; *bottom row:* Comes Again, age 86; Pemmican, age 85; John Sitting Bull, age 90.

Courtesy Illuminated Foto-Ad Service, Sioux Falls, S. Dak.

worst possible route. The scouts, however, overdid it, and the Lieutenant, who viewed their reluctance as nothing less than cowardice, called them together and "read them the riot act," telling them that the detachment would go to the Tongue River, regardless of obstacles, if it took a month. This warning had its intended effect, the Crows soon discovering a much easier route. Crossing the Rosebud and halting about nine miles beyond, they then rested until four o'clock on the morning of the sixteenth, when they moved forward again. After two or three hours more the command was halted and concealed in a grassy cove while Bradley and the Crows surveyed the country from a prominent peak. Although they could see for thirty miles or more up the valley of the Rosebud, there was no smoke or other sign of an Indian camp. Since the valley of the Tongue was cut off from view by a ridge of considerable elevation, Bradley decided to move still farther eastward in the hope of finding what he sought.

The march was then resumed, the command traveling with the greatest caution, marching through ravines and under cover of knolls wherever possible, and finally ascending and traveling along the crest of a wooded ridge whose pine timber effectively screened them from a distance of several miles. When it did become necessary to cross open ground, the group closed up into a fairly compact mass and dashed across as quickly as possible. Two of the scouts who were mounted on gray horses, which are hardest to see from a distance, were kept from two hundred to three hundred yards in advance of the others; they were always sent to the crest of the next ridge before the main body showed itself. So meticulous were the precautions taken that Bradley was fully justified in asserting that it would have required an especially vigilant enemy to have detected the presence of his detachment.

About four o'clock in the afternoon the Crows in advance signaled the discovery of a village. From a high hill Lieutenant Bradley was able to see a great cloud of smoke hanging over the valley some five or six miles in his front and about eighteen miles from the confluence of the Tongue and Yellowstone rivers. Owing to the intervening bluffs, not a single tepee could be seen, but from the smoke the Crows estimated that there must be at least three hundred lodges—later it was discovered that there were closer to four hundred—and probably some eight hundred to a thousand warriors. Bradley's plan was to wait until after dark, then to try to get closer to the village to ascertain its exact strength, but this proposal was vigorously opposed by the scouts, who were skeptical that any white man could successfully undertake such a task. Instead, they insisted that the best course was to return to the main body of troops as soon as possible, since their small detachment would have little chance of survival if they were discovered by the enemy. Although greatly disappointed in not being able to strike a blow against the enemy, Bradley deferred to the judgment of the scouts, and the return trip was begun shortly after six o'clock. They traveled now with less attempt at concealment, although cautiously, for no one had forgotten that a party of thirty or more warriors was somewhere in front of them. Now that they were headed in the direction they wanted to go, the Crows revealed an excellent detailed knowledge of the country and, despite the darkness of the night, led the detachment over an easy route, arriving on the south bank of the river, opposite Gibbon's camp, soon after sunrise on the seventeenth.

Bradley crossed at once to report the result of his scout to Colonel Gibbon. The command was under orders to march downstream, and preparations to that end were well advanced, but after deliberating for an hour, Gibbon canceled the orders, deciding to cross the river and attack the hostile village instead.

It was now two months to a day since the expedition had left Fort Shaw—and it coincided almost to the hour with the departure of the Dakota column from Fort Abraham Lincoln—two months of monotonous marching and resting in camp; therefore, the prospect of action was received generally with satisfaction, although there were a few chronic malcontents in camp who prophesied nothing but disaster. The Crows were especially pleased, for they saw an opportunity to get revenge for many past insults and humiliations at the hands of the Sioux, as well as to acquire some Sioux ponies; and while they loudly proclaimed their decision to fight side by side with the soldiers against the common foe, Bradley was of the opinion that the troops would do the fighting, and the Crows, reverting to their usual custom, would devote their major activity to stealing ponies.[9]

Captain Sanno and K Company of the infantry were to be left as a camp guard, while the remaining five companies of infantry and four troops of cavalry, a force of about 350 men and 34 officers, plus the Crow and civilian scouts, marched against the hostiles. Rations for seven days, one blanket, and 150 rounds of ammunition a man were to be taken along on thirty pack mules. It was believed that the entire command could be transported across the river before dark, then a forced night march would bring them to the vicinity of the camp, after which the time and method of the attack were to be governed by circumstances.

The crossing of the Yellowstone began about noon, the cavalry going first. From the very beginning everything went wrong, and all efforts seemed to be at cross-purposes. Accident succeeded accident, and there were several narrow escapes from drowning. Only about ten horses an hour were being taken over, and when four drowned, the entire project was abandoned, and the troops already across the stream were brought back to camp. Afterwards Lieutenant Bradley was to write, "What the trouble was I did not then understand, and I don't now, and I have never seen anybody that did."[10] The Crows were now as crestfallen as they had formerly been elated. Disappointed at losing the opportunity of acquiring horses for themselves at the expense of the Sioux, they professed to be unable to understand why the mere crossing of a river should present such an obstacle, and insisted on regarding it as merely an excuse to conceal the cowardice of the soldiers.[11]

During the forenoon a party of Sioux appeared on the south bank. At first it was supposed they were the war party known to have been in the vicinity for several days, and they were looked upon largely as a nuisance. However, when it was noticed that there were between seventy-five and one hundred warriors in the group, it was concluded that the trail of Bradley's scouting detachment had been discovered and that this group had set out to investigate and had followed him in. The Sioux remained in the vicinity all day, scattering whenever the troops moved against them. Al-

[9] Bradley, *Journal*, 189–93.

[10] *Ibid.*, 193; Marquis, *Memoirs of a White Crow Indian*, 232. Marquis, in an article in the *Billings Gazette*, May 15, 1932, says that one trooper and eleven cavalry horses were drowned in the attempted crossing.

[11] Bradley, *Journal*, 194.

though it is not certain whether they knew of the attempt to cross the river, it is probable that they did, in which case a successful surprise attack on the village would have been out of the question. This may have been a factor in Colonel Gibbon's decision to abandon the enterprise although he makes no mention of it, ascribing the abandonment simply to the fact that the "Yellowstone was a raging torrent."[12]

About ten o'clock that evening the camp was aroused by a false alarm. A guard posted on the riverbank over the boats saw what he thought were moving objects bearing a light. Receiving no answer to his whistled challenge and believing that they might be Indians signaling, he fired five shots at them. The command was immediately turned out, but was dismissed when investigation failed to disclose the proximity of an enemy. This incident, indicative of the jittery nerves of Gibbon's soldiers, caused one veteran of thirty years' service to comment: "Well, by God, I've lived a great many years, and seen lots of Indians and served a good deal in their country but these are the first Indians I ever knew to go hunting a camp of soldiers with a lantern."[13]

On the morning of the eighteenth Captain Thompson with his own and Captain Wheelan's company of the cavalry was ordered on a scout to a point opposite the mouth of the Tongue River, to discover, if possible, whether the hostiles were showing any intention of attempting to cross the Yellowstone.[14] If they could be kept on the south side of the river, they were sure to be attacked eventually by either Custer or Crook, or perhaps both, but if they once got into the vast open country between the Yellowstone and Missouri rivers, they would be able to escape pursuit indefinitely, and might even cross the border into the British possessions.[15]

In the evening four Crows started out on foot with the announced intention of proceeding to the Tongue River village, where they expected to provide themselves with ponies. At the same time Bradley, with his detachment, LeForge, and five Crows, started upstream on a three-day scout or until they met couriers expected from Fort Ellis. They met the messengers about nine o'clock on the

[12] *Ibid.*, 194; Gibbon, "Summer Expedition," 285; Gibbon's Report, 472.

[13] Bradley, *Journal*, 195.

[14] Gibbon, "Summer Expedition," 286.

[15] Bradley, *Journal*, 195.

following morning and six hours later were back in camp. From the dispatches which they brought it was learned that the Department commander, Brigadier General Alfred H. Terry, had taken the field in person, and that they might look for the arrival of Custer and the entire Seventh Cavalry in about a month. In the meantime Gibbon was to continue closely patrolling the north bank.[16]

On the day following, the twentieth, widespread excitement was created by the abrupt arrival back in camp of the four Crows who had gone pony stealing. They had acquired no horses, but they did have big news. They reported having almost been run over by a large war party headed toward the Rosebud from the Tongue. This report caused Gibbon to fear for the safety of Captain Thompson's scouting party and to conclude that the hostiles might be preparing to cross to the north bank.[17] So, leaving B Company to guard the camp, the remainder of the command started downstream on a forced march, Bradley's detachment as usual scouting ahead. A drenching rain was falling, so in order to increase the mobility of the command, ten wagons were taken along in which groups of the infantry rode by turns. After covering nine miles, they halted, since there were no signs to indicate that the hostiles had crossed at or near the mouth of the Rosebud, which, because of the nature of the banks, was the most logical place. Bradley reconnoitered for another thirteen miles downstream, discovering a cavalry trail leading back up the river that convinced him that the two commands had passed each other. However, he found in another place where the cavalry had again approached the river, and here discovered several empty cartridge cases and other evidences of preparation for a fight. There were no indications that an actual battle had taken place anywhere in the vicinity, and when the scouts were unable to shed any additional light on the problem, Bradley relinquished any further attempts at its solution and returned to camp.[18]

The mystery was solved the following day when Captain Thompson's command arrived and reported that on the nineteenth they had discovered a party of hostiles approaching the stream on

16 *Ibid.*, 196.
17 Gibbon, "Summer Expedition," 286.
18 Bradley, *Journal*, 197.

the south bank, apparently with the intention of crossing. The troops had concealed themselves in a ravine and prepared to give the Indians a hot reception, hence the empty cartridge cases that Bradley had found. But, after testing the depth of the water with poles, the Indians had decided not to cross and had withdrawn to the timber. Bouyer and one of the Crows then swam the stream, hoping to be able to make off with some of the enemy ponies, but they were discovered and barely escaped with their lives. Captain Thompson then continued his scout without any further alarms or signs of the Sioux until, on his return trip, he found Bradley's trail and discovered that he had been followed to within a short distance of the camp by a small war party that had evidently crossed the river farther downstream. After hearing this report, Gibbon decided to make camp where he was, and the wagons were sent back to bring down the tents and other equipment.[19]

On the twenty-third, word having been received that the Montana hauling contract had been given to E. G. Maclay and Company, all the wagons belonging to the former contractor, John W. Power, were ordered discharged and sent back to Fort Ellis. Company I of the infantry, Lieutenant English, and Troop C of the cavalry, Lieutenant Roe, were sent along as an escort, and with them went one of the Gatlings.[20] Lieutenant Roe's command was ordered to turn back at the end of the second day's march because it was considered that by then the zone of greatest danger would have been passed. Lieutenant English was to continue on until he met the new supply train coming from Fort Ellis with an escort under command of Lieutenant Kendrick, and was then to bring the train into camp. With the party also went Bravo and two of the Crow scouts, who were returning to their agency for the purpose of securing horses for the dismounted Crows, all but two of whom had agreed to send for them.[21]

During this period Sioux warriors often put in appearance on the bluffs opposite the camp, shaking their guns and lances and yelling taunts at the soldiers. The troops saw as many if not more Sioux when they were not looking for them than they did when

[19] *Ibid.*, 197–98.
[20] Gibbon, "Summer Expedition," 287.
[21] Bradley, *Journal*, 202.

they were actually searching.[22] On several occasions hunting parties had been fired on and driven back into camp. Late in the morning of the twenty-third the civilian scout, George Herendeen, saw Indians and heard firing, and upon investigation it was found that two troopers, Stoker and Raymemyer of H Troop, and a citizen teamster by the name of Quinn, who had gone hunting, had been ambushed and killed. The cavalry immediately took up the pursuit of the Indians, who were at first believed to number about forty warriors, but the discovery of a trail of a much larger body farther on prompted the speculation that the Indians had been trying to run off the herd when the hunting party walked right into them. The slain men were absent from camp without permission, for which there was no excuse, since Colonel Gibbon gave hunting passes to all who asked for them, believing that hunting improved the marksmanship of the soldiers, kept the messes supplied with fresh meat, and was also an excellent means of scouting. As Bradley noted, the same thing could have happened just as readily to men who had official permission to be absent.[23] From that day on, Colonel Gibbon felt that his camp was under the constant and careful scrutiny of the enemy, who undoubtedly had pickets hidden in the hills opposite the camp to give warning of any movement that the troops might make, especially across the river into Indian territory.[24]

In the afternoon, a Colonel Chestnut, described as a "Bozeman gentleman," with a crew of four men, arrived at the camp in a Mackinaw boat, having made the trip downstream from Benson's Landing without incident and without seeing any sign of the Sioux. They brought a cargo of vegetables, butter, eggs, tobacco, and other goods, including a keg of beer—all of which found a ready sale. Just before dark several Indians were seen on the southern bank, and one of them, who was wearing a large and elaborate war bonnet, shook it defiantly at the soldiers. This caused Colonel Gibbon to consider seriously the possibility of an attack on the camp. Accordingly, the twelve-pound "Napoleon gun" was rolled up to the bank to reply in case the hostiles opened fire; and since Indian attacks

22 Marquis, *Memoirs of a White Crow Indian*, 225.

23 Bradley, *Journal*, 202; Gibbon, "Summer Expedition," 286–87; *Helena Weekly Herald*, July 6, 1876.

24 Gibbon, "Summer Expedition," 287; Marquis, *Memoirs of a White Crow Indian*, 225.

usually took place at early dawn, the troops were ordered to "stand to" at two o'clock in the morning and to remain in formation until after daylight, a schedule that was adhered to until the camp was moved on the fifth of June.[25]

The next few days were uneventful; the weather was very warm and the troops remained quietly in camp. Despite some indications that the Sioux were still in the vicinity, few of them were seen.[26] The Crow scouts often observed signs that they did not report to the officers, because they felt that there were many more hostiles in the country than the troops could handle, and that a report would only mean a fruitless sally or, worse, a disastrous encounter.[27] On the twenty-sixth, Lieutenant Roe returned and reported that he had gone almost to Fort Pease without finding any sign of Indians.[28]

While the troops were camped opposite the mouth of the Rosebud, two incidents occurred that illustrate the nature of the campaign. About ten o'clock one night a guard mistook a floating log for a swimming Sioux and fired at it as it drifted past. The command was immediately turned out, and Bradley hurried the scouts over to the riverbank, where he had them "lie down and creep here and there through a brushy and reedy area where he knew there was an abundance of mosquitoes, frogs and snakes. He himself was scurrying back and forth while giving orders about the proper mode of locating the enemy." All this time he was carrying in his hands a lighted lantern, which led to much "talk about the humor of the situation, a well-educated army officer using a lighted lantern at night in a hunt for hostile Sioux," the humor of which was enjoyed by the scouts as much as by the soldiers.[29] At this time, too, LeForge and "Mitch" Bouyer carried on a talk in the sign language with some Sioux across the river. The hostiles are reported to have said:

> At the agencies they took away our horses and our guns. We then could not hunt and as they did not give us enough food, we were

[25] Bradley, *Journal*, 203.
[26] *Ibid.*, 203.
[27] Marquis, *Memoirs of a White Crow Indian*, 221–22.
[28] Bradley, *Journal*, 204.
[29] Marquis, *Memoirs of a White Crow Indian*, 229.

then starving. So we got other horses and guns, and we are now out hunting for food. Many of our women are walking because we have not enough horses, and our children are hungry. We do not want to fight the white people, and we wish the soldiers would stay on the north side of the river and leave us here. We will stay here and kill buffalo, where they are plentiful. Fighting takes away our energies that ought to be given to hunting for food and robes. Tell this to your chiefs.

The Sioux then asked for ammunition, saying they would send a man over for it, but LeForge and Bouyer refused this request. They claim to have reported the talk to Lieutenant Roe, but if they did, nothing more ever came of it.[30]

In order to discover whether this inactivity on the part of the hostiles had any particular significance, Lieutenant Bradley and his detachment were sent on another scout across the river. Fearing a possible trap, Gibbon sent Captain Clifford, Bradley's immediate superior, and his company to occupy the bluffs on the southern bank to support Bradley in case his detachment was attacked and had to fall back. Clifford's command crossed at daybreak, followed by Bradley's detachment of twenty men. The little force marched about a mile upstream and then turned inland, riding for several miles up a long dry ravine and then crossing the plain toward the Little Wolf Mountains, with abundant Indian signs on every side. There were many carcasses of freshly killed buffalo, skinned in a manner that showed the hides were wanted for lodge skins, and innumerable pony tracks—so many that when the Indians had been forced to travel close together, they had left a beaten path track like a well-traveled road. The signs indicated that hundreds of mounted Indians had been there within a very few days. The almost total lack of concealment made it a very nervous ride, the Crow scouts being especially apprehensive. The fact that most of the tracks were about a week old, with only a very few more recent ones, showed that the Crows had been telling the truth when they reported a great Sioux war party moving from the Tongue River towards the Rosebud.[31]

Bradley sheltered his command in the same grassy cove that

[30] *Ibid.*, 222.
[31] Bradley, *Journal*, 204.

had been used on the sixteenth, while he and some of the scouts, including Bouyer, LeForge, and White-Man-Runs-Him, proceeded to the same high peak that had served as an observation point on that previous occasion. But, whereas on the sixteenth they could see for thirty miles or more up the valley of the Rosebud with no sign of an Indian camp, they now saw heavy smoke ascending in many columns and forming a blanket over the valley, and with glasses Bradley was able to spot a great Indian village strung out along the stream for a distance of over two miles, the plain above the camp dotted with black spots that could only be horses. The better-trained eyes of the Crows were even able to make out the more decided colors. A sudden movement among the pony herd made the scouts fear that the presence of the detachment had been discovered and that the horses were being driven in, preparatory to the formation of a war party. The Crows became very much excited and wanted to leave at once, despite Bradley's desire to bring all the members of his detachment to the peak to show them the camp, a desire motivated by the fact that on the previous occasion some persons had been ungenerous enough to deny that he had seen a village; this time he wanted to accumulate corroborative evidence. Most of his men, however, as well as the scouts, preferred to return to camp. In returning, the command took only two hours to cover the same distance that had taken them five hours coming out.[32]

The result of this scout made it certain that the hostiles were in force, and that this was the same village that Bradley had seen earlier on the Tongue River.[33] Then they had been about thirty-five miles from Gibbon's position; now they were only eighteen, and the fact that they had moved closer to the soldiers rather than farther away made it obvious that they had no particular fear of the troops. Bradley judged that the movement from the Tongue to the Rosebud had taken place on the nineteenth and that the war party reported by the Crow scouts merely constituted the advance guard of the larger movement.

[32] *Ibid.*, 204–205; Marquis, *Memoirs of a White Crow Indian*, 229.

[33] Although Bradley estimated the strength of the village at from eight hundred to one thousand warriors and the number of lodges at four hundred, Lieutenant Roe, who was not with the scouting party, later expressed the opinion that between eighteen hundred and two thousand warriors were in this village. Roe, *Custer's Last Battle*, 2.

Many of the officers, on hearing of Bradley's latest discovery, expected Colonel Gibbon to cross the river and march to the attack; and when the expected order failed to come, there was much speculation as to the reasons. The difficulty in crossing the Yellowstone, which had caused the failure of a previous attempt, was not now as great since the condition of both banks of the Yellowstone at the mouth of the Rosebud made the crossing of the horses much easier. The difficulty could also have been overcome by leaving the horses behind, for, since the village was only eighteen miles away, the command could be ferried across the river in the afternoon and reach the village by a night march in plenty of time for the traditional "attack at dawn," the accepted procedure in Indian fighting. (No record has been preserved of the reaction of the cavalry to this particular scheme, but it may very easily be imagined.) In the absence of Lieutenant English's company, Gibbon would have had about 350 men available for the attack, but whether that number would have been sufficient is at least open to question.[34] On the one hand, an attack might have scattered the assembled tribes sufficiently to prevent that great concentration of Indian power that was to annihilate Custer and the members of his immediate command a few weeks later; on the other, it might have led to the massacre and destruction of all of Gibbon's force.

Just after dark on the evening of the twenty-seventh, a white scout by the name of Williamson and two privates of Company E, Bell and Stewart, who had volunteered for the duty, started downstream in a skiff, especially fitted out with extra oars, muffled oarlocks, and other equipment, in an attempt to communicate with General Terry, who was believed to be at the mouth of Glendive Creek or on the Powder River. In case they failed to find him, they were to continue on to Fort Buford, or until they met one of the river steamers.[35]

The next day another Mackinaw boat made its appearance. Like the first traders, its passengers had had no trouble and had seen no signs of the Sioux. In addition to the usual cargo of vegetables, butter, eggs, tobacco, and canned goods, it carried a quantity of whiskey and champagne cider, from which the officers concocted

[34] Bradley, *Journal*, 205.
[35] *Ibid.*, 206; Gibbon, "Summer Expedition," 287.

a new drink appropriately named "Rosebud" in honor of the stream across from which the command was camped. The operator of the boat, a Mr. McCormick, also brought a large mail, with new orders for Colonel Gibbon from General Terry. Stating that he had reason to believe that the hostiles were concentrating at a point above the mouth of Glendive Creek, Terry ordered Gibbon to march along the north bank of the Yellowstone toward that point, then to cross the river and co-operate with the Dakota column. Since such a movement would be impossible until the arrival of the supply train now en route from Fort Ellis, all government wagons in the camp were unloaded and sent back the next morning with an escort under command of Captain Sanno, the idea being to meet the new train, lighten its load, and thus hasten its progress. Bradley believed that a concentration such as Terry reported was unlikely since the hostile Indians appeared to be working the other way, but orders had to be obeyed. Colonel Gibbon apparently shared the opinion held by his subordinate, for in the days to follow he displayed little or no inclination to hasten his march down the river, a hesitation that at times amounted to nothing more than indolence, although the official reason was given as "bad roads and weather."[36]

On the thirtieth, two of the Crows started on another of their perpetual horse-stealing expeditions. Put across the river just after dark, they started to move inland up a small ravine. In a very short time, however, they were back on the bank calling lustily for a boat and announcing that the Sioux were close at hand. Safely back in camp, the Crows told of being almost run over by a large party of Sioux warriors but of escaping without detection, which caused Bradley to comment scornfully and sarcastically:

> It turns out that we have not wanted any Sioux villages, but had it been otherwise it seems likely that we would have continued to want them for all that the Crows would have found for us. They are mortally afraid of the Sioux, and even when they pluck up courage and start, the slightest misadventure suffices to convince them that their "medicine" is bad, and then back they come.[37]

[36] Gibbon, "Summer Expedition," 288; Gibbon, Report, 472.

[37] Bradley, *Journal*, 207. For the Indians' side of the story, see Marquis, *Memoirs of a White Crow Indian*, 215–16.

On June 1, the same snowstorm that was to delay both the Crook and Custer commands struck the camp of the Montana column, although it was less severe than in the other cases, despite the fact that Gibbon speaks of it as "a furious snow storm which raged all day."[38] The next day was stormy and so cold that a fire was necessary for comfort. The cold also had the effect of reducing the flow of water in the mountain tributaries of the Yellowstone, causing the latter stream to drop nearly three feet in as many days, thus making for renewed vigilance against any attempted crossing by the Sioux.[39]

On the third, Captain Ball's troop was started upstream with instructions to go as far as Big Porcupine Creek, find the best place for the wagons to cross that stream, and construct such bridges across any other streams as would be necessary to expedite the progress of the supply train. At the same time Captain Logan's company was started downstream ahead of the command for the purpose of bridging creeks and otherwise putting the road in shape for the contemplated movement.[40]

Lieutenant Kendrick, who had gone back with the first contingent of discharged wagons, arrived at Fort Ellis on May 5. Nine days later he began the return journey with a detail of fifteen men from the garrison at the fort, accompanying the Diamond R train carrying 100,000 pounds of freight. On the twenty-eighth, when six miles below Baker's battleground, they met the detachment and train commanded by Lieutenant English, who sent the discharged wagons on to the fort under the escort of the fifteen men from there.[41] Lieutenant English, as the senior officer, then took command of the train and brought it as far as Pompey's Pillar, where they met the wagons under command of Captain Sanno coming to their assistance. Some of the cargo was transferred to the empty wagons, and the combined force made all possible speed toward camp.

38 Gibbon, "Summer Expedition," 288.

39 Bradley, *Journal*, 207.

40 *Ibid*., 208.

41 "Diary of Mathew Carroll, Master in Charge of Transportation for Colonel John Gibbon's Expedition against the Sioux Indians, 1876," *Contributions to the Historical Society of Montana*, II (1896), 231 (hereinafter cited as Carroll, "Diary").

The entire march was without significant incident except for the accidental shooting of Sergeant Belecke of C Company of the Seventh Infantry, who was a member of the escort furnished Lieutenant Kendrick at Fort Ellis. The Sergeant, who was nearsighted and wore glasses, was shot in the head and killed by a sentry when, after having accidentally wandered outside the lines, he failed to respond to the whistled challenge—"a victim of this wretched method of challenging. There could be one thing worse: to fire on sight without challenging at all," as Bradley expressed it.[42] The Lieutenant was probably justified in his belief that the system would result in the death of one hundred soldiers for every Indian who was killed because of it.[43]

Bravo and the two Crow scouts also returned with the train, having secured horses for all of the dismounted scouts except the two who, in a fit of Indian obstinacy and ill humor, had failed to send for them. Bravo had succeeded in this task at considerable risk to himself, for he swam the almost ice-cold Yellowstone River at Pompey's Pillar, and then set off toward the Crow village, the exact location of which was a matter of conjecture, and traveled through an unknown region possibly infested with Sioux. But he reached the village, secured his horses, and on the return trip overtook the command about twenty miles below Fort Pease.[44]

The reunited column moved downstream about nine o'clock on the morning of June 5, Bradley's command as usual being several miles in advance. The command kept to the valley and halted after a march of only nine miles at the rate of two miles an hour. Captain Clifford's company was once again in charge of the boats, being careful not to get too far ahead of their more luckless comrades so that the command always camped together at night.

The next day, as the result of difficulties with the wagon train, the march covered only ten miles, but on the seventh the troops covered twenty-two miles, mostly across a flat tableland which was covered with a luxuriant growth of grass. The descent into the valley was through a narrow and dangerous defile, and here

42 *Ibid.*, 229; Bradley, *Journal*, 208.
43 Carroll, "Diary," 229; Bradley, *Journal*, 208.
44 Bradley, *Journal*, 209–10.

the wagons lost so much time that it was nine o'clock before the camp was fairly in shape and an hour later before supper was ready for a very hungry assortment of soldiers. This camp was made two miles below the confluence of the Tongue and Yellowstone rivers, but on the opposite bank. In three days the command had covered only forty-one miles because of the roughness of the terrain, and Bouyer told them that the country ahead was even worse.[45] The next morning the column moved before seven o'clock. A few miles farther downstream one of the Crow scouts discovered the tracks of two shod horses and a small sack containing sugar, bacon, and other articles of food, as well as cartridges, all wrapped in pieces of newspaper. Since the articles were fresh, Bradley reasoned that they must have come only recently from a large supply camp or steamer. Because the foods were not those that an Indian would be apt to carry and the tracks were those of soldiers' horses rather than of Indian ponies, the Lieutenant was convinced that couriers from General Terry were in the vicinity and that they had probably turned back on seeing the Crows, whom they had mistaken for Sioux.[46]

That morning, since Gibbon had intended to make his next camp on the high land rather than close to the river, Captain Clifford's company had drawn rations for two days before starting downstream. Gibbon had expected the boats to make the usual day's run before tying up at night, but Clifford had misunderstood and believed himself at liberty to make a two days' run in one, and so passed on with the intention of landing and fortifying a position opposite the mouth of the Powder River, there to await the arrival of the rest of the column.[47] With him were Major Brisbin, Lieutenant Doane, the scout George Herendeen, and two of the Crows. At the mouth of the Powder they found the steamer *Far West;* and later General Terry, with two companies of the Seventh Cavalry, put in appearance.

Gibbon's column had made camp at 7:40 P.M., after a march of sixteen miles, broken by a two-hour halt at midday. Here the valley was about three miles wide and fifteen miles long, with heavy

45 Gibbon, "Summer Expedition," 288; Carroll, "Diary," 232.
46 Gibbon, "Summer Expedition," 288–89; Bradley, *Journal,* 211.
47 Bradley, *Journal,* 211.

grass but quite destitute of timber, so that driftwood from the river had to be used in preparing supper. Shortly after midnight Herendeen and one of the Crow scouts arrived, bringing dispatches from General Terry stating that the Dakota column had reached the Powder and ordering Gibbon to leave the command in camp and proceed downstream to meet Terry coming up on the *Far West*.[48]

Gibbon started at seven o'clock in the morning, accompanied by Bradley's detachment and Captain Ball's troop. Eight miles downstream, at a place known ever since as Steamboat Point, they met the *Far West*, which was proceeding upriver with General Terry and staff and with Captain Clifford's company as passengers. The boat drew in to the shore, and Gibbon went on board. The steamer then continued its run upstream, while Bradley and Ball and their commands rode along the bank. This trip was costly in one respect, for, while chasing an antelope, LeForge fell from his horse, breaking his collarbone. Thus the command was deprived of the service of the better of its two interpreters just at the time when the real campaign was about to begin. The cavalry escort arrived back in camp at noon, a few minutes ahead of the boat. The *Far West*, after a stay of two hours,[49] during which time all of the officers went aboard to meet General Terry, cast off and started downstream for the mouth of the Powder, where Terry had decided to establish a base camp.

Future actions would depend upon developments. The existence of any large camps of Indians in the region was now more than ever a matter of doubt, for Terry and Custer had discovered none, and Gibbon had knowledge of only the one that Bradley had seen on the Tongue and later on the Rosebud. There had been no word from General Crook, and on the theory that the hostiles might be farther up the Yellowstone, Terry ordered Gibbon to retrace his steps to the camp opposite the mouth of the Rosebud. Gibbon planned to move immediately, but a torrential rainstorm caused delay, and the trip back upriver was made under conditions far worse than those that had prevailed coming down. Not until the fourteenth of June was the command reunited opposite the mouth

48 Gibbon, "Summer Expedition," 289.

49 Carroll says that the boat arrived at one o'clock and stayed only an hour. Carroll, "Diary," 232.

of Rosebud Creek, where they awaited the coming of the Department commander and continued their scouting activities both up and down the river. Although they were still in doubt concerning the location of the hostile tribes, there was evidence that they might be found on the Little Big Horn, and many of the officers still believed that the Sioux and Cheyennes, burdened with women and children, were desirous only of avoiding any contact with the soldiers.[50]

[50] Gibbon, "Summer Expedition," 289–91.

CHAPTER VIII

The Dakota Column

THE PRINCIPAL PART of the Terry command was one of the most, if not the most, famous regiments in the history of the United States Army—the Seventh Cavalry. Organized under an act of Congress of July 28, 1866, the regiment was activated at Fort Riley, Kansas, later in the same year, and from the beginning was intended for service against the Indians of the Great Plains. At first there were only eight companies,[1] but this number was soon increased to twelve, although the entire regiment had never been all together until the expedition of 1876 against the hostile Sioux and Cheyennes.[2]

The first colonel, Andrew J. Smith, was a veteran of both the Mexican and Civil wars and an able, experienced Indian fighter. Soon after completing the organization of the regiment, he was assigned to the command of one of the military districts created to police the states of the former Confederacy, and the real work of fashioning the regiment into an efficient fighting tool fell on the shoulders of the Lieutenant Colonel, George Armstrong Custer, with the result that the man and the regiment have been peculiarly identified in the American mind ever since. In 1869 Colonel Smith was succeeded in command of the regiment by Samuel D. Sturgis.

Sturgis had graduated from West Point in 1846, and after serving in the Mexican War, had been promoted to a captaincy in 1855. He fought in several Indian campaigns in the Southwest and during the Civil War displayed gallantry and courage at South Mountain, Antietam, and Fredericksburg. After being mustered out of the volunteer service in August, 1865, he became lieutenant colonel of

[1] DeLand, *The Sioux Wars,* 310.

[2] In fact, it was the first time in nineteen years, except during the Civil War, that an entire regiment had served together in one command. *New York Herald,* June 19, 1876.

the Sixth Cavalry, and in May, 1869, was assigned to the Seventh.[3] He and his subordinate, however, seldom saw eye to eye on any subject; Custer had undoubtedly expected the promotion for himself, his Civil War record being superior to that of Sturgis, even though the latter was Custer's senior by many years. The result was that the relations of the two men were never apparently friendly. As the best way out of a bad situation, General Sheridan, who may have sympathized with Custer and who seems always to have had a warm spot in his heart for him, resolved the dilemma by keeping Colonel Sturgis on detached service and recruiting duty "basking in the sunshine of a large city," while Custer remained where he much preferred to be—on the plains with his regiment.[4]

In 1867 the regiment got its baptism of fire when it was included in General Hancock's expedition against the Cheyennes. The Kansas Pacific Railroad was building westward, to the great alarm of the Indians, who retaliated in the only way they knew—by attacking the construction gangs. During the campaign the regiment covered nearly one thousand miles and got its first taste of Indian fighting—a new experience for officers and men alike. The strategy and tactics with which they were familiar, that of the Civil War, simply would not work against the wild tribes of the plains, and Custer received a lesson in the decoy and ambush strategy of the western tribesmen. In fact, the Indians actually succeeded in trapping a part of the regiment, but the lesson was not too costly to the troops since they had such a great superiority in both arms and numbers that the hostiles were forced to open the trap and let their captives go.[5] Towards the close of the campaign Custer committed a series of indiscretions, both major and minor, which led to his court-martial and conviction. As a consequence he was suspended from rank and command for one year with loss of pay.

The army was engaged in a campaign against the southern tribes, and while Custer fumed and fretted in his enforced exile, his successors fumbled and blundered in their operations against the hostiles. Finally, in exasperation, General Sheridan intervened, requesting that Custer's sentence be shortened, and Custer was re-

[3] *Dictionary of American Biography*, XVIII, 183.
[4] Bates, *Custer's Indian Battles*, 8; *New York Herald*, July 7, 1876.
[5] Hyde, *Red Cloud's Folk*, 155.

stored to duty in order to lead his regiment against the tribesmen of the Southern Plains. The result was the famous Battle of the Washita, which gave the regiment and its commander their reputations. Custer had always had a tendency toward the dramatic, a tendency which had been intensified by his months of idleness. So when, at dawn on the bitterly cold day of November 27, 1868, the Seventh Cavalry swept down on Black Kettle's sleeping village of Cheyennes located along the banks of the ice-covered Washita River, the trumpets not only shrilled the "Charge" but the bandsmen bravely tootled away at "Garry Owen," at least until their instruments froze. The attack was a complete surprise; before the Indians were aware that there were troops in the vicinity, the soldiers were riding through the village.

To Lieutenant Edward S. Godfrey and his platoon had been assigned the task of capturing the Indian pony herd. The completion of this assignment had taken them several miles down the river, and from the crest of a high bluff the Lieutenant saw other villages in the valley whose fighting men were preparing to come to the assistance of Black Kettle's band. Godfrey, aware that Custer believed that he had only the one village to fight, started back to warn his commander. Under attack by Indians all the way, he fought a slow withdrawing action and succeeded in rejoining the main command without the loss of a man.[6]

During the fight in the village, Major Joel Elliott, who had commanded the regiment during Custer's absence, rode, with a small detachment, in pursuit of a fleeing group of the hostiles. The group was apparently cut off by hostiles from the other villages who were coming up to join in the fight and never rejoined the rest of the regiment. The troops and the Indians were each uncertain about the other's exact strength. Custer was well aware that he could not fight all the Indians of the Southwest, but his action in destroying the village, plus his usual bold front, convinced the hostiles that his force was much larger than it really was. Elliott's absence was noticed, and several parties were sent in search of the missing men, but they failed to find any trace of them near the village and were prevented from going farther by the great number of Indians gathering downstream. Although there was plenty of reason to suspect

[6] Bates, *Custer's Indian Battles*, 13.

that the detachment had been cut off and trapped, there was also ground for believing, in the light of Lieutenant Godfrey's experience, that they might have been able to fight their way through and rejoin the main wagon train.[7] In any event, Custer, with night coming on, uncertain of the strength of the Indians and professing concern for the safety of his supply train, decided to withdraw, without determining for a certainty what had become of Elliott and his men. Their frozen bodies, badly mutilated, were found later a little more than two miles from the site occupied by the Cheyenne village.

While this battle made the reputation of Custer and the regiment, it also sowed the seeds of disaster. There were jeers mixed with the cheers, and the loss of Major Elliott was represented as a plain case of callous abandonment of a portion of the command. Most caustic and bitter of all the critics was Captain Fred W. Benteen, of Troop H. During the Civil War he had been a member of a cavalry brigade which had included Joel Elliott, and the loss of his former associate moved Benteen to rage that was nothing short of explosive. He even went so far as to write an anonymous letter to the newspapers, the authorship of which he later readily admitted, in which he ridiculed Custer and belittled the regiment.[8]

The Indians of the Southwest realized that the white man was too strong to be successfully resisted, and peace, of a kind, soon came to the region. The Battle of the Washita and the controversy following it became only a memory, and the public soon forgot everything except that it had been a glorious victory. In the army, however, especially among the officers of the Seventh Cavalry, it became a festering sore, destined to embitter the relationships of individuals as long as any of them remained alive and to complicate and obscure the facts of history down to the present day.

In 1870 the regiment was broken up into several detachments and scattered throughout the states of the former Confederacy. Quite a few years of idyllic existence followed, with duties no more onerous than apprehending violators of the revenue laws, putting

[7] The Battle of the Washita from the Indian point of view is described in Grinnell, *The Fighting Cheyennes*, 287–98. It contains an account of the death of Major Elliot and the members of his detachment.

[8] Bates, *Custer's Indian Battles*, 13.

down the violence brought about by the activity of the Ku Klux Klan, and in general trying to maintain for the former slaves that full and free social equality that a radical Congress was determined to give them. There was comparatively little to do, and the time passed pleasantly. But in 1872 there was a rude awakening, for in that year General Sheridan, alarmed by the growing strength and hostility of the Sioux, requested that the regiment be transferred to Dakota Territory with headquarters at Fort Abraham Lincoln. Later in that year it had constituted a part of the force which General Stanley led up the Yellowstone River, and the next summer Custer had led ten companies of the regiment on the Black Hills expedition. Since his rhapsodical reports of the riches of the last-named region started the stampede of miners and other settlers into the territory, it was perhaps poetic justice that in 1876 Custer, at the head of that same regiment, was being sent to quell the Indian disturbances which had been occasioned in part by the white man's desire to acquire those Hills and by the Indians' reluctance to part with them.

In the decade since its activation the Seventh Cavalry had acquired a reputation as the most experienced and capable mounted regiment in the armed forces, but it had also developed internal dissension; by 1876 there was more than the usual amount of jealousy and bickering among its officers. The many and varied causes of these hard feelings were partly what one should have expected in a service that was poorly paid and highly competitive, and in which the competitors were thrown in constant personal contact. It was intensified by the fact that the Civil War had brought a large number of new men into the service and that with the end of that conflict a corresponding reduction in personnel had become necessary. With this oversupply of trained personnel many officers found themselves reduced far below what they considered their appropriate rank and, what was worse, in many cases serving under men who had previously been their juniors. With such a vast reservoir, promotion was bound to be both slow and uncertain.

The situation was, of course, by no means peculiar to the Seventh Cavalry, but extended to all branches of the armed services. Jealousy and even hatred existed among the forces of both General Crook and General Gibbon, and both of those commands suffered from these conditions during the campaign against the Sioux, although apparently not to the same extent as Custer's forces.[9]

By far the most important cause of dissension in the Seventh Cavalry, and one which was limited to that regiment alone, was the character and personality of its lieutenant colonel. Custer was a supreme egotist, with boundless ambition and equally boundless faith in his own destiny, a faith that was not at all unwarranted in view of the remarkable successes of his early life.

Born in Ohio, apparently of Hessian ancestry,[10] he had moved with his family to Michigan, and from that state he received his appointment to the Military Academy at West Point. Here his lifelong addiction to practical jokes and his hatred of restraint rather than any deficiency of intelligence or ability caused "his roll of demerits to assume formidable proportions,"[11] and he graduated last in a class of thirty-four as well as under a disciplinary cloud. In fact, probably only the outbreak of the Civil War saved him from dishonorable dismissal. Having an investment of more than three years plus several thousands of dollars in his education, the War Department seems to have reasoned that the country was entitled to some return, so he was commissioned a second lieutenant and ordered to join the Army of the Potomac, arriving just in time for the disastrous encounter at Bull Run. Originally assigned to the Balloon Corps, our earliest example of an air force, Custer was soon transferred to the staff of General George B. McClellan. From that time on his rise was meteoric, and at the age of twenty-three he was commissioned a major general of Volunteers, youngest man ever to hold that rank in the history of the army. Admittedly a peculiar genius, Custer had a flair for catching the public eye, and by the end of the war he had not only won an undying popular fame but had captivated the imagination of the Northerners as few military leaders before or since have been able to do.[12] Nor was this

9 James P. Murphy, "The Campaign of the Little Big Horn," *Infantry Journal*, Vol. XXXIV (June, 1929), 24.

10 *Army and Navy Journal*, July 15, 1876. An item in the *Cheyenne* (Wyo.) *Daily Leader*, July 29, 1876, says that Custer was born near Baden, Germany, and that the family name was originally Kuester. Cited in Spring, *Cheyenne and Black Hills Stage and Express Routes*, 153.

11 Hanson, "The Civil War Custer," *Cavalry Journal*, Vol. XLIII (1934), 24.

12 *New York Herald*, July 11, 1876.

all; for his reputation for courage and dash won the admiration and excited the enthusiasm of the majority of the younger officers of the army, even those who had never met or even seen him.[13]

Custer was too uniformly successful, however, too much given to doing things that others felt could not be done, not to be envied and even hated.[14] There were not wanting those who believed—and not without some justification—that his success was due largely, if not entirely, to luck rather than to merit and ability, and the expression "Custer's luck" soon became almost a byword. People of this opinion insisted that he was a "pet" soldier who, because of Sheridan's influence and patronage, had risen not only above his merit but above men of equal merit.[15] On the other hand, Custer's defenders, and they were numerous, answered that what jealous rivals called "luck" was simply the result of downright hard work, unlimited energy, and dauntless courage.[16]

With the close of the war and the reorganization of the army that followed, Custer, who was a Democrat and did not approve of the administration's Reconstruction policies, apparently flirted with the idea of taking service in the Mexican army operating against the Emperor Maximilian. He finally decided against it and accepted the offer of the lieutenant colonelcy of the newly authorized Seventh Cavalry, taking it in preference to the colonelcy of the Ninth Cavalry, which was a Negro regiment.

By 1876 the situation in the regiment was such that not only did Custer have both devoted friends and bitter enemies in the regiment, but the officers seem to have been quite definitely split into pro- and anti-Custer factions. A few nonpolitically minded ones were members of neither faction and apparently attempted to preserve a strict, if somewhat precarious, neutrality. The opposition seems to have been centered around Captain Fred Benteen, of H troop, who was the ranking captain, and Marcus A. Reno, the junior major. Both men were considerably older than Custer and had seen

13 McClernand, "With Indian and Buffalo in Montana," *Cavalry Journal*, Vol. XXXVI (January and April, 1927), 23.

14 Edna L. Waldo, *Dakota*, 183.

15 *New York Herald*, July 7, 1876.

16 Charles Francis Bates, *The Westchester Horse and the Custer Trail* (pamphlet in Western America Collection, Denver Public Library), n.p.

service in the Civil War, service that, if not distinguished, was probably above the average.[17]

Major Reno, who told the Court of Inquiry that he had known Custer for a long time and had no confidence in his ability as a soldier,[18] had been appointed to the Military Academy by Senator Stephen A. Douglas and had graduated in 1857, four years ahead of Custer. The outbreak of the Civil War found him a captain. Twice brevetted for gallantry, he was colonel of the Twelfth Pennsylvania Volunteer Cavalry and the acting commander of a brigade at the close of the war. Benteen, despite the fact that in rank he was Reno's junior, was much the abler man and apparently the real leader of the opposition. A Virginian by birth, he had sided with the Union during the Civil War and had won a wide reputation as a cavalry leader. His brothers had served in the Confederate Army, and his father is said to have prayed for the death of his "disloyal" son.[19] Benteen had joined the Seventh Cavalry in 1866 and seems to have shown an immediate dislike for Custer, whom he regarded as a boastful upstart, although this animosity did not come out into the open until after the Battle of the Washita. From that time on, Benteen neither forgave nor forgot what he chose to consider Custer's "abandonment" of a portion of his command to the enemy. Benteen later claimed that he was always open and aboveboard in his criticism of Custer, that Custer liked him for it, and would have welcomed him as a friend. Benteen declared, however, that he knew the man too well to be friendly with him.[20] In fact, Benteen's dominant characteristic seems to have been jealousy of and hostility to almost everybody and everything. There were few of his fellow-officers for whom he had either liking or respect, and in particular he seems to have despised Major Reno, although he made common cause with him out of his inveterate hatred and jealousy of Custer.[21]

17 For a very devastating criticism of Reno's war record and his position in the regiment, see "Varnum, Reno and the Little Big Horn," by W. J. Ghent, in *Winners of the West*, April 30, 1936.

18 Reno *Court*, 730; *Proceedings of a Court of Inquiry in the Case of Major Marcus A. Reno Concerning his Conduct at the Battle of the Little Big Horn River*, June 25–26, 1876 (General Court-Martial Number Q. Q. 979. Records of the Judge-Advocate General, National Archives, Washington, D. C.), 1092 (hereinafter cited as *Official Transcript*).

19 Bates, *Custer's Indian Battles*, 16.

20 Graham, *The Custer Myth*, 190.

21 Fred Dustin, *The Custer Fight; Some Criticisms of General E. S. Godfrey's*

Others, outside the regiment, had unflattering opinions of Custer. During the Yellowstone expedition of 1874, General Stanley had written to his wife: ". . . I have seen enough of Custer to convince me that he is a cold-blooded, untruthful and unprincipled man. He is universally despised by all the officers of his regiment excepting his relatives and one or two sycophants."[22] Stanley's opinion may not have been entirely unprejudiced, and Custer had his side of the story. In several letters to Mrs. Custer he told of Stanley's misbehavior and especially of his addiction to alcohol, a weakness that caused Custer to anticipate official trouble between them.[23] Finally, Stanley had ordered Custer arrested for taking over as second in command when Stanley was unable to discharge his functions as the commanding officer. But according to Custer, Stanley had apologized within forty-eight hours, acknowledged that he had been in the wrong, and even offered to repeat the apology in the presence of Custer's officers.[24]

After the disaster, Colonel Sturgis, his long accumulated resentment against Custer intensified by the grief and shock caused by the death of his son, Lieutenant Jack Sturgis, described Custer as a brave but very selfish man, one who was "insanely ambitious for glory and the phrase 'Custer's luck' a good clue to his ruling passion."[25] Of Custer's reputation as an Indian fighter, Sturgis declared that while Custer had written much and therefore might have been supposed to have had great experience in savage warfare, such was not the case, his experience being exceedingly limited.[26]

Much of the enmity to Custer was caused by certain facets of his character, for he was not only a man of unusual personality and overwhelming ambition but mentally and physically a package of incessantly popping explosive.[27] Vigilant and almost tireless himself, he was able to endure hardships, such as forced marches and long periods of exposure to the elements, without apparent ill effect.

"Custer's Last Battle," . . . and Mrs. Elizabeth Custer's Pamphlet of 1921, 26. W. J. Ghent, "Varnum, Reno and the Little Big Horn," *Winners of the West*, April 30, 1936.

22 *Personal Memoirs of General D. S. Stanley*, 239.

23 Merington, *The Custer Story*, 252.

24 *Ibid.*, 265.

25 *Army and Navy Journal*, July 29, 1876.

26 *Army and Navy Journal*, July 22, 1876.

27 Marquis, *Sketch Story of the Custer Battle*, n. p.

Almost literally "a man of iron," he seemed to feel that the other members of his command were made of similar stuff; and when they failed to measure up to his expectations, he attributed the failure to a want of will rather than to a want of stamina.[28] A part of the enmity toward him, moreover, was caused by that jealousy which stodgy, unimaginative men always feel for the brilliantly successful, especially if the successful person be younger than they. One of the seldom mentioned and, indeed, little-known facts about the Seventh Cavalry in 1876 was that its commanding officer was younger than most of his "junior" officers.[29] The hard feelings were further intensified by Custer's having managed to secure the assignment of a younger brother and a brother-in-law to his regiment. Of the appointment of his brother, Tom, Custer wrote jubilantly that the "Custer luck" had again prevailed.[30] He had also secured the appointment of several other officers who had served with him during the war. Although this had the value of giving the commanding officer the companionship of men he liked and respected, it unfortunately caused some of the others to feel that they were outsiders and were discriminated against.[31]

The personnel of the regiment at the start of the campaign against the Sioux was about what anyone familiar with the army would have expected, and probably could have been duplicated in almost any other regiment of the day. Both officers and men represented a cross section of the conglomerate American population that had given the United States the appellation, "The Melting Pot."

The officers constituted a rather motley group. While the majority of them were native-born Americans who had either earned their military reputations during the Civil War or were recent graduates of the Military Academy, a few were veterans of foreign armies. Captain Keogh and Lieutenant Nowlan were both of Irish

28 William Rose Benét, review of Frederic F. Van de Water's *Glory Hunter*, in *Saturday Review of Literature* (December 1, 1934), 325; Dustin, *The Custer Fight*, 21n.; Frederic F. Van de Water, in *Glory Hunter, a Life of General Custer*, speaks of ". . . the tireless energy of Custer at which all men marvelled and some cursed" (p. 133).

29 Bates, *Custer's Indian Battles*, 8.

30 Merington, *The Custer Story*, 178. For the appointment of Calhoun, Custer's brother-in-law, see *ibid.*, 236.

31 Eli J. Huggins, "Custer and Rain-in-the-Face," *American Mercury*, Vol. IX (November, 1926), 338; Merington, *The Custer Story*, for the appointment of Captain Yates.

extraction and had served in the Papal Guard before coming to America. Keogh, who had been decorated by Pope Pius IX with the *Medaglia di Pro Petri Sede* and who is generally given credit for the adoption of "Garry Owen" as the marching song of the regiment, has been unfavorably pictured by some historians of the battle. He is said to have been almost continually inebriated when liquor was obtainable, which was most of the time, and to have systematically "caned" the enlisted men who incurred his displeasure. Two of them later described him as "an insolent, drunken brute," and since some of the noncommissioned officers were as dissolute as their captain, "Wild I," as a troop, had a drinking reputation throughout the army.[32] But these reports have been denied, and the probability seems to be that Keogh was little, if any, worse than most of his brothers-in-arms. As Kipling expressed it, "Single men in barracks don't grow into plaster saints."[33]

Lieutenant Mathey was a Frenchman who had become so addicted to blasphemy that he had been nicknamed "Bible-Thumper" by his associates.[34] Lieutenant William W. Cooke, the regimental adjutant, was a Canadian by birth and a soldier of fortune by choice. Fourth on the army list of first lieutenants, he was affectionately known as "The Queen's Own" because of his proud, stately bearing, not to mention the long and flowing Dundreary whiskers of which he was so proud. Considered the fastest runner as well as the best shot in the regiment, Cooke was probably one of its ablest and most efficient members.[35]

Lieutenant Charles Camilus DeRudio was an Italian with a genius for sculpture and a reputation as a teller of tall tales. In Europe he had been involved in the Orsini plot against the life of Napoleon III and had been saved from execution only by the personal appeal of Mrs. DeRudio to the Empress Eugénie. He had then fought with Garibaldi in the war for Italian liberation, afterwards migrating to the United States where he saw action in the last days of the Civil War. Continuing in the army, he had been made a lieu-

[32] Dustin, *The Custer Tragedy*, 236.

[33] The best account of Captain Myles Keogh is Edward S. Luce, *Keogh, Comanche and Custer*.

[34] Fougera, *With Custer's Cavalry*, 123.

[35] Bates, *Custer's Indian Battles*, 28.

tenant in the Second Infantry, transferring to the Seventh Cavalry in 1869.[36]

Of the other officers only a few need any special mention: Captains Moylan and Tom Custer were both "rankers," having come up from the ranks of the enlisted men. The latter had won two Congressional Medals of Honor during the Civil War. Lieutenant Algernon E. Smith had been a student at Hamilton College when Fort Sumter was fired upon, but the close of the war found him a captain in the Union Army. At the storming of Fort Fisher he had displayed a conspicuous gallantry and had suffered a shoulder wound which left him partially crippled, with the result that in 1876 he could not raise his arm above his head nor put on his coat without assistance. He was able and experienced, and in 1872 had served as quartermaster for the Stanley expedition.[37] Lieutenant Donald McIntosh was a half-blood Indian, his father having been a Canadian trader in Oregon who had married an Indian woman.[38] Lieutenant William Van W. Reilly was the son of a naval officer who in 1855 had been lost at sea.[39] Youngest of all the officers and the last to be regularly assigned to the Seventh Cavalry prior to the start of the campaign was Jack Sturgis, a recent graduate of West Point, who had requested assignment to his father's regiment.

The enlisted men comprised an even more conglomerate group than did the officers. Despite the fact that Custer's Civil War record and his reputation for getting the best of everything for his command was supposed to have attracted a superior type of recruit to the regiment,[40] the enlisted personnel was probably little if any above the level of the other regiments of the army. Many of the men were foreigners. Large numbers of Germans, who, ironically, had come to America to escape compulsory military service in the land of their birth, enlisted in the army as one of the easiest and quickest ways of learning the English language as well as of secur-

36 Jesse Brown and A. M. Willard, *Black Hills Trails . . .*, edited by John T. Milck, 199–200; Charles C. DeRudio, "My Personal Story," *Frontier and Midland*, Vol. XIV (January, 1934), 155.

37 *Army and Navy Journal*, July 15, 1876.

38 *Ibid.*; *The New York Herald*, July 10, 1876, said that McIntosh was an Indian of the Six Nations and a native of Canada.

39 *Army and Navy Journal*, July 22, 1876.

40 Mary Roberts Rinehart, "To Wyoming," *Saturday Evening Post*, Vol. CXCIX (October 2, 1926), 17.

ing employment in a new, strange land. There were also a good many Irish and some Italians, as well as a sprinkling of other nationalities.[41] Of the native Americans, many of the older men had served in either the Union or Confederate armies and had turned to professional soldiering when civilian life proved unattractive. Economics also played its part, for the Panic of 1873 was still much more than a bitter memory, and some Americans enlisted in the army not only to find a job but also as the best way of easing the financial burden of the hard-pressed families that they had left behind.

In those days it was a common belief that the only men who would enlist in the regular army were those who were either too lazy or too shiftless to accept regular employment, so many of the men, native and foreign alike, enlisted under assumed names. There is no denying that the Seventh Cavalry had its full quota of ne'er-do-wells, besides a number who had enlisted solely in the hope of finding adventure and excitement, as well as those who looked upon an enlistment period as one way of sowing the inevitable wild oats. One factor which made all regiments of the army somewhat nondescript in character was the lack of a severe penalty for desertion; therefore, many homeless men enlisted in the army in the fall merely to have a place to eat and sleep during the winter. Since they intended to desert in the spring, they were quite generally known as "snowbirds." While a regiment stationed on the Indian frontier was not plagued by this condition to the extent that those in more populated localities were, another situation prevailed that was equally annoying: Easterners then generally had the same peculiar ideas of western geography and distances that many of them still possess, and as a result large numbers of city boys enlisted, requesting to be sent to the western posts such as Fort Lincoln, with every intention of deserting at the first opportunity and making their way to the Colorado or Montana mines. Conditions such as these led Custer to remark at the opening of the campaign that if he had all the men who had been members of the regiment during the year, he would have been in command of a brigade.[42]

[41] The facts hardly bear out the statement of Brigadier General Charles King that the Seventh Cavalry was practically "an American regiment, one in which the soldier of foreign birth was almost a stranger." Colonel William A. Graham, *The Story of the Little Big Horn*, xx.

While many of the rank and file were undoubtedly of a rather low order, others, especially among the noncommissioned officers and older men, were of good character and quality[43] and constituted the hard central core around which the effective fighting strength of any military organization has to be fashioned. The command was at peace-time strength, which meant that it averaged about sixty men a company for the twelve companies, although absences brought the actual strength somewhat below that figure.

As the officers differed considerably in their evaluation of their commanding officer, so did the enlisted men. Martin was later to declare that he admired General Custer very much, as did all of the men since he was a fighter and not afraid of anything,[44] and some testified that he was the idol of his men.[45] Others have not been so charitable. Jacob Horner, the last survivor of the regiment, said that most of the men did not like Custer because he was too hard on the men and horses and changed his mind too often. Horner admitted, nevertheless, that Custer would not order a man to do what he was unwilling to do or send a soldier where he (Custer) himself was unwilling to go.[46] Other evidence indicates that Custer was tyrannical, with little or no regard for the soldiers under him, and, accordingly, not a popular man among his troops.[47] It has been said that no command he ever held esteemed Custer until it had followed him into battle, for it was then that the spectacle of his intrepid bravery provided "a partial compensation for the ordeal of serving under him."[48] That the enlisted men were not unaware of some of the currents and crosscurrents of the times, however, is shown by the fact that they believed that President Grant's treatment of Custer was traceable not only to spite over the Belknap

42 Vestal, *The Missouri*, 221; Bates, *Custer's Indian Battles*, 8.

43 Dustin, *The Custer Tragedy*, 236. John Burkman says that the Seventh Cavalry was filled mostly with Civil War veterans who had since been with Custer on the Stanley expedition and the Black Hills expedition. Glendolin D. Wagner, *Old Neutriment*, 121.

44 Colonel William A. Graham, "'Come On! Be Quick! Bring Packs!' The Story of Custer's Last Message . . . ," *Cavalry Journal*, Vol. XXXII (July, 1923), 310.

45 Adams, "Survivor's Story," 29; Huggins, "Custer and Rain-in-the-Face," *American Mercury*, Vol. IX (November, 1926), 338.

46 Roy P. Johnson, "Jacob Horner of the Seventh Cavalry," *North Dakota History*, Vol. XVI (April, 1949), 99.

47 *Army and Navy Journal*, July 29, 1876.

48 Van de Water, *Glory Hunter, a Life of General Custer*, 129.

affair but also to Custer's having once placed the President's son under military arrest for drunkenness.[49]

At the opening of the campaign some of the men in the ranks were merely recruits, and some of the recruits were scarcely older than boys, who had enlisted that spring and had never seen a hostile Indian nor heard a shot fired in anger.[50] Just how many recruits there were and how large a proportion of the command was without prior service are matters of dispute since no exact statistics are available; there is also disagreement over just what constitutes a recruit. In October, 1875, 150 new men had been added to the regiment. Of these, 60 had either served a previous enlistment or had seen service in the Civil War. By May, 1876, when the regiment marched on the campaign against the Sioux, all of these men had had more than six months of training.[51] On April 15, 1876, the superintendent of the Mounted Recruiting Service was ordered to forward 62 recruits to St. Paul to join the Seventh Cavalry. Of these, 25 were assigned to Company B, 19 to Company G, and 18 to Company K. They joined their respective organizations as the troops passed through St. Paul en route to Fort Lincoln.[52] None of these new men could have had any real training. Most of them were poor horsemen—some had never even been on a horse before—and they were even poorer shots. They were not in any sense ready to be taken into action.[53]

Almost equally important was the fact that many of the horses were new and untrained. Lieutenant DeRudio estimated that at least one-half of the horses were "green" and not accustomed to the noise of battle, the smell of powder, and the appearance of In-

[49] Brown and Willard, *Black Hills Trails*, 133.

[50] Dustin, *The Custer Tragedy*, 236.

[51] Luce, *Keogh, Comanche and Custer*, 87–88.

[52] *Army and Navy Journal*, April 22, 1876. Another account says that there were "about 78 recruits in St. Paul." Roy P. Johnson, "Jacob Horner of the Seventh Cavalry," *North Dakota History*, Vol. XVI (April, 1949), 79.

[53] Reno, *Court*, 96, 530; W. J. Ghent, "Varnum, Reno and the Little Big Horn," *Winners of the West*, April 30, 1936, declares categorically that the number of recruits in the regiment was shamelessly exaggerated to aid Major Reno in defending himself against the implied charge of incompetency at the Court of Inquiry in 1879. Ghent maintains that most of the recruits were left at the Powder River base camp. He says that in the Battle of the Little Big Horn River, Lieutenant Godfrey had only two recruits in his company, and that it is very unlikely that the other companies had more than that.

dians.[54] Despite his expressed belief that he would be a credit to the army if assigned to the command of the expedition, Major Reno had neglected the fundamentals of training while he was commanding the regiment in Custer's absence. Target practice had not been held, and many other matters had been neglected which, if properly taken care of, would have increased the regiment's efficiency.[55] Nevertheless, in 1876 the Seventh Cavalry still possessed much of the spirit and dash that had given it its reputation. In August, an officer of the Fifth Cavalry wrote:

> Each company as it comes forward opens out like a fan, and a sheaf of skirmishers is launched to the front. Something in the snap and style of the whole movement stamps them at once; no need of waving guidon and stirring call to identify them. I recognize the Seventh Cavalry at a glance. . . .[56]

On the eve of the starting against the Sioux, many of the officers were on leave or detached service of various kinds, a fact which could not but decrease the regimental potency. These included Colonel Sturgis, who since his assignment to the regiment had been almost continually on recruiting duty. Also absent were two majors, Joseph G. Tilford and Lewis Merrill, the latter having been detailed as chief of staff to the president of the Centennial Exposition. Since Major Merrill was an experienced Indian fighter, Custer had requested that he be ordered to rejoin his regiment for the campaign. Accordingly, Merrill had been relieved of duty with the Exposition,[57] but a few days later the order was revoked by President Grant,[58] a possibility which Custer had apparently foreseen, since he had written Mrs. Custer that "all the carpetbaggers" were bringing pressure on the President to take such action.[59] In the opinion of highly placed persons in the nation's capital, the campaign against the Sioux was apparently of less importance than the Exposition, by

54 Reno, *Court*, 448.

55 Bates, *Custer's Indian Battles*, 28.

56 Captain Charles King, "The Meeting of Terry and Crook," in Roe, *Custer's Last Battle*, 39.

57 *Army and Navy Journal*, April 1, 1876.

58 *Ibid.*, April 15, 1876.

59 Merington, *The Custer Story*, 283. That there were hard feelings between Custer and Merrill is apparent from an article in the *Army and Navy Journal*, May 6, 1876.

which the United States celebrated its first one hundred years of independence. The fact that four captains and seven lieutenants also were absent from duty necessitated some shifting of officers among the various companies, so that at the time of the battle a few officers were not too well acquainted with the men under their command.

This, then, was the regiment which was expected to play a major part in the subjugation of the hostile Sioux and Cheyennes. At the time it was believed to be one of the best-equipped and organized commands ever to be sent against the Indians,[60] and writers have too often pictured the Seventh Cavalry as a matchless regiment, without fault and above reproach, both in personnel and training. As a matter of fact it was not, but neither was it the forlorn hope that so many of Custer's detractors have pictured it as being. Under-officered and with some of the enlisted personnel not too well trained, it was, instead, an example of what a false economy, plus the jealousies and bickerings of petty and obscure men can do to bring chaos out of order.

In addition to the cavalry, there were three companies of infantry. These were Companies C and G of the Seventeenth Infantry, commanded respectively by Captains McArthur and Sanger, and Company B of the Sixth Infantry under Captain Baker, comprising a total of 8 officers and 135 men.[61] There was also a platoon of three Gatling guns, the machine guns of that day, handled by a detachment of 2 officers, Lieutenants Low and Kenzie, and 32 men from the Twentieth Infantry, with each gun drawn by four condemned cavalry horses.[62]

A drove of cattle to supply fresh meat on the march, a few extra horses, and a train of more than 150 wagons completed the

60 *New York Herald*, June 19, 1876; E. A. Brininstool, *A Trooper with Custer and Other Historic Incidents of the Battle of the Little Big Horn*, 23.

61 Hanson, *Conquest of the Missouri*, 241, says that Company B, Sixth Infantry, went aboard the steamer *Far West* at Fort Buford, but War Department records show that during the winter of 1875–76, this company was stationed at Fort Lincoln and that it was one of the three companies that marched overland to the Powder River with the Dakota column. See also the *Army and Navy Journal*, May 13, 1876, and *ibid.*, July 15, 1876.

62 James P. Murphy, "The Campaign of the Little Big Horn," *Infantry Journal*, Vol. XXXIV (June, 1929), 632.

expedition. Of the wagons, 114 were six-mule government wagons, each carrying about two tons of freight, while the remainder were two-horse contractors' wagons, each carrying less than a ton. Although each cavalryman carried his own equipment plus one hundred rounds of carbine ammunition either on his person or in his saddlebags, he carried no rations; rations, plus water for emergencies and forage for a month as well as the extra ammunition, were transported in the wagons. Also in the train were 250 aparejos and packsaddles, insurance against the day when the wagons could go no farther and a mule train would take over the transportation. To insure the proper functioning of the wagon and mule trains, there was a miscellaneous assortment of nearly two hundred packers, teamsters, and herders. Among these civilian employees were two other relatives of the Lieutenant Colonel commanding: Armstrong Reed, a nephew, who, as a herder, went along for a summer outing, and Boston Custer, youngest of the Custer brothers, who for reasons of health accompanied the expedition as forage master.

The territory included in the possible field of operations comprised a district approximately twice as large as New York State and one into which no railroad or military road had yet penetrated, largely *terra incognita* to everyone except the Indian and the occasional trapper. The northern limit of the region was marked by the Yellowstone River, but from its source to its mouth this stream did not boast of a single military post. While most of its tributaries had been named, there were no accurate maps of the region, and no one, not even the scouts, had any more than an elementary notion of the distances involved. On the map used by General Terry, which was the best obtainable, nearly all of the Tongue, Rosebud, and Little Big Horn rivers were indicated by dotted lines showing hypothetical courses, and the headwaters of Mizpah Creek were shown as being more than forty miles north of their actual location, while Pumpkin Creek was indicated as being about ten miles long, although actually it is more than seventy.[63]

For these reasons recourse was had to the services of Indian scouts, and nearly forty Arikaras, often called Rees, blood enemies of the Sioux, accompanied the expedition. Those who attained some fame or notoriety in subsequent proceedings included Bob-tailed

[63] Dustin, *The Custer Tragedy*, 60.

Bull, Soldier, Young Hawk, Stabbed, Little Brave, Red Star, Bull, Forked Horn, and Bloody-Knife. These scouts were paid $16 a month, and for each pony furnished were allowed $12 extra. They were given the same rations as the troops, and like the latter were paid every two months. The leader of the contingent was Bob-tailed Bull, who, as a consequence, wore three stripes on his sleeve, while Soldier, who wore two stripes, was the second leader.

The Arikaras were often called the Corn Indians from their habit of living in more or less permanent villages and of depending for their living partially upon agricultural pursuits. They raised corn, squash, pumpkins, and other vegetables. This the Sioux despised, for they considered farming such a degrading occupation that they would not even allow their women to engage in it.[64] Nevertheless, the Sioux did not make the mistake of underestimating their adversaries, for they knew the Arikaras as tough and brave fighters who would even plunge into the river and attack a wounded buffalo bull with knives.[65] The Arikaras had formerly been a large and warlike tribe, but were now badly decimated by disease. Their hostility to the Sioux, however, was undiminished, and they were now making common cause with the soldiers for the redress of ancestral wrongs, and for the money there was in it. The men of the tribe were mostly of medium size and very solemn, even the younger ones rarely being seen to smile. Quite dark in color, they had at all times a somewhat dirty appearance because they paid little attention to the cleanliness of either person or clothing. When mounted, they are said to have looked not unlike antiquated Negro washerwomen.[66]

Of all the scouts, Bloody Knife was the best known. A great favorite with Custer, he is often, for that reason, described as the leader of the group. His knowledge, skill, and courage were beyond question, and made him exceptionally useful. In 1876 he was a man of mature years with hair already graying at the temples. Said by some to have been half-Sioux and half-Ree, he had spent his entire life in battle and adventure, in the course of which he had developed a feud or vendetta with Gall of the Uncpapa Sioux, a

[64] Hyde, *Red Cloud's Folk*, 194.

[65] Vestal, *The Missouri*, 191.

[66] Captain Edward Maguire, Annual Report on the Expedition against the Sioux, May 17–Sept. 7, 1876, in the *Report of the Secretary of War*, 45 Cong., 2 sess., Vol. II, Part 2 (hereinafter cited as Maguire's Report).

feud which was to culminate disastrously in the bottoms along the Little Big Horn River. Bloody Knife's one serious failing, a fondness for the bottle, was one which, in common with many another tribesman, he had acquired from the whites.

One evening shortly before the expedition marched, Custer is said to have visited the camp of the scouts and to have presented Bloody Knife with several gifts, including a medal which Custer said had been given to him at Washington. Apparently on this occasion he told an attentive circle of Arikaras of his visit to the national capital, where he said that he had been informed that this would be his last Indian campaign and that no matter how small a victory he might win—even though against only six lodges of the Sioux—it would make him President or Great Father. He promised that when he went to Washington, he would take his brother, Bloody Knife, with him. But Bloody Knife would return and live among the Arikaras, where he would have a fine house. Those who were present on this campaign would be appointed to look after the work of which Bloody Knife would be in charge. Then Custer is said to have promised that he, as the Great Father, would always look after the welfare of his children, the Arikaras.[67]

In addition to the Rees there were some other Indian scouts, four of whom were members of the Sioux tribes and were thus serving against their own people. Also serving were two half-blood Blackfeet—the brothers Robert and William Jackson, who were more white than Indian. Acting as interpreter for the Rees was Fred Girard, who had held that post at both Fort Lincoln and Fort Rice and who, in addition to his other activities, supplemented the family income by selling eggs to the officers' families at the garrison.[68]

Two other civilians accompanied the expedition. One was another favorite of Custer's, the famous "Lonesome Charley" Reynolds, known to the Indians as "Lucky Man," who had accompanied both the Stanley expedition along the Yellowstone and the excursion

[67] Orin G. Libby, (ed.) *The Arikara Narrative of the Campaign against the Hostile Dakotas, June, 1876* (North Dakota Historical *Collections*, VI), 58–63. While this story is of doubtful authenticity, it may very well be true. Custer was ambitious beyond a doubt and with Grant's example before him probably felt that he was just as well qualified to be chief executive of the nation.

[68] Fougera, *With Custer's Cavalry*, 270. Despite his rather extensive experience Girard was making his first trip with the troops. *Official Transcript*, 156. There is a picture of Girard in North Dakota Historical *Collections*, I, 344.

into the Black Hills. Not least important was Isaiah, or Teat, Dorman, a Negro interpreter, who had spent many years in the Indian country. Having come up the Missouri River some time before 1871, he is said to have married an Indian woman and to have become an intimate friend of Sitting Bull. The Sioux apparently had great affection for him and had given him the name "Teat" because the Sioux word for it sounds very much like the name Isaiah. He had served as a government courier or mail carrier, and apparently accompanied the Custer expedition at his own request because he loved the wild country and wished to see the western land again before he died.[69]

It was May 10 before General Terry, accompanied by his staff and Lieutenant Colonel Custer, arrived at Fort Lincoln. The plans had been for the expedition to move early on the morning of the fourteenth, but the spring rains of late April and early May had turned the surrounding country into such a quagmire that a three days' postponement was decided upon. It was promised that, rain or shine, the command would move on the seventeenth, for somewhere to the west the hostile tribes would be found, and General Terry knew, as did everyone else, that the Sioux would not stand still, waiting for the army to catch them.

[69] Vestal, *New Sources of Indian History*, 340; Vestal, *Sitting Bull*, 170. See also Ronald C. McConnell, "Isaiah Dorman and the Custer Expedition," *Journal of Negro History*, Vol. XXXIII (July, 1948), 344–52.

CHAPTER IX

The Wanderings of the Tribes

In the meantime, the hostile tribes which were the object of so much activity and expense had wintered in the well-protected valleys of the Tongue and Powder rivers, and had gradually assembled a formidable force of warriors, whether purposely or accidentally it is difficult to say. When the smoke and excitement occasioned by the surprise dawn attack of Colonel Reynolds on March 17 had subsided, the Cheyennes and Ogallalas who had been in the camp of Old Bear began a forlorn journey eastward in search of the camp of Crazy Horse and his band of Ogallalas, who for several years had been the closest Sioux friends of the Cheyennes.[1] Many of the travelers were afoot; although the Indians had recovered some of their ponies, they lacked adequate food and clothing, especially since the ground was covered with snow and ice, and freezing temperatures prevailed. Finally, on the twentieth and twenty-first they found the camp they sought near Charcoal Butte. Furnishing little besides food and shelter, this haven of safety could be only a temporary one, for, although Crazy Horse was one of the two principal chiefs who had never accepted the treaty of 1868, he did not feel strong enough to tempt the wrath of the soldiers unassisted. Nor were the Ogallalas wealthy enough to furnish much material relief to the impoverished followers of Old Bear. Therefore, after considerable dis-

[1] This account of the wanderings and the gradual assembly into one camp of the numerous bands of Sioux and Cheyennes who defeated General Custer on the Little Big Horn River is based largely on Thomas B. Marquis, *A Warrior Who Fought Custer,* which also contains excellent maps of the wanderings, both before and after the battle, and on Marquis, *She* (Kate Bighead) *Watched Custer's Last Battle,* in addition to several other accounts found in the Montana Collection of the Billings Public Library.

cussion it was decided that the merged camp should request the aid of Sitting Bull and his band of Uncpapas.[2]

Accordingly, the two groups set out for the village of that great Sioux leader, located, according to the Cheyenne account, some fifty miles east of the Powder River on the headwaters of a small creek flowing westward to that stream and near a tall white rock formation which the white men called Chalk Butte, about twenty-seven miles from present Ekalaka, Montana. Here they found not only the Uncpapas, whose numbers were greater than those of the Cheyennes and Ogallalas combined, but also a large band of Minneconjou Sioux under the leadership of their famous chief, Lame Deer. These last had had no recent trouble with the soldiers, but are said to have made the pilgrimage to the Uncpapa camp as the result of vague feelings of dread and in the belief that the combined strength of the camps would be sufficient to deter the soldiers from attacking, thus keeping the Indians out of trouble.[3]

This assembling of the various tribes around the Uncpapas as a nucleus was not the result of either accident or chance. On the contrary, it resulted from several very valid reasons. The first was the fact that, while the Sioux were the most numerous and powerful nation of Indians on the North American continent,[4] the Uncpapas were the fiercest and most belligerent of all the Sioux.[5] Numerically they were also the greatest, with a much larger band of warriors than any of the others, and they were much wealthier because for several years past they had abstained from active warfare, devoting themselves to the building up of their material possessions. Secondly, Sitting Bull, the great leader of the band, was widely known among both red men and white as the great exponent of preserving the traditional Indian way of life by the simple expedient of living entirely isolated from the whites, thus avoiding possible contamination by their civilization. He had never broken a treaty with the

[2] Thomas B. Marquis, *Which Indian Killed Custer?*, n.p.; Marquis, *She Watched Custer's Last Battle*, n.p.; Marquis, *A Warrior Who Fought Custer*, 170.

[3] *Billings Gazette*, July 17, 1932; Vestal, *New Sources of Indian History*, 143; Vestal, *Sitting Bull*, 141–43; Charles Eastman, "The Story of the Little Big Horn," *Chautauquan*, Vol. XXXI (July, 1900), 355.

[4] William S. Brackett, "Custer's Last Battle on the Little Big Horn in Montana, June 25, 1876," *Contributions to the Historical Society of Montana*, IV (1903), 259.

[5] DeLand, *The Sioux Wars*,. 278.

whites for the simple reason that he had never signed one. In 1868 he had broken with Red Cloud over the question of peace with the whites and thereafter had lived away from the agencies, refusing to accept any gifts or presents from the government.[6]

Sitting Bull's[7] position in history has suffered appreciably at the hands of his friends as well as of his enemies, and probably more romantic nonsense has been written about him than about any other Indian. Certainly no saint, he was also far from being the coward and charlatan that some writers have claimed.[8] If Sitting Bull was something of a fakir,[9] he was such because that was necessary to the type of leadership that the Indians demanded, and if not "a first-class fighting man" he managed to compensate in cunning and resourcefulness for what he lacked in courage.[10] One of the greatest possible errors in historical study is to ascribe to one period or race the standards of another, yet that is precisely what his critics have done. The Indian did not have the white man's mentality or his outlook on life; the supernatural bulked large in everything he did, and the most effective appeal that could be made to him was one predicated on a religious myth.[11]

While the historical record of many Americans has been distorted by excessive adulation and "hero worship," that of Sitting Bull has suffered from both propaganda and falsehood. The "good Indians" were those who accepted the inevitable and decided to give in. Those who resisted were damned and misrepresented, and since, more than any other tribesman, Sitting Bull was the greatest instrument in uniting the various tribes of the Northern Plains in a campaign of resistance to the whites, his name has led all the others in the calendar of infamy.[12]

Of his real position among his people there is no better evidence

[6] Thomas B. Marquis, *Sitting Bull and Gall the Warrior*, n.p.; *Army and Navy Journal*, July 15, 1876.

[7] DeCost Smith, *Indian Experiences*, 184, 190; Britt, *Great Indian Chiefs*, 195–96; Charles Eastman, *Indian Heroes and Great Chieftains*, 109; Vestal, *New Sources of Indian History*, 91.

[8] McLaughlin, *My Friend, the Indian*, 141.

[9] Usher L. Burdick, *The Last Battle of the Sioux Nation*, 20.

[10] Percy Cross Standing, "Custer's Cavalry at the Little Big Horn," *Cavalry Journal* (British), Vol. IX (1914), 142.

[11] Burdick, *The Last Battle of the Sioux Nation*, 20.

[12] Marquis, *Sitting Bull and Gall the Warrior*, n.p.; *Army and Navy Journal*, July 15, 1876.

than his name, which literally translated means "Buffalo Bull Sitting Down." Among the Indians of the plains the buffalo bull was considered to be the most wise and powerful of animals, and, as the special animal next to man, the most favored by the Everywhere Spirit. They used the expression "sitting down" in the sense of locating permanently, so that the name really means that the animal having the highest status resided permanently among them.[13]

Sitting Bull, a medicine man, was also a chief, although not a warrior chief, for it was not at all unusual for an individual to be both; in the councils of the tribe Sitting Bull had a voice and vote the same as any other chief.[14] He was an old-man chief, the highest rank possible in his own tribe, and in 1876 he was not only the most influential of the hostiles but the most noted Indian of the day as well, being *the* old-man chief of the assembled bands.[15] There is not the slightest doubt of his position, for all of the old Indians attest to it. There is equally little doubt of the fact that Sitting Bull was a great chief—he had to be in order to maintain the position and respect that was his. Living as they did, constantly in the midst of danger and getting their living from day to day by their own efforts, the tribesmen had little if any room for sycophancy and "pull." Only more settled civilizations can afford such luxuries, a fact upon which some of Sitting Bull's present-day detractors might reflect with profit.

Finally, Sitting Bull's recalcitrance and his open invitation to the agency Indians to "come out and have one more fight with the soldiers," even if not expressed in so many words, could not have helped but have a distinct appeal to all the restless and ambitious young warriors who knew that the old, free, roving life of the tribes was almost a thing of the past—warriors who resented the intrusion of the white man and were vaguely disquieted without knowing precisely what to do about it. To reassure those doubters who believed that the white man was too strong to be successfully opposed, Sitting Bull is said to have explained the great cities and

[13] Marquis, *Sitting Bull and Gall the Warrior*, n.p.; Dustin, *The Custer Tragedy*, 161; Vestal, *New Sources of Indian History*, 142.

[14] Brigadier General Edward S. Godfrey, "Custer's Last Battle," *Century Magazine*, Vol. XLIII (1892), 363 (hereinafter cited as Godfrey, *Century*).

[15] Patrick E. Byrne, *Soldiers of the Plains*, 31; Dustin, *The Custer Tragedy*, 161.

other phenomena of the whites, which Red Cloud and others had reported, as illusions induced by the white man's "medicine."[16] As a result of all these factors:

> Sitting Bull had great power over the Sioux. He was a good medicine man. He made good medicine. Many Indians believed him. He knew how to lead them. He told the Sioux many times he was not made to be a reservation Indian. The Great Spirit made him a free Indian to go where he wanted to go, to hunt buffalo and to be a big leader in his tribe.[17]

Contemporary official white opinion, nevertheless, was inclined to minimize the chief's importance. Gibbon described him as "a rather notorious Sioux" who prided himself on standing aloof from the whites while trading indirectly with the agencies,[18] and Sheridan held that there was no real evidence that he was the leader of the hostile tribes. He believed, on the contrary, that Sitting Bull's influence was rather insignificant and largely the result of the accident of his unusual name, since the newspaper correspondents had given it so much importance that in time it came to be confused with "hostile" in the public mind, the two becoming almost synonyms. The General also believed that the Chief himself was unconscious of his great reputation among the whites since he had done nothing to acquire it, never having been anything more than an insignificant warrior with a few thieving followers.[19]

The net result of the journey of the Cheyennes and the Ogallalas to the Uncpapas was the decision of the tribes to travel and camp together for better protection from the soldiers. Because the Indians considered that the Cheyennes had been unjustly attacked—indeed, as the hostiles viewed it, the so-called Sioux War of 1876 was, in its inception, at least, a war of extermination waged by the whites against the Cheyennes—it was arranged that this tribe should always be first in the line of march, and that the others, as allies, should follow. Since the Uncpapas, especially, were said not to

[16] *New York Tribune*, July 15, 1876.

[17] This quotation is taken from an account given by a white scout, Lewis Dewitt. It is to be found in the Custer Scrapbooks in the Billings Public Library.

[18] Gibbon, "Summer Expedition," 273.

[19] Sheridan's *Report*, 447.

desire war and only wanted to be let alone, their position in the line was to be last.[20]

A camp as large as that of the combined Sioux and Cheyennes could not remain for very long in one location because of the simple problem of supply. Grass for the ponies and meat for the Indians disappeared in a short time, and the camp had to be constantly on the move. It was impossible to feed a large camp long from the proceeds of the daily hunt, since the Indians invariably frightened the game away, for even the unthinking buffalo would not "stay within earshot of an Indian drum."[21] Another important problem in that dry country was the water supply, which made it necessary for a large camp to follow the river most, if not all, of the time.[22] It was the prerogative of the Cheyennes, as the leaders, to choose the direction of the march and to decide where camp should be made. They would, naturally, choose those localities where there was the most grass, food for the ponies, and where the most buffalo were to be found.

The tribes moved northward towards the Yellowstone. This was due to the fact that the soldier attack had come from the south and that the troops had gone back in that direction, and the main desire of the hostiles was to keep out of trouble. They were soon joined by the Sans Arc Sioux (Without Bows) who, like the others, had come to believe that the greatest safety was to be found in numbers. These Indian professions of peaceful intentions and of a desire to be let alone have to be taken *cum grano salis*. They are conscious and unconscious rationalization, for in after years the well-known warrior Rain-in-the-Face confessed to his fellow-Sioux, Dr. Charles Eastman, that in the camp on the Tongue the Indians had decided to fight the white soldiers to the finish, "until no warrior should be left," as he expressed it,[23] and Crazy Horse told Two Moon that they were going to fight the white man again.[24]

Not only was the number of camp circles increasing, but the

20 *Billings Gazette*, July 17, 1932; Marquis, *Which Indian Killed Custer?* n.p.

21 Vestal, *Warpath and Council Fire*, 236.

22 Charles Eastman, "Story of the Little Big Horn," *Chautauquan*, Vol. XXXI (July, 1900), 354.

23 *Missoulian* (Missoula, Mont.), March 3, 1907.

24 Hamlin Garland, "Custer's Last Fight as Seen by Two Moon," *McClure's Magazine*, Vol. XI (September, 1898), 444.

number of Indians in each of the camps increased regularly as more and more tribesmen who had wintered at the agencies slipped away to the hunting grounds, bringing with them rifles and liberal supplies of ammunition. By mid-April, the Cheyenne circle, which was the smallest of all, probably consisted of more than fifty lodges. Largest was that of the Uncpapa, with probably more than three times as many, while each of the other circles included more than seventy lodges. Thus there were, in all probability, between four and five hundred lodges in the camp, and from twelve hundred to fifteen hundred warriors.

The numbers continued to increase. Next to join were the Blackfeet or Sihasapa Sioux of western South Dakota, so named because they wore black moccasins; they are to be distinguished from the tribe of a similar name who lived in northern Montana and who received their name because their moccasins were discolored in the ashes of prairie fires.[25] These made up the sixth circle. Also some Waist and Skirt Indians (Santees), some Assiniboins, Brulé, or Burned-Thigh Sioux, and other smaller groups attached themselves to the various circles, since their numbers were not great enough to justify a separate circle of their own.

When the combined camp reached the Powder River, the Cheyenne circle was greatly increased by the addition of a large band under the leadership of Lame White Man. These Indians had spent the winter at the White River Agency and were reportedly ignorant of the soldiers' attack on March 17.[26] Then the force continued its westward march, spending several days in the region between the Powder and the Tongue, and about the middle of May camped some thirty or forty miles below the confluence of Otter Creek and the river. Sitting Bull is said to have sent a message from the camp on the Tongue to the agencies calling for volunteers to fight the soldiers and to have designated Rosebud Creek as the place of rendezvous.[27] Here another big band of Cheyennes under Dirty Moccasins came in, making that circle almost double what it had been a month before, while the other circles were increasing in the same way and in about the same proportion. It was here, about ten

[25] Alter, *James Bridger*, 66n.; *Montana Guide Book*, 238.

[26] Marquis, *A Warrior Who Fought Custer*, 183.

[27] Vestal, *New Sources of Indian History*, 163; Grinnell, *The Fighting Cheyennes*, 344.

miles above the site of the present village of Garland, that the great Indian village was discovered on May 15 by Lieutenant Bradley and his Crow scouts, who reported smoke blanketing the valley of the Tongue. Responsible government officials were not unaware, however, that this concentration of the hostiles was taking place.[28] Not only did every Indian agent know that a large proportion of his charges had slipped away to join the hostiles, but the army knew it as well. The agent made no report because he made a profit selling the supplies intended for the absentees; and, because of difficulties of communication, the army reports did not reach the operating units in time. On May 7, Lieutenant Egan of Crook's command met a war party of one hundred lodges and from seven hundred to eight hundred warriors on the Powder River trail—all going north. Each side ignored the other, although the Indians had previously attacked a train. On the same day the Red Cloud Agency was reported to be practically deserted, with the young men generally going on the warpath.[29] On June 8, an Indian courier reported at Fort Laramie that there was a great concentration of hostiles at the mouth of the Tongue. The village, said to consist of 1,273 lodges, was under command of Sitting Bull and Crazy Horse, and was also said to be on its way to the Powder River to fight General Crook.[30]

Just when the hostiles became aware of the presence of Colonel Gibbon's forces to the north of the Yellowstone is uncertain, but it was probably about the end of April, while the Indian camp was on Tongue River. The discovery apparently made little difference in the Indians' way of life, for they continued to move steadily westward, toward the soldiers rather than away from them. They stopped briefly on Wood Creek, which is the first stream of any importance flowing into the Yellowstone west of the Tongue, and

[28] For the exodus of the Indians from the agencies see *Rocky Mountain News*, May 30, 1876; *Army and Navy Journal*, May 27, 1876; Hughes, "The Campaign Against the Sioux in 1876," *Journal of the Military Service Institution of the United States*, Vol. XVIII (January, 1896), 16–17; Spring, *Cheyenne and Black Hills Stage and Express Routes*, 147. These reports of a wholesale exodus were categorically denied in a letter written by Inspector Vandever from Red Cloud Agency. *New York Herald*, July 6, 1876.

[29] 44 Cong., 1 sess., *House Exec. Doc. No. 184*, 55; *The Army and Navy Journal*, June 10, 1876, gives a slightly different version.

[30] 44 Cong., 1 sess., *House Exec. Doc. No. 184*, 55–61.

a few days later made camp on Rosebud Creek, where they were seen by Bradley and Bouyer. Wooden Leg says that the first camp on the Rosebud was made only seven or eight miles from the mouth of that stream, but he may be mistaken, for the camp which Bouyer saw and to which he later led Major Reno's scouting force was about eighteen miles from the Yellowstone; we have no record of any campsite being discovered later between that place and the mouth of the stream. Another Cheyenne source says that this first camp on the Rosebud was located ten or twelve miles southeast of the present town of Forsyth,[31] and it may well be that the seeming discrepancy is just another case of Indians' estimates of distance being at variance.

Here still further accessions of strength were received by the hostiles. Charcoal Bear, the chief medicine man of the northern Cheyennes, and many of his people joined the hostiles at this place after having wintered at the agencies. As long as the two sides stayed where they were with the river between them, there would be no trouble, although the Sioux and Cheyennes could not forbear to take advantage of the convenient opportunity to launch horse-stealing expeditions and nuisance raids against the soldiers and their Crow allies.

This first camp seems to have been occupied for a period of about a week, and then that great village moved slowly up the Rosebud, traveling about twelve miles before making the next camp. A march of from ten to twelve miles on the following day brought the camp to the west and south of a pointed peak which the whites later called Teat Butte, while the fourth camp was made not far from where the present-day Forsyth road forks to go to Lame Deer and Ashland. From the Cheyenne circle at the mouth of Greenleaf Creek to that of the Uncpapas was more than one and one-half miles. At this camp for the first time on the journey one of the Sioux circles was set on the west bank of the Rosebud. Here they remained for several days and apparently learned for the first time that many soldiers, from the south and east as well as from the north, were in the field against them.[32]

The assemblage was a straggling one, since the hostiles did

31 Marquis, *Sketch Story of the Custer Battle*, n.p.
32 Marquis, *A Warrior Who Fought Custer*, 190.

not move in "Indian file" but in a wide, irregular column, each family traveling by itself, and the group was spread out probably one mile in width and over three miles in length. The line was so long that the Cheyennes in advance "would have their tents pitched and supper over before the Uncpapas in the rear had even reached the camping ground."[33] However, when occasion demanded it, this seemingly cumbersome organization could move with remarkable speed, being able to make fifty miles a day despite the presence of women and children and the fact that they were burdened with the lodges and miscellaneous baggage of the camp. This remarkable mobility, plus the fact that they were thoroughly familiar with the country and had scouts and hunting parties out most of the time, generally enabled them to keep out of the way of the soldiers.[34]

On May 27, Bradley had seen the smoke of this village. During the first part of June, the Indians, following their usual custom, had begun moving over into the valley of the Little Big Horn, where they camped on the same ground that they were later to occupy at the time of the Custer attack. A favorite resort of the Indians, this valley had luxuriant grasses, and as a result buffalo, deer, and elk were plentiful. At this time, however, the buffalo were scarce, and the Indians moved back to the Rosebud a few days later. Here, on the night of June 9, they first heard of the presence of General Crook's command to the south. It was as yet too far away to constitute any danger, but the Indians decided to go out and meet Crook as soon as he came within half a day's march of their camp. They also decided that he should be attacked by only half of the warriors, the rest remaining to guard the camp.[35] Here they held the Sun Dance[36] which Sitting Bull had vowed, during the course of which he was to have the vision which gave the Sioux the courage and confidence they needed to face the whites' attack.

The Sun Dance, a ceremony common to all the Indian tribes of the plains, was a semireligious festival and was apparently held

[33] Vestal, *Sitting Bull,* 157; Grinnell, *The Fighting Cheyennes,* 185–86.

[34] Crook's Report, September 25, 1876, p. 500.

[35] Charles Eastman, "Story of the Little Big Horn," *Chautauquan,* Vol. XXXI (July, 1900), 355–56.

[36] Vestal, *Sitting Bull,* 151 ff.; Vestal, *Warpath: True Story of the Fighting Sioux,* 97.

for two purposes. On the one hand, it resembled somewhat "commencement" or graduation exercises of civilized communities, for in its ceremonies the young Indian men were transformed into warriors, or "knighted," as it were. The various ordeals which gave opportunity for a wonderful display of heroism and the powers of endurance and suffering seem almost diabolical according to civilized standards, but their purpose was to test the fortitude and courage of the neophytes. Those who "passed" were received as warriors; those who "failed" were branded as women and cowards, and doomed to the association of the women and to permanent celibacy.[37] The second purpose was to placate the various tribal gods by personal torture and sacrifice. Among the Sioux the four great virtues which were taught by the dance were Bravery, Generosity, Fortitude, and Fecundity.[38] The early fur traders called it the "Medicine Lodge," which is, in some ways, the more accurate term, since dancing was not always the most important part of the ceremony. Inasmuch as the Indians believed that dreams were the actual experiences of the human soul or spirit while the physical body was inert, the object was by self-torture to placate the gods and induce a prophetic vision, and it was this feature which led to its being called O-Kan, or Vision, among the Blackfeet, while the Cheyennes gave it the name of the New Life Lodge.[39]

Among the Sioux the arena was a special Sun Dance lodge, approximately 150 feet in diameter and constructed of rough-cut poles which were tied together by rawhide thongs. In the center was the sacred pole, which was always selected, cut, and installed with considerable ceremony. About twelve inches in diameter at the base and about twenty feet in height, it was set firmly in the ground. From a crossbar near the top, rawhide lariats fifteen feet in length were suspended.

The warriors squatted in a circle around the arena, the women standing behind them. The neophytes entered the circle, and the medicine men proceeded to cut gashes in the breasts through which

[37] Godfrey, *Montana*, 161. With this Mr. Stanley Vestal disagrees.

[38] Vestal, *Warpath: True Story of the Fighting Sioux*, 87.

[39] George A. Dorsey, *The Sun Dance*, 57. There is a good picture of a Sioux Sun Dance in Schmitt and Brown, *Fighting Indians of the West*, 146, and another in McClernand, "With Indian and Buffalo in Montana," *Cavalry Journal*, Vol. XXXVI (January and April, 1927), 8.

skewer sticks were inserted just beneath the muscles which underlie the skin. Over the ends of these sticks a buckskin thong was lapped, and this was fastened to the end of the split lariats. Then the lines were drawn tight so that only by standing on his toes could the aspiring warrior escape being suspended by his breast and shoulders.[40] Sometimes the integument stretched three or four inches from the body. Each neophyte also had an ornamented whistle, shrill in tone, which he blew almost continually during the ceremony. Frantic with pain, he would dance, whistle, and yell, while staring almost constantly at the sun; and the dancing, prayers, and invocations, as may well be imagined, were fervent. Neither sleep, food, nor drink was permitted until the dance ended, which was only when the motions of the dancer had caused the skewer sticks to tear through the muscles, and the pain had sent him into a trance in which the sought-for vision appeared.

There were variations of the torture. It was considered more painful and therefore more admirable to have the skewer sticks placed beneath the muscles of the back rather than of the breast, and this was often done by individuals who had vowed the dance for a second time. Another form was to have the skewer sticks inserted in the cheeks just below the eyes.[41] Dancers often had several buffalo heads or skulls attached to their bodies by skewers and buckskin thongs and then ran and jumped about until the weight of the object caused the sticks to break through the flesh.[42]

On other occasions dancers offered so many pieces of skin or flesh, generally one hundred, although varying between fifty and two hundred, to the Great Spirit, and these were cut from the arms and shoulders at the height of the ceremony. On the occasion of Sitting Bull's dance on the Rosebud, the Chief sat on the ground with his back to the sacred Sun Dance pole while his adopted brother, Jumping Bull, lifted a small piece of skin with an awl and then cut it with a sharp knife. Fifty patches of skin, each about the size of the head of a match, were taken from the right arm, beginning

40 Dorsey, *The Sun Dance,* 175–76.

41 *Ibid.*, 176.

42 The number of these might be two, three, or four, but one dancer is known to have had eight. See the account of a Sun Dance held on Poplar River which was witnessed by Dr. T. T. Woodbridge, agency physician at Fort Peck, and which is described in the *Rocky Mountain News,* July 12, 1879.

at the wrist and working up to the shoulder, and then another fifty from the left arm. All the time Sitting Bull was singing, apparently composing the song on the spot, an appeal to the Everywhere Spirit to have mercy on the Sioux. The cutting lasted probably for about half an hour, and then Sitting Bull, with the blood streaming down his arms, danced around and around the pole, staring constantly at the sun. He is said to have danced for more than eighteen hours before falling into a trance. Then the vision he had hoped for came. Sitting Bull heard a voice saying: "I give you these because they have no ears," and at the same time saw soldiers and Indians on horseback falling upside down into the Sioux camp. This he interpreted as meaning that the soldiers were coming to attack the Sioux camp but that the Indians would be victorious over their enemies.[43]

Sitting Bull having had his vision, Black Moon, who held the office of Intercessor and was thus in charge of the dance, brought it swiftly to a close.[44] It was held on the west bank of the Rosebud, not far from where the Painted Rocks are, and all the people, both Sioux and Cheyennes, went into one big circle for the ceremony, although only the Uncpapas seem to have participated. The dance apparently came to an end on June 14;[45] Godfrey puts the date as the fifth, but this is probably too early.[46]

The hostiles moved back across the divide and into the valley of the Little Big Horn almost immediately, and were camped on Ash or Sundance Creek when the Cheyenne scouts reported the presence of Crook's troops on the upper Rosebud. After the warriors had left for the Crook fight, the village moved a short distance down the creek toward the Little Big Horn. It remained here for two nights and then moved to the mouth of the creek, where the tribes remained for five or six days.

While these events had been transpiring, General Crook, exasperated by the failure of his winter campaign, had been preparing another expedition against the hostiles. On May 29, while Terry's

[43] Vestal, *Sitting Bull,* 151–53. On the contrary, Grinnell says that Sitting Bull had his vision on Tongue River in 1875. See *The Fighting Cheyennes,* 334.

[44] Vestal, *Sitting Bull,* 153.

[45] *Ibid.,* 153; for the statement that it was the second week in June, see Schmitt and Brown, *Fighting Indians of the West,* 146.

[46] Godfrey, *Century,* 363.

column had been exploring the valley of the Little Missouri, while Gibbon was holding the north bank of the Yellowstone River against any attempt of the Sioux to cross, and while the Indians were moving slowly up the Rosebud, Crook left his camp at Fort Fetterman and marched northward, hoping to find the hostile village and destroy it. He had a force of forty-seven officers and more than one thousand men, consisting of detachments from the Second and Third Cavalry regiments under the command of Lieutenant Colonel W. B. Royall of the Third, and of the Fourth and Ninth Infantry under Major Alex Chambers of the Fourth.[47] He was accompanied by a wagon train of 120 wagons,[48] each drawn by six mules, and a train of more than one thousand pack mules.[49] This column, consisting of cavalry, infantry, wagon train, pack train, and ambulances, stretched out across the prairie for over four miles. By the time it reached hostile territory, the force had been augmented and was over thirteen hundred strong. Among the new accessions were civilian and Indian scouts, both Crow and Shoshone, but Crook had not been successful in enlisting the services of some vitally needed men from the Sioux agencies of Red Cloud and Spotted Tail because of the open opposition of the agents, principally Agent Hastings, who was incensed at what he considered Crook's wild and reckless statements about finding agency goods, chiefly ammunition, in the camp of Old Bear on the Powder River. This opposition of the agents was felt by some to constitute open warfare on Crook by the members of the "Indian ring."[50]

The expedition moved over the old Montana or Bozeman Road, experiencing many hardships and difficulties. On May 31, the thermometer stood at zero, and the velocity of the wind equaled that of a hurricane. The next two days saw a heavy snowfall, apparently the same storm that harassed both the Montana and Dakota columns, while the high wind made marching particularly disagreeable. About noon on June 5, the column reached the site of Fort Phil Kearny.

[47] *Report of the Secretary of War, 1876*, 29–30; *Rocky Mountain News*, May 28, 1876.

[48] For statements that Calamity Jane was with both of the Crook expeditions, see Mills, *My Story*, 401, and Spring, *Cheyenne and Black Hills Stage and Express Routes*, 86.

[49] Vestal, *Warpath and Council Fire*, 219.

[50] Hyde, *Red Cloud's Folk*, 259.

From here they marched toward the Tongue River, camping on the seventh at the junction of Prairie Dog Creek with the main stream. By this time the danger from the hostiles was so great that communication with the base camp was forbidden, and the column could neither receive supplies nor send back its sick and wounded.[51] The march was also impeded by very high streams. On the ninth, definite Indian signs were reported, and that evening some of the troops had a brush with a small party of Cheyennes, apparently from the main camp on the Rosebud. In this engagement two soldiers were wounded; the Indian casualties, if any, are unknown. Since the hostiles were constantly watching his command and he deemed it impossible to surprise them, Crook now fell back to the foot of the Big Horn Mountains and camped on Wild Goose Creek, near the present city of Sheridan, Wyoming.[52] He was now 154 miles from Fort Fetterman. Here he was joined by a detachment of Crow and Shoshone scouts.[53] "Spoiling for a fight" and being informed that hostiles were in the immediate vicinity, Crook decided on drastic measures in an attempt to force them to combat. Of the strength of the enemy the scouts professed to be uncertain, being confident only that they were in considerable force.

In order to secure greater mobility, Crook reorganized his command. One decision was to mount two hundred of the infantrymen on mules, an order against which Major Chambers protested vigorously but ineffectively.[54] Another was to leave the wagon train and everything miscellaneous behind, guarded by Major Fury and the remaining infantrymen and civilian employees, who could if necessary defend it until the return of the command. One day was used in breaking the mules to riders and in teaching the infantrymen to ride them, a procedure which furnished much amusement to everyone except those most concerned, and which also gave the Indian scouts an opportunity to display their superb horsemanship. Advantage was also taken of the delay to have the horses reshod and the guns and other equipment cleaned and repaired.[55]

[51] Mills, *My Story*, 400.

[52] Crook, *Autobiography*, 193–97; Crawford, *Rekindling Camp Fires*, 254.

[53] Cynthia J. Capron, "The Indian Border War of 1876," *Illinois State Historical Society Journal*, Vol. XIII (January, 1921), 486.

[54] Mills, *My Story*, 402; Vestal, *Warpath and Council Fire*, 219.

[55] Crook's Report, June 20, 1876, 504.

It was apparently at this place that Plenty Coups, a Crow scout who said that General Crook was expecting messengers from the troops on the Yellowstone River, claims to have discovered two dead cavalry horses with buzzards circling over them. He identified the horses as belonging to the soldiers by the iron on their hooves, and felt that this discovery explained why Crook had not received the expected news from General Terry.[56]

The morning of the sixteenth saw the command move out, the infantry, as usual when Crook was in charge, getting off an hour or two ahead of the rest of the command. Each man in the expedition had rations for four days and as much ammunition as his horse could carry. The men had been told that supplies would be replenished on reaching General Terry, for he was understood to have plenty of stores at his base on the Yellowstone River.[57] No led horses were allowed, officers and men were equipped alike, and every individual with the command, whether citizen, servant, or soldier, was armed with some fighting instrument.[58] Only two pack mules were allowed, one carrying tools and the other a small amount of hospital supplies.[59] Great care was exercised in the movement, for some of the scouts had reported the discovery of a trail obviously made by a large body of Sioux.[60] The direction of the march was north and west, the idea being to surprise the hostile camp which Crook now definitely believed to be located at the northern end of Rosebud Canyon,[61] although the scouts were apparently under the impression that it was located on Tongue River or one of its smaller tributaries and were confident of their ability to surprise it.[62]

The day's march lay through fine buffalo country, and in the afternoon the toiling column saw vast herds of these magnificent

[56] Linderman, *American*, 164. This story is of doubtful authenticity since there is no official record to show that the two commands ever were in communication. For a statement that one individual carried a message from Crook to Custer and returned with an answer, see David, *Finn Burnett*, 339.

[57] *Army and Navy Journal*, July 22, 1876.

[58] Crook's Report, June 20, 1876, 504.

[59] *Army and Navy Journal*, July 22, 1876.

[60] Grace R. Hebard, *Washakie, An Account of Indian Resistance of the Covered Wagon and Union Pacific Railroad Invasions of Their Territory*, 184 (hereinafter cited as *Washakie*).

[61] Crook, *Autobiography*, 194.

[62] Crook's Report, June 20, 1876, p. 504.

animals, described as the "truest brute representatives of the America of Columbus," which the Crow and Shoshone scouts proceeded to slaughter in great numbers, justifying their action on the ground that the more they killed, the fewer there would be for the Sioux. This conduct greatly annoyed General Crook, who knew that where there were buffalo there were apt to be Sioux not too far distant, but he did not dare even attempt to discipline his scouts at that crucial time. Near the divide which separates the waters flowing into Tongue River from those flowing into Rosebud Creek, some of the officers discovered that the soldiers had been seen by a small party of Indian hunters. Therefore Crook crossed the divide that evening and about eight o'clock made camp on the headwaters of Rosebud Creek, about forty miles due north of the camp on Goose Creek.[63] Here the Rosebud flows almost due east, but some distance farther on it makes a great bend to the north and then some miles beyond that enters a deep, rocky canyon. Plenty Coups claims that he considered this a poor camp and expected an attack before morning, since during the day he had seen several Sioux and had made signs to them which they had answered;[64] but, like all statements made long after the event, these claims must be accepted with considerable reserve.

The presence of Crook's command had been known to the hostiles for some time. Wooden Leg said that he and ten other buffalo hunters had seen soldiers on the Powder River near Lodgepole Creek, and that they then returned to the village, which was still located on the Rosebud. The news did not disquiet the Indians, for they continued to move upstream. While the Cheyennes were camped on the east bank just across from the mouth of Davis Creek, with the Uncpapa circle just below the site of the present Busby School, they learned definitely of the presence of pony and walking soldiers on Goose Creek, and from this time on Crook's movements were continually watched by spies from the big camp.[65] From here the camp, said to have contained twelve thousand individuals,[66] moved westward up Davis Creek, following the usual

[63] John F. Finerty, *Warpath and Bivouac, or the Conquest of the Sioux,* 118; Crook's Report, June 20, 1876, 504.

[64] Linderman, *American,* 163.

[65] "Crazy Horse's Story of the Custer Fight," South Dakota Historical *Collections,* VI, 228.

[66] *Billings Gazette,* July 17, 1932.

Indian trail to the valley of the Little Big Horn, camping for one night just east of the divide and about one mile north of the present road, the camp extending up a broad coulee full of thickets of wild plum. This was a dry camp, there being no water near by. The next day they crossed the divide and camped at the forks of Sundance or Reno Creek,[67] the campsite being about two miles in length and centered about where the present road crosses a bridge at the forks of the creek.

A small party of Cheyenne warriors led by Little Hawk, and including Yellow Eagle and Little Shield, had been on an expedition apparently for the dual purpose of stealing ponies and keeping an eye on the soldiers when they almost blundered into Crook's command. Believing that their presence had not been discovered by the soldiers, the young men hurried back to the main camp of the hostiles, where they reported that the upper valley of the Rosebud was "black with troops." These soldiers were supposed to be hunting for the Cheyennes, or they would not have come to that particular spot at that particular season since that was considered to be special Cheyenne hunting country. They were also supposed to be the same soldiers who had attacked the camp of Old Bear three months before.[68]

The Cheyennes and Sioux who had been camped for five nights at the forks of Reno Creek, only a few miles from the Little Big Horn, had, for some reason, begun to suspect the presence of troops in the Rosebud Valley—possibly Major Reno's scouting expedition—and they were on the alert with guards constantly riding around the camp. This, however, was the first definite information that they had concerning the strength and exact location of the troops, and it seems to have misled them—at least temporarily—into believing that Crook's forces were the only ones in the valley. The chiefs of the various bands after a lengthy conference assembled a force of between a thousand and fifteen hundred warriors and made an amazing night march across country to the vicinity of Crook's position. All of the groups were represented—Cheyenne,

[67] Vestal, *Warpath: True Story of the Fighting Sioux*, 185. The Indian camp was on Sundance or Reno Creek, about six or seven miles from its confluence with the Little Big Horn. Vestal, *New Sources of Indian History*, 163.

[68] *Billings Gazette*, July 17, 1932; Grinnell, *The Fighting Cheyennes*, 318.

Blackfoot, Ogallala, Uncpapa, Sans Arc, and Minneconjou.[69] During this march they proceeded in column formation, with the front, rear, and flanks guarded by members of the various warrior societies in order to prevent any overly ambitious tribesmen from slipping away in advance and putting the enemy on his guard by a premature attack. This particular formation was apparently used only on those occasions when a large party was on an unusually important expedition, and was probably copied from the old-time buffalo hunt where the hunters were kept under guard in order to prevent them from frightening away the game.[70]

At dawn the Indians were on the Rosebud at the mouth of Trail Creek. Here they stopped and let their ponies rest, while they proceeded to dress and paint themselves. Before battle, a Sioux warrior always painted himself carefully and dressed in his finest clothes, if at all possible. The painting was a form of "medicine" intended to insure the personal safety of the warrior. In addition to making a man more courageous, the fine clothes were a guarantee that if he were killed his prowess as a warrior would be appreciated, for, observing him lying there, even his enemies would know that he had been a brave man. Otherwise those who saw him might say, "This was a poor man. He must not have been a good warrior. See how shabby he lies there."[71]

On the morning of the seventeenth Crook's scouts were unusually reluctant to advance, a fair sign that they suspected the proximity of the enemy, although their reluctance may have been due to nothing more than a desire to feast still further on the buffalo killed the day before. Despite this difficulty, the command managed to get under way about three o'clock, in the expectation of making a fifty-mile march, with the scouts and the mule-mounted infantry ahead; however, they were soon passed by the cavalry, and after a march of five hours they halted in a small valley which was divided into two almost equal parts from north to south by Rosebud Creek, where they were ordered to unsaddle and let the horses graze. This halt was occasioned by the report of several scouts that hostile

[69] Marquis, *She Watched Custer's Last Battle*, n.p.; Vestal, *Warpath: True Story of the Fighting Sioux*, 187; Charles Eastman, "Story of the Little Big Horn," *Chautauquan*, Vol. XXXI (July, 1900), 356; Vestal, *Sitting Bull*, 155.

[70] Hyde, *Red Cloud's Folk*, 110.

[71] Vestal, *Warpath: True Story of the Fighting Sioux*, 186.

Indians had been discovered not far in advance, and by their request that the column be halted while they went forward to reconnoiter.[72] Chief Washakie, the great Shoshone leader, is said to have told General Crook at this time that there were too many Sioux ahead for him to fight.[73]

The Sioux and Cheyennes were drawn up behind a high hill on the west side of the Rosebud and some distance south of the canyon. Crook's command was only a short distance away—in fact, in the valley on the other side of the same hill, and his Indian scouts were moving cautiously ahead. About 8:30 A.M. the soldiers heard scattered shots fired behind the bluff to the north and at first thought that the scouts were again hunting buffalo. It so happened, however, that a few of the hostile warriors had started from the camp on Sundance Creek later than the main body and in the darkness had missed the trail. Ascending a hill to view the surrounding country, they discovered Crook's scouts coming over that same hill. A few shots were exchanged, and Crook was greatly surprised to see his scouts come tearing back with their horses on a dead run and their war bonnets streaming behind them, the Crows clapping their hands and shouting, "Sioux, Sioux," at the top of their lungs.[74] The Sioux war party was apparently equally surprised when their warriors came down the hill yelling. Recovering quickly, the Sioux pursued the Crow scouts almost into Crook's camp.[75]

Thus began the Battle of the Rosebud. Historians quite generally have repeated one another in calling this affair an attack on the village of Crazy Horse, whereas actually it was only a punitive attack, since there was no village there. It was obviously begun somewhat prematurely for both sides. In the fight the Indians seem to have been without either a plan or adequate leadership, although many of their more famous chiefs were on the battlefield. Crazy Horse[76] was there, as was also Sitting Bull, although to say that either was in command is to strain historical fact. Sitting Bull was

[72] Crook, *Autobiography*, 194–95; Crook's Report, June 20, 1876.

[73] Hebard, *Washakie*, 203.

[74] Crook, *Autobiography*, 194; Grinnell, *The Fighting Cheyennes*, 320.

[75] Charles Eastman, "Story of the Little Big Horn," *Chautauquan*, Vol. XXXI (July, 1900), 356.

[76] According to Plenty Coups, Crazy Horse and his warriors were on their way to join the great village on the Little Big Horn. Linderman, *American*, 162.

probably suffering too much from the tortures of the recent Sun Dance to do much more than shout advice, advice which for the most part was unheeded. The fact that Gall and Crow King seem not to have been present at this fight implies that the forces that were to destroy Custer were not completely concentrated at this time.[77] And the fact that the battle rapidly assumed the character of an old-time frontier barroom brawl, with every man for himself, has suggested to some writers that the Indians had a plan which failed—probably the familiar decoy-and-ambush trick. Since this plan of decoy and ambush, apparently the only strategy that the tribes of the plains ever devised, is suggested by the preliminary arrangements, if the Indians did have a plan of battle, this was probably it.[78]

George B. Grinnell, the leading authority on the Cheyenne Indians, denies that the hostiles had any such plan, pointing out that the terrain was not suitable, since it was all comparatively rolling prairie and offered little or no opportunity for ambuscade or approach under cover. Instead, he suggests that Crook's Indian scouts attempted to lead the hostiles into a trap between the two groups of soldiers but that the ruse failed when the Crows, in their excitement, fled down the wrong ridge.[79] A statement by John Finerty, a newspaper correspondent who was with Crook, to the effect that Crook's well-laid plans were destroyed by the timidity and obstinacy of the Crows supports this theory to a certain extent.[80] Finerty's explanation, however, seems rather farfetched, as the Crows were too surprised, and Crook too uncertain of the exact whereabouts of the enemy, for them to have planned anything of the kind. On the other side of the story, the celebrated warrior, Rain-in-the-Face, whose testimony is to be accepted only with definite reservation, said long afterwards that Crook was saved by his Indian scouts, for if the hostiles had been able to wait for the General to attack, his fate would have been the same as Custer's,

[77] Burdick, *The Last Battle of the Sioux Nation*, 39. Eastman says that Gall was at this battle. "Story of the Little Big Horn," *Chautauquan*, Vol. XXXI (July, 1900), 356. If Gall and Crow King were both missing from this fight and joined the village later, it would account for the heavy trail that Captain Ball later found.

[78] Hyde, *Red Cloud's Folk*, 130.

[79] Grinnell, *The Fighting Cheyennes*, 321.

[80] Finerty, *Warpath and Bivouac*, 135.

but as it was, Crook had too good a position and the Indians could do nothing with him.[81]

The fight took place on both banks of the Rosebud—very rough and broken ground, covered with rocks, trees, and bushes—and the Indian attack was made with such desperation that in advancing to meet it the command became badly separated. Crook was aiming at a village supposedly lying some six or eight miles down the Rosebud; he believed that the Indians, having discovered his presence, had not awaited his coming but had come out boldly to meet him.[82] Realizing that any real success would demand the capture and destruction of the village, Crook now attempted to close up the command, but had great difficulty in getting the battalions together, owing to the roughness of the ground and the fact that each element of the command was hard pressed by the enemy, who displayed a strong force at all points and fought with such tenacity as to convince Crook that they were fighting for time to get their village to a place of safety. Orders to Major Royall, who had previously been sent to the left, to return with the least possible delay were not carried out until two hours later, and the plan to charge the enemy in front could not be executed.[83]

Crook did succeed in sending a detachment of eight troops of cavalry, under Captain Anson Mills, down the so-called Rosebud Canyon for several miles toward the supposed site of the Indian village, with orders to take it and hold it until the General could come to his support. Mills's scouts, however, refused to enter the canyon, saying that to do so would mean certain death. Crook himself noticed that the sides and approaches were well covered with timber, a circumstance that would allow the hostiles to fire on the command at short range while the return fire would be ineffective. He also observed that the Indians on the hill who could have opposed the advance of the detachment did not do so, but instead sneaked off the hill, being careful to keep in advance of the troops. Convinced by their withdrawal that the soldiers were doing exactly what the Indians wanted them to do and were being drawn into a

[81] Hebard, *Washakie,* 186; Bourke, *On the Border with Crook,* 311; Grinnell, *The Fighting Cheyennes,* 317; *Missoulian,* March 3, 1907.

[82] *Report of the Secretary of War, 1876,* 30; Crook's Report, June 20, 1876, 504; Sheridan's *Report,* 442.

[83] Crook, *Autobiography,* 195.

trap, Crook sent an order by Captain Nickerson recalling the detachment,[84] an order which Mills believed saved his command from annihilation.[85]

The hostiles are said to have allowed Mills to go down the river unopposed not because there was no village to defend, but because he was going away from the fight.[86] Crook's explanation to Mills was that since the engagement was much more serious than he had expected, such a large force must be left to protect the wounded that he could not keep his promise to support Mills with the rest of the command.[87]

General Crook was under the impression that he had met the entire Sioux Nation instead of what was really only a large war party.[88] He soon realized that he had run into a regular hornets' nest, and believing his forces to be badly outnumbered, which probably was not the case, he began withdrawing his troops and fighting on the defensive before the day was half over.[89] The fighting was characterized by alternating charges back and forth with neither side winning a decisive advantage; toward evening the hostiles withdrew, leaving Crook in possession of the field. This withdrawal is said by some of the Indians to have been a ruse, the hostiles hoping that Crook would pursue and fall into a trap set by their great reserve force under Gall and Sitting Bull. The chiefs did not realize how glad Crook was to get out of the scrape into which he had blundered.[90]

Among the Cheyennes this battle is known as "Where the Girl Saved Her Brother," from the fact that during the fighting a Cheyenne, Chief Comes-in-Sight, was unhorsed and surrounded by enemies. He was saved from death by the bravery of his sister, Calf Road, who had accompanied her husband, Black Coyote, and was

[84] *Ibid.*, 195; Crook's Report, June 20, 1876, 504–505.

[85] Mills, *My Story*, 409.

[86] Vestal, *Warpath and Council Fire*, 229.

[87] Mills, *My Story*, 407–408.

[88] The exact strength of the Indians is unknown, and there are many guesses. See Lewis Crawford, *Rekindling Camp Fires*, 250; Bourke, *On the Border with Crook*, 311; and Vestal, *Sitting Bull*, 156.

[89] Charles King, "Custer's Last Battle," *Harper's*, Vol. LXXXI (August, 1890), 381.

[90] "Crazy Horse's Story of the Custer Fight," South Dakota Historical *Collections*, VI, 224.

riding and charging with the warriors.[91] It was also marked by the dash, singlehanded, of a small malformed Crow, known as Humpy, into a group of Sioux horsemen in order to rescue a cavalry sergeant named Van Mall, who had been cut off and surrounded by the hostiles. Although such performances were by no means rare among the Crows, those Indians have generally had a reputation for cowardice which was not deserved. In this case Humpy received no recognition for his bravery because he was only an Indian ally; had he been a white soldier, the story would undoubtedly have been different.[92]

The losses in the battle, considering the numbers engaged, were comparatively light. Crook reported casualties of ten killed, including one Indian scout, and twenty-one wounded. About the same number of enemy dead, thirteen in all, were picked up, having been left in close proximity to the position held by the troops, and undoubtedly the hostiles, in accordance with their custom, had carried away many others. Nor was the field, which extended over several miles of rough country, thoroughly searched after the battle. The Cheyennes claim that only one of their number, Black Sun, was killed, but number the Sioux dead as twenty or more, adding that there were many wounded, some of whom died later. All of which is rather infinitesimal, especially in view of the fact that Crook reported that his troops had fired away some twenty-five thousand rounds of ammunition.[93]

Crook's forces camped on the field that night. He felt that he was faced with two alternatives: to pursue the retreating enemy without rations and dragging his wounded on rough mule litters, or to return to the base camp on Goose Creek, where they could be cared for. Feeling that the Sioux village had probably been removed during the fight and satisfied that the number and quality of the enemy were greater than his command could handle, he buried his dead, and on the morning of the eighteenth began to retreat slowly

[91] Grinnell, *The Fighting Cheyennes*, 324; Vestal, *Warpath and Council Fire*, 224–25.

[92] Dustin, *The Custer Tragedy*, 3.

[93] Crook's Report, June 20, 1876, 505; Crook, *Autobiography*, 195; Vestal, *New Sources of Indian History*, 136. Although all of these accounts differ slightly, they add point to the statement that it cost the government about one million dollars for each Indian killed, women and children not counted. *New York Herald*, June 19, 1876.

up the west bank of the Rosebud.[94] Before leaving, he sent Frank Grouard and possibly one other scout to discover the true situation in the canyon. They reported all sorts of preparations on the sides of the Canyon, and in the cul-de-sac at the bottom, for a massacre if the troops had gone a short distance farther.[95] Much of this report was probably a newspaperman's yarn, for the facts of topography simply do not fit in with this account; furthermore, the Sioux and Cheyennes who were in the war party, on being interviewed in later years, insisted that there were no plans for an ambush in the valley of the Rosebud or anywhere else during the fight.[96]

Base camp was reached on the evening of the nineteenth, the detachment having, as Mills later wrote, "little pride in their achievement."[97] As intended when they started, they had been absent four days. A group of hostiles chiefly interested in stealing horses accompanied them on their return, and in the days following annoyed the soldiers in every possible way, setting fire to the grass, firing into the camp at long range, and especially attempting to stampede the horses and mules. Despite dispatches from the East urging Crook to strike and strike hard, the troops remained in their base camp for over a month, licking their wounds and awaiting the arrival of re-enforcements and additional supplies.[98] The General did not ask for re-enforcements, a procedure which he justified on the ground that large numbers of Indians in other areas would need the restraining hand of the military and he did not wish to embarrass the Division commander by calls for additional troops, since he knew they would be sent as soon as available.[99] Meantime, the troops settled down to the enjoyment of weeks of hunting and fishing, no doubt preferring these activities to the rigors of campaigning against the Sioux. An estimated fifteen thousand or more trout were taken from the waters of near-by streams, while the number of deer, elk, mountain sheep, and bear brought in by members of the command ran into the hundreds, so that the attitude of the soldiers has been

[94] *Report of the Secretary of War, 1876*, 30; Crook's Report, June 20, 1876, 500, 505; Crook, *Autobiography*, 197; *New York Herald*, July 6, 1876.

[95] E. A. Brininstool, *The Custer Fight: Captain F. W. Benteen's Story of the Battle of the Little Big Horn*, 35.

[96] Vestal, *Warpath and Council Fire*, 221, 229.

[97] Mills, *My Story*, 409.

[98] Crook, *Autobiography*, 197.

[99] Crook's Report, September 25, 1876, 499–500.

compared to that of summer picnickers rather than that of soldiers on a serious expedition against hostile Indians.[100]

Although reported to the American public as a victory for Crook, this battle, fought on the one-hundredth anniversary of Bunker Hill, was far from being that; in fact, Crook received a sound thrashing.[101] He had been on the offensive, and this fight stopped him dead in his tracks; even Sheridan admitted that the "victory" was barren of results since he had been unable to pursue the enemy.[102] It was a defeat, practical if not tactical, since it left the Indians in possession of the country and the work would all have to be done over again.[103] No amount of rationalization could change the fact that the fight had given the Indians new confidence and that it had prevented a junction with General Terry's command, an event which would have doubtless brought to a successful end the campaign against the Sioux.[104] The defeat rankled in Crook's memory, and he continued to insist that, had the battle been fought according to plan, he would have had a real victory and that the power of the Sioux would have been effectively broken. In 1886, in response to criticism that he had made a poor fight, Crook placed the responsibility for the failure on two subordinates, Royall and Nickerson, and expressed his regret that he had not had them court-martialed.[105]

The greater number of the hostile warriors returned immediately to their camp on Sundance Creek, which, according to Indian custom, was moved immediately after the battle.[106] The new camp was located on the east side of the Little Big Horn, an area which was largely *terra incognita* to the Sioux, but which had been a home

[100] Crawford, *Rekindling Camp Fires*, 254–61.

[101] Colonel T. M. Coughlan, "The Battle of the Little Big Horn," *Cavalry Journal*, Vol. XLIII (January–February, 1934), 13.

[102] Sheridan's *Report*, 442; Crook's Report, September 25, 1876, p. 500.

[103] *New York Herald*, July 11, 1876, quoting the *Helena Independent*. The *Army and Navy Journal*, July 1, 1876, waxed especially sarcastic in stating that the hostile tribes were somewhat badly off for field artillery but that in another year or so the mismanagement of the Interior Department could be depended upon to correct that deficiency and that the Indians would have several batteries of Gatling guns in time for the 1877 campaign.

[104] Crook, *Autobiography*, 195–96.

[105] *Ibid.*, 196.

[106] Dr. Charles Eastman, however, says that it was after the Rosebud fight that the Indian camp was moved westward across the divide to the Little Big Horn River. "Story of the Little Big Horn," *Chautauquan*, Vol. XXXI (July, 1900), 356.

spot to the Cheyennes for over ten years.[107] The Indians still being unsatisfied, they continued to await the fulfillment of Sitting Bull's vision which had promised soldiers falling right into the camp of the Indians, for General Crook had not come within miles of that great village on the Little Big Horn.[108] They were confident and unafraid, and Crook's refusal to seek contact again meant that, for the time being, the campaign from the south had collapsed completely and that the Indians were now free to devote their undivided attention to Gibbon, to Terry, and to Custer.

[107] *Billings Gazette*, July 17, 1876. This article, which is by Dr. Marquis, is contradicted by Stanley Vestal who says that in the spring of 1871 a large Sioux village had camped on what was later to be the Custer battlefield. He seems to imply that the valley was familiar territory to the Sioux. *New Sources of Indian History*, 161.

[108] Vestal, *Sitting Bull*, 156.

CHAPTER X

The Road to War

THE MORNING of May 17 dawned cold and raw, with a heavy mist hanging over the river.[1] At five o'clock, the "general," which was the signal to strike tents and break camp, was sounded, and the command started with a brave show of style. The Arikara scouts "beat their drums and sang their melancholy war songs"[2] while the Seventh's band played "Garry Owen" as the regiment marched across the parade ground. The scouts were the first to parade, forming themselves according to warrior societies, and were followed by the regiment in column of platoons. The families of the Ree scouts set up the wailing, mournful dirge that was customary when the Indians went to war, but the white children played at being soldiers, carrying flags made of bits of cloth tied on sticks and beating on tin pans for drums while they marched to and fro.[3] A brief halt was made as the married officers and enlisted men dismounted for a final leave-taking of their families. In the meantime the wagon train had been assembling on the plateau to the west of the fort, awaiting the order to advance. Shortly after seven o'clock the trumpets blew "to horse," and with the band giving forth bravely with "The Girl I Left Behind," the regiment marched towards the west.

Despite the panoply there was over all an oppressive feeling of dread, almost a foreboding of disaster to come, for the Sioux

[1] The story of the westward march of the Dakota column is based largely on General E. S. Godfrey, "Custer's Last Battle," in *Century Magazine*, Vol. XLIII (January, 1892) (hereinafter cited as Godfrey, *Century*). The article is reprinted with much additional material in *Contributions to the Historical Society of Montana*, IX (1923) (hereinafter cited as Godfrey, *Montana*).

[2] Vestal, *The Missouri*, 221.

[3] Bates, *Custer's Indian Battles*, 28.

were known to be formidable enemies, and there was little doubt that many of the troopers who marched away so gallantly would never return. Apparently in the hope of allaying this feeling, General Terry had ordered the march across the parade ground.[4] He seems to have felt that if the fearful ones could view the regiment in all its splendor and fighting strength, they would find new hope and courage. Instead, the gloom was intensified, for, as the expedition marched across the prairie, "the fog began to lift and the sun broke through causing one of the rarest phenomena of the plains, and the moving column was mirrored in the radiant mist," and through a mirage the line of troops and wagons seemed to march both on the earth and in the sky. To the weeping women at the fort, this transformation of both men and horses seemed to be of supernatural origin and an ill omen, a preview of the tragedy to come.[5]

The first day the troops marched about fourteen miles over rolling prairie before making camp at 1:30 P.M. on the banks of the Heart River. The campsite was almost ideal, being bottom land fenced on three sides by high bluffs. The grass was good and plentiful, and wood and water were abundant. Rattlesnakes also abounded, and a large number of the reptiles, some of them measuring two and one-half feet in length, were killed in the camp. Here the men were paid. This had not been done before leaving Fort Lincoln because of General Terry's well-grounded fear that the temptations of the fleshpots of the city of Bismarck would be too great,[6] and that the regiment would be weakened by desertion, debauchery, and disease.

At the campsite, the Heart River was only about thirty yards wide and three feet deep, with a fairly firm bottom and only a slight current. The banks, however, were both abrupt and slippery, and much corduroying was necessary in order to get the wagon train across; this resulted in a delay of nearly three hours in addi-

[4] Custer may have been responsible for this order. He is said to have told Bloody Knife that the march was for the purpose of reassuring the women. James W. Schultz, *William Jackson, Indian Scout, His True Story . . .*, 124.

[5] DeLand, *The Sioux Wars*, 325; Bates, *Custer's Indian Battles*, 28; Custer, *Boots and Saddles*, 263–64.

[6] Charles Windolph, one of the last survivors of the regiment, says that Custer was responsible for the order. Frazier and Robert Hunt, *I Fought with Custer*, 53.

tion to being extremely fatiguing to the troops, who were still soft from the winter months in garrison. As a result, the second day's camp was made at two o'clock, on a branch of the Sweet Briar River, with only eleven miles covered during the day.[7]

For greater efficiency of command, the Seventh Cavalry had been divided into a right and left wing, each consisting of six companies divided into two battalions. The right wing, consisting of Companies B, C, I, E, F, and L, was commanded by Major Marcus A. Reno, while the battalion commanders were Captains Keogh and Yates. The remaining six companies composed the left wing, commanded by the senior captain, Fred W. Benteen of H, with the battalions under the leadership of Captains Weir and French. On the march one battalion always constituted the advance guard, another the rear guard, while the other two were stationed on the flanks. Of the advance guard, one troop under Custer's personal command rode ahead, selecting the route to be followed, while the other two were detailed to General Terry for pioneering work, such as the construction of bridges and the corduroying of roads. These troops were accompanied by two light spring wagons carrying axes, pickaxes, shovels, and enough pine boards and scantlings for the construction of a short bridge. On account of the inadequacy of the materials, the crossing of even a small stream was apt to be tedious and difficult and to result in a delay of several hours.[8]

Behind the "pioneers" came General Terry and his staff, with an infantry company,[9] then the battalion of Gatling guns, and behind them the wagon train—four wagons abreast with an infantry company at each end of the column. One wagon was assigned to each troop and in it were carried rations and forage as well as the mess kits and other equipment of both officers and men. Each trooper's horse carried about eighty or ninety pounds of equipment in addition to its rider and one hundred rounds of ammunition. The

[7] Maguire's Report, 1341.

[8] Godfrey, *Century*, 359. The *Army and Navy Journal*, July 22, 1876, gives a slightly different distribution of the companies into battalions. The use of the word "squadron" to designate a battalion of cavalry did not come into official use until April 13, 1901, although General Custer had used the term as early as September 6, 1873. Merington, *The Custer Story*, 262. Similarly the word "troop" instead of "company" when speaking of cavalry was officially designated in September, 1883, although it had been used on cavalry muster rolls at least two years earlier.

[9] Terry's Report, 459.

beef herd and the extra horses and mules were driven alongside the wagon train by the packers and herders. Last of all came the cavalry battalion constituting the rear guard. Mrs. Custer claimed that the number of men with the expedition—soldiers, citizens, employees, and scouts—was about twelve hundred and that there were more than seventeen hundred animals in all. On the march the expedition strung out for more than two miles and from a distance seemed like a broad ribbon stretched smoothly over the prairies.[10]

The flanking battalions had to be especially vigilant, and in rough country were deployed in open formation. In order to guard against a surprise attack, no trooper was ever out of sight of the one next closest to the column. Under instructions to keep within five hundred yards of the trail, the soldiers were never to get more than one-half mile in advance or to the rear of the train. Far out in front and almost enveloping the command were the Arikara scouts under the command of Lieutenant Charles Varnum, whom they aptly called "Peaked-Face." They did their work carefully and painstakingly and yet managed to keep ahead of the crawling column without difficulty.[11]

Camp was always made in the form of a rectangle and close to a stream if possible. The longest sides were formed by the cavalry wings, and the end nearest the stream was occupied by the headquarters company of the infantry. The other end was closed by the remaining companies of the infantry, and the wagon train was contained within the enclosed space. The horses and mules were watered as soon as possible after halting and then were grazed outside the enclosure under the supervision of a stable guard detailed from all the cavalry troops. Great care had to be exercised in selecting the watering places, owing to the ever present possibility of quicksand as well as the precipitous, slippery banks of the prairie streams. The system of grazing at a distance from the camp was adopted in order to preserve the grass within the enclosure for night grazing. To guard against the possibility of a dreaded prairie fire, trenches were dug for the mess fires and grass burned off for quite a distance around. Fresh beef was distributed to all elements of the expedition and enough cattle slaughtered to take care of the next day's supply.

10 Custer, *Boots and Saddles*, 262–65; Bates, *Custer's Indian Battles*, 28.
11 Godfrey, *Century*, 359.

Shortly after sunset the roll was called in order to make sure that the men had their equipment in place, and the horses and mules were driven within the enclosure and tethered to picket lines. A "main guard" was posted around the camp, while the Indian scouts kept watch from small hills around and some distance from the column.[12]

The routine of the days became almost monotonous in its regularity: Reveille usually sounded a few minutes after four o'clock, breakfast was ready soon afterwards, and an hour or so later the regiment was again on the march. Camp was usually made in the late afternoon, but the distance covered varied greatly, depending upon the difficulties and obstacles encountered and upon the available supply of wood, water, and grass. Custer himself always selected the campsite and determined when the halt should be made.

The expedition struck straight across country, keeping a little to the north of the present main line of the Northern Pacific Railway. The first few days saw slow and difficult going, owing to the fact that late spring rains had left the ground soft and soggy so that the heavily laden wagons sometimes sank up to the hubs. As Burkman later wrote: "It don't sound much in the tellin' to say a wheel come off'n a wagon, or a wagon got stuck in the mud but for us that had to tug and sweat and cuss in the blazin' sun for maybe half a day, it meant a lot."[13] For this reason the lower areas along the streams were avoided as much as possible, and the command marched along the benches and plateaus which bordered the valleys.

On May 19 the Sweet Briar River had been reached. It was found to be a raging torrent fully fifty feet wide and ten feet deep. Since it could not be bridged with the material at hand, a detour to the south was necessary. The ground was very soft, so soft that in many places double teams were needed for the wagons, and progress was accordingly slow. Camp was made early at Buzzard's Roost, which the scouts named "Turkey Buzzard Camp." There was no wood closer than five miles, and the "buffalo chips" were too wet to burn. Little grass could be found, and the only water was that standing in coulees and buffalo wallows, with the result that a large portion of the command was unable to cook either

[12] *Ibid.*, 360.

[13] Glendolin Wagner, *Old Neutriment*, 86.

supper or breakfast. All in all, it was a cheerless camp with no redeeming characteristics. But the gloom which pervaded it was lightened somewhat by the arrival of mail from Fort Lincoln on the twentieth. Although the mail carriers had seen no signs of hostile Indians, the expedition was nonetheless in enemy country, and for that reason the scouts with the return mail were not sent out until after nightfall. Then they traveled by night, concealing themselves by day.[14] In his letter to his wife, Custer reported that the roads were fearfully bad, that it was raining and had been ever since the expedition started. In four days they had managed to cover only forty-six miles.[15]

Nevertheless, the march was far from being one of unrelieved hardship. In fact, in many ways it had some of the characteristics of a picnic. Game was plentiful, and the troopers were encouraged to hunt as a means of improving their marksmanship and also of adding variety to the army ration. The scouts, whose position in the advance gave them much better opportunities, earned considerable side money by killing game and then selling it to the soldiers. Custer, as was his custom on campaign, had taken at least four of his staghounds along,[16] and their pursuit of antelope who "sped away light as smoke, swift as cloud shadows"[17] proved an unending source of amusement to everyone.

On the twenty-first the column made only a little better than thirteen miles between six o'clock in the morning and five in the afternoon, and camped about eight miles north and one-half mile west of present Glen Ullin, North Dakota. Some twelve miles to the northwest were the twin buttes, picturesquely named "Young Maiden's Breasts." The next day the soldiers began to see large patches of alkali and to pass sage- and cactus-covered hills scarred by deep ravines. That night camp was made in some groves of box elder on Thin-faced Woman Creek, a branch of the Knife River, near the present town of Hebron. A short distance west of this place the present highway follows Custer's trail, and the deep ruts cut in the prairie by the heavily laden military wagons are still visible.[18]

[14] Libby, *Arikara Narrative*, 63–64; Custer, *Boots and Saddles*, 305.

[15] Custer, *Boots and Saddles*, 305.

[16] *Ibid.*, 210.

[17] Vestal, *Warpath: True Story of the Fighting Sioux*, 161.

[18] Kellogg, "Notes, May 17 to June 9, 1876 of the Little Big Horn Expedition," in *Contributions to the Historical Society of Montana*, IX (1923), 213.

On the twenty-third they made only eight miles, camping before nine o'clock in the morning at the headwaters of a branch of the Knife River. Here there was good water, and grass and wood were abundant. The ostensible reason for the early halt was to take advantage of these features as well as to give the horses and mules a chance to rest in preparation for the long march ahead on the next day. There was another and more compelling reason, however, for on this same day the expedition found the first evidence of the quarry it sought. Early that morning Custer, while chasing an elk far ahead of the column, came upon a fresh-burning campfire left by the hostiles, and at dusk Indians were observed on a bluff about three miles away watching the troops.[19] The region ahead was scouted carefully in the expectation that the Sioux might be in force, but no further evidence of the hostiles was discovered. Although the identity of this particular band was never established, they were apparently one of the numerous groups who were deserting the agencies and making their way to join the hostiles, and their presence here is further proof that the Sioux were not ignorant of the whereabouts of Custer's command from the day that the expedition left Fort Lincoln.

At nine o'clock on the morning of the twenty-fourth the column crossed the line of survey of the Northern Pacific Railroad and later the site of Dickinson was passed, camp being made on a hill to the south, where breastworks thrown up for protection are still visible.[20] This camp was one of the best that they had yet experienced, with plenty of wood and excellent grazing. The stream was cool, clear, and swift running, with an abundance of small fish.[21] Two days later the troops began to experience very sultry weather. Thousands of mosquitoes now began to annoy the command, while the ground was literally covered with young grasshoppers, so that

[19] Kellogg, "Notes, May 17 to June 9, 1876 of the Little Big Horn Expedition," in *Contributions to the Historical Society of Montana*, IX (1923), 215. Kellogg also said that on two occasions hunting parties had found warm embers of small campfires within easy distance of the camp of the soldiers, so that it was obvious that the hostiles were observing them, but that up until that, the command had not seen an Indian. *New York Herald*, June 19, 1876.

[20] *North Dakota, A Guide to the Northern Prairie State*, 296. An item in the Custer Scrapbooks in the Billings Public Library says that this camp was on Duck Creek just west of the present town.

[21] Kellogg, "Notes, May 17 to June 9, 1876 of the Little Big Horn Expedition," in *Contributions to the Historical Society of Montana*, IX (1923), 215.

it was impossible to walk without crushing several of them at every step.[22]

On the twenty-seventh, just ten days after leaving Fort Lincoln, the column came into full view of the *Mauvaises Terres* or Bad Lands of the Little Missouri River, and here the route of march turned almost due south.[23] In traversing this region, the expedition followed Sully's trail of 1864 down to the stream that is now known as Davis Creek. This follows a very tortuous course, and its high, perpendicular banks, which are skirted with cottonwoods, willows, and sagebrush, made progress slow and extremely difficult. In covering one stretch of eight miles, it was necessary to ford the stream ten times, and on the twenty-eighth and twenty-ninth not less than thirteen bridges had to be constructed. The creek bed varies from fifteen to seventy feet in width, while the soil, which is alternating sand and gravel, has only a light growth of grass. The entire outlook was dismal, an effect which was heightened by the enormous clouds of mosquitoes which plagued men and animals alike.[24]

At nine o'clock on the morning of the thirtieth, camp was made on the east bank of the Little Missouri River. Along its course were groves of cottonwood, elm, and pine, as a result of which the Sioux called it the Thick Timber River.[25] The troops found the water unexpectedly low and clear.[26] Camp was made on a grassy plain surrounded on three sides by high hills and separated from the stream by a thick belt of trees. There was wood in abundance, and the river teemed with fish, providing a welcome change from the beef and bacon diet of the march. This campsite was five miles south of the present site of Medora, at the confluence of Davis Creek and the Little Missouri, and the parapets erected for defense as well as deep cuts made by the wagons are still visible. The real task of the expedition now lay just ahead, and Custer forbade all discharge of

22 *Ibid.*, 216.

23 Vestal, *The Missouri*, 263–64. The region was first sighted south of the present town of Fryburg, in Billings County, North Dakota. "It was an amazing sight, lying in the distance like a great sunken city with high spires and buildings half-hidden in the mist." Roy P. Johnson, "Jacob Horner of the Seventh Cavalry," *North Dakota History*, Vol. XVI (April, 1949), 81–82.

24 44 Cong., 1 sess., *House Exec. Doc. 184*, 56; *Army and Navy Journal*, June 24, 1876.

25 Vestal, *The Missouri*, 264.

26 Kellogg, "Notes, May 17 to June 9, 1876 of the Little Big Horn Expedition," in *Contributions to the Historical Society of Montana*, IX (1923), 217–18.

firearms lest it should give warning to the Sioux, and soldiers and scouts who violated the order were drastically and effectively punished.

Before leaving Fort Lincoln, General Terry had expressed the belief that he might find the hostiles on the Little Missouri River since that stream, with its deep valleys and thickly timbered bottoms, was a favorite wintering place for the northern tribes, and in view of the lateness of the spring he was justified in feeling that the Indians might not have gone far away. But in this expectation he was disappointed. The region was thoroughly scouted without any recent Indian signs being found, and Custer, with Troops C, D, F, and M, guided by Lieutenant Varnum and twelve of the scouts, explored up the river for more than twenty miles without discovering any sign of the presence of Indians in the valley. The scout also established the fact that no significant number of hostiles had visited or even passed through the region within a period of six months.[27] The ruggedness of the country is apparent from the fact that, although the river valley is about a mile wide, it is so hemmed in by impassable terrain that in this march of some fifty miles it was necessary for the scouting party to ford the stream thirty-four times. This was especially hard on the horses, who had difficulty in clambering up the steep, smooth banks. The descent was almost as arduous and was even more dangerous, for they had to slide down with their legs braced.[28]

Finally, General Terry came to the reluctant conclusion that he had been mistaken and that the hostiles would be found still farther west; thus the high hopes of a speedy campaign that had been held by some of the officers faded for a time. The next day the march was resumed, the river being crossed without mishap at Sentinel Butte, which the scouts called "Two Buttes Facing Each Other,"[29] only a few miles south of the town of Medora, where today the Northern Pacific Railroad bridges the stream.

[27] "Diary of Captain [*sic*] E. S. Godfrey, Battle of the Little Big Horn, 1876" (Edward S. Godfrey MSS., Library of Congress), n.p. (hereinafter cited as Godfrey, "Diary"); Brown and Willard, *Black Hills Trails*, 137. Kellogg's dispatch from the camp on the Little Missouri River is in the *New York Herald*, June 19, 1876.

[28] Brown and Willard, *Black Hills Trails*, 137; Custer, *Boots and Saddles*, 306; Kellogg, "Notes, May 17 to June 9, 1876 of the Little Big Horn Expedition," in *Contributions to the Historical Society of Montana*, IX (1923), 217–18.

Before resuming the march, Terry had sent a dispatch to General Sheridan reporting on operations to date. Stating that he had found no hostile Indians nor any recent signs of any, Terry declared that progress, on account of conditions beyond the control of the officers, was much slower than had been anticipated but that the health and condition of the command was excellent and that he planned to push on westward, constantly scouting to the left in order to prevent the Sioux from passing around his flank on their way back to the agencies.[30]

On the twenty-ninth, Sheridan had sent a lengthy report to Sherman. In it he stated that Crook and Terry each had a force of about nine hundred men, while Gibbon had four hundred, which J. D. Cameron, the secretary of war, declared to be as strong as could be maintained in that inhospitable country or could be spared from other pressing necessities.[31] Regarding the numbers or whereabouts of the hostile Indians, there was little or no accurate information; but, since they could not keep the field in any great numbers for more than a week or ten days at a time, Sheridan believed—and the opinion was shared by both Terry and Crook—that each column would be able to take care of itself in chastising the Indians, should it have the opportunity. Sheridan was, however, very dubious concerning the results which were to be obtained from the campaign, since the military expeditions under way would cause many of the Indians to return to the reservations only to take the field again in the fall as soon as the troops came in. Although he feared that the expedition might have to be repeated, Sheridan felt that an attempt to settle the whole matter might as well be made; therefore, he renewed his recommendation for the erection of two forts on the Yellowstone River and for military control of the In-

29 Kellogg, "Notes, May 17 to June 9, 1876 of the Little Big Horn Expedition," in *Contributions to the Historical Society of Montana*, IX (1923), 217. In one of the Custer Scrapbooks in the Billings Public Library there is an account of the discovery of a rock upon which the names of several members of Custer's command had been carved. This rock was found twelve miles southwest of Fryburg, N. D., and on a ranch owned by William McCarty. It is about three miles north of Sentinel Butte. The names of W. C. Williams, Company H, and F. Neeley, of M, were still decipherable.

30 44 Cong., 1 sess., *House Exec. Doc. 184*, 56; *Army and Navy Journal*, June 24, 1876.

31 44 Cong., 1 sess., *House Exec. Doc. 81*, 3; *Army and Navy Journal*, July 15, 1876.

dians at the various agencies in order to prevent any of the hostiles from coming in except under terms of unconditional surrender.[32] The next day Sheridan apprised Sherman by telegraph of the disquieting news from Crook that all of the agency Indians capable of taking the warpath were then, or soon would be, in the field.[33]

West of the river, the route of Custer's march lay up the bed of a small creek and then over the bluffs. Travel was slow and difficult since extensive pioneer work was required. The country was very broken, with the trail zigzagging up and down the high, steep buttes. So difficult was the terrain that the expedition camped at two o'clock after having covered only thirteen miles. Terry had anticipated trouble from the hostiles in the Bad Lands or while traversing the broken country west of the Little Missouri, but there was still no sign of any of the hostiles being in the vicinity.[34]

It began to rain, and on June 1 the freakish Dakota weather produced a snowstorm which blocked the progress of the expedition. The snow was between one and two feet deep on the level, and some of the tents were drifted halfway to the top. It was quite cold, and wood was scarce and not easily accessible. The animals, especially, suffered from exposure and the lack of grazing. This storm disturbed the Arikara scouts very much. Disliking the way things were going, they were becoming more and more convinced that each new mishap was a fresh portent of the disaster which they believed awaited the command. The column was snowbound for two days, but on the afternoon of the second the forage and supply wagons were hauled up the next hill to be ready to start early on the following morning.[35] Camp was broken early on the morning of the third, and after a march of twenty-five miles, the longest yet made, they reached Beaver Creek in the early evening.

During the day messengers, one Indian and two white scouts, came in from Gibbon's command. They reported that the Sioux were south of the Yellowstone and in considerable force, and that two soldiers and one civilian had been killed while hunting on the upper reaches of that stream. Dispatches were also received from

[32] 44 Cong., 1 sess., *House Exec. Doc. 184*, 53–54.

[33] *Ibid.*, 54.

[34] Kellogg, "Notes, May 17 to June 9, 1876 of the Little Big Horn Expedition," 217–18.

[35] *Ibid.*, 219.

Major Moore, who was at Stanley's Stockade. He reported that the supply steamers, *Far West* and *Josephine*, had reached their destination and that the latter had already discharged its cargo and left the river, but that the former was at the stockade and would remain there until the Dakota column arrived. News that there were no hostiles between Beaver Creek and the Yellowstone and that the latter stream was full of water and easily navigable by steamers caused General Terry to abandon his decision to march to the mouth of Glendive Creek and to decide instead to move southward up Beaver Creek, then westward across the divide to the mouth of the Powder River. The Indians having been located, orders were sent to Gibbon to halt the eastward movement of his command and remain where he was until further orders. Instructions were also sent to Major Moore. He was to move a boatload of supplies from Stanley's Stockade to a new depot to be established at the junction of the Yellowstone and Powder rivers.[36]

That day the column made a very circuitous march, and the heat was so intense that General Terry suffered a sunstroke. Camp was made on Stanley's campground of 1872, and the next morning the column moved up Beaver Creek.[37] For two days they marched along that stream and then struck directly west. On and on they went and about noon on the third day passed Cabin Creek,[38] where the narrowness of the valley, the steepness of the descent, and the soft alkaline nature of the soil, complicated by deep washouts, provided the hardest going of the entire trip. After worrying through these Bad Lands, they finally reached a beautiful rolling country with fine grass.[39] During the day fresh buffalo and Indian signs were seen, but two of Benteen's men who went hunting got lost and remained in the Bad Lands overnight. Their absence caused some alarm and led to the issuance of an order against hunting parties.[40]

36 *Ibid.*, 219. Terry's Report, 460; *New York Herald*, June 27, 1876. Stanley's Stockade was located on the right bank of Yellowstone River some distance above the mouth of Glendive Creek.

37 Kellogg, "Notes, May 17 to June 9, 1876 of the Little Big Horn Expedition," in *Contributions to the Historical Society of Montana*, IX (1923), 219; Godfrey, "Diary," n.p.

38 Kellogg, "Notes, May 17 to June 9, 1876 of the Little Big Horn Expedition," in *Contributions to the Historical Society of Montana*, IX (1923), 220.

39 Godfrey, "Diary," n.p.

40 Maguire's Report, 1345.

On June 6 the command reached O'Fallon's Creek, a running stream with standing pools of water, which the Indians knew by the picturesque name of "Where the Woman Broke Her Leg," but still without finding any trace of their quarry. They had seen but few Indians—indeed, few traces of any—but they knew from the information sent by Colonel Gibbon that every mile they passed without trace of the hostiles increased by that much the possibility that the next mile would reveal them. From that night's camp on the south fork of O'Fallon's Creek the troops could see the hills which border the Powder River. The next day they crossed the divide between the two streams, moving through territory never before traversed by white men, and which few, if any, whites had ever seen before. It was very rough going, and the country, barren and uninteresting, appeared to be absolutely worthless. Here "Lonesome Charley" Reynolds, who was guiding, got lost, and Custer, who was "a born pathfinder, better even than Frémont,"[41] putting his "bump of locality" to use, found the only practicable route for miles on either side.[42] The descent to the valley of the Powder was a difficult and dangerous task, but after a march of thirty-two miles they camped on that stream about twenty miles from its mouth, Custer at 3:30 P.M.; Terry and the head of the column one and one-half hours later; and the rear of the column at eight o'clock in the evening.[43] Custer, who had scouted ahead with Weir's troop, had ridden over fifty miles during the day. Everyone was tired out—the stock completely so—and during the day several horses and mules had dropped out of the teams.[44]

The Powder River, located in the eastern part of the present Montana, has been called by one newspaper correspondent "the filthiest stream in America or elsewhere"; it is described as being "too thick to drink and too thin to plow" and also as "four hundred miles long, a mile wide, and an inch deep."[45] In its upper reaches

[41] Cyrus Townsend Brady, "War with the Sioux," *Pearson's Magazine*, Vol. XII (August, 1904), 171. However, Stanley Vestal says that the Indians applied this name to Mizpah Creek. Vestal, *Sitting Bull*, 131.

[42] Custer, *Boots and Saddles*, 307–308.

[43] Maguire's Report, 1345.

[44] Kellogg, "Notes, May 17 to June 9, 1876 of the Little Big Horn Expedition," in *Contributions to the Historical Society of Montana*, IX (1923), 221.

[45] John F. Finerty, *Warpath and Bivouac*, 233; *Montana Guide Book*, 367.

it is a stream of deep and narrow canyons fringed with cottonwood, ash, and various kinds of berry bushes which give fine protection against the winds of winter and made it another favorite camping place of the Sioux. The first white man to visit it was apparently Captain Clark in 1806, who called it the Red Stone River, but the name Powder is more appropriate, not because of the yellowish color of the water, as so many have supposed, but from the dark powder-like sand along its banks.

At the campsite the stream was only about two hundred feet wide and from two to three feet deep, but the problem of fording it was complicated by the fact that the bottom alternated between firm gravel and treacherous quicksand. General Terry decided to remain in camp there for a few days and rest the much-marched command while he decided upon the next step.[46]

Scouts sent to the mouth of the river the day before returned on the morning of the eighth, bringing mail and the news that Gibbon's couriers had not been able to return to him, having been driven back by the hostiles. The scouts also reported an encounter with four of the Sioux, who had run away upon seeing them.[47] That afternoon Terry, accompanied by Troop A under Moylan and Troop I under Keogh, proceeded to the mouth of the Powder. Here they found, as Terry knew they would, the river steamer, *Far West*, which had been chartered to carry supplies to the expedition.

This boat, one of the best known in western history, had been built in 1870 for the Coulsons in Pittsburgh. She was 190 feet long with a beam of 33 feet, 6 inches. Motive power was provided by two 15-inch diameter engines of 5-foot piston stroke. In addition, there were two steam capstans, one on each side of the bow, designed to help in negotiating rapids and other shallow places in the stream. This was an innovation at a time when most river steamers had only one capstan. Thirty passengers were all that her cabin could accommodate, and the absence of a large cabin and consequent lack of a "texas" (officers' quarters) resulted in a superstructure that

This description is given on a state historical marker on U. S. Highway 10, not far from the mouth of the Powder River.

46 Maguire's Report, 1346.

47 Kellogg, "Notes, May 17 to June 9, 1876 of the Little Big Horn Expedition," in *Contributions to the Historical Society of Montana,* IX (1923), 221.

offered little resistance to the wind and made the *Far West* a very manageable craft in the high winds which often prevailed in the Dakota and Montana country. Light, strong, and speedy, she was eminently a vessel for hard and continuous service, well deserving her reputation:

As speedy a craft as the river'd float,
She could buck the bends like a big horn goat.

As interesting as the boat was her captain, Grant Marsh, who until then was the only river captain to navigate the waters of the upper Yellowstone. Said to have known every foot of the river like most men know their own backyards, he was reputed to be able to navigate the *Far West* on a heavy dew, and to take her anyplace where there was enough water to keep her bottom damp.

The steamer had been laid up for the winter at Yankton. It had started upstream about the middle of May, loaded to capacity with government stores. Arriving at Fort Abraham Lincoln on the twenty-seventh, nearly twenty-four hours were spent in loading and transferring cargo, and then she sailed upstream for Stanley's Stockade. On board were two hundred tons of new cargo, including forage, commissary goods, medicines, ammunition, and general quartermaster supplies, for the wagon train had carried only enough supplies to last the Dakota column to the mouth of the Powder. At the fort Mrs. Custer and Mrs. Calhoun had asked to be taken along as passengers, but Marsh had wisely—so subsequent events proved—refused to accede to their request.

At Stanley's Stockade at the mouth of Glendive Creek, Marsh found Major Orlando Moore and three companies of the Sixth Infantry who had marched overland from Fort Buford. After landing some supplies, the *Far West* steamed for the mouth of the Powder to establish communication with the Dakota column. It arrived there on June 7.[48]

[48] The description of the *Far West* is summarized from that in Hanson, *Conquest of the Missouri*, 237–42. There is also some material in McLaughlin, *My Friend, the Indian*, 126–27. Grant Marsh was one of the legendary figures of the Yellowstone River region, and colorful stories about him are the proverbial "dime a dozen." There is some disagreement over whether it was Mrs. Calhoun or Mrs. Algernon Smith who requested, along with Mrs. Custer, to go along as a passenger. Both may have made the request.

Only a few hours later several skiffs were discovered floating downstream. This occasioned some alarm at first, but it disappeared when they were found to be manned by Major Brisbin, Captain Clifford, and the men of Company E of the Seventh Infantry. The next morning, General Terry and his staff arrived. Orders were immediately sent to Major Moore that all supplies be transferred from the stockade to the temporary base camp to be established at the mouth of the Powder, and to Colonel Gibbon directing him to move downstream for a conference with the other commanders.[49]

At the conference, General Terry, after listening to Gibbon's report regarding the encounters of his command with the hostiles and to his theory that the Indians were probably either on the Tongue River or on Rosebud Creek, announced his intention of thoroughly scouting the upper reaches of both the Tongue and Powder rivers before moving any farther west. This was not necessarily because he disbelieved what Gibbon had told him or because he in any way doubted the latter's ability to discover the whereabouts of the enemy, but because he wanted to clear the region of any small detached bands which might be lurking away from the larger village located farther west.[50] Another reason for the scout was to communicate, if possible, with General Crook, who, it was believed, might have reached the mouth of the Little Powder River.[51]

In order to aid in the projected reconnaissance, General Gibbon contributed the services of his famous half-blood scout, "Mitch" Bouyer, who went downstream with Terry on the *Far West*.[52] The Department commander and his escort companies rejoined the regiment on the morning of the tenth to find that during their absence all preparations for the projected cavalry scout had been made. At three o'clock that afternoon, with Bouyer as guide and accompanied by a contingent of the Arikara scouts, Major Reno set out with the six troops composing the right wing of the regiment, a Gatling gun and its crew under Lieutenant Kenzie, and a mule train of eleven mules per troop, to comb the Montana badlands for

49 Terry's Report, 461.

50 *New York Herald*, June 27, 1876.

51 *New York Herald*, June 27, 1876; *Army and Navy Journal*, July 15, 1876; Bates, *Custer's Indian Battles*, 29.

52 Gibbon, "Summer Expedition," 290.

traces of the hostiles. They had rations and forage for ten days and were under orders to proceed from the camp to the mouth of the Little Powder, then cross to the headwaters of Mizpah Creek, go down that stream almost to its junction with the Powder, then turn westward to Pumpkin Creek and follow it to its confluence with Tongue River. The scouting detail was then to descend the Tongue to its confluence with the Yellowstone. The detachment was not to go as far west as the Rosebud.[53] Although it was not expected that they would encounter any Indians, this course was to be followed unless some discovery should make a quicker return advisable in order to make plans for action and pursuit. It was expected that Terry, Custer, and the remainder of the command would be waiting at the mouth of the Tongue.

There is reason to believe that Custer was very much disappointed at not being selected to lead this reconnaissance in person and that he protested to Terry in no uncertain terms;[54] the matter became a subject of gossip among the officers, who, as Godfrey admits, were "unable to arrive at a satisfactory solution."[55] Terry remained adamant in his choice, possibly because Custer had led the scout up the Missouri River only a short time before, and also because the commander wished to divide both assignments and responsibility as well as to avoid any appearance of favoritism.

Although Major Reno seems to have believed that the main body of the hostiles would be found on the Powder River, his opinion was not shared by Custer or by many of the other officers, most of whom were opposed to the Reno scout. They believed that it was nothing but a "wild goose chase" and that the main hostile village would be found on the Rosebud or the Little Big Horn River. They also felt that the only result of the scout would be to keep the remainder of the regiment in idleness within a two days' march of where the main body of the Sioux could be found. But the greatest objection to the scout, in their opinion, was the danger that the hostiles—ever on the alert—might thus be made aware of the nearness of the punitive expedition.[56]

[53] Terry's Report, 461; *New York Herald*, June 27, 1876; *ibid.*, July 11, 1876; Bates, *Custer's Indian Battles*, 29; Coughlan, "The Battle of the Little Big Horn," *Cavalry Journal*, Vol. XLIII (January–February, 1934), 14–15.

[54] Dustin, *The Custer Fight*, 7.

[55] Godfrey, "Diary," n.p.

The *Far West* had been ordered back to Stanley's Stockade to transfer the supplies stored there to the mouth of the Powder, and Major Moore was ordered to move his troops to the same point. These orders had been carried into execution by June 15, and Grant Marsh and his steamer then stood by for further duty.[57]

In the meantime, Gibbon's much-marched command was again set in motion, this time retracing its route to a point opposite the mouth of Rosebud Creek. The remainder of the Terry command marched for the mouth of the Powder. The route which the commander had taken two days before was too rough for the wagons, and a new one had to be found. A detachment was sent out to discover a practicable road, but only succeeded in getting lost. At five o'clock on the morning of the eleventh, the command, with Custer as its guide, broke camp and started for the Yellowstone. For the first five miles the road was very rough, but Custer with his marvelous sense of topography soon discovered a good wagon route lying along the second bench above the stream. This route consisted of three successive plateaus, each between three and four miles in length and separated by alkaline creeks, whose soft and steep banks provided the only obstacles to the march. Since most of the officers, men, and mules alike had had no experience with transportation by muleback because no train of pack mules had ever been organized in the department,[58] advantage was taken of the opportunity for practical instruction in the art; as a result, Godfrey's troop, which constituted the rear guard, was often as much as three miles behind the rest of the command owing to difficulties with the packs. About ten o'clock Custer found the lost detachment of the day before which had spent the night in the Bad Lands, and the reunited command camped that night on the bank of the Yellowstone,[59] their twentieth camp since leaving Fort Lincoln and almost due west from that point. Since May 17 they had covered 318 miles, for an average of 15.9 miles a day.

From here Terry reported to Sheridan:

No Indians east of the Powder. Reno with six companies is now

[56] *New York Herald*, July 11, 1876.

[57] Terry's Report, 460–61; Hanson, *The Conquest of the Missouri*, 243.

[58] Terry's Report, 460; Godfrey, *Century*, 362.

[59] Godfrey, *Century*, 362; Custer, *Boots and Saddles*, 309.

well up the river on his way to the Forks, whence he will cross to and come down Mizpah creek, and thence by Pumpkin creek to Tongue river where I hope to meet him with the rest of the cavalry and fresh supplies. I intend then if nothing new is developed, to send Custer with nine companies of his regiment up the Tongue and then across to and down the Rosebud while the rest of the Seventh will join Gibbon and move up the Rosebud. Have met Gibbon and concerted movements with him.[60]

Following the return of the scouting party, it was expected that Custer, with nine troops selected from his own regiment, rationed for fifteen days, and accompanied by the scouts and a pack train, would start up Tongue River Valley, then move quickly across to the Rosebud and down that stream toward the Yellowstone. In the meantime, General Terry with the remaining three troops of the Seventh Cavalry would scout from the Tongue to the mouth of Rosebud Creek, and then, accompanied by Brisbin's four troops, would move upstream to a junction with Custer's command. This maneuver was expected to result in either a fight or a foot race, and the only question was whether Sitting Bull would "sit" long enough to allow the troops to close the trap around him.[61]

The ground at the mouth of the Powder was extremely soft and badly cut by ravines. Moreover, it abounded in sagebrush, cactus, and rattlesnakes. After much difficulty in finding a spot sufficiently firm, General Terry ordered the construction of a base camp, which, under the circumstances, was to prove almost worthless. This was not apparent at the time, however, and there was much more to the plan than a mere desire to keep the soldiers busy at something that might be considered useful. A trader, or sutler, by the name of James Coleman had come up on the *Far West* and now set up a tent and began selling whiskey to both officers and men. While Coleman acted as bartender, a man named John Smith seems to have been in charge.[62] A partition of canned goods separated the enlisted men from the officers, but prices were the same for all, one dollar a pint, and canteens which held three pints were filled only on an order from the captain. There was no guardhouse, and the drunk and dis-

[60] 44 Cong., 1 sess., *House Exec. Doc. 184*, 57; *New York Herald*, July 11, 1876.
[61] *New York Herald*, June 27, 1876; *Ibid.*, July 11, 1876.
[62] Dustin, *The Custer Tragedy*, 128.

orderly were simply herded out on the open prairie. As the men had been paid after leaving Fort Lincoln and had had little opportunity to spend their money, Coleman did a thriving business. Coleman, dark and swarthy, resembled an Arikara—so much so that the scouts dubbed him "Arrow Feathered with Crow Feathers."[63] It is largely from this sale of liquor to the troops that the stories that Custer's command was intoxicated at the Battle of the Little Big Horn have originated.

At this camp on the Powder, the Seventh Cavalry stripped for action. The infantry was to remain as camp guard under the command of Major Moore. Left also was the wagon train, and from now on the regiment would be serviced by a pack train, much to Custer's satisfaction, for he preferred the more mobile mules to the slower moving wagons. All nonessentials were to be discarded, and from now on the regiment would be traveling "light." Left behind were Custer's hunting dogs,[64] and officers and men alike gave up their sabers, which were packed in wooden boxes and stored. The movies to the contrary, there was not a single sword or saber in the Seventh Cavalry at the subsequent battle. This decision was probably attributable to the fact that sabers were of little use in Indian fighting since the Indians generally scattered when charged by cavalry. Although experienced army officers seldom took sabers into an Indian fight,[65] there are those who believe that this decision was a great mistake because the Sioux had such a horror of the "long knife" that it was too effective a threat to have been so casually left behind. The regimental band stayed behind, but Custer took their horses for remounts. The regiment had started from Fort Lincoln with between 85 and 110 dismounted men, most of them recruits, who had marched all the way to the Powder River, where it was expected that horses would be found. No horses were there, and the unmounted men, for the most part, remained behind, a course of action that was perfectly agreeable to the recruits, who, with sore and blistered feet, were glad for the opportunity to rest and recuperate. Ten or twelve members of the noncommissioned staff

[63] Libby, *Arikara Narrative*, 71.

[64] Edward S. Godfrey, "Letter to E. S. Paxson, painter, June 16, 1896," in Albart J. Partoll, "After the Custer Battle," *Frontier and Midland*, Vol. XIX, No. 4 (1938–39), 277.

[65] *Official Transcript*, 91, 238; Vestal, *Warpath and Council Fire*, 263.

were also left, and their horses, together with those of the band, furnished mounts for a few of the dismounted. Two recruits were in Company K when it left the mouth of the Powder River, and it is doubtful if any of the other companies had any more than that. Eight of the Indian scouts also stayed at the base camp because their horses were badly galled or otherwise out of condition.[66]

These arrangements completed, Custer, with the six troops of the left wing, the remaining Gatlings and their crews, the scouts and the pack train, marched for the mouth of the Tongue River on the morning of Friday, June 16, keeping about four or five miles back from the river. As the regiment marched out, the band from a convenient bluff serenaded the departing troops with a medley of martial airs, concluding with the regimental song, "Garry Owen."[67]

The terrain over which they passed was so rough that, although the members of the command were rested and in good condition, they made only about twenty-eight miles the first day and did not arrive at their destination until about midmorning of the seventeenth, although the total distance between the Powder and the Tongue is only about forty miles.[68] A part of the responsibility for their slow progress must be assigned to the pack mules, which continued to display the unmanageableness that was to characterize them throughout the entire campaign and to justify Godfrey's assertion that it is always the unexpected that happens with a mule. On the march the command passed the remains of several large abandoned Indian villages, none of which gave any signs of recent occupancy, although one of them, which was over two miles in length and had consisted of from twelve to fifteen hundred lodges, was estimated to be less than a year old.[69] On the site where Miles City was later to be established they found a Sioux camp which gave every indication of occupancy during the winter just passed, and whose rude shelters furnished fuel for the soldiers' campfires.[70] Here

66 Schultz, *William Jackson*, 426; James P. Murphy, "The Campaign of the Little Big Horn," *Infantry Journal*, Vol. XXXIV (June, 1929), 639; W. J. Ghent, "Varnum, Reno and the Little Big Horn," *Winners of the West*, April 30, 1936; Roy Johnson, "Jacob Horner of the Seventh Cavalry," *North Dakota History*, Vol. XVI (April, 1949), 82–83.

67 Godfrey, "Diary," n.p.

68 Terry's Report, 461.

69 *New York Herald*, July 11, 1876.

70 Godfrey, *Century*, 362; *New York Herald*, July 11, 1876.

under the ashes of an ancient fire they found the bones and skull[71] of a soldier, with buttons from his uniform indicating that he had been attached to a cavalry regiment. The signs indicated that he had died under torture. Custer stood silent for several moments looking down at the remains. On August 4, 1873, two troops of the Seventh had had a brush with the Sioux near this spot and had had one trooper reported missing and presumably killed; these may or may not have been his remains.

The troops also found a Sioux burial scaffold with the uprights colored alternately black and red, indicating that the occupant had been a very brave man. In some mysterious way this had escaped the earlier attentions of the Crows.[72] At Custer's direction the scaffold was taken down, and Dorman, the Negro interpreter, took the wrappings off the body. On the scaffold were rawhide bags, horn spoons, and partly finished moccasins, which officers and men claimed as souvenirs. Dorman threw the body in the river, and when he was later seen fishing at that same spot the Arikaras not unnaturally suspected that he was using the corpse as bait.[73]

At a spot two miles below the mouth of the Tongue, the battalions went into camp to await the return of Reno's scouting party. Coleman again set up shop, and Custer wrote what was to be his last article for the *Galaxy*.[74]

Up to this time the command had not seen an Indian that they could definitely identify as hostile; indeed, they had found few recent signs of any Indians at all. From all evidence that they had discovered the regiment would have been justified in regarding the red man as having belonged to a pre-existent race.[75] Some members of the command were of the opinion that they were on a "wild-goose chase," that the mere presence of the troops had been enough to persuade the erstwhile "hostiles" that peace was the best policy, and that even now they were making all possible haste to get back

[71] According to an account in the Custer Scrapbooks in the Billings Public Library, this skull was given to Major J. H. Brown for safe keeping. Its ultimate disposition is unknown.

[72] At the mouth of the Powder River there were a number of dead Indians on scaffolds and in trees. Godfrey, *Century*, 362.

[73] Libby, *Arikara Narrative*, 76.

[74] Godfrey, *Century*, 362.

[75] *New York Herald*, June 19, 1876.

to the reservations. Events would soon tell how badly mistaken they were.

The command waited at the mouth of the Tongue. Finally, on the nineteenth, two scouts came in with the news that the detachment under Major Reno was at the mouth of the Rosebud and marching toward Tongue River.

CHAPTER XI

Up the Rosebud

THOSE OFFICERS who expected a short campaign, in the belief that the very magnitude of the preparations against them had frightened the hostile tribes back to the agencies, were destined to have their hopes rudely shattered. For, on the afternoon of Sunday, June 18, Major Reno and his detachment returned from their scouting expedition, coming out at the mouth of Rosebud Creek instead of at the confluence of the Tongue and Yellowstone rivers as General Terry had specifically ordered. Reno immediately sent a courier to the Department commander, who, with Custer and the other six companies of the regiment, was waiting at the appointed meeting place, thirty-five miles away, stating that he was marching for the mouth of Tongue River.

Colonel Gibbon's command was in camp on the north bank of the Yellowstone opposite the mouth of the Rosebud. After identifying the detachment, he sent a Crow messenger across the stream with dispatches for Major Reno after the white scout Bostwick had attempted the crossing and failed, because of an attack of cramps. The Crow, after tying the message in his scalp lock and painting his body red as a protection against alligators—proof of the southern origin of the Crows as well as illustration of the way in which traditions perpetuate themselves after all reason for their existence has disappeared—swam the stream buoyed up by a piece of dry wood. As it turned out, the trip was unnecessary, for while it was being made some of Gibbon's officers improvised a signal flag from a handkerchief and a stick of wood, and using the army code of signals, secured the information that Colonel Gibbon wanted.[1]

[1] Marquis, *Memoirs of a White Crow Indian*, 238; Bradley, *Journal*, 214; Gibbon, "Summer Expedition," 290–91; McClernand, "With Indian and Buffalo in Montana," *Cavalry Journal*, Vol. XXXVI (January and April, 1927), 14–15.

The news of Reno's return reached General Terry about sunset of the next day. That he was thoroughly nettled by what he considered flagrant disobedience of orders is to state the case too mildly. Terry later wrote to his sisters that Reno "had done this in positive defiance of my orders not to go to the Rosebud, in the belief that there were Indians on that stream and that he could make a successful attack on them which would cover up his disobedience. . . . He had not the supplies to enable him to go far and he returned without justification. Of course this performance made a change in my plans necessary."[2] At the time, however, Terry contented himself with sending a peremptory note to Major Reno, ordering him to remain where he was and rest his animals. Custer, with the left wing, crossed Tongue River about three miles above its mouth and marched toward the Rosebud, while Terry and his staff went upstream on the steamer. Much of Custer's route was over "bad lands" in the extreme sense of that term, with ascents and descents so steep as to appear impassable, and the command alternately rode through deep, abrupt canyons and along narrow defiles.[3] The regiment was reunited on the evening of the twentieth and bivouacked together two miles below the mouth of Rosebud Creek about noon on the twenty-first. As they rode down from the bluffs to the Yellowstone, they could see the four troops of the Second Cavalry marching up the opposite bank.[4]

The news that Reno brought back furnished ample material for speculation and conversation among the officers and men. The scouting party reported that there were no hostile Indians on the Powder River nor on the upper reaches of the Tongue nor in the valley of the Rosebud, but that in the last named they had found a great Indian trail more than half a mile wide made by thousands of trailing lodgepoles. The trail led upstream and merely indicated the truth of what nearly everyone had suspected, that the Indians were moving up the Rosebud preparatory to crossing the Little Chetish or Wolf Mountains into the valley of the Little Big Horn. The news contributed nothing to General Terry's understanding of

[2] Bates, *Custer's Indian Battles*, 29; Hughes, "Campaign against the Sioux in 1876," *Journal of the Military Service Institution of the United States*, Vol. XVIII (January, 1896), 20; *Billings Gazette*, June 23, 1936.

[3] *New York Herald*, July 11, 1876.

[4] Godfrey, "Diary," n.p.

the situation, since he had been aware of this movement from the reports of Lieutenant Bradley and the Crow scouts before Reno left on his expedition.[5]

The itinerary of Reno's trip was kept by Lieutenant Sturgis and was apparently on his person when he was killed on the twenty-fifth, so that we do not have a detailed account of the movements of Reno's command. Lieutenant Kenzie, who was in command of the Gatling gun detachment, was also supposed to keep a daily account of the march, but the country traversed was so rough that he had all he could do to keep up with the cavalry and so kept no records.[6] However, it is not difficult to trace the probable movements of the scouting party if we remember that "Mitch" Bouyer was with them, for Bouyer knew where the hostile Indians were, since he and Lieutenant Bradley had seen the great Indian village about eighteen miles from the mouth of the Rosebud weeks before, and the fact that Major Reno found the trail when and where he did was probably due to a suggestion from Bouyer that he could show the Major plenty of Indians. Whether Reno did or did not carry out General Terry's instructions to determine whether any of the hostiles had slipped away to the east we have no means of knowing, nor are we safe in assuming that he had satisfied himself that the great body of the Sioux were moving westward before following the course that he did.[7] Nevertheless, he apparently saw no Indians, and there is no evidence whatever to indicate that he heard anything at all about General Crook's command.[8]

Bouyer seems to have led the command from the forks of the Powder across the Tongue and into the valley of the Rosebud, striking it two or three miles below the site of the deserted Indian village.[9] From that point the Arikara scouts were sent out, and from a hill one of them, Young Hawk, discovered the abandoned camp with birds flying over it and a horse standing near by. From the

[5] Coughlan, "The Battle of the Little Big Horn," *Cavalry Journal*, Vol. XLIII (January–February, 1934), 14; Dustin, *The Custer Fight*, 7.

[6] Maguire's Report, 1346.

[7] Critical of Reno's conduct is Sheridan's *Report*, 443, and Hughes, "Campaign against the Sioux in 1876," *Journal of the Military Service Institution of the United States*, Vol. XVIII (January, 1896), 22. Dustin defends Reno, however. See Dustin, *The Custer Fight*, 7, and Dustin, *The Custer Tragedy*, 60–61.

[8] *New York Herald*, July 8, 1876.

[9] Brown and Willard, *Black Hills Trails*, 140.

meat scaffolds and the arrangement of the tepees the Arikaras knew it was a Sioux camp, and from the number of fires they estimated that the village had contained some 360 lodges and probably upwards of 800 warriors.[10] Bouyer is said to have counted 360 lodge fires arranged in nine circles, all within supporting distance of each other. There was evidence, also, to indicate that the pony herd had been driven inside the circles at night, showing that an attack was expected and that the hostiles were prepared to meet it.[11]

There was considerable doubt concerning just how recently the camp had been occupied, and it was this uncertainty that was apparently responsible for Reno's failure to return immediately to the camp on the Yellowstone. His men made camp near the site of the village, and the next day moved upstream, following the Indian trail to the vicinity of what is now the village of Lee, Montana. Here the scouts found an entrenchment where a party of whites had had a fight with the Indians two years before and evidence that several of the whites had been killed. The trail was so wide and the ground so torn up by the trailing lodgepoles that the troops found a suitable camping place only with difficulty.[12] Reno is said to have asked Forked Horn, who was the leader of the scouts, what he thought of the trail. The Arikara answered that if the command was discovered by the Sioux "the sun will not move very far before we are all killed. But you are the leader and we will go on if you say."[13]

Reno apparently followed the trail for a day and a half until he reached a point some thirty or forty miles above the mouth of the Rosebud. Rations were running low, and since his orders were to turn back if he found an Indian trail, he apparently concluded that discretion was the better part of valor and so decided not to go any farther but to return to the base camp without delay.[14] Although he is generally believed to have turned back on June 17, the same day that General Crook was fighting the Indians on the upper

[10] Libby, *Arikara Narrative*, 70.

[11] DeLand, *The Sioux Wars*, 345.

[12] Brown and Willard, *Black Hills Trails*, 141. Lieutenant Godfrey thought that the trail was at least three weeks old. *Century*, 363.

[13] Libby, *Arikara Narrative*, 70–71.

[14] Daniel A. Kanipe, "A New Story of Custer's Last Battle," in *Contributions to the Historical Society of Montana*, IV (1903), 278.

Rosebud, the exact date is by no means certain. Since he arrived at the mouth of the Rosebud on the afternoon of the eighteenth, it is possible that he reached his highest position on the sixteenth, the day before Crook's fight on the Rosebud.[15]

Reno's detachment had covered some 240 miles or more, traveling over some very rough country with an average march of better than 25 miles a day, and the horses, men, and especially the pack mules were, as General Terry noted, tired and badly spent, a fact which was destined to be of great importance later on. Reno's report plus all the other information Terry had, including a recent report from the Crow scouts with General Gibbon that they had seen smoke in the valley of the Little Big Horn, made it seem probable that the hostiles would be found somewhere on the banks of that stream. The decision regarding the next move was now up to General Terry.

The Department commander, in common with most of the officers, seems to have been disgusted with Reno's actions and to have told the Major in unmistakable terms that he considered his conduct to be a violation of specific orders, and the possibility of a court-martial was strongly hinted.[16] Custer was even more outspoken, but he criticized his subordinate for not pursuing and attacking the hostile force, an action which would have constituted a further and more serious violation of orders. It was reported among the troops that Custer had upbraided Reno severely for not at least finding out the number of the Indians and the direction in which they were moving, instead of supposing and guessing. There were said to have been some sharp questions and short answers before Terry intervened.[17]

That Custer was very much disturbed by what he considered the failure of his subordinate cannot be doubted, for he wrote to his wife that Reno had found the trail of a village of about 380 lodges which was not over a week old, and that the scouts reported that

[15] For Reno's itinerary see Brown and Willard, *Black Hills Trails*, 140; *New York Herald*, July 8, 1876; McLaughlin, *My Friend, the Indian*, 126; Dustin, *The Custer Tragedy*, 62; Daniel A. Kanipe, "New Story of the Custer Battle," *Contributions to the Historical Society of Montana*, IV (1903), 278.

[16] *New York Herald*, July 11, 1876; Dustin, *The Custer Tragedy*, 62.

[17] Brown and Willard, *Black Hills Trails*, 143; Dustin, *The Custer Tragedy*, 62–63.

the hostiles could have been overtaken in one and one-half days.[18] The *New York Herald* quoted him as saying: "Few officers have ever had so fine an opportunity to make a successful and telling strike, and few have ever so completely failed to improve their opportunity."[19] Custer felt that, in addition to losing valuable time, Reno's failure had imperiled the success of the whole enterprise by giving the hostiles an intimation of the presence of the troops.[20]

What Custer and Reno did not know was that, with only one or two minor changes of circumstance, the Major might have made contact with the Indians. The hostile tribes knew that there were soldiers in the valley of the Rosebud and were watching for them when they learned of the approach of General Crook's command. The hostiles' camp was not too many miles to the west and south of Reno when he reached his highest point on the Rosebud. Not all of the warriors had gone to fight Crook, but how many remained in camp is, of course, uncertain. The attention of the Sioux and Cheyennes was focused on General Crook, but in view of the fact that the Indians always had hunting parties out, and also that there was a vast amount of miscellaneous roaming around and visiting, it must be accounted at least one of the minor miracles of western history that neither Reno nor the hostiles discovered the proximity of the other. Had Reno been discovered, or had he attacked the village as Custer felt he should have done, he might have struck and destroyed the greatly weakened village, or he might have led his command into ambush and massacre. Here again, as in so many other cases, it is difficult enough to know what actually happened without trying to ascertain what might have happened had things been different.

The reports convinced General Terry that the hostile tribes were moving toward the valley of the Little Big Horn. Also pointing in this direction was the fact that the large Crow village which had been located for several weeks on the Big Horn River had completely disappeared, sure evidence that the Sioux were headed that

[18] Custer, *Boots and Saddles*, 312; *New York Herald*, July 8, 1876; *Army and Navy Journal*, July 15, 1876. Bouyer is said to have believed that the Indians could have been overtaken in one day's march. Brown and Willard, *Black Hills Trails*, 142.

[19] *New York Herald*, June 11, 1876.

[20] Custer, *Boots and Saddles*, 312.

way and in considerable force.[21] It was also evident that the hostiles had no immediate intention of crossing to the north bank of the Yellowstone, or they would not go so far upstream.[22]

Terry wasted no time in vain regrets for what might have been. Having set the Seventh Cavalry in motion toward the mouth of the Rosebud, he started for Gibbon's camp on the north bank of the Yellowstone, but that commander, anticipating that a movement upstream would be ordered, had taken the necessary preliminary steps; on Terry's arrival the entire command was started toward a point opposite the mouth of the Big Horn, and was under way before Custer had reached his camp on the south side. Only Gibbon and Brisbin remained behind for a conference with Custer and Terry.[23]

Sometime during the morning, General Terry sent off a telegram to General Sheridan in Chicago which shows that the main outline of the strategy to be pursued had already been decided upon:

> No Indians have been met with as yet; but traces of a large and recent camp have been discovered twenty or thirty miles up the Rosebud. Gibbon's column will move this morning on the north side of the Yellowstone for the mouth of the Big Horn where it will be ferried across by the supply steamer, and thence it will proceed to the mouth of the Little Horn and so on.
>
> Custer will go up the Rosebud tomorrow with his whole regiment and thence to the headwaters and thence down the Little Horn.

The dispatch closed with the words: "I only hope that one of the two columns will find the Indians. I go personally with Gibbon." It should be noted that there was no word of any plan to have the two columns meet at any place or at any time, which was in accordance with Sheridan's idea that it was an absurdity to expect co-operation in such open and broken country, especially since each column was believed able to take care of itself if it met the Indians.[24]

21 DeLand, *The Sioux Wars*, 345; Hughes, "Campaign against the Sioux in 1876," *Journal of the Military Service Institution of the United States*, Vol. XVIII (January, 1896), 36.

22 Bradley, *Journal*, 214.

23 *Ibid.*, 214–15.

24 Old-timers of the region always referred to it as the Little Horn River. John K. Rollinson, "Brands of the Eighties and Nineties in the Big Horn Basin, Wyoming Territory," *Annals of Wyoming*, XIX (July, 1947), 65. For the details

In what was to be his last dispatch, Kellogg wrote:

> . . . tomorrow, June 22nd, General Custer with twelve cavalry companies will scout from its mouth up the valley of the Rosebud until he reaches the fresh trail discovered by Major Reno, and move on that trail with all the rapidity possible in order to overhaul the Indians whom it has been ascertained are hunting buffalo and making daily and leisurely short marches. Gibbon's part of the command will march up the Big Horn valley in order to intercept the Indians if they should attempt to escape from General Custer down that avenue.[25]

Later on that day, Terry held a council of war with Gibbon and Custer, at which Brisbin and some of the members of the General's staff were present. Just what happened at this conference we shall never know, for Custer's lips were soon sealed forever, and the accounts of the surviving participants are not entirely satisfactory, since they are marked by attempted justification of their subsequent actions. It is certain, however, that General Terry outlined in considerable detail the strategy which he had already decided to adopt, and concerning which he had wired Sheridan, strategy which he hoped would bring about the capitulation if not the annihilation of the Sioux Nation.[26] Since his idea was to get the hostile Indians between the two detachments of his command and thus force them to fight, it was arranged that Gibbon's command, after being ferried to the south bank of the Yellowstone at the mouth of the Big Horn, would move southward after first scouting the lower reaches of Tullock's Creek. This stream was a convenient route for the tribesmen traveling north and south through the Big Horn country, and might possibly be utilized by the hostiles. It was believed that the infantry would be able to march rapidly across the tablelands which separate Tullock's Creek from the Big Horn River since it was a fairly easy route and would also be shorter than the one which followed the course of the river. In the mean-

---

of Terry's plan see *New York Herald*, July 7, 1876; Bates, *Custer's Indian Battles*, 31; and Godfrey, *Montana*, 209. Colonel Hughes was of the opinion that the general features of the plan were clear in General Terry's mind before the regiment left Fort Lincoln, "Campaign against the Sioux in 1876," *Journal of the Military Service Institution of the United States*, Vol. XVIII (January, 1896), 36.

[25] *New York Herald*, July 11, 1876.

[26] Terry's Report, 461.

time Captain Grant Marsh was to push the steamer up the Big Horn as far as the mouth of the Little Big Horn if the river were found to be navigable for that distance. Captain Baker's company of the Sixth Infantry was to remain as a guard on board the steamer.[27]

Custer was not to press his march too rapidly and was also to scout the upper reaches of Tullock's Creek where the Crow scouts had reported seeing smoke. He was also to keep constantly feeling to the left in order to prevent the hostiles from escaping south and east around his flank. If the Sioux became aware of the troops and tried to run away, it was expected that they would go south toward the Big Horn Mountains. Custer would be moving in from the east, the Sioux knew of Gibbon's command to the north, and the west was closed to them since it was the home of their traditional enemies, the Crows.

Not only did the Big Horn Mountains furnish the Sioux's only avenue of escape, but once the Indians reached there, scattering and concealment would be easy, and the army would have the difficult task of rounding them up to do all over again. Therefore, General Terry suggested that if the trail seemed to turn westward and lead across the Wolf Mountains into the valley of the Little Big Horn—and he expected that it would—Custer should not follow it, but instead move farther south *toward* the headwaters of the Tongue River before turning west and north. The idea apparently was to give Gibbon's slower-moving infantry ample time to get into position, for he would need at least a day longer to reach any place on the Little Big Horn than would Custer. In this way Custer would also be able to intercept the hostiles in case they attempted to escape by passing around his left, and he could head them back into position where they would be caught between the two columns. At Terry's request, Major Brisbin is said to have traced the route of each column on the map and placed pins to show the approximate camping places en route.[28]

27 *Ibid.*, 462; Marquis, *Sketch Story of the Custer Battle*, n.p.

28 Gibbon's Report, 473; Terry's Report, 460–62. These ideas as expressed by General Terry would certainly have carried Custer farther to the south than he went. The views were expressed evidently with no concern "as to Custer's danger but solely to prevent the dreaded escape of the enemy." *Army and Navy Journal*, July 22, 1876. If Major Brisbin marked the camping places as claimed, Custer turned to the right approximately twenty miles short of his furthermost point on the Rosebud routing.

Although this is the traditional account, there is reason to believe that the plan of operations was somewhat different. An article in the *New York Herald*, July 8, 1876, written by a member of Gibbon's command, probably Major Brisbin, reads as follows:

> A consultation was held with Generals Gibbon and Custer and then General Terry definitely fixed upon the plan of action. It was believed the Indians were on the head of the Rosebud, or over on the Little Horn, a divide of about fifteen miles separating the two streams. It was announced by General Terry that *General Custer's column would strike the blow* [italics mine] and General Gibbon and his men received the decision without a murmur.
>
> There was great rivalry between the two columns and each wanted to be in at the death. General Gibbon's cavalry had been in the field since the 22nd of last February, herding and watching these Indians and the infantry had been in the field and on the march since early last March. They had come to regard the Yellowstone Indians as their peculiar property and have worked and waited five months until the Indians could be concentrated and General Crook and Terry get into position to prevent their escape. The Montana column felt disappointed when they learned that they were not to be present at the final capture of the great village but General Terry's reasons for affording the honor of the attack to General Custer were good ones. First Custer had all cavalry and could pursue if they attempted to escape, while Gibbon's column was half infantry, and in rapid marching in approaching the village, as well as pursuing the Indians after the fight, General Gibbon's cavalry and infantry must become separated and the strength of the column be weakened. Second, General Custer's column was numerically stronger than Gibbon's and General Terry desired the strongest column to strike the Indians; so it was decided that Custer's men were, as usual, to have the post of honor and the officers and men of the Montana column cheered them and bade them God-speed.[29]

Just how many Indians the attacking force was likely to encounter, no one seemed to know. The scouts insisted that the hostile warriors could not possibly number fewer than five thousand, but the officers favored their own supposition that there were not more than one thousand to fifteen hundred warriors—and Custer seems

[29] *New York Herald*, July 8, 1876; McClernand, "With Indian and Buffalo in Montana," *Cavalry Journal*, Vol. XXXVI (January and April, 1927), 14–15.

to have been the only one who put the estimate that high—and many estimated a much lower number. Custer believed that the number of lodge fires as reported by Bouyer indicated that they might meet a force of one thousand warriors, and that there might be enough young men from the various agencies visiting the hostile bands to bring the total to fifteen hundred, but he was confident from the reports of the Indian officials that the warriors in the hostile bands would not exceed that number. In fact, it seems to have been the general consensus that the village whose trail Reno had discovered was the only one in the country, and the troop dispositions were made accordingly.[30] Up to that "moment there was nothing official or private" to justify any expectation that either "detachment could encounter more than five hundred, or at a maximum, eight hundred hostile warriors."[31] While it was expected that either column would be able to defeat any hostile force that it might encounter, no one expected that the Indians would stand and fight a pitched battle unless they were forced to, and the entire campaign was accordingly based on the assumption that the Sioux must be surrounded and prevented from running away.

That there was, and could have been, no definite plan for the two commands to act in concert should be obvious from the nature of the country. There were no roads in the territory and no accurate maps of the region, and no one, not even the Indians, had anything more than a hazy idea of the distances involved. The region to be traversed was rough and broken, consisting of deep ravines, high bluffs, and arid plains, offering many obstacles to passage by white soldiers.[32] The position of the enemy, moreover, could only be guessed at. In addition, the Sioux had an excellent knowledge of the country, they were known to be vigilant as well as belligerent, and could move with speed and stealth when the occasion demanded. Thus there could have been no justification for any plan of operations which involved a co-operative attack delivered by the two

[30] McLaughlin, *My Friend, the Indian*, 127; Francis C. Holley, *Once Their Home or, Our Legacy from the Dakotas*, 228–29.

[31] *Report of the Secretary of War, 1876*, p. 30.

[32] *Army and Navy Journal*, July 15, 1876. ". . . the Rosebud was an unexplored and unmapped region." Hughes, "Campaign against the Sioux in 1876," *Journal of the Military Service Institution of the United States*, Vol. XVIII (January, 1896), 35.

commands "after a three or four days march from different points in the wilderness."[33]

Obviously much would depend upon the judgment used as the various contingencies developed and upon the ability to keep the enemy in the dark regarding just what was going on. Luck was also certain to play a large part in the ultimate success or failure of the plan, and luck was precisely what Custer was supposed to possess in abundance. Despite some rather obvious shortcomings, none of those present seem to have offered any objection to the plan as Terry presented it. Indeed, their only worries apparently were that the hostiles might escape without a battle or that General Crook might catch and annihilate the hostile tribes before the others had had a chance.

None of the three leaders seem to have even considered the possibility of defeat. This was all the more remarkable because Charley Reynolds, who had been sent out to scout during the winter and early spring, had become convinced that the Sioux intended to fight and that they would prove to be very troublesome customers. He reported that the hostile tribes had been preparing for war for a long time, supplying themselves with the best of Winchester repeating rifles and with plenty of ammunition, and that "every move they were making meant fight."[34] The Crows and the Arikaras were both constantly "making medicine" for protection. Even before leaving Fort Lincoln, the Rees had insisted that the regiment would meet a great many hostiles. They were fully aware that the number of Indians in the field was much larger than the soldiers supposed it to be, and while they professed to have no exact knowledge of the number that would be encountered, they could seldom be induced to get very far away from the soldiers.[35] To these warnings, however, the army leaders gave only grudging and disdainful attention. Custer seems to have been convinced that his regiment alone could whip any number of Indians which might be brought against it,[36] and this delusion—for delusion it certainly was—

[33] *Army and Navy Journal*, July 22, 1876.

[34] Byrne, *Soldiers of the Plains*, 86; Marquis, *Sketch Story of the Custer Battle*, n.p.

[35] Maguire's Report, 1346.

[36] Custer had spent the winter of 1875–76 in New York. While there he expressed to General G. M. Dodge the conviction that his regiment could defeat all

was apparently shared by the other members of General Terry's council of war.

The Arikaras were not familiar with the country that the regiment would have to cross in moving up the Rosebud, so Custer was provided with additional scouts from Gibbon's command. First and foremost there was the famous Bouyer who had guided Reno's detachment and who was one of the very few persons who knew the country of the Rosebud and Little Big Horn valleys thoroughly. In addition, since Terry had expressed a desire that the upper reaches of Tullock's Creek should be explored for traces of the hostiles and a messenger sent down that valley to him with any news that Custer might have, the civilian scout, George B. Herendeen, was attached to the Seventh Cavalry for that specific purpose. He stipulated that *if he were called upon to incur the additional risk of carrying dispatches down Tullock's Creek* [italics mine], he should receive additional compensation of $200, a stipulation to which General Terry agreed. Herendeen was well acquainted with the Tullock's Creek region, having lived in the country for several years, was considered to be a good and reliable scout, and had more than proved his worth to the Montana column.[37]

With the Seventh Cavalry, consisting of approximately 31 officers and 585 enlisted men, also went Charley Reynolds, who was almost completely incapacitated by a felon on his right hand, the Negro, Isaiah Dorman, the interpreter, Girard, and almost the entire delegation of Arikara scouts, the exceptions being those who, for one reason or another, had been left at the base camp on the Powder River. Also with the regiment were six of Gibbon's best Crow scouts who had volunteered for the task. These were Paints-Half-His-Face-Yellow, generally known as Half-Yellow-Face, who was the leader, or, as the Crows expressed it, "carried the pipe,"

the Indians on the plains, and despite Dodge's warnings Custer refused to concede that he might be mistaken. Jacob R. Perkins, *Trails, Rails, and War*, 193. With unconscious prophecy he had written to his brother, Tom Custer, "I expect to be in the field, in the summer, with the 7th, and think there will be lively work before us. I think the 7th Cavalry may have its greatest campaign ahead." Merington, *The Custer Story*, 277.

[37] Dustin, *The Custer Tragedy*, 89; Gibbon, "Summer Expedition," 292–93. Herendeen was sent with Custer for no other purpose than carrying dispatches from Custer to Terry, and Colonel Hughes implies that no discretion was allowed Custer. "Campaign against the Sioux," *Journal of the Military Service Institution of the United States*, Vol. XVIII (January, 1896), 31.

White Swan, White-Man-Runs-Him,[38] Goes Ahead, and—best known of all—Curly Hair or Curly, at that time a boy of only seventeen or eighteen years of age, who, despite his youth, had been selected by Gibbon as one of the best of the Crows.[39] Five or six civilian packers, later to be the cause of some difficulty, as well as Custer's youngest brother, Boston, his nephew, Arthur Reed, generally known as "Autie," and Mark Kellogg, the newspaperman, also went along.

Terry seems to have suggested the possibility that Custer might want to take Brisbin's battalion of the Second Cavalry with him, in addition to the platoon of Gatling guns, but Custer had declined both, explaining that he felt that his regiment could defeat any force of Indians it might meet, and that if it could not, the extra battalion would not make any difference. As for the Gatlings, he was afraid that the country to be traversed might be so rough that they would seriously impair his march and thus prove more of a liability than an asset. In this contention Custer was perfectly justified, for the Gatlings were each hauled by four condemned cavalry horses and unfitted for long, rapid marches. Had any demand been made for speed across rough ground, they would have been unable to keep up.[40] Lieutenant Kenzie had been unable to keep up with Reno's scouting detachment, and these same Gatlings that were offered to Custer were later to be the source of difficulty for the Montana column.

Later, Custer, to his officers, rationalized his reasons for declining additional forces more in detail, but there can be but little doubt that his real reason was selfishness: he wanted the coming encounter with the hostiles to be exclusively a Seventh Cavalry battle.[41] Later on that same evening of the twenty-first, Lieutenant J. H. Bradley wrote:

[38] Linderman, *Red Mother*, 225.

[39] Dustin, *The Custer Tragedy*, 88; Dixon, *The Vanishing Race*, 142; Custer, *Boots and Saddles*, 312.

[40] There is notable contradiction regarding just how serious this suggestion to join Brisbin's battalion to Custer's command really was. See *Army and Navy Journal*, July 15, 1876; McClernand, "With Indian and Buffalo in Montana," *Cavalry Journal*, Vol. XXXVI (January and April, 1927), 18, 24; Terry's Report, 462; Godfrey, *Montana*, 206. The idea of joining the two forces was probably suggested as a possibility but was merely an exploratory idea and was soon abandoned.

[41] *Army and Navy Journal*, July 15, 1876. Custer is said to have told Lieutenant Carland of Captain Baker's guard on the *Far West* that this was to be a Seventh Cavalry battle. Dustin, *The Custer Tragedy*, 88.

. . . it is understood that if Custer arrives first he is at liberty to attack at once if he deems prudent. We have little hope of being in on the death, as Custer will undoubtedly exert himself to the utmost to get there first and win all the laurels for himself and his regiment.[42]

This statement shows not only Lieutenant Bradley's understanding of Custer's orders but also a keen appreciation of his character.

When the conference broke up, both Gibbon and Terry walked to Custer's tent with him, spending a few moments of conversation there. Whether there was any elaboration or modification of Custer's order we do not know. Terry and Gibbon then returned to the steamer, which transferred the Gatlings and their crews across the river and brought back the Crow scouts who were to march with the Seventh Cavalry.[43] Custer called a meeting of his officers and informed them of the impending march. Wing and battalion formations were to be broken up, each troop commander being made directly responsible to Custer, thus leaving Major Reno without a command, possibly as a result of his disobedience of Terry's orders or on account of his failure to pursue the enemy whose trail he had discovered. What should not be overlooked, however, is the fact that, although Reno was now without a direct command, he was actually in the position of the acting lieutenant colonel of the regiment.

Custer ordered that fifteen days' rations of hard bread, coffee, and sugar, and twelve days' rations of bacon be provided. These, together with fifty rounds of carbine ammunition a man, were to be transported on the pack mules, while each trooper was to carry one hundred rounds of carbine and twenty-four rounds of pistol ammunition on his person and in his saddlebags. Twelve pounds of oats were also to be carried on each horse, and Custer suggested that extra forage should be transported on the mules. This last suggestion brought protests from both Moylan and Godfrey, who argued that the mules had been badly used up on the Reno scout and that this extra burden might cause them to break down. At this, Custer is said to have become very much excited and to have told the troop

[42] Bradley, *Journal*, 216; Coughlan, "The Battle of the Little Big Horn," *Cavalry Journal*, Vol. XLIII (January–February, 1934), 14.

[43] Coughlan, "The Battle of the Little Big Horn," *Cavalry Journal*, Vol. XLIII (January–February, 1934), 14; Hughes, "Campaign against the Sioux," *Journal of the Military Service Institution of the United States*, Vol. XVIII (January, 1896), 35.

commanders that they might take what supplies they pleased, but that they would be held responsible for their companies. He also promised that the regiment would follow the Indian trail for fifteen days no matter how far it might take them from their base of supplies, and that they might not see the supply steamer again. He suggested further that plenty of salt be taken along as the regiment might have to live on horse and mule meat before the campaign was over. He was taken at his word, and additional supplies of salt were included.[44]

Some writers have made much of the "black mood" that seemed to possess Custer after the two meetings, but in this he was not alone, for while he did seem to be "oppressed by his thoughts," it was also noted that "Terry was grave and anxious, and Gibbon silent and doubtful."[45] All three of them undoubtedly realized only too well the responsibilities which were theirs in the decisions that had just been made. The instructions to the officers also seem to have had a very bad effect on all concerned, for many of the officers and men now wrote letters home, some made their wills, and others gave verbal directions for the disposal of personal property and mementoes. Charley Reynolds, the scout, had a strong presentiment of disaster and twice attempted to get General Terry to release him from his position, so certain was he that he was going to his death, but Terry shamed him out of it.[46] This general atmosphere of gloom apparently did not last long, and it did not affect several of the younger officers, who took advantage of the occasion for one last big poker party aboard the *Far West*, a party that did not break up until well after dawn.[47]

On the morning of the twenty-second, General Terry sent written instructions to Custer, putting down in black and white the suggestions he had made the night before. Since controversy has raged, fierce and bitter, for more than seventy years over whether Custer did, or did not, violate his orders, they are here quoted in full.

[44] Godfrey, *Montana*, 162; Brown and Willard, *Black Hills Trails*, 142.

[45] Dustin, *The Custer Tragedy*, 89. "Yet something strange happened there [the cabin of the *Far West*]. Some spiritual blow was dealt Custer who entered expectant and emerged profoundly depressed." Van de Water, *Glory Hunter*, 314.

[46] Reno, *Court*, 224; *Official Transcript*, 175.

[47] Hanson, *Conquest of the Missouri*, 262–63.

Camp at the Mouth of Rosebud River.
June 22, 1876.
Lt. Colonel Custer, 7th Cavalry.
Colonel:—

The Brigadier-General commanding directs that as soon as your regiment can be made ready for the march, you proceed up the Rosebud in pursuit of the Indians whose trail was discovered by Major Reno a few days ago. It is, of course, impossible to give you any definite instructions in regard to this movement, and were it not impossible to do so, the Department Commander places too much confidence in your zeal, energy and ability to impose upon you precise orders which might hamper your action when nearly in contact with the enemy.

He will, however, indicate to you his own views of what your action should be, and he desires that you conform to them unless you see *sufficient reason for departing from them.* He thinks that you should proceed up the Rosebud until you ascertain definitely the direction in which the trail above spoken of leads. Should it be found, as it appears almost certain that it will be found, to turn toward the Little Big Horn he thinks that you should proceed southward, perhaps as far as the headwaters of the Tongue, and then turn toward the Little Big Horn, feeling constantly however to your left so as to preclude the possibility of the escape of the Indians to the south or southeast by passing around your left flank.

The column of General Gibbon is now in motion for the mouth of the Big Horn. As soon as it reaches that point it will cross the Yellowstone and move up at least as far as the forks of the Big and Little Big Horn. Of course its future movements must be controlled by circumstances as they may arise; but it is to be hoped that the Indians, if upon the Little Big Horn may be so nearly enclosed by the two columns that their escape will be impossible.

The Department Commander desires that on your way up the Rosebud you should thoroughly examine the upper part of Tullocks creek, and that you should endeavor to send a scout through to Colonel Gibbon's column with the information of the result of your examination. The lower part of this creek will be examined by a detachment from Colonel Gibbon's command.

The supply steamer will be pushed up the Big Horn as far as the forks if the river is found to be navigable for that space, and the Department Commander, who will accompany the column of Colonel Gibbon, desires you to report to him there not later than the time for which your troops are rationed, unless in the meantime you receive further orders.[48]

These were the suggestions, rather than orders,[49] which Terry gave Custer just before the expedition moved, and they are noteworthy for what they do not contain. No mention is made of co-operation between the two columns. Custer was to report to Terry, not necessarily in person, some time before the end of the fifteen days for which he was provisioned. Custer was to conform only until he saw sufficient reason for not doing so, and of that sufficiency he was to be the sole judge. It is pure idiocy to assume that Custer was to meet Terry at the mouth of the Little Big Horn on the twenty-sixth, since he was rationed for fifteen days and might not reach that point before the sixth of July. Terry hoped to hear from Custer in the days ahead, and he was merely letting Custer know where he might be found.[50]

These instructions show an unusual mingling of anxiety and forbearance, for Terry—knowing Custer's impetuous disposition and also that he was still smarting from his unjust treatment by the President—seems to have feared that Custer might act in a rash and precipitate manner, and yet to have hesitated to say anything that might still further wound the feelings of his subordinate or in any way reflect upon the latter's discretion. The Department commander seems to have recognized the impossibility of giving definite instructions at that moment when there were so many imponderables, so many unforeseen contingencies that might develop. A distinguished historian of the battle has written, "The character of Terry's instructions are positive and clear as to the strategical maneuver but avoid definite directions to his two subordinates as to the tactics to

[48] Terry's Report, 462. Godfrey was later to argue that the phrase, "when nearly in contact with the enemy," referred to the immediate time and place of writing the instructions, i.e.—the mouth of the Rosebud—hence Terry's orders were advisory only. Cyrus Townsend Brady, *Indian Fights and Fighters*, 389.

[49] General Nelson A. Miles, *Serving the Republic*, 186. On the contrary, Colonel Hughes argues that the orders could not have been more explicit, "more definite in purpose and more clearly prescient of what Custer would find on his march," and that the courtesy of their phraseology detracted nothing from their force. Hughes, "Campaign against the Sioux in 1876," *Journal of the Military Service Institution of the United States*, Vol. XVIII (January, 1896), 20, 26.

[50] Charles King, "Custer's Last Battle," *Harper's*, Vol. LXXXI (August, 1890), 381.

be employed when immediately confronted by the enemy";[51] while another has criticized these same instructions as being "a poor substitute for properly prepared orders" and as "leaving much to be desired for the operation of an exterior column."[52]

There is nothing in the orders to indicate that Custer was to co-operate with Gibbon in any way, and the best that can be inferred is that Terry did not want Custer to attack until the Montana column had had time to get into position to be able to cut off the retreat of the hostiles if they should flee to the north. If this was intended, Terry made a bad mistake, for, knowing that Gibbon had a longer line to travel than did Custer, and that the former's infantry would necessarily delay his march, Terry either should have given Gibbon more of a start than he did or else should have held Custer under a much tighter rein. That he did neither constitutes one of the major blunders of the campaign[53] and provides a basis for valid criticism of his conduct as a commanding officer.

The point of prime importance was to get Custer to the south of the enemy in order to prevent their escape to the Big Horn Mountains or their return to the agencies. Nothing in Terry's letter indicated that if Custer found the Indians he should delay fighting them until the infantry could come up. He expected Custer to attack the hostiles wherever he found them, and he left the method and manner of the attack to Custer's discretion and judgment.[54] Terry may have given Custer verbal orders supplementing the written ones, but if so they have been lost to history.[55]

During the march that lay ahead, Custer paid lip service to most

[51] Coughlan, "The Battle of the Little Big Horn," *Cavalry Journal*, Vol. XLIII (January–February, 1934), 15. On the other hand, Colonel Hughes believed that it would be very difficult to conceive of more explicit orders being given to a detached command. Hughes, "Campaign against the Sioux in 1876," *Journal of the Military Service Institution of the United States*, Vol. XVIII (January, 1896), 27.

[52] James P. Murphy, "Campaign of the Little Big Horn," *Infantry Journal*, Vol. XXXIV (June, 1929), 633, 639.

[53] General Sheridan is reported to have expressed the opinion that he was the only officer who could control Custer. Reno, *Court*, 17.

[54] Colonel James B. Fry, *Military Miscellanies*, 508. See also the letter of T. L. Rosser in *New York Herald*, July 11, 1876.

[55] General Nelson A. Miles, *Personal Recollections and Observations*, 204, has a story which has been widely quoted, of oral instructions given to Custer which practically gave the latter full freedom of operation. However, the story would not bear examination and was exposed by Colonel Graham in his *Story of the Little Big Horn*, 176–77.

of the suggestions, specifically violated one of them, but in general did probably almost exactly what Terry expected him to do, and probably what any other commander would have done in similar circumstances.

The only suggestion of a possible defeat came from the scouts. Bloody Knife communicated the news of the coming march to the Arikaras and emphasized that there were many enemies in the region just ahead of them. If the troops attacked the camp of the Sioux and were beaten, the retreat was to be made in small groups, and the scouts were not to run away or attempt to return to their homes. If the group was broken up into squads or single horsemen, the camp on the Yellowstone at the mouth of the Powder River was to be the appointed place for reassembling.[56] Just before the march started, Girard told the Arikaras that he wanted them to sing their death songs, whereupon they mounted their ponies and rode around singing these songs. Then they fell in and marched with the regiment.

The column moved at noon on the twenty-second. Sensing the inherent drama of the situation, the commander had issued orders for a regimental parade, with Terry, Gibbon, and Brisbin as the reviewing officers. Massed trumpeters played the regiment through, with General Terry taking the salutes and having a pleasant word for each officer as he passed. The regiment "was pronounced by all to be in splendid condition" and presented a good appearance. Gibbon noted especially the number of fine horses in the ranks, many of them being part-blooded horses from Kentucky. The men and officers alike were in high spirits, the "black mood" of the day before having vanished completely and given way to a feeling of pride that it was the Seventh that was being sent.[57] Lieutenant Edgerly wrote that a more eager command had probably never set out after the enemy; but they knew that a hard task lay ahead, they believed that the enemy would run, and then "the hard stern chase would begin."[58] The pack mules followed the regiment and after them came the rear guard. Custer lingered behind a little for any final

[56] Libby, *Arikara Narrative*, 74.

[57] Wagner, *Old Neutriment*, 141; *New York Herald*, July 8, 1876.

[58] General W. S. Edgerly, *Narrative of the March of General George A. Custer*, etc., 1. See also Edgerly's letter to his wife as given in Bates, *Custer's Indian Battles*, 31.

instructions from Terry, and then shook hands with the three officers and bade them good-bye. As he turned to leave, Gibbon, half in jest and half in earnest, suggested that he not be greedy but leave a few Indians for the rest of them, a remark actuated by the very real fear that Custer would allow his zeal to carry him forward too rapidly.[59] Custer, dead serious, refused to promise, and rode off after his command. "Little did we think that we had seen him for the last time, or imagine under what circumstances we should next see the command, now mounting the bluffs in the distance with its guidons gayly fluttering in the breeze."[60]

Terry and the other officers rode back to the deserted camp, and Girard, who says that he was detained there a short time by his official duties, claims that he overheard General Terry remark: "Custer is happy now, off with a roving command of fifteen days. I told him if he found the Indians not to do as Reno did, but if he thought he could whip them to do so."[61]

Custer soon overtook the regiment and halted it. Now the scouts were sent ahead, and the command marched the two miles to the mouth of Rosebud Creek. This stream, which got its name from the profusion of wild roses which grew in the meadows along its banks, was described by Lieutenant George Wallace, who as regimental engineering officer kept the itinerary, as a clear, running stream from three to four feet wide and about three inches deep with a firm gravelly bottom.[62] The troops crossed near its mouth, and then moved upstream, traveling along the high ground or second bench above the water. Here the soil was very poor, and the grass correspondingly thin and crowded out by sagebrush and cactus, although the bottom was timbered with large cottonwoods and in many places small willows grew thickly along the banks.

The Arikaras worked well ahead of the command. There were

59 There are several versions of this incident. See *inter alia* Brady, "War with the Sioux," *Pearson's Magazine*, August, 1904, 179; Hughes, "Campaign against the Sioux in 1876," *Journal of the Military Service Institution of the United States*, Vol. XVIII (January, 1896), 32; McClernand, "With Indian and Buffalo in Montana," *Cavalry Journal*, Vol. XXXVI (January and April, 1927), 16.

60 *New York Herald*, July 8, 1876. This article is believed to have been written by Major James Brisbin. See also Gibbon, "Summer Expedition," 141.

61 Holley, *Once Their Home or Our Legacy from the Dakotas*, 262.

62 Lieutenant George D. Wallace, Report, in *Report of the Secretary of War, 1877*, II, pt. 2, 1378 (hereinafter cited as Wallace's Report).

two groups, one led by Soldier, the other by Bobtailed Bull, and each was responsible for scouting one side of the stream. Ahead of them were Bouyer and the six Crows, who found themselves perfectly at home, although the Arikaras were getting away from the territory with which they were most familiar.

For the first eight miles the country sloped back gradually from the stream, but then it became more abrupt and was cut by deep ravines, while the surface was covered with stones and cactus. The weather was clear but not unpleasantly warm, and the troops rode leisurely. They halted at four o'clock, after having covered some twelve or fourteen miles from the mouth of the stream, the early halt being made largely because of delays with the pack mules, some of which did not reach the camping place until nearly sunset.

Camp was made at the base of a steep bluff, where wood, water, and grass were abundant. The water was only slightly alkaline and was not unpalatable. There were fish in the stream, and during the day some game had been seen, but the strict rules against the discharge of firearms prevented any hunting. After supper many of the officers and men went fishing.[63]

At sunset, Custer took the step, most unusual for him, of holding a council of the officers and detailing his plans for the campaign. This procedure was so unusual that practically all of those present commented upon it. Because they were in enemy country and the avoidance of detection was of primary importance, he ordered that in the future there be no trumpet calls except in case of emergency. He emphasized that all of the troop commanders were directly responsible for their companies, but two things would be decided by him: when to move out in the morning and when and where to camp at night. Everything else—grazing, watering, and stables—was to be left to the discretion of the troop commanders, all of whom, being veterans, should know what was necessary. At three o'clock the stable guards were to awaken the troopers, and the regiment was to be ready to march two hours later. During the march they were to be careful not to get ahead of the scouts, nor were they to lag too far in the rear, but were to keep closed up and within supporting distance of each other at all times. The marches, Custer said, would be by easy stages and would average from twenty-five to thirty miles each day.

During the day's march the pack train had given much trouble, some of the packs having even fallen off before the regiment was out of camp, and during the day the mules had straggled badly. The principal reason for this was the fact that the train was made up of mules taken out of the traces of the wagons, and was "the saddest burlesque" in the direction of a pack train that one could ever expect to see.[64] Custer now detailed Lieutenant Mathey to command the train, its 175 mules, 70 troopers, and 6 or 7 civilian packers.[65] He was to report at the end of each day on the relative efficiency of the troop packers. This helped to alleviate the situation, for the troopers suspected that if a detachment that required rapid marching was to be sent out, the troops with the most efficient packing records would draw the assignment. Also, the troops with the worst records were assigned to guard the train, so that in two ways Custer stimulated the ambition of the troop packers to excel in that particular field. However, the problem never was entirely solved, for the pack train continued to be a source of trouble and exasperation, and at least a contributing factor in the final disaster.

Custer then explained that Terry had offered him the platoon of Gatling guns as well as Major Brisbin's battalion of the Second Cavalry, but that he had refused both. Since the country that his command would have to cover was largely unknown and unexplored, he said, he felt that it might possibly be so rough that the Gatlings would seriously delay his march. Regarding Brisbin's battalion, he appealed to their regimental *esprit de corps* by explaining that, since he expected to meet not more than fifteen hundred warriors, he felt that if the Seventh Cavalry could not handle them, the extra battalion would not make any difference and might seriously weaken his command by creating jealousy among its component parts. It was obvious that Custer was rationalizing and that, smarting under the sting of his rebuke by President Grant, he wanted an independent command plus sole credit for any success that might

63 Wallace's Report, 1378.

64 Bourke, *On the Border with Crook*, 353; Godfrey, "Diary," n.p.

65 There is no general agreement about the number of mules in the train. While of little importance the disagreement illustrates some of the difficulties in studying the battle. The figure which I have used is a sort of average of various numbers which have been given. See Reno, *Court*, 600, 640, and the *Army and Navy Journal*, July 15, 1876.

be attained. Custer was all too human and sought vindication in the only way that he understood—the winning of a glorious success against the Sioux that would be so overwhelming as to make Grant's opinion of him immaterial and irrelevant.

He appealed for loyalty and co-operation from his officers and complained that some of his official actions had been criticized. He stated that he was quite willing to accept recommendations but wanted them to come in the proper form. Here Benteen broke in with the complaint that he was lashing all of them for the derelictions of a few and requested that he be more specific. Custer, apparently in some agitation, declared that he was not there to be catechized by anyone, but that for Benteen's information, none of the criticism had been directed at him.[66] He then requested that the officers feel free to bring him any criticisms or suggestions that they might have and announced his determination to pursue the hostiles until he caught them, even if it took him to the agencies in Nebraska or on the Missouri River.[67]

The whole tone of the meeting—so unlike the dashing, reckless, self-confident Custer whom the veterans knew—left the officers dumbfounded and amazed. After leaving the council, Lieutenant Wallace, who apparently had more than his share of superstition, confided to Lieutenants Gibson and Godfrey his belief that Custer was going to be killed and had a premonition of disaster, since he had never been known to talk that way before.[68]

On the way back to his station while checking on the preparations for the night, and especially on the security of the herd, Godfrey found Bouyer with a group of the Indian scouts, both Crow and Arikara, "talking" in the sign language of the tribes of the plains. In answer to questions concerning whether he had ever fought against the Sioux and how many Indians the command expected to meet, Godfrey "guessed" that the number would be about fifteen hundred, and when in reply to a further question he

[66] Lieutenant Edgerly has been quoted as saying that when Benteen inquired about the grumbling, Custer replied, "I want the saddle to go just where it fits," but added that he knew of no grumbling by Benteen. Merington, *The Custer Story*, 310.

[67] Godfrey, *Century*, 365.

[68] Edgerly, *Narrative of the March of General George A. Custer*, 1 (hereinafter cited as Edgerly, *Narrative*). See also Godfrey, "Diary," n.p.

expressed confidence that the regiment would be able to handle that number, Bouyer observed, "Well, I can tell you we are going to have a damned big fight."[69]

[69] Godfrey, *Century*, 364–65. Bouyer is reported to have made similar remarks on several prior occasions. McClernand, "With Indian and Buffalo in Montana," *Cavalry Journal*, Vol. XXXVI (January and April, 1927), 16.

CHAPTER XII

Following the Indian Trail

THE REGIMENT resumed the march again at five o'clock on the morning of the twenty-third.[1] The bluffs were very broken, so that it was necessary for the command to follow along the valley for a considerable distance, and in the course of the first three miles they had to ford the stream no less than five times. Then the soldiers moved up the right bank for about ten miles. Five miles after leaving camp, they found the large lodgepole trail that Major Reno had discovered, and the sight is said to have caused Custer to confide to Lieutenant Varnum his unflattering opinion that Reno had made the mistake of his life in not pushing on.[2] Three miles farther on they found the campsite which both Bradley and Reno had reported. The signs indicated that it had been a large village of many lodges. In addition, there had been a great number of wickiups, temporary shelters formed by drawing the tops of the bushes together so that a blanket or piece of canvas could be thrown over them. These were used for transient visitors who had no regular place in the lodges. How naïve even experienced army officers could be is shown by Godfrey's statement that at this time the wickiups were presumed to be shelters for the dogs and that it was only later that their real purpose was discovered.[3] This camp was about eighteen miles from the mouth of the Rosebud; it was un-

[1] The day-by-day marches of the Custer command are based on material found in Godfrey, *Montana;* Godfrey, "Diary"; the testimony of the interpreter, Girard, before the Reno Court of Inquiry, especially the *Official Transcript*, 180; and Holley, *Once Their Home.*

[2] Van de Water, *Glory Hunter*, 328; *New York Herald*, July 8, 1876. Lieutenant Gibson in a letter to his wife, dated July 4, 1876, said the trail was only two days old. Fougera, *With Custer's Cavalry*, 266.

[3] Godfrey, "Diary," n.p. Godfrey, *Montana*, 167. For another view see *Official Transcript*, 259.

doubtedly the one whose smoke Bradley had seen on the fifteenth of May, and which he had noticed again on the twenty-seventh.

After covering about fifteen miles, the regiment halted in order to allow the pack train to catch up. They then crossed to the left bank of the stream and followed that for about fifteen miles. During the day, three more Indian camping places were passed, brief halts being made at each. The number of lodges and the age of the pony droppings were the all absorbing topics of conversation. All of these camps were old, but the signs indicated a large body of Indians. The trail in some places was at least three hundred yards in width and deeply worn. The scouts said that it had been made by about fifteen hundred lodges, and since there were doubtless other trails, they agreed that it proved that enormous numbers of Sioux, Cheyennes, and Arapahoes had left the agencies to join Sitting Bull. But the officers, misled by the report that there were only five to eight hundred warriors in the hostile bands, missed the significance of the trail entirely and persisted in believing that these large camps—they were from one-third to one-half a mile in diameter—were a succession of camps of a single band, rather than what they were, the single camp of several large bands together. On several occasions, smoke signals were seen, indicating that the hostiles were aware of the presence of the troops.[4]

During the day the regiment covered some very rough ground. The soil was poor except along the creek, and there the Indian ponies had eaten all the grass so that little was left for the cavalry horses. The regiment went into camp about 4:30 P.M. on the right bank of the Rosebud at the mouth of Beaver Creek, a few miles above the present settlement of Lee, where the water was bad but where there was plenty of grass,[5] having covered better than thirty miles in approximately twelve hours. Once again the pack train had fallen far behind, its last units not arriving in camp until after sunset.[6] That the command was straggling badly is illustrated by the fact that Dr. Lord, the regimental surgeon, who was suffering from an indisposition, came in several hours after camp had been established. Tired out, he had halted several miles back to rest, and on

[4] Edgerly, *Narrative*, 2.
[5] Brown and Willard, *Black Hills Trails*, 146.
[6] Godfrey, *Century*, 366.

his arrival wanted only to sleep, being too tired to either eat or drink.[7]

On the day previous, Benteen's mules and packers, with those of two other companies, had been reported the most unmanageable and troublesome of the entire command. So, as the senior captain, Benteen had been given the command of a battalion composed of those three companies, and ordered to follow the pack train. In a march of seven or eight miles the train had scattered over two miles, and on one occasion it had taken more than an hour and a half to get all of the mules across a small creek. After considering the nature of the country being traversed and the danger of a surprise attack from ambush, Benteen had halted and closed up the command. Then he placed one company at the head, another at the rear, and the third on the right flank of the center of the train, and the march resumed. That night Benteen told Lieutenant Cooke of the changes he had made, but Cooke refused to mention them to Custer. The next morning, Benteen himself told Custer, who stammered and replied: "I am much obliged to you, Colonel, and I will turn over the same order of march for the rear guard to the officer who relieves you."[8]

The next morning, Saturday, the twenty-fourth, the valley narrowed, and once or twice smoke signals were again reported from the valley of Tullock's Creek, which was in general view from the divide along which the command was riding.[9] When Godfrey called Custer's attention to them, Custer replied that the scouts were well out on the divide and that if any signals had been made he was confident that the scouts would have reported them, but they reported that nothing had been seen. Subsequent observation convinced Godfrey that the so-called "smoke-puffs" were "cloudlets of mist formed during the night in the valleys and wafted over the hill-tops by the morning breeze."[10]

[7] Colonel F. W. Benteen, *An Account of the Little Big Horn Campaign*, 4 (hereinafter cited as Benteen, *Account*). This material is reprinted in Graham, *The Custer Myth*.

[8] *Ibid.*, 3; E. A. Brininstool, *The Custer Fight, Captain F. W. Benteen's Story of the Battle of the Little Big Horn*, 7 (hereinafter cited as *Captain Benteen's Story*). According to this Custer stammered and replied, "I am very much obliged to you, Colonel Benteen; I will direct the officer who relieves you to guard the train in the manner you have done."

[9] This statement has been contradicted by Colonel Hughes, "Campaign against the Sioux in 1876," *Journal of the Military Service Institution of the United States*, Vol. XVIII (January, 1896), 31.

There can be but little doubt that both Sioux and Cheyenne warriors watched the command from the time it left the camp at the mouth of the Rosebud. Despite the fact that the regiment was marched in several columns, the dust kicked up by the horses rose in enormous clouds which were visible for miles, and it would have been remarkable if the hostiles had not discovered the presence of the troops. On several occasions the Crow scouts saw fresh Sioux signs, indicating that every move made by the troops was under enemy surveillance. On one particular occasion, White-Man, who, as one of the oldest scouts who knew the country well, did most of the advance scouting,[11] claims that he was close enough to a Sioux scout for each to know the identity of the other and to communicate by means of the sign language.[12]

There was a genuine alarm about 6:00 A.M. when the Crow scouts reported having discovered fresh tracks of the Sioux, the tracks of three or four ponies, and of one Indian on foot. On the theory that these might be scouts from a band camped near by, Custer with two troops rode ahead while the remainder of the regiment waited about half a mile back, but no further discoveries were made.[13] This incident, in connection with the smoke signals reported during the day, may have caused Custer to conclude that his presence had been discovered by the hostiles. If so, it would explain his actions later in the evening.

Throughout the day many Indian camping places were passed. "Every bend of the stream bore traces of some old camp, and their ponies had nipped almost every blade of grass. The ground was strewn with broken bones and cuttings from buffalo hides,"[14] in

10 Godfrey, *Century*, 366; Godfrey, *Montana*, 163. Lieutenant Edgerly said that "on the 24th we saw their smoke signals and knew that their scouts saw us." *Narrative*, 10.

11 *Accounts of the Custer Fight Given to General Hugh L. Scott by Two Crow Scouts, "White-Man-Runs-Him" and "Curley,"* (Aug. 24, 1919), 17 (hereinafter cited as *Account to Scott*).

12 "From the time Custer's command left the military camp at the mouth of Rosebud Creek, it was under the surveillance of Sioux scouting parties." "Custer's Battle from the Indian Viewpoint," *American Indian Journal*, Vol. I [1928], 15. The copy used was found in the Montana State Historical Library, Helena, Montana. This seems to have been the only issue of the magazine.

13 Godfrey, *Century*, 366–67; Godfrey, *Montana*, 168; *New York Herald*, July 8, 1876. Although never positively identified, this was probably the Cheyenne band of Little Wolf.

14 Wallace, Report, 1377.

addition to the carcasses of dead buffalo that had been killed and skinned only a short time before.[15] Even so, the officers persisted in their delusion that these were the successive camping places of one small band rather than the single camp of a much larger group.[16] One cannot have a very high opinion of the intelligence of experienced cavalry officers who failed to be impressed by the fact that the various camps were all of the same age. But the scouts, both Crow and Arikara, were under no illusions and were quite aware that a great many hostiles—possibly several thousand—were somewhere ahead.

One campsite was much larger than the others, and still standing was the framework of a large sun-dance lodge in which hung the scalp of a white man, presumably that of a trooper of Brisbin's Second Cavalry.[17] There was abundant evidence that the Sioux had held their great religious ceremony here and had made "much medicine." The sand had been arranged and smoothed, and pictures had been drawn. The Dakota scouts with Custer said that this meant that the Sioux knew that the army was coming. In one of the sweat lodges there was a long heap or ridge of sand, and on this figures had been drawn indicating by hoofprints Custer's men on the one side and the Indians on the other. Between them were drawn pictures of dead men with their heads toward the Sioux, which the scouts said meant that the Dakota medicine was too strong and that the white men would be defeated. In another lodge there were three stones all in a row: in the sign language this meant that the Great Spirit had given victory to the Sioux and that if the soldiers did not come the Indians would seek them. Another evidence of the number and confidence of the Sioux was the arrangement of a pile of stones with the skull of a buffalo bull on one side and that of a buffalo cow on the other, a pole set slanting toward the cow skull serving as a pointer. The Arikaras said this meant that when the Sioux were overtaken they would fight like a buffalo bull and that the soldiers would run from them like women.[18] Apparently it was

[15] William A. Graham, "'Come on! Be quick! Bring packs!' The Story of Custer's Last Message . . . ," *Cavalry Journal*, Vol. XXXII (July, 1923), 305.

[16] Godfrey, *Century*, 366.

[17] Edgerly said there were two fresh scalps of white men dangling from the center pole. *Narrative*, 2.

[18] Libby, *Arikara Narrative*, 79. Dustin claims that this was a symbolic asser-

while the officers were conferring here that Custer's flag blew down facing to the rear. Picked up and stuck in the ground, it soon blew down again. Then it was placed so that it was supported by some sagebrush, and no further trouble was encountered, but Lieutenant Wallace, ever superstitious, regarded this incident as an omen of disaster to come.[19]

The day was long and tedious. The weather had turned unpleasantly warm, and the troops rode constantly in a cloud of choking dust. Many halts were made in order not to get ahead of the scouts, who were doing their work carefully and well, especially on the right toward Tullock's Creek. Two running tributaries of the Rosebud were passed, the first seen since the beginning of the march, and Lieutenant Wallace noted that while the hills were rough and broken, the soil was very good and the grazing fine. The regiment halted about one o'clock, approximately four miles north of the present town of Lame Deer. Here coffee was made, and the troops rested until the scouts came back to report a fresh Indian camp at the forks of the Rosebud.

Shortly after the command again moved forward, they crossed a large Indian trail coming from the south, and from this and other signs they deduced that many newcomers—probably Indians who had wintered at the various agencies—had joined the hostiles here. Even the men in the ranks were fully aware that many warriors had been in the group, for the trail, where it crossed the Rosebud, was more than a mile wide. The trail was now comparatively fresh, and the whole valley so scratched up by thousands of trailing lodgepoles that it gave the appearance of a poorly plowed field. It was now apparent that the long-sought quarry was not far ahead.[20]

The civilian scout, George Herendeen, who had been attached to the regiment for the purpose of scouting Tullock's Creek and then possibly riding down it with dispatches for General Terry, was anxious to earn the extra compensation that had been promised

tion that the troops had been defeated, and probably referred to Crook's fight on the Rosebud. *The Custer Tragedy*, 95. The fight on the Rosebud took place after the Sun Dance, however.

19 Godfrey's "Diary," n.p.

20 Henry Brinkerhoff, *Account of the Custer Battle*, n.p. Brinkerhoff was a sergeant in G troop. This item is to be found in the Scrapbooks in the Billings Public Library.

him, so he now reported to Custer, saying, "General here is where I leave you to go to the other command." Custer merely looked at him, making no answer. Herendeen rode alongside for some distance, then seeing that his services were not wanted, fell back and followed along. There was really no reason why Herendeen should have been sent from here since no new positive evidence had been discovered.[21] Later in the evening Custer is said to have discussed with Herendeen the question of sending him down Tullock's Creek to communicate with General Terry, but both felt that they had better wait until they were farther along on the trail. The next day, after it became apparent that the Indians had discovered the presence of the command, Custer knew that the scout could not get through.[22]

Custer did openly and flagrantly violate his orders in one particular—he failed to scout the upper reaches of Tullock's Creek. Not only was no special attention devoted to that area, but Lieutenant Varnum said afterwards that in all of his instructions from Custer he never heard of Tullock's Creek but was instructed to devote close attention to the opposite side and that if any examination was made of the Tullock Valley, it was made without his knowledge and by someone not under his control.[23] Custer's failure in this regard was justified by Lieutenant Edgerly, who believed that any good officer would have acted similarly under the same circumstances, for when the regiment arrived in the region of Tullock's Creek, it was on a hot trail, and it would have been useless to scout the valley when the Indians were obviously in front of the command.[24] In any event Custer's violation probably did not affect the subsequent tragedy in any way, although he has been severely criticized for this neglect.[25]

Custer was especially vigilant in guarding against the possibility of the enemy's passing around his left flank and escaping into the

[21] Cyrus Townsend Brady, "War with the Sioux," *Pearson's Magazine* (August, 1904), 390; Dustin, *The Custer Tragedy*, 97–98.

[22] Charles F. Bates and Fairfax Downey, *Fifty Years after the Little Big Horn Battle*, 12. In a memorandum to Cyrus Townsend Brady, Godfrey said that in his opinion the reason Herendeen was not sent down Tullock's Fork was Custer's belief that the scout could not get through. *Indian Fights and Fighters*, 372.

[23] Coughlan, "The Battle of the Little Big Horn," *Cavalry Journal*, Vol. XLIII (January–February, 1934), 16.

[24] Lieutenant Colonel Otto Louis Hein, *Memories of Long Ago*, 144–45.

[25] Coughlan, "The Battle of the Little Big Horn," *Cavalry Journal*, Vol. XLIII (January–February, 1934), 14; Dustin, *The Custer Tragedy*, 97; Godfrey, *Montana*, 209.

vast region around the middle courses of the Tongue, Powder, and Little Missouri rivers. The scouts were ordered to follow every trail that led to the left, no matter how small. Varnum was ordered to investigate one small trail which the scouts had not reported, but which upon investigation was found to lead up a ravine, then across the prairie and back at last to the main trail.[26]

The regiment went into camp not far from the present town of Busby—perhaps at the junction of Thompson's Creek with the Rosebud, for here the water was clear and good,[27] but more probably a few miles to the north and approximately twenty-two miles east of the Little Big Horn River. Camp was made a few minutes before eight in the evening, the command having covered nearly thirty miles during the day, a very good performance in view of the many halts. This camp was about eighteen miles distant from the site of Crook's defeat of the week before at the hands of the selfsame Indians that Custer was seeking. It was obvious to all that the Sioux in large numbers were not far ahead, for there were Sioux signs on every side and evidence to indicate that some of the fires left by the hostiles were still smoldering.[28]

Custer was now fully twenty-four hours ahead of schedule, and both men and horses were tired. He could have waited and rested the command, in the meantime scouting carefully ahead, especially around the headwaters of Tullock's Creek as General Terry had suggested, but for some reason he decided against doing so. Instead of giving his regiment the rest that it needed so badly, he had sent ahead three of the Crows—White-Man, Goes Ahead, and Hairy Moccasins—even before the command reached the site of Busby. The scouts were not sure which way the Sioux would go, although they knew the trail and the direction in which the Sioux were mov-

[26] Cyrus Townsend Brady, *Northwestern Fights and Fighters*, 357.

[27] Linderman, *Red Mother*, 233–34.

[28] Herendeen said that the camp was made two miles below the forks of the Rosebud. *New York Herald*, July 8, 1876; *Army and Navy Journal*, July 15, 1876. Burkman said it was a mile below the present town of Busby, Montana, and on the site of a ranch now owned by Willis Rowland. Wagner, *Old Neutriment*, 245. Marquis, *Sketch Story of the Custer Battle*, n.p. The fact that all three of these accounts put the camp in approximately the same place would seem to settle the matter despite the contrary testimony of Goes Ahead. It must be remembered that the camp of twelve troops of cavalry plus a pack train would cover considerable territory.

ing.[29] A general understanding prevailed that if the trail was found to turn west across the divide into the valley of the Little Big Horn, a night march might be ordered. The officers were apparently certain of the result since the mules were not unpacked except to obtain the necessary supplies for supper.[30] Custer had been told of the Crow's Nest, a high, rounded hill almost exactly on the center of the divide, from which almost everything of note in the valley could be seen, and it was understood that the three Crows would try to locate the Indian camp from there.[31]

The last bivouac on the Rosebud was in one of the most beautiful spots that the troopers had yet seen. On the right there was a high and almost perpendicular cliff which partially concealed the regiment from prying eyes. Two or three hundred yards away was the river, and in the intervening space great masses of wild rose bushes were in full bloom, with here and there a tree to add to the parklike effect. It is doubtful, however, that many of Custer's tired troopers gave any attention to the beauty of their surroundings, doubtless preferring after their frugal supper of hardtack, bacon, and coffee to roll up in their blankets and try to sleep.[32] The fires had been put out as soon as supper was over, and the orders were to be ready to move again at eleven-thirty.[33]

It was nearly nine o'clock when the three Crows returned and reported that the hostile Indians had crossed the divide, but that they had been unable to locate their camp.[34] Custer immediately decided on a night march, and told Lieutenant Varnum that he would move the regiment to the base of the divide starting at eleven o'clock. He then ordered Varnum, Bouyer, and Reynolds with four of the Crows and five or six of the Rees to the Crow's Nest to see if they could locate the enemy from the smoke of his campfires. Varnum was to send Custer a note as early as possible detailing what he had discovered, but if the hostiles had not been found by noon the next

[29] *Account to Scott*, 7.

[30] Brown and Willard, *Black Hills Trails*, 146.

[31] Hughes, "Campaign against the Sioux in 1876," *Journal of the Military Service Institution of the United States*, Vol. XVIII (January, 1896), 29.

[32] *Billings Gazette*, May 28, 1916. There are also numerous clippings in the Custer File of the Billings Public Library, as well as an original poem entitled "Up the Rosebud."

[33] Godfrey, *Century*, 366.

[34] Wallace, Report, 1377.

day, the party was to return.[35] At a council of the officers, Custer detached Lieutenant Hare from K troop and placed him on duty with the scouts. This step was necessary because Lieutenant Varnum's presence with the advance scouting party left the rest of the scouts without supervision, but it also left K troop with only one officer. Custer, who was not blind and who was becoming increasingly certain that great numbers of the enemy were ahead, told his officers that they were about to go into the fight of their lives,[36] and ordered the regiment to march again at eleven o'clock, following the Indian trail in order to get as close as possible to the summit of the divide before daybreak. They would hide there all day on the twenty-fifth while the scouts reconnoitered the country preparatory to a surprise attack on the hostile village at dawn on the twenty-sixth.[37] This was a good plan and if adhered to would have eliminated much of the subsequent criticism of Custer. The trouble is that it was not adhered to.

In deciding to follow the Indian trail, Custer was flouting General Terry's suggestion. Just why he did so has ever since been a matter of conjecture. To know and understand the motives of another person is practically impossible even when those concerned live in daily contact with each other, and to evaluate correctly the motives behind the action of the Lieutenant Colonel of the Seventh Cavalry on this occasion is well-nigh impossible. A fair guess would be that Custer was determined that the credit for winning the great victory over the hostile tribes should go to him and his regiment alone. To delay too long meant that the glory might have to be shared with Terry and Gibbon. To continue south towards the headwaters of the Tongue River—as Terry had suggested—meant that he might encounter General Crook, in which case he would be outranked and would become merely a subordinate commander in a larger enterprise, so that the credit for crushing the Sioux would

35 Libby, *Arikara Narrative*, 86; Hughes, "Campaign against the Sioux in 1876," *Journal of the Military Service Institution of the United States*, Vol. XVIII (January, 1896), 29; Dustin, *The Custer Tragedy*, 98.

36 Roe, *Custer's Last Battle*, 8. Custer was undoubtedly impressed by the attitude, if not the reports, of the Crow scouts. That they were not anxious for a fight is one of the certainties of the campaign. McLaughlin, *My Friend, the Indian*, 128.

37 Godfrey, *Montana*, 169; Godfrey, *Century*, 366; Holley, *Once Their Home*, 234.

go to others. There was no room for a division of honor for the great victory that he fully expected to win. While this conclusion is wholly inferential, it seems fair and logical in view of all the attendant circumstances.

There is another aspect to consider—Custer's character or disposition. Throughout all of his military career Custer had been distinguished by a wild and reckless bravery, which, together with an utter lack of fear, was largely responsible for the military reputation that he enjoyed. Custer on a hot trail was like a bloodhound: he could not leave it, he could not even rest until he had brought his quarry to bay.

> Like the hunter in the chase, knowing full well that the discovery of his presence would disperse the objects of such long and eager pursuit, and that failure to attack, in case the game brought to bay should escape, would mortify his command and possibly bring professional reproach, Custer seems to have been impelled as on the Washita, to dare the risks for a crowning victory.[38]

After the conference at Custer's tent, a group of the younger officers, including Sturgis, Moylan, and Edgerly, held an impromptu concert, singing "Annie Laurie" and "Little Footsteps, Soft and Gentle," among other songs, and closing with the Doxology. Then, apparently feeling that their repertoire had been too somber and gloomy, they added, at the risk of being considered irreverent, "For He's a Jolly Good Fellow," before dispersing to their commands.[39] While the troops were in camp here, they were observed by Big Crow and Blackwhiteman, two of Little Wolf's band of Cheyennes. They did not know who the soldiers were or what they were there for, however, and Little Wolf did not reach the hostile camp until after the battle.[40]

[38] Margaret I. Carrington, *Ab-sa-ra-ka, Land of Massacre*, 330. There has been widespread argument over whether Custer here wilfully disobeyed Terry's orders, and the point of view of each disputant generally depends upon his opinion of Custer. The case against Custer, that he wilfully disobeyed the positive orders of his superior, is most ably presented by Colonel Robert P. Hughes, who was a member of Terry's staff. His article "The Campaign against the Sioux in 1876," is one which should be read by every serious student of the battle. Originally published in the *Journal of the Military Service Institution of the United States*, Vol. XVIII, January, 1896, it can perhaps be found most conveniently in the appendix to the second edition of Colonel W. A. Graham, *The Story of the Little Big Horn*.

[39] *Billings Gazette*, May 28, 1916.

The orders were to move at eleven o'clock, and the regiment moved at that hour. Captain Keogh's troop, which was in charge of the pack train, used up nearly an hour and a half in getting its charges across Mud Creek, while the remainder of the regiment waited impatiently on the other side. This delay caused Benteen to record his belief that Job had never had very much to do with pack mules.[41] A change was made in the procedure, so that each company now led its own mules since it was too dark to see to drive them.[42] Thus it was between midnight and one o'clock in the morning of that fateful twenty-fifth of June before the regiment finally got under way, moving up one of the many small streams which flow into the Rosebud from the right. There is some dispute concerning the line of march followed—Was it Davis Creek, or Thompson's Creek, which is two miles farther to the south?—since no one who later described the march bothered to pay too much attention to such geographical features as gradient, width of ravine, steepness of the slopes, and so forth, which would enable us to identify the route positively.[43] The prevailing darkness, since there was no moon and the troops had only a faint starlight to guide them, undoubtedly had much to do with this oversight, but Lieutenant Wallace reported that they followed a dry ravine where the soil was poor, the grass short, and the hills low, a description that fits either route.[44]

Although most writers are inclined to favor the Davis Creek route, there is a possibility that the regiment followed Thompson's Creek for a short distance, then turned up the dry bed of Little Thompson Creek, which comes in from the north, and followed it to its source near the summit of the divide. From that point there is an easy pass over to the headwaters of Davis Creek, so that the regiment would have crossed the divide at the same place regardless of the route taken to get there. The evidence in favor of the Thomp-

40 "Story of White Elk as told to Willis Rowland at Lame Deer, Montana, May 25, 1927," Custer Scrapbooks, Billings Public Library.

41 Benteen, *Account*, 5. Brininstool, *Captain Benteen's Story*, 8–9.

42 Brown and Willard, *Black Hills Trails*, 127.

43 DeLand, *The Sioux Wars*, 396. Godfrey's description fits the Thompson Creek route better than the one by Davis Creek, but in later years he was dubious concerning whether the Thompson Creek route was the one actually taken. *Ibid.*, 411.

44 Wallace, Report, 1378.

son Creek route includes the following facts: Goes Ahead claimed that the last bivouac was made near its mouth; old-timers among the cattlemen of the vicinity still point out the spot where they say the ashes of Custer's campfires were visible for many years afterwards; the only water in the vicinity that is heavily impregnated with alkali is on that route; and, most important of all, by following Thompson's Creek, Custer would have obeyed the letter, if not the spirit, of General Terry's instructions. He would not have followed the Indian trail when it was found to turn westward up Davis Creek, but instead would have continued southward *toward* the headwaters of the Tongue—for only a short distance, to be sure—before turning to the west and north. When Custer turned, he was about twenty miles north of where Terry expected him to turn as shown by Brisbin's markings, and he was about twenty miles from the Little Big Horn River; but, by the route he followed, it was about thirty-three miles from his camp of the twenty-fourth to the hostile village.

On the other hand, and in favor of the Davis Creek route, is the declaration of White-Man that Custer followed the regular Indian trail from the Rosebud over to the Little Big Horn. This trail, which is fairly smooth, follows up Davis Creek and through a pass to the headwaters of Reno Creek.[45] Moylan illustrated the general uncertainty on the subject when he told the Reno Court of Inquiry that on the night march the command was "supposed to be moving up the Dry Fork of the Rosebud."[46]

A night march is always much more difficult and tiring than one made by day, and this particular one seems to have been attended by excessive noise and confusion. No lights were permitted, and about the only way that the troops in the rear had of knowing that they were following those ahead was by the dust cloud which they raised. If they could not smell dust, they knew they were off the trail. Also, the men in the rear of a troop pounded their tin cups on the horns of their saddles in order to guide the men behind them. Although it seems scarcely possible under the circumstances, two of the participants insist that this march was made at a trot or gallop.[47] According to Lieutenant Wallace, the regiment covered

45 *Account to Scott*, 4–7.

46 Reno, *Court*, 328.

47 Daniel A. Kanipe, "A New Story of Custer's Last Battle," in *Contributions*

only about six miles[48] before halting, near the head of the creek whose course they had been following, shortly after two o'clock at the first streaks of dawn, when the scouts told Custer that they could not possibly hope to cross the divide before daybreak and that they could not cross after daylight without being discovered by the Sioux.[49]

On this march Girard, Half-Yellow-Face, and Bloody Knife rode with Custer at the head of the column. When Custer kept insisting that he did not want any of the Sioux to escape, Bloody Knife told him that he need not be too particular about the small camps, for when they struck the main village, the regiment would find all of the Indians it wanted. In reply to a question Girard then estimated that they would find not less than twenty-five hundred warriors[50] and possibly three thousand, although later he corrected himself and declared that he had overestimated the number of Indians by one thousand.[51]

While this night march was not tactically unsound—for it must be remembered that no enemy had been met with and there was little evidence to indicate that the Sioux knew of Custer's location or disposition—it probably contributed greatly to Custer's later misfortunes,[52] for men and horses were already tired and the march only intensified that condition. Peter Thompson of Troop C noted that most of the horses appeared poor and gaunt; and later in the day many of them, including his own, broke down, and their riders had to be picked up by the rear guard.[53] This condition, however, was by no means general, for others testified that the horses were

to the Historical Society of Montana, IV (1903), 279. Benteen said that "the gait was a trot and was kept up for eight or ten miles although the night was pitch dark." Benteen, *Account*, 6. But there is another account, written by an officer who was not present which says, "Leading their horses much of the time, groping their way forward over treacherous rocky declevities, their progress was provokingly slow." Colonel William W. Edwards, "The Battle of the Little Big Horn," *Outdoor Life*, Vol. LXXI (February, 1933), 7.

48 Wallace, Report, 1378; Godfrey, *Century*, 367; Reno, *Court*, 144.

49 Reno, *Court*, 144; *Official Transcript*, 336; Holley, *Once Their Home*, 234.

50 Reno, *Court*, 143.

51 *Ibid.*, 191.

52 James P. Murphy, "Campaign of the Little Big Horn," *Infantry Journal*, Vol. XXXIV (June, 1929), 633.

53 Brown and Willard, *Black Hills Trails*, 148–49; E. A. Brininstool, *A Trooper with Custer*, 47.

in fair condition.[54] The grazing had not been too good on the march, and as the regiment was traveling light, the horses had had but little grain.[55]

After halting, the troops found concealment in a wooded ravine situated between two high ridges. Some of the mules were unpacked and some troopers unsaddled, although some did not. Most of them simply dropped down with the reins over their arms and went to sleep, which, as one of them afterwards noted, was not at all an unusual thing for a cavalryman to do on campaign.[56] This campsite was a poor one; there was little grass for the horses, the water was so heavily impregnated with alkali that the horses refused to drink it, and coffee made from it was unpalatable.[57]

It is altogether probable that Custer, following the plan announced to his officers only a few hours before, fully intended to remain here throughout the day, resting and reconnoitering, preparatory to an attack on the hostile village at dawn on the twenty-sixth. Subsequent developments were to force a change in that plan.

The Wolf or Little Chetish Mountains, which form the divide between the valleys of the Rosebud and the Little Big Horn, are, in the strict sense of the term, not mountains at all, but rather a rough, broken country of marked elevation, with precipitous sides and deep, narrow gullies and ravines. In all probability these "mountains" were formed not so much by a volcanic upheaval as by water and wind erosion which cut and gullied the land and sandstone rock. The rocky promontory which the Indians called the Crow's Nest—we do not know precisely which hill, but in all probability it was the fourth peak south of the pass which connects the valley of Davis Creek with that of Sundance or Reno Creek—was a well-known place of observation. It was located almost exactly on the divide, and from its summit the greater part of the valley of the Little Big Horn could be seen. Its value was not the result of any great elevation, for it was little if any higher than some of the other

[54] There is extensive disagreement regarding the condition of the horses. See Reno, *Court,* 197, 324, 469, 600, and 634.

[55] Brininstool, *A Trooper with Custer,* 26.

[56] *Hardin* (Montana) *Tribune,* June 22, 1923; Edgerly, *Narrative,* 3; Godfrey, "Diary," n.p.; Reno, *Court,* 328–29, 401.

[57] Wagner, *Old Neutriment,* 147; *Army and Navy Journal,* July 15, 1876; *Official Transcript,* 180, 317.

Gall,
fighting chief of the Uncpapas, most "warlike and recalcitrant of all the Sioux tribes."

Two Moon,
war chief of the Cheyennes, " 'fiercest of all the frontier cavalry.' "

Both courtesy Custer Battlefield National Monument

"Camp of Sitting Bull in the Big Horn Mountains, 1873."
From a painting by Henry H. Cross.

points near by, but resulted largely from its location in regard to the bluffs and other topographical features of the valley.[58]

Varnum, Bouyer, and the other scouts who had been sent ahead in an attempt to discover the exact whereabouts of the enemy reached this promontory about 2:30 A.M. on the twenty-fifth.[59] Before dawn Varnum managed to catch a nap of about forty-five minutes, but the others maintained an unceasing vigilance. The sight that the increasing light revealed made them gasp in astonishment. Intervening bluffs cut off a full view of the hostile camp, but the flat was white with lodges, and to the northwest the smoke from many campfires made a murky haze, while nearer at hand and on the benches on the other side of the Little Big Horn, the greatest pony herd that any of them had ever seen covered the earth like a carpet as far as they could see.[60] Lieutenant Varnum was awakened, but with his eyes heavy from many sleepless hours he could distinguish nothing of what the scouts pointed out to him. They said that it was like "looking for worms crawling in the grass," and so the Lieutenant looked for worms but could not see any.[61]

It was now nearly five o'clock, and Varnum sent two of the Arikaras, Red Star and Bull, back with a note to Custer stating that he could see the smoke from the hostile village about twenty miles away in the valley of the Little Big Horn.[62] The scouts knew the location of the regiment from the smoke ascending from Custer's campfires, about ten miles off, smoke which made the Crows very angry and caused them to question the judgment of the white leaders who seemed to operate on the principle that the Sioux were blind. Shortly after the two Rees left, the remaining scouts saw mounted hostiles at the foot of the hill about one and one-half miles to the west. When they soon disappeared, riding down Davis Creek toward the soldiers, the scouts feared that they might cut off the messengers, especially since Bull was very poorly mounted, his pony being little larger than a large Newfoundland dog. The scouts also

58 For another description of the Crow's Nest, see Dustin, *The Custer Tragedy*, 101. See also Robert M. Utley, *Custer's Last Stand*, 20n.

59 *Account to Scott*, 5–7.

60 *Ibid.*, 6; Linderman, *Red Mother*, 235.

61 Reno, *Court*, 292; *Official Transcript*, 260; see also Hughes, "Campaign against the Sioux in 1876," *Journal of the Military Institution of the United States*, Vol. XVIII (January, 1896), 29.

62 Maguire's Report, 1377.

saw six Sioux to the northeast, over near Tullock's Creek, and made a dash for them, but the Sioux escaped in the direction of the village. That the hostiles would be advised of the nearness of the troops there was little doubt, for on their way back to the village the Sioux began to circle.[63]

During the early morning Bloody Knife had approached Custer and begged him to use extreme caution, declaring that there were more hostiles ahead than there were bullets in the belts of the soldiers, and that the regiment would find enough Sioux to keep it fighting for two or three days, but Custer brushed the warning aside, saying that he guessed they could get through them in one day.[64] Later, witnesses were to assert that he smiled sadly as he made the remark,[65] but this assertion is at least open to question. Both Bloody Knife and Charley Reynolds were pessimistic about the outcome of the impending battle. The night before, Reynolds had opened his "war-sack" and divided its contents among his friends. Many had refused his presents, while others had accepted them only with reluctance.[66]

While Custer was talking to Bloody Knife, Martin, who had been assigned to Custer as an orderly for the day, reported.[67] Shortly afterwards Red Star rode into camp with Varnum's message[68]—Bull's pony had "played out" and he had lagged far behind—and told Custer that the Indian village had been located, pointing out the butte from which he said it could be seen. Without finishing his breakfast, Custer, mounted bareback, rode around the camp telling the officers what he wanted them to do.[69] Custer was dressed that morning in a blue-gray flannel shirt, buckskin trousers, and long boots, and wore a regular company hat over his close-cropped hair.[70]

63 Hughes, "Campaign against the Sioux in 1876," *Journal of the Military Service Institution of the United States*, Vol. XVIII (January, 1896), 29; *Account to Scott*, 5–6; Edgerly, *Narrative*, 3; *Army and Navy Journal*, March 25, 1882. This last account was written by Lieutenant Charles F. Roe, who got his information from the scout Curly, LeForge being the interpreter.

64 Godfrey, *Century*, 367.

65 McLaughlin, *My Friend, the Indian*, 128–29.

66 Dustin, *The Custer Tragedy*, 101.

67 William A. Graham, "'Come on! Be quick! Bring packs!' The Story of Custer's Last Message . . . ," *Cavalry Journal*, Vol. XXXII (July, 1923), 304–305.

68 Burkman says that it was Isaiah Dorman, the Negro interpreter, who came back looking for Custer, Wagner, *Old Neutriment*, 148–49.

69 Godfrey, *Montana*, 170. In his "Diary," however, Godfrey gives a slightly different account of this series of incidents. See also Benteen, *Account*, 6.

By eight-thirty the command was ready, and the scouts moved out ahead, the regiment following about fifteen minutes later.[71] Everyone was in high spirits, with much laughing and bantering among the men.[72] After marching at a walk for more than an hour, they came to a deep, well-wooded ravine where they halted and hid, with orders to keep quiet and stay concealed. The sun having risen clear and bright, it was already obvious that another extremely hot day was in prospect.[73] Custer hurried ahead to the Crow's Nest to confirm the report of the discovery of the village. Near the butte he met Lieutenant Varnum, who told him that the presence of the troops had been discovered and that the scouts had seen messengers ride off in the direction of the hostile camp. Arrived at the Crow's Nest, which was several hundred feet above the trail, Custer climbed up far enough to see over and into the valley.[74] He looked in the direction indicated, but declared that he could see no signs of a hostile encampment.[75] The explanation for his failure to discover it probably lies in the fact that the scouts saw the smoke of the village and the pony herds in the valley shortly after dawn through a clear, calm atmosphere with the early morning sun at their backs, while Custer's observations were made several hours later with the sun almost directly overhead and the distant view obscured by the haze which accompanies summer heat.[76] Assured by Bouyer that there was a huge hostile camp about fifteen miles distant in the valley

[70] William A. Graham, "'Come on! Be quick! Bring packs!' The Story of Custer's Last Message . . . ," *Cavalry Journal*, Vol. XXXII (July, 1923), 305.

[71] Godfrey, "Diary," n.p.; Edgerly, *Narrative*, 3; DeRudio, "My Personal Story," *Frontier and Midland*, Vol. XIV (January, 1934), 155.

[72] Brown and Willard, *Black Hills Trails*, 149.

[73] Usher L. Burdick, *Tragedy in the Great Sioux Camp*, 12.

[74] *Account to Scott*, 4–5. Girard said that they rode as far as they could, dismounted and walked to the summit. He added that on the side which he and Custer went up, there was a little ravine with timber in it and part of the way up there was a spring. *Official Transcript*, 187.

[75] Coughlan, "The Battle of the Little Big Horn," *Cavalry Journal*, Vol. XLIII (January–February, 1934), 16; Wallace, Report, 1377; William A. Graham, "'Come on! Be quick! Bring packs!' The Story of Custer's Last Message . . . ," *Cavalry Journal*, Vol. XXXII (July, 1923), 305; Godfrey, *Century*, 367.

[76] Coughlan, "The Battle of the Little Big Horn," *Cavalry Journal*, Vol. XLIII (January–February, 1934), 16; William A. Graham, "'Come on! Be quick! Bring packs!' The Story of Custer's Last Message . . . ," *Cavalry Journal*, Vol. XXXII (July, 1923), 316. White-Man-Runs-Him later told General Scott that Custer viewed the valley at six o'clock and that the sun was just up. *Account to Scott*, 5–6. This would seem to be far too early.

of the Little Big Horn, Custer still remained skeptical even after looking through his field glasses. Bouyer also told him that it was the largest village which had ever collected in the Northwest, and reminded him that he (Bouyer) had known these Indians for over thirty years.[77] Custer then rode back and rejoined the regiment.

After Custer had left, Varnum and the scouts saw a dark mass, which they knew to be a band of Indians with their lodges and other equipment, moving downstream. The inference was that, the presence of the soldiers having been reported, the great Indian encampment was beginning to break up and scatter, and the news was promptly sent on to Custer. Actually, as was learned afterwards, this was a much smaller village of about sixty lodges which had been located not far from the mouth of Reno Creek. Having learned of the proximity of Custer's command from their returning scouts, they had hastily packed up and started to join the larger village farther down the valley.[78] It is easily apparent how a village of this size, with all of its ponies and camp impedimenta, moving at a fast gait could give the impression that a much larger one was in flight.

During Custer's absence some of the scouts had come in with the report that the presence of the regiment had been discovered by the Sioux, for two small parties had seen the regiment and were even then riding toward the village. Examination revealed fresh pony tracks in a near-by ravine, and Herendeen saw an Indian only a few hundred yards away watching the soldiers. During this halt Sergeant Curtis and two men of Troop F received permission to ride over the regiment's back trail in search of some boxes of hard bread which had been lost from one of the packs. They found the lost boxes and an Indian trying to open one of them, who, upon seeing the soldiers, galloped away out of range and then moved leisurely along the ridge.[79] On his return Curtis reported the incident to Captain Yates, who told Keogh, who in turn related the story to a group of the officers who had gathered to await Custer's return. Upon hearing it, Captain Tom Custer jumped up with the remark

[77] Coughlan, "The Battle of the Little Big Horn," *Cavalry Journal*, Vol. XLIII (January–February, 1934), 16.

[78] Brady, *Indian Fights and Fighters*, 383, quoting Lieutenant Woodruff who was with Gibbon's column.

[79] Godfrey, *Century*, 368; *New York Herald*, July 8, 1876; *Official Transcript*, 318.

that he was going to report that to the General, and left the group, soon returning with his brother, who ordered officers' call sounded. Charlie Reynolds probably reflected the opinion of the scouts when he said: "I knew well enough that they had scouts ahead of us but I didn't think that others would be trailing along to pick up stuff dropped by our careless packers."[80]

Custer is said to have told his officers that he had just come down from the Crow's Nest and that while the scouts had reported a great Indian camp in the valley below, with ponies, tepees, and smoke, he had been unable to see anything of the kind even after looking through his glasses; he declared that he did not believe there was a village there,[81] although Godfrey later expressed much surprise that Custer should have made any such statement.[82] However, Custer did admit that the hostile Indians had discovered the presence of the regiment and that the scouts had seen Indians moving along the ridges overlooking the valley through which the regiment had recently marched.[83] Accordingly, he felt that any further attempts at concealment were unnecessary, and he had therefore decided to cross the divide immediately, ride down into the valley, and attack any Indians who might be there, for otherwise the Sioux, if they were where the scouts said they were, would soon scatter in all directions, and the work of rounding them up would have to be done all over again.[84]

The effect of the news brought back by Sergeant Curtis is difficult to assess. It seemed to indicate that at least two different bodies of Indians were involved, with the possibility that the command might be surrounded, and that if Custer did not attack the Sioux, the Sioux might attack the troops. This news may have been the determining factor in Custer's decision to attack, or it may merely have re-enforced a decision already made. We know now that the breadbox incident did not mean a thing. The Indians who discovered it and who were seen by the soldiers were Little Wolf's

80 Schultz, *William Jackson*, 132.

81 Reno, *Court*, 545; *Official Transcript*, 648; Benteen, *Account*, 6.

82 Graham, "'Come on! Be quick! Bring packs!' The Story of Custer's Last Message . . . ," *Cavalry Journal*, Vol. XXXII (July, 1923), 305.

83 *Ibid.*, 305; Godfrey, *Century*, 368; Reno, *Court*, 387.

84 Edgerly, *Narrative*, 3; see also the article by General Scott in the *Custer* (So. Dak.) *Chronicle*, July 23, 1936.

band of Cheyennes. They were the same ones the discovery of whose tracks on the morning of the twenty-fourth had caused so much excitement in the regiment, and who had seen the troops in the camp near Busby but did not know who they were or their purpose in the country. After being fired on by Sergeant Curtis and his men, they did not hurry down to give the alarm but followed along behind the troops and arrived after the fight was over.[85]

The time selected for the attack was unusual, but the conditions which confronted Custer were also unusual and not at all what had been anticipated in General Terry's letter of instructions.[86] Custer's original plan had been to attack at dawn on the twenty-sixth, the time of day ordinarily selected for an attack on an Indian village. That plan was now impossible. Custer probably suspected that the Indians would be expecting the attack then. If he did, he would have been correct, for that was their expectation as soon as they learned of the proximity of the troops. Or the Indians might have sallied forth and made an attack on the Seventh Cavalry as they had on Crook's command. Thus, to his way of thinking, Custer had two alternatives: an immediate attack in the middle of the day with the Indians on the alert and with no chance of concealment or surprise, or a delayed attack, risking the possibility that the Indians would scatter and make good their escape and perhaps cause him to be severely punished for failing to bring them to battle.

Custer's decision to attack at once has been harshly criticized, and perhaps justly so; it may very well be that in his eagerness to force a fight, he violated the principle of surprise, thus destroying his only chance of success. It is difficult to see, however, what other course he could have followed, after having made the fateful decision to turn west at Busby. The wisdom or lack of wisdom of his tactics must be determined not by what we know now but in the light of the information that was available to him at the time. Indian fighting was always a touch-and-go proposition, and Custer knew

[85] Marquis, *A Warrior who Fought Custer,* 248–50. For the story that this band was Sioux rather than Cheyenne and that news of the affair reached Sitting Bull only a few moments before Reno's attack developed, see Vestal, *Sitting Bull,* 164.

[86] For a defense of Custer's action see Edgerly, *Narrative,* 16. For a criticism of that action, Hughes, "Campaign against the Sioux in 1876," *Journal of the Military Service Institution of the United States,* Vol. XVIII (January, 1896), 27, 41.

that he had lost the element of surprise. He did not know of Crook's defeat or of the great numerical strength of the Sioux and Cheyennes, or he might have waited. It probably would not have made any difference if he had, for we must remember that a leader of Custer's disposition was not apt to weigh the various possibilities too carefully. Nor must it be forgotten that Custer's mind was in a turmoil. He had incurred the displeasure of the President, and failure against the Sioux would give Grant the excuse to end the Custer military career—and Custer knew full well that outside of the army there was little possibility of a brilliant career for him. Furthermore, since it was seldom the habit of the Indians to give battle, the only chance of failure that he could see was that the Sioux might scatter and escape. Thus his entire future may have seemed to hang on a brilliant victory, a victory so overwhelming that even the hatred and animosity of the President of the United States would be unable to stand against it. On the other hand, Custer's management of the affair would probably have been just about what it was had he had no difficulty with the President. He regarded attack and victory as synonymous, and his only concern seems to have been to keep the Indians where they were until he could strike them.[87]

The number of hostiles caused him no concern, for he knew that a large camp could scatter as easily as a small one,[88] and he had not the slightest doubt of the ability of his regiment alone to defeat the entire Sioux Nation. He is reported to have answered the contention that there were too many Indians ahead for the command to handle with the remark that there were not too many Indians on the whole North American continent for the Seventh Cavalry to handle.[89] Delay for the purpose of reconnoitering would only give the hostiles that much more opportunity to escape, and he seems to have decided to risk everything on this one desperate maneuver. There can be little doubt that he had few, if any, illusions regarding the strength of the enemy, and was perfectly aware that there were great numbers of hostiles ahead. He was too astute and too experienced an Indian fighter not to have read the message so plainly

[87] *Army and Navy Journal*, July 22, 1876; Fry, *Military Miscellanies*, 509–11.
[88] Godfrey, *Montana*, 210.
[89] *Oregon Journal* (Portland, Oregon), August 3, 1923. A large part of Custer's confidence was attributable to the fact that the Indians were poor marksmen. Bates and Downey, *Fifty Years after the Little Big Horn*, 9.

pictured in the various Indian camps that the regiment had passed.[90] Furthermore, he had been warned specifically by Bloody Knife, Girard, Bouyer, Reynolds, and the Crow scouts. Reynolds had reported to him that the biggest bunch of Indians he had ever seen was ahead,[91] and Custer informed his officers that "the largest Indian camp on the North American continent is ahead and I am going to attack it,"[92] and is said to have told Burkman, "I think we are going in to a real fight. . . . There'll be plenty of Indians for us all."[93]

But Custer's decision to attack also had the sanction of his Crow scouts, for White-Man had counseled hiding in the ravine during the day and surprising the camp at dawn. When the command had been discovered by the Sioux, however, he agreed that Custer did as he would have done: "Hurry and get there and get an even fight with them."[94] General Sherman later declared that in his opinion the attack was neither desperate nor rash in view of all the circumstances or according to the rules of Indian fighting, and that Custer "could do nothing but attack when he found himself in the presence of the Indians."[95]

The scouts were ordered ahead and told to ride hard, to stop for nothing, and to steal or stampede the Sioux pony herd. Custer told them that they would have a hard day but reminded them of the great importance of their task, for, without their horses the Sioux would be unable to move rapidly or to escape—an important part of Custer's plan. This order was doubtless congenial to the scouts, who had developed the stealing of horses to the status of a fine art. But the scouts were thoroughly convinced in their own minds that the regiment was going to encounter a lot more hostiles than it expected to find, and as a result they had been constantly "making medicine" which they hoped would bring them good luck. One of the older ones, Stabbed, who knew that most of the other Arikaras were young and inexperienced, now rode around among

[90] *Billings Gazette*, August 13, 1933. Mr. James Gatchell believes that from the trail Custer knew that at least thirteen thousand Indians were ahead but that he did not know that the Northern Cheyennes were in the assemblage.

[91] *Billings Gazette*, January 6, 1934.

[92] *Oregon Journal*, August 3, 1923; Roe, *Custer's Last Battle*, 8.

[93] Wagner, *Old Neutriment*, 37.

[94] *Account to Scott*, 6–9.

[95] Brackett, *Custer's Last Battle*, 262; *Army and Navy Journal*, July 22, 1876.

them exhorting them to be brave and attempting to prepare them for what lay ahead. He rubbed some clay which he had brought from Fort Lincoln between his hands while he prayed over it. Then he rubbed a little of it on the body of each Arikara in the hope of assuring their safety in the coming battle.[96]

Custer ordered each company commander to select one non-commissioned officer and six privates from his troop and detail them to the pack train, each man to lead two of the pack mules. Pretty Face, one of the Ree scouts, was assigned to the same duty, and there may have been other men whose horses were unfit for hard service who also stayed with the train. Thus the train, with its guard, accounted for about 130 men, or fully 20 per cent of the command.[97] Each commander was also ordered to inspect his troop and to satisfy himself that men and horses were ready for any contingency.[98] As a stimulus Custer promised that the troops would march in the order in which their commanders reported them ready. First to report was Captain Benteen, who did not visit his company but may have received a signal from Lieutenant Gibson; and to H troop fell the privilege of leading the advance. It took the commanders less than two minutes to report their troops, and Lieutenant Godfrey, who was among the last to report and marched in position number ten, complained to his diary that some of the officers reported "all ready" without seeing to anything and so got the lead.[99] Last to report was Captain McDougall, and to Troop B fell the unenvied task of guarding the slow-moving pack train commanded by Lieutenant Mathey, who was ordered to march the train off to one side of the trail on account of the dust cloud which it would raise. The packs were also not to get under way until twenty minutes after the remainder of the regiment had marched.[100] Because Dr. Lord, the senior surgeon, was not well, Custer suggested that he remain with the packs while Dr. Porter accompanied the column. Dr. Lord refused to hear of

[96] Libby, *Arikara Narrative*, 84.

[97] Coughlan, "The Battle of the Little Big Horn," *Cavalry Journal*, Vol. XLIII (January–February, 1934), 16–17; Holley, *Once Their Home*, 244.

[98] Brininstool, *Captain Benteen's Story*, 10–11; *Official Transcript*, 649.

[99] Godfrey, "Diary," n.p.; Edgerly, *Narrative*, 2.

[100] William A. Graham, "'Come on! Be quick! Bring packs!' The Story of Custer's Last Message . . . ," *Cavalry Journal*, Vol. XXXII (July, 1923), 316; Godfrey, *Montana*, 174.

this, insisting that as long as he was able to ride, he would remain with the regiment and go wherever it went.[101]

Shortly before twelve o'clock all was ready, and it was almost exactly noon, June 25, 1876, when the regiment rode over the divide[102] and started down into the valley of the Little Big Horn—for many of them the Valley of the Shadow—riding into regimental immortality to become a part of one of the most glorious epics of the West!

[101] *New York Herald*, July 11, 1876; *Army and Navy Journal*, July 15, 1876.

[102] The spot where the regiment crossed is now indicated by a marker which reads, "General George Custer and the Seventh Cavalry crossed the Divide at this point, June 25, 1876." The marker was placed by the late Walter M. Camp with the help of the Crow scout Curly and George Herendeen, acting independently. See a letter written by Mr. Camp, October 29, 1917, which is in the files of the Montana State Historical Society.

CHAPTER XIII

Gibbon's March

ANTICIPATING that, in the face of Major Reno's discovery, an advance up the Yellowstone River would be ordered, and a cavalry scout up that stream having reported the side streams almost impassable as the result of floods caused by the recent rains, Colonel Gibbon had issued orders on the twentieth for Captain Freeman with companies E, H, and K of the infantry to start upstream on the morning of the twenty-first for the purpose of bridging the creeks and otherwise putting the road in order.[1] The detachment got under way at six o'clock that morning, but shortly thereafter the *Far West* was discovered steaming upriver, and orders for the entire command to prepare to move were immediately issued. General Terry arrived at eight o'clock, and less than two hours later all of Gibbon's much marched command was again in motion up the Yellowstone River with Fort Pease as their immediate objective.

Both Colonel Gibbon and Major Brisbin remained behind for the conference with General Terry, so that the immediate command of the column devolved upon the ranking officer, Captain Ball. Also remaining behind were six of the best of the Crow scouts who had volunteered for the duty and who, together with "Mitch" Bouyer, were to assist Custer in the coming campaign. As the Montana column moved out, word circulated among the soldiers that Custer and his command were close at hand, and shortly afterwards the twelve troops of the Seventh Cavalry appeared in view on the south bank of the river, riding along the tablelands toward the mouth of the Rosebud.[2]

1 Gibbon's Report, 473; Gibbon, "Summer Expedition," 291.

2 McClernand wrote that "compared to the showing made by Gibbon's force when on the march, Custer's column looked large and imposing." "With Indian and

Sixteen miles up the Yellowstone River, Gibbon's command was reunited. Captain Freeman's companies had gone into camp and were just getting settled for the night when the rest of the column appeared, and Freeman was ordered to break camp and resume the march along with the others, a most unwelcome order for which there appears to have been but little excuse except perhaps Captain Ball's desire to exhibit his authority. Camp was barely formed, a short distance below the mouth of Big Porcupine Creek, when a terrific storm arose, characterized by winds of great velocity and by hailstones as large as walnuts.[3] Tents were blown down, and it was only with difficulty that the horse and mule herd was kept from stampeding. Fortunately the storm, as summer storms in that region often are, was of short duration and the weather soon cleared.[4]

About midnight, Lieutenants Low and Kenzie with the battalion of Gatling guns arrived,[5] having been detached from Custer's command because of the latter's belief that they might impede his progress. They had been ferried across the river by the steamer and had then set out by a forced march to overtake the Montana column. The two officers were openly indignant at not having been allowed to accompany the Seventh Cavalry and voiced the belief that the transfer had robbed them of any opportunity to see action, an opinion which seems to have been almost unanimous among both officers and men of the infantry and cavalry.[6]

At six o'clock the next morning the cavalry and the Gatling battalion started with orders to push on to Fort Pease as speedily as possible. The infantry was to follow at as rapid a rate as they could since the storm of the night before had left the road so muddy that it seemed that the progress of the foot soldiers would be greatly impeded. But the expected order was soon reversed. The infantry, starting an hour behind the cavalry, took the lead when the cavalry's

Buffalo in Montana," *Cavalry Journal*, Vol. XXXVI (January and April, 1927), 16. Godfrey said in his "Diary" that as the Seventh Cavalry approached the Rosebud they could see Gibbon's men on the north bank of the Yellowstone just beginning their march up that stream.

[3] Bradley, *Journal*, 215. Mathew Carroll said some of the hailstones were as large as pigeon's eggs. Carroll, "Diary," 233.

[4] Bradley, *Journal*, 215.

[5] Carroll speaks of two pieces of artillery and a lot of sorebacked mules. "Diary," 233.

[6] Bradley, *Journal*, 215.

wagon train mired in the heavy mud. The two detachments crossed Big Porcupine Creek at different points, the infantry following the bench lands back from the river while the cavalry companies kept to the valley. Despite the fact that on at least one occasion Captain Freeman halted his detachment and allowed the cavalry to go ahead, the two groups camped that night within two miles of each other. During the day the infantry had covered twenty-nine miles—very fast marching under the circumstances.[7]

The next day the infantry broke camp first and soon came up with the horsemen who were just saddling up. But the cavalry train had taken the road ahead of that of the infantry, and the latter was unable to gain the lead despite a purse put up by some of the sportive infantrymen in the interest of a race. During the day, Lieutenant Doane and "Muggins" Taylor, who were scouting ahead of the column, saw several mounted hostiles on the south bank of the Yellowstone River, apparently observing the troops.[8] They also saw thousands of buffalo and killed a good many of them, so that the cavalrymen supplied themselves liberally with meat. They left some buffalo meat for the infantrymen, even going so far as to leave a subordinate to show where it had been cached, but Lieutenant Jacobs, the quartermaster, "with unaccountable obstinacy and disregard for the men's welfare objected to the train halting for the few moments necessary to take it on." As Captain Freeman refused to overrule his subordinate, that night the command ate bacon instead of the fresh buffalo steaks that they might have enjoyed. Camp was made after a march of twenty-two miles, the infantry being a mile below Fort Pease and the cavalry two miles above.[9]

The Montana column had thus covered, in three days going upstream, a distance that had required ten days going down. Consideration of this rate of travel may temper the enthusiasm of some critics who have accused Custer of needlessly tiring his men by hurrying them along at too rapid a gait, merely to get there first and secure all of the glory for himself and his regiment. The plain fact is that Gibbon was hurrying, Custer was hurrying, everyone was hurrying, the all-consuming fear uppermost in the minds of all

[7] *Ibid.*, 216.

[8] *Ibid.*, 216. Carroll says that these mounted Indians were supposed to be scouts from the boat. "Diary," 233.

[9] Bradley, *Journal*, 216–17.

being that the Sioux would take fright at the approach of the troops, scatter, and escape.[10]

A cold wind was blowing from the north when at four o'clock on the afternoon of the twenty-second, the *Far West*, with Terry, Gibbon, and Brisbin on board, pulled away from the campsite near the mouth of the Rosebud. The steamer ran upstream until dark, when it tied up for the night.[11] The next day the boat steamed steadily upstream, but was unable to reach Fort Pease or to overtake the troops before darkness again made it necessary to tie up alongside the bank.[12] Although the men on board the steamer probably did not know it, they were only a few miles below the camp of the infantry, and the scouts with the column had discovered the smoke of the steamer a short time before sundown. A few minutes after four o'clock the next morning the *Far West* passed the infantry bivouac and moved up opposite the cavalry. The infantry column marched at six o'clock, and a few hours later the command was again reunited. Orders were immediately issued to all the companies except B of the infantry, commanded by Lieutenant Kirtland, to prepare to march at once. Following the system of rotation in vogue since the beginning of the campaign, Company B was to be left to guard the wagons and the surplus stores. All of the others were to take rations for eight days. These, the extra ammunition, and some forage were to be transported on a train of pack mules, four mules being assigned to each infantry company and six to each cavalry troop.[13]

At eleven o'clock, twelve of the Crow scouts were put across the river, and started up Tullock's Creek, a small tributary which flows into the Big Horn River near its mouth, with orders to keep going until they found a Sioux village or a recent trail. An hour later the steamer began ferrying the troops across, the cavalry going on the first three trips, the Gatlings, Bradley's detachment, and a part of the infantry on the fourth, and the remainder of the infantry on the fifth, and last, trip. The place where the expedition crossed

10 *Billings Gazette*, May 15, 1932.
11 Gibbon, "Summer Expedition," 293.
12 *Ibid.*, 294.
13 Bradley, *Journal*, 217.

was the site of Montana's first fur-trading post, built by Manuel Lisa in 1807, and of the present town of Big Horn. Expected to require about three hours, the transfer, as is usually the case, took longer, and it was not until after four o'clock that the last soldier was ashore on the southern bank of the Yellowstone. Then the march up the Big Horn River began, with Bradley's detachment, as usual, scouting ahead. The command turned and began to ascend the valley of Tullock's Creek, halting at six o'clock and going into camp at the foot of a perpendicular wall of rock on the banks of that stream. They had covered approximately six miles in the two hours since leaving the boat.[14] About an hour later General Terry and his staff arrived at the camping place. Colonel Gibbon, who had been taken seriously ill the night before, remained on the steamer, the immediate command of the column thus devolving upon Major Brisbin.[15]

Just before dark the twelve Crows who had been sent ahead came tearing down the valley, behaving in such an extravagant fashion that everyone concerned expected that they had made some startling discovery, although by this time Gibbon's officers should have known better. When the scouts reached camp almost breathless with excitement, it was merely to report that some six miles farther up the valley they had found a buffalo bull freshly wounded with arrows, which had caused them to suspect that they were in the immediate proximity of a Sioux village. Bradley registered his disgust at this exhibition of what he considered flagrant cowardice on the part of the scouts, who, "after wasting eight hours in advancing ten miles," had returned to the safety of the command on such a slight excuse. The Crows themselves knew better than anyone else that no importance was to be attached to their discovery, since the animal might have been wounded by a small hunting party, and that there was no village, large or small, within fifty miles. On being reminded of this fact, the scouts rather lamely explained that they had returned because there was no one in charge to tell them what to do. Bradley also derived a measure of amusement from the incident in listening to the comments and speculations of the "pil-

14 *Ibid.*, 217.

15 Gibbon, "Summer Expedition," 294; Gibbon's Report, 463; Maguire's Report, 1348.

grims"—newcomers who were ignorant of the ways and hardships of the country—and who saw in the report of the scouts proof positive that an enemy camp could not be far distant.[16]

The night passed without further incident, and at four o'clock in the morning, Bradley started six of the Crows up Tullock's Creek, the Lieutenant following with the rest of the scouts and his detachment about half an hour later. After traveling for about nine miles, they halted to wait "for some definite indication that they were being followed by the rest of the command,"[17] which had broken camp at five-thirty and marched a little more than three miles up the stream before turning to the right along a dry creek bed and beginning to ascend the divide that separates the valley of Tullock's Creek from that of the Big Horn River, expecting to find a fairly level tableland leading to the valley of the Little Big Horn.[18] Lieutenant McClernand, who had been attached to General Terry's staff, had been ordered to select a trail across to the Little Big Horn River. He had decided to move up the valley of Tullock's Creek to a point only a few miles north of where Captain Ball's scouting party had struck it on the return from their scouting trip, then turn to the right and cross the divide, striking the Little Big Horn about five miles above its mouth. This route would have made several crossings of the stream necessary, but would have caused no hardship to anyone except the battery of Gatling guns, who were already encumbering Terry's march as Custer had known they would encumber his, and moreover would have had the advantage of keeping the entire command within easy distance of a sufficient supply of water during the greater part of the march.[19]

A change of route was decided upon, however, apparently at the suggestion of Major Brisbin and Lieutenant Doane, who in turn acted on the advice of the civilian scout, "Muggins" Taylor, who was not too familiar with either route but believed that the summit of the divide would furnish a better road than the creek valley.[20]

16 Bradley, *Journal*, 217.

17 *Ibid.*, 218.

18 For a somewhat different version see Roe, *Custer's Last Battle*, 4. Lieutenant McClernand's Report is in the *Report of the Secretary of War, 1877*, II, Part 2, 1370.

19 McClernand, "With Indian and Buffalo in Montana," *Cavalry Journal*, Vol. XXXVI (January and April, 1927), 19–20.

20 *Ibid.*, 20.

For this change of route Colonel Hughes blames Custer, on the ground that had he sent a messenger to General Terry, as instructed, the change would not have been made. Had Gibbon's column followed the valley of Tullock's Creek, which offered "a fair route directly to the Indian village," instead of making the march across "to the Big Horn," which was "most arduous and exhausting," it would have been possible for it "to appear on the field of action on the afternoon of the 25th" in time to have been of assistance to the Custer column.[21]

In this sequence of events is to be found abundant refutation of the oft repeated claim that General Terry lost valuable time on Tullock's Creek waiting for the scout, George Herendeen, who was expected to descend that stream with dispatches from Custer, who had bivouacked the night before approximately thirty-three miles from where Bradley waited. In any event, he certainly wasted no time waiting for a courier, and if Bradley expected to meet Herendeen or anyone else, it is strange that he makes no mention of the fact.

A detachment of the cavalry was sent to overtake Bradley and inform him of the change in direction. The Lieutenant and his men then rejoined the main command by taking a "short cut" across the hills and found the soldiers "hopelessly involved in a labyrinth of bold hills and deep precipitous ravines, entirely destitute of water."[22] The men were greatly fatigued from clambering over the rough ground, and thirst added to their discomfort. Believing that the day's march would lie along the banks of Tullock's Creek, many of them had not taken the precaution to fill their canteens. The scouts were soon able to set the command on a better road, though one that was far from level, for the divide itself was high, crooked, uneven, and narrow, being broken by ridges and deep ravines, the steep sides of which were covered with a thick growth of small brush so that the Gatling-gun battalion, especially, had much trouble. Around the worst of these obstructions it was necessary to detour, thus increasing the difficulties of the march, for the surface was covered with small boulders and a thick growth of cactus.

The day was very warm and the air so still and sultry that the

[21] Hughes, "Campaign against the Sioux in 1876," *Journal of the Military Service Institution of the United States*, Vol. XVIII (January, 1896), 28.

[22] Bradley, *Journal*, 218.

sun seemed to concentrate its rays and literally pour down its heat on that plateau. The air was also filled with the heavy alkaline dust kicked up by the marching soldiers which produced phantasies and mirages and seemed to overpower the senses, affecting an individual something like sailing over a very rough sea. Maguire noted that it was only when the sharp rattle of the snakes aroused the almost somnolent column that there seemed to be any life in the troopers.[23]

Finally, after a march of about sixteen miles, they turned toward the Big Horn River, which was about four or five miles away. Then as the infantrymen began to collapse from fatigue, thirst, and heat, a shuttle service was organized, the canteens being loaded on the horses of some of the cavalrymen, who rode to the river and brought back water for the suffering infantry.[24] The column reached the Big Horn River about three o'clock, having marched more than twenty-one miles under the worst possible conditions. Many of the infantrymen were on the verge of complete exhaustion and could go no farther. Here the river was about two hundred yards wide with a swift current of clear and cold water, and a temporary camp was made in order to give the men a rest.[25]

Lieutenant Bradley had been sent ahead with the scouts and ordered to explore a distant ridge on the left of the line of march, from which it was hoped that the valley of the Little Big Horn River could be seen. But after arriving at the summit after a toilsome trip, the Lieutenant discovered that the hoped-for view was obstructed by another and higher ridge a few miles farther on. Since his orders were not to go beyond the first ridge, the detachment reluctantly turned back and joined the rest of the command, which was just going into camp.[26]

After resting for about two hours, the infantrymen had begun to move upstream to the place where the cavalry had halted in a thick grove of trees about a mile farther on. They arrived at the campsite just as the four cavalry troops were moving out. Some

[23] Maguire's Report, 1348; *Report of the Secretary of War, 1876*, 463; *New York Herald*, July 13, 1876; McClernand, "With Indian and Buffalo in Montana," *Cavalry Journal*, Vol. XXXVI (January and April, 1927), 20.

[24] Roe, *Custer's Last Battle*, 4; McClernand; "With Indian and Buffalo in Montana," *Cavalry Journal*, Vol. XXXVI (January and April, 1927), 20.

[25] Bradley, *Journal*, 218; Roe, *Custer's Last Battle*, 4.

[26] Bradley, *Journal*, 218.

of the Crow scouts who had started earliest of all had come in and reported seeing a heavy smoke in the direction of the valley of the Little Big Horn. Since this was believed to indicate the presence of a Sioux village—some of the officers were of the opinion that the smoke was caused by Custer burning the village—General Terry had ordered a night march of the cavalry and the Gatling-gun battalion in order to get as close as possible to the valley that night. Then at daybreak the scouts could be sent ahead into the valley of the Little Big Horn. The infantry was to follow in the morning.[27] Bradley expressed the belief that the Indian village was a large one and that the coming battle would be one of the greatest and most decisive ever fought on this continent. And he reflected that while there was little enough glory in Indian fighting, it would be worthwhile to have been present on such an occasion.[28]

Bradley's detachment now joined the cavalry, and the column —minus the infantry companies—started up the Big Horn River. During the late afternoon a brisk rain had set in, and frequent heavy showers continued throughout the night.[29] The rain not only caused physical discomfort but added to General Terry's uneasiness arising from the superstition that rain always follows a great battle. There can be no doubt that Terry was honestly worried at having received no word from Custer, for he knew only too well the dashing and impetuous character of the latter and was properly concerned lest his subordinate had encountered more Indians than his regiment could handle alone.

This night march was very difficult—it was so dark that nothing could be seen at any distance, and it would have been impossible to follow a straight course even had the nature of the terrain permitted. In addition, there was rain and wind together, as bad a night for duty as could be imagined. Besides being unknown, the country was rough and broken; on several occasions long halts were necessary in order to find the way out of some topographical trap into

[27] *Ibid.*, 218; Terry's Report, 463.

[28] Bradley, *Journal*, 218. Colonel Gibbon wrote, somewhat cynically, that glory was "a term upon the frontier, which has long since been defined to signify 'being shot by an Indian from behind a rock, and having your name spelled wrong in the newspaper.'" General John Gibbon, "Hunting Sitting Bull," *American Catholic Quarterly Review*, Vol. II, No. 3 (October, 1899), 691.

[29] McClernand, "With Indian and Buffalo in Montana," *Cavalry Journal*, Vol. XXXVI (January and April, 1927), 21.

which the command had blundered. On occasion the troops found themselves bunched up into a dense mass, and then again stretched out like an "attenuated thread" which was in grave danger of being broken into fragments and scattered. Once the Gatling-gun battery, which had had great difficulty in keeping up with the rest of the command, did get separated and wandered a mile or so off the trail, and was only brought back by repeated trumpet calls.[30] Lieutenant Roe's troop also got lost and in the darkness fell into a ravine and wasted more than an hour wandering around before rejoining their fellows.[31]

For want of anyone better, the cavalry officers who had scouted the region in April were acting as guides and doing a poor job of it, as Roe's experience illustrates. Finally, when the column found itself on a very high precipice, at the foot of which the roaring waters of the Big Horn River could be seen 150 feet below, with similar declivities on both the right and the left, Bradley ventured to suggest to General Terry, who seemed uncertain about just what should be done, that the services of Little Face, one of the Crow scouts who had roamed the region as a boy some fifty years before and said he knew every foot of it, should be utilized. The merits of this suggestion were so obvious that one wonders that no one had thought of it before. The explanation probably is to be found in the stubborn reluctance of most army officers to make full use of their Indian allies, preferring to disparage their services and to use them only when all other alternatives had been exhausted.[32]

The suggestion was accepted, and Little Face, called up, led off without the slightest hesitation and as confidently as though he had been operating at noonday rather than at midnight. He led the thoroughly fatigued and rain-soaked troops by an easy route some two miles to a sheltered cove, where there was enough water for drinking purposes but little grass for the horses. Here, at midnight, the weary soldiers halted, unsaddled, and literally threw themselves

[30] *New York Herald*, July 8, 1876.

[31] Bradley, *Journal*, 219; Roe, *Custer's Last Battle*, 5.

[32] For instance, in his Report Maguire makes no mention of the services of Little Face. Nor does McClernand, who merely says that General Terry decided that he was taxing the strength of the command to little purpose and at midnight ordered a halt. "With Indian and Buffalo in Montana," *Cavalry Journal*, Vol. XXXVI (January and April, 1927), 21.

down on the ground "in a perfect slough of mud and disgust."[33] During the day the cavalry had covered more than thirty-five miles, while Bradley's detachment, because of its many diversions from the main column, had ridden at least twenty miles more.[34]

Despite these extra miles, Major Brisbin aroused Bradley at daybreak and ordered him on scout at once, without giving him or his men time to eat breakfast. Bradley considered such treatment rather rough since both horses and men were tired and hungry. So he engaged in what in modern parlance would be called a "slow-down," refusing to make too much haste, and it was not until half-past three that six of the Crows were sent ahead, the remainder of the detachment following half an hour later. During this period of morning twilight Indians could be seen on the surrounding hills,[35] and Bradley was instructed to search carefully for any signs of the Sioux and to send back word of any significant discoveries. He was to go as far as the valley of the Little Big Horn River, which was thought to be the site of a possible battlefield since a heavy smoke could be seen in front, probably some fifteen or twenty miles distant, a smoke which caused General Terry a great deal of uneasiness.[36]

General Terry and his staff had left the *Far West* about six o'clock on the evening of the twenty-fourth, about the same time that Custer was going into camp near the site of Busby. The steamer apparently moved upstream a short distance, then wooded and tied up to the left bank of the river for the night. Near noon of the next day it entered the mouth of the Big Horn River, which runs about two hundred miles approximately north and south and drains, with its tributaries, an immense area of country, carrying almost as much water as the Yellowstone.[37] Four miles from the mouth, Tullock's Creek enters the main stream. After passing this tributary, the steamer began working its slow and tedious way up the Big Horn.[38]

[33] Maguire's Report, 1348.
[34] Bradley, *Journal*, 219.
[35] Roe, *Custer's Last Battle*, 5.
[36] Bradley, *Journal*, 220.
[37] Gibbon, "Summer Expedition," 271.
[38] For the account of the trip of the steamer *Far West* up the Big Horn River, see especially the Report of Sergeant James E. Wilson, in the *Report of the Secretary of War, 1877*, II, Part 2, 1378–81.

In many cases the main channel was broken by rapids which were too shallow to navigate by means of the wheel alone. Here use was made of the long warping cable, one end of which was fastened to a tree on the bank, and the other to one of the boat's capstans. The latter was then set in motion and, by rolling up the cable, slowly dragged the boat forward. "Through all of that long, hot Sunday afternoon of June 25th, the soldiers and the crew, sweaty and weary, coaxed and hauled their cumbersome charge up the mountain stream, past dark overhanging cliffs and through ranges of broken and naked bad lands."[39]

The steamer tied up to the bank at eight-thirty that night and resumed the voyage seven hours later. Not long afterwards a messenger, Lieutenant Burnett, arrived with orders from General Terry directing Captain Marsh to reach the mouth of the Little Big Horn if possible, but under no circumstances to pass any point where the water was less than three feet deep lest a sudden fall in the river strand the boat. If the mouth of the Little Big Horn could not be reached, the steamer was to return to the place where the orders had been received and wait there.[40]

From Burnett, Colonel Gibbon learned that the infantry camp of the night before was only two miles distant and that General Terry had started on a night march with the cavalry, so he decided to join his command at once, although not yet fully recovered from his illness. After a ride of four or five miles, Gibbon overtook the infantry column marching across a plateau which was not particularly rough but was badly cut up by the numerous deep ravines and gullies which had made the night march of the cavalry so slow and difficult.[41]

The *Far West* continued its course upstream and about ten o'clock on the morning of the twenty-sixth reached the mouth of a sizable tributary entering the Big Horn River from the east. Although Captain Marsh was positive that it was the Little Big Horn, Captain Baker, who commanded the infantry guard, disagreed, and even went so far as to land his company and march them some four or five miles upstream, returning with the positive statement that

[39] Hanson, *Conquest of the Missouri*, 270.
[40] *Ibid.*, 271.
[41] Gibbon, "Summer Expedition," 294.

the river was not the Little Big Horn. Baker saw no Indians, and the Sioux, who were very much occupied in attempting to demolish the command of Major Reno, were apparently not in the least aware of his excursion. Marsh then took the *Far West* some fifteen miles farther up the Big Horn to Sitting Bull's Rapids, where two islands divide the river into three channels, and here they tied up for the night, being an estimated sixty-six miles from the mouth of the stream. Soundings were taken to ascertain the depth of the water, which Marsh is said to have reported falsely to be less than the required three feet, but in the morning at least one attempt was made to ascend these rapids before Marsh decided to drop downstream to the mouth of the eastern tributary, which Captain Baker now admitted to be the Little Big Horn, although what caused him to change his mind will forever remain a mystery. Because of the many quagmires at the junction of the two streams as well as for greater safety in case of an Indian attack, the steamer tied up to the shore of an island just opposite the mouth of the smaller stream, and there remained all day awaiting further developments.[42]

A few miles after leaving the cavalry campsite, Bradley's scouts discovered the fresh tracks of four Indian ponies. The tracks were in a narrow valley cut by a dry creek bed and led toward the river. Bradley, immediately suspecting that they had been made by scouts from the Sioux village, sent back a written report of his discovery and then followed the trail toward the Big Horn River, finding that it crossed that stream a few miles farther on. Here the Indians had abandoned a horse and several articles of personal equipment, which upon examination were found to be items which had belonged to the Crow scouts who had accompanied the Seventh Cavalry on the march up the Rosebud, and who were now presumed to be bringing dispatches to General Terry from Custer.[43]

Then some of the Crows discovered three Indians on the farther bank of the river, apparently watching the soldiers. The Crows signaled with blankets that they were friends, but received no response. When they were about to give up and seek some other

[42] Wilson, Report, 1378–80; Hanson, *The Conquest of the Missouri*, 272.

[43] Bradley, *Journal*, 221; Gibbon, "Summer Expedition," 295. For a slightly different version, see *New York Herald*, July 8, 1876.

means of communication, the three built a fire and by means of the smoke signaled that they trusted Bradley's assurances, and soon after came down to the bank of the river. They proved to be Goes Ahead, White-Man-Runs-Him, and Hairy Moccasins,[44] who had left Reno the evening before and, after detouring around the hostile camp, had ridden down the ridges between Tullock's Creek and the Little Big Horn, traveling through the same rainstorm that had brought so much discomfort to the troops. They now talked across the stream to Pretty Face and two or three of the other scouts, the remainder of Bradley's detachment remaining on the bluffs while the interview was going on.

Presently our Indians turned back and as they came shouted out at the top of their voices a doleful series of cries and wails that the interpreter, Bravo, explained was a song of mourning for the dead. That it boded some misfortune there was no doubt; and when they came up shedding copious tears and appearing pictures of misery, it was evident that the occasion was no common sort. Little Face in particular wept with a bitterness of anguish which I have rarely seen. For awhile he could not speak but at last composed himself and told his story in a choking voice broken by frequent sobs. As he proceeded the Crows one by one broke off from the group of listeners and going aside a little distance sat down alone, weeping and chanting that dreadful mourning song, and rocking their bodies to and fro. They were the first listeners to the horrid story of the Custer massacre, and outside of the relatives and personal friends of the fallen, there were none in this whole horrified nation of forty millions of people to whom the tidings brought greater grief. The three men over the river were in truth a portion of the six scouts furnished to General Custer from my detachment. . . .[45]

The three survivors told Little Face that Custer, after leaving the mouth of the Rosebud, had followed the Indian trail and "yesterday struck the village on the Little Big Horn, the Sioux warriors letting him get close to the village and then sallying forth in overwhelming numbers to meet him, defeating his command and destroying all but a small portion who had been driven into the hills and surrounded by the Sioux, where the Crows had left them fight-

[44] Maguire says that there were only two Indians, but this is in error. Report, 1348.

[45] Bradley, *Journal*, 221.

ing desperately."[46] They also said that when they left, Custer was surrounded by Sioux, "who covered all the plain" as thick as they could stand and too numerous to count.[47] They told the soldiers that Custer had divided his command and that the remnant of the other group was on the top of a high hill surrounded by the hostile Indians. The corpses of Custer's troopers were said to be strewn all over the countryside; and of the other three Crow scouts, White Swan and Half-Yellow-Face were killed and Curly was missing and probably killed. Pressed for details regarding where the fight had taken place, they pointed to a column of smoke rising about twenty miles away and urged Gibbon's men to go no farther, saying that the Sioux would probably kill all of them.[48]

Bradley, who says that he instinctively believed the story, no longer wondered at the demonstrative grief of the Crows and remarks that, while his soldiers listened to the recital without betraying any marked emotion, it was obvious that they were too much affected by it to do more than look at each other in pained silence. The news was so terrible, and so different from what they had expected, that the Lieutenant could only hope that the account of the three fugitives was badly overdrawn.[49]

The infantry had camped about twelve miles back of the cavalry and had resumed the march at five o'clock in the morning. But trouble with their pack train caused several delays, so that it was not until about noon that they came up with the horsemen. Since some of the officers thought they had seen Indians on the surrounding hills, the combined command now pushed cautiously ahead in the direction taken by the scouts. They crossed the dry creek bed where the tracks had first been discovered and then mounted a small ridge, beyond which they met Bradley riding toward them, obviously with important news. As one who heard his report later wrote, "Had a bolt from heaven fallen into the midst of the group of officers, it could not have more completely astounded or overwhelmed

[46] *Ibid.*, 221.

[47] Reno, *Court*, 14; *New York Herald*, July 8, 1876.

[48] Bradley, *Journal*, 221; Roe, *Custer's Last Battle*, 5; Gibbon, "Summer Expedition," 295; McClernand, "With Indian and Buffalo in Montana," *Cavalry Journal*, Vol. XXXVI (January and April, 1927), 22.

[49] Bradley, *Journal*, 221.

them."[50] General Terry remained quiet and thoughtful on hearing the news, but the members of his staff were not so reticent and in no uncertain fashion expressed their doubts of the report, declaring that a disaster of such magnitude was improbable if not impossible and denouncing the scouts as cowards who had fled the field and had now invented this story as an excuse for their cowardice.[51] A part of the skepticism was undoubtedly due to the low esteem in which Bravo, the only interpreter with the command, was held, for the injured LeForge had been left at the base camp on the Yellowstone.

General Terry took no part in the skeptical comments of his staff, but sat "silent and thoughtful, biting his lower lip" and looking at Bradley as though to contradict some of the remarks of the younger officers.[52] But Lieutenant Roe later quoted the Division commander as saying in his hearing, "I find it impossible to believe that so fine a regiment as the Seventh Cavalry should have met with such a catastrophe,"[53] and the consensus was that, while the report was not to be altogether believed, there was a possibility that something had happened to the Custer command. But the worst that anyone could conceive as possible was that the regiment had been defeated and driven from the field,[54] and that the sooner Gibbon's command could reach Custer the better.[55]

The three fugitives had at first declared that both they and their ponies were too tired to join Gibbon's men, but finally consented to do so, provided that some of the others would wait for them. The other scouts, ever since hearing the news, had stayed close to the troops, refusing to work ahead of the command, proof to Gibbon that they believed the story.[56] So when the troops passed the point where he had first received the news of the disaster, Lieutenant Bradley permitted all of the Crows to remain behind, partly

[50] *New York Herald*, July 8, 1876.

[51] Bradley, *Journal*, 221–22; *New York Herald*, July 8, 1876.

[52] Bradley, *Journal*, 221.

[53] Roe, *Custer's Last Battle*, 5; McClernand, "With Indian and Buffalo in Montana," *Cavalry Journal*, Vol. XXXVI (January and April, 1927), 23. Captain Clifford later wrote, somewhat naïvely, "How these scouts managed to obtain such accurate information as they imparted to us on the 26th, is a puzzle." Burdick, *Tales of Buffalo Land*, 57.

[54] *New York Herald*, July 8, 1876.

[55] Gibbon, "Summer Expedition," 295.

[56] *Ibid.*, 295.

in the hope that they would be able to persuade the three to join them and partly to allow the entire group to overcome its fears.

Bravo, who stayed with the Crows, is said to have been so much excited and demoralized by the news that he was almost out of his wits, and the command was not out of sight before he persuaded the scouts to abandon the expedition, representing that the officers had told him that the services of the Crows were no longer needed. Years later White-Man was to relate that he had told the officers that he had no more clothes and was going home and that they had replied, "All right," and so he went.[57] In any event, some of the officers who were at the rear of the column saw all of the scouts mount and gallop away together,[58] never stopping, according to Gibbon, until they reached their agency a hundred miles away.[59] Later, some of the Crows attempted to excuse their action on the ground that they believed that the war was over, but it was apparent that they were more concerned with the fact that it had just begun.[60]

The detachment pushed on, crossing a rugged divide and at last entering the valley of the Little Big Horn, some distance up which heavy columns of smoke could now be plainly seen.[61] At this point the valley is about one and one-half miles wide, and the grass was noted as being very good, with little cactus or sage. The river, which meanders all over the valley, was from thirty to seventy-five yards in width, its banks well lined with cottonwoods, many of which were of substantial size. The water was described as sweet, clear, and cold, and flowed over a gravelly bottom.[62] Here, Roe with F troop was ordered to march along the bluffs, parallel with the river, keeping out of sight as much as possible, but being ever alert for any and all signs of the Sioux. After about an hour he was ordered into the valley to attempt to find a ford where the infantry could cross.[63] A few miles above the mouth of the stream he found

57 *Account to Scott*, 9.

58 Bradley, *Journal*, 222; Gibbon, "Summer Expedition," 296.

59 Gibbon, "Summer Expedition," 296.

60 Marquis, *Memoirs of a White Crow Indian*, 248–49.

61 McClernand says that it was here that the infantry and cavalry joined, and puts the time at eleven o'clock. "With Indian and Buffalo in Montana," *Cavalry Journal*, Vol. XXXVI (January and April, 1927), 47.

62 Maguire's Report, 1349.

63 Roe, *Custer's Last Battle*, 6; McClernand, "With Indian and Buffalo in Montana," *Cavalry Journal*, Vol. XXXVI (January and April, 1927), 47.

a ford, and the infantry was obliged to strip and wade. The entire command crossed to the left bank and moved a short distance up the stream befort halting about three o'clock in order to allow the men to rest and make coffee, and to water and graze the animals.[64]

The nearest smoke was now from twelve to fifteen miles distant. But the command could see nothing of interest, for in their front the stream cut across the valley from right to left, the timber and brush which bordered it cutting off the view of everything farther down the valley.[65] During this rest period the two white scouts, Bostwick and Taylor, were sent forward in an effort to open communication with General Custer or some other member of the Seventh Cavalry. As an additional incentive they were promised an extra $200 in pay if they succeeded in getting through to him. Both were given the same message, and they were instructed to separate and follow different routes. Therefore, Taylor crossed over to the right bank while Bostwick remained on the left.[66]

At four o'clock the column again moved forward. Now they noted mounted Indians in their front, and a few Indian ponies, mostly strays, were captured and driven in. The troops had moved but a short distance when they met Bostwick galloping down the valley at full speed. He said that he had proceeded cautiously for several miles up the valley when all at once he came on a large number of Indians. Not wishing to make their acquaintance further, he had retreated and now declared that the command would find all the Sioux they wanted.[67]

Taylor also returned and told of having ridden across the hills until he came to a point which afterwards proved to be within five miles of the village. Here he saw a line of horsemen whom he at first supposed to be members of Custer's command because of the flags flying in the middle of the line. But when some of the men started in his direction, he discovered that they were Indians and then supposed them to be Custer's scouts. So he dismounted and

[64] Reno, *Court,* 14; Bradley, *Journal,* 22–23; Maguire's Report, 1349; Roe, *Custer's Last Battle,* 6.

[65] Gibbon, "Summer Expedition," 296–97.

[66] Bradley, *Journal,* 222.

[67] *Ibid.,* 222; Roe, *Custer's Last Battle,* 6. Vestal says that on the afternoon of the twenty-sixth the Sioux raided Gibbon's horse herd and captured seven cavalry horses. *Sitting Bull,* 179.

ordered one of them to advance. This Indian was a boy of about fourteen years of age, armed with a long rifle. Taylor, his suspicions at last aroused, leveled his gun at the boy, whereupon one of the other Indians fired at Taylor's horse. Without further ado, the scout mounted and made his way back to the command. The Sioux pursued, firing over one hundred shots, and did not give over the chase until Taylor was about a mile from Roe's troop.[68] Taylor declared wrathfully that he recognized the Indian who fired at him as one of Custer's Ree scouts, and that he would kill him when they next met.[69] The report by both scouts of a large number of hostiles moving across the Little Big Horn Valley from the direction of Tullock's Creek gave rise to the belief that they had been planning to ambush Terry's command in the pass between the two streams and had failed because of the change in route.[70]

Bostwick also pointed out a section of bench land which extended into the valley about six miles beyond and declared that the Indians were concentrating there. In the face of all these indications that the enemy was developing in force, General Terry deployed his troops in battle formation. On the left and nearest the river were the Gatling batteries and four companies of infantry, while the cavalry covered the right. The center was made up of the pack train, with one platoon of the remaining infantry company in front and the other behind. At the head rode Terry, Gibbon, Brisbin, and the members of the staff. Scouting along the bluffs half a mile or so in advance and on the right flank was Roe's troop, while Bradley and his small detachment of mounted infantry did similar duty on the left, passing through the timber that grows in occasional clumps along the stream.[71]

Bradley could see many Indians ahead both in the valley and on the bluffs. There was one group of seventy-five or a hundred on a distant hill who exchanged a few long-range shots with members of Roe's command with no apparent damage to either side. The

[68] *Bozeman* (Montana) *Avant-Courier*, July 7, 1876.

[69] Gibbon, "Summer Expedition," 297; McClernand, "With Indian and Buffalo in Montana," *Cavalry Journal*, Vol. XXXVI (January and April, 1927), 25.

[70] Burdick, *Tales of Buffalo Land*, 51. This is possibly open to question. What the scouts may have seen were the preparations for the flight of the hostile village which was taking place at about this time.

[71] Bradley, *Journal*, 223.

hostiles also seemed to be massing in the timber at a particularly narrow spot in the valley through which Bradley and his detachment would have to ride. Lieutenant Bradley later observed: ". . . in my whole career as a soldier never did anything call for as much nerve as that riding slowly up with eleven men, half a mile from the rest of the column, on a body of ambushed warriors."

His men also fully realized the danger of the situation but neither flinched nor faltered, but "with pale faces and compressed lips rode steadily forward with stern determination expecting in a few minutes more to be shot down. . . ."[72]

From the bluffs Roe could see a long line of dark objects defiling across the prairie toward the south. Between his company and this line of objects were hundreds of Indians, some of them dressed in blue uniforms, and cavalry guidons were also in evidence. For a time these men were thought to be members of Custer's command, but a sergeant and three troopers sent forward to investigate were fired on and compelled to retreat.[73]

The nonmilitary person may be pardoned for having doubts regarding the competency of high army officers in view of Gibbon's comment at this time:

> The condition of affairs regarding Custer's command was now more involved in doubt than ever. If he had defeated the Indians and destroyed their camp, as the fires seemed to indicate, it was difficult to account for the presence of those Indians in our front, who were evidently watching us; whereas, if the report of the Crows was correct and the Indians had defeated Custer, their bearing was equally inexplicable.[74]

From his position on the extreme left, Bradley saw the column halt and followed suit, his detachment being then less than a quarter of a mile from the place in the timber where he believed a large force of Indians to be concealed. Several horses emerged from the thicket, apparently an Indian ruse to tempt the troops to a further advance. If so, it did not succeed, and the horses were captured by Bostwick and young Will Logan, thus putting the soldiers in pos-

[72] *Ibid.*, 223.
[73] Roe, *Custer's Last Battle*, 6.
[74] Gibbon, "Summer Expedition," 297.

session of four good Indian ponies. Lieutenant Burnett soon rode over and told Bradley that camp was forming for the night and that he was to remain where he was until the cavalry had finished watering, when he was to join the main command.[75] Similar orders were sent to Roe.

Camp was made about twenty minutes to nine, in the form of a square, with the horses and mules picketed inside the line of troops. It was about eleven miles in a straight line from the mouth of the Little Big Horn and eight or nine miles from Major Reno's position on the bluffs.[76] The soldiers were about midway between the bluffs and the river, being about a mile distant from each and well out of rifle range from either. The camp was probably on the site of the present town of Crow Agency, Montana, with the center about where the schoolhouse now stands.[77] No fires were permitted, and the troops slept on their arms, but they presented a very weak face down the river, not over twenty or thirty men being on that side. The troops were very tired, despite the fact that during the last stages of the march they had been animated by the prospect of a fight, for the infantry had covered between twenty-nine and thirty miles during the day and had been on the move for sixteen hours, while the other units had put about eighteen miles behind them.[78]

Critics who have condemned the speed with which Custer marched his regiment to the battlefield should pause and consider that Terry's force had also been in rapid movement. Custer had all cavalry, while Gibbon's infantry on the twenty-fifth had covered about twenty-three miles, most of them under the worst imaginable marching conditions, and had covered almost thirty miles on the next day, which was more spirited crowding than that of which Custer had been guilty. Nor must we overlook the fact that Bris-

[75] Bradley, *Journal*, 224. McClernand says that Colonel Hughes objected to the halt being made and wanted to push on, but that General Terry refused, believing that in the dusk and uncertainty the two columns might fire into each other. "With Indian and Buffalo in Montana," *Cavalry Journal*, Vol. XXXVI (January and April, 1927), 25.

[76] Bradley, *Journal*, 224; Maguire's Report, 1349.

[77] Terry's Report, 463–64; Reno, *Court*, 21; Gibbon, "Summer Expedition," 297; Marquis, *Two Days after the Custer Battle*, n.p. *Billings Gazette*, May 15, 1932.

[78] Bradley, *Journal*, 224; McClernand, "With Indian and Buffalo in Montana," *Cavalry Journal*, Vol. XXXVI (January and April, 1927), 28.

bin's cavalry in covering thirty-five miles also included a night march. Custer's night march has been severely criticized, and perhaps justly so, but his Department commander was guilty of the same error, if error it was. Brisbin's cavalry had had a longer rest than Custer's on the day following the night march, but that was due solely to the fact that the Second Cavalry had to wait for the more slowly moving infantry to come up, while the Seventh did not. If anything, Terry's advance must have been accomplished with much greater effort, since his route was longer than Custer's and over terrain that was much more difficult, especially for infantry.[79]

That there were fully a thousand well-armed and belligerent warriors in front of General Terry's command when it bivouacked that night is beyond doubt. The Indians were concealed in the timber, on the bluffs, and in other positions of great strength which would have given them a decided advantage and from which it would have been difficult to dislodge them. Yet this formidable force was only the rear guard of the hostile village, which was already in full withdrawal toward the Big Horn Mountains. Had Terry been an hour earlier, he would have had abundant opportunity to test for himself the fighting power of the Sioux and Cheyennes. That he did not have to lead his tired troops into battle was not the result of his planning, for had he marched five hundred yards farther, he would, in all probability, have been attacked.[80] He has been criticized for halting and going into camp "in the face of the enemy and without attempting to satisfy himself as to the character of a large body of men who crossed his front."[81]

General Terry, especially, was very uneasy about Custer, not only because of the story told by the Crow scouts but because Custer had not communicated with him. Terry had told Custer that he would be at the mouth of the Little Horn (the Little Big Horn) on the twenty-sixth, and would expect couriers from him.[82] This statement apparently referred to Herendeen, who was expected to come down Tullock's Creek with dispatches, and is undoubtedly respon-

[79] Marquis, *Memoirs of a White Crow Indian,* 246.

[80] Brady, *Indian Fights and Fighters,* 383.

[81] *Field Artillery Journal,* Vol. XXXVI, No. 4 (July–August, 1936), 356; Letter of Lieutenant H. O. Paulding, July 8, 1876.

[82] *New York Herald,* July 8, 1876; McClernand, "With Indian and Buffalo in Montana," *Cavalry Journal,* Vol. XXXVI (January and April, 1927), 25.

sible for the legend that Custer and Terry were to meet at the mouth of the Little Big Horn on the twenty-sixth. Obviously nothing of the kind was planned, and Custer was merely to report to Terry, by courier, letting him know what had occurred to date.

The officers were much divided in their opinions. Some believed that Custer in a desperate fight had captured the village and was now in pursuit of the foe, and insisted that there was not an Indian in the valley, being able to explain away ingeniously any and all contradictory circumstances. While these individuals, who were mostly from the cavalry, continued to scoff at the story told by the Crows, there were others who furtively surmised that Custer and his entire command had been destroyed, reasoning that if he had merely been defeated, he would have retired to the mouth of the Little Big Horn, where he was sure to meet General Gibbon's command. Furthermore, if he had been victorious, why had he not sent messengers as ordered to the same point?[83] No agreement or reconciliation of these two views was possible, and the command lay down that night full of anxiety for Custer and convinced that whatever the result of Custer's fight had been, Gibbon's command could expect to be in one on the morrow.[84]

[83] *New York Herald*, July 8, 1876; Burdick, *Tales from Buffalo Land*, 51.

[84] *Ibid.*, 55; McClernand, "With Indian and Buffalo in Montana," *Cavalry Journal*, Vol. XXXVI (January and April, 1927), 25.

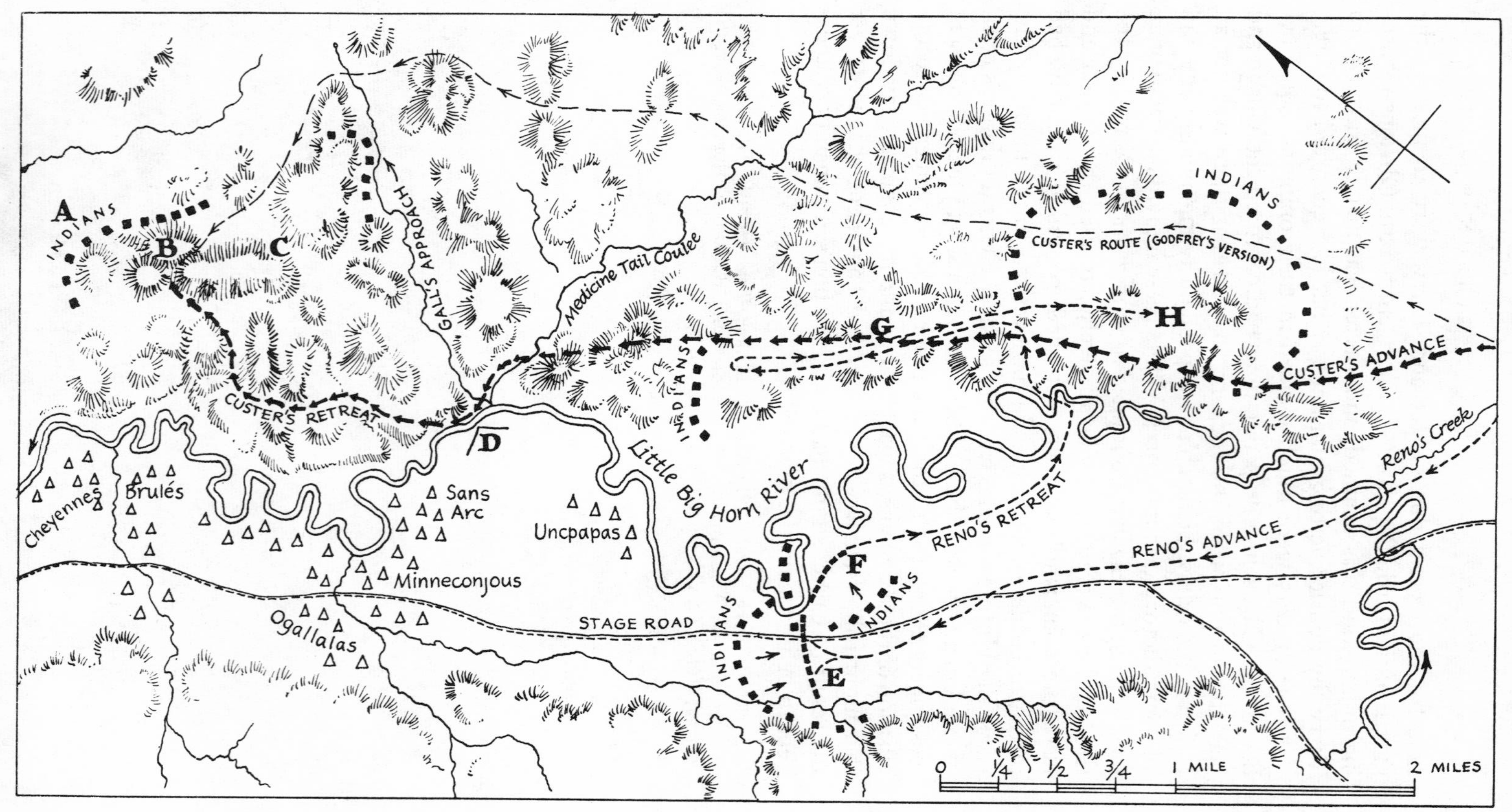
A
B
C
D
E
F
G
H
INDIANS
INDIANS
INDIANS
INDIANS
INDIANS
CUSTER'S ROUTE (GODFREY'S VERSION)
CUSTER'S ADVANCE
CUSTER'S RETREAT
GALL'S APPROACH
Medicine Tail Coulee
Little Big Horn River
Reno's Creek
RENO'S RETREAT
RENO'S ADVANCE
STAGE ROAD
Cheyennes
Brulés
Sans Arc
Uncpapas
Minneconjous
Ogallalas
0
1/4
1/2
3/4
1 MILE
2 MILES

This map is based on one made by Lt. Edward S. Godfrey, whose conception of the Custer route is indicated in light arrows. Heavy arrows show the route of Custer's advance and retreat according to early accounts by Indian eyewitnesses. The latter route is deemed more probable by Edward S. Luce (in the official pamphlet distributed by the Custer Battlefield National Monument), George E. Hyde (in *Red Cloud's Folk*), and the author. Custer was last seen (by Reno's men) on an elevation before he entered Medicine Tail Coulee and descended to the Minneconjou Ford (D); there he turned for some reason and retreated to Custer Ridge (B). At approximately the time of Custer's fight at the ford, Reno began his retreat, freeing many warriors for the final battle with Custer.

The Battle of the Little Big Horn
(June 25, 1876)

A) Crazy Horse's attack
B) final positions on Custer Ridge of Capt. Tom Custer, Capt. Yates, Lt. Smith, and Lt.-Col. Custer
C) near-by positions of Capt. Keogh and Lt. Calhoun
D) Minneconjou Ford
E & F) Major Reno's first and second positions
G) Capt. Weir's reconnaissance attempt to locate Custer
H) bluff to which Reno retreated and where he, Capt. Benteen, and the rest of the command spent the night of June 25.

CHAPTER XIV

Journey into Battle

THE STREAM which the Indians, according to some writers, called the Greasy Grass,[1] but which the white man knows as the Little Big Horn River, was, and is, a stream of some singular characteristics. Scarcely more than a creek, its clear and cold waters flow between banks that are both abrupt and soft. These banks keep the stream from being easily fordable at almost any point, their steepness being the principal hindrance. This is particularly true of the east bank, for although in some places the river winds in great coils across the valley and almost touches the western hills, in others it runs close to the eastern bluffs which rise so abruptly they are impassable in most places. These bluffs are cut at infrequent intervals by creek beds in which brush and scrub timber grow. The river bottom is flat, but with little timber except along the stream where the cottonwoods grow thickly. The river is about two miles in width at its widest point. The bank and bluff line is very irregular; in fact, some of the northern promontories push so far to the west that they effectively obscure the view of the valley from points of observation farther to the south.[2]

At ordinary stages the river was from two to five feet in depth, and at the place where the hostile Indians were encamped it ranged

[1] McClernand, "With Indian and Buffalo in Montana," *Cavalry Journal*, Vol. XXXVI (January and April, 1927), 12; Colonel W. H. C. Bowen, "Custer's Losing Battle Re-Fought," *Winners of the West*, September 30, 1926; and DeCost Smith, *Indian Experiences*, 230; all speak of the valley as "the Greasy Grass of the Sioux," and the *Montana State Guide Book*, 264, says that "the Crows knew the place by a name which probably meant 'rich grass' but was sometimes interpreted as 'Greasy Grass.' " An article in the *Billings Gazette*, August 13, 1933, says that the name Greasy Grass was used to designate present Lodge Grass Creek, a tributary of the Little Big Horn River. These explanations derive weight from the fact that the Crow words for "lodge" and "grease" are very similar, and apt to be confused.

[2] Vestal, *Warpath: True Story of the Fighting Sioux*, 192.

from twenty to forty yards in width and correspondingly deeper where narrower.[3] But there were places where the current was quite sluggish, and in these places the water was generally deep enough to swim a horse. At various intervals between these sluggish areas the water became quite shallow, enough so for easy fording, and "went rippling along to the next deep spot below."[4] But the summer of 1876 had begun exceptionally late, and the tardily melting snows of the mountains had caused all the streams of the region to run bank full until well into the summer. Thus the Little Big Horn was probably wider and deeper than was usually the case at that season of the year. Although the general features of the stream are the same, it has changed appreciably since that memorable day and is today probably both straighter and swifter than then, as well as somewhat to the westward of its former course. The changes that have taken place make it difficult, if not impossible, to identify some of the places described by participants in the battle, especially those places west of the stream. Today much water is taken from the upper reaches of the river for irrigation purposes so that in the summer months it is undoubtedly shallower than it was in 1876. The region to the west is largely undulating prairie, along the first bench of which the hostile Indians were encamped.

The site of this great Indian camp was several feet higher than the river, the land behind it rising gradually to the west to an upland plateau some two hundred feet above the stream. Here the vast pony herds of the hostiles grazed. To the south stretched flat, open bottoms broken by sloughs which showed where the river formerly ran. In the farther distance rose the Big Horn Mountains, and along the river ash-gray bluffs rose above the rank growth of green cottonwoods.[5] The Indian camp lay along the western bank, approximately fifteen miles south of the junction of the Little Big Horn with the Big Horn River, and only a few miles south of the present town of Crow Agency, Montana.

The village was large—it may have been the largest gathering

[3] Stuart, *Forty Years on the Frontier*, II, 119, says that in 1880, four years after the battle, the river was fifty to sixty yards wide, about three feet deep, and very swift.

[4] Colonel John Gibbon, "Hunting Sitting Bull," *American Catholic Quarterly Review*, Vol. II, No. 3 (October, 1877), 668.

[5] Vestal, *Sitting Bull*, 160.

of Indians ever on the North American continent—and extended for several miles along the stream. Following the usual Indian custom, it was arranged in the form of tribal circles in which each lodge had its regularly assigned place: "Each circle was in its appointed place, each band had its allotted place within the circle; each tent its relative position within the band. Every Indian had his known address in that great city of buffalo hunters."[6]

Just how many circles there were is a matter of disagreement, but farthest down the river and on the extreme northern end of the camp were the Cheyennes, "fiercest of all the frontier cavalry,"[7] despite the fact that they have received much less notoriety than the better-publicized Sioux tribes. Their circle was about two miles north of the present railway station of Garryowen and straddled a small creek flowing in from the west.[8] Their chiefs were the famous Two Moon, Little Horse, and White Bull, the last to be distinguished from Sitting Bull's belligerent nephew of the same name who was married to a Sans Arc Sioux. Only a very few of the Northern Cheyennes were not there, and Kate Bighead said that there were more Indians there than she had ever seen anywhere else.[9]

Next to the Cheyennes were the Ogallalas under Crazy Horse,[10] while farther to the south were the Sans Arcs, whose chiefs were Spotted Eagle and Fast Bear. Between them and the Minneconjous, whose war chiefs included Hump, or High Back-bone, Lame Deer, and Fast Bull, was another insignificant stream. To the west and southwest was the circle of the Blackfeet Sioux,[11] while farthest to the south, because traditionally last in the order of march and therefore in the greatest danger of attack, were Sitting Bull's Uncpapas,

[6] *Ibid.*, 158; McLaughlin, *My Friend, the Indian*, 132.

[7] Graham, *Story of the Little Big Horn*, Introduction, *vii*.

[8] *Billings Gazette*, July 17, 1932.

[9] Marquis, *She Watched Custer's Last Battle*, n.p.

[10] Although Crazy Horse is supposed to have been the leader in the fight against General Crook on the Rosebud, there is the possibility, despite Indian allegations to the contrary, that he had joined the big camp on the Little Big Horn after the battle. Edwin W. Deming, "Custer's Last Stand; the Indian Version of the Massacre," *Mentor*, Vol. XIV (July, 1926), 56–57.

[11] The Blackfeet, or Siksika, were probably so named because their moccasins were discolored from the ashes of prairie fires. Their habitat was Alberta and northwestern Montana. The Blackfeet, or Sihasapa, Sioux, were so called because they wore black moccasins. Their habitat was western South Dakota. These are the ones who were in the hostile camp on the Little Big Horn River. Cecil Alter, *James Bridger*, 6n.

most recalcitrant and warlike of all the Sioux tribes. Their war chiefs included Gall, Crow King, and Black Moon.[12] "The tipi of their great leader, Sitting Bull, stood on the southwest side of the camp circle about fifty yards south of the lane which today leads east from the main road to the cottage on the river bank near the slough."[13]

There seem to have been a few Arapahoes in the Cheyenne camp, and the various Sioux circles included some Cuthead, Two Kettle, and Brulé Sioux, although Gall said afterwards that the last-named had a circle of their own. There were also a few Santees under Inkpaduta of Spirit Lake infamy, while other miscellaneous tribesmen were scattered throughout the camp. All the malcontents of the prairies were there. In addition, there were hundreds of young men who had spent the winter at the various agencies and streamed out to join the hostiles as soon as the grass was up in the spring and the news of Crook's fiasco on the Powder had emboldened them to the point where they felt that they could safely defy the government. Thus we have the anomaly of the army's being met in the summer by hostile Indians who had been fed, sheltered, and armed during the previous winter at the expense of another department of the government.[14]

How many hostiles there were in that great camp no one knew, and the matter is still one of speculation and argument. The persons who could have given the most accurate information, the agents of the various Sioux and Cheyenne reservations, were silent for reasons of their own, although it did not necessarily follow that all of the young men missing from the agencies had joined the hostile village. The number of Indians in the village has been variously estimated, the guesses ranging all the way from twenty-five hundred to nine thousand warriors, and since there is little conclusive evidence upon which an estimate could be based, one person's opinion is almost as good as another's.[15] The probability is that there were not more

12 Other arrangements of the circles were given by Gall in 1886, see Vestal, *Warpath and Council Fire*, 131; by Crazy Horse, see South Dakota Historical *Collections*, VI, 226; and by Charles Eastman, see "Story of the Little Big Horn," 354. The discrepancies, and there are many, will never be reconciled.

13 Vestal, *Sitting Bull*, 159.

14 *Report of the Secretary of War, 1876*, 6.

15 On this subject there is no agreement whatever. Of the soldiers who participated in the campaign, Anson Mills, who was with General Crook, believed that

Custer attacked a village of from fifteen to twenty thousand souls, of whom four to five thousand were warriors. He believed that only about half of these had been in the fight with Crook's command on the Rosebud eight days before (Mills, *My Story*, 409). Colonel Gibbon put the number much lower and expressed the opinion that there were between twelve hundred and twenty-five hundred warriors in the hostile camp [*Contributions to the Historical Society of Montana*, IV (1903), 285] while Lieutenant Hare, who helped burn the tepee poles after the battle, counted where forty tepees had stood and from this estimated that there had been about fifteen hundred lodges in the camp besides four hundred wickiups, which at a low estimate would mean a fighting force of about four thousand (Reno, *Court*, 434; *Official Transcript*, 389). A year after the battle General Scott attempted to count the sites of the Sioux lodges, and counted more than fifteen hundred without having counted them all. From this he estimated that there were nearer seven thousand than six thousand Indians in the camp (Scott, *Some Memories of a Soldier*, 49). But the number of places where lodges had stood did not mean too much since for sanitary or other reasons the Indians frequently moved the lodge site (*Official Transcript*, 784). The scout, George Herendeen, who said that he had seen innumerable Indian camps and that this was the largest one he had ever seen, believed that the Indians had moved camp that morning before the arrival of the troops, and that the village covered extensive ground that they were not using (*Official Transcript*, 334). Shortly after the battle he estimated that the village contained six thousand people of whom about one half were warriors (*Army and Navy Journal*, July 15, 1876), but he told the Reno Court of Inquiry that there were about eighteen hundred lodges and thirty-five hundred fighting men (Reno, *Court*, 399–400). Lieutenant DeRudio put the number of warriors at between three and four thousand and admitted that at the time of the battle his estimate would have been higher (Reno, *Court*, 457). In addition to the lodges there were a good many wickiups, most of which had been left standing, which were occupied by men who had left their families at the agencies and by others who had no regular place in the lodges. Captain Moylan, who put the Indian fighting force at between thirty-five hundred and four thousand men (*ibid.*, 365) said that there was a separate and distinct camp of wickiups (*Official Transcript*, 308) while Lieutenant Varnum said they were quite thick along the edge of the timber, on the stream, and at the lower end of the village (Reno, *Court*, 292).

Stanley Vestal, who has examined the subject carefully, especially from the Indian point of view, quotes White Bull as saying that there were about twenty-five hundred Indians fit to bear arms, but puts the number of lodges in the village at more than two thousand with from one to three warriors to a lodge (Vestal, *Sitting Bull*, 157). In another place the same writer, who is one of the most able and conscientious students of Indian history, puts "the top estimate of the effective man-power of the Western Sioux when all together" at three thousand (*Warpath: True Story of the Fighting Sioux*, 80) and in a third place says that there were all of two thousand tepees, each with one or two or three warriors, more than one-half of them seasoned fighters (*Warpath and Council Fire*, 235). Brackett believed that there were between twelve and fifteen thousand Indians in the camp of whom about one-third were warriors (*Contributions to the Historical Society of Montana*, IV, 263), but Barron Brown believed that these figures were absurd and that there were not more than two thousand, of whom not more than one half had modern firearms (Brown, *Comanche*, 27). Frazier Hunt put the number of warriors at between eighteen hundred and two thousand (Hunt, *Custer, the Last of the Cavaliers*, 174), while Lewis Crawford estimated the number to be between two thousand and twenty-five hundred and pointed out that the country could not have sustained that number for very long if they had stayed together. *Rekindling Camp Fires*, 259, and *Arikara Narrative*, 24, also put the number of warriors at between twenty-five hundred and three thousand, while Fred Dustin estimated the probable population of the village at ten or twelve thousand, of whom three thousand to thirty-five hundred were warriors. He did not believe that more than twenty-five hundred participated in the battle (*The Custer Tragedy*, 106). Dr. Marquis, who spent many years among the Cheyennes, felt that there were about twelve thousand Indians in the camp since most of the tepees were family lodges (*Sketch Story of the Custer Battle*, n.p.).

Indian accounts are equally at variance, and even Gall, whose following in 1876 numbered sixty lodges (Taylor, "Bloody Knife and Gall," *North Dakota Historical Quarterly*, Vol. IV [April, 1930], 165) and who was very intelligent and truthful, could not tell how many warriors there were (McLaughlin, *My Friend, the Indian*, 134). Red Cloud said that there were four thousand Indians in the camp (Dixon, *The Vanishing Race*, 170), while Chief Runs-the-Enemy, who participated in the battle, estimated that two thousand warriors took part (*ibid.*, 179). Flat Iron, the last surviving Cheyenne chief who was also a participant, was quoted as saying that there were fourteen thousand Indians in the camp, of whom eight thousand were fighting men (*Helena Independent*, October 15, 1915). Flying Hawk said there were about twelve hundred warriors in the camp but that only about one thousand took part in the battle since many were out hunting (*Flying Hawk's Tales*, 40). Crazy Horse said that there were eighteen hundred lodges and four hundred wickiups and at least seven thousand warriors although he believed that that number was too low since there were a good many transients and hangers-on, warriors who had no permanent shelter (South Dakota Historical *Collections*, VI, 227).

Dr. Charles Eastman, who was a full-blood Sioux, did not believe that there were more than five thousand Indians all told. After years of careful research (and he spent several years in exile with Sitting Bull's band in Canada), he came to the conclusion that the Uncpapa had 224 lodges, the Sans Arcs, 85, Inkpaduta's band, 15, the Brulés, 140, the Minneconjou, 190, the Ogallalas, 240, and the Cheyennes, 55, for a total of 949 lodges. At five persons to a lodge this would mean 4,945 Indians, and assuming that one-fourth of them were warriors, which is too high a percentage, as Dr. Eastman admits, and allowing for an extra two hundred unattached young men from the various agencies, which is probably too low, he argues that Custer did not have more than 1,411 warriors in front of his command, which was a smaller number than he had expected to meet. Elimination of the old men and boys would reduce the number to eight or nine hundred (Eastman, "The Story of the Little Big Horn," *Chautauquan*, Vol. XXXI [July, 1900], 354). He concludes that it is unnecessary to overestimate the number of Indians engaged in the fight, that Custer was outnumbered, although not as badly as he had expected to be, and that his mistake lay not in underestimating the number of the Indians to be encountered as much as in failing to give them credit for the military ability that they possessed (*ibid.*, 358. See also the *Review of Reviews*, Vol. XXII, p. 219).

His figures have been criticized by equally competent scholars. George Bird Grinnell points out that there were at least two hundred lodges in the Cheyenne circle—Two Moon said that his band consisted of fifty lodges (Thrall, "The Sioux War," Kansas State Historical *Collections*, Vol. XVI, p. 573), and his band was only one of several Cheyenne bands—and six villages of Sioux each as large or larger than the Cheyenne, which would have meant at least fourteen hundred lodges besides the multitude of strangers who occupied the wickiups and whose number cannot even be estimated. Grinnell adds that Cheyennes have told him that at three or four fighting men to a lodge there would have been between forty-five hundred and six thousand warriors present (Grinnell, *The Fighting Cheyennes*, 343–44). With these figures Stanley Vestal agrees (*Sitting Bull*, 147), and Major McLaughlin indicates general agreement by his statement that the Uncpapas' circle did not contain "over four hundred lodges" (*My Friend, the Indian*, 136–37). When these

than four thousand warriors—and possibly not that many—but even at that, Custer's forces were outnumbered at a ratio of about eight to one. Although not all the Indians had guns, they were probably as well armed as the troops; indeed, there are some who insist that they were better armed, but this is another disputed point.[16]

On that twenty-fifth of June there were three fords which could have been used conveniently in attacking the village. In their order from south to north, and also in the chronological order in which they enter the narrative, they were: (1) the Reno ford which

---

three scholars agree, the matter might almost be considered settled were it not for the fact that George E. Hyde says that fifty lodges of "the wildest of the Northern Cheyennes" were the only ones of the tribe present at the Custer battle (*Red Cloud's Folk,* 182) although the accuracy of this statement is to be doubted (Marquis, *A Warrior Who Fought Custer,* and Marquis, *She Watched Custer's Last Battle*).

After the battle, under the pressure of an aroused public opinion, a survey of the various Indian agencies was ordered. This showed that thousands of Indians were unaccounted for. While a great many of them had undoubtedly left the reservations in the flush of enthusiasm following receipt of the news of the Custer disaster (Dunn, *Massacres of the Mountains,* 618), and certainly not all of the others were in the camp on the Little Big Horn River, there were others who had left a week or so before the battle and returned in about the same number of days after it had been fought (Roe, *Custer's Last Battle,* 11). In addition there were probably about three thousand roaming Indians who were always off the reservation, and the most of these were undoubtedly in the hostile camp (Dunn, *Massacres of the Mountains,* 618). Although surprise has been expressed that so many Indians could absent themselves from their reservations without being reported (Godfrey, *Century,* 383), the explanation is by no means difficult. Many of the absent Indians were not reported for the simple reason that the agents made a profit from selling the supplies intended for the use of those absentees. Many of the absent Indians were reported, but too late for the information to be forwarded to the commanders in the field. For instance, General Terry learned from Sheridan, after the battle, that eighteen hundred lodges had set out to join the hostile bands (Godfrey, *Montana,* 157).

Taking into consideration all of the highly contradictory evidence, the fact that the Indians moved their camp at least once during the battle and probably had moved shortly before, and that the game resources of the region were inadequate to support an extremely large number for any extended period of time, it seems fairly certain that most accounts of the battle have exaggerated the number of Indians engaged. Probably a fair estimate would be that there were three thousand warriors in the hostile camp, and the proportion of warriors to noncombatants was higher than was usually the case in a camp of that size. While most of the tepees were undoubtedly family, rather than war, lodges the number of wickiups was unusually large, and these were occupied almost exclusively by fighting men. Custer certainly met more Indians than he had expected to, but he did not meet as many as the survivors of the regiment thought they had.

[16] Frazier and Robert Hunt, *I Fought with Custer,* 92; Dixon, *The Vanishing Race,* 171; Marquis, *She Watched Custer's Last Battle,* n.p.

was just above the mouth of Reno, or Sundance, Creek and which was the one used by Major Reno's battalion in advancing to the attack on the village which opened the battle. About two miles farther north and down the river, and about one mile south of the southern limit of the hostile village, there was a crossing of the river which cannot by any stretch of the imagination be designated as a ford. It was used by the Major's men in their retreat or "charge" from the timber to the bluffs. The second ford was the Minneconjou or middle ford, which was opposite the Minneconjou circle and approximately at the foot of Medicine Tail Coulee. To the left of this coulee as one faces it from the river, there was an unnamed creek running from back in the hills and originating at a place marked "spring" on the maps, the two creeks thus forming a rough *V*. It was toward this ford that Custer moved with the five companies under his command and where he apparently intended to cross the river and attack the village. Last and most northerly of all was the so-called Cheyenne ford, about a mile north of the Minneconjou and a short distance north of the Cheyenne circle.[17]

The Indians had occupied this camp ground for only a few days, although they had been in the vicinity for a much longer time. On the twenty-second the camp had been on the east side of the Little Big Horn, and the plan seems to have been to move up that stream after buffalo, but the plan was changed when scouts brought back reports of great herds of antelope grazing on the tablelands to the west and north. On the twenty-third the tribes moved west, crossing the river and going downstream about five miles. The Cheyenne circle was placed in the position that it occupied at the time of the Custer attack. One report says that they planned to stay there only one night, and at best the camp was a temporary one; on the night of the twenty-fourth the Indian women are said to have packed up preparatory to moving the next day, the intention being to move northward and across to the Big Horn River.[18]

17 In addition to the crossings used by the troops there were several others that could have been utilized.

18 Dixon, *The Vanishing Race*, 170; Marquis, *She Watched Custer's Last Battle*, n.p. One Indian account says that an Indian had started to return to the Red Cloud Agency that morning but had gone only a few miles when he saw a large cloud of dust. He turned back to the village and reported a large herd of buffalo. "Story of Red Horse," *Colorado Transcript* (Denver), March 21, 1877.

The time spent in the vicinity had been passed in the ordinary pursuits of peace as well as in preparing for eventualities. Buffalo-hunting parties had been sent out, and their luck had been uniformly good. The bodies of the dead from the Rosebud battle had been disposed of, the wounded cared for, and guns and knives cleaned and made ready for the attack that all felt was sure to come.[19] The Indians insist that all preparations were purely defensive, and Sitting Bull is said to have expressed their attitude: "A bird, when it is on the nest spreads its wings to cover the nest and eggs and protect them. It cannot use its wings for defense but it can cackle and try to drive away the enemy. We are here to protect our wives and children, and we must not let the soldiers get them."[20] Throughout the circles social dances were held in the evenings, but the Indians insist that there were no war dances, and that no war parties were sent out,[21] although this denial must be viewed with caution.

The Indian camp was poorly situated for defense, and the only indication that an attack might be expected was that it was more concentrated than was usually the case. The fact that there were so many women and children present has been cited as proof that an attack was not expected. While under ordinary conditions this would be good circumstantial evidence, it is not in this case for the simple reason that there was no place of safety to which the noncombatants could be sent.[22] The scouts had been keeping a close watch on General Crook's forces, but did not anticipate any trouble from that direction for some time to come. The hostiles were well aware of Gibbon's presence north of the Yellowstone and were not at all ignorant of the fact that there were other "pony soldiers" in the valley of the Rosebud. There is evidence to indicate that the Sioux knew when the Terry expedition left Fort Abraham Lincoln and that they had been kept fairly well informed of its western progress,[23] but they do not seem to have expected an early attack from that quarter.

[19] Vestal, *Sitting Bull*, 159.

[20] Dixon, *The Vanishing Race*, 174.

[21] Marquis, *A Warrior Who Fought Custer*, 215.

[22] DeLand, *The Sioux Wars*, 458; Albert Britt, *Great Indian Chiefs*, 218; McLaughlin, *My Friend, the Indians*, 131.

[23] See above.

The Dakota column apparently reached the Little Big Horn before the Indians expected them, for Gall stated years afterward that he was very much surprised when the buffalo scouts came in and reported the camping place of the soldiers on the night of the twenty-fourth. Even then the hostiles apparently did not expect an attack the next day. Custer's night march upset their calculations as well as tiring his men and horses. There can be no doubt, however, that by ten o'clock on the morning of the twenty-fifth—two hours before the troops crossed the divide—the Indians knew where Custer was, his approximate strength, and also that his force was the only one within striking distance of their camp.[24]

Like the soldiers, the Indians had some prophets of doom. Box Elder, a Cheyenne warrior, who was also known as Dog-on-the-Ridge, warned his people to keep their horses picketed close to the lodges, while another warrior of that tribe howled like a wolf and when a wolf howled back at him from the bluffs, interpreted it to mean meat—meat for the wolves—and soon. Many individuals had dreams and visions which they announced to the camps, but most of the Indians seem to have regarded them as what they probably were—merely cheap attempts to gain personal notoriety—and to have paid little attention to them. On the night of the twenty-fourth, while Custer's troopers were toiling up the eastern slopes of the Little Chetish Mountains, the Indians, as usual, held social dances in all of the circles; and, as one of the leading Cheyenne participants in the next day's fighting later expressed it, "It seemed that peace and happiness were prevailing all over the world and nowhere was any man planning to lift his hand against his fellowman."[25]

It was high noon when the regiment crossed the summit of the divide. Here Lieutenant Varnum and the scouts who had remained at the Crow's Nest rejoined the command. They brought the additional information that after Custer had left the lookout point to ride back to the regiment, a group of Indians who were in that

[24] David F. Barry, *Indian Notes on the Custer Battle*, edited by Usher L. Burdick, 26–27. Sitting Bull later claimed that he had known for days that the soldiers were coming. *Billings Times*, September 10, 1925; Wagner, *Old Neutriment*, 127; DeLand, *The Sioux Wars*, 370; McLaughlin, *My Friend, the Indian*, 137.

[25] Vestal, *Sitting Bull*, 158; Marquis, *A Warrior Who Fought Custer*, 215.

part of the hostile camp closest to the soldiers had been observed to break camp and start moving downstream. This was considered positive proof that the presence of the troops had been discovered and that the Indian village was beginning to break up and scatter.

From the summit of the divide the troops could see only a small part of the Little Big Horn Valley, but some fifteen or twenty miles to the northwest there was a light blue cloud which the scouts said was smoke that marked the location of the great Indian camp. The regiment rode for about a mile down the western slope and halted just before reaching the headwaters of Reno Creek. According to Benteen, he had led the advance for only a short distance when Custer rode up and told him that he was setting too fast a pace, and soon after, the order to halt was given. Then Custer and Lieutenant Cooke withdrew to one side, and after figuring on paper for a while, divided the regiment into battalions.[26] They were then about one mile from the divide and some ten or eleven miles from the Lone Tepee and possibly fifteen miles from the place where Reno later crossed the Little Big Horn to the attack.[27] During this halt Bouyer again warned Custer that there was a great Indian camp ahead, and that he would find more Sioux than he could handle, a warning which was seconded by Bloody Knife.[28] Custer, exasperated, accused Bouyer of being afraid. To this preposterous accusation the scout merely replied, "If we go in there we will never come out," and told the others that they were going to have a terrible fight.[29] Custer refused to be convinced, and after a moment or two of reflection, Bloody Knife is said to have looked up and, using the sign language of the plains, bade farewell to the sun, saying, "I shall not see you go down behind the hills tonight."[30]

No division of the regiment had been made since the march up the Rosebud began, but Custer had told Reno that he would assign commands on the march.[31] Now three troops, H, D, and K,

[26] Benteen, *Account*, 7. In one place Lieutenant Wallace says that this halt was made shortly after noon, and in another confirms it by giving the specific time as 12:05 P.M. Reno, *Court*, 88, 672–73.

[27] Reno, *Court*, 753.

[28] Reno, *Court*, 89; Adams, "Survivor's Story," 228.

[29] Dustin, *The Custer Fight*, 9.

[30] Schultz, *William Jackson*, 133–34. This story is probably apocryphal, but it reflects Custer's faith in the regiment and his determination to risk everything upon the coming battle.

commanded by Benteen, Weir, and Godfrey, respectively, with a total of about 125 men were formed as one battalion under the command of Benteen, as the senior captain, and ordered to diverge to the left at an angle of about forty-five degrees.

This division of the command was made at about 12:05 P.M., and it was about ten minutes later that Benteen started his march to the left.[32] Widespread disagreement exists concerning precisely what this detachment was expected to do. The orders were verbal and possibly indefinite, leaving much to the discretion of the officer commanding. But as he passed Major Reno, who was still without a specific command, Benteen told him that he was being sent to the left with orders to pitch into anything he might come across.[33] Beyond that, Reno seems to have had no knowledge of Benteen's orders; and as things then stood, there was no reason why Reno should have been told anything about what this detachment was expected to do, since subsequent co-operation between the various units of the command would depend upon developments. As the situation clarified, Reno could be informed of any orders about which it might be necessary for him to know. In fact, at this time Custer probably did not expect anything more than a running fight to develop, and he certainly did not anticipate a battle of the magnitude of the one that did develop, being apparently fully occupied with the obsession that the hostiles might escape and he would be denied the brilliant victory that he apparently believed could alone save his military career.

While Benteen's column was still in sight, Custer sent two suppletory orders. The first, carried by Henry Voss, the chief trumpeter, apparently instructed Benteen to go on to the second line of bluffs if he found nothing on reaching the first; the other, carried by the regimental sergeant major, told Benteen, to go on into the valley if he found no Indians on the second line of bluffs. Apparently in order to guard against ambush or surprise he was also commanded to keep a well-mounted officer with five or six men well

[31] 44 Cong., 2 sess., *House Exec. Doc. 1,* Part 2 (Report of Major Marcus A. Reno), 32 (hereinafter cited as Reno's *Report*).

[32] Reno, *Court,* 672–73, Benteen, however, put the time at 12:10 P.M. *Ibid.,* 549.

[33] *Ibid.,* 564. Reno testified that Benteen added that he was to sweep everything before him, but that he did not recall the exact words. *Ibid.,* 699.

in advance of the rest of the detachment to report whether any Indians could be seen.[34]

In the years following the battle, the orders to Benteen suffered not a little from conscious and unconscious distortion, from rationalization, and from faulty memories. What the actual orders were we do not know. We have only Benteen's word for them since all of the others—Voss, Sharrow, and Cooke—died on the heights with Custer,[35] and it would have been comparatively easy for the orders to have been misunderstood or misrepresented, either deliberately or otherwise.[36]

Years afterward Benteen was to declare that from the orders he received he might have gone on for twenty miles without finding a valley. He insisted that the orders required no interpretation at all, and admitted that he felt he was being sent on rather a senseless errand, one possibly designed to keep him out of the battle that seemed to be shaping up. It was his belief, he said, that the regiment was then on the trail of from eight to ten thousand Indians, and he felt that it was hardly necessary to attempt to scare up any more. But it was not his business to reason why—Benteen was ordered to the left and to the left he went.[37] In his *Report*, written only a few days after the battle, he declared that he was ordered to move to the left with his battalion to explore a line of bluffs some four or five miles away, to pitch into anything he might find, and to send word to Custer.[38] A letter written to his wife at the same time says substantially the same thing, with the addition that he was sent "over the immense hills to the left in search of the valley which was supposed to be very near by."[39] He also told a representative of the *New York Herald* that he was sent to a line of bluffs about five

[34] 44 Cong., 2 sess., *House Exec. Doc. 1*, Part 2 (Report of Captain F. W. Benteen), 476 (hereinafter cited as Benteen's *Report*); Reno, *Court*, 546, 562; Godfrey, *Montana*, 175.

[35] Reno, *Court*, 542, 546.

[36] W. J. Ghent, "Windolph, Benteen, and Custer," *Cavalry Journal*, Vol. XLIII (November–December, 1934), 65. Compare the story that Benteen told at the Court of Inquiry and that given in his *Account* with the one published in the *New York Herald*, August 8, 1876, or the one given in his letter written to Mrs. Benteen only a few days after the battle. This, in an incomplete form, is to be found most conveniently in Frazier and Robert Hunt, *I Fought with Custer*, 186–90.

[37] Reno, *Court*, 546–63; *Official Transcript*, 650–51.

[38] Benteen's *Report*, 476.

[39] Hunt and Hunt, *I Fought with Custer*, 188.

miles to his left to look for Indians. If he found none, he was to go on until he had satisfied himself that it was useless to go farther in that direction, at which time he was to rejoin the main trail. He added that the supplemental orders merely permitted him to use his own discretion in case he found no Indians, but in case he found any trails or other evidence of the presence of the hostiles, he was to send word to Custer immediately.

This fact is confirmed by another letter written about the same time by Lieutenant Gibson of Benteen's troop, in which he said that the battalion was ordered to the left in an attempt to discover whether any Indians were trying to escape up the valley of the Little Big Horn. As soon as they had satisfied themselves that the Sioux were not moving in that direction, the battalion was to rejoin the main command as quickly as possible.[40] While there is the distinct possibility that both Benteen and Gibson, writing so soon after the event, confused what the detachment did with what it was ordered to do, the probability is that these statements represent an approximate summary of the actual orders to Benteen, and that all of the rest is an excrescence gathered through the years for the purpose of maligning or defending some of the actors in the ensuing tragedy.

Although Custer did not, so far as we know, explain its purpose or the reasons behind it to anyone, this division of the command undoubtedly originated in that part of General Terry's instructions which directed Custer to keep feeling constantly to his left in order to keep the hostiles from passing around that flank and escaping to the south and west. Other purposes were probably to be served as well, and it may possibly be that Benteen was sent to scout the ridges on the left in order to prevent a surprise attack from that direction while the regiment marched down the valley. If so, it was probably the protection of the pack train that Custer had in mind, for the regiment could not move fast enough to keep the Indians from scattering and still protect the slow-moving packs. Custer undoubtedly expected the affair to be settled very quickly since speed was the essence of the problem's solution, but the pack train with its precious cargo of ammunition had to be protected at all costs. Another possible reason may be found in the fact that the

[40] *New York Herald*, August 8, 1876.

hostile warriors had gone up the south fork of Reno Creek on their way to the Rosebud battle, and while Custer did not know of this engagement, the scouts may have told him of the great trail they had left as well as of Indians moving in the valley. If so, he could have sent Benteen to discover whether or not another camp was located farther up the stream.[41]

Custer has been severely criticized for this division of his command.[42] No village had been sighted, no notable number of hostiles had been seen, and there was obviously no plan of battle in Custer's mind; indeed, there could have been none simply because he had not yet established the position and strength of the enemy. There was no diverging trail of the Sioux for Benteen to follow—indeed, Bouyer and the other scouts were positive that the village would be found in the opposite direction. But experienced Indian fighters knew that for sanitary reasons and to secure better grazing for the pony herds, Sioux villages would often consist of a series of groups of lodges, sometimes separated by quite a distance, scattered up and down the banks of a stream. While Custer did not necessarily intend that Benteen should attack the village from the left while he and Reno attacked from the right and center respectively, as many writers have assumed from these orders, he probably was so uncertain of the exact whereabouts of the enemy that he may have felt that Benteen might even strike the southern or upper end of a great camp, and experience had shown that the only way to defeat Indians was to strike from two or more sides at the same time.

In any event, if the Indians attempted to escape, they would have to go north or south; if they went north, they would run into Gibbon, who would drive them back, while Benteen would be able to turn back any who attempted to escape by fleeing up the valley toward the Big Horn Mountains. None of the white commanders believed for a moment that the Indians would stand for a daylight attack. Since Custer did not know exactly where the Indians were, there was great danger that if he kept the troops together he might lead them to the wrong place.[43] Since Custer could not have had

41 Article in the Custer File, Billings Public Library.

42 Coughlan, "The Battle of the Little Big Horn," *Cavalry Journal*, Vol. XLIII (January–February, 1934), 17.

43 Godfrey, *Montana*, 175; Graham, " 'Come on! Be quick! Bring packs!' The

at that time any definite plan of approach or attack because, as has been pointed out, he was uncertain of the exact strength and precise location of the enemy, he was probably attempting to guard against as many eventualities as possible.[44]

About a quarter of an hour after the troops divided, Benteen's three troops passed from the sight of the main column, which continued to ride down toward the valley of the Little Big Horn. Custer, in the meantime, had assigned Major Reno to the command of a battalion composed of Troops A, G, and M, while the remaining five troops stayed under the personal command of Custer. These five seem to have been divided into two battalions, commanded respectively by Keogh and Yates, the latter having only two companies, C and E. But any such division was largely meaningless since they continued to operate as a single command. Custer has been criticized for this on the ground that by tying himself to one unit of the command he sacrificed some of the over-all supervision that was necessary if the various units were to co-operate in support of one another.[45] But in so doing he was merely following his customary practice of staying directly on the front line, "where he could see with his own eyes the rapid changes of cavalry situations and instantly form and execute his plans."[46] When the Indians began their expected scatteration at the approach of the troops, Custer would be able to place the five companies where they could be used to the best advantage.[47]

The troops in a column of fours followed down the small creek which had its origin near the place where the regiment had crossed the divide and which flowed in the general direction of the smoke which the scouts said marked the approximate location of the hostile camp. This was the middle fork of Reno Creek, which empties into the Little Big Horn some two or three miles above the southern limit of the Indian camp.[48] The country was broken and the creek

Story of Custer's Last Message . . . ," *Cavalry Journal,* Vol. XXXII (July, 1923), 317; *Billings Gazette,* August 13, 1933.

44 Coughlan, "The Battle of the Little Big Horn," *Cavalry Journal,* Vol. XLIII (January–February, 1934), 17.

45 *Ibid.,* 18; Fougera, *With Custer's Cavalry,* 266.

46 Joseph Mills Hanson, "The Civil War Custer," *Cavalry Journal,* Vol. XLIII (1934), 30.

47 Edgerly, *Narrative,* 4.

48 Reno, *Court,* 59.

bed was thickly bordered with timber, but the progress of the soldiers was apparently not impeded to any great extent since they rode at a trot most of the time. A few miles farther on, the valley widened, so Reno's command crossed over to the left bank, and the two commands rode almost abreast, although on opposite sides of the stream, sometimes close at hand and sometimes as much as a hundred yards apart. While the scouts were riding in and out, Custer would listen to them and sometimes gallop a short distance to one side and look around.[49]

The command could have been seen at any time coming down the rough country from the divide, and it was at some time during this stage of the march that the Indians in the village first became aware of the proximity of the troops. Some of the women were digging tipsin or wild turnips east of the river and sighted the dust cloud kicked up by the horses.[50] The ground throughout the entire battle area was so dry that it sent up enormous clouds of dust from any movement of horses and mules, and on one occasion during the march, Lieutenant Cooke ordered a portion of the command off to the side of the trail so that they would not raise so much dust.[51] The soldiers were then about eight miles from the village. As the two columns came down into the lower valley and closer to the river, the creek bottom widened out considerably, and Custer with his hat motioned for Major Reno to cross to the right bank. The columns continued to ride side by side, only a few yards apart, so close in fact that the troopers in the two detachments easily talked back and forth, although there seems to have been no conversation between the two commanders.[52] A mile or so farther on, and eleven

[49] *Ibid.*, 90; Graham, 'Come on! Be quick! Bring packs!' The Story of Custer's Last Message . . . ," *Cavalry Journal*, Vol. XXXII (July, 1923), 306; *Account to Scott*, 7.

[50] Article in Custer Scrapbooks, Billings Public Library. Years later Gall is supposed to have said that the troops had been seen crossing the divide. D. J. Benham, "The Sioux Warrior's Revenge," *Canadian Magazine*, Vol. XLIII (September, 1914), 462.

[51] Marquis, *Two Days after the Custer Battle*, n.p.; Reno, *Court*, 721–22.

[52] Reno, *Court*, 91. Lieutenant Wallace said that it was about two o'clock when Custer called Reno's battalion across the creek to the same side that Custer was on. *Official Transcript*, 51.

[53] Graham, *Story of the Little Big Horn*, 30. Dr. Charles Kuhlman has located the site of the Lone Warrior Tepee, and it is one of the few things about this battle of which we are really certain. Girard said that it was about eleven miles

miles from the divide, they reached the Lone Warrior Tepee, which stood on the south bank of the middle fork of Reno Creek.[53] It was now about two-fifteen.[54]

The Lone Tepee was a valuable and handsomely decorated burial lodge which had been left standing by the Sioux. It is said to have contained the corpse of a warrior, the brother of Chief Circling Bear, who had died as the result of wounds received in the Battle of the Rosebud. There is some uncertainty as to whether there was more than one tepee—for instance, Captain Moylan described it as "a couple of abandoned Indian lodges"[55]—but the evidence is not inconclusive, and the point is immaterial.[56] The tepee is also said to have been covered with Indian hieroglyphics, and some of the soldiers later declared, probably with more imagination than veracity, that these had been put there as a warning to the whites of what would happen to them if they attacked the Indian village.[57] This idea probably arose from the fact that it was the custom of the Sioux to decorate their lodges with paintings of buffalo hunts, battles, and other events of importance to the tribe,[58] and, under the circumstances, these ornamentations could very well have been mistaken for a warning.

The site of the Lone Warrior Tepee not only marked the place of a great general encampment of only a few days before; it had also been the overnight camp of a small group of hostiles who were then on their way to join the larger camp farther down the river. It was this group breaking camp that Lieutenant Varnum and the others had seen from the Crow's Nest, causing the scouts to conclude that the camp was scattering on the approach of the troops. The smaller camp had, in fact, become alarmed at the reports

from the Crow's Nest to the knoll from which he saw the Indians. *Official Transcript*, 189; *Account to Scott*, 11; Kuhlman, *Legend into History*, 51.

54 Graham, *Story of the Little Big Horn*, 30; *Official Transcript*, 1000.

55 *Official Transcript*, 301. Lieutenant Varnum said that from the Crow's Nest he "saw the two tepees spoken of so often, on the branch down which we went to the fight." Colonel Robert P. Hughes, "Campaign against the Sioux in 1876," *Journal of the Military Service Institution of the United States*, Vol. XVIII (January, 1896), 29.

56 There is also disagreement concerning how many dead Indians were inside the tepee. See *Official Transcript*, 423, 966; Grinnell, *The Fighting Cheyennes*, 336; and Holley, *Once Their Home*, 264.

57 DeLand, *The Sioux Wars*, 666.

58 Sullivan, *Jedediah Smith*, 17.

brought back by the young men who had first discovered the proximity of the soldiers, and the group had broken camp so hurriedly that they even left cooking utensils on the fires. They were moving downstream when the Crows and Arikaras discovered them. Lieutenant Hare, who was with the scouts, said later that they had seen some forty or fifty hostiles as they approached the tepee. The Sioux were on a rise between him and the river, and from the fact that they disappeared almost immediately he concluded that they had also seen the soldiers.[59]

Some of the scouts had been sent on in advance of the column, not only to reconnoiter the country but to find any hostiles who might be in the valley and to steal and stampede their horses. These scouts were supposed to be about an hour ahead of the troops, but they had stopped at the Lone Tepee, whether from curiosity or fear is uncertain, but possibly from a combination of both. After some examination they apparently set fire to the tepee, although the Crows insisted afterwards that this was done by some of the soldiers, and not by the scouts.[60]

As the head of the column rode up, they could see into the valley of the Little Big Horn and observed a heavy cloud of dust some four or five miles farther down that stream, which caused Custer and many of the officers to believe that the hostiles were already in flight,[61] an opinion which was reinforced by Girard, who had ridden up a knoll some forty or fifty yards to the right of the tepee. At the summit he took off his hat, waving it to attract attention, and then called out to the command in general and to Custer in particular, "There go your Indians, running like devils,"[62] thus calling the commander's attention to a group of some forty or fifty warriors—apparently the same group seen by Lieutenant Hare—who were in flight downstream, being some three miles away and on the right bank of the river.[63] These Indians undoubtedly constituted the rear guard of the smaller camp and were covering the withdrawal of the women and children with the heavily laden ponies. The warriors seemed to be neither afraid of the troops nor

59 Reno, *Court*, 412; Brininstool, *A Trooper with Custer*, 59.
60 *Account to Scott*, 11.
61 *Army and Navy Journal*, July 15, 1876.
62 Reno, *Court*, 142, 203.
63 *Ibid.*, 201; *Official Transcript*, 156.

surprised at seeing them, but cantered ahead slowly, simply keeping far enough in advance to encourage pursuit. All of the evidence indicated that the Indians had vacated the village suddenly and recently, and this was enough to justify Custer's assumption that the Indians were doing what he had feared they would do. Therefore, he decided to hasten his attack, even though it meant bringing on the battle before he had all of his men up.[64]

Custer now ordered the scouts to pursue the fleeing hostiles, but they refused to go,[65] and he berated them soundly for cowardice. According to the scouts, Custer reproved them for having disobeyed his orders not to stop and told them, "If any man of you is not brave, I will take away his weapons, and make a woman of him." At this one of the Rees cried out, "Tell him if he does the same to all his white soldiers who are not as brave as we are, it will take him a long time indeed." The scouts all laughed at this sally, and indicated by signs that they were ready for battle.[66] Bouyer and the Crows may at this time have made another effort to dissuade Custer from the attack, telling him that there were more Sioux ahead than there were bullets in the belts of the soldiers,[67] but again Custer would not be convinced.

The scouts having refused to go in pursuit of the fleeing Indians, Custer decided to send Reno's battalion ahead to attack the enemy. While an order to this effect would undoubtedly have followed in the natural sequence of events, it was probably hastened by the action of the scouts. While Reno was riding up, Custer told Lieutenant Cooke to order him to take his three troops, cross the river, and attack the Indians. He added that he (Custer) would support with the rest of the command. According to Martin, who as Custer's orderly may have been close enough to hear the conversation, Custer told Cooke that he would go down to the other end of the village and drive the hostiles, and that he would have Benteen hurry up and attack in the center.[68] This report implies

[64] General Terry's Second Report, July 2, 1876, as given in Graham, *Story of the Little Big Horn*, 113.

[65] *Official Transcript*, 355, 1049.

[66] Libby, *Arikara Narrative*, 121–22.

[67] "But Son-of-the-Morning-Star (the Crow's name for Custer) was going to his death and did not know it. He was like a feather borne by the wind and had to go." Linderman, *Red Mother*, 235.

[68] Graham, "'Come on! Be quick! Bring packs!' The Story of Custer's Last Message . . . ," *Cavalry Journal*, Vol. XXXII (July, 1923), 306.

that Custer already knew the approximate location, although not necessarily the size, of the Sioux village, an implication which is obviously untenable since Custer did not as yet know of the existence of a village. Reno was merely to harass and delay a fleeing enemy, and Custer probably did not believe that the detachment would be called on to do any serious fighting.[69]

Lieutenant Cooke apparently told the Major that the hostile village was two and one-half miles below and that the Indians were reported to be running away. Reno was to attempt to overtake the fleeing Indians with his battalion and bring them to battle, and was apparently told that he would be supported by the remainder of the regiment. Again the order was verbal and was given to Reno by the Adjutant, and there is some disagreement over just what was said, although all parties seem to agree that it contained the expression, "You will be supported by the whole outfit," or words to that effect. Reno stated later in his official report that Cooke came to him and said that the village was only two miles ahead and was running away and that he was "to move forward at as rapid a gait as he thought prudent, and to charge afterwards and that the whole outfit would support."[70]

Both Girard and Herendeen later testified that Custer gave the order to Reno in person. Herendeen stated that he was standing right beside the Lone Tepee, which he had helped to cut open, when Custer told Reno to lead out and that he (Custer) would be with him.[71] Although Herendeen conceded that Cooke could have given Reno the order without the scouts' having been aware of it,[72] Girard insisted that Custer called to Reno and beckoned him with his hand, and as the Major rode up, Custer ordered, "You will take your battalion and try to bring them to battle and I will support you." Then Custer added, "Take the scouts with you."[73] Recorder Lee thought that this discrepancy in the testimony regarding whether Cooke or Custer actually delivered the orders might

[69] Dr. Charles Kuhlman, *Custer and the Gall Saga*, 9.

[70] Reno's *Report*, 32; *Official Transcript*, 1049. In a letter dated July 30, Reno insisted that "there was no mention of any plan, no thought of a junction, only the usual orders to the advance guard to attack by the charge." *New York Herald*, August 8, 1876. Reprinted in Graham, *The Custer Myth*.

[71] Reno, *Court*, 387, 401; *Official Transcript*, 336.

[72] Reno, *Court*, 404.

[73] *Ibid.*, 144–45; *Official Transcript*, 156–57.

have arisen from the similarity of their dress—they were both wearing buckskin—or from the fact that Girard and Herendeen might have overheard Custer give the order to Cooke and later confused the identity of the two men.[74]

Reno apparently interpreted his order to mean that the five companies under Custer's direct command would act in close coöperation with him, supporting him from the rear and not by a flank attack at some distant point. Reno said later that from the manner in which Cooke's order was given, he could not imagine any other method of support, and that he asked Cooke no questions since he had all of the official information he needed.[75] Not only was Reno justified in his assumption, but it was undoubtedly what Custer had in mind at the time the order was given.[76] None of the witnesses mention Benteen and the plan to have him come up and attack in the center, if there was any such plan, except Trooper Bob Davern, who says that he was acting as Reno's orderly. (Congestion would seem to have been too mild a term for the condition of the region immediately around the Major.) Davern further complicates the situation by insisting that he heard Lieutenant Cooke tell Reno that Custer had directed that Reno take his three companies and sweep everything before him. Then, says Davern, Cooke added that Captain Benteen would be on Reno's left and would have the same instructions. Under questioning Davern stuck to his story and insisted that he was sure those were the orders, and that he believed those were the exact words.[77]

Two things about these orders should be noted: (1) they were the first orders given to Reno after the division of the command, and perhaps the only orders received by him from Custer,[78] al-

[74] Reno, *Court,* 758.

[75] *Ibid.,* 729. But Dr. Porter testified that he was by Reno's side when the order was given and heard Reno ask Lieutenant Cooke if Custer was going to support him. Cooke answered in the affirmative. Reno then asked if the General was coming along and was told that he was. *Official Transcript,* 276–77, see also Brininstool, *A Trooper with Custer,* 99. For General Rosser's views on Custer's plan of action see *New York Herald,* July 11, 1876.

[76] Reno, *Court,* 721; Coughlan, "The Battle of the Little Big Horn," *Cavalry Journal,* Vol. XLIII (January–February, 1934), 17. To support an attack, however, it is not necessary to get behind it since a flank attack or a demonstration in force from some other direction may be just as effective. Brady, *Indian Fights and Fighters,* 235.

[77] *Official Transcript,* 480; Reno, *Court,* 269.

[78] Reno, *Court,* 91.

though on this point there is disagreement,[79] and (2) the only discretion given Reno was in the rapidity of his advance. There was no provision for a retreat at anyone's discretion. Reno was to charge the enemy—and the order was positive and peremptory.[80]

At the time the order was given, Captain Benteen was probably between two and five miles to the left and rear, McDougall and the pack train a little farther away, and neither was, in any sense of the term, within co-operating distance. No village was in sight and no hostile warriors were visible, the small group which Hare and Girard had seen earlier having already disappeared downstream. There was absolutely nothing to warn Custer of the immediate proximity of several thousand very belligerent Indians, except the repeated warnings of the scouts that "the Sioux were too many," warnings which Custer refused to heed. In defiance of even the most rudimentary and elementary rules of warfare, Custer had made no adequate reconnaissance to discover the strength and position of the enemy, but assumed, on the basis of insufficient evidence, that the village was already in flight. Now he added another mistake, that of sending Reno on too fast when he did not know the distances involved.[81] Under the circumstances, he could have no real plan of battle, and was apparently relying on the proverbial "Custer's luck" when he decided to send Reno ahead in an attempt to bring the enemy to battle. His idea undoubtedly was to follow up Reno's charge and hurl the remainder of the regiment on a hostile force which had been broken and disorganized by the impact of that first onslaught.[82] Custer's great mistake was "acting in mingled ignorance of, and contempt for, his enemy." To his mind attack and victory were synonymous, and the only contingency against which he guarded was the escape of the hostile tribes.[83]

Reno had been told to take the scouts with him, and as a result all of them except Bouyer, four of the Crows, and one or two of the Rees went with the Major. While the command had halted, Custer

[79] See below.

[80] Reno, *Court*, 786.

[81] William "Billy" Jackson later said that Reno was told to wait thirty or forty minutes before attacking, probably in order to give Custer time to get into position. "The Story of William Jackson" as told to Jack Burton Munroe.

[82] Coughlan, "The Battle of the Little Big Horn," *Cavalry Journal*, Vol. XLIII (January–February, 1934), 316.

[83] *Army and Navy Journal*, July 22, 1876.

had seen dust rising down the valley, which led Half-Yellow-Face, the leader of the Crow scouts, to suggest that the Sioux must be running away. Bouyer, at Custer's suggestion, ordered Half-Yellow-Face and White Swan to go up on the ridge to see if they could discover the enemy camp. But just then Reno's battalion began to move, and the two scouts, apparently confused or misunderstanding their orders, turned to the left and rode off with the battalion. Therefore, Bouyer and the remaining four Crow scouts started toward the ridge while Custer and his five troops followed the trail that Reno's battalion had taken.[84]

In addition to his three troops, Reno had an uncertain number of Ree scouts, since some had fallen behind because they were so poorly mounted, the two Crows, Girard and Dorman, the interpreters, Reynolds, Herendeen, and the two Jackson brothers, who were half-blood Pikunis. There were also a few troopers from other companies, who for one reason or another happened to be on detached service with the battalion.[85]

It seems obvious that so far Custer had been acting on the assumption that the Lone Tepee marked the site of the great Indian encampment of which the scouts had told him. But just as Reno's command rode off, Lieutenant Varnum, who had been working ahead of the regiment, brought the news that from the top of the bluffs he had seen a large force of Indians and a large village farther down the valley. Custer had every confidence in Varnum's integrity and intelligence, and his report was apparently the first intimation—from what Custer considered a responsible source—of the immediate proximity of a large number of hostiles. Varnum does not seem to have given any indication of the exact whereabouts of these Indians except that they were somewhere down the stream. And the expression "a large force" might have meant two hundred warriors or several thousand.[86] Varnum, having reported to Custer, now joined the scouts and rode with Reno's battalion toward the river.

84 *Account to Scott*, 1–2. For the story that Half-Yellow-Face was sent with Reno as punishment for having argued with Custer, and that the scout told Custer, "You and I are both going home today and by a road that we do not know," see Linderman, *Red Mother*, 175. The story is probably apocryphal since Custer did not speak Crow nor the scout English.

85 See below.

86 Kuhlman, *Custer and the Gall Saga*, 11; *Official Transcript*, 193–94, 232.

As Varnum rode off, he is said to have swung his hat around his head and sung out, "Thirty days' furlough to the man who gets the first scalp."[87]

It was apparently the information brought by his chief of scouts which caused Custer to change his plans, and instead of following Reno across the river as he had probably intended, he followed the trail for about two miles until he passed the slight elevation of land which lies between the main stream of Reno Creek and the small tributary which flows in from the north, and then turned abruptly to the right and began to ride down the Little Big Horn. The sight of a large and well-defined lodgepole trail—larger than the one Reno had followed—leading over the ridges to the right,[88] as well as the presence of a number of mounted Indians on those ridges, may have been contributing factors in that they may have caused him to consider the possibility that the main body of the hostiles had turned north here and not crossed the river at all.[89] Another factor may have been that inasmuch as Custer believed the Indians to be in flight, he felt that their complete destruction could better be brought about by a flank attack. Ten years after the battle Lieutenant Edgerly ascribed the change in plan to the fact that Custer saw that Reno was meeting with slight opposition, and that since the water was only knee-deep to the horses, he swung to the right in the belief that the river could be crossed anywhere.[90] Or Custer may have planned for a simultaneous attack and believed that he would be in position soon after Reno was.

How far it was from the Lone Warrior Tepee to the place where Reno crossed the river is a matter of dispute. The estimates of the officers who rode behind the Major varied greatly, ranging all the way from three-quarters of a mile to five miles.[91] Since the three troops rode at a trot or gallop and apparently covered the dis-

[87] *Hardin* (Montana) *Tribune*, June 22, 1923.

[88] Graham, *Story of the Little Big Horn*, 55; Reno, *Court*, 151. Martin also told of seeing a trail near where Custer had turned off, and said it looked as though tepee poles had been dragged along there. *Official Transcript*, 637.

[89] Daniel A. Kanipe, "New Story of Custer's Last Battle," in *Contributions to the Historical Society of Montana*, IV (1903), 280.

[90] Hein, *Memories of Long Ago*, 144–45.

[91] The estimates of the officers concerning the distance to the ford varied greatly. See Edgar I. Stewart, "Variations on a Minor Theme," *Montana Magazine of History*, Vol. I, No. 3 (July, 1951), 25–26.

tance in about fifteen minutes (although three officers say from twenty minutes to a half-hour),[92] the fairest guess would seem to be that it was from three to four miles.[93] Because the river has changed course several times since then, present distances mean nothing. Both Captain Keogh and Lieutenant Cooke rode with the battalion for some distance, Cooke telling Major Reno in a bantering way, "We are all going with the advance, and Miles Keogh is coming too." Reno soon lost sight of them when his attention was taken up in getting his battalion across the river, and he never saw either alive again, but Cooke at any rate went as far as the river before turning back to join Custer. Lieutenant Wallace was not aware that they had turned back and thought that they rode into the fight with Reno.[94] Cooke at the crossing ordered the stragglers to close up, promising them that there was plenty of hot work ahead.[95]

The three troops crossed without opposition, with M ahead, A following, and G bringing up the rear, riding in the column of twos which was the usual order for moving over a stream.[96] The crossing was made at a natural ford which had been used by the Indians and which was a short distance upstream from where Reno Creek enters the Little Big Horn. The water was fairly deep and swift, and the river from twenty-five to thirty feet wide.[97] There was a delay of some ten or fifteen minutes in crossing. The horses had gone without watering since the evening before, and now thrust their muzzles deep into the clear and cold waters of the stream. Although there was no formal halt, some of the officers and men took advantage of the delay to fill their canteens.[98] There was much

92 The gait at which the battalion rode is also disputed, the officers differing over whether it was a trot or a gallop. Similarly the time consumed in reaching the ford varied, according to the officers, from ten to thirty minutes. See *Official Transcript*, 232; Reno, *Court*, 63, 142, 341, 388, 412, 470, 504, 570, and the *Army and Navy Journal*, July 15, 1876.

93 At the present time the distance from the site of Lone Warrior Tepee to where Reno crossed is approximately four and one-half miles. But the river has changed course since 1876 and is now farther to the west than it was then.

94 *New York Herald*, August 8, 1876; Reno, *Court*, 95.

95 Reno, *Court*, 523.

96 *Ibid.*, 94; *Official Transcript*, 92, 424.

97 Reno, *Court*, 232n; *Official Transcript*, 44, 198; *Hardin Tribune*, June 22, 1923.

98 Reno, *Court*, 93, 412, 504; E. A. Brininstool, "The Custer Battle Water Party," *Hunter-Trader-Trapper*, Vol. LXV (August, 1932), 10.

confusion on the farther bank as the excitement of the troopers communicated itself to the horses, and since the command was somewhat disorganized, Reno halted briefly to close up the column.[99] It was now a little after two-thirty.

Just when the hostiles became aware of the danger from the south is uncertain. Both Wallace and Moylan believed that the Indians discovered Reno's approach before his command crossed the river, for the approach was several feet higher than the valley where the Indian camp was located, and that if they did not see the troops, they saw the dust cloud and knew what it meant.[100] Trooper Morris afterwards said that Reno's men pursued a party of about one hundred hostiles before they reached the river,[101] while others claimed to have seen several Indians before the battalion crossed. These, who were presumably from the hostile village, were not far from the ford and were riding in circles.[102]

While the command was crossing, the scouts told Girard that the Indians were coming upstream, and one of the Crows called out that the Sioux were coming to meet them. Girard said that he reported this fact to Major Reno, saying, "Major Reno, the Indians are coming up the valley to meet us."[103] Herendeen said that he also heard the Crow scouts warn that the Sioux were coming, and he called out to no one in particular, "Hold on, the Sioux are coming."[104] But Reno testified at the Court of Inquiry, and repeated his statement a second time, that he would have listened to Girard if the latter had had any official information, but that he would not have believed him.[105] Moylan declared that he had no recollection of seeing Girard speak to Reno, in fact that he had no recollection of seeing Girard at the ford,[106] and he insisted further that at the time the regiment crossed no Indians were coming up—that he was in a position to see them had there been any.[107]

99 Reno, *Court*, 504.

100 *Ibid.*, 66, 340–41.

101 Brady, *Indian Fights and Fighters*, 408.

102 Reno, *Court*, 447, 470. On the other hand, Sergeant Culbertson said that he saw no Indian before the column crossed but that he did see a cloud of dust. *Ibid.*, 504.

103 Reno, *Court*, 146; *Official Transcript*, 158–59.

104 Reno, *Court*, 388; *Official Transcript*, 319.

105 Reno, *Court*, 735; *Official Transcript*, 1094.

106 Reno, *Court*, 368.

107 *Ibid.*, 341.

Even though the hostiles were some three miles downstream, Girard thought that the information he had was important and that Custer should know of the development since it might cause a change in his plans. Therefore, without orders from anyone, he started back, but some seventy-five or eighty yards from the river he met Lieutenant Cooke and told him[108] that the Indians were in large numbers and were about two and one-half miles down the valley.[109] The adjutant promised to carry the news to Custer, who Girard believed might have been only a short distance away—possibly on the other side of a small knoll—at the time.[110] This development was also probably responsible for Reno's sending his first messenger, Trooper McIlhargy, to Custer with the news that he had the enemy in front and that they were very strong.[111]

A short distance after turning to the right, Custer halted at a small stream to water his horses, cautioning his men against letting them drink too much as they would have to travel far. This stream was probably the north fork of Reno Creek,[112] which establishes the approximate point at which he turned to the north. Here both Lieutenant Cooke and Private McIlhargy reached him with the report that the Sioux were swarming upstream to meet Reno, which report, supplementing that of Lieutenant Varnum, probably reinforced his earlier belief that the village was running away and that the rear guard was coming up to cover the retreat by fighting a delaying action as far from it as possible. Since it is always easier to flank an advancing enemy than a retreating one, Custer apparently decided to continue down the river and then cross to the left bank, thus catching the Sioux between the two detachments and rolling them up. He may be justly criticized for dividing his forces when so nearly in contact with the enemy, and while such tactics are not in accordance with the best teachings of the military art,

[108] *Ibid.*, 151; *Official Transcript*, 161–62.

[109] Reno, *Court*, 207. Girard's apprehensions were not aroused by the large number of Indians but by the fact that he knew Custer was acting on the assumption that the village was in flight whereas actually the warriors were coming out to meet the troops. *Official Transcript*, 161.

[110] Reno, *Court*, 146.

[111] Reno's *Report*, 32. Lieutenant Wallace said that he was not aware that Reno sent back a messenger. Reno, *Court*, 93.

[112] According to what Martin later told the Reno Court of Inquiry, Custer may have watered his horses in the main stream of Reno Creek before turning to the right. Reno, *Court*, 531.

nevertheless experience on the frontier had shown the advantage of attacking an Indian camp from several directions at the same time. Although the situation was not the same, the stratagem had proved highly successful at the Battle of the Washita. Experience had demonstrated also that under proper conditions of surprise the Indians would stampede like a herd of buffalo, a large village scattering as easily as a small one.[113]

Custer has been criticized for not informing Major Reno of his change in plan. He had committed the Major's battalion to action on the assumption that the Sioux were in flight and that it would be supported by the "whole outfit," and the fact that with every opportunity to do so he "failed to acquaint Reno with this sudden and variant change in his expressed intention" has been held to constitute a lack of good faith.[114] In acting thus, Custer probably reasoned that his detachment would reach the valley of the Little Big Horn before a messenger could overtake the Major's command.[115] Moreover, he still believed that the main village was in flight and that the Major would have only a rear-guard action with which to contend.

It must be added that we do not know definitely that Reno was not informed of the change in plan. The Crow scout Curly said afterwards that just before the command turned to the right, Custer sent him to Reno with a message, the contents of which were unknown to him, a statement corroborated by another of the Crows, Goes Ahead.[116] Here also probably occurred, if it occurred at all, the incident related by Theodore Goldin. According to his story, Goldin, who was a member of G troop, had been detailed that morning as an orderly and assigned to Lieutenant Cooke. On the ride down the Little Big Horn, Custer talked with Cooke, who wrote a message and called for an orderly. Goldin, the first to get there, was given the dispatch and told to deliver it to Major Reno, to remain with him until the two commands effected a junction, and

113 Coughlan, "The Battle of the Little Big Horn," *Cavalry Journal*, Vol. XLIII (January–February, 1934), 17, points out that the situation was not the same as at the Washita and that battle should have taught Custer a lesson in the value of adequate reconnaissance.

114 *Ibid.*, 18.

115 Kuhlman, *Custer and the Gall Saga*, 12.

116 Dixon, *The Vanishing Race*, 163–67.

then to report to Lieutenant Cooke at once. Although Goldin declared that he did not know the contents of the message,[117] there is one account which says that it read: "Crowd them as hard as you can. We will soon be with you."[118] Goldin claimed that he rode back over the trail that the command had followed, crossed the Little Big Horn, and delivered the message after a ride of five or six miles. Reno is said to have glanced at the dispatch somewhat hurriedly and then stuck it in the pocket of his shirt.[119] Major Reno later denied ever having received such a message, and no trace of it has ever been found.

Some historians accept the Goldin story as genuine;[120] others reject it entirely on the ground that it has too much of the aspect of a "last survivor" yarn.[121] While there is nothing inherently improbable about the story, it is certainly open to question. Reno had sent two messengers to Custer informing him of the situation on the Major's front, and it would not be beyond the realm of probability for Custer to have sent an answer, and, as Lieutenant Godfrey suggested, the message might have contained important instructions and been hastily glanced at, then "pocketed, ignored, destroyed, and never revealed."[122] But Major Reno, while denying that he received any message from Custer after being ordered to the front, apparently did not feel that his commanding officer was at all remiss in not notifying him of the change in plan, for in his *Report*, made only a few days after the battle, he said, "General Custer was fully confident that [the Sioux] were running or he would not have turned from me,"[123] an opinion which was fully shared by General Terry.[124]

117 Brady, *Indian Fights and Fighters*, 271.

118 Article in the Custer Scrapbooks, Billings Public Library.

119 Brady, *Indian Fights and Fighters*, 271.

120 DeLand, *The Sioux Wars*, 572.

121 Coughlan, "The Battle of the Little Big Horn," *Cavalry Journal*, Vol. XLIII (January–February, 1934), 18; Dustin, *The Custer Tragedy*, 149. In his earlier book, *The Custer Fight*, as he readily admits, Mr. Dustin had accepted Goldin's account as factual. Probably the best account of the Goldin story is the unpublished manuscript by W. J. Ghent, "Theodore Goldin and the Ride to Reno." It is in the Ghent Papers in the Library of Congress.

122 William A. Graham, "'Come on! Be quick! Bring packs!' The Story of Custer's Last Message . . . ," *Cavalry Journal*, Vol. XXXII (July, 1923), 316.

123 Reno, *Report*, 34.

124 General Terry's dispatch of July 2, 1876, from the mouth of the Big Horn River, as cited in Graham, *Story of the Little Big Horn*, 110–14.

After watering, Custer led his five troops up and across the ridge, skirting along through the ravine behind and parallel to the line of bluffs which front the right bank of the Little Big Horn. Custer was wasting no time, and the troops rode rapidly, being at a trot or a gallop most of the way.[125] There has been much speculation regarding the exact route that Custer followed—did he take the first valley lying just east of the bluffs which line the eastern bank of the river, or did he ride along the slope of the range of hills beyond this valley, or follow the second valley behind this second range of hills? The answer to this question will never positively be known since the only people who could answer it are dead. For, of the men who rode with Custer after the Lone Tepee was passed, the four Crow scouts, Sergeant Kanipe of Troop C, Trumpeter Martin of Troop H, and Privates Peter Thompson and James Watson alone came back, and their testimony is contradictory and unsatisfactory.

The probability is that Custer followed down slightly behind the line of bluffs, passing behind the hill upon which Reno and Benteen's troopers were later to be besieged, that he then passed to the right of the sharp point which bears the name of Weir's Point, and on beyond to the ravine which we now know as Medicine Tail Coulee. Terry in his official report said that Custer's trail passed "along and in the rear of the crest of bluffs on the right bank for nearly three miles,"[126] and there seems to have been little question of the route until Godfrey, writing years after the battle, presented a theory of his own concerning it. And Benteen, who had followed the trail of Custer's battalions only a few days after the fight, later publicized some of his ideas regarding the route followed, ideas which were probably conscious rationalization designed to support a theory of the battle which he had developed. At this time Benteen

[125] Gibbon, "Summer Expedition," 303; Graham, "'Come on! Be quick! Bring packs!' The Story of Custer's Last Message . . . ," *Cavalry Journal*, Vol. XXXII (July, 1923), 306; Brown and Willard, *Black Hills Trails*, 153. Martin told the Court of Inquiry that Custer went about three hundred yards from the watering place, then turned to the right a little more for another four or five hundred yards, then came to the hill and went on top of the ridge. Reno, *Court*, 531.

[126] *Report of the Secretary of War, 1876*, 463; Gibbon, "Summer Expedition," 303. McLaughlin, however, believed that Custer rode down the crest of "the long high ridge" which was in full view of the Indian camp for a distance of about six miles. *My Friend, the Indian*, 138.

expressed the opinion that Custer went to the right of the second divide,[127] while Godfrey, who was with Benteen's detachment, speaks of Custer's marching along and well up the slope of the bluffs forming the second ridge back from the river and nearly parallel to it.[128] Both statements are sheer inference; no one will ever really know the exact route followed by the five troops.

On at least two occasions Custer left the command and rode up on the bluffs, either looking for a place to cross and attack or else to learn the force and disposition of the enemy.[129] Probably the latter explanation is correct since Bouyer and the Crows were perfectly familiar with the country, and could—and probably did—tell him how far he would have to go before finding a suitable ford. The first of these side excursions was apparently made near the site of the Hodgson marker, and the second from the high point about a mile farther down the stream. What he saw was not at all reassuring. He got his first look at the hostile village, and even then he did not see all of it because a part was cut off from his view by intervening bluffs. There were, however, several hundred lodges in plain sight, and he began to realize that this was not a village at all but a good-sized city, and to appreciate the magnitude of the task that he had set for his small command.[130] But whatever else he may have been, George Armstrong Custer was not a coward in any sense of the term, and his disposition was such that he welcomed great odds against him since then there was the more credit in overcoming them. He apparently was undaunted by what he saw, although the Crows continued to insist that the Sioux were too many; and counting on the success of Reno's charge to direct the expected scattering—he could see Reno's men riding down the valley—Custer decided to press rapidly forward and be ready to attack the fleeing enemy.[131]

127 Brininstool, *Captain Benteen's Story*, 23.

128 Godfrey, *Montana*, 139.

129 It has also been suggested that Custer went up on the bluffs in order to let Reno know where he was, since the Major would be looking for the promised support and would guess at a diversion farther down the river. Kuhlman, *Custer and the Gall Saga*, 15.

130 Graham, " 'Come on! Be quick! Bring packs!' The Story of Custer's Last Message . . . ," *Cavalry Journal*, Vol. XXXII (July, 1923), 306; *Account to Scott*, 12; Reno, *Court*, 532–33.

131 Godfrey, *Montana*, 195; McClernand, "With Indian and Buffalo in Montana," *Cavalry Journal*, Vol. XXXVI (January and April, 1927), 44.

He did conclude that with a battle of unusually large proportions imminent, the concentration of the badly scattered units of the regiment was advisable, and his first move was to see to the safety of the pack train. The pack train was especially vulnerable; yet, since it carried the extra ammunition, it had to be protected at all hazards, and the best way to do so was to bring it under the protection of the largest element of the command. Thus Captain Tom Custer, at his brother's direction, sent Sergeant Kanipe of his own troop with an oral order to Captain McDougall to bring the train straight across country instead of following the trail of the regiment and, if any of the packs came loose, to cut them away and hurry on with the remainder.[132] Somewhere between Reno Hill and the bluff, which we know today as Weir's Peak, Kanipe left the command and rode back, the first of the few survivors of the men who followed Custer beyond the Lone Tepee.

The two battalions then continued northward at a gallop, probably riding along the high ground directly behind the bluffs.[133] It was apparently during this stage of the march that the horses of four troopers, all of Troop C, became exhausted and dropped from the column. Two of the riders, Privates Thompson and Watson, subsequently joined Reno's command on the hill, but the other two, Fitzgerald and Brennan are unaccounted for and were undoubtedly killed by the Indians.[134] The Arikara scouts also told of seeing several of Custer's men trying to get their fallen horses up again.[135] What became of these troopers is unknown, although it is probable that some of them were picked up by the rear guard.

About a mile north of where he had first ridden out on the bluffs, Custer halted his five companies under the shadow of a towering ridge, and accompanied by Tom Custer, Lieutenant Cooke, Autie Reed, and Martin, whose testimony is not too reliable but is about all that we have to go on, again rode out to the edge of the bluffs. The village seemed deserted, with only a few women, chil-

[132] Daniel A. Kanipe, "A New Story of Custer's Last Battle," in *Contributions to the Historical Society of Montana*, IV (1903), 280; Kuhlman, *Custer and the Gall Saga*, 14–15.

[133] Kuhlman, *Custer and the Gall Saga*, 22.

[134] Brown and Willard, *Black Hills Trails*, 155; Dustin, *The Custer Tragedy*, 149; Graham, *Story of the Little Big Horn*, 86.

[135] Libby, *Arikara Narrative*, 116.

dren, ponies, and dogs in sight. Custer is supposed to have said, "We've got them this time," and to have expressed the belief that the Indians were in their lodges asleep. (It is more likely that he said that the Indians had been "caught napping," and Martin's English was inadequate to the idiom.)[136] Custer is then said to have turned in his saddle, taken off his hat and waved it to attract the attention of the members of the command who had halted at the base of the hill, and called out, "Hurrah, boys, we've got them. We'll finish them up and then go home to our station."[137] It was probably this waving of the hat that Reno's troopers in the valley saw and interpreted as intended to urge them on, whereas it probably meant nothing of the sort. Martin, in fact, says that they could see nothing of Reno's command, although they looked for it especially,[138] and they may possibly have been concealed by the timber, for Kanipe mentioned having seen them earlier "moving at full speed down the valley."[139] Custer, from what he could see, would have had no reason to believe that there was any particular danger; he anticipated that there would be a hard fight, but was justified in believing that Reno would hold his own and that things were proceeding according to plan. Custer then rode down to the troops and, after talking for a moment with Lieutenant Cooke, again set the command in motion riding down the ravine which skirts the eastern edge of Weir Point until they came to "a big ravine which led in the direction of the river,"[140] and which could only have been Medicine Tail Coulee.

Custer had learned many things as a result of his observations from the bluffs. He had been able to see up the valley of the Little Big Horn and knew that there were no Indians there and that Ben-

136 Graham, *Story of the Little Big Horn*, 84. The story told by the Crow scouts supports Martin's statement that no Indians were to be seen, for Bouyer is said to have explained the almost deserted camp by saying they were probably out campaigning somewhere. *Account to Scott*, 2–3.

137 Graham, "'Come on! Be quick! Bring packs!' The Story of Custer's Last Message . . . ," *Cavalry Journal*, Vol. XXXII (July, 1923), 306; Reno, *Court*, 533; Kuhlman, *Custer and the Gall Saga*, 14.

138 Graham, "'Come on! Be quick! Bring packs!' The Story of Custer's Last Message . . . ," *Cavalry Journal*, Vol. XXXII (July, 1923), 306.

139 Daniel A. Kanipe, "A New Story of Custer's Last Battle," in *Contributions to the Historical Society of Montana*, IV, 280.

140 Graham, "'Come on! Be quick! Bring packs!' The Story of Custer's Last Message . . . ," *Cavalry Journal*, Vol. XXXII (July, 1923), 307–308.

teen's mission had been unnecessary. From the dust kicked up by the detachments he knew that Benteen had also realized that fact and had turned to follow the trail of the regiment and was now only a short distance ahead of the pack train. He also apparently knew that the Indians were not leaving the village, and since his entire strategy up to this point had been predicated on the theory that the village was in flight, a change became necessary. Because the number of Indians was much greater than he had expected to meet, he concluded that the entire strength of the regiment would be needed.[141]

Martin, the lone surviving participant, gave two versions of what happened. According to the traditional account, Custer summoned him and said:

> "Orderly, I want you to take a message to Colonel Benteen. Ride as fast as you can and tell him to hurry. Tell him it is a big village and I want him to be quick, and to bring the ammunition packs." He didn't stop at all when he was telling me this and I just said "Yes, sir" and checked my horse, when the Adjutant said, "Wait, orderly, I'll give you a message," and he stopped and wrote it in a big hurry in a little book and then tore out the leaf and gave it to me.[142]

However, Martin told the Reno Court of Inquiry in 1879 that after going down a ravine that led to the river Custer told the adjutant to send a message to Captain Benteen, and that he (Martin) did not know what it was.[143] He added that Lieutenant Cooke told him that he was to take the message to Captain Benteen and to go as fast as he could over the same trail that the five companies had followed. If there was no danger and Martin had time, he was to return; otherwise he was to join his own troop and report to Lieutenant Cooke when he did return.[144]

Martin was a green Italian lad—he had been a drummer boy with Garibaldi at Villafranca and had been in the United States

[141] Edgerly, *Narrative,* 11.

[142] Graham, " 'Come on! Be quick! Bring packs!' The Story of Custer's Last Message . . . ," *Cavalry Journal,* Vol. XXXII (July, 1923), 308; Graham, *Story of the Little Big Horn,* 85.

[143] Reno, *Court,* 616.

[144] Graham, " 'Come on! Be quick! Bring packs!' The Story of Custer's Last Message . . . ," *Cavalry Journal,* Vol. XXXII (July, 1923), 308; Godfrey, *Century,* 373.

only a few years—and his intellectual and language difficulties were many; indeed, this is not the only incident of which he gave different accounts at different times. The now famous message which Cooke gave him read: "Benteen—come on—big village—be quick—bring packs. W. W. Cooke, P. S. Bring packs."[145] Critics of Custer have contended that this repetition of the final instructions indicated that the leader was already worried about the outcome of the approaching conflict, without bothering to notice that the message was written by Cooke and not by Custer, although it may safely be inferred that the adjutant was excited.

As the trumpeter started back, the command turned toward the river and rode down into Medicine Tail Coulee at a gallop, the gray-horse troop being in the center of the column.[146] Martin's horse was tired, but he rode as fast as he could. A short distance away he met Boston Custer, who was riding at a run in an attempt to overtake the command. The younger Custer checked his horse and asked, "Where's the General?" Martin pointed back and answered, "Right behind that next ridge you'll find him." And Boston Custer rode on. It was then about three-thirty o'clock.

Almost at the same time, Martin later claimed, he heard firing behind him. He looked around and saw a number of Indians who had been in ambush—how many he does not say. Some were shooting at the soldiers, while others were waving buffalo robes and blankets in an attempt to frighten and stampede the horses. They saw Martin and fired several shots at him, one of which struck his horse, although he did not know it at the time.[147] Martin rode on, and before going three-quarters of a mile he found himself on the same ridge from which Custer had surveyed the valley only a few minutes before. He looked down into the bottom and saw that Reno's command was engaged. Although Martin later claimed that there were hundreds of Indians riding around and shooting at Reno's men, who were dismounted and on a skirmish line which was slowly

[145] This message may be found in a number of places. The original is now in the Library of the United States Military Academy at West Point. A photostatic copy is reproduced in the Handbook distributed at the Custer Battlefield National Monument.

[146] Reno, *Court*, 532.

[147] Graham, "'Come on! Be quick! Bring packs!' The Story of Custer's Last Message . . . ," *Cavalry Journal*, Vol. XXXII (July, 1923), 308.

falling back, he told the Court of Inquiry that he noticed the fighting in the valley but paid no attention to it and went on about his business.[148]

[148] *Official Transcript*, 617–18; Reno, *Court*, 535. In his testimony before the Court, Martin also made no mention of meeting Boston Custer.

CHAPTER XV

Reno's Fight

ACROSS THE RIVER, Reno's battalion—consisting of about 134 officers and men and 16 scouts[1]—was between two and three miles upstream from the lodges of the Uncpapa and Blackfeet Sioux, the southernmost of the circles. From the ford they entered a narrow belt of timber and halted there to re-form.[2] This apparently took from five to ten minutes,[3] and it was while here that Major Reno sent Trooper McIlhargy, his "striker," back with a message to Custer reporting that he had the enemy in his front and that he was very strong.[4] Then the order to advance was given, and, for a distance of about half a mile in columns of fours with the heads of the three companies on a line,[5] the battalion rode down the valley. The formation was then changed, Troops A and M forming a line, with G troop in reserve. The pace at first had been a brisk trot but had increased to a gallop.[6] The scouts under Lieutenants Varnum and Hare were slightly ahead and on the extreme left of the command, while Major Reno rode in the center about twenty yards in advance.[7]

The ground was broad, level prairie, but the soil was sandy and full of wild sage; the grass had all been eaten off by the Indian ponies and the surface so badly cut up by their hooves that Lieu-

1 Just how many men Reno had in his battalion is one of the most hotly disputed subjects pertaining to the battle. Reno claimed that he had 114 men in the saddle when he rode toward the ford; some of his critics have claimed that the number was closer to 140. For a full discussion see Stewart, "Variations on a Minor Theme," *Montana Magazine of History*, Vol. I, No. 3 (July, 1951), 27. The muster rolls of the regiment are to be found in Luce, *Keogh, Comanche, and Custer*.

2 Reno, *Court*, 60–61.

3 *Ibid.*, 304; *Official Transcript*, 49.

4 Reno, *Court*, 498; Graham, *Story of the Little Big Horn*, 36.

5 Reno, *Court*, 367.

6 Godfrey, *Century*, 370.

7 Reno, *Court*, 63; *Official Transcript*, 48.

tenant Wallace compared it to an ash bed; it was difficult terrain for cavalry to cross, but the line kept in good order.[8] On the right was the crooked, tortuous bed of the Little Big Horn River, its banks covered with a growth of tall cottonwoods and thick bushes, while on the left there were slowly rising barren benchlands, and behind them a line of low, round hills, rising slowly toward the distant mountains.[9] Farther down the stream the valley widened out substantially,[10] and the troops could see great clouds of dust and, in the dust, Indians—just how many was uncertain, and still is a matter of dispute. One trooper, an inexperienced recruit, estimated that at least 2,000 hostiles were swarming upstream to meet the small command,[11] but Sergeant Culbertson, who was more experienced in such matters, put the number at between 100 and 150.[12] The dust cloud in the distance was caused by the great number of animals in motion, and both Lieutenant Hare[13] and Dr. Porter noted that the Indians were driving the pony herd downstream toward the village, Dr. Porter adding that there were few Indians and many ponies.[14]

A few of the hostiles, possibly to the number of forty or fifty, had been in the valley on miscellaneous errands, although Major Reno later insisted that they were there as decoys,[15] and they now fled before the cavalry advance. In an effort to confuse and frighten the troopers, and possibly to cover their own retreat, the Indians began to fire the grass, and other fires were observed springing up down the valley.[16] The hostiles were also riding madly back and forth kicking up the dust as a defensive maneuver which was a forerunner of the modern smoke screen,[17] but it is doubtful if, for two miles, the detachment "pursued close on the verge of an immense and blinding cloud of dust raised by the madly flying savages ahead,"[18] since practically all the Indian accounts agree that Reno encountered no opposition as he galloped toward the village.[19]

[8] Reno, *Court*, 248; *Official Transcript*, 426.
[9] *Army and Navy Journal*, July 15, 1876.
[10] Reno, *Court*, 516.
[11] Brady, *Indian Fights and Fighters*, 402.
[12] Reno, *Court*, 516.
[13] *Ibid.*, 413.
[14] *Ibid.*, 297.
[15] *Ibid.*, 731.
[16] *Ibid.*, 389.
[17] *Ibid.*, 232n.

The original plan had been to charge with two companies and have the third on which to rally, but about halfway to the point where he finally halted, the belief that there were large numbers of Indians ahead caused Reno to bring Troop G up into the line. However, the battalion did not break its fast gallop down the valley, riding faster than some of the troopers had ever ridden before,[20] and it became increasingly difficult to keep the line straight.[21] The troops began to cheer in answer to the whoops and yells of the Indians until the dour, unimaginative Reno ordered them to "stop that noise,"[22] telling them not to get excited for they would have quite enough work to do, or words to that effect.[23] He is also said to have promised one of the younger troopers that he would give him all of the fighting he wanted before the day was over.[24]

There was apparently no need for haste, and it has been contended that Reno attacked prematurely, without allowing Custer time to get into position. It has also been alleged that Reno acted as he did in the hope and expectation of winning a great victory, entirely by himself, and thus attaining revenge on Custer for many real and fancied wrongs and grievances. This is sheer and unadulterated nonsense, for the Major was still proceeding on the assumption that he would be "supported by the whole outfit." Although there is one account that says that Custer told Reno to wait thirty or forty minutes before attacking,[25] there is no other evidence to support it, and hence no reason to believe that Reno had any way of knowing that Custer needed any time to get into position. Reno did not, and indeed could not, know that his commander had ap-

18 DeRudio, "My Personal Story," *Frontier and Midland*, Vol. XIV (January, 1934), 155.

19 *New York Times*, June 20, 1926.

20 Reno, *Court*, 695; Brady, *Indian Fights and Fighters*, 403.

21 Reno, *Court*, 96.

22 Godfrey, *Montana*, 178.

23 Reno, *Court*, 516.

24 *Ibid.*, 368. In a letter dated July 8, 1876, Dr. Paulding said that as the battalion galloped across the plain they heard several volleys from where Custer was supposed to be. "New Light on the Little Big Horn" (two letters of Captain H. O. Paulding, then a Lieutenant, Medical Corps, with Gibbon), *Field Artillery Journal*, Vol. XXXVI, No. 4 (July–August, 1936), 352 (hereinafter cited as Paulding, *Letters*). Paulding was with the Montana column but had many friends among the officers of the Seventh Cavalry from whom he doubtless derived his information.

25 MS, "Billy Jackson's Story as told to Jack Burton Monroe," Montana State Historical Library, Helena, Montana.

parently changed his original plans and was at that moment riding just on the other side of the bluffs that line the eastern bank of the Little Big Horn. Major Reno had been ordered to pursue an enemy who was believed to be running away and to attempt to bring him to battle. He was doing just that.

It is doubtful that the dust cloud that Girard and the scouts had observed was what they took it to be, since almost all of the Indian accounts of the battle agree that the attack on the village came as a complete surprise. Indeed, if the surprise had been less complete, there might have been no battle, for the Indians would have had time to collect their belongings and strike camp, and the expected scatteration would then have taken place. In fact, Gall later went so far as to declare that, when Custer's command was observed coming down into the valley, orders were given for the village to move. But Reno swept down so rapidly upon the upper end of the camp that the order could not be executed and the Indians were forced to fight.[26] Although the hostiles knew that there were troops in the vicinity and that they were only fifteen miles away at ten o'clock that morning, they expected that an attack, if it came, would come at daybreak.

The hunters who had started out earliest that morning had already brought in their game, but a good many others had not yet returned. A number of warriors were still in their tepees; in fact, some of the Sioux say that the troops made their appearance when the laziest of the tribesmen were just getting up[27] and the pony herd was about a mile distant from the camp, although in most cases a favorite horse was picketed near his owner's lodge.[28] Some of the men and boys were fishing, while others were playing games and racing their ponies on the flat benches near the stream, and east of the river women were digging tipsin. Earlier, some of the warriors had seen dust clouds in the east and had suspected their cause, and later some of them had noticed soldiers about two miles east of the camp. They had seen Custer's command riding along the eastern ridges toward the lower end of the camp as though

[26] *Army and Navy Journal*, July 3, 1886; Brady, *Indian Fights and Fighters*, 373.

[27] *Account to Scott*, 7; Dr. Charles Eastman, "Story of the Little Big Horn," *Chautauquan*, Vol. XXXI (July, 1900), 356.

[28] Edgerly, *Narrative*, 5–6.

on dress parade, and had noticed particularly the number of white (gray) horses. This had caused widespread comment, and Chief Gall said later that it was a nice sight to see "the parade across the river to our east."[29] In other words, while the Indians seem to have been aware of the earlier division of the regiment, they claim to have had no suspicion of an attack from the south. They were speculating about the identity of these pony soldiers and thought that they might be those of General Crook, the Gray Fox, whom they had beaten a few days before on the Rosebud, except that these soldiers had more gray horses than his command.[30] It was a hot day and almost windless, and the hooves of Reno's horses raised a great cloud of dust which seemed to hang in the air and could have been seen for miles. It was apparently this huge dust cloud rolling rapidly down the valley toward them which interrupted the hostiles' speculation regarding the identity of the soldiers across the river and first warned them of their danger. The Sioux also maintain that a few young men rode into the camp and reported the advance of the troops just a few moments before carbine shots began to rattle among the tepees, setting some of them on fire and inflicting a few casualties. Among the dead were the two wives of Gall, as well as three of his children.[31] According to the Sioux, Reno's soldiers were almost in the camp before they were discovered: "All through that great camp was the confusion of complete surprise. . . . White Bull [Sitting Bull's daredevil nephew] saw young girls clutching shawls over their frightened heads, fat matrons puffing and perspiring, old women, shrivelled as mummies, hobbling along on their sticks, trying to save themselves."[32] Then the Indians began to get organized, and while most of the warriors rushed in the direction of the pony herd, a few went out to face Reno, some on foot and the others on ponies that, luckily, had been picketed in the village. It was probably the young men who only a few moments before had been play-

[29] Barry, *Indian Notes on the Custer Battle*, 9; Dr. Charles Eastman, "Story of the Little Big Horn," *Chautauquan*, Vol. XXXI (July, 1900), 356; Edgerly, *Narrative*, 3. See also McLaughlin, *My Friend, the Indian*, 139.

[30] This statement is open to question since Captain Egan's troop of the Second Cavalry, which was with Crook, had gray horses. *Army and Navy Journal*, April 15, 1876.

[31] *Army and Navy Journal*, July 3, 1886.

[32] Vestal, *Warpath: True Story of the Fighting Sioux*, 193; Vestal, *Sitting Bull*, 165; McLaughlin, *My Friend, the Indian*, 138–39.

ing on the flats who provided the first resistance that Reno encountered.[33]

The Indian protestations of surprise must be taken with a much larger quantity of salt than the proverbial grain. Custer could have been seen at any time coming down the western slope of the divide, and there is evidence that he was seen and his approach reported.[34] Five or six miles east of Reno's crossing, Lieutenant Varnum[35] had noticed that the pony herd was being driven into the village, and Dr. Porter[36] was of the opinion that the dust cloud observed from the Lone Tepee was caused by the Indian women driving the ponies toward the camp and estimated that about a thousand animals were in motion. Among the Indians, One Bull later declared that the hostiles had known the day before that the soldiers were coming and were ready for them, and that he was dressing and painting himself in the lodge of his uncle, Sitting Bull, at the time Reno attacked.[37] It is not at all improbable that the Indians knew of the approach of the soldiers before the troops were aware of the proximity of the hostile camp.[38]

Moreover, if the Sioux and Cheyennes were surprised, their recovery was almost instantaneous. According to Gall, they had been speculating about whether the troops across the river intended to attack the village, but Reno's action removed all doubt from their minds. Not many minutes had passed before another dust cloud was sweeping up the valley from north to south as the warriors swarmed out like angry hornets to do battle with the soldiers. Nor was it the full power and strength of the Sioux and Cheyenne Nations that confronted Major Reno, for, regardless of how many warriors there were in that hostile camp, probably not more than one-fourth of the available fighting strength rode upstream to oppose the Major's detachment, the remainder staying where they were to guard the village against the expected attack of those soldiers seen earlier riding northward along the bluffs. Just how many

[33] Dr. Charles Eastman, "Story of the Little Big Horn," *Chautauquan*, Vol. XXXI (July, 1900), 356; see also Edgerly, *Narrative*, 5–6.

[34] *Army and Navy Journal*, July 3, 1886.

[35] *Official Transcript*, 352.

[36] *Ibid.*, 263.

[37] Item in the Custer scrapbooks, Billings Public Library.

[38] Burdick, *Tragedy in the Great Sioux Camp*, 12; *Army and Navy Journal*, July 3, 1886.

Indians rode out to meet Reno we do not know, but certainly not as many as he thought there were, although probably more than he had expected to meet. For their part, the hostile chiefs apparently were not too sure of the strength of the attacking force, and the women began to strike the lodges in preparation for a retreat, should one become necessary.[39] In the midst of the confusion Sitting Bull is said to have stood by his tepee and advised his people: "Warriors, we have everything to fight for, and if we are defeated we shall have nothing to live for, therefore let us fight like brave men."[40]

Each moment that passed saw the arrival of additional warriors, and ahead of Reno's command the dust was so thick that the soldiers could see for only a short distance. The hostiles were racing their ponies back and forth as they always did before a battle in order to give them their second wind. The maneuver also served to stir up the dust and provide a cover for their movements. On the left the dust was even thicker; here the Arikaras, following the traditional Indian style of fighting, broke and scattered as they approached the village[41] in an attempt to run off the hostiles' pony herd, and the Sioux were fighting back desperately.

The activities of the scouts on this occasion have been almost universally misunderstood. Custer, like most other commanders of his day, never used the scouts for line fighting. Instead, they were employed for trailing the enemy, for skirmishing, and for capturing or running off the pony herds of the enemy. In this battle he had depended upon the scouts to bring him into contact with the enemy, and now their purpose was, if possible, to cripple the mobility of the Sioux. The Arikaras made a vigorous effort to carry out the difficult task that Custer had assigned them, and that they failed was not due so much to a want of courage as to the fact that they were badly outnumbered. Indians are very realistic. In war, defeat generally meant death, and since there was no alternative, retreat was preferable to defeat. The failure of the scouts was also partially due to Reno's failure to hold his skirmish line, as this released many of

[39] Barry, *Indian Notes on the Custer Battle,* 11; Dr. Charles Eastman, "Story of the Little Big Horn," *Chautauquan,* Vol. XXXI (July, 1900), 357; McLaughlin, *My Friend, the Indian,* 138.

[40] Dr. Charles Eastman, "Story of the Little Big Horn," *Chautauquan,* Vol. XXXI (July, 1900), 357.

[41] *Billings Gazette,* August 13, 1933.

the Sioux, who were then able to recapture the pony herd and force the scouts to retreat without having accomplished their mission.[42] The story that the scouts fled the field in wild terror and confusion is pure fantasy, a tale manufactured from whole cloth, but repeated with such persistence that in the course of time it came to be accepted as a fact. Nor must it be overlooked that at least three of the scouts were killed and two others wounded, a proportion of loss greater than that suffered by the troopers.[43]

The smoke and dust made it very difficult for Major Reno to see anything, but he could see that the village was still standing. This, plus the ease with which he drove the Indians, made him fear a trap, but there was also the possibility that the lack of resistance was due to the extreme demoralization of the few warriors who opposed him.[44] Uncertain about what confronted him, uncertain about Custer's whereabouts or intentions except for the rather vague promise of general support, Reno made the first of several fateful decisions and halted his command. He said later that he could see a ravine or ditch ten yards wide and three or four yards deep some three hundred yards ahead and that large numbers of Indians were emerging from it, while other parties of hostiles were coming toward him at a rapid gait and cutting around his left toward the rear.[45] This statement was confirmed by Lieutenant Wallace, who said that on the right there was a bend in the river, then open prairie for a few rods, and then a ditch or ravine through which the hostiles were coming;[46] and Lieutenant Hare, who admitted that he did not know why the halt was made, added that several hundred hostiles emerged from this ravine after the troops had halted. But Hare also said that the Major could not have seen the Indians in the coulee ahead when the halt was ordered and that the halt was made before the Indians started to emerge. His version was contradicted by Lieutenant Varnum, who testified that the ground ahead of the command was open prairie and that, although he was told afterward

[42] Libby, *Arikara Narrative*, 12–14.

[43] Dustin, *The Custer Tragedy*, 111; Byrne, *Soldiers of the Plains*, 99; *Winners of the West*, April 30, 1936.

[44] Reno, *Court*, 16; Edgerly, *Narrative*, 3–4.

[45] Reno, *Court*, 695. See also the account in the *New York Herald*, August 8, 1876, in which no mention is made of a ditch or ravine.

[46] Reno, *Court*, 65; McLaughlin, *My Friend, the Indian*, 139.

that there were ravines there, as he saw it at the time the ground was open and very like that over which they had just passed.[47]

Reno, who later attempted to justify his action on the ground that he had become convinced that he could not make a successful offensive charge because the great number of Indians had forced him on the defensive, now decided to dismount his command and fight on foot. It must have been at this time that he sent back to Custer his second messenger, Trooper Mitchell, a cook, with the same report that McIlhargy had carried. We know that both messengers reached the general, for the bodies of both were found on battle ridge.[48]

It was Reno's first taste of Indian fighting,[49] and while he had earned a reputation as a brave and competent officer during the Civil War, he seems to have been one of those individuals who, while personally stalwart and honest, lack the ability to make decisions under fire; and he seems, further, to have been totally lacking in the capability to command. Under the immediate supervision of a superior officer, Reno would probably have performed his duties as a subordinate in a satisfactory manner; as matters stood, however, he demonstrated that the courage to follow is one thing, while the courage to lead is something very different.[50]

The Major has been severely, and not entirely unjustly, criticized for not obeying his orders, which incidentally gave him no discretion, and charging the village. Lieutenant Edgerly later wrote: "If Reno had charged through the village, Custer would have joined him in a very short time, and Benteen later, and we might have had an expensive victory."[51] Mrs. Spotted Horn Bull, who was in the hostile camp, agreed that Reno struck too soon and that if he had charged the camp as ordered, the power of the Sioux would have been broken.[52] Colonel Charles King, one of the severest of

[47] Reno, *Court*, 413; *Official Transcript*, 201, 414.

[48] Coughlan, "The Battle of the Little Big Horn," *Cavalry Journal*, Vol. XXXXIII (January–February, 1934), 18. Colonel Graham, however, says that Mitchell was sent back before the battalion halted. *Story of the Little Big Horn*, 41.

[49] Vestal, *Sitting Bull*, 169. Lieutenant Godfrey said, "I doubt if Reno had ever before seen a hostile Indian, he certainly had not in any campaign with the Seventh Cavalry." McClernand, "With Indian and Buffalo in Montana," *Cavalry Journal*, Vol. XXXVI (January and April, 1927), 36.

[50] *Ibid.*, 48.

[51] Hein, *Memories of Long Ago*, 145.

[52] McLaughlin, *My Friend, the Indian*, 170.

Reno's critics, maintains that Custer expected a bold and dashing charge into the heart of the Sioux encampment, but that "Reno had no dash to speak of, and the sight that burst upon his eyes eliminated any that might have been latent. He attacked but the attack was spiritless and abortive."[53] Another critic has written: "He [Reno] was not well fitted to lead such an attack and his conduct that day was more like one bereft of reason than that of a fighting major of cavalry."[54]

In contrast to these writers, who maintain that a spirited charge would have thrown the village into confusion and allowed Custer's command to strike a decisive blow, Reno's defenders contend that the battalion could not have gone half a mile farther without being destroyed, in view of the number of hostiles opposing them. Reno himself was of the opinion that if he had carried out his orders and charged, most of the saddles would have been empty and most of the troopers and horses dead before he had advanced very far.[55] Lieutenant Hare agreed, saying that if the command had gone three hundred yards farther mounted, they would not have lasted five minutes and not a man would have been able to get out alive,[56] while Lieutenant DeRudio believed that in another five hundred yards they would all have been butchered.[57] The fairest conclusion seems to be that it was a problem for the judgment of the officer commanding, and that while some of the hostile accounts indicate that Reno lost a chance for a brilliant victory when the Indians saw his irresolution and acted upon it,[58] it may very well be that he did the only sensible thing in the light of his knowledge of the situation. In the years that have elapsed since the battle, every action, almost every word, has been so surrounded by controversy and dispute that it is well to remember, in this case as in so many others, that it is difficult enough to discover what really happened without trying

53 Charles King, "Custer's Last Battle," *Harper's Monthly Magazine*, Vol. LXXXI (August, 1890), 383.

54 Olin D. Whelan, "The Custer Battle Field," *Smalley's Magazine*, Vol. XXII, No. 1 (July, 1903), 7.

55 Reno, *Court*, 738.

56 *Ibid.*, 438.

57 *Ibid.*, 465.

58 Olin D. Whelan, "The Custer Battle Field," *Smalley's Magazine*, Vol. XXII, No. 1 (July, 1903), 7.

to speculate too much over what might have happened had the course of action been different.

At the time Reno made his fateful decision there had been no contact with the enemy. Only a few scattering shots had been fired by the Indians, and apparently only one trooper had been wounded, although the Major insisted that this had no relation to his action.[59] The troops had fired a few shots, and Private Davern, who was on the left of the line with Lieutenant Hare, said he got a shot at some hostiles about four or five hundred yards away.[60] But there had been no regular or sustained fire on either side.[61]

The order to dismount was given to Troop G by Lieutenant Hodgson, and to the other two troops by Major Reno in person. Before it could be executed, the horse of Trooper George F. Smith bolted and ran away, carrying his rider straight into the Indian camp. Smith was never seen again, his body was never recovered, and his fate is unknown, though it is almost certain that he was killed by the Indians. On the site of the village Brisbin's troopers later found the head of a white man which had been severed from the body by dragging the man around at the end of a lariat until the head was pulled off. This may have been the head of this unfortunate trooper, or it may have been that of any one of several other members of Custer's command whose bodies were never identified. Three other horses are reported to have bolted and run away. In two cases, their riders, J. R. Meyer and Roman Rullin, succeeded in rejoining the battalion, although both had been wounded. The third trooper, James Turley, is said to have suffered the same fate as Smith.[62]

The troops dismounted, coming down accurately and in good order, somewhat to the surprise of Lieutenant DeRudio.[63] Along the riverbank about forty or fifty yards away[64] and several feet lower than the surrounding prairie[65] was an extensive growth of small

59 Reno, *Court,* 738; *Official Transcript,* 97, 1096. See also McClernand, "With Indian and Buffalo in Montana," *Cavalry Journal,* Vol. XXXVI (January and April, 1927), 37.

60 Reno, *Court,* 471.

61 *Ibid.,* 99, 232v, 449.

62 *Official Transcript,* 1053; Edgerly, *Narrative,* 13; *Hardin Tribune,* June 22, 1913; Brady, *Indian Fights and Fighters,* 402.

63 Reno, *Court,* 448; *Official Transcript,* 426.

64 Reno, *Court,* 147.

65 *Hardin Tribune,* June 22, 1913.

timber and underbrush. Acting under orders from Captain French, Sergeant John Ryan and ten men skirmished it thoroughly for hostiles who might be hiding there.[66] When none were found, the horses were taken here for protection, there being one horse-holder for every four horses.

With the horse-holders out, Reno had about ninety men forming a skirmish line of only a few hundred yards in length. At five-yard intervals these men would have covered about one-quarter of a mile.[67] The command had originally halted some 150 yards from the river, but before dismounting had advanced to where it made a quick change of course. The hostile village was across the bend, and it was seemingly only seventy-five or a hundred yards to the first tepee, the troops facing north, with the line curving slightly to the left where the scouts were posted, Bob-tailed Bull being the last man on the left of the line. The right flank rested on the edge of a dry, thickly wooded creek bed, and the left extended toward the bluffs.[68] There was a prairie dog town where the skirmish line formed and some of the men are said to have used the mounds for breastworks.[69] Once afoot, the line of troopers steadied and even advanced a short distance, Captain Moylan insisting that the line progressed about one hundred yards after it was deployed, the advance being a movement separate and distinct from the deployment.[70]

Just how many hostiles were in front of Reno at this time is unknown. Reno himself said that he saw between five and six hundred Indians, and had the same idea as the scouts that there were great numbers in front.[71] While Lieutenant Wallace estimated that there were only from two to three hundred Indians in and near the ravine which was just ahead, he also insisted that the number steadily increased.[72] Girard, who was notoriously anti-Reno but was un-

[66] Reno, *Court*, 389; Brady, *Indian Fights and Fighters*, 402.

[67] Lieutenant Wallace said there were seventy-five men on the skirmish, Private Morris said seven officers and ninety men plus a few scouts and civilians. Reno, *Court*, 98; Brady, *Indian Fights and Fighters*, 402.

[68] DeRudio, "My Personal Story," *Frontier and Midland*, Vol. XIV (January, 1934), 155.

[69] *Hardin Tribune*, June 22, 1923.

[70] For the dispute over whether or not an advance was made, see Reno, *Court*, 64–65, 99, 345, 450; *Official Transcript*, 50, 165–66, 202, 429.

[71] Reno, *Court*, 696.

[72] Reno, *Court*, 65; *Official Transcript*, 52–53, 272, 320–21.

doubtedly a more competent judge, said that where the skirmish line formed, the ground was flat and level prairie, that he could see down the valley for a distance of from twelve to fifteen hundred yards, that the nearest hostiles were fully one thousand yards distant, and that they did not come up to the line until some time after it had been formed. Girard also testified that he did not see more than fifty to seventy-five Indians in front of the line. Herendeen, who was on the extreme left of the line and therefore had a good vantage point for observation, saw only a few Indians in the valley and none immediately in front of Reno. The few that he saw were sitting on their horses and did not move until the troops got near the point where they halted. Then the Indians began moving out as skirmishers.[73]

Dr. Porter's testimony supported that of the two scouts. He said that the nearest Indians were from eight to nine hundred yards away and that when the line deployed there were not more than fifty hostiles confronting Reno,[74] an estimate with which Lieutenant Hare agreed.[75] But Captain Moylan asserted, on the contrary, that there were above five hundred hostiles less than a quarter of a mile in front of Reno when he halted, and that at least two hundred others had passed around the left flank.[76] With this statement Lieutenant Varnum agreed. He believed that there were from three to four hundred Indians—possibly more—in Reno's front. Lieutenant Hare probably provided a key to the widely varying estimates when he testified that it was almost impossible to estimate the strength of mounted Indians since they were always on the move and did not stand still to be counted.[77]

On the skirmish line the troops kept up a rapid fire. Many of them were without actual experience in Indian fighting, and it was difficult to keep them from firing too fast. There was little attempt at fire control since most of the officers were firing themselves rather

[73] Reno, *Court*, 152–53. Girard said that at the time not more than fifty Indians were near Reno's command. *Official Transcript*, 183.

[74] Reno, *Court*, 304–305; *Official Transcript*, 267–68.

[75] *Official Transcript*, 356. Herendeen was of the opinion that the number of Indians who attacked Reno in the valley did not exceed two hundred warriors. *New York Herald*, January 22, 1876; McClernand, "With Indian and Buffalo in Montana," *Cavalry Journal*, Vol. XXXVI (January and April, 1927), 36.

[76] Reno, *Court*, 343.

[77] Reno, *Court*, 435; *Official Transcript*, 205.

than attempting to regulate the fire of their men.[78] As a result, some of the troopers began to exhaust the supply of ammunition carried in their belts, so each alternate trooper was ordered to fall out and go back to get ammunition from his saddlebags, then to return to the line so that the others could go back.[79] In addition, the troopers did not keep their intervals well, but had a tendency to bunch up like frightened sheep, despite the best efforts of the officers to prevent it.[80] The contest was not entirely one-sided, however, for some of the Sioux lodges were destroyed and several Indians killed.[81] Although it has been alleged that the soldiers' carbines were outranged by the guns of the Indians, this has been denied,[82] and the controversy probably arose from the fact that the Indians were equipped with all sorts of weapons—from bows and arrows up to Winchesters of a very recent design, along with old Sharps, Spencers, and Ballards, which were inefficient as well as ancient.[83] But it is certain that the troopers' carbines soon began to overheat and that after firing only a few rounds the men began to experience difficulty in extracting the empty cartridges.[84]

A new danger now revealed itself as the Sioux, trying to get at the horses, began to infiltrate along the riverbank and into the timber. To meet this new threat, Reno took G company off the line and sent it back to the banks of the river, while the soldiers remaining on the skirmish line attempted to compensate for the withdrawal by extending their intervals. But the line was now too thin, and, with the left flank "in the air" as the result of having been turned by the hostiles, the command was in grave danger of being surrounded and cut to pieces. Moylan asked Reno what to do, and the skirmishers were ordered withdrawn to the timber and around the horses.

[78] *Official Transcript*, 511; Brady, *Indian Fights and Fighters*, 402.

[79] Reno, *Court*, 67, 232p., 354.

[80] *Ibid.*, 343, 505–506. The late W. J. Ghent, one of the most competent and conscientious students of the battle, always insisted that the surviving officers of the Seventh Cavalry deliberately exaggerated the numbr of recruits in the regiment in order to help Major Reno. See *Winners of the West*, April 30, 1936. The question of recruits is also discussed in Luce, *Keogh, Comanche, and Custer*.

[81] Mari Sandoz, *Crazy Horse, the Strange Man of the Oglalas*, 326.

[82] Reno, *Court*, 450; *Official Transcript*, 429. Lieutenant Varnum insisted that the Indian guns did not outrange the troop carbines. Reno, *Court*, 287. *Official Transcript*, 253, 1089.

[83] Britt, *Sitting Bull*, 216.

[84] Reno, *Court*, 488; *Official Transcript*, 572.

The troops had apparently been on the skirmish line about fifteen or twenty minutes.[85] According to one account, Reno gave the abrupt command, "Retreat to the timber," but it was countermanded by Captain French, and the line retired slowly with faces to the enemy while continuing the fire.[86] This story is to be doubted, for while the retirement, which consisted of Troops A and M executing a flank movement to the right, was carried out quickly and efficiently, the command apparently ceased to fire, and no measures were taken to keep back the enemy or protect the movement while it was being executed.[87] About one-half of M company had to face the left again in order to change front in the direction of the hills because the Indian attack was being made from that quarter.[88] Sergeant Culbertson, although he described this movement, said he did not know who ordered it, since his position had been on the left of the skirmish line.[89] This version of the change of position has been challenged, and it may be that instead of ordering the change, Major Reno, through the lack of an aggressive and controlling leadership, merely allowed his battalion to slip from the offensive to the defensive.[90]

The line now faced west and southwest, and the troops were in the shelter of the trees and behind a cut-bank which had been left when the Little Big Horn made one of its frequent changes of course. The hostile Indians had almost if not entirely surrounded the command. That the troops had reached the timber just in time was evident from the fact that soon afterwards a large number of Sioux came around the edge of the woods.[91] It was apparently at this stage of the battle that either Wallace or Moylan suggested to Billy Jackson, the half-blood scout, that he attempt to carry a mes-

[85] Reno, *Court*, 333, 454; *Official Transcript*, 1055. Estimates concerning how long the soldiers had been on the skirmish line vary from fifteen to thirty-five minutes. See Reno, *Court*, 402, 506; *Official Transcript*, 100, 166–67, 301, 342.

[86] Brady, *Indian Fights and Fighters*, 402.

[87] Reno, *Court*, 789.

[88] *Ibid.*, 333. Lieutenant Wallace said the line remained in position until the left was forced to fall back, then the entire line retired to the woods. *Official Transcript*, 98.

[89] Reno, *Court*, 505–506.

[90] McClernand, "With Indian and Buffalo in Montana," *Cavalry Journal*, Vol. XXXVI (January and April, 1927), 36.

[91] Reno, *Court*, 517, 525.

sage to Custer, but he refused, waving his arms toward the hostiles and declaring that no man could get through.[92]

Shortly after the fight in the valley began, Lieutenant Varnum saw the gray-horse troop moving north along the bluffs on the opposite side of the river. He caught only a momentary glimpse of a portion of the troop and did not know that it was Custer's command. They were some distance back from the actual edge of the bluff and were moving at a trot but not a fast trot, and Varnum estimated that it would have taken them another twenty or thirty minutes to reach the ford, as the ground was very uneven and they had to cross some ravines.[93] Lieutenant DeRudio later claimed that he saw Custer on the eastern bluffs and that he was accompanied by two other men, one of whom was Lieutenant Cooke. DeRudio identified them by their dress—blue shirts and buckskin pants—and by Cooke's immense beard. No part of the column was visible, but DeRudio judged that it was probably behind the bluff. The officers were on the highest point on the right bank and just below where Dr. DeWolf was later killed. DeRudio said that it was not Weir's Point, but one nearer the river, where the Little Big Horn comes right under the bluffs. Although they were fully one thousand yards from DeRudio, he insisted that he could recognize them at that distance and was positive about the identification, even though they remained on the bluffs for only about a minute when Custer waved his hat and disappeared.[94] General Hugh Scott always doubted the authenticity of this story, declaring that it rested on the statement of a not too reliable person and expressing the opinion that, if anyone appeared on the bluffs, it was probably Bouyer.[95]

The timber in which Reno's men had taken refuge was growing on what had once been the bottom of the Little Big Horn River. About twenty-five yards wide and in the general form of a crescent,

[92] *Ibid.*, 103, 385; *Official Transcript,* 102, 315–16.

[93] Reno, *Court,* 238–39, 272–74; *Official Transcript,* 219, 236. Varnum, "I Was There," *Winners of the West,* March 30, 1936. There are some discrepancies in these various accounts.

[94] Reno, *Court,* 476–84; *Official Transcript,* 491–93, 503, 505. Lieutenant DeRudio estimated that it was six or seven minutes after the troops reached the timber, and five or six minutes before they left that he saw Custer on the bluffs. *Official Transcript,* 498–502.

[95] *Custer Chronicle,* July 23, 1936. DeRudio's reputation for veracity does not seem to have been very high.

one point of which was within a thousand feet of the village,[96] the woods provided an excellent position defensively, since most of the timber was young and was filled in with a thick growth of underbrush.[97] But it did not constitute any threat to the hostile village, for the Indians could always pull down their lodges and move away.[98] Nor could the soldiers have done very much damage to the village, since the timber was lower than the ground on which the lodges stood, and the troopers would have overshot.[99] Nevertheless, it probably could have been held for several hours without any difficulty, and, by the use of axes, shovels, and other entrenching tools, it could have been made into a defensive position which could have been held indefinitely; in fact, it would have been a much better one than the subsequent position on the hill.[100] The command did not have the necessary tools, however, and Reno soon began to realize that it would take more men than he had to cover it adequately enough to keep the Indians from creeping up, sheltering themselves in the timber, and firing on the troops.[101] The problem of provisions and ammunition also promised to be serious. Reno's men had no rations, and their ammunition would not last for more than three or four hours, no matter how carefully handled.[102] There was no sign of Custer, for despite the fact that he had been seen across the river by members of the battalion, apparently no one had thought that it was important enough to tell Major Reno; at least no one had taken that responsibility.

The plight of the battalion was by no means desperate, although there was the possibility that it might become so at any time. As a possible forerunner of what might come, the Sioux now began to infiltrate the woods from the eastern bank of the stream. There was thus the ever increasing danger that Reno's right would be turned and the troopers surrounded and cut off from their horses.[103]

Reno, bedeviled and uncertain of what to do next, seems to have considered the possibility of making a sally from the woods

96 Reno, *Court*, 455, 472.
97 *Ibid.*, 71.
98 *Ibid.*, 557.
99 *Ibid.*, 360.
100 *Ibid.*, 557, 580.
101 *Ibid.*, 235, 281, 732.
102 *Ibid.*, 479.
103 *Ibid.*, 462, 697.

against the nearest part of the Indian village but decided against it.[104] Believing himself to be surrounded, he is said to have asked the advice of French, the senior captain. One account maintains that French advised getting out of the river bottom,[105] but, in a letter to Mrs. Cooke written in 1880, French indicated that he was tempted to shoot Reno when the order to retreat was given, and that since that time he had come to the conclusion that he would have been fully justified in doing so.[106]

Reno decided that the best chance of safety lay in gaining the high bluffs on the opposite side of the river and later justified his judgment on the ground that he had every reason to believe that the regiment had been scattered since Custer was not carrying out his promise of support and no one had brought him any further orders. Since in his situation he could render assistance to no one, the first requisite, in his opinion, was to reunite his command with Custer's instead of leaving him unsupported. To this end Reno planned to move to the bluffs, where he could not only hold his own but also be seen by the other detachments. He felt that it was his duty and responsibility to unite his battalion with the others, since he, not being in command, could not expect them to come to him. Therefore, he decided to move his battalion through the surrounding Indians.[107] After asking Captain Moylan's opinion about the best point to which to retreat, he designated a point to which the command would move, there establish itself, and await developments.[108] It was certainly not cowardice or timidity that prompted this action, nor do the losses suffered up to that point provide the motive. Supporters of Major Reno have argued that the retreat was made not so much because of the casualties already suffered as it was to prevent further casualties.[109]

Just how many casualties the detachment had suffered up to that time is—like so many other facts about the Custer fight—a matter of disagreement. Reno himself told the Court of Inquiry that he could not remember how many men he had lost before he left

[104] *Ibid.*, 100.
[105] Brininstool, *A Trooper with Custer*, 30.
[106] *Winners of the West*, April 30, 1936.
[107] Reno, *Court*, 697–98, 739, 741; *Official Transcript*, 1055.
[108] Reno, *Court*, 334.
[109] *Ibid.*, 712, 776, 792.

the timber, although he believed that the interpreter, Isaiah Dorman, had been killed and several troopers wounded.[110] Lieutenant Wallace insisted that two men had been killed on the skirmish line and one in the timber, and that several had been wounded.[111] Captain Moylan, apparently referring to his own company, said that one man had been killed and one wounded before the order to leave the timber was given.[112] Sergeant Culbertson declared that he knew of only one man wounded on the skirmish line but four others had been hit before the battalion left the position in the woods.[113] Dr. Porter, whose evidence should have considerable weight, said that to his knowledge only one man had been wounded up to the time the battalion left the timber.[114] Later writers are equally at variance. Dustin says that Reno had lost eight or nine men killed, including Smith whose horse had run away,[115] but he lists both Dorman and Reynolds as killed on the skirmish line, whereas both apparently lost their lives after the retreat from the timber began. On the other hand, Sergeant Kanipe claims that up to the time that the retreat from the timber began, Reno had not lost a man;[116] and Graham says that Reno had lost one man, Sergeant Hynes of Troop A, who had been killed as the battalion made its change of front.[117] At this late date it is extremely unlikely that these discrepancies ever will be reconciled.

Reno gave an oral order—there was no trumpet call—for the troops to leave the timber. He later claimed that he sent the order to Captain French by Lieutenant Hodgson, and gave it to Captain Moylan and Lieutenant McIntosh in person.[118] The company com-

110 *Ibid.*, 731; *Official Transcript*, 1092. Reno was mistaken about Dorman.

111 Reno, *Court*, 106. Lieutenant Wallace said that he saw two men killed or disabled and heard of one other before Reno left the timber. *Ibid.*, 67.

112 *Ibid.*, 353–54. Lieutenant DeRudio, who was temporarily detailed with A troop, said he saw one man killed on the line and two or three others wounded. *Official Transcript*, 438.

113 Reno, *Court*, 506, 526.

114 *Ibid.*, 309; *Official Transcript*, 263, 272. Lieutenant Varnum put the casualties even lower and said he knew of none either on the line or in the timber. *Official Transcript*, 204. The wounded man mentioned by Porter was left in the timber.

115 Dustin, *The Custer Tragedy*, 117.

116 Daniel A. Kanipe, "A New Story of Custer's Last Battle," in *Contributions to the Historical Society of Montana*, IV (1903), 281.

117 Graham, *Story of the Little Big Horn*, 42.

118 Lieutenant Edgerly said the only order was, "Mount and get to the bluffs." *Narrative*, 6.

manders were told to withdraw their men and horses to a small clearing in the timber and to mount in columns of four, with the head of the column headed upstream and away from the Indian camp.[119] Troop A seems to have been the first to form, followed closely by M, which took position on the left of Troop A. While this was going on, Major Reno sat on his horse, supervising the formation.[120] Although Captain Moylan said later that the whole of his command was formed before starting from the timber,[121] there is some reason to doubt the accuracy of his statement, and it certainly was not true of the others, for G troop, which was scattered through the woods, seems to have received no definite orders to leave and had no information beyond hearing a rumor that the others were leaving the timber.[122] Lieutenant Wallace, its second in command, said the word was passed that they were going to charge, but where or how he did not know.[123] Accordingly, a part of the troop was not formed until too late to accompany the rest of the battalion.[124]

It was owing to the noise of the firing and the fact that their attention was concentrated elsewhere that many—officers, men, and scouts—failed to hear of the decision to retreat to the bluffs.[125] Davern, despite the fact that he was Reno's orderly, first knew that the command was leaving when he saw some of the members of Troop G running through the timber toward their horses,[126] and Lieutenant Hare first heard of the movement when his orderly brought him his horse and told him they were leaving. This orderly was Private Clare of K troop, who was killed during the retreat. But for his action, Hare admitted, he would have been left in the timber.[127] Sergeant Culbertson heard no orders.[128]

119 *Official Transcript*, 1056.

120 *Ibid.*, 1180; Reno, *Court*, 334, 698.

121 Reno, *Court*, 357; *Official Transcript*, 307.

122 Reno, *Court*, 790.

123 *Ibid.*, 68; *Official Transcript*, 105.

124 Godfrey, *Montana*, 179.

125 Reno, *Court*, 507.

126 *Ibid.*, 474.

127 *Ibid.*, 414; *Official Transcript*, 358. The roster of the regiment as given in Luce, *Keogh, Comanche, and Custer*, and the list of dead and wounded given in Burdick, *Last Battle of the Sioux Nation*, do not list a soldier by this name. Both of them list a Private Clear as killed. Since he was a member of Troop K, this was undoubtedly the man referred to.

128 Reno, *Court*, 507.

Nor did all of those who knew that the battalion was leaving succeed in joining it in time to get out of the timber, as several troopers were unable to mount their frightened and excited horses.[129] A goodly number of these were members of Troop G, which seems to have suffered from demoralization much more than either of the other two troops.[130]

While the troops were gathering in the clearing, the fire of the command almost entirely ceased, and no means were taken to keep back the Indians or to cover the movement in any way. Before the formation had been completed, a large party of Sioux broke through the timber to within thirty feet of the command and fired a volley point-blank into the troops. Private Lorenz, or Lawrence, of Troop M was hit and "hollered," "Oh, my God, I have got it,"[131] and toppled from his horse. He was caught by Privates Neeley and Morris and concealed in the brush.[132] The same volley killed the scout Bloody Knife, who was eight or ten feet to the right and front of Major Reno, while the latter was trying to get from him by signs information about what he thought the Indians were going to do.[133] The bullet struck the scout between the eyes, spattering blood and brains in the face of the Major.[134] According to Herendeen, this occurrence so disconcerted Reno that he ordered the troops to dismount, only to order them immediately to remount.[135] It also frightened a number of the men, and in Herendeen's opinion was the principal factor in causing them to stampede.[136] Apparently Reno gave no further orders, but got out of the timber ahead, his horse jumping as though he had had the spurs put to him and, with the troopers following, rode toward the river.[137] How long the battalion had been in the river bottom no one knows exactly, and the estimates of the amount of time that had elapsed from the mo-

129 *Ibid.*, 733.

130 *Ibid.*, 474.

131 *Official Transcript*, 1180; Reno, *Court*, 423. Another account says that the man shot was Kotzbucher. Brininstool, *A Trooper with Custer*, 31.

132 Dustin, *The Custer Fight*, 16.

133 *Official Transcript*, 1059.

134 Reno, *Court*, 423; Holley, *Once Their Home*, 250.

135 Reno, *Court*, 309.

136 *Ibid.*, 423–24; *Official Transcript*, 365–67. At the Reno Court of Inquiry Herendeen was quite emphatic in his account of the incident, and vigorous cross-examination failed to shake his story.

137 Reno, *Court*, 423; *Official Transcript*, 367, 1056, 1059.

ment they deployed as skirmishers until they left the timber vary from twenty minutes to three-quarters of an hour.[138]

Although the battalion is usually represented to have ridden in a column of fours with Troop A ahead, G following, and M bringing up the rear, this does not seem to have been quite the situation.[139] Rather, the three companies formed the three angles of a triangle with A on one side constituting the right flank and slightly ahead of the others, while G was on the left, and M behind. They were described as being "individually together—well closed up" and going at a fast gallop,[140] although Sergeant Davern later recalled that the troops were strung out all the way between the woods and the river.[141]

Behind him Reno left his dead and wounded, no effort being made to take them out, and he also deserted Lieutenant McIntosh, several of the scouts, and from twelve to fifteen troopers.[142] Abandonment of the strong position in the timber came as a surprise to some who were of the opinion that it could have been held almost indefinitely. When Girard heard Moylan give the command, "Men, to your horses. There are Indians in our rear," he exclaimed to Reynolds, "What damn fool move is this?" because he thought that they were safer in the timber and that if the command moved out on the prairie, it would not last five minutes.[143] Although Reno has been criticized for this move, one writer going so far as to say that he was routed not by force of numbers but by inexperience and panic,[144] most of the officers who were with him believed that the action was justified by the existing situation. Captain Moylan justified it on the ground that the command was virtually, although not actually, driven from the timber.[145] Lieutenant Wallace believed that the withdrawal was dictated by the fact that the command was sur-

138 McLaughlin says, "How long he [Reno] remained there in the timber is a question. The Indians are not very clear about it at all, and the military is not very much clearer." McLaughlin, *My Friend, the Indian,* 142. For the views of some of the officers see *Official Transcript,* 55, 236, 273, 359, 436, 530.

139 *Official Transcript,* 210, 1060.

140 *Ibid.,* 360; Reno, *Court,* 105, 355, 415.

141 *Official Transcript,* 518–19.

142 Reno, *Court,* 733; *Official Transcript,* 438.

143 Reno, *Court,* 149, 223; *Official Transcript,* 167.

144 J. L. Beardsley, "Could Custer Have Won?" *Outdoor Life,* Vol. LXXI (March, 1933), 57.

145 *Official Transcript,* 307.

rounded and in a bad position to defend itself,[146] and that the decision to seek higher ground was the only one possible under the circumstances, since to remain where they were could only have meant the annihilation of the battalion.[147] This opinion was shared by Lieutenant Hare, Sergeant Culbertson, Private Morris, and the Crow scout, White-Man-Runs-Him.[148] On the other hand, Lieutenant Edgerly felt that the withdrawal from the timber was Reno's fatal error,[149] that there was little excuse for the movement, and none for the manner in which it was executed.[150] Lieutenant Godfrey, who, like Edgerly, was with Benteen, believed that Reno could and should have held the position.[151]

The hostiles themselves seem to have felt that Reno had a strong position and to have been taken by surprise when the soldiers left it so hurriedly. Later some of them told General Miles that if Reno had not retreated, the Indians would have fled, since the soldiers could not have been dislodged.[152] The Indians would have been compelled to divide their forces and would therefore have been unable to concentrate all of their fighting strength against Custer's two battalions. The order had already been given for the village to break up and scatter and the women had begun to strike the lodges, but as soon as Reno fled toward the bluffs, the order was countermanded. Had he not retreated, the order would have been carried out, with the fighting efficiency of the hostiles correspondingly decreased.[153]

Lieutenant DeRudio was also of the opinion that the presence of the battalion in the timber constituted a major threat to the village, since a short charge would have gone right through it. By remaining there, Reno could have held the attention of a large number of the enemy, for the Indians would not have dared leave his

146 *Ibid.*, 56.

147 Reno, *Court*, 103.

148 *Ibid.*, 433, 439, 517; Brady, *Indian Fights and Fighters*, 405; *Account to Scott*, 8.

149 Hein, *Memories of Long Ago*, 145; *Winners of the West*, April 30, 1936.

150 Edgerly, *Narrative*, 6.

151 "Letter of E. S. Godfrey to Superintendent C. H. Asbury, Crow Agency, Montana." (Original in Montana Historical Collection, Billings Public Library).

152 Miles, *Serving the Republic*, 191, 289; Grinnell, *The Fighting Cheyennes*, 344.

153 Miles, *Serving the Republic*, 191; Godfrey, *Century*, 383–84.

battalion unchecked in a position so near the lodges.[154] At this distance in time it appears that the troops could have held out longer than they did, although in the end the result might have been total annihilation. There is the possibility that had Reno held the position, it would have enabled Benteen to carry out Custer's last orders: to "come on" and hurl his three comparatively fresh companies on the rear of the enemy between Reno and Custer. However, there is also the possibility that, instead of following Custer's trail, Benteen would have elected to join Reno in the timber. Whether he could have done so or not and taken the pack train through is highly problematical, but such a move would at least have created a diversion and perhaps enabled Custer to extricate his command from the ambuscade into which he had ridden. Had the commands of Reno and Benteen been able to effect a junction, they might have been able to take the offensive and ride through the village.[155] Thus Reno, by his action in leaving the valley, may have tossed aside the chance at least of a partial victory.[156]

For Reno's failure to remain longer in the timber, Coughlan blames Custer, reasoning that if he had told Reno to expect support from the flank, rather than leaving the matter indefinite, the Major might have remained longer in the bottom waiting for Custer's attack to develop, an attack "that did a little later draw the foe from his [Reno's] front as he gained the bluffs."[157] When all is said, the fact remains that the question of whether to remain longer in the timber in the face of mounting danger was one for the judgment of the battalion commander, and in the opinion of most of his officers, Reno exercised proper discretion and good leadership up to the time that the retreat to the bluffs began. None of them had any criticism of his troop movements and disposition. However, when Bloody Knife was killed at his side, Reno seems to have lost entirely his nerve and judgment, and his demoralization communicated itself to the men.

154 Reno, *Court*, 459–60; *Official Transcript*, 217.

155 Reno, *Court*, 254–55. McClernand criticized Reno for not advancing rather than retreating. "With Indian and Buffalo in Montana," *Cavalry Journal*, Vol. XXXVI (January and April, 1927), 38–39.

156 Miles, *Personal Recollections*, 289; Reno, *Court*, 794–95.

157 Coughlan, "The Battle of the Little Big Horn," *Cavalry Journal*, Vol. XLIII (January–February, 1934), 18.

In any case, the effect of his action on the subsequent fate of Custer was decisive. It not only released several hundred Indians for the attack on Custer's two battalions, but enabled them to be thrown into the battle at just the time and place that made their addition most effective, since the attack on Custer did not begin until about the time Reno reached the bluffs.[158]

As the soldiers emerged from the timber and headed for the river, which was from one-half to three-quarters of a mile away and over level ground,[159] the several hundred Indians[160] who had been fighting the command but had already started to leave Reno and go down the river[161] thought it was an attack and scattered.[162] However, they soon discovered their mistake and realized that the soldiers were running away. There were no hostiles directly in front, but as the troops headed for the river, they were pressed closely on both flanks and in the rear,[163] and the Indians ranged in alongside, hunting the troopers as though they were buffalo. They did not charge into the rear end of the column but stayed on the flank, generally some fifty yards or so out—occasionally closer—pumping their Winchesters into the troops.[164] Had they closed in, they would probably have made short work of the battalion.[165] That so many troopers were able to escape was probably due to the immense clouds of dust which hung in the air, making it impossible to see fifty feet in any direction.[166] At every moment

[158] Godfrey, *Century*, 384; James P. Murphy, "Campaign of the Little Big Horn," *Infantry Journal*, Vol. XXXIV (June, 1929), 636.

[159] Reno, *Court*, 69–70, 232. Dr. Porter, however, put the distance at between one-half mile and a mile. *Official Transcript*, 273.

[160] Reno said there were from six to nine hundred Indians at his left and rear with plenty of others between him and the village and on the far bank of the river. Reno, *Court*, 731. Other officers put the estimate even higher. *Ibid.*, 415, 507. But Dr. Porter said there were only between two and three hundred Indians in the immediate vicinity. *Ibid.*, 323.

[161] Reno, *Court*, 275; *Official Transcript*, 217–18.

[162] Dr. Marquis makes the amazing statement that the Indians thought Reno had attacked them in the belief they were Cheyennes and retreated when he found they were not, and Custer had then attacked the Cheyennes. *Billings Gazette*, July 17, 1932.

[163] Reno, *Court*, 790.

[164] *Ibid.*, 289–90. In later years Private Slaper recalled that an Indian had ridden so close to him that he could have reached him with his saber if he had had one. Brininstool, *A Trooper with Custer*, 50–51.

[165] Reno, *Court*, 68, 293, 434; *Account to Scott*, 3.

[166] Brininstool, *A Trooper with Custer*, 34.

the rate of speed increased: at first the troopers had been riding at a trot, then a gallop, with the retreat finally resolving itself into a desperate run for the ford.[167] Not only was there little or no resistance, either organized or individual, but Major Reno made no attempt to cover the withdrawal in any way. The troopers were seeking merely to escape, and every man seemed to be running on his own hook, having little or no concern for anyone else.[168] With this conclusion, Lieutenant Hare, who admitted that he had never seen a demoralized column or panic-stricken body of men, disagreed. In his opinion the retreat was not a demoralized rout, for there was always more or less disorder in a force of cavalry moving at a fast gait.[169] Private Slaper added that while the retreat did not have a very military appearance, he saw nothing disorderly about it.[170]

Major Reno rode at the head of the column.[171] He was apparently very much excited, and after exhausting the shots in his revolvers is said to have thrown them away,[172] although this story has been denied and is merely another of those myths which haunt the battle. He had lost his hat—a cheap affair of the same kind that many of the officers had purchased for fifty cents or less from the trader on the *Far West*[173]—and he may have had a red handkerchief tied around his head, but it is doubtful if his face was bloody and that he yelled orders which no one could understand, as Burkman, who was not there, says he did.[174] We can also discount the Arikara testimony that his mouth and beard were white with foam and his eyes wild and bloodshot.[175] Although censured for being in the

167 Reno, *Court*, 334, 346; *Army and Navy Journal*, July 15, 1876. In his summation at the Reno Court of Inquiry, Recorder Lee inquired, "Was this movement a charge, a retreat or a stampede?" *Official Transcript*, 1185.

168 Reno, *Court*, 310; *Official Transcript*, 360; Godfrey, *Century*, 371. For further evidence on the disorganized nature of the retirement see King, "Custer's Last Battle," *Harper's*, Vol. LXXXI (August, 1890), 384; Grinnell, *The Fighting Cheyennes*, 337; Vestal, *Sitting Bull*, 169.

169 Reno, *Court*, 439.

170 Brininstool, *A Trooper with Custer*, 31; Reno, *Court*, 259.

171 *Official Transcript*, 307.

172 Godfrey, *Century*, 371; McClernand, "With Indian and Buffalo in Montana," *Cavalry Journal*, Vol. XXXVI (January and April, 1927), 38. On the hill Davern told Reno that he had lost his carbine. The only answer was that Reno had lost his carbine and pistol, but he did not say how or where. *Official Transcript*, 642–46.

173 *Official Transcript*, 1078.

174 Article by Glendolin Wagner in Clipping File, Billings Public Library.

175 Libby, *Arikara Narrative*, 128.

The Valley of the Little Big Horn.

Where Reno's troops first attacked the Indians. Later Reno retreated across the river and climbed the bluffs in the foreground.

Roahen Photograph

Major Marcus A. Reno.

"... he demonstrated that the courage to follow is one thing, while the courage to lead is something very different."

Courtesy Custer Battlefield National Monument

forefront of this race for the ford, Reno had some justification for his action. In the first place he considered it a charge and not a retreat, and it might also be argued that, since the river and the country ahead were both unknown, it was proper for him to be at the head of the column in order to supervise the crossing of the stream and select a new position.[176]

But while the retreat, which Captain French referred to as the "*sauve qui peut* movement,"[177] was largely characterized by blind panic and was a desperate fight for life every inch of the way, there were deeds of heroism as well in those six or seven minutes that it took the detachment to reach the river. About halfway to the stream, Captain Moylan checked his company and attempted to close it up in order to protect the men in the rear as much as possible. One of the men had his horse shot from under him, but succeeded in catching another one—a sorrel belonging to G troop, whose rider had apparently been killed—and coming up with the command.[178] Lieutenant Varnum's orderly was wounded and his horse killed. Varnum stopped, and with the help of two or three others caught up a loose horse and remounted his orderly before riding on.[179] Lieutenant Wallace also tried to pick up one of his men who had been wounded and unhorsed. In this attempt he was unsuccessful, for the trooper was killed by the Indians before Wallace was able to assist him.[180] Bob Davern's horse also fell, and he was dismounted. Near by two G company men on foot were being attacked by two Indians, who in their excitement ran their horses together. In the resulting confusion, Davern was able to recover his horse, mount, and escape, although the two G company men were killed.[181]

"Lonesome Charley" Reynolds, who had had premonitions of disaster, had been left behind in the timber but attempted to overtake the others and was killed as he rode up the slope at the west, near the present railway station of Garryowen. Isaiah Dorman was slain a little farther on. Reynolds had been surprised at the order to leave the timber, but after the retreat had begun did all he could

176 Reno, *Court,* 763.
177 Edgerly, *Narrative,* 6; Grinnell, *The Fighting Cheyennes,* 336.
178 Reno, *Court,* 335, 339; *Official Transcript,* 307.
179 Reno, *Court,* 232r, 261.
180 *Official Transcript,* 124.
181 *Ibid.,* 520.

to hold the Indians in check, in order to give the soldiers a better opportunity to escape.[182] His horse was apparently shot from under him, for after the battle his body was found behind it with a large number of empty cartridge shells near by, showing that he had fought valiantly to the last, and Chief Runs-the-Enemy thus describes the death of Dorman: "We passed a black man in a soldier's uniform and we had him. He turned on his horse and shot an Indian right through the heart. Then the Indians fired at this one man and riddled his horse with bullets. His horse fell over on his back and the black man could not get up. I saw him as I rode by. I afterwards saw him lying there dead."[183]

The Indian scouts also suffered during the retreat, for the soldiers could not distinguish the different tribes. To them an Indian was an Indian—they all looked alike. One of the Arikaras, Goose, had his right hand severely mangled by a soldier, and White Swan was also wounded.[184] This retreat from the timber was one action in which Reno's lack of experience in Indian fighting was a positive detriment, for all the frontiersmen and old soldiers knew that to run from an Indian in battle was almost the equivalent of death.[185]

When the column left the timber, Lieutenant Varnum, uncertain about just what was happening, spoke to some of the men at the head of the column. The classic account has it that he called out, "For God's sake, boys, don't run. Don't let them whip us," and that Major Reno, whom Varnum had not seen, replied sharply, "I am in command here, sir," whereupon the Lieutenant fell in alongside Troop A and said no more.[186] Varnum later told the Court of Inquiry that when he got out of the woods, the head of the column was a couple of rods toward the river. He assumed that a general charge had been ordered, that the head of the column had seen some Indians and had started for them, and that the rest of the command had followed. Seeing no officer at the head, he yelled at the men to stop, then discovered Major Reno's presence

[182] Grinnell, *Two Great Scouts*, 18; as against Graham, *Story of the Little Big Horn*, 44.

[183] Dixon, *The Vanishing Race*, 173.

[184] Dustin, *The Custer Tragedy*, 131.

[185] Stanley Vestal, *Short Grass Country*, 12.

[186] Van de Water, *Glory Hunter*, 349. Graham says that Varnum exclaimed: "For God's sake, men, don't run, we have got to go back and save the wounded." *Story of the Little Big Horn*, 46.

so said no more.[187] But Dr. Porter described Varnum as attempting to check the retreat by saying, "For God's sake, men, don't run. There is [*sic*] a good many officers and men killed and wounded and we have got to go back and get them."[188] This remark was apparently made after the command had crossed the river but before it had reached the top of the bluffs.[189] Herendeen also told of hearing an unidentified officer trying to rally his men. The scout thought that the officer said, "Company A, halt; let us fight them; for God's sake, don't let us run," or something like that.[190] This officer may have been Lieutenant DeRudio, who tried to stop the retreat of his men. They, however, refused to listen to him or to obey his commands.[191]

Major Reno and his defenders have always referred to this movement not as a retreat but as a "charge," which prompted one writer to comment sarcastically that it should be studied carefully by everyone interested in military history, because "it is probably as original, unique, and peculiar a 'charge' as any known in military tactics," and that it should become immortal in our military annals since it was led enthusiastically by the Major himself, and was directed not against the Sioux but against the clay banks on the other side of the river. The fact that a few Indians complicated the matter by getting in the way is held to have been entirely coincidental and should not in any way reflect discredit upon the Major.[192]

The troopers were headed for the ford by which they had crossed to the attack, but as the pressure of the hostiles was almost entirely from the right, the column was forced to the left and along a narrow, little-used pony or buffalo trail leading to the nearest bluffs and a crossing about a mile downstream from the mouth of Reno Creek. This was not a regular ford; indeed, the stampede is said to have been so demoralized that the soldiers did not cross at any particular place,[193] but simply moved on the trail and into the

187 *Official Transcript*, 196.
188 Reno, *Court*, 299.
189 *Official Transcript*, 196.
190 Reno, *Court*, 394.
191 *Ibid.*, 450–52; *Official Transcript*, 434.
192 Olin D. Whelan, "The Custer Battlefield," *Smalley's Magazine*, Vol. XXII, No. 1 (July, 1903), 7; Brady, *Indian Fights and Fighters*, 272.
193 *Account to Scott*, 12.

river and got out on the other side.[194] The water was not too deep, although Dr. Porter, who felt that it was a good crossing and about the best that could have been found in the immediate vicinity, said that it came up to the saddles.[195] The width of the river here varied from twenty-five to fifty feet, and the western bank was about five feet above the water—some make it even more.[196] The only way to get into the stream was to jump, and while the leaders hesitated, they were forced by the pressure of those behind. The bank was a straight cut-bank, but after some of the horses had gone down it, it caved in, making a fairly good crossing for those behind.[197]

The eastern bank was about eight feet high[198] and, in the opinion of Colonel Smith, one of the steepest ever ascended by horse or mule.[199] It was a steep, abrupt, and slippery bluff intersected at short intervals by equally steep and narrow ravines. The sides of these were of rough clay and were too perpendicular for a direct ascent, but up them the members of the command scrambled and rode, Lieutenant Varnum relating afterwards that his horse nearly threw him off by jumping up so straight.[200] As a result of these obstacles the battalion got jammed and soon lost all semblance of organization. The horses were frantic with fear and excitement, many out of control, and several of the troopers jumped into the stream never to be seen again.[201] The crossing, which would have been difficult enough under ordinary conditions, was made doubly so by the fact that it was made under the sniping fire of the Indians on the bluffs,[202] and a few of the hostiles even rode across the stream in pursuit of the fleeing enemy, clubbing the troopers and pulling them from their saddles.[203] But the fight was not all one-

[194] Reno, *Court*, 335.

[195] *Official Transcript*, 294. For testimony concerning the depth and width of the stream see Gibbon, "Summer Expedition," 300; *Hardin Tribune*, June 22, 1913; Reno, *Court*, 70, 310–11.

[196] Col. William W. Edwards, "The Battle of the Little Big Horn," *Outdoor Life*, Vol. LXXI (February, 1933), 6; Burdick, *Tragedy in the Great Sioux Camp*, 55.

[197] Reno, *Court*, 310–11.

[198] *Ibid.*, 70.

[199] *Ibid.*, 13.

[200] *Ibid.*, 232y.

[201] Dr. Charles Eastman, "Story of the Little Big Horn," *Chautauquan*, Vol. XXXI (July, 1900), 357.

[202] Reno, *Court*, 232 o.

[203] *Army and Navy Journal*, July 8, 1876; Brininstool, *A Trooper with Custer*,

sided, for a corporal of Troop G followed one of the Indians across, shot him, and took his scalp.[204] And Davern delayed long enough in getting to the top of the bluff to catch up a loose Indian pony as well as to take three or four shots at some of the hostiles on nearby ridges.[205]

Indicative of Reno's complete loss of control is the fact that no attempt was made by those who had gained the eastern bank to cover the crossing in any way or to protect and aid the men whose horses were still plunging and rearing in the stream,[206] although Indians on both the right and left banks were firing at the men in the water[207] and succeeded in killing several of them[208] in the three or four minutes that it took the battalion to cross.[209] Sergeant Culbertson thought that an attempt should at least be made to protect the wounded who were coming across, and spoke to Captain French about it, who replied, "I'll try, I'll try," and then rode up the hill. At no time was there any organized firing on the hostiles to prevent them from sniping at the troopers in the stream.[210] Panic had seized the command to such an extent that nearly everyone thought only of himself and gave no thought whatsoever to the safety of his comrades.[211]

Lieutenant "Benny" Hodgson, who was Reno's adjutant and a great favorite in the regiment, had tendered his resignation from the army in the spring of 1876 but had withdrawn it when the regiment had been ordered against the Sioux.[212] He was as surprised as anyone else at the order to leave the timber, and during the "charge"

33. Adams, "A Survivor's Story," 230, says that several of Reno's men were lassoed from their horses and later burned at the stake.

204 Reno, *Court*, 502–503; *Official Transcript*, 46.

205 *Official Transcript*, 557–58.

206 Reno, *Court*, 791.

207 *Ibid.*, 309, 415.

208 *Ibid.*, 476.

209 *Ibid.*, 70.

210 *Ibid.*, 508. According to the *Official Transcript*, 566, it was Sergeant Lloyd who spoke to French about covering the crossing, and he did so at Culbertson's suggestion. But Luce states that the only sergeant by the name of Lloyd was Frank Lloyd of Company G, who is listed as not having participated in the battle. Luce, *Keogh, Comanche, and Custer*, 108.

211 Reno, *Court*, 232y; King, "Custer's Last Battle," *Harper's*, Vol. LXXXI (August, 1890), 384.

212 Fougera, *With Custer's Cavalry*, 70; *Army and Navy Journal*, July 15, 1876.

he is said to have asked a fellow-officer, "What is this, a retreat?" receiving the answer, "It looks most damnably like a rout."[213] While in the river he had his leg broken by a bullet which killed his horse. As he floundered in the water, a trooper thrust out a stirrup, which Hodgson seized. He was then towed across the stream and succeeded in getting up the steep eastern bank only to be picked off by an Indian sharpshooter firing from the bluffs when Hodgson was about fifty yards up the ravine.[214] Illustrative of the extreme state of confusion prevailing, the trooper who towed him across has been variously identified as Trumpeter Henry Fisher, Sergeant Benjamin Criswell, Private William Morris, and a bugler by the name of Myers. Ryan gives the credit to Fisher, although stating that it was claimed by several others.[215]

Although several troopers were killed and others wounded at the crossing, the dead were apparently pretty well scattered along the line between the timber and the top of the bluffs, and the casualties were by no means all suffered at the crossing, where there was so much crowding and confusion. In fact, it was possible later to trace the line of the retreat by the dead men and horses lying along it, which showed that Reno had, intentionally or otherwise, just skirted the edge of the timber.[216] Most of the wounded were members of Moylan's troop, which was in the lead and thus suffered less delay than the others at the crossing. It is a fair inference that the more seriously wounded of the other two troops never reached the river at all but fell into the hands of the Indians, for Reno admitted that no effort was made to take care of them.[217]

The hostiles singled out the scouts for special attention, since nothing delighted an Indian more than to kill another Indian who fought on the side of the whites. At least three of Reno's dead were Arikaras, Bob-tailed Bull having apparently been killed on the skirmish line and Bloody Knife in the timber. The Cheyennes tell of chasing a Ree across a wet slough and into some timber, where he

[213] Roe, *Custer's Last Battle*, 9.

[214] Reno, *Court*, 13, 107; *Official Transcript*, 107, 521. See also Graham, *Story of the Little Big Horn*, 47, and Brady, *Indian Fights and Fighters*, 273.

[215] *Hardin Tribune*, June 22, 1913; Brininstool, *A Trooper with Custer*, 33.

[216] On the distribution of Reno's casualties see Dustin, *The Custer Tragedy*, 182; Reno, *Court*, 105; Edgerly, *Narrative*, 5; *Winners of the West*, March 30, 1936.

[217] Reno, *Court*, 355, 733; *Official Transcript*, 79.

was killed. They identify this warrior as Bloody Knife, which is obviously wrong, although it may have been Little Brave, who is generally supposed to have been killed just below Reno's crossing and on the left bank of the river, or it may have been another scout whose name we do not know.[218]

Not all of the soldiers attempted to cross the river. At least three of them continued to ride southward along the west bank, and were pursued by Sun Bear, Eagle Tail Feather, and Little Sun, all Cheyennes, and several Sioux. Two of the soldiers were finally surrounded and killed, but the third, who is described as riding a gray horse and who may possibly have been Sergeant James T. Reilly, finally escaped across the river after being wounded and joined the others on the bluff.[219]

Lieutenant McIntosh had been left in the timber attempting to rally and collect his men. At the edge of the timber his horse was shot from under him, but he succeeded in getting another from a trooper named McCormick, who gave it up with the remark that they were all dead men anyway and that he might as well be killed on foot as on horseback.[220] The Lieutenant left the timber far behind the other members of the battalion and, alone as he apparently was, with his horse wounded, had little or no chance of escaping and was killed on the riverbank.[221] McIntosh may possibly have been the officer described by the Crows as being dragged by his horse as he attempted to remount.[222] By an odd quirk of fate, McCormick, who surrendered his horse, later was able to rejoin the battalion and came safely through the battle.

Lieutenant DeRudio, who had made an unsuccessful attempt to halt the men of his company, noticed a company guidon which had been left behind on the riverbank. Believing that that was not a proper place to leave it and that it was the duty of a soldier to preserve his colors even at the risk of his life, he attempted to recover it, an action which he admitted was influenced by the fact that he

218 Dustin, *The Custer Tragedy*, 131.

219 Marquis, *A Warrior who Fought Custer*, 222–23.

220 Brady, *Indian Fights and Fighters*, 272.

221 Reno, *Court*, 12; *Army and Navy Journal*, July 15, 1876. The first account of the disaster published in the *Bismarck Tribune* said that Lieutenant McIntosh was armed only with a saber.

222 Linderman, *Red Mother*, 244.

did not think there was any danger since he did not know that the battalion's rear had been cut off. But the Indians saw him and fired at him so that, in his own words, he "dropped right down plump." By this time most of the men had gotten out of the river bottom, and DeRudio, believing himself left behind, wasted no time in taking refuge in the timber.[223] Here he found Private O'Neil, Girard, and the scout Billy Jackson, the last two being still mounted. They watched the Indians pursue Reno's men almost to the river, then noticed that the hostiles were watching something or someone upstream, and saw a column of troops ride down close to the river as though intending to cross. Instead, the column turned to the right and disappeared behind a bluff. This checked the Indian pursuit, and they continued to watch this new body of soldiers for about ten minutes. Then more than half of the hostiles left the river bottom when they heard the sound of heavy firing farther downstream.[224] Of the Indians who remained, some went up on the high bluffs, while the others picketed their horses in the underbrush along the river and lay down flat watching Reno's men.[225] The firing which the four men heard apparently commenced between the time Reno left the timber and the time he reached the top of the bluffs. Girard said that it began as a few scattering shots which continued for about fifteen or twenty minutes before the firing became general.[226] The first volleys were very plain but then got farther off, but not too far off, and the firing was steady for a long time—probably for from one and one-half to two hours—and then died away with a small scattering of shots which lasted only for a short period.[227] The four remained together in the timber for some time but separated when they ran into a band of Indians, Girard taking off to the left at full speed.[228] After a day and night of skulking and hiding in the river bottom and of several narrow escapes, all of them succeeded in joining Reno on the hill.

Once on the right bank of the stream, Reno's troopers were comparatively secure since they were screened from the fire of their

[223] Reno, *Court*, 451; *Official Transcript*, 431.
[224] Reno, *Court*, 461, 467; *Official Transcript*, 460.
[225] *Official Transcript*, 436.
[226] *Ibid.*, 184.
[227] *Ibid.*, 440, 465–66.
[228] *Ibid.*, 478.

pursuers by the spur of the bluff which extended out between the two parties.[229] Here, on the side of the hill, the command halted for a time, but Reno decided that it was no place to form, and after a few minutes' rest they straggled on toward the top of the bluffs.[230] They straggled up, it is said, in a very unmilitary manner,[231] for only in this way can a detachment of cavalry climb a steep hill.[232] Major Reno was one of the first to reach the top.[233]

Lieutenant Varnum started up a ravine to his left but was called back by some of the men who could see Indians at the top of the bluff. Before starting to retrace his steps, he called to Dr. DeWolf, who, dismounted, was ahead of him and going in the same direction. But the surgeon was too close to the summit and just as he started back was killed by a shot from above. The Indians then proceeded to scalp him in full view of his comrades.[234] Also killed were several troopers, including Private Clare, who, like Varnum, had started up the wrong ravine and had not been warned in time.[235] Just how many men were killed at the crossing is unknown. Captain Moylan later admitted that a great many men might have been dragged or thrown into the stream, but doubted if anything of the kind did occur since there was no evidence of it.[236]

The point on the bluffs to which Reno took the battalion was about four hundred yards from the crossing[237] and up a hill so steep that most of the troopers had to lead their horses.[238] It was probably between three-thirty and four o'clock and some fifteen minutes after the command had ridden out of the timber when the main part of the battalion reached the summit of the ridge.[239] Here the

229 Edgerly, *Narrative*, 6.

230 Reno, *Court*, 234, 768.

231 Charles Eastman, "Story of the Little Big Horn," *Chautauquan*, Vol. XXXI (July, 1900), 357.

232 Reno, *Court*, 768.

233 *Ibid.*, 791–92.

234 *Ibid.*, 107, 232y, 508.

235 *Official Transcript*, 362. There is also some evidence that Clare was killed at the edge of the stream. Reno, *Court*, 416. Graham says both men were killed a few feet up the ravine to the left. *Story of the Little Big Horn*, 47–48.

236 Reno, *Court*, 279–80.

237 *Ibid.*, 232x.

238 Brininstool, *A Trooper with Custer*, 34.

239 Reno, *Court*, 69. Liuetenant Wallace had the following timetable:
2:20 P.M.—crossed the Little Big Horn River
2:30 P.M.—on the skirmish line and in the woods, forty-five minutes

troopers deployed along the edge preparatory to another stand if that should be necessary, a movement that was apparently carried out under the direction of the troop commanders with little or no assistance from Major Reno.[240] The Indians had begun to leave Reno's front about the time that the troops emerged from the timber,[241] and the troopers now noticed them riding off downstream in great numbers. Many others had crossed the river above and were riding down on Reno's position when for some reason their attention was diverted elsewhere, and they joined the multitudes going downstream, although there were still a few occupying strategic high points on the eastern bluffs and others circling about in the valley below.[242] Although surprised at this unexpected withdrawal, the troops were too much concerned with their own troubles even to speculate about its probable cause. Most of the troopers seem to have felt that they had been fairly well licked and were fearful of even worse things to come. Dr. Porter, who had been in several Indian fights, reported to Reno that the men were quite demoralized, only to have the Major reply, apparently somewhat testily, "That was a cavalry charge, Sir!"[243]

One does not need to be possessed of an overly vivid imagination to appreciate the feelings of those battered and bedeviled troopers of Reno's command, when a few moments later they saw Benteen's battalion come riding toward them along the ridges.

3:15 P.M.—left the timber
3:30 P.M.—on the bluffs
Official Transcript, 106.
That these times are only approximate is apparent from the fact that Lieutenant Varnum thought it was about thirty minutes from the time they deployed on the skirmish line until they left the timber (Reno, *Court*, 232w, 271), while Lieutenant Hare said they were on the skirmish line and in the timber from thirty to forty minutes. Reno, *Court*, 415. Graham says that the battalion reached the top of the bluffs about four o'clock. *Story of the Little Big Horn*, 49.

240 McClernand, "With Indian and Buffalo in Montana," *Cavalry Journal*, Vol. XXXVI (January and April, 1927), 39.

241 Reno, *Court*, 275.

242 Graham, *Story of the Little Big Horn*, 49.

243 *Official Transcript*, 264.

CHAPTER XVI

Benteen Rescues Reno

ALTHOUGH the remainder of the regiment soon lost sight of Benteen's detachment, Benteen was able to catch occasional glimpses of them riding down the creek valley toward the river, his last sight of the column being the gray-horse troop riding at a dead gallop.[1] On one or two occasions after this his troopers heard loud cheering and some scattered shots, although they never learned the reasons for these demonstrations.[2] The battalion apparently went over the first ridge to the left after leaving Custer's trail and into a small valley down which they rode. About a mile and a half off the trail they crossed an insignificant branch of the Little Big Horn River and rode toward the bluffs which they had been ordered to explore. Although Benteen later made a great deal of complaint about the rough and broken nature of the country across which his detachment had to ride, examination of the region discloses that the terrain was not nearly as bad as he represented it. True enough, the bluffs were difficult to climb, but they were ascended by only a small detail and not by the entire battalion. The command did, however, wind through some narrow and tortuous ravines and around rugged hills which were too steep to climb, and this, plus the rocky nature of the ground, was extremely hard on the horses. As a result, many of them became somewhat jaded and fell to the rear of the column.[3]

Custer had instructed Benteen to send a well-mounted officer with a small detail of men ahead to scout the country and report whether any Indians could be seen. Lieutenant Gibson, of Benteen's

1 Reno, *Court*, 547.
2 Godfrey, *Century*, 369; Godfrey, *Montana*, 176.
3 Godfrey, *Montana*, 175.

own troop, was the officer selected for this duty, and his group was followed by the rest of the battalion, riding mostly in a column of twos, although upon occasion the narrow ravines necessitated a single-file formation. Benteen, who had a very fast-walking horse, occasionally got ahead of the scouting detail, often forcing the column to trot in order to keep up. About a mile or so on they came to the bluffs which Custer had designated, and Gibson with a few men was sent to the top to report what he could see. There was nothing in sight except more bluffs, equally large and precipitous, and no Indians. But orders were orders, and, although Lieutenant Edgerly said that they made no further attempt to go to the left as the country was reported to be very rough and broken, Benteen claimed that he kept on to the next line of bluffs only to find the country the same, no valley of any kind being sighted on any side, although Lieutenant Gibson was sent to the top of the bluffs four times while the battalion was covering six miles. The farther they proceeded, the more convinced Benteen became that the detachment was on a wild-goose chase, that nothing was to be found in that direction, and that the Indians had too much sense to travel over such rough country unless there was no other way for them to go.[4]

After they had proceeded several miles with no sign of Indians, "wandering among hills without any possibility of accomplishing anything," as Lieutenant Godfrey expressed it,[5] Lieutenant Gibson was again sent to the top of a high ridge to make an observation. From there he was able to obtain, with the aid of glasses, a view of the country for several miles up the valley of the Little Big Horn; but downstream, which was the direction of the Indian village, his view was obscured by the irregular course of the stream and by the high westward-jutting promontories. In the entire valley he could see not one single living thing. On hearing the report of his lieutenant, Benteen decided to take advantage of the discretion allowed by his orders that if in his judgment there was nothing to be seen of Indians, valleys, and so on, in the direction he was going, he was to return to the trail that was being followed by the rest of the regiment.[6]

[4] Benteen, *Report*, 479; Reno, *Court*, 547; *Official Transcript*, 652, 747–48.

[5] Godfrey, "Diary," n.p.

[6] In a letter to Godfrey dated August 8, 1908, Gibson said that he had a view of the Little Big Horn Valley "for a long distance" and that as a result of his

Many accounts of the Custer fight state that the terrain was so rough that Benteen was forced more and more to his right until the command finally came out on Custer's trail. This idea probably originated from Lieutenant Edgerly's statement that, after receiving Gibson's report, the battalion skirted the hills in an attempt to find a way out of the valley without a climb that would be too fatiguing for both men and horses, and this course brought them to the right and into Reno's trail in less than an hour.[7] But the plain truth of the matter is that Benteen turned to the right because he had decided to do so, and not because of the difficulty of the terrain, which was not much worse than that covered by the remainder of the regiment. Benteen himself admitted that the roughness of the country did not force him to the right, and said that he could have gone in a straight line all the way to Fort Benton had that been necessary, but that "as there were no Indians in the valley," he felt that it was his duty "to go back to the trail and join the command."[8]

Although he later stated that he was probably guilty of at least a technical violation of his orders when he turned to the right to rejoin Custer,[9] his admission was sheer nonsense, since it is difficult, if not impossible, to see what other course he could have followed. He had gone as far as he felt was necessary, and he was more than reasonably certain that there were no Indians in the region he had been ordered to explore. In his judgment, more good was to be accomplished by rejoining the regiment, and such a decision had been left entirely to his discretion. In fact Benteen probably did exactly what Custer wanted and expected him to do, and there was no sense in his saying that he felt he had violated his orders.[10]

The battalion kept on skirting the hills until they came into a small valley bordered by low hills separating it from another valley, which the pack train on Custer's trail was following.[11] Just be-

report Benteen altered his course in order to pick up the trail of the regiment. Graham, *Story of the Little Big Horn*, 131.

7 Edgerly, *Narrative*, 5.

8 Brininstool, *Captain Benteen's Story*, 28; Reno, *Court*, 547, 569; *Official Transcript*, 715.

9 Reno, *Court*, 567.

10 Benteen told the Court of Inquiry that he turned to the right because he felt he would be needed, his idea being that there was fighting going on or soon would be, and that he had done just about what Custer expected him to do is shown by the findings of the court. *Ibid.*, 1212.

11 *Ibid.*, 748.

fore they joined the main Indian trail, from the age of which Lieutenant Godfrey estimated that it would be at least fifteen miles to a village,[12] Boston Custer rode by. He waved good-naturedly and called out a greeting to Lieutenant Edgerly as he passed. The youngest of the Custers had been with the pack train and was now hurrying to overtake his brother's command in order not to miss any of the excitement.[13] About a mile farther on, the troops came to an old village site and beyond it a morass or spring hole where a stream of running water had its source. Here they halted to water the horses, which had gone without a drink since about eight o'clock the night before.[14] Some of the troopers may have filled their canteens, despite the fact that one of them said later that the water "was alkali and would take the hide off your tongue but it was wet."[15]

Although Benteen stated that it was about half-past one when his detachment reached the morass,[16] this seems hardly possible since he had diverged shortly after noon. Godfrey makes it fully half an hour later,[17] which is more probable, although it is possible that it was even later. In any event Benteen was probably at or near the morass at the same time that Major Reno's battalion was crossing the Little Big Horn River to the attack. Also it should be noted that Boston Custer had passed Benteen's detachment just as it reached the main Indian trail, and he was able to overtake his brother's command just after Martin had been sent back with the message to Benteen. Thus it is fairly obvious that Benteen's detachment was not too far behind the remainder of the regiment, probably not more than five miles at most, so that his later recital of having made a long detour is to be viewed with definite skepticism.

Just how far the battalion had ridden is a matter of some disagreement. Lieutenant Godfrey was of the opinion that they had traveled about twelve or fifteen miles from the time they left Custer until they again struck the trail, but he qualified the statement some-

12 Godfrey, "Diary," n.p.

13 Edgerly, *Narrative*, 5.

14 Benteen, *Account*, 8; Reno, *Court*, 547.

15 Usher L. Burdick, *The Army Life of Charles "Chip" Creighton Who Participated in the Engagement with the Sioux Indians . . . and in the Battle of the Little Big Horn . . .*, 27.

16 *New York Herald*, August 8, 1876.

17 Godfrey, "Diary," n.p.; *Official Transcript*, 846; Graham, *Story of the Little Big Horn*, 52, says three-thirty o'clock.

what by adding that the gait had been so irregular that it was difficult to gauge the distance.[18] Benteen himself said that they had covered "about fully ten miles"[19] when he determined to return to Custer's trail, while Lieutenant Edgerly believed that they had made a circuit of about fourteen miles.[20] As the battalion moved out after watering, the head of the pack train reached the morass, and several of the mules, crazed at the sight and smell of the water, came tearing down the hill, rushed into the spring, and were mired. At the time of divergence the pack train was up with the command and had halted in the rear. The morass was about six miles from the divide and five miles from the place where the commands had separated.[21] Since the packs could easily make three miles an hour downgrade over this kind of terrain and were only about a mile behind Benteen's men when the latter reached the morass, it is obvious that Benteen's detachment, which should have averaged between four and six miles an hour, had not covered too much ground, probably not more than ten miles at the most. Benteen's statement that his command had marched at a trot all the way is somewhat peculiar in view of his complaints about the extremely rough nature of the country[22] and statements made by other members of his command.[23] Moreover, he could not hurry his troopers and expect to have them in an effective condition when they arrived at the scene of action, and the pace had to be constantly slowed down in order to keep the command closed up.

The battalion probably spent somewhere between ten and twenty minutes at the spring.[24] While there, some of the officers thought they heard the sound of distant firing—the first intimation that the regiment might be in action. This "sound of battle," which probably came from Reno's first contact with the enemy, caused Captain Weir marked uneasiness, and he urged Benteen to move out immediately. When his entreaties went unheeded, he sought

18 *Official Transcript*, 846.

19 Benteen's Report, 479.

20 *Official Transcript*, 751.

21 *Ibid.*, 930; Reno, *Court*, 640.

22 *Official Transcript*, 727–28.

23 Lieutenant Godfrey said that his troop, which was in the rear, often had to trot to keep up. *Official Transcript*, 845. For a statement that the command had walked all the way, see Brady, *Indian Fights and Fighters*, 404.

24 *Official Transcript*, 754.

Godfrey's assistance, and failing to obtain it, announced that he was going anyway, mounted his troop, and moved off on the trail of the regiment. Shortly after, Benteen gave the order to mount, and the other two companies followed the path that D troop had taken.[25] After going about three miles at a slow trot,[26] they came to the Lone Warrior Tepee, which was still burning. Benteen said that he rode around it but could not recall whether or not he dismounted.[27] The battalion did not halt, however, and only a short distance—probably less than a mile—farther on they met Sergeant Kanipe.[28] He had verbal orders to the commander of the train to bring it to the front with as much speed as possible, and since Captain McDougall was in command of the train and its escort, Benteen did not feel that it was any of his affair. He therefore sent the Sergeant on after telling him that the packs were several miles in the rear, since he believed that the mules were probably still stuck in the mud at the morass.[29] Kanipe was jubilant and as he rode down the line of troopers called out, "We've got them, boys."[30] From this and other remarks the men and officers alike inferred that Custer had attacked and either captured or destroyed the hostile village.[31]

Another mile or so farther on, about a mile south of Reno Hill and just before reaching the place where Custer had halted to water the horses, the battalion, which was still riding at a trot, met the trumpeter, Martin.[32] Benteen later put the place of meeting about two miles from where Reno had crossed the river in advance and about two and a half miles from the Lone Tepee.[33] He estimated that it was approximately fifteen miles from where he had diverged

[25] McClernand, "With Indian and Buffalo in Montana," *Cavalry Journal*, Vol. XXXVI (January and April, 1927), 41.

[26] Reno, *Court*, 547; *Official Transcript*, 731; Brininstool, *Captain Benteen's Story*, 14. Although Benteen consistently makes the distance from the watering place to the Lone Tepee seven miles, it is not quite half that far.

[27] *Official Transcript*, 653.

[28] Benteen, *Account*, 8; *New York Herald*, August 8, 1876; Daniel A. Kanipe, "New Story of Custer's Last Battle," in *Contributions to the Historical Society of Montana*, IV (1903), 280.

[29] Reno, *Court*, 579.

[30] *Ibid.*, 618.

[31] Benteen's Report, 480; Godfrey, *Montana*, 180.

[32] *Official Transcript*, 638, 732; McClernand, "With Indian and Buffalo in Montana," *Cavalry Journal*, Vol. XXXVI (January and April, 1927), 39.

[33] Brininstool, *Captain Benteen's Story*, 29; *New York Herald*, August 8, 1876; Reno, *Court*, 547.

from the main column to where he met the trumpeter, and declared that the command had ridden at a trot all the way except for the time it took to water the horses.[34] Benteen believed that it was about three o'clock and expressed the opinion that at the time of the meeting Custer and all the members of his command were dead.[35]

The fact that Benteen saw Martin coming when the latter was about a mile away might indicate that he had seen Martin before he met Kanipe, although at the time he did not know who he was or what he wanted. The country was so very irregular and broken that Benteen could see the rider on the ridges but then would lose sight of him as he rode down into a coulee or gully. The trumpeter, his horse badly spent and also severely wounded, although he was not aware of the latter fact until Benteen called it to his attention, came at a jog trot. He met Benteen, who with his orderly was riding some two or three hundred yards ahead of Captain Weir and his troop,[36] and gave him Lieutenant Cooke's message. Martin later estimated that it was about forty-five minutes from the time he saw Reno fighting in the valley until he met Benteen.[37] The senior captain must have been somewhat of a stickler for detail as well as a captious critic since he noted that the adjutant's message was not dated.[38] Benteen showed the message to Captain Weir, but he asked no questions and apparently Weir offered no comment.

It has been suggested that neither officer could believe that the message meant what it said,[39] and Lieutenant Edgerly, who says that they met Martin before reaching the Lone Tepee, declares that Benteen showed the message to him as well as to Captain Weir, and that one of them—he could not remember which one—remarked that Custer could not possibly want them to go back for the packs since Captain McDougall was there and would bring them.[40] It was obvious that if Custer were attacking he would have no use for the packs because supplies could not be distributed at such a time. And if he was concerned about the safety of the pack train, he knew

[34] *Official Transcript*, 701–703.

[35] Reno, *Court*, 573; *Official Transcript*, 721.

[36] *Official Transcript*, 732; Graham, " 'Come on! Be quick! Bring packs!' The Story of Custer's Last Message . . . ," *Cavalry Journal*, Vol. XXXII (July, 1923), 309.

[37] Reno, *Court*, 535–36.

[38] *Official Transcript*, 654.

[39] *Ibid.*, 655; Benteen's Report, 480; Kuhlman, *Custer and the Gall Saga*, 20–21.

[40] *Official Transcript*, 747–48.

that even Benteen's entire battalion would be insufficient to defend the train against a determined Indian attack in force. Thus the message just did not seem to make sense. That Weir was as surprised as Benteen is shown by the fact that he made no protest when the order was ignored.[41] On the other hand, Benteen apparently felt that if Custer were engaged with a strong enemy force, every man would be needed, and in such circumstances he could not consider keeping his battalion out of action with the pack train. In his own words, "It savored too much of 'coffee-cooling' to return when I was sure that a fight was progressing in the front."[42]

In answer to Benteen's questions about what had taken place, the trumpeter replied that the Indians had "skedaddled" and by his language gave the very definite impression that the troops were in possession of the Indian village.[43] Martin in his account, however, says that he told Benteen that the Indians he saw were running and that he supposed that by this time Custer had charged through the hostile camp.[44] Although he told the Court of Inquiry that he said nothing about Reno's battalion because Benteen asked no questions about it,[45] he later said that he was going to tell Benteen about seeing Reno's men in action but did not get a chance to do so, for just then Benteen pointed out that his horse was severely wounded. Even this did not jog Martin's memory, for he not only did not tell Benteen of the Reno action in the valley but also neglected to inform him of the ambush and attack upon Custer's command.[46] All of which adds up to the conclusion that Martin not only had language difficulties but was also lacking in general intelligence and justifies Benteen's statement that he was a "thick-headed, dull-witted Italian, just as much cut out for a cavalryman as he was for a King."[47]

Martin was not sent back to the pack train, as the Reno Court of Inquiry later reported him as saying he was, an error which arose from his very faulty command of English. Instead, he joined

[41] Kuhlman, *Custer and the Gall Saga*, 20–21.

[42] Benteen's Report, 480.

[43] Godfrey, *Montana*, 181; Reno, *Court*, 577; *Official Transcript*, 655, 727.

[44] Graham, "'Come on! Be quick! Bring packs!' The Story of Custer's Last Message . . . ," *Cavalry Journal*, Vol. XXXII (July, 1923), 309.

[45] *Official Transcript*, 619.

[46] Graham, "'Come on! Be quick! Bring packs!' The Story of Custer's Last Message . . . ," *Cavalry Journal*, Vol. XXXII (July, 1923), 309.

[47] Benteen, *Account*, 9.

Benteen's battalion, and Lieutenant Edgerly heard him talking to the orderly behind, telling him that it was the largest Indian village that he (Martin) had ever seen, and that Major Reno was charging it and killing everybody—men, women, and children.[48] Martin's message, together with the one shouted by Sergeant Kanipe, shows how obsessed the entire regiment was with the idea that the Indians would break and run as soon as they caught sight of the troops. It also caused general excitement among the younger members of the battalion, since it seemed probable that what everyone believed would be the last great Indian fight on this continent would be over before they would even get close enough to see it—certainly before they could take an active part in it.[49] They were of the opinion that it must have been only a small village and that there would be little for them to do other than congratulate the others and help destroy the plunder.[50]

The packs were now in sight, only a mile or so behind the battalion, some of the mules walking, others trotting, and a few running. But the troops moved on faster than the packs could go, and soon the train was out of sight, although its position was known from the dust it kicked up. Now for the first time the battalion heard unmistakable sounds of firing, and the gait quickened.[51] The only living thing in sight was a riderless horse on a distant hill,[52] whether Indian pony or cavalry horse we do not know. The sound of firing increased in intensity and seemed to be coming toward them. The battalion took a gallop with pistols drawn, expecting to meet the enemy which they assumed the victorious Custer was driving before him. The troops were just forming into line to meet the supposed enemy when they rode out into full view of the valley of the Little Big Horn River.[53]

48 *Official Transcript*, 752; Reno, *Court*, 586. In its account the *Chicago Times* inserted parenthetically that when Martin referred to Reno, he probably meant Custer.

49 Edgerly, *Narrative*, 7.

50 Godfrey, "Diary," n.p.

51 Godfrey, "Diary," n.p. Benteen, however, said that no firing was heard until he got to the ford, and then he both saw and heard it. Reno, *Court*, 570.

52 Benteen's Report, 480.

53 Byrne, *Soldiers of the Plains*, 96–97; Godfrey, *Montana*, 181; Graham, " 'Come on! Be quick! Bring packs!' The Story of Custer's Last Message . . . ," *Cavalry Journal*, Vol. XXXII (July, 1923), 309.

As Benteen's detachment came in sight of the river near the place where Major Reno's battalion had first crossed, they saw many horsemen in the valley as well as a heavy smoke from the burning prairie. They did not halt long enough to get a good view of the situation, but Lieutenant Godfrey, whose company was at the rear of the column, believed from what he could see and from what the two messengers had said that Custer's troops were burning the Indian village and that a small party of men observed on a bluff to the right were a picket guard set out by Custer to protect the working parties.[54] But Captain Benteen, who went as far as the ford—although the battalion did not go with him[55]—noticed that two fights seemed to be going on at the same time, one in the valley and the other on the bluffs. The plain seemed to be alive with Indians attempting to demolish some twelve or fourteen men on a skirmish line which ran parallel to the river, the Indians charging and recharging them.[56] These were troopers who had been dismounted and consequently abandoned during Reno's retreat from the valley. Their ultimate fate is unknown, but there is the possibility that some of them took refuge in the timber, later making their way to safety. Other troopers were observed running for the bluffs on the right-hand bank of the stream.[57] The Indians saw Benteen's detachment about the same time he saw them and checked their pursuit of Reno's men. Benteen estimated that there were about nine hundred Indians circling about in the river bottom while about half that number could be observed on a point farther down the stream. It was obvious to him that whatever "skedaddling" was being done, was not being done by the Indians,[58] and the question now was what to do in a situation so greatly different from the one that the officers of the battalion had expected.

A group of Arikara scouts—both Benteen and Godfrey made the mistake of calling them Crows, and the mistake has been repeated by several subsequent writers[59]—who were driving off a number of captured Sioux ponies, pointed to the right in answer to a question

[54] *Official Transcript*, 851.
[55] *Ibid.*, 661.
[56] *Ibid.*, 655, 717.
[57] Benteen's Report, 479.
[58] Brininstool, *Captain Benteen's Story*, 16.
[59] Dustin, *The Custer Tragedy*, 131.

concerning the whereabouts of the soldiers. At the same time they called out "Otoe Sioux, Otoe Sioux," meaning innumerable Sioux or "heaps of them"[60] and told Benteen that there was a big "pooh-poohing" going on in the valley, which, as Benteen said, he had already seen for himself. He had no alternative other than to conclude that an attack had been made and repulsed, although he was in error in believing that the entire regiment had been engaged, since he did not know—in fact, had no way of knowing—of Custer's second division of the command. He decided not to cross the river, but instead turned his battalion to the right and rode toward the bluffs. For this decision Benteen later gave conflicting explanations. In 1879 he simply stated that he believed that the entire command had been thrashed and that it was not a good place to cross,[61] but earlier, in his *Report*, he had written that his decision was due to the fact that he felt that, with the great number of recruits, his battalion would stand absolutely no chance as mounted men against the nine hundred or so veteran warriors he estimated were in the valley.[62]

Benteen's battalion then moved across a hill to the place where the members of Reno's badly battered battalion were gathering. Benteen was very close to them before they saw him—Lieutenant Wallace estimated that it was not over two hundred yards[63]—and Reno rode out to meet him exclaiming breathlessly, "For God's sake, Benteen, halt your command and help me. I've lost half my men." He did not explain why he had retreated from the valley, and apparently Benteen did not ask. But Reno does seem to have told Benteen of receiving the order to charge the Indians and of Lieutenant Cooke's statement that he would be supported.[64] Benteen also apparently showed Reno his last order from Cooke, but it made little, if any, impression upon the Major, who was completely absorbed with getting the packs together and resolved not to move until that had been accomplished.[65] Benteen also inquired concerning Custer's whereabouts, but Reno could only state that Custer had started downstream with five companies and that nothing

60 Benteen's Report, 480; Benteen, *Account*, 9; Reno, *Court*, 548.
61 *Official Transcript*, 656.
62 Benteen's Report, 480.
63 Reno, *Court*, 480.
64 Benteen's Report, 480; Reno, *Court*, 549.
65 Reno, *Court*, 724; *Official Transcript*, 1084.

had been heard of him since.[66] In defiance of his orders, which were to join Custer as speedily as possible—or perhaps on the assumption that he had complied with them—Benteen halted his advance, uniting his command with that of Major Reno. Why Benteen did not go on is problematical. While he may have been prevented by Major Reno,[67] it is more likely that he felt he had complied with the letter, if not the spirit, of his orders, and was not concerned with what might happen to Custer and his detachment.[68]

The members of Benteen's three companies thus witnessed the recrossing of the Little Big Horn by a part of Reno's battalion. In fact, they were united with the remnant of the Major's command before all of his men had taken position on the bluff. Some of them were still coming up the hill—some mounted and some dismounted—the most of them rather disorganized and excited, although there were a few exceptions, especially among the veterans. One soldier—a corporal of G troop—who was himself badly wounded, swung a fresh scalp as he walked.[69]

It was probably between three-thirty and four o'clock in the afternoon when the two commands were united.[70] Benteen had about 125 men, all of them comparatively fresh, since they had seen no action, although some of the horses were badly tired as a result of the morning's march. Reno had lost about the strength of a troop, or approximately one-third of his battalion, in killed, wounded, and missing. Three officers and twenty-nine enlisted men were dead, and the number of wounded probably amounted to ten or eleven.[71] In addition, one officer, three scouts, and fifteen troopers were missing, most of whom subsequently rejoined the command. As a result

[66] Graham, " 'Come on! Be Quick! Bring Packs!' The Story of Custer's Last Message . . . ," *Cavalry Journal*, Vol. XXXII (July, 1923), 310; Graham, *Story of the Little Big Horn*, 62–63.

[67] James P. Murphy, "Campaign of the Little Big Horn," *Infantry Journal*, Vol. XXXIV (June, 1929), 640.

[68] J. L. Beardsley, "Could Custer Have Won?" *Outdoor Life*, Vol. LXXI (March, 1933), is quite emphatic in expressing the belief that Benteen was guilty of a flagrant violation of his orders.

[69] Graham, *Story of the Little Big Horn*, 59.

[70] Coughlan, "The Battle of the Little Big Horn," *Cavalry Journal*, Vol. XLIII (January–February, 1934), 20. Graham, *Story of the Little Big Horn*, 62. For other estimates concerning the time of Benteen's arrival on the hill see Reno, *Court*, 311, 549, and *Official Transcript*, 74, 657.

[71] Reno, *Court*, 110.

of these losses, most of the battalion were apparently on the verge of demoralization, although Major Reno insisted that the majority were in good order. He did admit that they were almost exhausted as a result of their mad ride across the valley, and Dr. Porter insisted that the command was badly demoralized and that the troopers knew they had been whipped.[72] Benteen, admitting that the command seemed shaken, denied that it was demoralized. He conceded that when he came up he did not find the troopers drawn up in any line of battle, but scattered around. "They all thought there was a happier place than that, I guess," was the way he expressed it.[73] Lieutenant Hare, who agreed with Benteen and denied that the Reno battalion was demoralized as was shown by the prompt way in which they rallied and formed,[74] came over to his company commander, Lieutenant Godfrey, and grasping his hand, said, with great emphasis, "We've had a big fight in the valley, got whipped like hell and I am—damned—glad to see you,"[75] a description which at least had the merit of accuracy. Reno was apparently very much excited and is said to have discharged a pistol at some Indians who were about a thousand yards off, fully nine hundred yards out of pistol range. Lieutenant Varnum, also very much excited, was crying, and seizing a carbine, began firing wildly at the hostiles.[76]

Immediately after Benteen's command arrived, a few Indians began firing into the soldiers from positions in ravines and hills on the near-by bluffs. They were doing no damage and were more of a nuisance than anything else, but D troop—the strongest company in the regiment—was dismounted and formed as skirmishers by Captain Weir, and in a very few moments drove the hostiles away. At the same time Godfrey was ordered to dismount his men and form them in a skirmish line on the bluffs toward the river.[77] But for the most part the Indians had begun riding off downstream about the same time that Benteen's men came in sight of the valley, and the few who remained were mostly between Reno and the place where

[72] *Ibid.*, 299.

[73] *Ibid.*, 549; *Official Transcript*, 659.

[74] Reno, *Court*, 416.

[75] *Ibid.*, 619.

[76] Graham, *Story of the Little Big Horn*, 58. However, Reno denied firing his pistol from the top of the hill, a statement in which he was supported by Benteen. Reno, *Court*, 599, 712, 734.

[77] Edgerly, *Narrative*, 8; Reno, *Court*, 703; *Official Transcript*, 757, 852.

Custer's command was later found. The troops were at a loss to explain this abrupt departure of their foes, although Benteen later tried to rationalize it by declaring his belief that it was done with the idea of drawing the troopers into a trap and ambushing them if they tried to move downstream.[78] Nothing could be seen of the movements of the hostiles, since the high bluffs cut off the view of the lower valley.[79] However, there was little doubt, and both officers and men knew it, that had the Sioux followed up their advantage they might, in the confusion, have rolled over the two combined commands with comparatively little effort and less loss. In fact, Benteen's battalion had reached the bluff just in time to prevent the complete annihilation of Reno's command.[80] But the troopers wasted little time in speculations such as these. They were thankful for the brief respite afforded them, with nearly everyone taking advantage of the opportunity to go down to the river to fill his canteen.[81]

In the meantime some firing had been heard downstream—just how much is a matter of dispute. Both Davern[82] and Sergeant Culbertson claim that they heard volley firing shortly after Reno's command reached the hill. Culbertson spoke of it to Varnum, who replied that "Custer is heavily engaged," or "Custer is giving it to them hot," or used some similar expression. Just then Major Reno came over and began talking to Varnum. Reno was facing down the river and stood only a few feet from the Sergeant, who said that he could still hear the firing.[83] Varnum apparently said nothing to Reno about what he heard, for the latter insisted that he heard no firing of the kind described, but admitted that if he had heard it, he would have known that Custer was fighting farther down the valley.[84] Reno said that he heard a few scattering shots, which he

[78] Graham, "'Come on! Be quick! Bring packs!' The Story of Custer's Last Message . . . ," *Cavalry Journal*, Vol. XXXII (July, 1923), 309; Dustin, *The Custer Tragedy*, 122; Reno, *Court*, 583. Benteen said the Indians stayed around for about half an hour after the two commands joined.

[79] Reno, *Court*, 79, 433.

[80] Daniel A. Kanipe, "A New Story of Custer's Last Battle," in *Contributions to the Historical Society of Montana*, IV (1903), 281.

[81] Reno, *Court*, 232r.

[82] *Ibid.*, 492–95; *Official Transcript*, 525–28.

[83] *Ibid.*, 512–13. Lieutenant Hare and Churchill, one of the packers, both said they heard firing down the river soon after arriving on the hill. Hare had his attention called to it by Godfrey. *Official Transcript*, 374, 869.

believed came from the direction of the Indian village, but that there were not enough of them to suggest a general engagement.[85] Reno must have been rationalizing, for in his *Report*, written only a few days after the battle, he said, "We could hear firing in that direction and knew that it could only be Custer,"[86] and the Bozeman *Avant-Courier* of July 7, 1876, in a story based on the dispatches brought by the scout "Muggins" Taylor, reported that the attack on Custer began "about 3 P.M. and lasted about three hours in the judgment of Major Reno who heard the first and last volleys of the firing."[87]

Captain Benteen supported Reno, maintaining that he heard no firing from the direction of the Custer battlefield and had no intimation that an engagement was taking place at any point,[88] although admitting that he heard about fifteen or twenty shots which seemed to come from near the ford.[89] Lieutenant Wallace said he heard no firing from the direction which Custer had taken, although he did hear a few scattering shots from the left. But he insisted that there were no volleys or any other evidence of extensive fighting.[90] His statement was contradicted by Lieutenant Varnum, who claimed that he had borrowed a carbine from Wallace and was just handing it back when he heard firing downstream, which caused him to exclaim, "Jesus Christ what does that mean?" A heavy firing but not a volley, it seemed to come from near the lower end of the village. Varnum said it made him think that Custer was having a pretty warm time of it.[91]

Just how heavy this firing was is also disputed. Dr. Porter described it as heavy and sharp,[92] Captain Moylan as very faint,[93] while Lieutenant Edgerly contented himself with saying that it was of sufficient distinctness to be heard by the command.[94] Sergeant Cul-

[84] Reno, *Court*, 737.

[85] *Ibid.*, 713.

[86] Reno's *Report*, 477.

[87] *Bozeman Avant-Courier*, July 7, 1876.

[88] Reno, *Court*, 566.

[89] *Ibid.*, 550. Benteen claimed that he heard no volleys but admitted that he heard officers disputing among themselves about hearing volleys. *Official Transcript*, 663.

[90] Reno, *Court*, 111; *Official Transcript*, 73.

[91] Reno, *Court*, 224.

[92] *Ibid.*, 300.

[93] *Ibid.*, 363.

[94] *Ibid.*, 588.

bertson believed that it was no heavier than that heard on Reno's skirmish line and said that it did not appear that Custer was having any more serious trouble than Reno had had,[95] while Churchill, one of the civilian packers who had joined the expedition at the Powder River base, declared that the firing was not very plain and sounded as if it were from two and a half to three miles away.[96] Most of the officers were quite generally satisfied that Custer was fighting the Indians somewhere and that "the command ought to do something or Custer would be after Reno with a sharp stick."[97] The men in the ranks were of the same opinion, believing that the firing indicated that Custer was whipping the Indians and they ought to join him.[98] Some of the officers, especially among the pro-Custer faction, believed that the troops should march to the sound of the firing either to help out or to discover what was going on,[99] but Major Reno claimed that his men were almost out of ammunition and so refused to order an advance until the pack train could be brought up and the men given a chance to replenish their supply.

Lieutenant Godfrey was later to question whether the shortage was an actual fact or merely an excuse for procrastination, since it seemed unbelievable to him that in the short time the command had been fighting "most of the men" could have fired away 150 rounds of carbine ammunition apiece.[100] Godfrey's suspicions find support in the fact that Major Reno never gave the shortage of ammunition as an excuse for the retreat from the timber, and also that when the ammunition mules were brought up, with each mule carrying two thousand rounds in four boxes of five hundred rounds each, Lieutenant Wallace saw only one box opened, the men then helping themselves to what cartridges they needed.[101] This would

95 *Ibid.*, 519.

96 *Ibid.*, 599.

97 Godfrey, *Century*, 373.

98 Graham, "'Come on! Be quick! Bring packs!' The Story of Custer's Last Message . . . ," *Cavalry Journal*, Vol. XXXII (July, 1923), 310.

99 Reno, *Court*, 293.

100 Godfrey, *Montana*, 182. But in his "Diary" Godfrey simply said that they were waiting anxiously for the packs since Reno's men had exhausted nearly all their ammunition. He added that at this time the command could hear volley and the rattle of the guns.

101 Reno, *Court*, 797; *Official Transcript*, 1002. Lieutenant Wallace said flatly that the command was out of ammunition. Reno, *Court*, 62–63. But Churchill said that the boxes of ammunition were not opened until the troops arrived back on the hill after the move down the river. *Official Transcript*, 821.

seem to indicate that Reno's command was not so badly in need of ammunition after all.

There had been a lapse of between thirty and forty-five minutes since the arrival of Benteen and his battalion, but no steps had been taken towards establishing contact with the rest of the regiment. Throughout this period of inactivity the officers seem to have alternated between trying to decide what to do next and trying to justify their failure to do anything whatsoever. During this time, with not an Indian in sight, Reno and Benteen are said to have "strode up and down their lines swearing and damning."[102] Whether this incident is true or not, the fact remains that there was every indication that Custer was heavily engaged, and yet there was a total lack of support by Reno,[103] who thus violated one of the most elementary precepts of miltary science: in the absence of orders, march to the sound of firing. That such a move might have resulted in the complete destruction of his command does not absolve Reno from blame, since his neglect was not predicated on any such possibility.[104] For this lack of initiative and action on the part of the two subordinates, pro-Custer critics have laid the blame on President Grant, maintaining that but for his action in humiliating Custer, neither Reno nor Benteen would have dared to flout their commander's orders as they did.[105]

The exact chronological order of happenings while the troops were on the hill is a matter of dispute. Reno was determined not to move until the packs were up, and while waiting for them to arrive, he decided, apparently for lack of something else to do, to make an attempt to recover and bury the body of Lieutenant Hodgson. Some ten or twelve troopers, in addition to Dr. Porter, went with the Major to the river, where they found several bodies. Examination of Hodgson's body, which they found lying on a little bench some distance above the river, revealed that someone had already

102 Brown and Willard, *Black Hills Trails*, 191.

103 James P. Murphy, "Campaign of the Little Big Horn," *Infantry Journal*, Vol. XXXIV (June, 1929), 636.

104 Lieutenant Edgerly later expressed the belief that they should have marched to the sound of the firing, although conceding that an attempt to join Custer might have meant that the rest of the regiment would have shared his fate. Edgerly, *Narrative*, 11. See also Graham, *The Custer Myth*, 217.

105 Hunt, "A Purposeful Picnic," *Pacific Monthly*, Vol. XIX (March–May, 1908), 234.

taken his watch and chain, but Reno did manage to recover the Lieutenant's class ring, as well as his keys and a small, gold bar pin. Porter secured Dr. DeWolf's pocketbook, along with several other small articles that were on his person, and the entire group took advantage of the opportunity to fill their canteens.[106] A few Indians were still in the valley and on the bluffs to the right, and their firing on the burial party made Reno decide not to attempt to move Hodgson's body to the hill. On the way back to the position on the bluffs they found a trooper of G company hiding in the brush. He had lost his horse and had concealed himself there in the hope of escaping detection by the Indians.[107] About thirty minutes had been consumed in Reno's expedition, and when they rejoined the main body of troops, they found that the pack train had not yet arrived. Therefore Major Reno decided to send back Lieutenant Hare, who had been pressed into duty as acting adjutant, to hurry it up.[108] Hare borrowed Lieutenant Godfrey's horse, which seemed to be the freshest, and rode back over the trail.[109]

In the meantime, Captain Weir was becoming increasingly disgusted with what he considered Reno's timidity, if not downright cowardice, in refusing to march in the direction that Custer's command had taken, and finally determined to do something about it himself. He told Lieutenant Edgerly that he thought they ought to go to Custer's assistance. When Edgerly agreed, Weir apparently went to Major Reno to secure permission to make a reconnaissance downstream. Just what happened is obscure, but apparently Reno refused permission, and Weir made some angry retort. Then the two seem to have engaged in a hot exchange of uncomplimentary language in which threats were made on both sides.[110] There can be little doubt that the conferences of the officers on Reno Hill were marked by excitement and rancor and that at times they bordered on actual quarreling.[111] But with the passage of time the "honor

[106] Reno, *Court*, 321, 544; *Official Transcript*, 290.

[107] *Official Transcript*, 572, 585.

[108] *Ibid.*, 1061–63.

[109] Reno, *Court*, 108, 620; *Official Transcript*, 855–57.

[110] Dustin, *The Custer Fight*, 21–22. There is much disagreement regarding just when Weir moved down the stream, but it was apparently at least half an hour after Benteen's arrival on the hill. See *Official Transcript*, 573–75, 664–65, 762, 859.

[111] Marquis, *Sketch Story of the Custer Battle*, n.p. Lieutenant McClernand saw the Weir Point episode as of importance chiefly because it showed that some

of the regiment" became uppermost, and much of what many, if not most, of the officers knew was allowed to be quietly forgotten.

Weir finally decided to make a personal survey from the high bluffs to the north of the position held by the troops and, followed by his orderly, rode off in that direction, traveling along the edge of the bluffs where some of Reno's officers had declared that they last saw Custer. Lieutenant Edgerly, having no orders, but presuming from Captain Weir's actions that permission for the reconnaissance had been given, mounted D troop and started north down the ravine which lies to the right of the position on the hill. Weir advanced for a distance of between a mile and a mile and a half,[112] and from the high point which he reached—now known as Weir's Peak—could see the Custer battlefield obscured by a great cloud of dust and smoke with the Indians riding around and shooting at objects on the ground.[113] Years later Gall was to reveal that by the time Weir reached the high point, Custer and all the members of his command were dead. Indian activity was confined to galloping around and over the bodies, putting bullets and arrows into them.[114] From his point of vantage Weir saw the Indians in sizable force start for Edgerly, who, being in the ravine, could not see them. Weir signaled his lieutenant to change direction and continued his signaling until he had swung the troop completely around and brought them over to the high point, where they remained for some time, not seriously molested.[115]

At the morass the pack train had experienced no delay, despite the fact that several of the mules had floundered into the mud and got stuck. The rest of the train simply went on, and Captain McDougall dismounted his company in order to help get the mired mules back on the trail, the only disadvantage being that the train was scattered a bit more than previously.[116] They kept on following the trail of the regiment. After going only a short distance,

of the officers appreciated the situation at its true value, and also appreciated their duty to their commander. "With Indian and Buffalo in Montana," *Cavalry Journal*, Vol. XXXVI (January and April, 1927), 44.

[112] Weir probably moved a little over a mile downstream. Reno, *Court*, 501.

[113] Reno, *Court*, 588–89. Graham, *Story of the Little Big Horn*, 64.

[114] *Army and Navy Journal*, July 3, 1886.

[115] Edgerly, *Narrative*, 8–9.

[116] *Official Transcript*, 929, 965–66.

Kanipe came on. Although Lieutenant Mathey[117] and Captain McDougall[118] each insisted that the Sergeant did not report to him, the train, in obedience to the orders which Kanipe brought, ceased to follow the trail of the regiment and cut straight across country toward the bluff where the Sergeant said he had left the five troops of Custer's command.[119] At the Lone Warrior Tepee, which was still burning, a heavy cloud of dust ahead and to the right[120] convinced Captain McDougall that the regiment was in action. Therefore the train was halted and closed up, while the escort deployed in preparation for any eventualities. A short distance beyond the Lone Tepee they met one of the half-blood scouts going back. Although sometimes identified as Curly, who was not a half-blood but a full-blood Crow Indian, this is more apt to have been Robert Jackson. Asked if Custer were whipping them, he replied in the negative, adding that the Sioux were too many.[121] A mile or so farther on they met Lieutenant Hare, who brought orders to move up as quickly as possible and to get the ammunition out. Accordingly, two of the ammunition mules were cut out of the train and sent forward at a run.[122] Each mule was led by one trooper, while another whipped it from behind. When they arrived on the hill, only one box was opened, and the troopers helped themselves to what cartridges they needed. Despite the fact that the ammunition had arrived and that there were at least three thousand rounds in reserve, Reno still refused to order a movement downstream and insisted on waiting until all of the packs had arrived.[123] For this he has been severely criticized and with abundant justification, for, as General Nelson A. Miles pointed out, no commander can win a victory "with seven-twelfths of the command remaining out of the engagement when within sound of his rifle shots."[124] The best justification for Reno's refusal was given by Sergeant Culbertson, who

117 Reno, *Court*, 641; *Official Transcript*, 931.

118 Reno, *Court*, 652; *Official Transcript*, 971.

119 Daniel A. Kanipe, "New Story of Custer's Last Battle," in *Contributions to the Historical Society of Montana*, IV (1903), 280.

120 Reno, *Court*, 649–50.

121 *Official Transcript*, 931.

122 Reno, *Court*, 427–28.

123 Graham, " 'Come on! Be quick! Bring packs!' The Story of Custer's Last Message . . . ," *Cavalry Journal*, Vol. XXXII (July, 1923), 310.

124 Miles, *Personal Recollections*, 290.

felt that it was on account of the wounded, for it was necessary to wait until the packs were up in order to get blankets in which to carry the wounded who were unable to ride.[125]

The pack train accelerated its progress, and when some of the packs became loose, no attempt was made to repack, the troopers being ordered to cut the ropes and let them go, but they were not bothered by the Indians in any way.[126] About five o'clock Captain McDougall brought the head of the train in, but they did not come in all at once, and it was nearly six o'clock before all of the packs were up.[127] About a mile from Reno Hill, Captain McDougall saw and heard things which made him believe that a first-class battle was being fought a few miles farther down the river. He reported his observations to Major Reno as soon as he arrived on the bluff,[128] but Reno later claimed that he had no recollection of any such report having been made to him.[129] According to McDougall, Reno made no direct reply, but merely said, "Captain, you have lost your lieutenant [Hodgson]. He has been killed down there."[130] This firing was also heard by Captain Moylan, who mentioned it to McDougall and received the reply that in all probability it was Custer fighting at the other end of the village.[131] Having failed to interest Reno in the battle that Custer was apparently fighting, McDougall, according to his story, went back to his company and deployed them as skirmishers.[132]

Herendeen and the other troopers, left in the river bottom, had heard heavy firing from downstream. There were only a few Indians in the upper end of the valley, and, as the heavy firing began to die away, the scout, realizing that it meant that the Sioux would soon be coming back, told the others they had better be getting out. After some discussion all but two of them apparently decided to make an attempt to rejoin Reno's command. Those two stayed behind in the timber, apparently without Herendeen's knowledge,

125 *Official Transcript*, 597.
126 *Hardin Tribune*, June 22, 1923; Reno, *Court*, 601.
127 Reno, *Court*, 363; Graham, *Story of the Little Big Horn*, 65.
128 Reno, *Court*, 653; *Official Transcript*, 967.
129 Reno, *Court*, 737.
130 *Ibid.*, 650; *Official Transcript*, 967.
131 *Official Transcript*, 308.
132 Reno, *Court*, 650; *Official Transcript*, 967.

and were almost certainly killed by the hostiles, since they were never heard of again. They had all turned their horses loose, and the twelve, on foot and deployed as skirmishers, moved toward the river. Near the stream they met five mounted Indians who fired on them, but the fire was returned and the Indians ran. The troopers forded the river, the water being up to their armpits, but they were not molested further and got across safely, although two of them were slightly wounded. They then headed for Reno's command, which they could see drawn up on the bluffs some distance off. Farther on they saw a small detail of men descending the slope and presumed that these men were coming to their assistance.[133]

Actually Lieutenant Varnum, having been ordered by Major Reno to take a detail and go down to the riverbank to bury the body of Lieutenant Hodgson, had been forced to wait for the arrival of the packs in order to secure the necessary tools. Finally, starting with a detail of six troopers, he was only about halfway to the riverbank when he saw Herendeen and his companions make their way across the stream and move toward the soldiers. After Varnum had stopped to see what was up, the two groups returned to the command, which had begun to move downstream,[134] and there was another delay while the newcomers were provided with ammunition.[135]

As soon as the ammunition mules were up, Reno sent Lieutenant Hare to tell Captain Weir that the rest of the command would follow him as soon as all of the pack train were accounted for. He also sent orders directing Weir to open communication with Custer, if possible, and to tell him the location of the remainder of the command.[136] But Weir had been checked and had ceased his forward movement before the adjutant reached him. Lieutenant Hare

[133] *Army and Navy Journal*, July 15, 1876; *Official Transcript*, 331–32. As McClernand has pointed out, the mere fact that Herendeen and others were able to make their way from the timber, to ford the stream, and to ascend the bluffs, dismounted, is sufficient evidence that Reno had no serious opposition confronting him. "With Indian and Buffalo in Montana," *Cavalry Journal*, Vol. XXXVI (January and April, 1927), 44. For a slightly different account of this same incident see Brady, *Indian Fights and Fighters*, 274.

[134] Reno, *Court*, 232r; McClernand, "With Indian and Buffalo in Montana," *Cavalry Journal*, Vol. XXXVI (January and April, 1927), 44.

[135] Godfrey, *Century*, 374; Godfrey, *Montana*, 184; *Official Transcript*, 307.

[136] Reno, *Court*, 427–28, 725.

Lieutenant Luther Hare of the Reno Battalion.

" 'We've had a big fight in the valley, got whipped like hell and I am—damned—glad to see you [Lieutenant Godfrey of Benteen's command].' "

Captain Frederick W. Benteen.

" 'Who became the commanding officer in fact if not in name, who gradually took over the direction of events, and who admittedly looked after things more than was his business or his duty.' "

Both courtesy Custer Battlefield National Monument

Lieutenant Edward Godfrey.

"Lieutenant Godfrey, convinced that Custer had been repulsed . . . suggested to Captain Weir that Reno try to effect a junction with the rest of the regiment."

Curly Head,
Custer's Crow scout.

"Probably the victim of more apochryphal tale-telling than any other character in western history, with the exception of Buffalo Bill."

Both courtesy North Dakota Historical Society

estimated that there were at least fifteen hundred warriors in plain sight and admitted that on account of the rough nature of the ground a much larger number could have been hidden.[137] He also observed that the Sioux were advancing to the attack with an enthusiasm which neither he nor any of the others was able to understand.[138]

Just how the movement downstream came to be undertaken is uncertain. With Captain McDougall's detachment Reno had a force of seven companies, four of which had seen no action. In addition there were some 35 or 40 men from the companies that were with Custer, men who had been detailed to service with the train. There were also a few scouts and packers. Probably all told, Reno had somewhere between 325 and 350 men.[139] But for some reason he was still somewhat reluctant to order an advance.

The advance was apparently forced by Captain Benteen, who was desirous of seeing more of "the lay of the land" and who was also fully cognizant of some of the latent possibilities involved in the situation. Within ten or fifteen minutes after D troop had moved out, and acting on his own responsibility and entirely without orders, Benteen led a battalion consisting of Troops H, K, and M downstream in the direction that Captain Weir had taken.[140] One participant said that in an attempt to apprise Custer of their whereabouts, the troops, whenever they reached a height of any kind, were brought "front into line," while the men cheered and waved their hats.[141] That some such effort was made is apparent from Benteen's testimony that he had the troops in file on the river bluffs and a company across at right angles, with the intention of showing General Custer the approximate location of the rest of the command.[142]

This movement downstream was followed by the rest of the command, most of whom acted without specific orders.[143] The movement apparently started at no one time, and the various units

137 *Ibid.*, 440; *Official Transcript*, 404.

138 Brininstool, "The Custer Battle Water Party," *Hunter-Trader-Trapper*, Vol. LXV (August, 1932), 11.

139 Holley, *Once Their Home*, 326; Reno, *Court*, 528, 556.

140 Reno, *Court*, 113; *Official Transcript*, 762.

141 Brininstool, "Custer Battle Water Party," *Hunter-Trader-Trapper*, Vol. LXV (August, 1932), 11.

142 *Official Transcript*, 664.

143 Sergeant Culbertson felt there was no unnecessary delay between the arrival of the pack train and the movement downstream. What delay there was was caused by the necessity of caring for the wounded. Reno, *Court*, 518.

seem to have operated almost independently of one another. But it was nearly six o'clock before the entire command was in motion, probably from half an hour to an hour after sounds of firing had ceased coming from Custer's position.[144] Although Reno later went so far as to say that after the packs came up he formed the command in three columns, with three companies on the left, the pack train in the center, and two companies on the right, and started down the stream,[145] this statement was undoubtedly pure rationalization, concocted in an attempt to justify his own conduct.

Many of the men were on foot, their horses having been either killed or stampeded. The wounded who were unable to ride were carried in horse blankets, six troopers being detailed to carry each improvised stretcher. Most of the wounded were from A troop, and the task of carrying them accounted for all the rest of Moylan's men. These were men who had been wounded during the retreat from the valley, since no attempt had been made to remove any of the wounded from the woods. They had been able to hang on to their saddles after being hit and so had managed to reach the comparative safety of the bluffs.[146]

It was a slow and arduous march, for the wounded could not be carried very far at a time.[147] Moylan's troop was soon far behind the others, and he had to ask Captain McDougall for assistance, at which time the second platoon of B troop was detailed to assist with the wounded.[148] The problem of the wounded in Indian warfare was one for which no adequate provision could be made. In civilized warfare the wounded could be left in hospitals on the field of battle, but in Indian fighting this was impossible, since an Indian considered that neither he nor his foe had been defeated until one of them was dead. Accordingly, the presence of only a few wounded men would be sufficient to paralyze the operations of a sizable number of troops.[149] In this case, however, the presence of the wounded need not have impeded the operations of Reno's detachment since, as

144 Reno, *Court*, 518, 550, 620, 654, 703.

145 *Official Transcript*, 1064.

146 Reno, *Court*, 302, 701.

147 *Ibid.*, 511.

148 *Ibid.*, 336, 650.

149 Gibbon's Report, 476; Gibbon, "Hunting Sitting Bull," *American Catholic Quarterly Review*, Vol. II, No. 3 (October, 1899), 694.

Lieutenant Hare pointed out, the wounded could have been left with the pack train while the rest of the command moved toward Custer's position. Captain McDougall had some 120 men all told, and the remaining six companies were strong enough to have operated alone.[150]

Just how far the troops went is uncertain, for many of the officers expressed highly contradictory views on the subject, probably partly because different parts of the command went farther downstream than others. Most of them went as far as the high point where Weir's troop waited. Here the view was unsatisfactory, the air being full of dust and smoke. Nonetheless, the soldiers could see plenty of Indians in the valley, which had a reddish-brown appearance and looked as though fire had scorched the foliage, an appearance later found to be caused by the immense herds of many-colored ponies ranging the river bottom.[151] Some of the troops are said to have gone about half a mile beyond Weir's Peak,[152] but it was here that Benteen set up a guidon on the highest point to show Custer the location of the rest of the command and to let him know that they were trying to reach him,[153] although it was also intended as a guide for any scattered detachments or men who might be in hiding.[154] Benteen's explanation of this action disposes, once and for all, of the contention that the Reno-Benteen officers had no suspicion of what had happened to Custer. They were fully satisfied that his command had been beaten, and beaten badly, the only question being to the magnitude of the disaster.

In after years, Private Edward Pigford of Troop M claimed that at the suggestion of Captain French, he, with two other soldiers, advanced ahead of the rest of the battalion to a small hill from which they could see the Custer battlefield, and that they saw the last of the fight in which the Custer command was annihilated. The other

[150] Reno, *Court*, 429.

[151] Godfrey, *Montana*, 185.

[152] Reno, *Court*, 564–65; *Official Transcript*, 706. Godfrey said that some of the troops went farther down the stream than Weir had gone, but how far he was unable to say. *Ibid.*, 864.

[153] Brininstool, *Captain Benteen's Story*, 23. Benteen told the Court of Inquiry that this guidon was planted to attract the attention of Custer's command since at that time no one had any idea that Custer and his men were not still alive. *Official Transcript*, 706–707.

[154] Reno, *Court*, 713; *Official Transcript*, 1079.

two men were killed by the Indians, but Pigford, though wounded, managed to escape.[155] The story may or may not be true—there is no way of checking it—but it appears almost too fantastic to believe, although Pigford was a member of Troop M and was wounded during the battle.

Just what the officers and men could see from the high point is uncertain, since their statements are somewhat at variance. Lieutenant Wallace insisted that he could see all over the Custer battlefield and that there were lots of Indians—he put the number at several thousand—riding around but not firing, who seemed to be moving upstream.[156] Opposed to this is the statement of Lieutenant Godfrey that he could see the general lay of the land and the place where Custer's body was later found, but that he did not see any Indians or any bodies and that there were no indications that any fighting was going on there at the time.[157] But he also said that he saw a lot of Indians who seemed to be going downstream, and, from the faint firing that he could hear, he suspected that Custer's attack had been beaten back and that these Indians were watching him.[158] To add to the general confusion, Lieutenant Roe, who got his information from various officers of the Seventh Cavalry, wrote that the troops could see Indians on Custer Hill shooting into objects lying on the ground, which at the time were supposed to be buffalo but were later found to be the bodies of the Custer command.[159] Benteen declared that there was no sign of the presence of troops nor any indication that a fight was going on anywhere in the vicinity,[160] although he said he could see the Indian camp in the river bottom and estimated it as being three or four miles long and consisting of eighteen hundred tepees.[161] He also insisted that the Custer battlefield was not in sight from the high point[162]—sheer nonsense,

155 Colonel William H. C. Bowen, "Custer's Last Fight," in Joe E. Milner and Earle R. Forrest, *California Joe . . .*, 364.

156 Reno, *Court*, 112.

157 *Ibid.*, 633; *Official Transcript*, 903.

158 Reno, *Court*, 622; *Official Transcript*, 864–65.

159 Roe, *Custer's Last Battle*, 11. At this distance in time, this explanation seems somewhat asinine because Lieutenant Roe failed to explain why the Indians would be shooting into the carcasses of buffalo.

160 Reno, *Court*, 565; *Official Transcript*, 706.

161 Brininstool, *Captain Benteen's Story*, 23; Reno, *Court*, 551; *Official Transcript*, 666.

162 Reno, *Court*, 565; *Official Transcript*, 706.

as any visitor to the battlefield today can easily prove for himself.

It was the sight of this great Indian encampment that brought Benteen to an acute realization of the immensity of the task that confronted what was left of the regiment.[163] Major Reno remained in nominal command, but in Gibson's phrase, he "did not know which end he was standing on"[164] and was too busy waiting for someone to send him orders to take any initiative.[165] It was Benteen who became the commanding officer in fact if not in name, who gradually took over the direction of events, and who admittedly looked after things more than was his business or his duty.[166] It was Benteen who, more than anyone else, saved the regiment from an even greater disaster.

But the troops did see the Sioux coming in full force against them, and Lieutenant Varnum was of the opinion that all the Indians in the country were coming from out of that prairie as fast as they could travel.[167] The position of the troops was admittedly poor defensively, although there is no agreement regarding just how they were arranged. Lieutenant Edgerly said that H troop was on top of a narrow bluff with M a little in its rear, while D troop was at right angles to H. Troop K was said to be holding a narrow spur of bluff alongside D.[168] But Lieutenant Wallace described the position occupied by the command as consisting of two almost parallel ridges with no way of defending the space between them and said that the troops were in two lines with the end toward the Indians open.[169] Benteen said that he wanted to try to check the Indians so as to select a better defensive position, but Reno thought that it would be better for them to return to the place where they first got on the hill.[170] No orders for the retirement were given,[171] and the first intimation that some of the troop commanders had of the withdrawal was finding their troops almost alone in the face of

163 Holley, *Once Their Home*, 252.

164 Fougera, *With Custer's Cavalry*, 272.

165 Brady, *Indian Fights and Fighters*, 375.

166 *Official Transcript*, 668.

167 Reno, *Court*, 232s.

168 *Official Transcript*, 767.

169 *Ibid.*, 125.

170 *Ibid.*, 666.

171 *Ibid.*, 668. However, Lieutenant Edgerly said that orders were given to fall back and insisted that the Indians did not drive the command from the advanced position. *Ibid.*, 766.

the enemy. Even so, the retreat does not seem to have been too precipitate or hard pressed, despite Benteen's statement that he left one company with orders to send their horses back and hold their position at all hazards, and that they disobeyed orders and came back as fast as any of them.[172] Lieutenant Wallace said that while the retirement was made actively, it was done quietly and with little confusion, his own men moving back at a walk.[173]

This successful withdrawal in the face of a very considerable force of the enemy was due largely to the fact that it was a planned retirement, Troops M and D apparently covering it until it was within a few hundred yards of the position on the hill, when K troop was dismounted and deployed as skirmishers, holding the Indians in check until the rest of the troops could get into position. Godfrey's men then began to withdraw slowly. When their commander noticed that their fire was slackening and that they were beginning to bunch up, he halted the line, made the men take their proper intervals, and cautioned them against bunching, which made them better targets for the Indians, before again beginning the slow withdrawal.[174] This covering of the retreat undoubtedly was responsible for the almost complete lack of casualties suffered during the movement, and illustrates what might have happened in the retreat from the valley had Major Reno not been overcome by blind panic, or had an abler officer been in command.

As D troop was withdrawing toward Godfrey's skirmish line, Lieutenant Edgerly saw a wounded man of the troop lying on the ground. Apparently in answer to the trooper's request for aid, Edgerly told him to get into a hole and that he (Edgerly) would form a line and come back to rescue him. As soon as the troop had reached K's skirmish line, the Lieutenant told Captain Weir, who had gone back ahead of his troop, about the wounded soldier and of his promise to return for him. Weir replied that he was sorry but that the orders were to go back on the hill. Edgerly protested that he had promised to save the man, but Weir remained adamant, declaring that the orders were to go back and that they must be obeyed. So the troop continued its retirement, leaving the wounded trooper to

172 *Ibid.*, 668.
173 Reno, *Court*, 115.
174 Godfrey, "Diary," n.p.

his fate, which was certain death—perhaps by torture—at the hands of the Sioux.[175] For this callous action, of which Major Reno seems to have been unaware, there appears, at this distance, to have been but little excuse, and it is in marked contrast to Lieutenant Varnum's action in saving the life of his orderly during the retreat from the valley.

When H troop arrived back at the first position on the hill, Captain Benteen ordered a halt, declaring that it was the best position he had seen, a conclusion with which Major Reno agreed.[176] Benteen ordered Lieutenant Wallace to place his company along a certain line, and when Wallace complained that he had no company, only three men, Benteen told him to place himself and the three men along the line. The Lieutenant did as ordered, and from this nucleus the line was formed.[177] Shortly after seven o'clock, with almost three hours of daylight remaining, the command was back on the hill, closely invested on all sides by the victorious and highly exultant Sioux.

175 *Official Transcript*, 764–65. For a slightly different version see Reno, *Court*, 591.

176 Reno, *Court*, 431.

177 *Official Transcript*, 669.

CHAPTER XVII

Reno Hill

THE POSITION occupied by the seven troops, selected primarily for defense, was not well suited for that purpose,[1] although Captain McDougall believed that it was the best that could have been found within a radius of several miles.[2] Located fully one hundred feet above the river, it consisted of two approximately parallel ridges running roughly east and west, separated by a small valley or swale. Although it has been compared to a saucer with a part of the rim broken away, and also to "the arc of a circle rather irregularly described,"[3] it can probably be best compared to a large, rather irregularly shaped horseshoe with one prong projecting farther than the other and with the shorter line turned in at, roughly, a right angle. The two ends rested on the bluffs above the river.[4]

The retirement had been well covered, and the troops had had time to herd the horses and mules into the swale and to place the wounded in the most protected position. Boxes and packs were placed across the open end of the coulee in order to furnish some slight protection to the troopers assigned to that part of the line which was formed by Captain Benteen on one side and Major Reno on the other. So closely did the Indians pursue that the troopers barely had time to get on the line dismounted before the hostiles were upon them in force, and K troop, the last one in, formed no separate part of the line, its members being mixed in with the other troops.[5] So formidable was the Indian attack that all the soldiers

[1] *Official Transcript,* 1035.

[2] *Ibid.,* 991.

[3] Benteen, *Account,* 11; *Official Transcript,* 667.

[4] *Official Transcript,* 667. Lieutenant Wallace said that "in a vague sort of way" it could be described as an elevated piece of ground with a little rise in the center and the men grouped around that. *Ibid.,* 1003.

[5] *Ibid.,* 870–71, 938, 1067–68; Reno, *Court,* 552.

were ordered to the line, the protection and care of the animals being left entirely to the civilian packers.[6]

The hostiles, encouraged by their success against Reno in the valley and by their wiping out of the Custer command—of which Reno's men were not yet aware—and convinced that their "medicine" was "good," now swarmed to the attack with an enthusiasm that both startled and dismayed the soldiers. Little protection was afforded on that saucer-like hilltop, even the sparse sagebrush being useless for anything other than concealment. Some benefit was derived from saddles, packs, and other equipment, but for the most part the men simply lay down on the bare ground and hoped for the best.[7] Of the weakness of the position and the ferocity of the Sioux attack, there is abundant evidence in the fact that in the three hours before the coming of darkness the command lost eighteen men killed and forty-six wounded, many of them being from the companies that had been with Reno.[8]

Three of the Crow scouts who had been with Custer—White-Man-Runs-Him, Hairy Moccasins, and Goes Ahead—claim to have joined Reno's command sometime during the late afternoon. According to their story, they told the soldiers that Custer and his command had been annihilated. Then they stayed and fought until nearly sundown, after which they left the command on the pretense of going for water. They rode eastward, following Reno Creek until they reached the pine timber. Apparently only a few of the enemy were in this direction, but the scouts claim to have killed one Sioux and to have captured his horse. Then they circled to the north toward the Yellowstone River, riding through the same heavy showers that made the night march of Gibbon's column so unpleasant. Concerning the other three Crow scouts, they professed ignorance of the whereabouts of Curly but insisted that Half-Yellow-Face and White Swan had been left in the valley where they were fortifying and fighting,[9] although both of these scouts were on the hill with the Reno-Benteen forces, White Swan, in particular, received the unstinted praise of the soldiers for his courage in fight-

[6] *Official Transcript*, 938.

[7] Reno, *Court*, 116.

[8] *Ibid.*, 80; Edgerly, *Narrative*, 10.

[9] *Account to Scott*, 4, 8, 11; Linderman, *Red Mother*, 239–40.

ing to the last, despite the fact that he had one hand almost entirely shot away.[10]

With the coming of darkness the fire of the Sioux slackened and finally ceased altogether except for the shot of an occasional sniper, for most of the hostiles returned to the village to feast, to dance, and to brag of their exploits during the day. But while the Indians held high carnival in the valley below, there was some rest and much work for the almost exhausted troopers on the bluffs.

The horses were all unsaddled and the mules relieved of their burdens. Quite a few of the animals had been killed during the fighting, and Lieutenant Mathey, acting on his own authority and without orders from anyone, now got ropes and lariats to improvise a sort of picket line, tying it to the legs of the dead mules and horses.[11] It was arranged so as to place the animals where they were at least partially protected from the fire of the hostiles in all directions except the east,[12] and at the same time to furnish the greatest possible protection to the fast-growing number of wounded, who were placed inside the circle formed by the horses and mules and further protected with bags and boxes taken from the packs.

The troops were then deployed around the crest of the ridges and across the end of the swale, each company being put in regular order and assigned to a definite part of the line.[13] Occupying the bluff on the extreme right as one stands with his back to the river was Benteen's H troop, while the other and shorter end of the *U* was held by McDougall's men, who faced the Indian village which was to the north and down the river. McDougall's left and Benteen's right thus rested on the edge of the high bluffs along the Little Big Horn River, Benteen's position being a little higher than the ground where the others were.[14] Fortified behind saddles and boxes from the packs, Captain Moylan's men were placed across the swale covering the corral.[15] There is some disagreement over just how the other four troops were placed, but apparently D troop was at the northern angle of the swale next to Troop A and perhaps

10 Burdick, *Last Battle of the Sioux Nation*, 10.
11 *Official Transcript*, 941–42; Reno, *Court*, 253.
12 Graham, *Story of the Little Big Horn*, 67.
13 *Official Transcript*, 872.
14 *Ibid.*, 231.
15 Reno, *Court*, 337.

also across it. Then came K, M, and G in that order.[16] Troop H, in holding the southern ridge by itself, thus occupied almost as much of the line as four of the other troops combined[17]—an arrangement that was probably due to the belief that the strongest attacks would come from the north, since the Indians would be fairly sure to keep the main body of their warriors between the troops and the village.

Major Reno later claimed that he had ordered the troop commanders to protect their men all they could because the command would probably have to stay there until help came. But he added that he knew that this would not be very long as General Terry could not be far away.[18] The result was that during the night most of the troopers worked with the few spades and axes[19]—probably not more than five of each—that were in the packs, with cups, with mess kits, and even with their bare hands to erect defenses against the intensified attack that would probably come with the first streaks of dawn. Their task was made doubly difficult by the light, porous nature of the soil and by the fact that both officers and men were tired to the verge of exhaustion from all that had taken place since they left the mouth of the Rosebud three days before. Despite the fact that some of the officers made serious efforts to keep the men awake,[20] it is probable that all of them got some sleep during the night,[21] since it was cloudy and cool with a few sprinkles of rain.[22] Pickets were put out in front of the line,[23] and the tired troopers dug a few rifle pits, constructing the best barricades they could with the means at their disposal.[24]

The only troop which failed to dig pits and construct some sort of a breastwork was H. Although Reno had ordered their construc-

[16] *Ibid.*, 337, 553. Benteen gives a slightly different arrangement as do both Varnum and Wallace. *Ibid.*, 119, 253, 553. Graham also gives a different order. *Story of the Little Big Horn*, 67–68.

[17] Benteen, *Account*, 11.

[18] Reno, *Court*, 705; *Official Transcript*, 1070.

[19] Wallace said there were three spades in the command. *Official Transcript*, 47. Benteen said five spades and "a very few axes." *Ibid.*, 685.

[20] Brininstool, *A Trooper with Custer*, 39.

[21] Reno, *Court*, 253, 706. Wallace said that the men worked all through the night of June 25. *Official Transcript*, 47. Varnum testified that the majority of the command slept during the same period. *Ibid.*, 231. As is usually the case the truth was probably somewhere in between.

[22] Reno, *Court*, 250.

[23] *Official Transcript*, 587.

[24] Reno, *Court*, 82.

tion, Benteen was very tired and knew that his men were also. Moreover, he had an idea that the Indians would leave rather than renew the attack. An order was an order, however, so he sent for spades, and when he found that they were all in use gave that fact as an excuse for disregarding the order.[25] Captain McDougall's troopers were also unable to obtain proper entrenching tools, and used butcher knives and tin cups to throw up the dirt and make some kind of barricade. McDougall admitted that it was not much in the way of breastworks, being merely a shelter for their heads, but felt that it was better than nothing.[26] There was no need to fortify or to occupy the western side of the position towards the river, since it had good natural protection in the form of a steep slope extending down towards the stream—which, moreover, could be swept by a cross fire from north to south. While the entrenchments left much to be desired and furnished little protection, the miracle was that the troops, considering their limited resources and extreme fatigue, had been able to accomplish so much in so short a time.

The weakness of the position was apparent in several ways. The surrounding country was rough and broken—"bad lands" in the full sense of that term—consisting of a series of small hills and ridges falling away gradually to a ravine in which the attacking Indians concealed themselves.[27] More serious was the fact that there were several ridges on the left which were higher than the ones occupied by the troops and from which the hostiles were able to pour a rather heavy volume of fire in upon the soldiers, who were unable to make any effective return. Other disadvantages were that the animals were exposed to the fire of the enemy,[28] that the position did not threaten the Indian village in any way since it was entirely out of range, and that Reno's forces could not create any diversion, if indeed they had been in any condition to do so, as they certainly were not.[29]

The major topic of conversation among both officers and men was speculation regarding the location of Custer. As is usually the case with American fighting men, wild rumors flew about recklessly. Despite the conjecture over the whereabouts of the commanding

25 *Ibid.*, 554; *Official Transcript*, 674.

26 *Official Transcript*, 977.

27 Reno, *Court*, 70, 687; Gibbon, "Summer Expedition," 301.

28 Reno, *Court*, 687; *Official Transcript*, 1035.

29 *Official Transcript*, 218–19.

officer and his detachment, there seems to have been little anxiety or uneasiness, since he had five troops with him and was presumably able to take care of himself.[30] Evidently there was some swearing at him for having gone off and left them, and the opinion was expressed that Custer had ordered them to the attack and then abandoned them. Some officers believed that he had made an attack himself, been repulsed, and had then started downstream to join General Terry without any further thought of what might happen to the men under Reno and Benteen.[31] Others indignantly rejected the suggestion that Custer would do such a thing.[32] Doubtless some of the veterans, both men and officers, recalled the rumors current after the Battle of the Washita, but the consensus seems to have been that the Indians in great force had gotten between the two segments of the regiment, that Custer had some wounded, and that, being surrounded just as Reno was, he was unable to come up.[33] This theory even found expression in a rumor that Lieutenant Calhoun was among Custer's wounded, which caused Captain Moylan to ask who had brought the news. Told that the information had been brought by some scout, the Captain expressed disbelief.[34]

Lieutenant Godfrey, convinced that Custer had been repulsed and was unable to come to them, suggested to Captain Weir that Reno try to effect a junction with the rest of the regiment, since they had fewer casualties than they would have later.[35] But there seems to have been no fear—at least no expressed fear—that Custer's command had been destroyed. In his *Report*, Reno said: ". . . the awful fate that did befall him never occurred to any of us as within the limits of possibility."[36] Benteen added that "not a soul in the command imagined that Custer had been destroyed until General Terry came up. That was the first intimation."[37] That his attitude was shared by the enlisted men is shown by Sergeant Culbertson's testimony.[38]

30 Reno, *Court*, 550, 706; Edgerly, *Narrative*, 7.
31 Reno, *Court*, 79, 112, 568.
32 *Ibid.*, 644.
33 *Ibid.*, 521.
34 *Ibid.*, 519; *Official Transcript*, 584.
35 Reno, *Court*, 625.
36 Reno's *Report*, 34.
37 Brininstool, *The Custer Fight*, 26; Reno, *Court*, 565.
38 Reno, *Court*, 521.

On the other hand, the none too reliable John Burkman, for years Custer's devoted personal orderly, says that Reno had been drinking with another officer in his tent on the hill when Burkman, who was on guard duty, overheard the Major say, "I wonder where the Murat of the American army is by this time." Then both officers laughed. Burkman did not understand the reference to Murat, but he knew they were talking about Custer, and from the sneer in the laugh he suspected that both of them hoped for the worst.[39] This story is difficult to evaluate. Burkman was not imaginative enough to have invented it, and, while it sounds almost too fantastic to be possible, there is circumstantial evidence to indicate that it might be true. Reno and Benteen both disliked Custer exceedingly; furthermore, under the circumstances it was only natural that they should have discussed the whereabouts of the commanding officer, as Reno admitted they did.[40] They were probably not too much concerned over what might have happened to him; in fact, they might have been glad to see him whipped, on the theory that it would "take some of the conceit out of him." While it is probable that neither suspected anything like the disaster that had occurred, it is possible that both were indifferent to the fate of large numbers of their comrades-in-arms in the satisfaction of their personal grudge.[41]

Although Benteen thought it would be impossible to open communication with Custer even if they knew where he was,[42] Reno seems to have felt that an attempt should at least be made. Several of the Arikaras[43] and two of the Crows were still with the command, and it occurred to him that since they were well acquainted with the Indian method of fighting they might be able to get through the encircling lines of the Sioux and Cheyennes and establish contact with either Custer or General Terry. Convinced that it would be certain death for a soldier to make the attempt, he would not even ask for volunteers from the ranks.[44] According to the Major,

[39] Wagner, *Old Neutriment*, 170.

[40] *Official Transcript*, 1071.

[41] Wagner, *Old Neutriment*, 232.

[42] *Official Transcript*, 711.

[43] Marquis, *Rain-in-the-Face and Curly the Crow*, n.p., says there were sixteen of the Arikaras, but this number is too high. From other evidence it would seem that only four of the Arikaras and the two Crows remained with Reno.

[44] Reno, *Court*, 719, 736.

this effort was made not only for the welfare of the men in his command but also to let Custer know the location of the rest of the regiment.[45] Just how serious the attempt was we do not know. Both Lieutenant Godfrey and Captain McDougall said they had heard that scouts were sent out on the night of the twenty-fifth in an attempt to communicate with Custer but did not know that such was the case,[46] while Lieutenant Mathey failed to remember any attempt to communicate with Custer, although he understood that Reno had tried to get someone to go out with the scouts.[47]

In any event, the endeavor was apparently halfhearted—the scouts, being fired on, soon returned to the lines, declaring that the country was full of Sioux,[48] probably an accurate statement. Major Reno, who had no very high opinion of the scouts to begin with, now apparently lost faith in them entirely, although it is doubtful if anyone could have penetrated the hostile lines. There was some talk of Lieutenant Varnum's being sent out with a message to Custer, and he was apparently willing to make the effort but wanted Sergeant McDermott to accompany him. The latter, however, refused to volunteer but said he would go if ordered.[49]

The night was one of frequent alarms for that portion of the command which was awake, for they seem to have suffered to some extent from delusions and hallucinations. Among these was the belief that they could make out columns of men riding across the ridges presumably coming to the relief of the beleaguered battalions, a delusion so strong that on one occasion all the trumpeters were assembled and ordered to sound their instruments to let the rescuers know their location.[50] In Lieutenant Godfrey's opinion these aberrations were due to "the long shadows of the hills and the refracted light which gave a supernatural aspect to the surrounding country."[51] That it may not have been entirely a delusion is evidenced by the testimony of Lieutenant DeRudio, who spent the night hiding in the bushes along the Little Big Horn River. About

45 *Ibid.*, 718.
46 *Ibid.*, 633; *Official Transcript*, 986.
47 Reno, *Court*, 644; Libby, *Arikara Narrative*, 104–105.
48 Godfrey, *Montana*, 188.
49 Reno, *Court*, 521.
50 Gibbon, "Summer Expedition," 302.
51 Godfrey, *Century*, 375.

daybreak on the twenty-sixth, he heard a number of horsemen fording the stream. Thinking that the soldiers were coming back, since he was sure that by that time the forces under Custer and Reno had been reunited, the Lieutenant left his place of concealment and walked out on the riverbank to see what was happening. He saw several gray horses ridden by men whom he believed, in the uncertain light, to be soldiers. One man, dressed in buckskin, wearing a white hat, and riding a sorrel he took to be Captain Tom Custer. DeRudio called out, "Tom, send your horse across here." But he was partially concealed by the bushes, and although the horsemen stopped and looked all around, they could not see him. He called again, "Here I am, don't you see me?" This time the Indians saw him, yelled, and fired a volley in his direction, causing him to scramble madly for a place of safety.[52]

Much bravery and self-sacrifice were exhibited by the members of the command on that fatal hill, and there was also widespread malingering, skulking, and just plain fear. Major Reno's conduct, in particular, has been a subject of controversy ever since the battle. Lieutenant Godfrey, at the time, wrote that "it was evident that Reno carried no vigor or decision and his personal behavior gave us no confidence in him."[53] Peter Thompson of Troop C, who declared that he was personally aware of all the movements of Reno's command from the time his command retreated from the valley, characterized the Major's conduct as "cowardly in the extreme."[54] According to him, Reno set a poor example to his men, remaining in a protected position where there was no danger of being hit, cowering in his hole, and acting as though he "would have pulled the hole in after him" had that been possible.[55] Captain French said that from the evening of the twenty-fifth until about noon on the twenty-sixth, by which time the Indian attack had begun to weaken, Reno was hidden. French declared that he himself was walking about most of the time when the fighting was hardest and that he not only did not see the Major but could not find anyone who did;[56] and Lieu-

[52] *Official Transcript,* 459; Reno, *Court,* 461.

[53] Godfrey, "Diary," n.p.; Reno, *Court,* 627.

[54] Brown and Willard, *Black Hills Trails,* 207.

[55] *Ibid.*, 191–92.

[56] Reno, *Court*, 177–78. Captain French did not testify at the Reno Court of Inquiry. These statements were made in a telegram from Bismarck, D. T.

tenant Godfrey added that he could not recall having seen Reno during the night or having received any orders from him.[57]

However, other officers contradicted these reports. Lieutenant Edgerly testified that he saw the Major lying on a blanket and that when he admitted he had been sleeping, Reno exclaimed, "Great God, I don't see how you can sleep."[58] Dr. Porter saw Reno once during the night,[59] and Benteen, who asserted that he was with Reno during most of the night of the twenty-fifth, declared that Reno was cool and collected during that time.[60] Lieutenant Wallace, who admitted that he did not see the Major from early evening of the twenty-fifth until the next morning, testified that Reno spent the greater part of the twenty-sixth on that section of the line where it was expected that the heaviest Indian attack would come;[61] and Godfrey related how, on the morning of the twenty-sixth during some particularly heavy Indian fire, Reno ducked and said in a laughing manner that he would be damned if he wanted to be killed by an Indian, that he had been through too many fights for that.[62] Most of the other officers agreed that Reno's conduct of the defense was competent though not heroic.

In addition to being indicted as a poltroon and a coward, Reno has also been accused of being drunk on the night of the twenty-fifth, which might account for the fact that Captain French was unable to find him during that time. When the regiment left the mouth of the Rosebud, it had rations for fifteen days, eleven days' food being carried on the mules. With the pack train affording the best protection to be found on the hill, skulkers were constantly tempted to hide there and steal from the packs. Although Lieutenant Mathey declared that he had had no trouble with the packers, whom Benteen believed to be primarily responsible,[63] he admitted that anyone could have taken rations at almost any time and suspected that many had availed themselves of the opportunity.[64] In fact,

57 Reno, *Court*, 625.
58 *Ibid.*, 591.
59 *Ibid.*, 320.
60 *Ibid.*, 555.
61 *Official Transcript*, 1004, 1010.
62 *Ibid.*, 878.
63 Reno, *Court*, 617.
64 *Ibid.*, 640.

Captain McDougall later confessed that after nightfall he went to the train and secured rations and ammunition for his men.[65]

So much complaint arose about the stealing of rations and other articles from the packs that both Reno and Benteen were there frequently to drive out marauding soldiers and packers who suddenly professed great solicitude for the safety of the horses and mules.[66] A civilian packer by the name of Frett, who said his own saddlebags had been stolen when his horse was shot, related the following story. He went to the pack train between nine and ten o'clock on the evening of the twenty-fifth for the purpose of obtaining some hardtack and blankets.[67] There he met Major Reno, who asked him, "Are the horses tight?" Frett said that he did not understand and asked Reno what he meant. The Major replied, "Tight, God damn you, tight," and struck him in the face with his hand. Reno had a flask of whiskey in his hand, and as he struck Frett some of the liquor spilled over him. Then Reno leveled a carbine, and was threatening to shoot Frett, when another packer by the name of Churchill pulled his comrade back and led him away.[68] Churchill substantiated Frett's story in all important details, saying that Reno gave the appearance of being under the influence of liquor.[69] Frett insisted that the Major was very drunk.[70]

Reno's explanation of the incident was that he had gone to the train to look for skulkers and found the two men there. Annoyed at finding them there, he was angered still more by what he considered Frett's insolent attitude. Feeling that this was no place for moral suasion, he struck Frett and possibly warned him that if he found him there again he would shoot him.[71] He insisted that he was not drunk, although he did admit having a drink on the night of the twenty-fifth—he thought with Captain Weir, but he was not sure—but said that it had no effect upon him, for he was in such circumstances that a drink would not make any impression.[72] He further declared that he was perfectly sober on the afternoon

[65] *Official Transcript*, 969.
[66] *Ibid.*, 924–25; Reno, *Court*, 716.
[67] Reno, *Court*, 636.
[68] *Ibid.*, 636.
[69] *Ibid.*, 607.
[70] *Ibid.*, 637–38.
[71] *Ibid.*, 716.
[72] *Ibid.*, 715.

and evening of the twenty-fifth. Lieutenant Edgerly substantiated his statement, declaring that the Major was perfectly sober at nine o'clock and again at two o'clock and that there was no suspicion among the officers that he was otherwise. If there had been, Edgerly declared, Reno would not have been allowed to retain command.[73]

This whiskey—carried in a flask containing closer to a pint than a quart—had been secured from the trader at the mouth of the Rosebud and was believed to be the only whiskey in the command besides that which the doctor carried. Reno said that the flask was not emptied until the morning of the twenty-eighth when the command was on Custer Ridge. The sight and odor of the dead bodies had a most disagreeable effect on both officers and men, and Reno gave Captain French a drink at the latter's request in order to steady his nerves.[74] But Lieutenant Mathey contradicted him, saying that he saw Reno take a drink on the morning of the twenty-sixth and that at that time there was very little whiskey left, although he did not consider Reno drunk.[75] Godfrey said that Reno had a half-gallon keg of whiskey which he took with him in the field, but added that he did not believe that any other officer sampled its contents,[76] although on another occasion he expressed the opinion that there was not enough whiskey in the command to make a man drunk,[77] an opinion shared by Benteen, who admitted that he also had some whiskey.[78] Of the others who were present, Burkman insisted that Reno was drunk,[79] Slaper that he was not.[80] Captain McDougall testified that he saw nothing in Reno's conduct to indicate intoxication,[81] but Girard asserted that while McDougall was an honest and competent officer, he simply did not dare to tell the truth about the matter.[82] Many years later the Reverend Arthur Edwards claimed that Reno told him that his strange actions at the Little Big Horn were due to the fact that he was drunk.[83] The sub-

73 *Ibid.*, 616–17.
74 *Ibid.*, 714–15.
75 *Ibid.*, 644–45; *Official Transcript*, 950.
76 Godfrey, *Montana*, 210.
77 Brady, *Indian Fights and Fighters*, 376.
78 Reno, *Court*, 617.
79 Wagner, *Old Neutriment*, 49.
80 Brininstool, *A Trooper with Custer*, 42.
81 *Official Transcript*, 991; Holley, *Once Their Home*, 246.
82 Holley, *Once Their Home*, 266.
83 Brady, *Indian Fights and Fighters*, 399.

ject cannot be resolved; it is simply another of those minor controversies that complicate the study of history. The Reno Court of Inquiry was more of a whitewash than an attempt at a serious investigation of the responsibility for the disaster; Burkman's bias is well known and is such as to make him a most unreliable witness, while Girard, who was notoriously anti-Reno, and not without reason, assumes throughout that the Major was incompetent and unfit to handle his command.[84]

During the night of the twenty-fifth, whether in panic or from an honest belief that such action was necessary to save the command, Reno suggested to Benteen that all men able to ride should be mounted, that such property as could not be carried be destroyed, and that the regiment should then make a forced march over their back trail in an attempt to reach the base camp on the Powder River. Those of the wounded who were able to ride were to be taken along; the more seriously wounded were to be left to the tender mercies of the Sioux. Although this proposition was indignantly and decisively rejected by Benteen, the news of it spread among the officers,[85] and rumors that such a plan was being considered circulated among the wounded with results which may very easily be imagined.[86]

While the men of Reno's command slept fitfully or worked in preparation for the anticipated attack, the Indians celebrated in the valley.[87] The troopers could see the great fires and hear the rhythmic beating of the tom-toms and the high-pitched wailing of

[84] Reno had discharged Girard from his post at Fort Lincoln in the fall of 1874 because he thought Girard was stealing from the government. Custer did not agree, and Girard was reinstated. Reno, *Court*, 721.

[85] On January 18, 1929, Godfrey wrote: "After the firing had ceased on the night of the 25th he [Reno] proposed to abandon the position, destroy property that could not be transported, mount all men who could ride and retreat to the supply camp at the mouth of Powder River. When asked what he proposed to do with the wounded, he said they would have to be *abandoned* [italics in the original], and Benteen then told him he would not do it." "Letter of E. S. Godfrey to Superintendent C. H. Asbury, Crow Agency, Montana." The first printed mention of the incident was in an article by Lydey Sloanaker in the *Boston Post*, June 20, 1926. For a full discussion of the affair see Hunt and Hunt, *I Fought with Custer*, 203–207.

[86] Gibbon, "Hunting Sitting Bull," *American Catholic Quarterly Review*, Vol. II, No. 3 (October, 1877), 667.

[87] Rain-in-the-Face said there was a big feast and scalp dance that night. *Montana* (Helena) *Lookout*, December 24, 1910; Brady, *Indian Fights and Fighters*, 290. For a denial of this story see Marquis, *A Warrior Who Fought Custer*, 256–57; Vestal, *Sitting Bull*, 176.

the women as the Sioux and Cheyennes celebrated their victory and lamented their dead. The sound struck terror to the hearts of the soldiers, who knew only too well that their defeat and death would be the occasion for a similar celebration on the following night.[88]

Daybreak came between two and three o'clock and with it the renewed onslaught. The Indians surrounded the command and invested it closely, keeping the soldiers under a steady and heavy fire. Lieutenant Varnum said that the Indians were from one hundred to five hundred yards away, and at times there was just one line of smoke around the whole line. Sometimes the troops made no reply, and the hostiles, presuming that they had inflicted much damage, would make a rush, then the troopers would open up on them and the Indians would go back. These tactics lasted for a long time, and occasionally the Sioux would ride up on their ponies close to the line of troopers.[89] Troop H suffered the most because of their failure to build breastworks or dig rifle pits and also because their position was commanded in reverse by a much higher ridge to the north. As a result Benteen had great difficulty in keeping his men on the line.[90] His position was the weakest and yet constituted the key to the whole defense so that it had to be held at all costs.[91]

There were few, if any, places on that hilltop that were safe from the enemy's fire. Even the slightest movement there was attended by danger, since it was almost certain to draw a bullet from an unseen foe.[92] As a result, the troops kept fairly close to the trenches and rifle pits, although some resorted to other expedients for protection–Lieutenant Godfrey, for instance, covering himself entirely with his bedding.[93] All of the troopers had trouble with their carbines, and Captain French seems to have spent the most of his time in extracting shells which had jammed in the barrels. He would extract a spent cartridge with a knife, load the carbine, and pass it back before turning his attention to another one.[94]

Just how many Indians there were around Reno's position we

[88] Hunt and Hunt, *I Fought with Custer*, 102.

[89] *Official Transcript*, 230.

[90] Reno, *Court*, 554.

[91] Graham, "'Come on! Be quick! Bring packs!' The Story of Custer's Last Message . . . ," *Cavalry Journal*, Vol. XXXII (July, 1923), 71.

[92] Reno, *Court*, 337.

[93] *Official Transcript*, 1082.

[94] Brininstool, *A Trooper with Custer*, 37.

do not know, but the number was probably in the thousands. Captain Benteen stated later that there were "picnic parties" of Indians as large as a regiment standing around the river bottom looking on, and that fully two thousand hostiles were idling about, waiting for a place from which to shoot. He declared, probably with understandable exaggeration, that there was not a foot of unoccupied land anywhere and that there were Indians everywhere from twelve feet to twelve hundred yards away, and estimated that the command was surrounded by from eight to nine thousand hostiles.[95]

On the Indian side, Little Buck Elk observed that the Indians were as thick as bees, and in such great numbers that all of them could not participate.[96] With this statement Lieutenant Varnum concurred, saying that the entire force of the Indians was never engaged and the men on the hill could see great crowds of hostiles a long way off.[97] He put the number at not less than four thousand and declared quite frankly that he would not like to take the number of men in Reno's command and fight half the number of warriors who opposed them on the hill.[98] Major Reno contended that his command was fighting not only all of the Sioux nation but also "all of the desperadoes, renegades, half-breeds and squawmen between the Arkansas and Missouri rivers."[99] At the time he estimated the number of hostiles at twenty-five hundred, but later came to believe that his estimate was below the mark.[100] Like Varnum and Benteen, Reno did not think that there was enough room on the hill for all the Indians to engage the command simultaneously. He believed that a circle with a circumference of two or three miles and a radius of from one thousand to twelve hundred yards from his position was almost completely covered with Indians.[101] Captain Moylan was more moderate. Since the Indians had such perfect cover that only a few of them could be seen, he estimated from the firing that there were from nine hundred to a thousand Indians around the command.[102] But the scout George Herendeen, who

[95] Reno, *Court*, 553–54; *Official Transcript*, 689.

[96] Thomas M. Newson, *Thrilling Scenes among the Indians with Graphic Description of Custer's Last Fight with Sitting Bull*, 190.

[97] Reno, *Court*, 237.

[98] *Ibid.*, 279.

[99] Reno, *Report*, 33.

[100] Reno, *Court*, 707.

[101] *Ibid.*, 728.

was undoubtedly a much more competent judge than any of the officers, placed the number at between four and five hundred, although admitting that there were enough to hold every position.[103] Benteen probably summed it up best when he wrote in after years that he did not know "how many of the miscreants there were—but there were enough."[104]

Several explanations have been offered for the Indians' failure to take advantage of their great numerical superiority by charging from all sides and overwhelming the troops. It is possible that the chiefs could not control their young men, although it is hardly probable because the younger warriors were generally given to deeds of reckless daring and the influence of the chiefs was all in the direction of restraint. Gall later explained that the medicine men were responsible by declaring that their medicine was not right for an attack. According to him, their advice was accepted by most of the warriors, although Gall himself said that he believed a good gun was the strongest form of medicine,[105] and the Sioux had had plenty of evidence during the few days just passed that their medicine was exceptionally good. No Indian charges or mass attacks occurred, although several individuals did distinguish themselves by personal acts of bravery and daring. Perhaps the most likely explanation of the Indians' failure to attack is that the chiefs thought that a charge would cost the lives of too many warriors and knowing that there was no water on the hill, believed that sooner or later thirst would force the soldiers to attempt to get to the river, when they could be killed with little or no risk to the Indians.[106]

For Reno's men the problem of water did become serious. Although many of the troopers had had full canteens at the beginning of the siege, that amount could not last indefinitely, and men and animals alike soon began to suffer severely, for the sun was hot and the dust choking on that sagebrush-covered hill.[107] "Our throats were parched, the smoke stung our nostrils, it seemed as if our

102 *Ibid.*, 339.

103 *Official Transcript*, 335.

104 Benteen, *Account*, 11.

105 Barry, *Indian Notes on the Custer Battle*, 29.

106 Eastman, "Story of the Little Big Horn," *Chautauquan*, Vol. XXXI (July, 1900), 358.

107 Brininstool, "Custer Battle Water Party," *Hunter-Trader-Trapper*, Vol. LXV (August, 1932), 10.

tongues had swollen so we couldn't close our mouths, and the heat of the sun seemed fairly to cook the blood in our veins,"[108] was the way one of them described the situation. Pebbles held in the mouth gave the illusion of helping, and a few raw potatoes were distributed. The suffering of the wounded was especially great, but Major Reno is said to have refused to allow the use of some canned fruits and vegetables in the packs for even the most severely wounded.[109]

Just a few yards in front of Benteen's line a small ravine headed. This ravine, or coulee, led down to the river, which was about six hundred yards from the line. However, the ravine was occupied by Indians who, although in force all around the oval with the exception of the west side, seemed to be concentrating more and more in front of Troop H. Observing this maneuver and aware of the necessity of securing water, Captain Benteen ran ten or twelve soldiers and a few packers out of the comparative safety of the pack train and also ordered Troop M out of their rifle pits to reinforce his company. Then, turning the command of his portion of the line over to Lieutenant Gibson, the Captain led a charge of the combined troops and drove the Indians from their positions—there were only four of them in the ravine proper, but they were right on Benteen's line—the Indians scattering in surprise at this unexpected offensive movement after the troopers had killed several of them. This action, taken entirely on Benteen's own authority and without orders from Reno,[110] caused a great deal of dissatisfaction among the members of Troop M, who believed that the whole difficulty was the result of Benteen's failure to extend and fortify his position the night before. M's troopers had been somewhat slow in leaving the shelter of their pits, and it was claimed later that Benteen refused to endorse Captain French's recommendation of Sergeant Ryan for a Medal of Honor because of his slowness in reinforcing Troop H at Benteen's order.[111] In this charge not a trooper was lost, but as the soldiers returned to their positions Private Thomas Meadows was shot and killed.[112] Immediately an Indian ran forward and at-

108 "Account of Edwin Pickard," *Oregon Journal*, July 31–August 4, 1923; *Winners of the West*, June 24, 1926.

109 Marquis, *Two Days after the Custer Battle*, n.p.; Godfrey, "Diary," n.p.

110 *Army and Navy Journal*, July 15, 1876; Reno, *Court*, 554; *Official Transcript*, 674–75.

111 Brady, *Indian Fights and Fighters*, 404.

tempted to strike the trooper's body with his coupstick only to be shot dead for his efforts, his body falling so close to the cavalry lines that his fellow-hostiles were unable to recover it.[113]

To get to the ravine, the soldiers had to go a short distance across a comparatively open space under the long-range fire of the Sioux, but once in the ravine they were comparatively safe until they reached the foot, where it opened out to the river. Here they had about thirty feet to go across a space which was exposed to the fire of hostiles concealed in the bushes on the opposite bank.[114] All available cooking pots, camp kettles, canteens, and other vessels were collected, and many of the troopers volunteered to make the attempt to reach the river, an attempt that the officers realized would be so risky that they refused to order anyone to make it. After one group had made the trip without any efforts being made to protect them, Benteen detailed four of the best shots in the command to form a skirmish line to cover the approach of the water-carriers to the river.[115] These were Sergeant George H. Geiger, Blacksmith Henry Meckling, Saddler Otto Voit, and Private Charles Windolph. They kept up a constant fire into the bushes on the opposite side of the stream, but despite their best efforts one man was killed and six or seven wounded, one of the latter, Mike Madden of Troop K, suffering a double leg fracture below the knee so that amputation was necessary.[116] Private J. J. Tanner of Troop M was killed at the stream, and Wooden Leg, a Cheyenne warrior, later claimed the somewhat dubious distinction of having killed him.[117] There is some doubt about whether Tanner was one of the regular water-carriers and it may have been that he was killed before the skirmish line to protect them had been established.

Many unorganized efforts to reach the river were made by troopers grown reckless and desperate by the agony of an ever

112 This trooper has also been identified as Private Tanner, *Hardin Tribune*, June 22, 1923.

113 Adams, "Survivor's Story," 232. The dead Indian was apparently a Sioux warrior named Long Robe. Vestal, *Sitting Bull*, 178.

114 Reno, *Court*, 119; *Army and Navy Journal*, July 15, 1876.

115 Holley, *Once Their Home*, 238; *Winners of the West*, October, 1942; *Hardin Tribune*, June 27, 1923.

116 Brininstool, "Custer Battle Water Party," *Hunter-Trader-Trapper*, Vol. LXV (August, 1932), 12; Benteen, *Account*, 13; *Army and Navy Journal*, July 15, 1876; Brady, *Indian Fights and Fighters*, 405; *New York Herald*, August 8, 1876.

117 Marquis, *A Warrior Who Fought Custer*, 259–60.

increasing thirst. The Indians tell of one soldier who, stripped to his underwear, ran down the ravine to the river. In one hand he had a quart cup and in the other a canteen. He threw himself face down in the river, drinking, while at the same time filling the two vessels. Although he was there for two or three minutes and under the constant fire of the hostiles on the opposite bank, he was not hit. Most of the time the Indians could not see him because of the water splashing from the bullets. He then arose and ran back to the ravine, finally reaching the parapet at the top in safety.[118]

By noon most of the heavy firing against the troops had ceased, and Benteen, having succeeded in getting the spades, had his troopers throwing up breastworks and building redoubts,[119] while the other companies utilized the opportunity to fill all available receptacles with water. The officers, however, feared some kind of trick and vigilance was not relaxed. The Indians may have hoped by this ruse to lure the soldiers from their defensive position and, failing, returned to the attack; or they may have been aware of the advance of the Terry-Gibbon column and withdrawn from the attack on Reno when news that the Montana column had entered the valley reached them, only to renew it when their scouts reported that Gibbon had halted for the noon bivouac.[120]

McDougall's troop, which faced north, had opposite it a high ridge, from the summit of which the hostiles were able to fire into the rear of Benteen's position. So effective was this fire that about two o'clock in the afternoon Benteen went to either Reno or McDougall or both, made a complaint, and asked permission to drive those Indians away. After some discussion, permission was given and a charge was made, apparently by Troops B and D and a few other troopers. But the Indian fire was so heavy that after going about sixty yards the troops were compelled to retire to their original position. In this sortie not a man was lost.[121] Just who led

[118] Grinnell, *The Fighting Cheyennes*, 342. William D. Nugent of Troop A said later that he went to the river with some others and "fell into the water and drank until suffocation broke my hold on that river. . . . In lowering my head to continue I received a rap on the head accompanied by a deluge of water." *Winners of the West*, June 24, 1926.

[119] Reno, *Court*, 555; *Official Transcript*, 699.

[120] McClernand, "With Indian and Buffalo in Montana," *Cavalry Journal*, Vol. XXXVI (January and April, 1927), 47.

[121] Reno, *Court*, 630, 651; Holley, *Once Their Home*, 245.

the charge is a matter of dispute, Benteen saying that he gave the order and went with the troops but Reno did not,[122] while both Godfrey and Edgerly said that Reno accompanied the soldiers but Benteen did not.[123]

From then on, the Indian fire was lacking in both vigor and volume, and within an hour it had practically ceased altogether except for a few isolated sharpshooters who annoyed the command until late in the evening.[124] During the afternoon Reno made an attempt to send a dispatch to General Terry telling him where he was and how he got there, and expressing his belief that he could hold his position. He admitted that he had no knowledge of Custer's whereabouts. What other information the message conveyed is not known, but apparently there was a request for medical assistance, although it is not certain whether any mention was made of medical stores. The scouts were reluctant to go out, but finally the Crows said they would go if the Rees would. Four copies of the note were prepared and given to the scouts, who either failed to get through the hostile lines or else did not even try to do so, for they soon returned, and the messages were subsequently lost or destroyed.[125] In this incident there is circumstantial evidence to indicate that Reno had a fairly strong intimation that Custer had been destroyed, for since Custer was his commanding officer, the notes should have been sent to him unless Major Reno had good reason to believe that Custer was unable to come to his relief.

In the late afternoon officers and men noticed widespread excitement in the hostile camp—the Sioux were making another attempt to fire the grass in the valley. Although Reno's men could not understand the reason for this action, we know now that it was occasioned by the receipt of news of the close approach of the steamer and of the Montana column. In the late afternoon the camp was broken up;[126] by sunset or shortly before, the Indians were again on the move, with the Cheyennes, as usual, in front and the Uncpapas bringing up the rear. The hostiles are said to have marched in for-

122 *Official Transcript*, 677.

123 *Ibid.*, 794, 890.

124 Reno, *Court*, 118, 707.

125 *Official Transcript*, 230, 252, 1083, 1095.

126 Charles Eastman, "Story of the Little Big Horn," *Chautauquan*, Vol. XXXI (July, 1900), 358.

mation southward up the valley of the Greasy Grass towards the Big Horn Mountains.

Most of the officers who saw the column go declared that it was from two to three miles long, comprising from three to four thousand warriors and innumerable ponies. Benteen, who was qualified to judge, estimated the strength of the hostiles as being equal to that of a full cavalry division. "It [the Indian column] started about sunset and was in sight till darkness came. It was in a straight line about three miles long, and I think half a mile wide, as densely packed as animals could be. They had an advance guard and platoons formed, and were in as regular military order as a corps or division."[127] Lieutenant Edgerly, who also watched from the hilltop, stated that it was the densest body of animals he had ever seen, estimating at least twenty thousand ponies.[128] He declared that the unridden ponies being herded up the valley looked like "a great brown carpet being dragged over the ground,"[129] while Captain Moylan compared their appearance to that of a huge herd of buffalo.[130] Lieutenant DeRudio, who was hidden in the woods only about fifty or sixty yards from the moving village, said that the procession lasted for several hours, and that in some places the marchers were very thick while in others they were scattered. He also noted that there were many women and children in the assemblage.[131] And yet this mighty host was not the full power and glory of the Sioux and Northern Cheyennes, for at that moment large numbers of warriors, possibly more than a thousand, were deployed in front of Terry and Gibbon—ready, if necessary, to contest their advance up the valley—while a few others were still around Reno's position. It is beyond doubt that the hostile camp on the banks of the Little Big Horn River had been one of the greatest gatherings of Indians ever seen upon the plains.

Reno's men, who gave them three cheers,[132] the tribute of one

[127] Brininstool, *Captain Benteen's Story*, 23–24; *Official Transcript*, 697–98.

[128] Reno, *Court*, 593.

[129] Edgerly, *Narrative*, 12; *Official Transcript*, 780.

[130] *Official Transcript*, 309.

[131] Reno, *Court*, 456. In contrast to this usually accepted version of the departure of the Indian camp, Dr. Eastman says that the hostiles departed "in several smaller parties and in different directions," "Story of the Little Big Horn," *Chautauquan*, Vol. XXXI (July, 1900), 358.

[132] *Official Transcript*, 981; Holley, *Once Their Home*, 246.

group of fighting men to another, saw them leave with mingled emotions—joy and relief being mixed with the fear of a trap. They could not understand why the Indians should leave, and the fear of some kind of treachery was uppermost in every mind, so the troopers were held in readiness to occupy their pits again at a moment's notice. Reno, vacillating as always, seemed unable to decide on anything except to remain where he was. Occasionally the bullet of a sniper concealed on the hill disturbed the cogitations of the commander, but not an Indian was in sight, although a few ponies were observed grazing in the valley.[133]

At dusk the horses and mules were led down to the river and watered, then put out to graze.[134] The animals had suffered severely. Many of them had been killed, and of the survivors many were so badly wounded that they had to be destroyed. All were hungry and thirsty, for there had been no opportunity to water or graze them since the early afternoon of the twenty-fifth. The men were in bad straits, too. The cooks prepared as good a supper as was possible under the circumstances, and the troopers relaxed for the first time in almost two days. That night the camp was moved a short distance upstream so as better to command the approaches to the river, to get away from the accumulated filth of the old position, and to escape the stench arising from the bodies of the dead men and horses, which it was feared might affect the health of the survivors.[135] The upstream flank of the old position now became the downstream flank of the new, which was higher than the former one. It was extended toward the river and carefully fortified by the troopers, whose self-confidence was rapidly returning.[136] The bodies of the men who had lost their lives during the fighting on the hill were buried in a common grave, the location of which is still unknown. Captain McDougall, with the help of Privates Ryan and Moore of B troop, finally recovered the body of Lieutenant Hodgson from the ravine, and after sewing it in a blanket buried it on a little knoll midway between McDougall's position and the works on the hill.[137]

Sometime during the evening the scout "Billy" Jackson and

133 Reno, *Court*, 119.
134 *Army and Navy Journal*, July 15, 1876.
135 Reno, *Court*, 119.
136 *Army and Navy Journal*, July 15, 1876.
137 Reno, *Court*, 682; *Official Transcript*, 1030.

Girard, the interpreter, rejoined the command, and about three o'clock in the morning, Private Thomas O'Neil came in. All three had been separated from the command and left in the valley during Reno's "charge" and had spent the intervening time hiding in the timber not far from the Indian camp. In the thirty-odd hours that they had spent in the bottom, they had had many hair-raising adventures and close escapes.[138] O'Neil was followed within a few moments by Lieutenant DeRudio, from whom he had separated at the bottom of the bluffs only a short time before. As he came in, DeRudio stumbled over the body of an Indian lying close to the parapet. The officers were by no means convinced that the Sioux were not attempting some sort of a trick; consequently, the troopers slept on their arms, and a close watch was kept. But the night passed quietly and without alarm, and the dawn of the twenty-seventh found the small command refreshed, confident, and ready for whatever the day might bring.

[138] DeRudio, "My Personal Story," *Frontier and Midland*, Vol. XIV (January, 1934), 159.

CHAPTER XVIII

The Last Stand

THE QUESTION asked by Reno's officers and men, "What has happened to Custer?" is one that has been echoed ever since and which still waits for a reply. And it has never been answered, for, of the members of that command who followed the Lieutenant Colonel of the Seventh Cavalry after Trumpeter Martin was sent back, not one returned, so that of the details relating to the complete destruction of the five companies with Custer we know almost nothing.[1]

Not only do we have no adequate evidence upon which to base any definite conclusions, but the entire subject has been overlaid with such a mass of supposition and theory that it is often difficult, if not impossible, to separate the few facts that there are from the much greater mass of conjecture. Professional romanticists have spun high-flown theories about the battle—some of them without even bothering to examine the battlefield—and have pontificated at length on what must have been without even bothering to notice whether or not it was geographically possible. As a result there are almost as many theories about the battle as there are people to have theories. And as a general rule one is as good as another, for, while we may lack sufficient evidence to prove that such and such a thing happened, we also lack, except in a few cases, enough evidence to prove that something else did not happen. If we cannot prove one theory, neither can we disprove another.

All the information we have, and it is little enough, is based on the testimony of the four Crow scouts who escaped and who apparently witnessed at least a part of the battle even if they did not participate in it; on the accounts of the Indians in the hostile

[1] Colonel John Gibbon, "Hunting Sitting Bull," *American Catholic Quarterly Review,* Vol. II, No. 3 (October, 1899), 667.

camp, who alone know anything resembling a complete story of the disaster; and on the mute evidence of the "remains": the trails, tracks, position of the bodies, and the general topography of the land. Even then, whether the distribution of the bodies of the command reveals anything beyond the fact that the bodies were found at certain points is open to question.[2] Of the human testimony, much is contradictory and unreliable. The Crow scouts told different stories at different times, and not one of them was in a position to give more than a general description of the opening phases of the battle. The army officers and others who examined the field at various times afterwards in many cases tailored their testimony to suit their prejudices, and told stories on one occasion which were quite at variance with the accounts given at another time. And, as Flying Hawk observed, "The white men's accounts are guess work, based on circumstantial evidence for no white man knows. None left."[3]

The stories of the Indians who were in the hostile camp suffer from several drawbacks. Recorded at various times after the events which they described, their accounts are marked by forgetfulness, both real and assumed, and by pronounced rationalization. For the Indian had learned early and from bitter experience that it was much better for him to tell what he knew his auditors wanted to hear, and if he didn't know, to keep still. Moreover, many of the Indians were afraid of being punished should they admit taking part in the battle in which the Long Hair lost his life. Also, we must not forget that the Indian in battle is an individualist, and not being bound to any particular group, is free to come and go as he pleases. Indians did not have commanders and subcommanders as the white man does. Each tribe had its various warrior societies, each of whom had its chief and subchiefs. Some of them were great warriors, but in battle they could not give an order and have it obeyed. Their authority was thus much more apparent than real, for they could do nothing with even the members of their own society when their blood was up. Any influence which the chiefs had was based on their personal prowess, and they risked losing this prestige every

[2] Olin D. Whelan, "The Custer Battlefield," *Smalley's Magazine*, Vol. XXII, No. 1 (July, 1903), 8.

[3] *Chief Flying Hawk's Tales: a True Story of Custer's Last Fight, as Told by Chief Flying Hawk to M. I. McCreight*, 31 (hereinafter cited as *Flying Hawk's Tales*).

Minneconjou Ford.

Where it is believed Custer may have attempted to cross the Big Horn.

Courtesy National Archives

"Custer's Last Fight."

From a painting by W. R. Leigh.

"The Indians who fought mounted indulged in the usual wild charges, warriors intoxicated by excitement rushing in on individual soldiers and fighting hand-to-hand combats. Many of the hostiles rode around and around the little group of soldiers, 'swirling like water around a stone.' "

Courtesy Woolaroc Museum, Bartlesville, Oklahoma

time they failed in an undertaking. It was this lack of discipline which was responsible for the Indians' seldom being able to triumph over trained troops.[4] Although Gall is sometimes said to have "commanded" the combined tribes at the Battle of the Little Big Horn River, he really did nothing of the sort, and he himself discounted inferences to that effect.[5]

Given these limitations, it is obvious that the Indian sees a battle from the point of view of an individual, and is not much interested in group movements and activities.[6] He will relate the actions of one warrior or soldier in detail without being able to tell what the other members of the group were doing at that particular time. The Indian also suffers from the all too human tendency to magnify his own part in the proceedings, unless he deems it expedient for reasons of personal safety to deny participation altogether. And the Indian narratives, being somewhat vague and full of allusion rather than precise data,[7] fall a long way short of meeting the white historian's definition of reliability. One writer even went so far as to say: "The Sioux who did take part in it [the battle], on being questioned gave very conflicting accounts of it, and being such infernal liars drew on their imaginations to a large extent, so that no satisfaction was to be had from them."[8] Lieutenant Edgerly was also of the belief that the average Indian would rather lie than tell the truth, and would tell the questioner what he thought the latter wanted to hear.[9] As a result, there are many white students of the battle who will give little or no credence to the hostile accounts, forgetting that in this case the Indians alone know and also that in many ways their stories are no more unreliable than those of the white soldiers. In both cases a wholesome amount of skepticism is the essential ingredient of consideration.

Since there is no such thing as a coherent and unbiased account of the Custer disaster, and even the best evidence that we have is fragmentary and incomplete, as well as being contradictory,

4 Grinnell, *Two Great Scouts,* 243–44; Vestal, *New Sources of Indian History,* 201.

5 Marquis, *Sitting Bull and Gall the Warrior,* n.p.

6 Graham, " 'Come on! Be quick! Bring packs!' The Story of Custer's Last Message . . . ," *Cavalry Journal,* Vol. XXXII (July, 1923), 317.

7 Britt, *Great Indian Chiefs,* 197.

8 Harry Young, *Hard Knocks; a Life Story of the Vanishing West,* 207.

9 Reno, *Court,* 593; *Official Transcript,* 783.

the account that follows is based upon the few facts we have, plus some possibilities and a large amount of speculation.

The Indians were not at all surprised at the appearance of Custer's command. They had known for some time—perhaps for days—the approximate location of the regiment. In fact, Flat Iron, one of the Cheyenne chiefs, later went so far as to declare that plans for the entrapment of Custer and his men had been worked out at a council the night before the battle.[10] Sitting Bull also claimed that Custer had been under the constant surveillance of the Sioux scouts for several days and that the last three of the scouts watched the regiment until the morning of the battle.[11] The Indians had seen the troopers riding down the western slope of the divide and must have known that they were coming to attack the camp. They also knew of the division of the command which had sent Benteen to the left, but apparently did not know of the existence of the pack train and its escort until Captain McDougall joined the other troops on the bluff. The hostiles were probably aware of the second division of the command and had watched the troops until they came down into the valley. They saw Custer's five companies riding along the bluffs towards the lower end of the camp[12] and knew that they were not on dress parade or staging a performance for the amusement of the Indians, but were, on the contrary, seeking a ravine or coulee by which they could descend from the bluffs to the river, cross, and attack the village. They also knew just how far Custer would have to go before reaching the ravine which would take him down to the ford opposite the Minneconjou circle, and they could calculate almost to the moment just how long it would take him to reach it. Thus plans to meet the attack could be made with deliberation and without undue haste.

The sight of Custer's column had either distracted their attention from Reno—which was possibly what Custer intended—or else the hostiles expected a synchronized attack by the two detachments, for it was not until they saw the dust cloud raised by Reno's advance that they became aware of their danger. Thus, before Custer's

[10] *Helena Independent*, October 15, 1915.

[11] Britt, *Great Indian Chiefs*, 217; *New York Herald*, September 9, 1876.

[12] Barry, *Indian Notes on the Custer Battle*, 23; *Army and Navy Journal*, July 3, 1886.

attack could develop, the battalion under Major Reno provided a temporary diversion, the camp was thrown into confusion, and Gall led a small force of warriors, mostly Uncpapas and Blackfeet, upstream to meet the new danger. Preparations were also made for moving the camp in case that should become necessary. Widespread confusion resulted from the lodges being taken down and the pack horses loaded, while at the same time many of the noncombatants were fleeing to a place of safety and the warriors were riding off to battle. Seeing this confusion from the bluffs, and because of it probably deceived about the size and extent of the village, Custer likely concluded that the camp was beginning to break up and, throwing discretion aside, hastened his attack.[13] But comparatively few warriors went upstream to meet Reno, for despite the Major's belief that he had the entire fighting force of the Sioux and Cheyennes in front of him, such was not the case, and little attention was paid to his detachment until after the force under Custer had been disposed of. As far as the Indians were concerned, the fight against Reno was a holding action, pure and simple, and the main fighting force of the hostiles—probably at least three-fourths of the warriors—was held in readiness to meet the attack which they knew was coming from across the river.[14]

The crossing towards which Custer was riding is located near a butte which is almost surrounded by two deep ravines or coulees.[15] Some distance apart at the river, these ravines gradually approach each other as they get farther away from the stream so that they form a great arc which completely encloses the ridge upon which the last stand was made. But from where Custer was, he probably could not see into the ravine nearest him or down to the river bank because of the long row of high bluffs and the full leafage of the cottonwood trees.[16]

Soon after Custer's command was seen on the bluffs, Crow King led several hundred of his fellow-Sioux across the river and

13 Hughes, "Campaign against the Sioux," *Journal of the Military Service Institution of the United States,* Vol. XVIII (January, 1896), 33.

14 Reno, *Court*, 38, 44. *Cavalry Journal*, July, 1923, 133; Burdick, *Last Battle of the Sioux Nation*, 80. Stanley Vestal disagrees. He says that all the warriors who could get there (1,000) defended the camp against Reno but that not half of all the warriors (2,500) joined in the attack on Custer. *Sitting Bull*, 171.

15 McLaughlin, *My Friend, the Indian*, 171.

16 Marquis, *She Watched Custer's Last Battle*, n.p.

up the gully to the south.[17] The main body of the Ogallalas and Cheyennes moved down the stream until they reached a ford a short distance below the Cheyenne circle. These Ogallalas and Cheyennes were led by the fanatical Crazy Horse—the "Stonewall Jackson of the Sioux"—who apparently had started for Reno's fight and then turned about, rushing down the valley through the comparatively small numbers of warriors riding upstream, calling out, "Today is a good day to fight, today is a good day to die: cowards to the rear, brave hearts follow me."[18] He led his followers across the ford and up the long coulee that goes east from the crossing until it passes Battle Ridge, when it turns to the right and follows a southerly direction around to the east and southeast, there meeting the coulee up which Crow King had led his warriors. Another group under the leadership of Iron Star and Low Dog had followed Crazy Horse across the river, but turned southward as soon as they were on the left bank, thus getting between the ridge and the river.[19] Other smaller parties of warriors crossed the Little Big Horn and moved up various ravines and gullies towards the benchland above the river, resembling nothing so much as "ants rushing out of a hill."[20] The terrain was admirable for concealment, the broken country cut by many small gullies and dotted with tiny hummocks and ridges, its patches of sagebrush and grass, which was much taller then than now, affording perfect cover for the Indians but making the terrain little suited to the formations necessary for the successful maneuvering of cavalry.[21] That the ground was ideal for the Indian style of fighting is apparent from the following description: "Coulees intervened, trees and shrubbery masked the Indians retreat along the river bank below; tall, heavy sagebrush, since cropped by sheep, covered the battlefield at a height that would conceal a lurking savage."[22] All of which gives weight to the contention that the

[17] McLaughlin, *My Friend, the Indian*, 174; Burdick, *Last Battle of the Sioux Nation*, 109.

[18] Joseph Henry Taylor, "Bloody Knife and Gall," *North Dakota Historical Quarterly*, Vol. IV, No. 3 (1930), 165. See also McGillycuddy, *McGillycuddy, Agent*, 46, and Sandoz, *Crazy Horse*, 319. 328.

[19] Charles Eastman, "Story of the Little Big Horn," *Chautauquan*, Vol. XXXI (July, 1900), 357; Garland, "Custer's Last Fight as seen by Two Moon," *McClure's Magazine*, Vol. XI (September, 1898), 447.

[20] Grinnell, *The Fighting Cheyennes*, 338.

[21] *Ibid.*, 345; *Official Transcript*, 313.

[22] Edna L. Waldo, *Dakota*, 197.

topography of the country in the vicinity of the hostile village had more to do with Custer's defeat than any other factor.[23]

Many warriors were concealed behind the ridge along which the Custer command was riding, so that when the time came to spring the trap the soldiers would be attacked from all directions.[24] A number of the warriors, especially those at the heads of the two ravines, were very close to the soldiers, but the latter were apparently unaware of the close proximity of the enemy.[25] At the same time a goodly number of hostiles seem to have gathered on the west bank opposite the ford to resist any attempt of the soldiers to cross. Here, apparently, the Sioux had first decided to make their stand. This group was under the leadership of Black Moon,[26] who was killed in the fighting, and Gall,[27] before the latter went upstream to meet Reno.

While nearly all of the officers, from General Terry down, had taken it for granted that the Indians would begin to scatter as soon as they caught sight of the troops, and Reno had been committed to action in the belief that such scatteration was already taking place, Custer, from the bluffs, was able to see things that were not at all reassuring. It was only too obvious that the Indians were not running, but on the contrary were confident and eager for a fight. He also began to realize that there were more Indians than he or anyone else had expected.[28] At that, he could not see all of the village, for his view of the section farthest downstream was cut off by the bends in the river and the timber growing along the banks.[29] But he was probably not at all disheartened, and little disturbed. He had superb faith in his regiment and welcomed great odds against him, since the greater the odds, the greater the credit for successfully overcoming them. From the bluffs as the five troops rode down the stream, Custer had undoubtedly been able to see Reno's detach-

23 Burdick, *Last Battle of the Sioux Nation*, 40.

24 Graham, "'Come on! Be quick! Bring packs!' The Story of Custer's Last Message . . . ," *Cavalry Journal*, Vol. XXXII (July, 1923), 317; McLaughlin, *My Friend, the Indian*, 173; Marquis, *Two Days after the Custer Battle*, n.p.

25 Barry, *Indian Notes on the Custer Battle*, 13.

26 Grinnell, *The Fighting Cheyennes*, 278n.

27 Hyde, *Red Cloud's Folk*, 270n.

28 Albert Britt, "Custer's Last Fight," *Pacific Historical Review*, Vol. XIII, No. 1 (1944), 17.

29 *Official Transcript*, 194.

ment moving down the valley.[30] He knew that Reno was outnumbered[31] and that he was dismounting and deploying instead of charging the village as he had been specifically ordered. Whatever he may have thought of the Major's action, however, Custer certainly had no reason to believe that Reno's battalion was in any danger or that it would not hold its position long enough to create the diversion so necessary to the success of his plan of battle,[32] since a commander seldom, if ever, goes into battle counting on the failure of his lieutenant to carry out his positive and peremptory orders.[33]

Martin was probably sent back about three o'clock or shortly thereafter. At approximately the same time the Indian attack on Reno was beginning to develop. The five companies were then about two miles from where Custer's body was later found. Just as Martin left, the column, with Troop F in the lead, and followed in order by C, E, I, and L,[34] rode down a swale that leads into Medicine Tail Coulee and within a few minutes was under attack by a few Sioux warriors who were waving blankets and buffalo robes in an attempt to stampede the horses. We know little of the strength of this attacking party, but it certainly was not formidable and possibly did not consist of more than a dozen warriors. In fact Cheyenne accounts say that the troops "were following five Sioux" who were running towards the camp but "who gradually circled away and the soldiers did not follow"[35]—a circumstance that might indicate that it was a part of the old decoy and ambush trick which Custer should have recognized and possibly did.

Martin saw the attack, and although the hostiles fired at him and wounded his horse, they were certainly not in sufficient strength to cause him any concern, since he apparently did not relate the incident to Benteen. Also, the strength of the hostiles was not enough to prevent Boston Custer from joining the troops, for Martin

30 *Ibid.*, 241.

31 *Ibid.*, 416.

32 *Ibid.*, 313.

33 Godfrey, *Montana*, 183.

34 Lieutenant Roe in the *Army and Navy Journal*, March, 1882, expressed the opinion that the gray-horse troop was in the lead. There is some Indian testimony to the same effect.

35 Grinnell, *The Fighting Cheyennes*, 337–38. The Cheyennes also say that at first only ten Indians were present at the ford to oppose any charge that might be made. *Ibid.*, 345.

met him and in answer to a question about the location of "the General" pointed out the route that the five troops had taken. Furthermore, Boston Custer's body was later found a short distance from Custer Hill, between the hill and the river at the foot of the ridge that runs up from the stream.[36]

Whether Custer rode down Medicine Tail Coulee towards the river or whether he led his command across the ridges towards the long hogsback, where they were to perish to a man, is a subject still hotly disputed. Many of the Cheyennes who were in the fight later declared positively that Custer's troops were never in Medicine Tail Coulee at all and were not at any time near the ford. They insisted that the five companies approached the battlefield from a high ridge nearly two miles east of the river, and said that several of their warriors rode out to meet the soldiers and exchanged a few long-distance shots with them. When the column reached the lower ridge and it was found, so these Cheyennes say, that further progress was blocked by the large number of Indians in their front, the troops halted and deployed along the ridge.[37] This account is contradicted by one of their own fighting chiefs, Brave Wolf, who insisted that Custer's men came down close to the stream but did not succeed in crossing.[38]

Another theory assumes that Custer, on reaching Medicine Tail Coulee and realizing that his command was badly outnumbered, turned to the right and led his command away from the river rather than toward it. A short distance on, he turned to the left and again rode parallel with the stream. This maneuver was designed apparently to serve several purposes: to draw the Indians away from their village and to gain time in which to allow Benteen to come up and attack in the center while Reno and Custer were pushing their attacks from the ends. Then Custer turned again to the left and rode in the direction of the Little Big Horn and the ridge where he met his death.[39]

36 Albert J. Partoll, "After the Custer Battle," *Frontier and Midland*, Vol. XIX, No. 4 (1938–39), 278.

37 Marquis, *Sketch Story*, n.p.; Olin D. Whelan, "The Custer Battlefield," *Smalley's Magazine*, Vol. XXII, No. 1 (July, 1903), 8; Dixon, *The Vanishing Race*, 181.

38 Grinnell, *The Fighting Cheyennes*, 340.

39 This thesis, with which I am unable to agree, has been very ably developed by Dr. Charles Kuhlman in *Custer and the Gall Saga*. Usher L. Burdick, *Tragedy*

Against this theory there are several arguments. First, the country back from the river is badly cut up and not at all suitable for cavalry, and no competent cavalry commander would take his troops there except in case of dire necessity. Secondly, to ride away from a fight was not in keeping with the Custer character or disposition. It is almost inconceivable that he, believing, as he did, that attack and victory were practically synonymous terms, would execute such a maneuver. Furthermore, he was seeking a ford by which he could cross the river and attack the Indian village, and this was the first opportunity that presented itself.

Two of the Crow scouts who were with him say that Custer led his two battalions down the coulee toward the camp as though expecting to cross the river there,[40] and all of the contemporary evidence indicates that he did just that. The nature of the terrain that the soldiers had to cross was probably not too easy. Herendeen described the creek which flowed into the Little Big Horn near the ford as "being bad with cut banks and difficult to get across" unless a trail cut by buffalo could be found, since the best place to ford it was not far from its junction with the larger stream.[41] He also said, however, that it was nice traveling down the swale that led to the creek, and from there the detachment could have followed the stream bed down to the ford. Nevertheless, he stated that he was not certain of the route that Custer followed.[42]

Whether Custer ever reached the ford is one of the most perplexing of all the questions concerning this much-argued-about battle. It might be that if we had the answer, the solution of some of the other questions would be easier. Several Indian accounts insist that the troops never reached the river at all, but were driven back by the large number of Indians in the ravine.[43] Flying Hawk said that Custer started down the coulee but stopped because the Indians

---

in the Great Sioux Camp, has a map showing that Custer did not go to the river at all but kept on along the ridges back from the stream. According to this map, Crow King crossed the river below the Indian camp while Crazy Horse crossed still farther down and came up behind Custer Ridge, while Gall, after chasing Reno to the bluffs, crossed just below the place of Reno's second crossing, and followed the trail left by Custer's column.

40 Dixon, *The Vanishing Race*, 155.

41 Reno, *Court*, 404.

42 *Official Transcript*, 330–31, 351.

43 Burdick, *Last Battle of the Sioux Nation*, 175.

were all around him,[44] while Gall maintained that Custer did not reach the river, but stopped about half a mile up the ravine and was then gradually forced back and to his right, away from the direction from which the command had come.[45]

Earlier Indian reports contradict this account of so early a retreat and insist that there was some sharp fighting at the ford,[46] Brave Wolf, a Cheyenne, stating emphatically that they fought there for quite a long time and that the soldiers were right down close to the stream but none of them were on the side of the village. George Bird Grinnell, who got his information from the Cheyennes, was of the opinion that a part of Custer's command did come down nearly to the ford, and that two companies—one being the gray-horse troop—reached that point. Here they apparently halted and dismounted, an example which was followed by the companies behind them and which apparently constituted a tragic blunder, for the Indians state that had Custer kept on and crossed the river the Indians would have fled and a great victory would have followed.[47] Dr. Eastman, whose informants were Sioux, supports this conclusion by saying that Custer, having found that it was impossible to cross the river, dismounted his men. Some of them began to fire into the camp at fairly long range, while others examined the banks.[48] Other historians believe that Custer reached the ford only to find several hundred Indians in his front, threw out dismounted skirmishers, and when they were unable to advance, remounted and began to retreat;[49] Granville Stuart, who examined the field not long after the battle, speaks of the place where Custer tried to cross the river and was driven back.[50]

White-Man-Runs-Him, who, with the other Crow scouts, remained on the high point of the bluffs, said that he knew for sure that Custer went to the ford, for he saw him go that far. He added

44 *Flying Hawk's Tales*, 29.

45 D. J. Benham, "The Sioux Warrior's Revenge," *Canadian Magazine*, Vol. XLIII (1914), 462; Barry, *Indian Notes*, 13.

46 Hyde, *Red Cloud's Folk*, 269.

47 Grinnell, *The Fighting Cheyennes*, 337–40, 344–45.

48 Charles Eastman, "The Story of the Little Big Horn," *Chautauquan*, Vol. XXXI (July, 1900), 357.

49 King, "Custer's Last Battle," 365; Newson, *Thrilling Scenes among the Indians*, 187. See Curly's account in the *New York Herald*, July 26, 1876.

50 Stuart, *Forty Years on the Frontier*, II, 120.

that there were thousands of Sioux on the opposite bank who began moving as soon as Custer reached the river, some going downstream and others up the valley to where the Crows could see Reno, who in full retreat had already reached the foot of the bluffs.[51] Then Custer opened fire and soon afterwards started to retire to the ridge back from the river, whereupon Bouyer told the Crows to go back to the train while he started down to join Custer.[52]

Edwin Pickard, whose testimony is none too reliable, but who was a member of F troop and claims that he was serving as Captain Yates's orderly, said that at the ford the troops were formed in company front. Here he was ordered to return to the pack train, and as he started back, the leading company began to move across the river.[53] But Herendeen believed that there was no fighting at the ford, since it was so near the place where he was hiding in the timber that he could have heard the firing more plainly than he did.[54]

Of the army officers who examined the field after the battle, Lieutenant McClernand could recall no dissenting opinion concerning Custer's having descended from the bluffs by following the coulee which led to the river. He conceded that Custer might never have reached the stream, but insisted that the command did enter the coulee and turn towards the river, apparently with the intention of crossing.[55] Lieutenant Godfrey later went to the ford, saw evidence that shod horses had gone across, and concluded that Custer had at least attempted to cross there, although he admitted that the tracks might have been made after the battle when other units of the regiment examined the field.[56] Dr. Paulding was of the opinion that Custer had charged down the coulee over ground that was rough and uneven, and, failing to strike the ford exactly, was forced to move for some distance downstream and along a cut-bank under the heavy fire of hostiles on the opposite shore. At the ford

[51] *Account to Scott*, 3. But in another place the scouts say that they saw Reno fighting across the river and did not know that he had retreated back to the bluffs. *Ibid.*, 13.

[52] *Ibid.*, 8.

[53] *Oregon Journal*, July 31–August 4, 1923.

[54] *Official Transcript*, 350.

[55] Edward J. McClernand, "The Fight on Custer Hill," in Roe, *Custer's Last Battle*, 38; McClernand, "With Indian and Buffalo in Montana," *Cavalry Journal*, Vol. XXXVI (January and April, 1927), 51.

[56] *Official Transcript*, 350.

the troops were met by a large number of Indians on foot, and the soldiers succeeded in crossing only to be driven back,[57] a hypothesis that has Indian support, for several Sioux later declared that Custer succeeded in reaching the edge of the Indian village before being compelled to retire.[58] Paulding believed that on reaching the east bank, the troopers dismounted and put in two stiff volleys, then remounted and began to retreat toward Custer Ridge.[59]

That no bodies were later found near the ford, a fact for which Benteen said he never could account,[60] in itself means nothing since the highly mutilated bodies of several soldiers were later found on the site of the village, and those which were nearest to it would be the ones which the Indians would be most apt to drag into their camp. There were some indications on the field that bodies had been dragged off, but these may have been those of hostiles since the Indians of the Great Plains never allowed their dead to fall into the hands of the enemy if they were able to prevent it. The bodies of several soldiers were found on the site of the Indian village after the battle, but whether the men were alive or dead when taken there we do not know.

There is also the possibility that a detachment of the troops rode into the stream in order to test the practicability of a crossing place. In fact, Lieutenant Roe asserts that a sergeant of Troop E had ridden into the stream before the Indians opened fire,[61] while others say that it was the gray-horse troop that attempted to ford the river at the foot of the ravine.[62] But Lieutenant Roe believed that no portion of Custer's command succeeded in crossing the river.[63] Corporal Ryan, who was one of the first white men to visit the scene, states that several bodies were found at the ford,[64] while another contemporary observer declares that there were several bodies in the river although no evidence that any of the soldiers had reached the opposite bank.[65]

57 Paulding, *Letters*, 351.
58 Finerty, *Warpath and Bivouac*, 453.
59 Paulding, *Letters*, 351.
60 *Official Transcript*, 695.
61 Roe, *Custer's Last Battle*, 10.
62 *Winners of the West*, October 30, 1926.
63 Roe, *Custer's Last Battle*, 10.
64 *Hardin Tribune*, June 22, 1923. To this, however, Dr. Charles Kuhlman takes violent exception. See *Custer and the Gall Saga*.
65 Adams, "Survivor's Story," 229.

Since there were several hundred hostiles on the opposite bank, several troopers might have been killed at the river without any record of the fact being left, since their bodies would have fallen into the water and been swept away by the current. There is also some reason to believe that several dead troopers may have been scattered along the route between the river and the hill but that these bodies later sank into the ground and disappeared.[66] An account by Pretty Shield, a wife of the scout Goes Ahead, says that Custer, with Bouyer on one side and his flag on the other, rode into the water of the Little Big Horn River and was killed by a bullet fired by a Sioux named Big Nose who was on the opposite bank, Custer's body falling into the stream and being swept away. The death of their leader is said to have resulted in confusion and demoralization throughout the command, making their complete annihilation comparatively easy. While this story is almost generally disbelieved, it at least has the merit of opening up some interesting possibilities.[67]

At first both Major Reno and Captain Benteen went further than most of the others and declared their belief that Custer not only came to the ford but crossed the river and penetrated the village with at least a part of his command before being driven out. In a letter to his wife, written on Fourth of July, just nine days after the battle, Benteen said in part:

Whether the Indians allowed Custer's column to cross at all is a mooted question, but I am of the opinion that nearly,—if not all of the five companies got into the village—but were driven out immediately—flying in great disorder and crossing by two instead of the one ford by which they had entered, "E" company going by the left and "F I and L" by the same one they crossed. What became of "C" company no one

[66] *Billings Gazette*, August 13, 1933. Concerning the reliability of the markers see Marquis, *Custer Soldiers Not Buried*, n.p. Sergeant Butler's marker—the one closest to the river—was moved in 1949 to a point farther back from the stream.

[67] Linderman, *Red Mother*, 236–38, 247. Marquis expressed the belief that this story was in error, that it was some other soldier, not Custer, who was killed in the river. "Custer is said to have been killed in the river in the story of Goes Ahead to his wife, from her to the interpreter and from the interpreter to Linderman there must have been a mix-up in persons. It was some other soldier, not Custer, who was killed in the river." This is on a typed note attached to the frontispiece of the copy of *Red Mother* in the Big Horn County Branch Library, Crow Agency, Montana.

knows—they must have charged them below the village, gotten away—or been killed in the bluffs on the village side of the stream—as very few of "C" company horses are found.[68]

Benteen later changed his mind and declared that in his opinion Custer never even reached the ford,[69] although he apparently could not decide how close the column approached the river but estimated that it might have been within three furlongs,[70] which would agree pretty well with Gall's testimony.

Major Reno concluded that Companies C and I, and perhaps a part of E, had crossed at the village or attempted to cross at the charge, but that they had been met by such a staggering fire that they had been forced to fall back.[71] However, in a letter to General Rosser written shortly after the battle, Reno expressed the opinion that Custer had ridden to the attack in the belief that he would strike a retreating enemy, but when he arrived at the ford, expecting to ride through the village with ease, he rode instead into an ambuscade of at least two thousand warriors.[72]

In his telegram of June 27, sent via Fort Ellis, General Terry reported:

> Custer's trail from the point where Reno crossed the stream passed along and in the rear of the crest of bluffs on the right bank for nearly or quite three miles. Then *it comes down to the bank of the river, but at once diverges from it as if he had unsuccessfully attempted to cross* [italics mine]; then turned upon itself, almost completes a circle and ceases. It is marked by the remains of his officers and men and the bodies of his horses, some of them dotted along the path, others heaped in ravines and upon knolls, where halts appear to have been made.[73]

Sheridan also spoke of "the point where Custer reached the river,"[74] and a dispatch in the *New York Herald* reported that Custer had

68 Hunt and Hunt, *I Fought with Custer*, 189.
69 Brininstool, *The Custer Fight*, 23.
70 Reno, *Court*, 558–60.
71 Reno, *Report*, 479; Holley, *Once Their Home*, 240.
72 *New York Herald*, August 8, 1876; Reno, *Court*, 31.
73 *Report of the Secretary of War, 1876*, 463.
74 *Ibid.*, 464.

apparently tried to ford the stream but had been repulsed and driven back, his trail leading back to the bluffs and northward.[75]

Of the other officers who examined the field, Lieutenant Wallace thought that Custer's command had never reached the river, the Indians meeting them as they came down the coulee and not giving them time to make a stand. Both Lieutenant Edgerly and Godfrey stated that they had found the tracks of shod horses leading toward the ford and from this evidence concluded that Custer had gone to the river and attempted to cross, despite the fact that they saw no sign of fighting there. Lieutenant DeRudio also saw the marks of shod horses and thought that they might have been left when the column made a change of direction. The entire area was so badly cut up by the hooves of the horses and ponies that this evidence is of doubtful value, a fact which Lieutenant Godfrey conceded in his admission that the tracks might have been made by captured horses which the Indians were driving into the village.[76]

While Girard thought that the ford was a very poor one, the left bank being a foot or more above the water and miry and precipitous as well,[77] he was almost alone in his estimate, practically everyone else agreeing with Captain J. S. Payne that, while the ford was not good, it was a practicable one such as cavalry on the plains was accustomed to use,[78] and the officers of the regiment also agreed that there were plenty of places where the command could have crossed easily except for the opposition of the Indians.[79] The probability, although by no means certain, is that Custer's command, or at least a part of it, reached the Little Big Horn River at the ford; some of them may even have succeeded in crossing, but that they did so is even less certain. If so, they were driven back. In any event, Custer turned his five companies to the right and began to move downstream.

Several other possibilities deserve consideration. If Custer's command was attacked in the coulee a short distance before reaching

[75] *New York Herald*, July 8, 1876. This was in a dispatch from the mouth of the Big Horn River, via Chicago. The date suggests that it was written by some one with the expedition, possibly Major Brisbin, and was sent out on the *Far West*.

[76] Reno, *Court*, 127, 464, 593, 628, 631.

[77] *Ibid.*, 232j.

[78] *Official Transcript*, 352.

[79] Reno, *Court*, 73, 405, 440, 506, 523, 529, 575.

the ford, the attacking force may have been in such numbers as to force him to the right and down the river. Or it may have been that the sight of the belligerent and overeager Sioux riding to meet him convinced him that a major battle was in the making, and since a country broken into narrow and choppy ravines with steep sides is not a good place in which to maneuver cavalry, he simply ordered his command to the right in an attempt to secure more room to fight.[80] Cavalry is very weak on defensive. Almost entirely an offensive arm, it can defend itself best only by attacking; thus room in which to maneuver is essential. Or Custer may have moved downstream in search of an unprotected crossing since the ground on the other side of the stream was broad, level prairie, ideally suited for one of those dashing cavalry charges which had given both commander and regiment their reputation. Or he may have realized the inability of his small command to handle successfully the forces opposed to it and have sought a defensive position which could be held until Benteen could "come on." Furthermore, by moving downstream, he was drawing the great mass of Sioux after him and away from the ford, getting them between his own command and the expected reinforcements, thus making possible a later attack from both directions.

Or the sight of the dust cloud moving down river on the opposite bank may have made Custer aware of the movement of Crazy Horse and his followers. Obsessed as he was with the idea that the Indians would not stand and fight but would run away if given even half a chance, it was only reasonable for him to assume that the village, or at least a large part of it, was in flight. As a result, he would quite naturally have turned downstream in the hope of being able to intercept and destroy it. Or Custer may have sensed the movement for what it really was, an attempt to flank and destroy his command, and in order to forestall such a maneuver, turned at about a forty-five-degree angle to the right and begun the movement downstream.

The character of this movement is conjectural. It may be, as it has been argued, that the command was already in full retreat, since they did not go back over the trail by which they had advanced

[80] Albert Britt, "Custer's Last Fight," *Pacific Historical Review*, Vol. XIII, No. 1 (1944), 17.

to the attack.[81] There may have been disorder in the retirement, although we do not know. Adams was of the opinion that when the retreat from the ford began Custer's men had lost all semblance of organization,[82] and Benteen spoke of it as being "a regular buffalo hunt,"[83] a simile also used by the Crow scouts, who told Lieutenant Bradley that the Sioux were chasing Custer's men and killing them like buffalo.[84] While some later writers believe that there was no organized resistance,[85] the Indians say that Custer's men retired gradually, being forced back step by step[86] and that they "kept fighting and falling from their horses—fighting and falling—nearly all the way" up to where the monument now stands.[87] Recorder Lee later argued that Custer's capability and bravery entirely ruled out the possibility of a panic and a rout,[88] and Lieutenant Wallace, who had no love for Custer, believed that the arrangements of the bodies gave every evidence of a running fight.[89]

The command was apparently in two battalions, the one farthest back from the river consisting of Troops I and L in solid formation, probably in a column of fours. They seem to have gone up a ravine towards the high ridge or hogsback only a few yards from the ford, which runs obliquely from the river, rising very gradually until it terminates in a small knoll at a place where it joins the larger ridge, which is in reality only a continuation of the one along which the soldiers had moved down the river. The other three troops, F, C, and E—probably in that order and apparently in echelon formation—moved north along the western slope of the ridge, and were probably under attack from the very beginning.[90] This ridge rises steeply for about thirty feet, forming a bench, and then slopes back gradually. Not steep—a horse could be galloped over nearly any part of it—it was covered with sagebrush and grass.[91] It was possibly as the

[81] Reno, *Court*, 766–67.
[82] Adams, "Survivor's Story," 230.
[83] Hunt and Hunt, *I Fought with Custer*, 189.
[84] Dustin, *The Custer Tragedy*, 172.
[85] Dustin, *The Custer Tragedy*, 186.
[86] Charles Eastman, "Story of the Little Big Horn," *Chautauquan*, Vol. XXXI (July, 1900), 357. D. J. Benham, "The Sioux Warrior's Revenge," *Canadian Magazine*, Vol. XLIII (1914), 462.
[87] Grinnell, *The Fighting Cheyennes*, 340.
[88] Reno, *Court*, 797.
[89] *Official Transcript*, 707.
[90] Hyde, *Red Cloud's Folk*, 270–71.

change in direction was made and the soldiers began to move downstream that Sergeant Butler of Troop L was killed.

By this time Custer had probably decided that all he could do was to take up the strongest defensive position available and wait for assistance, so the troops headed for the north end of the ridge, a position which offered some possibilities, however slight, for a defensive stand. It was here that Reno's flight from the valley contributed most disastrously to Custer's defeat. Gall and a large number of his warriors had crossed the river below the place of Reno's second crossing and had made their way up the bluffs intending to cut off the fleeing troopers before they reached the top. But Gall was hailed by one of his warriors, Iron Cedar, and told of Custer's increasingly close approach to the village. So, almost immediately, most of the warriors were called from the attack on Reno's demoralized detachment, and began to hurry downstream toward the new battle which was rapidly shaping up, riding north along the ridge and following Custer's trail.[92] Custer was now threatened with an attack from the south, and to meet the new danger, he ordered Lieutenant Calhoun's troop dismounted and deployed as skirmishers, their task being to hold the oncoming enemy in check until the rest of the command could get into position. A short distance farther on, Troop I was also dismounted, not so much because Troop L had failed to stem the savage onslaught as to cover the retirement of Calhoun's men when that should become necessary or feasible. That there was an appreciable interval of time between the order to Calhoun and the similar order to Keogh is apparent from the fact that the dead horses of the two companies were found some distance apart. Had the orders to the two troops been given at approximately the same time, the horses would have been much closer together.[93]

In the meantime the three troops closest to the river were being forced by Indian pressure up the side of the ridge. Troop F being in advance, probably suffered the fewest casualties, but Troop E was being slowly but surely cut to pieces by the Indians who had

[91] Stuart, *Forty Years on the Frontier*, II, 121.

[92] Barry, *Indian Notes*, 13. Gall said that as soon as Reno was beaten and driven across the river, the whole force turned on Custer and destroyed him. *Army and Navy Journal*, July 3, 1886.

[93] McClernand, "With Indian and Buffalo in Montana," *Cavalry Journal*, Vol. XXXVI (January and April, 1927), 51.

previously hidden in the ravines. Lieutenant Smith may have dismounted some of his men and deployed them as skirmishers, and some of them may even have killed their horses and fought behind them in order to cover the retreat of the remainder of the battalion. Many of the men of this company were later found in and near a ravine—about half of them in the ravine and the rest on a line outside. While there is the distinct possibility that they had gone into the gully in an attempt to hide or to escape, it is more probable that they tried to make a stand; and since most of them had been shot in the side of the head, it is altogether likely that they had been attacked from both sides almost simultaneously.[94] By this time the command was surrounded on at least three sides, if not completely encircled, and there were probably so many Indians that there was little unoccupied ground in the vicinity. Some Indians probably opposed the advance of the column so that Custer found himself fighting an offensive action at the front and a defensive action in the rear.

Just how long the action lasted is another of those matters of conjecture. Two years after the battle some of the Sioux participants insisted that the contest was quite even, lasting for about two hours before a massed charge turned the left of the line and the command was rolled up.[95] Other evidence suggests that the fight did not last anywhere near that long, and some evidence seems to show that a number of Calhoun's men did not even have time to dismount before being overwhelmed by the red avalanche.[96] In any event it is apparent that the main attack came from the south and was delivered by the hostiles who had just left Reno, and that Calhoun's troop was the first to be disposed of, the initial step being to take care of the led horses, which were stampeded by the old familiar device of waving blankets and buffalo robes as well as by the whooping and firing of the hostiles.[97] Then Gall gave his war whoop and a charge was made, the massed Sioux rolling over the little detachment with the troopers offering determined resistance and holding their positions in the regular order of skirmishers until the last. All of the evidence

[94] *Official Transcript*, 469, 938.

[95] Miles, *Personal Recollections*, 286–89.

[96] Albert Britt, "Custer's Last Fight," *Pacific Historical Review*, Vol. XIII, No. 1 (1944), 17.

[97] *Army and Navy Journal*, July 3, 1886.

indicates that they did not break, but died to the last man in the positions where they had been placed.[98] General Terry's men found them there two days later, "showing that they had hardly stirred from the spot where they reined their horses in and turned to meet the oncoming wave."[99] Calhoun's body was found in the rear of the first platoon, while Crittenden's lay twenty or thirty feet away.[100] One cannot help but wonder, with the twilight of eternity closing down over his command, if Calhoun recalled a letter he had written five years before, thanking Custer for his assistance in securing a first lieutenant's commission in the Seventh Cavalry for him. On that occasion Calhoun had written: "I shall do my best to prove my gratitude. If the time comes you shall not find me wanting."[101]

Troop I's turn was next. Their horse-holders may have been killed at the same time as those of Troop L, but there was apparently at least a short interval between the destruction of the two companies. The bodies of Keogh's men were found in a slight depression or "sag" on the north side of the slope about halfway between Calhoun's and Custer's positions. The bodies were scattered along, beginning only twenty or thirty yards from the place where Calhoun's body was found, and they occupied much of the ground well on toward Custer.[102] From this it would seem that the troopers of I company may have been closer to the position on Custer Hill when killed than when they first dismounted, and that they were in the process of carrying out an order from Custer to withdraw and form a junction with the rest of the command.[103] Lieutenant Edgerly thought that the arrangement of the bodies gave evidence of an irregular line and ventured the opinion that they had formed a line on the left of Calhoun's company;[104] Lieutenant Wallace disagreed,

98 Reno, *Court,* 124, 364, 458; Graham, "'Come on! Be quick! Bring packs!' The Story of Custer's Last Message . . . ," *Cavalry Journal,* Vol. XXXII (July, 1923), 317; D. J. Benham, "The Sioux Warrior's Revenge," *Canadian Magazine,* Vol. XLIII (1914), 462.

99 Albert Britt, "Custer's Last Fight," *Pacific Historical Review,* Vol. XIII, No. 1 (1944), 17.

100 *Official Transcript,* 788.

101 Merington, *The Custer Story,* 236–37.

102 Reno, *Court,* 125; Stuart, *Forty Years on the Frontier,* II, 120.

103 McClernand, "The Fight on Custer Hill," in Roe, *Custer's Last Battle,* 38; McClernand, "With Indian and Buffalo in Montana," *Cavalry Journal,* Vol. XXXVI (January and April, 1927), 52.

104 Reno, *Court,* 593; *Official Transcript,* 788.

concluding that the men had been killed while running in file.[105] Evidently Captain Keogh had been wounded—his leg had been broken—and the company sergeants had gathered around him and been killed with him.[106] A later visitor to the field, drawing his conclusions from the fifteen markers placed around the spot where Captain Keogh fell, expressed the belief that these men had been shot down in one volley of fire delivered from a cluster of wild cherry bushes a few yards away,[107] and Keogh's may have been the company mentioned by Gall as having been shot down in one bunch.[108]

The surviving troops, principally members of C and F with a few from E, had by this time been forced by hostile pressure to the summit of the ridge. They had almost reached its northernmost point (where the monument now stands) where the ground slopes sharply to the northwest, when any hopes of safety or rescue that they may have entertained were banished from the minds of the doomed troopers by the sight of the warriors under Crazy Horse coming over the point of that same ridge. Gall, emboldened by his success against Calhoun and Keogh, was pressing from the left, Crow King, Low Dog, and others who held the flank towards the river pushed relentlessly in, and Crazy Horse enveloped the right. All of the survivors fell back in the direction of the crest of the ridge in an attempt to unite with the group around Custer, where the last stand was to be made.

The accepted theory has been that, owing to the suddenness and ferocity of the Indian attack, Custer did not have the opportunity to form a regular line of battle as each unit of the command found itself with a separate fight on its hands. Captain Benteen, who was one of the first to make a detailed examination of the field, was impressed by this lack of battle lines, which he described by saying that one could scatter a handful of corn on the floor and get as close a resemblance to lines as were to be found. He also believed that the troops had been as much the victims of panic as of the Indians, and was positive in his declaration that the only evidence of a stand was

105 Reno, *Court*, 125.

106 *Official Transcript*, 788.

107 Frank M. Canton, *Frontier Trails*, edited by Edward Everett Dale, 31.

108 *Army and Navy Journal*, July 3, 1886; D. J. Benham, "The Sioux Warrior's Revenge," *Canadian Magazine*, Vol. XLIII (1914), 462.

to be found on Custer Hill.[109] With his opinion Lieutenant Hare agreed, stating that there was no evidence of the command's having made a stand;[110] and the fact that the bodies were found scattered over some ten acres of ground—here, there, and everywhere—has indicated to some observers that the officers had completely lost control of their men and that there was little or no organized resistance.[111]

With this theory there has been considerable disagreement. Calhoun's men were admittedly on a skirmish line, and Edgerly thought that Keogh's men were.[112] Edgerly also pointed out that in a desperate struggle, such as the fight on Custer Hill, it could not be expected that the bodies of the slain would be found lying in perfect order.[113] Some of Lieutenant Smith's men lay dead in skirmish order and at about the regular skirmish intervals,[114] and some military writers have since concluded that there was a line of dismounted skirmishers along the ridge with F on the right flank, E on the left, and C in the center.[115] Indian testimony inclines to this latter point of view. Gall spoke of the soldiers as fighting in line along the ridge,[116] and of Calhoun's and Keogh's men as being beaten back step by step until all were killed. He said that they never broke but were shot down in line where they stood.[117] Flying Hawk claimed that Custer's men made at least four separate stands,[118] while other hostile accounts put the number at five, and Red Horse said that on one occasion the Indians charged right in until they scattered the group, fighting among the soldiers hand to hand.[119] And an early visitor to the field wrote: "In the ravines lying as they had fought, line behind line showing where defensive positions had been successively taken up and held until none was left to fight, there, huddled

[109] Reno, *Court*, 558–59; Godfrey, *Montana*, 199.

[110] Reno, *Court*, 441.

[111] Canton, *Frontier Trails*, edited by Edward Everett Dale, 30.

[112] *Official Transcript*, 790–91.

[113] *Ibid.*, 790–91.

[114] *Ibid.*, 407; Reno, *Court*, 441.

[115] James P. Murphy, "The Campaign of the Little Big Horn," *Infantry Journal*, Vol. XXXIV (June, 1929), 636.

[116] D. J. Benham, "Sioux Warrior's Revenge," *Canadian Magazine*, Vol. XLIII (1914), 462.

[117] *Army and Navy Journal*, July 3, 1886.

[118] *Flying Hawk's Tales*, 28–29.

[119] *Colorado Transcript*, March 21, 1877. (This is a reprint from the *Chicago Times*, March 15, 1877).

in a narrow compass, horses and men were piled promiscuously. . . . The companies had successively thrown themselves across the path of the oncoming enemy and been annihilated."[120]

Although there was admittedly no evidence of company organization on Custer's position,[121] Lieutenant McClernand expressed the opinion that the line Custer established on the ridge showed greater care in deploying and placing the men than was shown on any other part of the field, not excluding Reno's several positions.[122] He declared that no thoughtful and unprejudiced person could have examined that position without being convinced that Custer was thinking clearly and courageously to the very last.[123] Again, in this case as in so many others, surmise has to take the place of fact and the truth never will be known.

Just why Custer had moved his command downstream we do not know, but it was undoubtedly for perfectly valid reasons. He made his last stand where he did, in a position that was not too favorable for defense, for reasons which are equally unknown, although the probability is that the Indians, having surrounded the command, forced him to halt and fight right where he was. But there is a theory that his horse was shot from under him and that this circumstance was responsible for his decision to make his stand where he did. Lieutenant McClernand, who went over the field only a few days after the battle, said that a dead horse some 150 feet, more or less, from the knoll, was pointed out to him as the animal ridden by Custer. The head was toward the knoll, and from the position of the legs McClernand judged that the animal was traveling rapidly when it was shot down.[124] In opposition to this theory is the positive statement that Custer's mare, "Vic," was not found on the battlefield and the tradition that she was in the possession of an Indian in the hostile camp after the battle.[125]

[120] *New York Herald*, July 8, 1876; Burdick, *Tales from Buffalo Land*, 56. See also Granville Stuart, *Forty Years on the Frontier*, II, 120.

[121] *Official Transcript*, 788.

[122] McClernand, "With Indian and Buffalo in Montana," *Cavalry Journal*, Vol. XXXVI (January and April, 1927), 52.

[123] *Ibid.*, 54.

[124] *Ibid.*, 54; William W. Edwards, "The Battle of the Little Big Horn," *Outdoor Life*, Vol. LXXI (February, 1933), 57.

[125] Albert J. Partoll, "After the Custer Battle," *Frontier and Midland*, Vol. XIX, No. 4 (1938–39), 277; Vestal, *Sitting Bull*, 175. See also Elmo Scott Watson, "What Was the Fate of Custer's Horse?" *Westerners Brand Book* (June, 1951), 30.

While the loss of his horse could have been one factor in causing Custer to make his stand, it is probable that by this time the pressure of the Indians had become too great to permit any further delay in the establishment of a defensive line. The flanking move by the hostiles under Crazy Horse making any further advance towards the top of the ridge impossible, the remainder of the command halted, and the troopers prepared to sell their lives as dearly as possible, for Custer and the men with him must have realized that the command was doomed. Just how many there were in the final group that gathered near the summit of the dusty ridge just above the Little Big Horn we shall never know, but the number was probably about seventy-five, although there may have been as few as forty or as many as one hundred troopers and civilians. Some of the men apparently turned their horses loose, with or without orders, while others shot theirs and arranged the bodies in a circle about thirty feet in diameter, a circle which seems to have been rather carefully formed.[126]

The dust and smoke made the afternoon almost as dark as evening, so dark as to thoroughly obscure the view of the fight from the village across the river, and the soldiers fighting valiantly to the end with "a desperation known only to the God of Battles"[127] could do but little damage against an unseen foe.[128] The visibility was so limited that friend could hardly be distinguished from foe, and the Indians in their excitement knocked one another from their horses and even killed their own warriors, as is attested by the fact that several of the hostiles were killed by arrows.[129]

A good many of the Indians fought dismounted, creeping up on foot under cover of the favorable terrain, concealing themselves in the brush and tall grass, and shooting the troopers one by one.[130] Many of the Sioux and Cheyennes were using bows and arrows, both from necessity and from choice. While a number of them had the latest improved guns, the majority had very inferior guns or nothing

126 Miles, *Personal Recollections*, 288; *Official Transcript*, 695, 1017–18; *Army and Navy Journal*, July 15, 1876.

127 Holley, *Once Their Home*, 232.

128 Barry, *Indian Notes*, 13.

129 South Dakota Historical *Collections*, VI, 227. An article in the Clipping File, Billings Public Library, quotes Little Knife as saying that the soldiers were wild and inaccurate in their firing.

130 Reno, *Court*, 560; Adams, "Survivor's Story," 230.

more than the usual bow and arrows and a war club.[131] But the bow was preferable to the gun in many respects: there was no smoke to indicate the firer's position, one did not have to expose himself in order to shoot, and the arrows had a much better trajectory, often striking in the back men and horses who were otherwise protected.[132]

The Indians who fought mounted indulged in the usual wild charges, warriors intoxicated by excitement rushing in on individual soldiers and fighting hand-to-hand combats. Many of the hostiles rode around and around the little group of soldiers, "swirling like water around a stone."[133] But both Sioux and Cheyennes insist that most of the soldiers were not killed by riding over them, but rather by shooting them from behind the hills, since every ravine and every bit of brush hid one or more Indians who kept up an almost incessant fire.[134] Many of the soldiers were later found to have been shot in the back. From their positions, it appeared that it was very easy for the Indians to crawl up and kill them while they were resisting in front.[135] It was probably only after all the troops in the main body had fallen and only stragglers were left that the Indians charged, literally sweeping everything before them and killing the few survivors with clubs and tomahawks,[136] although Flat Iron later said that most of the soldiers were killed by clubs rather than by shots.[137] "The soldiers toward the river backed away and after that the fight did not last long enough to light a pipe."[138] Few shots were fired by either side in these last moments, war clubs and clubbed carbines being the usual weapons, and in a few short moments all was over on the hill.[139]

Just how long the battle lasted we do not know, the range of conjecture being extremely wide. Lieutenant Hare believed that it did not take the Indians more than forty-five minutes to wipe out

131 Charles Eastman, "Story of the Little Big Horn," *Chautauquan*, Vol. XXXI (July, 1900), 355.

132 Marquis, *She Watched Custer's Last Battle*, n.p.

133 Garland, "Custer's Last Fight as Seen by Two Moon," *McClure's Magazine*, Vol. XI (September, 1898), 447.

134 Grinnell, *The Fighting Cheyennes*, 339.

135 Reno, *Court*, 441.

136 D. J. Benham, "Sioux Warrior's Revenge," *Canadian Magazine*, Vol. XLIII (1914), 463.

137 *Helena Independent*, October 15, 1915.

138 Grinnell, *The Fighting Cheyennes*, 341.

139 Burdick, *Last Battle of the Sioux Nation*, 80.

Custer's command[140] and thought that the initial attack on Custer occurred about the time Reno left the timber or a little before.[141] Lieutenant Wallace agreed with him, being of the opinion that Custer was heavily engaged by the time Reno reached the bluffs,[142] and Lieutenant Varnum believed that Custer was in action before Benteen joined Reno.[143] Other members of Reno's command had other ideas. Edgerly thought that the fight did not last more than fifteen or twenty minutes, or half an hour at the most,[144] while "Mike" Sheridan (who was not there) put it at not more than an hour.[145] Benteen, who seems to have had a very positive opinion about almost everything else, said that the fight might have lasted fifteen minutes, half an hour, or, on a guess, about an hour.[146] Herendeen, who heard volleys and scattering shots from the direction of the battlefield, stated that the fight began after he had been in the timber about thirty minutes and lasted for an hour,[147] while Girard, who also heard the firing from the woods, estimated the duration of the fight as twice as long, and declared that the single scattering shots lasted until dark.[148] Trooper O'Neil said that it was about five o'clock when they heard the last shots from Custer's position,[149] while the fourth member of the Seventh Cavalry who was in the timber declared that the firing started about two minutes after Reno reached the top of the bluffs. He described it as an immense volley fire which came from the other side of the river, downstream and somewhat north of the hostile village and recalled that the sound grew more distant and indistinct, but did not go very far away. He estimated that it lasted about an hour and then died off in small scattering shots, soon ceasing altogether. He believed that the firing was about four or five miles from his hiding place and in the direction of the Custer battlefield.[150]

Of the hostiles, Flying Hawk said that the fight was over in

140 Reno, *Court*, 441.
141 *Ibid.*, 436.
142 *Ibid.*, 78, 797.
143 Graham, *Story of the Little Big Horn*, 135.
144 Reno, *Court*, 596.
145 *Ibid.*, 676–77.
146 *Ibid.*, 566–67.
147 *Ibid.*, 395.
148 *Ibid.*, 164–67.
149 Brininstool, *A Trooper with Custer*, 69.
150 Reno, *Court*, 455, 463, 483.

an hour after the Indians got the troops surrounded,[151] although Gall declared that the fight lasted only half an hour, or perhaps a very little longer.[152] An old Cheyenne warrior told Linderman that the sun traveled only "the width of a lodge-pole" (perhaps twenty minutes) while the fight lasted,[153] and other Cheyennes have estimated that the actual wiping out of the Custer command did not take more than fifteen minutes.[154] One warrior reported that he saw a great cloud of dust come over the hill as Crazy Horse and his braves charged over the ridge from the north, and that as soon as the dust settled the white soldiers were all gone.[155] There can be little doubt that the final stand of Custer's men was of brief duration, and the discrepancies in the Indian stories are probably due to differences in estimating just when the fight started. The scattering shots heard by the soldiers in the valley probably came from the Indian's habit of putting a bullet into the body of a fallen enemy as they rode by, and since the Sioux and Cheyennes did a very thorough job of looting after the battle, this desultory firing may well have continued until dark.

Regardless of the lapse of time, there is no doubt that the final extinction of the Custer command was hastened by another factor which is often overlooked—the carbines became overheated and began to jam, the extractors cutting through the rims of the shells as though they were putty and leaving the exploded cartridges wedged in the chambers and rendering the weapons useless until the shells could be removed with a knife. For this, two factors were responsible: the carbines were defective and had a reputation for fouling after the second or third firing,[156] a condition that was apparent to the Indians, for both Gall and Rain-in-the-Face related afterwards that the soldiers got shells stuck in the guns and had to throw them away.[157] In addition, it has been claimed that the cart-

[151] *Flying Hawk's Tales*, 29.

[152] Barry, *Indian Notes*, 21.

[153] Linderman, *American*, 179.

[154] This information was given to me by Mr. James Gatchell of Buffalo, Wyoming, who had it from several Cheyenne warriors who were in the fight.

[155] Burdick, *Last Battle of the Sioux Nation*, 83.

[156] D. J. Benham, "Sioux Warrior's Revenge," *Canadian Magazine*, Vol. XLIII (1914), 462.

[157] *Army and Navy Journal*, July 3, 1876; Brady, *Indian Fights and Fighters*, 285.

ridges, being made with copper casings, were too soft, and as they were generally carried in leather belts with leather loops, the chemical reaction of the leather and the copper caused verdigris to develop, which made the shells difficult to extract.[158] Although the hostiles did a rather thorough job of looting after the battle, the men of Gibbon's command found a number of carbines with defective shell extractors as well as a few that had been loaded but not fired.[159] Regardless of other, controversial, points, one thing is certain: exhaustion of the ammunition supply was not a factor in the Custer defeat, for several nearly full cartridge belts were captured by the Indians, and no completely empty ones were found on the field.[160]

Most of the Indians bear witness to the courage of Custer's men. Gall speaks of the extreme bravery of the soldiers, who were right down on their knees loading and firing until the last man was killed; and Sitting Bull later declared: "I tell no lies about dead men. Those men who came with the 'Long Hair' were as good men as ever fought."[161] Brave Wolf concurred in saying: "It was hard fighting; very hard all the time. I have been in many hard fights, but I never saw such brave men."[162] According to the Sioux, none of the soldiers offered to surrender, and they do not mention any suicides,[163] but the Cheyennes tell of several troopers committing suicide, thus following the code of the frontiersmen—in fighting Indians, save the last bullet for yourself.[164]

Two Moon, the Cheyenne chief, told of one member of the detachment, apparently an officer, riding a sorrel horse with a white face and white forelegs, who led a group of about forty men in a sortie towards the river in an apparent attempt to escape. He and

158 Mills, *My Story*, 334. On the contrary, the James Gatchell Collection at Buffalo, Wyoming, includes a cartridge belt purportedly taken from the body of a trooper by Weasel Bear, a Cheyenne who was fifteen years of age at the time of the battle. This is a web belt and not leather at all.

159 James P. Murphy, "The Campaign of the Little Big Horn," *Infantry Journal*, Vol. XXXIV (June, 1929), 638.

160 Marquis, *Warrior Who Fought Custer*, 264; Army and Navy Journal, July 3, 1886.

161 *Rocky Mountain News*, November 21, 1877.

162 Grinnell, *The Fighting Cheyennes*, 340.

163 D. J. Benham, "The Sioux Warrior's Revenge," *Canadian Magazine*, Vol. XLIII (1914), 462. See also Vestal, *Warpath and Council Fire*, 247.

164 Marquis, *Warrior Who Fought Custer*, 231–32; *Billings Gazette*, September 3, 1913.

about four or five others are said to have been mounted while the remainder were on foot. Two Moon described him as wearing a buckskin shirt and having long black hair and a black mustache,[165] but we know of no officer of the Seventh Cavalry answering that description. The Indians say that he was one of the bravest men they ever fought and that he was killed near the river. One writer[166] has argued that this was Captain Myles Keogh. The description fits Keogh and his horse, "Comanche," fairly well; however, Keogh was not killed near the river but in the ravine behind Battle Ridge. Other officers who wore buckskin were the two Custers, Yates, Cooke, Calhoun, Smith, and Porter. Smith partly meets the description, but his body was found near that of Custer on the hill; in the case of Yates and the two Custers the description does not fit, although the horse could have been General Custer's "Vic," which he rode into the fight. Cooke had an enormous beard, which Two Moon probably would have mentioned, and his horse was white, although the fact that he led several charges against the Indians and the horse need not have been his own are points in his favor. Captain French also wore buckskin, but he was with Reno and not in the fight on Custer Hill; furthermore, he was not killed near the river or anywhere else. It is possible that the individual described was Bouyer. The description is not too far off, and his body was found near the river. But it seems hardly probable since he was well known to the Indians and they should have recognized him.

Red Horse, who describes what was probably the same incident, gives some indication that the officer may have been Custer.[167] He says that the horse had four white feet and that its rider wore a wide-brimmed hat and a buckskin coat. This officer saved his command on several occasions by turning on his horse during the retreat. Red Horse, who says that he saw the man several times during the battle, described him as being the bravest man the Indians had ever fought, but said that he did not know whether or not it was

165 Garland, "Custer's Last Fight as Seen by Two Moon," *McClure's Magazine*, Vol. XI (September, 1898), 447. J. M. Thralls quotes Two Moon as saying that nineteen men broke away from the group on the hill, evidently after Custer's death, under the command of a brave officer. "The Sioux War," Kansas State Historical *Collections*, XVI (1923–25), 573–76.

166 Luce, *Keogh, Comanche, and Custer.*

167 *Colorado Transcript*, March 21, 1877.

General Custer since he did not see his body, adding that he understood that Custer was killed by a Santee, who took possession of his horse.[168] Kate Bighead says that when the shots quit coming from Custer Ridge, the Indians got up and ran towards it, at which time seven of the soldiers sprang to their feet and went running for the river.[169] Another version relates that there were ten men, two of whom were wounded—one bleeding from the mouth—and that they, the last of Custer's men, were killed before reaching the river.[170] The Indians also tell that some of the men on gray horses attempted to escape and that the dismounted soldiers on the hill fired into them to try to make them come back,[171] but whether or not this was the same incident is unknown.

Of the many descriptions of this attempt to escape, none gives a satisfactory description of the leader, and his identity must forever remain one of the unsolved mysteries of the Custer battle. The bodies of these troopers, mostly of Troops C and E, were found scattered between the ridge and the river. The conclusion is fairly obvious that with their officers dead they sought to escape by seeking refuge in the trees and brush along the river, but were met and killed by the Indians. Looking at the markings which today designate the places where the bodies of these men were found, it seems apparent that they died in a last desperate effort to escape.[172]

Two Moon also told of one man who, all by himself, rode towards the river and then up over the hill. The Cheyenne chief thought that the soldier was going to escape, but he was finally shot through the head and killed by a Sioux warrior. Two Moon said that this trooper was the last one of Custer's command to die and that he had braids on his arms, which raises the possibility that it might have been Sergeant Butler of Troop L, who is believed by some to have been the last of the soldiers to die.[173] But, at about the

168 See below.

169 Marquis, *She Watched Custer's Last Battle*, n.p.

170 Vestal, *Warpath and Council Fire*, 248.

171 Brady, *Indian Fights and Fighters*, 331. To this is added the statement, "Of course this was never told in public."

172 Jacob P. Dunn, *Massacres of the Mountains; a History of the Indian Wars of the Far West*, 612. Godfrey, *Century*, 380; Godfrey, *Montana*, 196–99; Miles, *Personal Recollections*, 286–89.

173 Garland, "Custer's Last Fight as Seen by Two Moon," *McClure's Magazine*, Vol. XI (September, 1898), 448.

same time, another soldier was running away towards the east but was overtaken and killed by Crazy Horse about half a mile from the ridge,[174] and as nearly as we can tell from the stories told by the hostiles, he died several minutes after the soldier mentioned by Two Moon.

Another Indian story relates that eleven or more soldiers escaped from the battlefield and made their way eastward towards Rosebud Creek, in the direction from which the regiment had come. The Crow scout Curly said later that as he rode off he saw a dozen or more soldiers in a ravine about a mile from the battlefield. Completely surrounded, they were fighting desperately in an attempt to cut their way out.[175] No remains of these men have ever been found, but the Crows claim to have found the bodies of dead soldiers far from the battlefield for more than a year after the battle.[176]

The hostiles also tell of an officer riding a large white horse who broke through the ring of warriors surrounding the doomed command and started on a wild ride toward the north, down the valley of the Little Big Horn. A few Indians pursued him, but his horse was swift and apparently in good condition and he seemed to be making his escape, for the Indians had given up the chase and were sitting on their ponies watching to see what the man would do. Suddenly, to their surprise he drew his revolver and shot himself through the head. The Indians explained his action by saying that he did not wish to bear the odium of having saved his life by deserting his comrades.[177] Although the dead body of one lieutenant was said to have been found two miles away with that of his horse, this officer has never been positively identified, and has been variously supposed to have been either Lieutenant Harrington, Lieutenant Porter, or Dr. Lord, the regimental surgeon.

Others have concluded that Lieutenant Harrington was the soldier who, riding a sorrel horse, broke away and rode back up the river in the direction from which the soldiers had come. Several of

[174] *Flying Hawk's Tales*, 29. This soldier's marker can be seen today to the east of the monument.

[175] *New York Herald*, July 26, 1876; Colonel John Gibbon, "Hunting Sitting Bull," *American Catholic Quarterly Review*, Vol. II, No. 3 (October, 1877), 673.

[176] Linderman, *Red Mother*, 245–47.

[177] Frazier Hunt, *Custer, the Last of the Cavaliers*, 438; E. A. Brininstool, "Unwritten Seventh Cavalry History," *Middle Border Bulletin*, IV (1945), 1–2.

the Indians pursued and kept firing at him without result. Finally, Old Bear, a Cheyenne, fired, and a few moments later the soldier tumbled from his horse. When the Indians rode up, they found that he had been killed by a bullet in the back and concluded that Old Bear had killed him.[178] This is more likely to have been Lieutenant Porter, whose body was never found but whose buckskin shirt, with a bullet hole in the back and indications that he had been wearing it when shot, was found in the Indian camp.[179] Thus there was probably no definite time when the fight on the hill can be said to have ended.

The little band who had survived the retreat from the ford and up the long hogsback gathered around a few of their officers for the last stand. Custer may or may not have been there, the evidence is too conflicting to allow a positive statement, but the men who were there gradually melted away as the Indian fire took its toll. Finally the shots almost ceased coming from the hilltop, the hostiles made a rush, and there was a brief flurry of activity as men attempted to escape or went down fighting, and in a few short moments all was over. Custer had made his last stand—and lost.

178 Canton, *Frontier Trails*, 32; Grinnell, *The Fighting Cheyennes*, 341.
179 See below.

CHAPTER XIX

The Dregs of Defeat

GENERAL TERRY'S camp was astir early on the morning of the twenty-seventh, and anticipation mingled with anxiety over the developments that the day was expected to bring. In marked contrast to the evening before, not an Indian was in sight in that vast region.[1] But even if there were no Indians, there were abundant signs of Sioux on every hand, and at seven o'clock, when the small command moved cautiously forward, it was in battle formation with the scouts even farther out on the flanks than was customary. About a mile or a mile and a half beyond the campsite the river swept completely across the valley from the high bluffs on the east to the benchlands on the west, its banks covered with a thick growth of brush and cottonwoods which cut off the view of everything beyond. Here there was some delay while the advance guard reconnoitered among the trees in order to guard against a possible ambush. The column was forced to detour far to the right, covering some very rough ground and ascending the low sandstone bluffs on the west and on to the first bench above the stream.[2] From this vantage point they could see a couple of abandoned skin tepees in the valley and some stray horses grazing in the timber near the stream.[3] Nearly all of the river bottom was black and smoking from the fire which had swept over it, and grass existed only along the banks of the river.[4]

Where the great Indian camp had stood, there were now only the funeral tepees and a great mass of debris which the hostiles had abandoned.[5] Buffalo robes, dried meat, camp equipage of every

[1] Marquis, *Two Days after the Custer Battle*, n.p.

[2] McClernand, "With Indian and Buffalo in Montana," *Cavalry Journal*, Vol. XXXVI (January and April, 1927), 25–26; *New York Herald*, July 8, 1876.

[3] Gibbon, "Summer Expedition," 297; Burdick, *Tales from Buffalo Land*, 52.

[4] Gibbon, "Summer Expedition," 300.

Graves of Custer's unknown soldiers and the ridge where the last stand was made.

Courtesy National Archives

Present-day Custer Battlefield National Monument. The first stone at the right denotes the place where Custer supposedly fell.

Roahen Photograph

The method used to transport the wounded to the steamer *Far West* after the Battle of the Little Big Horn.

Courtesy National Archives

kind and description, saddles, blankets, cooking utensils, axes, guns, horn spoons, and new china dishes all lay scattered about in the wildest confusion.[6] Although the soldiers felt that this abandonment of so much property had been the prelude to a hurried stampede, the Indian custom was to abandon the tepee and all other household property in a family where a death had occurred. Thus the soldiers drew completely erroneous conclusions about the great mass of debris.[7]

Arriving at the lodges, the soldiers found them surrounded by a circle of dead horses, while many nondescript dogs prowled the vicinity like wolves, snarling at the approach of the whites. Inside the lodges were the bodies of eight warriors—five in one tepee and three in the other—all dressed in their finest clothes and lying in state on scaffolds.[8]

Everyone, officers and men alike, was possessed of a burning curiosity to examine the various articles which were scattered about in such profusion, and despite repeated commands for silence in the ranks a low and continuous hum of voices could be heard. Despite instructions to the contrary, many of the soldiers left the ranks to pick up various articles such as knives and pistols of an antique pattern. A great many such articles were collected from the Indian dead by the troopers for souvenirs,[9] although a large proportion of them, especially the heavier items, were carried for only a short distance before being thrown away.[10]

In searching among the abandoned material, the troopers found much white man's goods, goods which the Indians had either acquired from the agencies or as the result of past depredations.[11] One of the men picked up a pair of bloody drawers with the words "Sturgis—Seventh Cavalry" lettered across them,[12] and Captain Clifford found a pair of cavalry officer's pantaloons stained with blood. Dr. Paulding discovered a buckskin blouse which had belonged to Lieutenant Porter. From the bullet holes it was apparent that he

5 Roe, *Custer's Last Battle*, 11.
6 Burdick, *Tales from Buffalo Land*, 52.
7 Marquis, *Two Days after the Custer Battle*, n.p.
8 Burdick, *Tales from Buffalo Land*, 52.
9 Marquis, *Two Days after the Custer Battle*, n.p.
10 Burdick, *Tales from Buffalo Land*, 52.
11 Marquis, *Two Days after the Custer Battle*, n.p.
12 Gibbon, "Summer Expedition," 298.

had been wearing it when hit, and that he had been shot from the rear left side, the bullet coming out the left breast near the heart.[13] A number of beheaded white bodies so mutilated as to be unrecognizable were also found[14] as were the heads of three men fastened together with wires and suspended from a lodgepole. The hair had all been burned off, and the heads could not be identified.[15] Dr. Paulding believed that the heads had been dragged from a distance, while the bodies were perhaps those of wounded or captured men who had met death by torture.[16] Also found was the pocketcase which Dr. Lord had carried, together with cavalry saddles, parts of uniforms, and other equipment. Slowly the officers began to realize, albeit unwillingly, that there must be some truth in what the Crow scouts had told them and that the Seventh Cavalry had been defeated, if not destroyed.[17]

While the soldiers were still rummaging through the abandoned loot, Lieutenant Bradley, who, with his mounted infantry detachment, had been scouting along the range of hills to the left, rode up to Terry and Gibbon, and in a voice trembling with emotion said, "I have a very sad report to make. I have counted 197 bodies lying in the hills." In answer to the question, "White men?" he replied in the affirmative, and added that while he had never met General Custer, from pictures he had seen he believed one of the bodies to be that of the General.[18] The last reason for any valid doubt was gone. The Crows had been right, and the only question now remaining was the extent of the disaster. It immediately became the duty of the Terry-Gibbon command to discover what had happened and to rescue any units of the regiment that might have survived the defeat.

[13] Albert J. Partoll, "After the Custer Battle, *Frontier and Midland*, Vol. XIX, No. 4 (1938–39), 278; Brady, *Indian Fights and Fighters*, 385; Burdick, *Tales from Buffalo Land*, 52.

[14] Edward S. Godfrey, "Address on the Fortieth Anniversary of the Custer Battle." However, Herendeen, who scouted the country for ten or twelve miles around the battlefield looking for possible survivors, says no bodies were found in the village. Reno, *Court*, 404–405. Neither he nor Godfrey was with Gibbon, so it is a moot question which one was mistaken.

[15] *Hardin Tribune*, June 22, 1923.

[16] Paulding, *Letters*, 349.

[17] Burdick, *Tales from Buffalo Land*, 53.

[18] Gibbon, "Summer Expedition," 299; Roe, *Custer's Last Battle*, 11. Gibbon's Report says 194 bodies. There are several versions of this incident. See Paulding, *Letters*, 349; McClernand, "With Indian and Buffalo in Montana," *Cavalry Journal*, Vol. XXXVI (January and April, 1927), 27; *Winners of the West*, October, 1924.

Once again the column was set in motion marching south along the western bank of the Little Big Horn and proceeding more rapidly and less cautiously than before, uncertain regarding whether they were going to rescue the survivors of the Custer command or to give battle to the enemy that had annihilated it.[19]

On the hill Reno's men had taken advantage of the respite to strengthen their position and to make better provision for the care of the wounded. About nine o'clock a column of dust was observed down the valley, and the fear that it might be the Indians returning again gripped the command. But the slowness of the advance—a sufficient commentary upon some of the practical difficulties involved in fighting Indians—indicated that it was a column of troops, and soon Varnum and French with their field glasses were able to confirm the fact and quiet the anxiety of Reno's men.[20] Opinion was divided about the identity of the approaching soldiers, Major Reno sure that it could not be General Terry unless he was ahead of schedule,[21] and that it could not be Custer since there were no gray horses. Therefore it was reasoned that it must be at least a part of General Crook's command, although he was expected to arrive from the opposite direction.[22] The Major prepared a communication for General Terry, and three volunteers were sent out in an attempt to reach him. They were instructed that if the advancing column consisted of troops, they were to return; otherwise they were to push on and attempt to reach the Terry-Gibbon forces.[23] Major Reno also apparently overcame his reluctance to the use of the Arikara scouts and sent two of them, Forked Horn, and Young Hawk, to investigate the dust cloud.[24] They were followed by Lieutenants Hare and Wallace, who were ordered to tell General Terry who was on the

19 Gibbon's Report, 473.

20 Schultz, *William Jackson,* 154; *Army and Navy Journal,* July 15, 1876.

21 If Custer was to meet Terry at the mouth of the Little Big Horn on the twenty-sixth, then Terry was not ahead of schedule. There are several possibilities, among them that Terry expected a messenger from Custer on that date, and that Reno did not know what the plans were.

22 Godfrey, *Montana,* 201.

23 Holley, *Once Their Home,* 239.

24 Dustin, *The Custer Tragedy,* 176.

bluffs and to show him how to ascend them since the country was very rough.[25]

Gibbon's advance contacted the two scouts, from whom little could be learned, and then the two lieutenants were seen approaching. The first question that the two officers asked concerned the whereabouts of Custer, who had last been seen going along the high bluffs toward the lower end of the village. They sat their horses aghast at the reply and seemed slow to grasp the impact of what they heard,[26] since up until then they had believed that their detachment had fought the major engagement of the two days just passed.[27] When the two commands joined, questions concerning the fate of Custer were mingled with criticisms of Major Reno's conduct by the officers of the Seventh, criticisms that in many cases were extremely severe.[28]

The men of the Terry-Gibbon command went into camp on the west bank of the river at the foot of the bluffs which had been in a state of siege for the better part of two days, just east of the present Garryowen post office.[29] On the highest point of the ridge and along what had been the northern line of defense they found a number of shelter tents, and under and around them some fifty wounded men under the care of the courageous and self-sacrificing Dr. Porter and volunteers from among the enlisted men.[30] Utilizing blanket slings, carriers brought the wounded men down the bluff and across the river to a hastily improvised field hospital. By nightfall all of the wounded had been transferred and made as comfortable as was possible under the circumstances.[31]

[25] Reno, *Court*, 120.

[26] Roe, *Custer's Last Battle*, 11; McClernand, "With Indian and Buffalo in Montana," *Cavalry Journal*, Vol. XXXVI (January and April, 1927), 27; Byrne, *Soldiers of the Plains*, 123. For two slightly variant accounts, see James P. Murphy, "Campaign of the Little Big Horn," *Infantry Journal*, Vol. XXXIV (June, 1929), 638, and *New York Herald*, July 8, 1876.

[27] James P. Murphy, "Campaign of the Little Big Horn," *Infantry Journal*, Vol. XXXIV (June, 1929), 638.

[28] Ghent, "Varnum, Reno and the Little Big Horn," *Winners of the West*, April 30, 1936. By the time of the Reno Court of Inquiry most of the officers had conveniently "forgotten" their criticisms on this occasion. Lieutenant Mathey did, however, refer to the criticisms in his testimony. *Official Transcript*, 953.

[29] Maguire's Report, 1349; Marquis, *Two Days after the Custer Battle*, n.p.

[30] Gibbon, "Summer Expedition," 302.

[31] Marquis, *Two Days after the Custer Battle*, n.p.; Gibbon, "Hunting Sitting Bull," *American Catholic Quarterly Review*, Vol. II, No. 3 (October, 1899), 655.

In the meantime detachments of both commands had been sent out to search for any members of Custer's detachment who might still be alive and either wounded or in hiding, while others were given the unenviable task of attempting to identify the dead. Captain Benteen was assigned the responsibility of following Custer's trail, which lay just behind Reno's position, and attempting to ascertain what had happened and how the battle had been fought. He followed down through a canyon-like ravine or coulee which lay just back of the crest of the bluffs for a distance of three miles. This was the same gorge up which the Indians had rushed when Reno made his advance down-river. This ravine, which was from fifty to one hundred yards in width, was very irregular, and the bottom was badly cut up by smaller ravines and the marks left by the hooves of many horses.[32] From the gorge the trail swung towards the river and then turned back on itself, but still bore down the river. About three-quarters of a mile from the stream they found the remains of Troop L and behind them the other companies, and on the high point of the ridge they found the body of Custer surrounded by the bodies of most of his officers and about forty troopers. Yates, Smith, Tom Custer, Cooke, and Reilly lay dead near the General, while in a ravine just north of or below Calhoun's position was the body of Captain Keogh. His body, like that of Custer, was stripped except for the socks, and these had had the name cut away, but his body was not mutilated in any way, possibly because of the Catholic medal, *Pro Petri Sede*, which he wore and which had not been removed.[33] The bodies of Lieutenants Lord and Harrington were never found, or at least never identified, and no one knows exactly what happened to them,[34] although the opinion was expressed that they and the enlisted men who were never identified were buried with the others.[35] Bouyer's badly mutilated body was found near the

[32] *Official Transcript*, 690; Reno, *Court*, 558; Dunn, *Massacres of the Mountains*, 611–12.

[33] Albert J. Partoll, "After the Custer Battle," *Frontier and Midland*, Vol. XIX, No. 4 (1938–39), 278; Luce, *Keogh, Comanche, and Custer*, 63. Although most writers refer to this medal as an *Agnus Dei*, it was really a *Medaglia di Pro Petri Sede* which had been conferred by Pope Pius IX.

[34] Terry's Report. Today's visitor to the battlefield will note a marker bearing Lieutenant Harrington's name inside the enclosure that marks the place where the last stand was made. Despite this, his body was never recovered, or at least never identified.

[35] Reno, *Court*, 364.

river, fulfilling his prediction to Custer that "If we go in there, we will never come out."[36]

The task of identification of the enlisted men was much more difficult. All of the troop roll-lists were on the persons of the first sergeants and had been taken by the hostiles so that the accounting of the dead depended entirely on memory. Identification was made next to impossible by the fact that the Indian women had finished off most of the wounded by knocking them in the head with axes, which one officer surmised had probably been furnished by the government of the United States.[37] In addition to being bloody and dirty, the bodies were swollen and discolored from the two days' exposure to the merciless Montana sun, "with thousands of flies macerating the features into further decay."[38]

Whether or not the bodies of Custer's men were mutilated and to what extent is another subject of controversy, and authorities can be found to support almost any point of view. Godfrey said long afterwards that all of the bodies except that of Custer were scalped and mutilated,[39] while Burdick added that hands, heads, feet, and legs were cut off and scattered here and there.[40] His contention is supported by Godfrey's further assertion that the Indians had taken everything of value except for an occasional undershirt or pair of socks and that here the names had been cut out. "The naked mutilated bodies, with their bloody wounds were nearly unrecognizable, and presented a scene of sickening, ghastly horror."[41] And a trooper named Harmon, of F troop, who had been on duty with the pack train, had a brother in L whose body he was unable to identify because of the mutilations.[42] On the other hand, Lieutenant McClernand declared that on the part of the field around Custer there was very little mutilation,[43] and William F. White, who was also with

[36] Colonel John Gibbon, "Hunting Sitting Bull," *American Catholic Quarterly Review*, Vol. II, No. 3 (October, 1877), 665–94.

[37] Burdick, *Tales from Buffalo Land*, 57.

[38] Marquis, *Two Days after the Custer Battle*, n.p.

[39] Godfrey, "Address on the Fortieth Anniversary of the Custer Battle."

[40] Burdick, *Tales from Buffalo Land*, 57.

[41] Albert J. Partoll, "After the Custer Battle," *Frontier and Midland*, Vol. XIX, No. 4 (1938–39), 279.

[42] *Winners of the West*, June 26, 1926. However, the roster of the regiment as given in Luce, *Keogh, Comanche, and Custer*, fails to list a Harman in either F or L Troops.

Gibbon, said that while most of the bodies were stripped, only a few were mutilated. Some of them had been hacked and pounded with a tomahawk or a club, and he judged that the Indians had taken that method of disposing of the wounded.[44] Lieutenant Bradley, probably the first to visit the field, agreed that there was little mutilation in a majority of cases, that many of the bodies were not even scalped, and that some of them, including that of Mark Kellogg, were not stripped.[45] While it is probably safe to say that the majority were scalped, the mutilations probably consisted largely of disfiguration brought about by blows with a club or an axe, and from slashing the right thigh, the Sioux custom for marking their dead.[46]

Although it is generally agreed that Custer was not scalped, there is disagreement about why he was not, and the matter has become the subject of much romantic nonsense. The probable reason is a very simple one—his hair was too short and he was getting bald[47] —although Godfrey claims that Gall told him in 1886 that Custer was not scalped "because he was the big chief and we respected him,"[48] but there are those who feel that he was the last officer in the army to be respected by the Sioux,[49] since he had made "the thieves road" into the Black Hills and was known as "the chief of the thieves." There is also disagreement over whether or not his body was mutilated in any way. Godfrey said that it was not mutilated,[50] and Bradley agreed, adding that the wounds which had caused Custer's death were so minute as to be scarcely discoverable.[51] One wound was in front of the left temple, the other in the left breast at or near the heart, and either would have been fatal. However, Kate Bighead later told Dr. Marquis that Custer's body was

[43] McClernand, "With Indian and Buffalo in Montana," *Cavalry Journal*, Vol. XXXVI (January and April, 1927), 53.

[44] Wagner, *Old Neutriment*, 236.

[45] *Helena Weekly Herald*, July 27, 1876.

[46] James P. Murphy, "Campaign of the Little Big Horn," *Infantry Journal*, Vol. XXXIV (June, 1929), 638; *Helena Independent*, October 15, 1915.

[47] Vestal, *Sitting Bull*, 174; Vestal, *Warpath: True Story of the Fighting Sioux*, 203.

[48] *Denver Post*, June 23, 1918; Burdick, *Last Battle of the Sioux Nation*, 87.

[49] Vestal, *Sitting Bull*, 175.

[50] Albert J. Partoll, "After the Custer Battle," *Frontier and Midland*, Vol. XIX, No. 4 (1938–39), 278.

[51] *Helena Weekly Herald*, July 27, 1876.

mutilated—that the Cheyennes cut off one of his fingers and stuck awls in his ears "to enable him to hear better."[52] Then there are those who maintain that the statement that the General's body was not mutilated was a fabrication, deliberately concocted in order to spare the feelings of Mrs. Custer.[53]

Near Custer was found the body of Sergeant Robert Hughes of Troop K, who carried the General's battle flag.[54] According to the Indians this flag was captured by Yellownose, a Cheyenne warrior, before Hughes was killed. The hostiles treated it as an object of superstition, believing it to be "big medicine" because they had observed that the soldiers never allowed it to touch the ground.[55]

Almost everyone agrees that the body of Captain Tom Custer was mutilated, almost beyond recognition, his skull crushed and nearly all of his hair scalped. In addition, a number of arrows had been shot into various parts of his body.[56] In his case the mutilations were so extensive that they led to the story that Rain-in-the-Face had not only carried out his vow to cut the Captain's heart out but had eaten a part of it in the belief that to eat the heart of a brave man imparted some of his virtues to the eater.[57]

In the valley there had been much mutilation of the dead of Reno's command, which was only natural since they were the ones closest to the Indian camp. This disfigurement, plus the bloating and discoloration from the extreme heat and the activities of swarms of flies, made identification impossible in most cases.[58] The body of Lieutenant McIntosh, found lying on its face, was horribly mutilated because the Indians always devoted particular attention to those of their own race who fought on the side of the whites. The

[52] Marquis, *She Watched Custer's Last Battle*, n.p.

[53] This is a familiar story. I have heard it orally from several persons. There is no way of checking its authenticity.

[54] Albert J. Partoll, "After the Custer Battle," *Frontier and Midland*, Vol. XIX, No. 4 (1938–39), 278.

[55] "Story of White Elk as told to Willis Rowland at Lame Deer, Montana, May 25, 1927."

[56] Albert J. Partoll, "After the Custer Battle," *Frontier and Midland*, Vol. XIX, No. 4 (1938–39), 278.

[57] In this connection Captain Benteen commented that Tom Custer's heart had not been cut out and that if Rain-in-the-Face had been interpreted correctly, he must have been on "his high horse and lying like a Sioux." Hunt, "A Purposeful Picnic," *Pacific Monthly*, Vol. XIX (March–May, 1908), 244.

[58] Marquis, *Two Days after the Custer Battle*, n.p.; *New York Herald*, July 8, 1876.

body was partially clothed and was identified by Lieutenant Gibson, who was McIntosh's brother-in-law, apparently from certain articles of clothing.[59]

Also discovered was Keogh's horse, "Comanche,"[60] long advertised as the only living thing found on the Custer battlefield, although who found him, where, when, and under what circumstances is not at all certain. Some writers maintain that the animal was discovered by Lieutenant Henry J. Nowlan, who had served with Keogh in the Papal Guard and later in the Civil War, in a ravine back of where the monument now stands, half-dead from loss of blood from several wounds.[61] However, Gustave Korn, a blacksmith in Troop I and later detailed as Comanche's personal attendant, claimed that he discovered the horse, bleeding from six wounds, on the battlefield. A trooper by the name of Brown wanted to cut the animal's throat and put an end to his misery, but Korn refused to allow him to do so, and with some help from other troopers got Comanche down to the river, bathed and dressed his wounds, and got him into condition to be taken to the steamer.[62] Henry Brinkerhoff, of Troop G, later claimed to have discovered the badly wounded horse in a clump of trees and, on reporting his discovery, was told to shoot him. But on Brinkerhoff's return to carry out the order, Comanche whinnied and went to him. Ascertaining that none of the wounds were deep, Brinkerhoff led the animal back to camp.[63] A further claimant to the discovery is Captain McDougall, who in a letter to Godfrey written May 18, 1909, claimed to have discovered the horse standing in the small bushes along the river near the Indian camp. This discovery, he said, was made on the twenty-eighth while searching for implements with which to bury the dead.[64] But

59 Gibbon, "Summer Expedition," 300.

60 William J. Ghent describes Comanche as a "clay-bank sorrel," and adds that Godfrey called him a "buckskin," which is pretty much the same thing. *Winners of the West*, February 28, 1934. Captain Luce says that he was a light bay or buckskin. *Keogh, Comanche, and Custer*, 7. Korn describes the horse as dark cream in color with a black mane and tail. *Winners of the West*, January 30, 1936.

61 Luce, *Keogh, Comanche, and Custer*, 64; Hanson, *Conquest of the Missouri*, 296.

62 *Winners of the West*, January 30, 1936. This account is on the back of a large picture of Comanche and was purportedly written by Korn at Fort Meade, South Dakota, May 21, 1888.

63 *Winners of the West*, April 30, 1934.

64 *Winners of the West*, February 28, 1934.

others, while stating that the horse was found on the twenty-eighth, insist that he was not on the battlefield but on the site of the Indian village and that the discovery was made by Terry's men.[65] As W. J. Ghent remarks, it is evident that the student has a choice among several claimants for the honor of having discovered Comanche after the battle.[66]

Nor was Comanche the only living survivor of the Battle of the Little Big Horn. On the morning of June 27, while the troopers were examining the site of the great hostile encampment, several wounded Seventh Cavalry horses were found. Although we do not know definitely what happened to them, they were probably shot—perhaps they had been left behind because they were too badly wounded to be of use to the Indians. Both Girard and Benteen also told of finding a wounded horse lying in a pool of mud and water on the right bank of the stream a short distance below the ford where it was believed that Custer had attempted to cross to the attack, and hanging on a limb projecting from a near-by stump were the trousers of an enlisted man. Benteen, who shot the animal on the twenty-eighth to put an end to its suffering, described it as a white horse,[67] in which case it probably belonged to either Lieutenant Calhoun or Lieutenant Cooke, both of whom rode white horses. But Girard said that it was a gray,[68] in which case there are many more possibilities. Troop E was the gray-horse troop, and the trumpeters also rode horses of that color. The band also was mounted on grays, and while the bandsmen had been left at the base camp, their horses had been distributed among the other troops in order to mount as many men as possible.

On the morning of the twenty-eighth, several of the scouts were sent out to explore the surrounding country in the hope of finding possible survivors of the battle, but their efforts were without result. At the same time detachments of the Seventh Cavalry proceeded to the battlefield to bury the dead, each troop being assigned to a definite portion of the field. There were no more than a half dozen spades and shovels and as many picks and axes in the entire

[65] Colonel W. H. C. Bowen, "Custer's Losing Battle Re-Fought," *Winners of the West*, September 30, 1926.

[66] *Winners of the West*, February 28, 1934.

[67] *Official Transcript*, 695; Reno, *Court*, 560.

[68] *Army and Navy Journal*, August 5, 1876; Reno, *Court*, 166.

command,[69] so that burial would have been an impossible task had it not been for the discovery in the debris of the village of a large number of shovels and spades.[70] Even with these, the task was extremely difficult on account of the dry and porous nature of the soil. As a result, most of the burials were nothing more than respectful gestures. Left lying where they were found, the bodies were covered with sagebrush or a little dirt[71] and abandoned there "in that vast wilderness, hundreds of miles from civilization, friends and home—to the wolves."[72] Only the bodies of officers definitely identified as such were given anything that even approximated real burial.[73]

Also on the morning of the twenty-eighth, Captain Ball, with his company of the Second Cavalry, was sent out on reconnaissance to discover if possible what had become of the retreating Indians. He followed their trail directly south toward the Big Horn Mountains for a distance of twelve or fifteen miles. Here the trail divided, one group going to the southeast and the other to the southwest. In those directions the whole country was filled with the smoke of countless fires, for the hostiles were burning the grass behind their retreating camps. That the Indians were in great force is shown by the fact that a few days later Crook's scouts discovered one of the abandoned campsites and found that the Sioux had been in seven circles covering nearly four miles in length.[74] In returning, Captain Ball's detachment struck across to the Little Big Horn and discovered a large and heavy lodgepole trail that at best was only a few days old, leading down the river. This trail was distinct from the one that Custer had followed and seemed to indicate that at least three large bands of hostiles had united just prior to the time Custer struck

[69] Albert J. Partoll, "After the Custer Battle," *Frontier and Midland,* Vol. XIX, No. 4 (1938–39), 279.

[70] Colonel John Gibbon, "Hunting Sitting Bull," *American Catholic Quarterly Review,* Vol. II, No. 3 (October, 1899), 665.

[71] Marquis, *Custer Soldiers Not Buried,* n.p.; McClernand, "With Indian and Buffalo in Montana," *Cavalry Journal,* Vol. XXXVI (January and April, 1927), 54.

[72] Albert J. Partoll, "After the Custer Battle," *Frontier and Midland,* Vol. XIX, No. 4 (1938–39), 279.

[73] Marquis, *Custer Soldiers Not Buried,* n.p. In *Two Days after the Custer Battle,* the same author says, "I think that in no case was a body buried entirely below the surface of the earth where it had been lying when found."

[74] Bourke, *On the Border with Crook,* 350.

their camp,[75] so that the Seventh Cavalry had fought not only the party whose trail they had followed up the Rosebud, but also the warriors of a camp which had come in from the east and joined the hostile band near Busby, plus this third group which had come in from the south and was probably as large as either of the others. While there is the possibility that this trail had been made by the warriors returning from the Crook fight on the Rosebud, that apparently was not a lodgepole trail, and the trail that Captain Ball found was too recent.

The remainder of Gibbon's command had spent the day in making preparations to move the wounded to the *Far West*, which General Terry expected to find at the mouth of the Little Big Horn. Twelve of the wounded were able to ride, but litters had to be constructed for the others.[76] In the late afternoon the command started, eight men being detailed to carry each litter, so that of the more than eight hundred men in the combined commands, nearly half were required to carry the wounded. The start was made at this particular time in order to escape the terrific heat of midday, which would be exhausting to both the patients and their bearers.[77] From the beginning many difficulties were experienced, and it soon became apparent that some other means of transporting the wounded would have to be found. The unevenness of the ground and the differences in the heights of the bearers made their duty terribly hard work. It was even harder on the wounded, and the cries of pain from the sufferers were frequent. There was much jostling and bumping, especially after the coming of darkness, for the bearers would often step into a hole or stumble over a rough stretch of ground, and there was always considerable difficulty when one group of bearers was relieved by another. Because of the frequent halts and the delays incident to any movement of this kind, the column made slow progress. In addition, it also straggled badly, soon spreading over a large expanse of territory.[78] Shortly after midnight

[75] Gibbon's Report, 474; *Report of the Secretary of War, 1876*, 464; Colonel John Gibbon, "Hunting Sitting Bull," *American Catholic Quarterly Review*, Vol. XIX, No. 4 (1938–39), 666–67.

[76] Burdick, *Tales from Buffalo Land*, 56.

[77] Marquis, *Two Days after the Custer Battle*, n.p.

[78] Colonel John Gibbon, "Hunting Sitting Bull," *American Catholic Quarterly Review*, Vol. II, No. 3 (October, 1899), 666.

a halt was made and the command went into camp, having covered only four and a half miles, but with "the wounded worried and feverish and the bearers completely exhausted."[79]

Gibbon believed that a much more feasible method of transportation could be had through the construction of rafts from the dry cottonwoods along the stream bed, by means of which the sufferers could be floated down to the boat with little trouble. The scheme had merit—there were trees in abundance—and the timber for the rafts had even been selected, when for some reason—possibly the fact that the course of the Little Big Horn is winding and tortuous—the order was changed and the scheme abandoned.[80] Instead, Lieutenant G. C. Doane was detailed to supervise the construction of mule litters.[81]

The command laid over for the purpose of destroying the property left in the Indian camp so that it would be useless to the hostiles should they return to the valley,[82] but the greater part of the day was spent in the construction of horse and mule litters. Lodgepoles, twenty feet or so in length, were selected and laid in pairs. Then two crosspieces about three feet long were lashed to them about six and a half feet apart. The wounded horses and mules which had been destroyed were now skinned, the hides cut into strips, and the space between the crosspieces filled with a lattice work of horse hide. On this, buffalo robes and blankets were spread, and the wounded rode quite comfortably. Motive power was furnished by two horses or mules, one in the lead and the other in the rear, working as a horse does in the shafts of a buggy. One attendant was needed for each horse, which was a great improvement over the eight bearers formerly required for each wounded man. These litters worked nicely, although the fastenings on one of them did give way, spilling its occupant to the ground but not causing any further injury.[83]

One of the Crow scouts, White Swan, had been severely wounded, and for him his Indian friends built a travois consisting of a number of springy poles lashed to the side of a pony and trail-

79 Burdick, *Tales from Buffalo Land*, 58.

80 *Ibid.*, 58.

81 Gibbon's Report, 474.

82 Colonel John Gibbon, "Hunting Sitting Bull," *American Catholic Quarterly Review*, Vol. II, No. 3 (October, 1899), 668.

83 Burdick, *Tales from Buffalo Land*, 59.

ing along the ground. When one of the poles struck an uneven piece of ground, the others acted as a support and thus broke the force of the shock to the occupant. The whole thing was covered with robes and blankets on which the patient rested.[84] This contrivance, which was an improvement even over the mule litters, again illustrates the failure of the white man to learn from the natives who, from living in the country, had developed means and methods admirably suited to their environment.

The march downstream was resumed at about six o'clock in the evening. The original plan was to proceed for only a short distance in order to test the litters and then go into camp. But everything worked nicely, and the column had moved several miles during which they had made a second crossing of the river when they were met by couriers with the news that the *Far West* was waiting at the mouth of the Little Big Horn.[85] These messengers, Private Goodwin of the Seventh Infantry and Henry Bostwick, the post guide at Fort Shaw, had been sent out forty-eight hours earlier to carry the news of the disaster to the steamer and to order her crew to make preparations to receive the wounded. But they had missed the *Far West* at the mouth of the stream because it had gone farther up the Big Horn. The couriers, not knowing where to locate it, had ridden to the base camp on the Yellowstone River, where they had secured food and forage and then started back. This time they found the *Far West* about half a mile above the mouth of the Little Big Horn and discovered that the Crow scout Curly had gotten ahead of them and brought the news of the battle to the men on the steamer. But as Curly was unable to speak English and there was no interpreter aboard, very little reliable information had been obtained except that the troops had been defeated. It was noted, however, that while Curly's countenance was dejected and woebegone, his appetite was in first-class shape.[86]

This Indian scout has probably been the victim of more apocryphal tale-telling than any other character in western history, with the exception of Buffalo Bill. For a long time hailed as the only survivor of the "massacre," he was subsequently called a liar, a coward,

[84] *Ibid.*, 59.

[85] Colonel John Gibbon, "Hunting Sitting Bull," *American Catholic Quarterly Review*, Vol. II, No. 3 (October, 1899), 672.

[86] Wilson, Report, 1380.

and a poltroon, among other things, when he was actually none of them. He never claimed to have been in the battle; in fact, he admitted from the beginning that he was not present when the Custer fight began, but was on a hill some distance away. Earlier in the day, apparently about the time the command was approaching the Lone Tepee, he and Black Fox, one of the Arikaras, left the regiment and went a few miles east of the battlefield to where Curly claimed some hardtack was concealed. This may or may not have been the same box that figured in the earlier incident of the lost packs. By the time Curly returned the fight was on, and he watched it for a time and then went still farther away to another hill, where he watched the battle for a while longer. Now convinced that the soldiers were beaten, he started to leave. Somewhere he acquired a blanket from a dead Sioux and kept it, not for the purpose of concealment, but because it was a good blanket. He also captured two stray ponies but soon turned them loose when he found that they impeded his progress, and he was beyond a doubt anxious to get out of the vicinity. He then rode down Tullock's Creek to the Yellowstone River to a point opposite Gibbon's base camp and built a fire, probably in order to attract attention. He was observed from the camp by LeForge, and the two of them talked by signs across the river. This was the morning of the twenty-sixth, the day after the battle, and the time was approximately the same as when the other three Crow scouts were talking to Lieutenant Bradley. Curly inquired the whereabouts of Gibbon and was told that he had gone up the Big Horn on the steamboat. The scout then rode off, heading upstream. He did not tell LeForge about the battle and explained this oversight later by saying that he was so dull and sleepy that he fancied that by that time the entire world knew what had occurred.[87]

Sometime during the next afternoon three members of the crew of the *Far West* were fishing about a mile up the Little Big Horn River when the bushes back from the shore suddenly parted and Curly appeared. The three men were James Sipes, said to have been both a barber[88] and a cowboy,[89] and two stewards, Reuben Riley and James Boles. It was to them that Curly gave the first news of

[87] Marquis, *Rain-in-the-Face and Curly the Crow*, n.p.; Marquis, *Memoirs of a White Crow Indian*, 250–51.

[88] *Billings Gazette*, December 16, 1925.

[89] *Helena Independent Record*, January 13, 1946.

the Custer defeat. Curly said later that it was not his intention to carry the news to Gibbon, that he was merely looking for the soldiers to report for further duty.[90] This rather simple story has been considerably embroidered by later interpreters and fiction writers, but the tales were apparently the fabrications of others and not of Curly himself. The classic story that he offered Custer a Sioux blanket in order to help him escape and that Custer indignantly rejected it, preferring to die with his men, is only the worst of a series of idiotic romanticisms. Curly was riding the same pony when he appeared at the *Far West* that he had been riding when he left the mouth of the Rosebud with Custer's regiment. What did he do with it while offering the blanket to Custer and while working his own way through the hostile lines disguised as a Sioux? And how does one reconcile the facts that the Sioux and Crow painting, style of hair dressing, moccasins and other features of habiliment are so different as to make subterfuge impossible?[91]

The two couriers, after resting for an hour or so on the boat, rode on to find the Terry command and report the location of the steamer. The crew of the *Far West* had discounted, if they did not actually disbelieve, what they could understand of Curly's story, but the news brought by the couriers was another matter. Accordingly, preparations were made to receive the wounded, and at the same time the steamer was barricaded and placed in a position to resist an Indian attack in case that should become necessary.

On receipt of the news of the proximity of the boat, General Terry decided to press on and attempt to reach it that night if possible. The soldiers followed the valley for several miles and then turned across some rolling hills to a plateau, where large cactus plants proved very annoying to both men and animals. The moon went down about midnight, leaving the column in darkness and confusion, because cavalry, infantry, and litters were jumbled together in almost hopeless disorder. There were no lights, and to add to the general discomfort it began to rain; there was no road, even the scouts confessing their inability to find a way down to the river; and the location of the steamer, as respected the position of the col-

90 Marquis, *Memoirs of a White Crow Indian*, 248.
91 Marquis, *Rain-in-the-Face and Curly the Crow*, n.p.

umn, was a matter of mystery. "The wounded were helpless, the attendants tired, and everybody out of sorts and ill-tempered. One could hear such expressions as, 'Look out there, d——n you.' 'Where are you going?' 'Keep off those litters.' 'Move those pack mules away from here.' 'Now see that damned fool of a cavalryman. I wish I had my bayonet, blast you, I'd make you keep your distance.' "[92] But finally a road to the boat was discovered, fires to illuminate the path were lighted along the ravine leading down to the river, and shortly after two o'clock, just before sunrise on the thirtieth of June, the wounded were placed safely on the steamer, after a day's march of nearly fifteen miles.[93]

No sooner were the wounded on board than the *Far West* began landing supplies for Gibbon's command and for the remaining seven companies of the Seventh Cavalry under Major Reno, who had gone into camp along the bank and were to march overland to the base camp at the mouth of the Big Horn. Shortly after dawn, just as Captain Grant Marsh was preparing to cast off, he received a request to confer with General Terry in the latter's quarters. After closing the door, Terry is said to have told him:

> Captain, you are about to start on a trip with fifty-two wounded men on your boat. This is a bad river to navigate and accidents are liable to happen. I wish to ask of you that you use all the skill you possess, all the caution you can command, to make the journey safely. Captain, you have on board the most precious cargo a boat ever carried. Every soldier here who is suffering with wounds is the victim of a terrible blunder; a sad and terrible blunder.[94]

This statement, delivered with a great deal of emotion and emphasis by the usually very unemotional Terry, made a deep impression on Captain Marsh, who promised to do the best he could, and soon after began the dangerous, fifty-three-mile journey to the mouth of the stream. Late that afternoon he tied the steamer up to the bank of the Yellowstone, where the base camp had been established. Here it was to await the arrival of Gibbon and Reno and ferry their commands across to the north bank. Early the next morning, July 1,

[92] Burdick, *Tales from Buffalo Land*, 59.
[93] Roe, *Custer's Last Battle*, 28.
[94] Hanson, *Conquest of the Missouri*, 298.

"Muggins" Taylor started on a long and dangerous ride to Fort Ellis, carrying dispatches from both Terry and Gibbon.

In the meantime the combined commands of Gibbon and Reno had moved at five o'clock in the afternoon of the thirtieth, crossing the Little Big Horn and camping on the north bank near its mouth. The next morning they were under way before five o'clock, and after an uneventful march of twenty miles camped on the Big Horn in approximately the same place that the infantry had camped on the night of the twenty-fifth. On July 2, they marched the remaining twenty-three miles to the Yellowstone and were ferried across. Here they went into camp to await the arrival of reinforcements and supplies.

Fourteen of the wounded men had so far recovered as to be able to be put ashore with the expectation of being returned to duty in the near future. Also landed was Captain Baker's company of the infantry which had served as the guard on the boat, their places being taken by seventeen dismounted troopers of the Seventh Cavalry, who, having lost their horses, were temporarily useless in the field. Moreover, on the boat they could be of use in helping to care for their wounded comrades.[95] On July 3, at five o'clock in the afternoon, the *Far West* started for Bismarck under a full head of steam. Early the next morning, Private William George of H troop died of his wounds, and a brief stop was made at the Powder River base to inter his body and to take on the private property of the officers killed which had been left there for safekeeping. The steamer also brought orders to Major Moore to move his garrison up to the main camp at the mouth of the Big Horn.

A few days after the battle some three or four of the Arikara scouts had appeared at the supply depot with news of the disaster. Since their language could not be understood and there was no interpreter, they had asked for a piece of canvas on which they attempted, by drawings, to describe the battle. However, they were no more successful in conveying their message, and while the troops understood that there had been a fight, they felt sure that Custer had won, any other conclusion being unthinkable.[96] But there was

[95] *Ibid.*, 302.

[96] Roy P. Johnson, "Jacob Horner of the Seventh Cavalry," *North Dakota History*, XVI, No. 2 (April, 1949), 82.

no denying the news that the steamer brought, and Major Moore immediately began preparations to put his command in motion up the river.

At Fort Buford, the *Far West* stopped long enough to land a wounded scout, probably Goose, and on the afternoon of the fifth there was a brief stop at Fort Stevenson. Here, Captain Marsh, in accordance with the prevailing sentimentality of the day and in obedience to General Terry's specific orders, draped the derrick and jack staff in black and put the steamer's flag at half-staff. At eleven o'clock the *Far West* reached Bismarck, just fifty-four hours after leaving the mouth of the Big Horn, during which time she had covered 710 miles and set a speed record for the river which still stands.[97] The boat had no sooner touched the bank than members of the crew were ashore, spreading the news through the town. Captain Marsh hurried to the telegraph office, and the operator, J. M. Carnahan, began sending over the wire the news that was to confirm reports already circulating throughout the nation.

The question of who brought the first news of the disaster is still a matter of dispute. "Muggins" Taylor had left the base camp at the mouth of the Big Horn and ridden as far as Horace Countryman's ranch on the Stillwater. Too exhausted to continue farther, Taylor had prevailed on Countryman to take the news on to Bozeman. Arriving there, he found the government telegraph line down and rode on to Helena, where he arrived on the afternoon of July 4. Although all of the business houses were closed in honor of the Centennial Fourth, the editor of the *Helena Daily Herald* was able to get enough of his staff together to get out an extra, and that evening the news was sent east over Western Union. A group of discharged freighters returning to the Montana settlements had also been given the news by Taylor, and their somewhat garbled accounts also reached the outside in various ways. The *Far West* did not reach Bismarck until the late evening of the fifth, and the official dispatches sent by General Terry did not reach Sheridan's headquarters in Chicago until the morning of the sixth. Long before that time the publisher of the *Helena Daily Herald* had been deluged with telegrams begging for more details.[98]

[97] Hanson, *Conquest of the Missouri*, 306.

[98] Brininstool, "A Great Newspaper Scoop," *Hunter-Trader-Trapper*, Oc-

But the Indians had known it first of all, for immediately after the battle, the hostiles, by means of mounted messengers and signal smokes—the famous "moccasin telegraph" of the Great Plains—had sent the news of their great victory to all of the agencies. The Indians at Fort Abraham Lincoln had known of the battle for days before the *Far West* reached Bismarck, and one Indian had ridden night and day to carry the news to Standing Rock. The whites at the fort knew that something had happened and from the attitude of the Indians suspected that it was bad news for the soldiers.[99]

The *Far West* remained at Bismarck only a short time and then dropped downstream to Fort Lincoln, where the wounded were to be landed and where Mrs. Custer and the other widows had to be told of their bereavement.[100] For them the Seventh had ridden into the Valley of the Shadow, never to emerge.

Many unsolved questions remain to plague and bewilder, and at the same time fascinate, the student of the battle. Was Custer the last of that little group on the hill to die, which Indian killed him, and was there a white survivor of the fight? To all of these questions the answer must be the same, that no one knows and no one probably ever will know, but there are several interesting possibilities.

While there are many stories to the effect that Custer was the last to die and that his body was found just a few feet below where the monument now stands, neither fact is capable of verification. The legend has perhaps grown—and it has certainly received abundant currency—from the fact that the most famous of all western pictures[101]—"Custer's Last Stand," distributed by the Anheuser-

---

tober, 1919, 32–34; *Billings Gazette*, August 21, 1906. For a contrary point of view see Hanson, *Conquest of the Missouri*, 309–11.

[99] Crawford, *Rekindling Camp Fires*, 259; Vestal, *Sitting Bull*, 184.

[100] Hanson, *Conquest of the Missouri*, 312.

[101] Professor Robert Taft of the University of Kansas has an interesting article on pictures of Custer's Last Stand in the *Kansas Historical Quarterly*, Vol. XIV, No. 4 (November, 1946). While he does not list all of the pictures by any means, he gives a valuable account of the background of those that he does list. See also the same author's, *Artists and Illustrators of the Old West, 1850–1900*, especially Chapter X. One particularly horrific picture of the battle is displayed in Harold's Club, Reno, Nevada. Another picture of a much higher quality, however, is that of Elk Eber, a half-blood Indian whose mother was in the hostile camp at the time of the battle. The original is in Dresden, Germany, but a copy is reproduced on the cover of a pamphlet for sale at the Custer Battlefield National Monu-

Busch Company—depicts the General, saber in hand, fighting almost alone at the end. But this is a picturization of the artist's fancy and not a photographic reproduction; according to the best evidence that we have, there was not a saber in the command on that fatal Sunday. Although Sitting Bull[102] and Curly[103] both told stories that would indicate that Custer was among the very last of the soldiers to die, other accounts are at variance. There is much Indian testimony—and we must remember that after all the Indians are the only ones who really know—to indicate that Custer was killed early in the fight and that his body was found some distance down and back of the ridge near Keogh's position.[104] It must also be remembered that the day was hot and that officers and soldiers alike had removed their coats and top shirts, and that all insignia and rank were obliterated. Moreover, they were undoubtedly so caked with dust and perspiration that it is doubtful if a person could have recognized his own brother at a distance of more than a few feet. So, in view of these circumstances, all stories of Custer's being the last survivor, must be viewed with decided skepticism.[105]

Concerning which Indian actually killed Custer, there are many romantic yarns, well exemplified by Longfellow's poem, "The Revenge of Rain-in-the-Face," to whom is generally accorded the dubious distinction of having killed the "Long Hair." Rain-in-the-Face himself told many contradictory stories, at times denying and at others claiming credit for the deed, so that it appears that his version of the affair may have depended upon the person to whom he was talking at the time. On his deathbed, after he had been assured that the government would not punish him, he is said to have told Miss Mary C. Collins, a missionary to the Sioux, that he had killed Custer

ment. In many respects probably the best picture of the fight is that of William Reusswig, published in *Collier's,* June 30, 1951.

102 *Rocky Mountain News,* November 21, 1877.

103 *New York Herald,* July 26, 1876.

104 *New York Times,* June 19, 1927. Medicine Bear, a Cheyenne, told Mr. James Gatchell that Custer was with Keogh's troop when he was killed and that his body was found back of the ridge a hundred feet or more from where the monument now stands. This story was supported by one told by a trooper who helped bury the dead and who independently pointed out to Mr. Gatchell the place where Custer's body was found. The position he indicated was only a few feet from the one pointed out by Medicine Bear. This information was given me by Mr. Gatchell in the summer of 1949.

105 Burdick, *Last Battle of the Sioux Nation,* 82.

and that he was so close that the powder from his gun blackened the General's face. Miss Collins believed that he was telling the truth.[106] But the Sioux did not have a very good reputation for veracity, and there are those who maintain that Rain-in-the-Face was merely keeping up a tribal reputation. For there is substantial evidence from the hostiles themselves that Rain-in-the-Face was not on the battlefield at all during the fight, but instead was miles away in charge of the pony herd.[107] There were others among the Indians who said that Custer was killed by Rain-in-the-Face after he (Custer) had killed three Indians with his pistol and three with his saber.[108] In his official denial Rain-in-the-Face stated that it was a young Cheyenne warrior, Tce-tan, or Hawk, who shot the General, and explained that he and the Cheyenne were painted alike and were close enough together for him to see what happened.[109]

Long afterwards, Flat Hip, an Uncpapa Sioux, claimed credit for the deed,[110] and in 1879, Little Knife, another Uncpapa said that Custer was killed by a boy of fifteen years, whose brother had just been slain. According to this story, Custer was cheering his men and firing his pistol in the air—the cavalry signal to charge—when a stray bullet killed a young buck not far from the General. The slain warrior's brother then seized the latter's gun and shot Custer.[111] However, Flat Iron, a Cheyenne, said that the plan was to capture Custer and not to kill him, and he blamed Two Moon for Custer's death on the theory that he had a grudge against the General.[112] One of the most persistent of the stories is that Custer was the last to fall of the group with whom he was fighting and that the last shots fired upon this group of soldiers were from rifles in the hands of two sons of Inkpaduta, or Scarlet Top, a Santee,[113] while others go even farther and identify the individual as Red Horse.[114]

106 Smith, *Indian Experiences,* 247.

107 Joseph H. Taylor, "Inkpaduta and Sons," North Dakota Historical *Collections,* IV, No. 3 (April, 1930), 163.

108 *Rocky Mountain News,* July 13, 1876.

109 Smith, *Indian Experiences,* 234ff.

110 Warren K. Morehead, "The Passing of Red Cloud," Kansas State Historical *Collections,* X (1907–1908), 306.

111 Article in Clipping File, Billings Public Library.

112 *Helena Independent,* October 15, 1915. This is partially confirmed by the fact that Two Moon is said to have been the first to count "coup" on Custer. Hunt and Hunt, *I Fought with Custer,* 223.

One of the most interesting stories is that of the Cheyennes, whose camp Custer had attacked on the Washita, and with whom he had later smoked the peace pipe on a branch of the Red River in Texas. When he attacked their end of the village on the banks of the Little Big Horn, they felt that the pledge of peace had been broken, and their medicine men laid a curse on him which the Cheyennes say was responsible for his death and destruction, maintaining that his death was brought about by the Everywhere Spirit for having broken his oath.[115] Since one of the Cheyennes, Brave Bear, had been present on all three occasions—the Washita, Red River, and the Little Big Horn—he was "given the honorary distinction of having killed Custer."[116]

The Cheyennes also say that they recognized Custer's body after the fight and moved it to a point near Reno's entrenchments. Then they tried to open communication with the Major's command with the intention of turning the body over to them. But the Cheyennes were fired upon and gave over the attempt, returning the body to the place where they had originally found it. Although we know that there was an attempt to open communication with the Major by means of a white flag—it was not respected since the troops feared some kind of treachery—the two incidents do not necessarily fit together, for, while the Cheyennes might conceivably have carried Custer's body to Reno Hill, it is absolutely beyond the realm of possibility to expect them to have carried it back to where they found it.[117] In all this welter of conflicting and confusing testimony perhaps the most intelligent conclusion is that of the chiefs who declared that no one knew who killed Custer.[118]

All of these stories indicate that they knew they were fighting Custer and the Seventh Cavalry. Such may or may not have been

[113] Taylor, "Inkpaduta and Sons," North Dakota Historical *Collections,* IV, No. 3 (April, 1930), 164; Smith, *Indian Experiences,* 236.

[114] *New York Times,* June 19, 1927. See also Vestal, *Sitting Bull,* 175, and Elmo S. Watson, "What Was the Fate of Custer's Horse?" in *Westerners Brand Book,* III, No. 4 (June, 1951), 30.

[115] "Story of White Elk as told to Willis Rowland at Lame Deer, Montana, May 25, 1927."

[116] Marquis, *Which Indian Killed Custer?* n.p.; *Billings Gazette,* March 29, 1933.

[117] Marquis, *Two Days after the Custer Battle,* n.p.

[118] *Hardin Tribune-Herald,* November 8, 1929; Marquis, *Which Indian Killed Custer?* n.p.

the case. Again the evidence is contradictory, and again one must make allowance for possible rationalization by the Indians. In most cases in the Indian wars the hostiles knew little or nothing concerning the identity of the soldiers against whom they were fighting,[119] and there seems to be no reason why this battle should have been an exception. The smoke, dust, and confusion of the struggle probably would have made the identification of best friends difficult if not impossible, so that it was probably some time after the battle—perhaps after the return to the agencies—before the Indians learned against whom they had been fighting. Many of the hostiles declared that they did not recognize Custer during the battle or afterwards while they were rummaging over the field in search of spoil.[120] Sitting Bull, from his exile in Canada, told a reporter that the Indians had no knowledge of Custer's presence during the fight or immediately after it.[121] Others maintain that some of the Cheyennes recognized Custer's body after the fight, having seen him in the south.[122] The story of the Sioux is that after the battle a half-blood, Big Leggins, who could read numerals, told the Indians that they had been fighting the Seventh Cavalry. Then one of the Sioux, Bad Soup (or Bad Juice)—who has been called "that lean and hungry looking man"[123]—who had been around the Seventh at Fort Lincoln and knew that Custer was their leader, pointed out his body to White Bull.[124]

Another controversy concerns whether Custer committed suicide. It is often maintained that he took his own life and that his body was not mutilated because the Indians had a peculiar reverence for a suicide. Here again, obviously, the truth will never be known. Although the first news of the tragedy reaching Fort Rice was that Custer had shot himself at the end[125] and there is a story that Custer took his own life to avoid the certain torture that would have followed had he been taken alive,[126] neither account can be substanti-

119 Marquis, *Two Days after the Custer Battle,* n.p.; Vestal, *Sitting Bull,* 174.

120 *Cut Bank* (Montana) *Pioneer-Press,* October 6, 1923; Dustin, *The Custer Tragedy,* 159.

121 Reno, *Court,* 43.

122 Marquis, *She Watched Custer's Last Battle,* n.p.; "Story of White Elk as told to Willis Rowland at Lame Deer, Montana, May 25, 1927."

123 Vestal, *Sitting Bull,* 135.

124 *Ibid.,* 174; Vestal, *Warpath and Council Fire,* 203.

125 Fougera, *With Custer's Cavalry,* 264.

ated. The fact that neither of his wounds had powder burns[127] means little or nothing because he was dressed when the wounds were inflicted and his body stripped when found. In regard to the reverence which Indians have for a suicide and their avoidance of his body, it can be said that they differ on this subject the same as white men do. The Crows express disbelief in the suicide story, stating that while Custer was extremely foolish to attack such a large village, he was "too brave to take his own life like a coward."[128] But even if the Indians did hold such "an awesome reverence for self-destruction," how could all of those in the battle have known which soldiers committed suicide and which did not?[129] Several of the Cheyennes insisted, although the Sioux did not agree, that many soldiers took their own lives, but there is nothing to indicate that it was these bodies which were not mutilated. Why should Custer's body alone have been afforded such recognition?

Another mystery is provided by the body of Sergeant Butler of L troop, which was found about a quarter of a mile away from the ford where Custer is thought to have attempted to cross. It was thus the body farthest from Custer's and closest to Reno's position. A good soldier, Butler had served in the British Army, in the Northern forces during the Civil War, and had been a member of the Seventh Cavalry ever since its activation. It has been surmised that he was a courier from Custer attempting to get through to either Reno or Benteen,[130] but against this theory it may be pointed out that first sergeants are seldom if ever used as messengers. It could also be argued that since, as first sergeant, his position during the march would have been at the rear of the troop in order to keep the ranks closed up as much as possible, and that since Troop L was apparently last in the column, he may have been wounded or unhorsed as the command moved away from the ford. If so, he was probably one of the very first of Custer's detachment to die. In any case he apparently fought to the bitter end, as his several wounds and the many empty shells found scattered about his position seem to attest.

126 Hunt and Hunt, *I Fought with Custer*, 437.

127 Godfrey, "Address on the Fortieth Anniversary of the Battle."

128 Linderman, *American*, 176.

129 *Cut Bank Pioneer-Press*, October 6, 1933.

130 Godfrey, *Montana*, 199.

There are several Indian stories which apparently refer to Butler. One of them says that one company was pursued along the ridge to the south, and that out of it one soldier got away and rode off in the direction of Reno's position, but was chased back by some of the hostiles who had left Reno and were going to join the fight on Custer. Some say that this soldier, who may have been Butler, took his own life when he found the Indians all around him and all avenues of escape closed.[131] Another story says that he was on a hill to the southwest of Custer's position still firing when the battle ended and that the Indians had a hard time killing him. Finally, after he had killed several braves, the warriors crawled up the hill on all four sides of him, and while those in front distracted his attention he was killed by those in the rear.[132] There is another Sioux story to the effect that he ran out to one side and singlehanded stood off the Indians for a long time. That man with the three stripes on his sleeve, say the Sioux, was the bravest of them all.[133]

The most persistent and the most interesting, in many ways, of all the questions is whether there was a Custer survivor. During the early part of the present century, hardly a year passed without some individual winning a degree of temporary notoriety by claiming that he was a survivor of the little band that had followed George Armstrong Custer down into the valley of the Little Big Horn. There was invariably a very ingenious explanation of how he happened to escape from the field of carnage and an equally ingenious reason for having remained silent so long. Had Custer had all of those who claimed to be "the lone survivor" of his two battalions he would have had at least a brigade behind him when he crossed the Wolf Mountains and rode to the attack. None of the reports were ever substantiated, and while there is a possibility that there may have been a survivor, the probability is that there was not.

Rain-in-the-Face, in one of the many stories attributed to him, related that one soldier escaped when his horse ran away and carried its rider through the Indian camp. Rain-in-the-Face said that he did not see the incident but heard the women talking about it

131 Charles Eastman, "A Review of the Account of the Custer Fight in the *Chautauquan* for July, 1900," *Review of Reviews*, XXII (1900), 219.

132 Barry, *Indian Notes on the Custer Battle*, 29.

133 Vestal, *Sitting Bull*, 174.

after the fight. He added that he had forgotten all about it until he went to Chicago and saw the man there.[134] Curly also told of one trooper who got away although desperately wounded, and expressed the belief that the man either died of his wounds, starved to death in the bad lands, or was followed and killed by the Sioux.[135] Willis Rowland tells that, some years after the battle, he and another Cheyenne found the bones of a man in a thicket about fifteen miles east of the battlefield. There were no buttons, buckles, or other remnants of clothing by which even a partial identification could be made, but Rowland concluded that they were the remains of a soldier who, having been knocked out and stripped by the Sioux, recovered and wandered away, only to die of wounds, starvation, or exposure.[136] This could have been the soldier mentioned by Curly, or it could have been some individual who had no connection whatever with the battle.

In September of 1923, John Stout died in Delaware, Oklahoma, claiming to have been a scout for General Custer and to have escaped from the "Indian massacre in which his comrades were slain" by hiding in the carcass of a dead buffalo.[137] In the same year there appeared the story of Charles Hayward, who said that he had been a member of Troop I, claiming to have been wounded and to have gone "half out of his mind." In attempting to flee the field, his horse was shot, fell, and pinned its rider underneath. Hayward insisted he remembered nothing of what happened after that but that later he was told that he had been found by the Indians, who spared his life because of his impaired mentality. He was put to work and kept in servitude until 1900, when his mind suddenly cleared. Then he made his escape, carrying with him, he said, the old headquarters' flag of the Seventh Cavalry wound around his waist.[138] Examination of the regimental roster reveals the fact that there was a Haywood in Troop I, but his given name is George rather than Charles, and he is listed as not having participated in the battle, having been on detached service, probably at the Powder River base camp.[139]

134 Brady, *Indian Fights and Fighters*, 391.
135 *New York Herald*, July 26, 1876.
136 Vestal, *Sitting Bull*, 183.
137 *New York Times*, September 5, 1923.
138 *New York Times*, February 4, 1923.
139 Luce, *Keogh, Comanche, and Custer*, 109.

One other claimant to "last survivor" honors was Frank Finkel, who lived for many years in Dayton, Washington. His story was that on account of family difficulties he had left home and enlisted in the army under the name of Frank Hall, and had been assigned to the Seventh Cavalry. During the battle his horse bolted and ran away, carrying its rider through the Indian lines and up a ravine. After several hours of riding, he came to a trapper's cabin, where he was taken in and cared for. After several weeks he learned from the trapper the way to Fort Benton and made his way there to request a discharge from the officer commanding, only to be told that that individual had no authority to give him a discharge. He then made his way back to the family home in Iowa, but conditions there being no better than formerly, he again left and went to Washington Territory, arriving in Dayton in 1877. People who knew him state that he was honorable and truthful and apparently believe his story. But the roster of the regiment discloses no one by the name of Frank Hall. Troop D, which was not with Custer, had a Curtis Hall and an Edward Hall, the latter of whom is listed as not having participated in the battle. Since memory is notoriously fickle, this trooper might have enlisted under some other name than the one he gave, for had he been a member of the regiment under the name of Hall, he would be listed among those killed in action, while both of the Halls are listed as having survived the battle.[140] There was a garrison at Fort Benton at that time and there may have been some trappers' cabins in the region, although it is extremely doubtful if there were any within a day's ride of the site of the Custer defeat. While on the face of it Mr. Finkel's story appears to be somewhat improbable, it could be true, and a great deal more research would be necessary to establish beyond a doubt its authenticity or falsity.[141]

One incident which has never been explained and which possibly might point to a survivor of the regiment was the finding of a dead Seventh Cavalry horse on the south side of the Yellowstone just above the mouth of Rosebud Creek several weeks after the battle. The body was somewhat decomposed, and it was impossible

[140] *Ibid.*, 107.

[141] There is considerable newspaper and personal letter material in the Oskosh (Wisconsin) Public Museum on the claims of Frank Finkel to be a survivor of the Battle of the Little Big Horn River. It was largely collected through the efforts of the late Arthur Kannenberg.

to tell whether it was a sorrel or a light bay. Although the bridle was missing, the halter, lariat, saddle, saddle blanket, and saddlebags were intact, while a small grain bag, in which the oats had not been disturbed, was tied to the cantle. Godfrey was told that when it was first discovered, the carbine of the rider was there, and he noted that the saddlebags were empty. The animal had been shot in the forehead, death probably having been instantaneous.[142] Although Godfrey felt that this represented the possibility of some trooper's having escaped the fate of his comrades—he admitted that he had never met or heard of any of the reputed survivors who identified himself by this incident—he seems to have overlooked the possibility that the horse belonged to a deserter or a straggler from the command. On the twenty-second of June, the regiment had crossed the Rosebud near its mouth and marched up that stream. During that day and the one following, the troops had straggled badly, and there was plenty of opportunity for a trooper who had fallen far behind to take "French leave" and attempt to make his way back to civilization and leave the "glories" of Indian fighting for others. The possibility that something of this sort may have occurred is strengthened by the fact that the oats in the grain bag were undisturbed. But straggler or survivor, his name and his fate are things that we will never know—two other enigmas of the mystery-ridden Battle of the Little Big Horn River.

Speculation and controversy—much of it acrimonious in the extreme—over the responsibility for the disaster began almost as soon as the *Far West* docked at Bismarck. In the intervening years, every person involved has had his defenders and detractors, and the only thing that can be stated with certainty is that no assessment of responsibility will ever be made which will be entirely satisfactory to everyone. But at this distance in time, the following statements seem to be justified:

(1) Reno disobeyed orders on his scout, and compelled General Terry to revise his plan of campaign.

(2) Custer disobeyed the spirit if not the letter of his orders in following the Indian trail across the Wolf Mountains and getting himself into a position where he could do nothing but attack.

142 E. A. Brininstool, "Unwritten Seventh Cavalry History," *Middle Border Bulletin*, Spring, 1945. The same story appears under the title "Was There a Custer Survivor?" in *Hunter-Trader-Trapper* for April, 1922.

(3) The extremely large number of Indians in the hostile camp was not a deciding factor. Custer knew that enormous numbers of Sioux were ahead—he probably did not know that the Northern Cheyennes were with them—and he firmly believed that the Seventh Cavalry could handle the situation. And it might have done so—since if rightly handled, a large village will scatter as easily as a small one—had its various units been competently led.

(4) Reno disobeyed orders in not charging the Indians. His orders were not discretionary—the only thing that was left to his discretion was the rapidity of his advance—and his decision to halt and fight on foot made ultimate victory impossible.

(5) Reno's flight from the valley, or "charge" as he insisted on calling it, released a large number of Indians under Gall, who, by a stroke of luck, were able to follow Custer's trail and fall upon the flank held by Calhoun and Keogh and overwhelm it before a line could be established. Also this retreat gave a powerful boost to the morale of the Indians, convincing them that their "medicine" was good.

(6) Benteen, by disobeying orders, which were to unite with Custer and not with Reno, sealed the fate of Custer's men. Had Benteen gone on, instead of stopping to help Reno, he could have been in Medicine Tail Coulee within fifteen minutes. The appearance of his battalion would have created a diversion which might have enabled Custer to extricate himself and to save a large portion of his command.

(7) Custer was at fault in breaking up the regiment into so many parts and scattering them so widely. Then when the time came for concerted action, the scattered fragments could not be reassembled in time to avert disaster.

The Little Big Horn was a battle badly planned and in some ways badly fought.[143] Practically every principle of war was violated; in particular, the audacious spirit of the cavalry failed to manifest itself.[144] And the finale, as Colonel Coughlan has pointed out, "was meaningful sardonic," for, from General Terry on down, all members of the command had been obsessed with the idea that as

[143] McClernand, "With Indian and Buffalo in Montana," *Cavalry Journal*, Vol. XXXVI (January and April, 1927), 192.

[144] James P. Murphy, "The Campaign of the Little Big Horn," *Infantry Journal*, Vol. XXXIV (June, 1929), 640.

soon as the Indians caught sight of the soldiers, they would seek to escape. And the Indians did escape, but they waited until they had done to Custer just what he planned to do to them. They did it, moreover, not by an overmastering strategy of their own but simply by taking advantage of the mistakes of the soldiers. Then they escaped, "withdrawing leisurely and with savage dignity," leaving Custer and every member of his five companies dead on Battle Ridge, with Reno, marooned and impotent, on his hill, and Terry and Gibbon, uncertain and confused, stalemated in the valley.[145]

[145] Coughlan, "The Battle of the Little Big Horn," *Winners of the West*, March 30, 1934.

Bibliography

This bibliography is not intended to be all inclusive, but merely to list some of the more significant items dealing with the Battle of the Little Big Horn River.

I. MANUSCRIPT MATERIALS

"Accounts of the Custer Fight given to General Hugh L. Scott by two Crow scouts, 'White-Man-Runs-Him' and 'Curly,' August 24, 1919." (Typescript in William J. Ghent Papers in the Library of Congress, Washington, D. C.) Printed in Graham, *The Custer Myth.*

Benteen, Colonel Frederick W. "An Account of the Little Big Horn Campaign." (Typescript copy in William J. Ghent Papers, Library of Congress, Washington, D. C.) This is printed and to be found most conveniently in Graham, *The Custer Myth.*

"Diary of Captain E. S. Godfrey, Battle of the Little Big Horn, 1876." (In Edward S. Godfrey Papers in the Library of Congress, Washington, D. C.)

Edgerly, General Winfield S. "Narrative of the March of General George A. Custer. . . ." (Typescript copy in William J. Ghent Papers in Library of Congress, Washington, D. C.)

Godfrey, Edward S. "Address on the Fortieth Anniversary of the Custer Battle." (Manuscript in Billings, Montana, Public Library.)

"Letter of E. S. Godfrey, to Superintendent C. H. Asbury, Crow Agency, Montana. (Manuscript in Billings, Montana, Public Library.)

Reno Court of Inquiry. Proceedings of the Court of Inquiry in the case of Major Marcus A. Reno, concerning his conduct at the Battle of the Little Big Horn River, June 25–26, 1876. (National Archives, Washington, D. C.) This was privately printed by Colonel W. A. Graham, in a very limited edition in 1951, using an offset process.

A very good abstract of the testimony is to be found in Colonel Graham, *The Reno Court of Inquiry*, Harrisburg, Pa., 1954.

Reno Court of Inquiry. Stenographic Reports of the Testimony, Editorial, and Miscellaneous Articles from the *Chicago Times*, January 14 to February 12, 1879. (In the William J. Ghent Papers in the Library of Congress, Washington, D. C.)

"Story of White Elk as told to Willis Rowland at Lame Deer, Montana, May 25, 1927." (Manuscript in Billings, Montana, Public Library.)

"Story of William Jackson as told to Jack Burton Munroe." (Manuscript in Montana State Historical Library, Helena, Montana.)

2. GOVERNMENT PUBLICATIONS

Index to Reports of Committees of the House of Representatives for the First Session of the Forty-Fourth Congress, 1875–1876.

Jenny, Walter P. *Report on the Mineral Wealth, Climate and Rainfall and Natural Resources of the Black Hills of South Dakota.* 44 Cong., 1 sess., *Exec. Doc. 51.*

Kappler, Charles J. (compiler and editor). *Indian Affairs, Laws and Treaties. . . .* I–II: 57 Cong., 1 sess., *Sen. Doc. 452.* III: 62 Cong., 2 sess., *Sen. Doc. 719.*

Report of the Expedition to the Black Hills under Command of Brevet Major General G. A. Custer. 43 Cong., 2 sess., *Sen. Exec. Doc. 32.* This is also to be found in South Dakota Department of History, *Collections*, VII, 583–94.

Report of the Secretary of War . . . Communicated to the Two Houses of Congress at the Beginning of the Second Session, Forty-Fifth Congress, Vol. II, Part 2. This contains reports of the Battle of the Little Big Horn, from Lieutenant Wallace, Lieutenant Maguire, and Sergeant Wilson.

United States Army. *Letter . . . transmitting . . . Report of the Commissioner of Indian Affairs in relation to the present situation of Indian disturbances in the Sioux reservation.* 44 Cong., 1 sess., *Sen. Exec. Doc. 52.*

United States War Department. *Military Expedition against the Sioux Indians, Report, July 14, 1876.* 44 Cong., 1 sess., *House Exec. Doc. 184.*

United States War Department. *Annual Report, 1876.* Contains the reports of the Secretary of War, General of the Army, Major General Philip H. Sheridan, General Terry, General Gibbon, General

Crook, Major Reno, and Captain Benteen. This material is also to be found in 44 Cong. 2 sess., *House Exec. Doc. 1*, Part 2.

3. BIOGRAPHIES AND MEMOIRS

Some of the most valuable and readily obtainable books and articles on the Battle of the Little Big Horn have been indicated by an asterisk.

Alter, J. Cecil. *James Bridger, Trapper, Frontiersman, Scout and Guide; a Historical Narrative*. Salt Lake City, Shepherd Book Co., 1925.

Britt, Albert. *Great Indian Chiefs*. New York, Whittlesey House, 1938.

David, Robert B. *Finn Burnett, Frontiersman: The Life and Adventures of an Indian Fighter*. Glendale, Calif., Arthur H. Clark Co., 1937.

De Barthe, Joe. *Life and Adventures of Frank Grouard*. Buffalo, Wyo., *Buffalo Bulletin*, n.d.

Eastman, Charles. *Indian Heroes and Great Chieftains*. Boston, Little, Brown and Co., 1919.

*Linderman, Frank Bird. *American: The Life Story of a Great Indian*. New York, World Book Co., 1930.

——. *Red Mother*. New York, John Day Co., 1932.

*Marquis, Thomas B. *A Warrior Who Fought Custer*. Minneapolis, Midwest Publishing Co., 1931.

——. *Memoirs of a White Crow Indian*. New York, Century Co., 1928.

Miles, General Nelson A. *Personal Recollections and Observations*. New York, The Werner Co., 1896.

——. *Serving the Republic*. New York, Harper and Brothers, 1911.

Mills, General Anson. *My Story*. Washington, D. C., privately printed, 1918.

Milner, Joe E., and Earle R. Forrest. *California Joe . . . with an Authentic Account of Custer's Last Fight* by Col. H. C. Bowen. Caldwell, Idaho, The Caxton Printers, 1935.

Nevins, Allan. *Hamilton Fish, the Inner History of the Grant Administration*. New York, Dodd, Mead and Co., 1936.

Phillips, Paul C. *Forty Years on the Frontier, as Seen in the Journals and Reminiscences of Granville Stuart*. 2 vols. Cleveland, Arthur H. Clark Co., 1925.

*Schmitt, Martin F. *General George Crook: His Autobiography*. Norman, University of Oklahoma Press, 1946.

*Schultz, James Willard. *William Jackson, Indian Scout....* Boston and New York, Houghton Mifflin Co., 1926.

*Van de Water, Frederick F. *Glory Hunter: A Life of General Custer.* Indianapolis and New York, Bobbs-Merrill, 1934.

*Vestal, Stanley. *Jim Bridger, Mountain Man: A Biography.* New York, William Morrow, 1946.

*———. *Sitting Bull, Champion of the Sioux.* Boston and New York, Houghton Mifflin Co., 1932.

Wagner, Glendolin Damon. *Old Neutriment.* Boston, Ruth Hill, 1934.

4. GENERAL HISTORIES

Bourke, John Gregory. *On the Border with Crook.* New York, Charles Scribner's Sons, 1891.

*Brady, Cyrus Townsend. *Indian Fights and Fighters.* New York, Doubleday, Page and Co., 1904.

———. *Northwestern Fights and Fighters, 1876–1900.* New York, McClure Co., 1907.

Brown, Jesse, and A. M. Willard. *Black Hills Trails.* Edited by John T. Milck. Rapid City, S. Dak., Journal Publishing Co., 1924.

Burt, Struthers. *Powder River, Let 'er Buck.* (Rivers of America Series.) New York, Farrar and Rinehart, 1938.

Byrne, Patrick E. *Soldiers of the Plains.* New York, Minton, Balch and Co., 1926.

Canton, Frank M. *Frontier Trails.* Edited by Edward Everett Dale. Boston, and New York, Houghton Mifflin Co., 1930.

Carrington, Margaret Irvin. *Ab-sa-ro-ka, Land of Massacre.* Philadelphia, J. B. Lippincott, 1878.

Crawford, Lewis F. *Rekindling Camp Fires.* Bismarck, N. Dak., Capital Book Co., 1926.

*Custer, Elizabeth B. *Boots and Saddles.* New York, Harper and Brothers, 1885.

DeLand, Charles Edmund. *The Sioux Wars.* South Dakota Department of History *Collections,* XV. Pierre, S. Dak., 1930.

Dixon, Joseph K. *The Vanishing Race.* Garden City, N. Y., Doubleday, Page and Co., 1913.

Finerty, John F. *Warpath and Bivouac, or the Conquest of the Sioux.* Chicago, Donohue and Henneberry, 1890.

Fougera, Katherine Gibson. *With Custer's Cavalry.* Caldwell, Idaho, The Caxton Printers, 1940.

Fry, Colonel James B. *Military Miscellanies*. New York, Brentano's, 1889.

*Grinnell, George Bird. *The Fighting Cheyennes*. New York, Charles Scribner's Sons, 1915.

———. *Two Great Scouts and Their Pawnee Battalion*. Cleveland, Arthur H. Clark Co., 1928.

*Hanson, Joseph Mills. *The Conquest of the Missouri: Being the Story of the Life and Exploits of Grant Marsh*. New York, Murray Hill Books, Inc., 1946.

Hebard, Grace Raymond, and E. A. Brininstool. *The Bozeman Trail. . . .* 2 vols. Cleveland, Arthur H. Clark Co., 1922.

Hein, Lieutenant Colonel Otto Louis. *Memories of Long Ago*. New York, G. P. Putnam's Sons, 1925.

Holley, Frances C. *Once Their Home*. Chicago, Donohue and Henneberry, 1890.

Hunt, Frazier. *Custer, the Last of the Cavaliers*. New York, Cosmopolitan Book Co., 1928.

*Hyde, George E. *Red Cloud's Folk: A History of the Oglala Sioux Indians*. Norman, University of Oklahoma Press, 1937.

*McLaughlin, James. *My Friend, the Indian*. Boston and New York, Houghton Mifflin Co., 1910.

Montana: A State Guide Book. New York, Viking Press, 1939.

North Dakota: A Guide to the Northern Prairie State. Fargo, N. Dak., Knight Printing Co., 1938.

Perkins, Jacob Randolph. *Trails, Rails, and War*. Indianapolis, Bobbs-Merrill, 1929.

Rister, Carl Coke. *Border Command: General Phil Sheridan in the West*. Norman, University of Oklahoma Press, 1944.

Smith, DeCost. *Indian Experiences*. Caldwell, Idaho, The Caxton Printers, 1943.

*Vestal, Stanley (compiler). *New Sources of Indian History, 1850–1891; the Ghost Dance—the Prairie Sioux: A Miscellany*. Norman, University of Oklahoma Press, 1934.

———. *The Missouri*. (Rivers of America Series.) New York, Farrar and Rinehart, 1945.

*———. *Warpath: True Story of the Fighting Sioux*. Boston and New York, Houghton Mifflin Co., 1934.

*———. *Warpath and Council Fire: The Plains Indians' Struggle for Survival in War and in Diplomacy*. New York, Random House, 1948.

Wyoming: A Guide to its History, Highways, and People. New York, Oxford University Press, 1941.

5. SPECIAL MONOGRAPHS

Barry, David F. *Indian Notes on the Custer Battle*. Edited by Usher L. Burdick. Baltimore, Proof Press, 1937.

*Bates, Charles Francis. *Custer's Indian Battles*. Bronxville, N. Y., privately printed, 1936.

*Brininstool, E. A. *The Custer Fight: Captain F. W. Benteen's Story of the Battle of the Little Big Horn*. Hollywood, Calif., privately printed, 1940.

*———. *Troopers with Custer, Historic Incidents of the Battle of the Little Big Horn*. Harrisburg, Pa., Stackpole Co., 1952. In this volume Mr. Brininstool has collected many of his shorter essays, most of which were in widely scattered publications—many extremely difficult to obtain—and has made them readily available. This is a most valuable book for the study of the battle.

Burdick, Usher L. *The Last Battle of the Sioux Nation*. Stevens Point, Wis., Worzalla Publishing Co., 1929.

———. *Tales from Buffalo Land*. Baltimore, Wirth Brothers, 1940.

*———. *Tragedy in the Great Sioux Camp*. Baltimore, Proof Press, 1936.

Dorsey, George A. *The Sun Dance*. Chicago, *Field Columbian Museum Publication*, No. 103, *Anthropological Series*, Vol. IX, No. 2, 1905.

*Dustin, Fred. *Echoes from the Little Big Horn Fight*. Saginaw, Mich., privately printed, 1953.

*———. *The Custer Fight*. . . . Hollywood, Calif., privately printed, 1936.

*———. *The Custer Tragedy*. Ann Arbor, Mich., Edwards Brothers, 1939. One of the very best books on the battle, and one that is almost "required reading."

Flying Hawk. *Flying Hawk's Tales: A True Story of Custer's Last Fight*. New York, Alliance Press, 1936.

*Graham, Colonel William A. *The Custer Myth: A Source Book of Custeriana*. Harrisburg, Pa., The Stackpole Co., 1953.

*———. *The Reno Court of Inquiry*. Harrisburg, Pa., The Stackpole Co., 1954.

*———. *The Story of the Little Big Horn*. New York, Century Co., 1926 (Second Edition, Harrisburg, Pa., Military Service Publishing Co., 1941). Colonel Graham was one of the ablest students of the battle. Anything that he wrote is worth reading. *The Custer Myth*, especially, is a treasure house of material dealing with the battle.

*Hunt, Frazier and Robert. *I Fought with Custer: The Story of Sergeant Windolph*. New York, Charles Scribner's Sons, 1947. This book is especially valuable for the documentary material that it contains.

*Kuhlman, Charles. *Custer and the Gall Saga*. Billings, Mont., privately printed, 1940.

*———. *Legend into History: the Custer Mystery*. Harrisburg, Pa., The Stackpole Co., 1951. Dr. Kuhlman, who has devoted many years to an analytical study of the Battle of the Little Big Horn presents in these two books the results of his researches. While there are many who will not agree with him, his ideas are worth consideration, and the depth and breadth of his scholarship must be respected even by those who disagree.

Libby, Orin Grant (editor). *The Arikara Narrative of the Campaign Against the Hostile Dakotas, 1876*. North Dakota Historical *Collections*, VI. Bismarck, 1920.

*Luce, Edward S. *Keogh, Comanche, and Custer*. St. Louis, John S. Swift Co., 1939. Especially valuable for the documentary material that it contains.

Marquis, Thomas B. *Custer Soldiers Not Buried*. Hardin, Mont., privately printed, 1933.

———. *Rain-in-the-Face and Curly the Crow*. Hardin, Mont., privately printed, 1934.

———. *She Watched Custer's Last Battle*. Hardin, Mont., privately printed, 1933.

———. *Sitting Bull and Gall the Warrior*. Hardin, Mont., privately printed, 1934.

———. *Sketch Story of the Custer Battle*. Hardin, Mont., privately printed, 1933.

———. *Two Days after the Custer Battle*. Hardin, Mont., privately printed, 1935.

———. *Which Indian Killed Custer?* Hardin, Mont., privately printed, 1933.

*Roe, Charles F. *Custer's Last Battle*. New York, Robert Bruce, 1927. This is especially valuable for accounts of various participants in the battle, and for its maps.

6. ARTICLES AND ESSAYS

Adams, Jacob. "A Survivor's Story of the Custer Massacre on the American Frontier," *Journal of American History*, Vol. III (1909), 227–32.

Arnold, Lieutenant Colonel Frazier. "Ghost Dance and Wounded Knee," *Cavalry Journal*, Vol. XLIII (May–June, 1934).

Beardsley, J. L. "Could Custer Have Won?" *Outdoor Life*, No. 71 (March, 1933), 10–11, 56–57.

Benham, D. M. "The Sioux Warrior's Revenge," *Canadian Magazine*, No. 43 (September, 1914), 455-63.

Bourke, John Gregory. "General Crook in the Indian Country," *Century* magazine, Vol. XLI (March, 1891), 643-660.

Brackett, William S. "Custer's Last Battle on the Little Big Horn in Montana, June 25, 1876," *Contributions to the Historical Society of Montana*, IV (1903), 259-76.

*Bradley, Lieutenant James H. "Journal of the Sioux Campaign of 1876 under the command of General John Gibbon," *Contributions to the Historical Society of Montana*, II (1896), 140-226.

Brininstool, E. A. "A Great Newspaper Scoop," *Hunter-Trader-Trapper*, No. 39 (October, 1919), 32-35.

———. "Unwritten Seventh Cavalry History," *Middle Border Bulletin* (Mitchell, South Dakota), Vol. IV (1925), 1-2.

———. "With Colonel Varnum at the Little Big Horn," *Hunter-Trader-Trapper*, No. 54 (June, 1927), 15-17, 67; No. 55 (July, 1927), 13-16. (Also in *Winners of the West*, Vol. XIII [March 20, 1936].)

Brinkerhoff, Henry. "Account of the Custer Battle," n.d., n.p. In *Custer Scrapbooks*, Billings Public Library.

Britt, Albert. "Custer's Last Fight," *Pacific Historical Review*, Vol. XIII (1944), 12-21.

Byrne, Patrick E. "The Custer Myth," *North Dakota Historical Quarterly*, Vol. VI (April, 1932), 187-200.

Coughlan, Colonel T. M. "The Battle of the Little Big Horn," *Cavalry Journal*, No. 43 (January-February, 1934), 13-21.

"Custer's Battle from the Indian Viewpoint," *American Indian Journal*, Vol. I (1929). This was apparently the only number of this magazine issued. The copy used was in the Billings Public Library.

DeRudio, Charles C. "My Personal Story," *Frontier and Midland*, Vol. XIV (January, 1934), 155-59.

"Diary of Mathew Carroll, Master in Charge of Transportation for Colonel John Gibbon's Expedition against the Sioux Indians, 1876," *Contributions to the Historical Society of Montana*, II (1896).

Donaldson, A. B. "The Black Hills Expedition," South Dakota Historical *Collections*, Vol. VII (1914), 554-80.

Eastman, Charles A. "The Story of the Little Big Horn; Told from the Indian Standpoint by One of Their Race," *Chautauquan*, No. 31 (July, 1900), 353-58.

Garland, Hamlin. "General Custer's Last Fight as Seen by Two Moon," *McClure's* magazine, Vol. IX (September, 1898), 443-48.

*Ghent, William J. "Varnum, Reno and the Little Big Horn," *Winners of the West*, Vol. XIII (April 30, 1936), 1, 4.

*———. "Windolph, Benteen, and Custer," *Cavalry Journal*, No. 43 (November–December, 1934), 65–66.

Gibbon, Colonel John. "Hunting Sitting Bull," *American Catholic Quarterly Review*, Vol. II (October, 1877), 665–94.

*———. "Last Summer's Expedition against the Sioux," *American Catholic Quarterly Review*, Vol. II (April, 1877), 271–304.

*Godfrey, General Edward Settle. "Custer's Last Battle," *Century* magazine, No. 43 (January, 1892), 358–87.

*———. "Custer's Last Battle," *Contributions to the Historical Society of Montana*, IX (1923), 141–225. The same as item listed above with some additional material.

*Graham, Colonel William A. " 'Come on! Be quick! Bring packs!' " *Cavalry Journal*, No. 32 (July, 1923), 303–17. This is reprinted in Graham, *The Custer Myth*.

*Hagerty, Leroy W. "Indian Raids along the Platte and Little Blue Rivers, 1864–65," *Nebraska State Historical Quarterly*, Vol. XXVIII (1947), n.p.

*Hanson, Joseph Mills. "The Civil War Custer," *Cavalry Journal*, No. 43 (May–June, 1934), 24–31.

*Hughes, Colonel Robert Patterson. "The Campaign against the Sioux," *Journal of the Military Service Institution of the United States*, Vol. XVIII (January, 1896). Reprinted in Graham, *Story of the Little Big Horn*, Second Edition.

Hull, Myra E. (editor). "Soldiering on the High Plains: The Diary of Lewis Byram Hull, 1864–66," *Kansas Historical Society Quarterly* (February, 1938).

Hunt, Fred A. "A Purposeful Picnic," *Pacific Monthly*, No. 19 (March–May, 1908), 233–45, 431–48.

*Johnson, Roy P. "Jacob Horner of the Seventh Cavalry," *North Dakota Historical Quarterly*, Vol. XVI (April, 1949), 75–101.

Kanipe, Daniel A. "A New Story of Custer's Last Battle; Told by the Messenger Boy Who Survived," *Contributions to the Historical Society of Montana*, IV (1923), 213–25.

*Kellogg, Mark. "Notes, May 17 to June 9, 1876, of the Little Big Horn Expedition, *Contributions to the Historical Society of Montana*, Vol. IX (1923), 213–25.

King, Captain Charles, "Custer's Last Battle," *Harper's*, No. 81 (August, 1890), 378–87.

Larson, Arthur J. "The Black Hills Gold Rush," *North Dakota Historical Quarterly*, Vol. VI (January–April, 1927), 302–19.

*McClernand, Edward J. "With the Indians and the Buffalo in Montana," *Cavalry Journal*, No. 36 (January–April, 1927), 7–54.

McConnell, Ronald C. "Isaiah Dorman and the Custer Expedition," *Journal of Negro History*, Vol. XXXIII (July, 1948), 344–52.

*Murphy, James P. "The Campaign of the Little Big Horn," *Infantry Journal*, No. 34 (June, 1929), 631–40.

*Partoll, Albert J. "After the Custer Battle," *Frontier and Midland* (1939), 277–79.

Ryan, Benjamin. "The Bozeman Trail to Virginia City, Montana, in 1864; A Diary," *Annals of Wyoming*, July, 1947.

Taylor, Joseph Henry. "Bloody Knife and Gall," *North Dakota Historical Quarterly*, Vol. IV (July, 1947), 163–73.

———. "Inkpaduta and Sons," *North Dakota Historical Quarterly*, Vol. IV (April, 1930), 153–63.

———. "Lonesome Charley," *North Dakota Historical Quarterly*, Vol. IV (July, 1930), 227–38.

Wemett, W. M. "Custer's Expedition to the Black Hills in 1874," *North Dakota Historical Quarterly*, Vol. VI (1932), 292–302.

7. NEWSPAPERS AND MAGAZINES

Army and Navy Journal
Billings Gazette (Montana)
Billings Times (Montana)
Bozeman Avant-Courier (Montana)
Colorado Transcript (Denver)
Custer Chronicle (South Dakota)
Denver Post
Hardin Tribune (Montana)
Hardin Tribune-Herald (Montana)
Helena Independent (Montana)
Missoulian (Montana)
Montana Lookout (Helena)
Nation (New York)
New York Herald
New York Times
New York Tribune
Oregon Journal (Portland)
Rocky Mountain News (Denver)
Time (New York)
Winners of the West (St. Joseph, Missouri)

8. MISCELLANEOUS

Custer Files. Western Collection, Billings, Montana, Public Library. This is a great mass of miscellaneous items dealing with the Battle of the Little Big Horn and related subjects.

Custer Scrapbooks. Western Collection, Billings, Montana, Public Library. This contains newspaper clippings and other items, some with source indicated, and others not.

Johnson, Allen (editor). *The Dictionary of American Biography*. New York, Charles Scribner's Sons, 1928.

*Merington, Marguerite. *The Custer Story: The Life and Intimate Letters of General George A. Custer and His Wife Elizabeth*. New York, Devin-Adair Co., 1950.

Index

Custer's Luck has been set on the Linotype in the type face known as Janson, which in its modern recutting traces to the original work of Anton Janson, a punchcutter and type-founder evidently of Dutch origin but at the time (1660–1687) practicing in Leipzig. It is distinguished by its fine clarity and excellence of drawing, and by the quality which typographers call "character." The Linotype recutting was made direct from type cast from the original matrices in possession of the Stempel Foundry in Frankfurt am Main.

UNIVERSITY OF OKLAHOMA PRESS : NORMAN